1001 WINDOWS *95* TIPS

GREG PERRY

JAMSA
P·R·E·S·S ™
...a computer user's best friend™

a division of Kris Jamsa Software, Inc.

1001 Windows 95 Tips

Published by
Jamsa Press
2975 S. Rainbow, Suite I
Las Vegas, NV 89102
U.S.A.

For information about the translation or distribution of any Jamsa Press book, please write to Jamsa Press at the address listed above.

1001 Windows 95 Tips

Copyright © 1995 by Jamsa Press. All rights reserved. Except as permitted under the Copyright Act of 1976, no part of this publication may be reproduced or distributed in any format or by any means, or stored in a database or retrieval system, without the prior written permission of Jamsa Press.

Printed in the United States of America.
98765432

ISBN 1-884133-15-0

Publisher	**Technical Advisor**	**Cover Design**
Debbie Jamsa	Phil Schmauder	Phil Schmauder
Composition	**Cover Photograph**	**Proofers**
Phil Schmauder	O'Gara/Bissell	Rosemary Pasco
		Jeanne Smith
		Heather Grigg
Indexer	**Copy Editors**	**Technical Editor**
Linda Linssen	Tammy Funk	Steve Weakley
	Heather Grigg	
	Larry Letourneau	
	Rosemary Pasco	

This book identifies product names and services known to be trademarks or registered trademarks of their respective companies. They are used throughout this book in an editorial fashion only. In addition, terms suspected of being trademarks or service marks have been appropriately capitalized. Jamsa Press cannot attest to the accuracy of this information. Use of a term in this book should not be regarded as affecting the validity of any trademark or service mark.

The information and material contained in this book are provided "as is," without warranty of any kind, express or implied, including without limitation any warranty concerning the accuracy, adequacy, or completeness of such information or material or the results to be obtained from using such information or material. Neither Jamsa Press nor the author shall be responsible for any claims attributable to errors, omissions, or other inaccuracies in the information or material contained in this book, and in no event shall Jamsa Press or the author be liable for direct, indirect, special, incidental, or consequential damages arising out of the use of such information or material.

This publication is designed to provide accurate and authoritative information in regard to the subject matter covered. It is sold with the understanding that the publisher is not engaged in rendering professional service or endorsing particular products or services. If legal advice or other expert assistance is required, the services of a competent professional should be sought.

Table of Contents

GETTING STARTED WITH WINDOWS 95

- Starting Windows 95 1
- What You'll See 2
- The Welcome Window Features 3
- What's New in Windows 95 4
- Where is MS-DOS? 5
- A Window is Still a Window 6
- Starting a Program 7
- Ending a Program 8
- Running Multiple Programs 9
- Switching Between Windows 10
- Minimizing a Window 11
- Minimizing All Open Windows at Once ... 12
- Maximizing a Window 13
- Restoring a Window's Original Size 14
- Using the Taskbar 15
- Moving a Window 16
- Dragging the Window Frame to Size a Window 17
- Moving the Taskbar 18
- Getting to Your Windows 3.1 Program Groups 19
- Shutting Down Your Computer 20
- Rebooting Your Computer 21
- Taking a Look at My Computer 22
- Understanding Files and Folders 23
- Traversing Drives inside My Computer 24
- Getting to Know Your Network Neighborhood 25
- Retrieving Objects from the Recycle Bin .. 26
- Surfing Cyberspace with Microsoft Network 27
- Using the Windows 95 Inbox 28
- Understanding and Using Documents 29
- Taking Advantage of the Documents Menu 30
- Running a Program Using the Run Option 31
- Getting to an MS-DOS Prompt 32
- Windows 95 Doesn't Need AUTOEXEC.BAT and CONFIG.SYS 33
- Windows 95 and INI Files 34
- Using the Taskbar to Cascade or Tile Open Windows 35
- Using a Local Reboot to End an Application 36
- Understanding Plug and Play 37
- Requesting the Windows 95 Startup Tips 38
- Understanding Wizards 39
- Registering Windows 95 40
- Using AutoPlay to Play Music CDs 41
- Using the Taskbar to Control Sound Card Volume 42
- File Manager is Now Explorer 43
- Understanding and Using Long Filenames 44
- Getting to the Windows 95 Control Panel 45
- Clearing the Documents Menu 46
- Adding an Option to the Start Menu 47
- Online Sources of Windows 95 Information 48
- Acquire the Windows 95 Resource Kit 49
- Read and Print the Windows 95 Release Notes 50

GETTING THE MOST FROM WINDOWS 95 ON-LINE HELP

- Starting Windows 95 Online Help 51
- Selecting and Viewing a Help Topic 52
- Understanding Help Topic Links 53
- Moving Back to a Previously Displayed Help Topic 54
- Using Browse Buttons to Traverse Help Topics 55
- Printing a Help Topic 56
- Using the What's This? Option 57
- Using Help to Find Definitions 58
- Annotating (Adding Your Own Notes to) a Help Topic 59
- Locating Information Using Help's Topic Index 60
- Selecting the Help Topics You Desire 61
- Copying a Help Topic to the Clipboard 62
- Finding Information Using Find within Help 63
- Building a Topic Index for Help 64
- Fine-Tuning Help Find Options 65
- Keeping your Help Windows Visible 66
- Customizing the Help Window Font Size 67
- Starting an Operation From Within Help 68
- Placing and Jumping to a Bookmark within Help 69
- Finding Similar Topics within Help 70
- Finding Out About Toolbar Buttons 71

Fundamental Windows Operations

- Using Scroll Bars to View a Document 72
- Working with Pull-Down Menus 73
- Understanding Menu Option Hot Keys 74
- Understanding Sheets, Pages, and Tabs 75
- Highlighting a Dialog Box Option 76
- Using Check boxes to Select Multiple Options 77
- Using Option Buttons 78
- Selecting Items from a Pull-Down List 79
- Using a Text Box to Type in Data 80
- Using the OK, Cancel, and Apply Buttons 81
- Organizing Your Files Using Directories 82
- How Windows 95 Folders Relate to Directories 83
- Creating and Removing Folders 84
- Understanding the Open Dialog Box 85
- Using the Open Dialog Box to Locate and Open Files 86
- Listing Files of a Specific Type Using the Open Dialog Box 87
- Using the Save and Save As Options 88
- Saving a File in a Specific Folder Using the Save In Field 89
- Saving a File to a Specific Format 90
- Quickly Move Up One Level of Folders 91
- Creating Folder within a File-Related Dialog Box 92
- Listing Folder Icons or Details within a File-Related dialog Box 93
- Using the Browse Dialog Box 94
- Understanding Program and Document Windows 95
- Using the Control Menu 96
- Using the New, Open, Save, and Print Icons 97

Windows 95 Desktop Operations

- Understanding the Windows 95 Desktop 98
- Tracking a Large Number of Programs on the Taskbar 99
- Making the Taskbar Wider 100
- Arranging Icons on the Desktop 101
- Lining Up Icons on the Desktop 102
- Insuring the Taskbar is Always Visible 103
- Hiding the Taskbar After Each use 104
- Displaying or Hiding the Taskbar Clock 105
- Controlling the Size of Start Menu Options 106
- Understanding and Creating Shortcuts 107
- Copying Objects Using Copy and Paste 108
- Moving Objects Using Cut and Paste 109
- Using Drag and Drop to Move and Copy Objects 110
- Using Drag and Drop Printing 111
- Creating Your Own Folders 112
- Organizing your Folders Using Subfolders 113
- Renaming a Folder 114
- Understanding Desktop Properties 115
- Installing a Screen Saver 116
- Password Protecting your Screen Saver 117
- Customizing your Screen Saver Settings 118
- Using a Color Scheme to Control Desktop Colors 119
- Assigning a Specific Color to a Desktop Item 120
- Assigning a Specific Font to a Desktop Item 121
- Creating a Custom Color 122
- Saving Your Color Scheme 123
- Assigning a Pattern to the Desktop 124
- Assigning a Wallpaper to the Desktop 125
- Assigning a Graphic to the Desktop using a New Bitmap 126
- Understanding and Using Energy Star Features 127
- Using Drag and Drop to add a Program to the Start menu 128
- Using Drag and Drop to Delete a File or Folder 129
- Recovering Files and Folders from the Recycle Bin 130
- Using Drag and Drop to Restore a Specific File or Folder 131
- Removing a Specific File or Folder from the Recycle Bin 132
- Emptying (Flushing) the Recycle Bin 133
- Using the Properties Menu to Undo a Delete Operation 134
- Using Alt-Tab to Select a Running Program 135
- Using **Ctrl-Esc** to Access the Start Menu 136
- Changing the Number of Colors Your Monitor Displays 137
- Changing Your Screen Resolution 138
- Changing Your Screen Font Size 139
- Changing Your Video Card or Monitor Type ... 140
- Displaying the Day and Date 141

Changing Your System's Date or Time 142
Changing the Time Zone 143

WINDOWS 95 AND MS-DOS

Windows 95 Replaces MS-DOS 144
Opening an MS-DOS Window 145
Sizing an MS-DOS Window 146
Closing an MS-DOS Window 147
Running an MS-DOS Program 148
Some MS-DOS Programs May Not Run 149
Starting Your Computer in MS-DOS Mode 150
How Windows 95 Uses AUTOEXEC.BAT 151
How Windows 95 Uses CONFIG.SYS 152
Using the MS-DOS Window Toolbar 153
Controlling the Font Size in an MS-DOS
  Window 154
Copying Text from an MS-DOS
  Window to the Clipboard 155
Pasting Text into an MS-DOS Window 156
The Properties Sheet Replaces the PIF Editor . 157
Controlling an MS-DOS-based
  Program's Command Line 158
Controlling an MS-DOS-Based
  Program's Working Directory 159
Running a Batch File Immediately Before
  an MS-DOS—Based Program 160
Using a Shortcut Key to Activate an
  MS-DOS- Based Program 161
Controlling an MS-DOS-Based
  Program's Window 162
Changing an MS-DOS-based Program's
  Icon 163
Preventing an MS-DOS-Based Program
  from Knowing It's Running within
  Windows 164
Suggesting that an MS-DOS-Based
  Program Run in MS-DOS Mode 165
Controlling a Program's
  AUTOEXEC.BAT and
  CONFIG.SYS Settings 166
Controlling an MS-DOS-Based
  Program's Font 167
How MS-DOS-Based Memory
  Management Differs from
  Windows 95 168
Controlling an MS-DOS-Based Program's
  Conventional Memory 169
Controlling an MS-DOS-Based Program's
  Expanded Memory 170
Controlling an MS-DOS-Based Program's
  Extended Memory 171

Controlling an MS-DOS-Based Program's
  DPMI Memory 172
Controlling an MS-DOS Program's Screen
  and Window Usage 173
Improving an MS-DOS-Based Program's
  Video Output 174
Controlling Screen Saver Operations for
  MS-DOS Programs 175
Suspending or Allowing MS-DOS Programs
  in the Background 176
Using Idle Sensitivity to Improve System
  or Program Responsiveness 177
Controlling Mouse Operations in an
  MS-DOS-Based Window 178
Controlling Termination of an
  MS-DOS-Based Program 179
Controlling Windows Shortcut Keys for
  an MS-DOS-Based Program 180
Windows 95 Does Not Use the
  Command Path 181
MS-DOS-Based Windows Support
  Long Filenames 182
Exchanging Files with Non-Windows 95
  Users 183
Starting Your Computer to a
  Non-Windows 95 Prompt 184
Logging Your System Startup Using
  BOOTLOG.TXT 185
Starting Your System in Safe Mode 186
Step-by-step Confirmation of Your
  System Startup 187
Starting Your System to a Command
  Prompt 188
You No Longer Need to Use SmartDrive 189
Windows 95 May Load Old TSR Programs
  During Startup 190
Understanding IO.SYS and MSDOS.SYS 191
Default System Settings in IO.SYS 192
Understanding and Using File Entries
  in MSDOS.SYS 193
Can't Find an MS-DOS Command? Try
  C:\WINDOWS\COMMAND 194
Finding Your Old System Files 195
Moving Up Multiple Directory Levels
  Using the CD Command 196

USING THE WINDOWS 95 CONTROL PANEL

Why You Need to Customize 197
Understanding Control Panel Icons 198
Installing New Hardware 199
Using the Add New Hardware Wizard 200

Installing and Removing Software 201
Understanding the Differences between the Windows 95 Setup Options 202
Adding and Removing Windows 95 Components 203
Viewing Details about a Component 204
Creating a Startup Disk 205
Understanding Apply Versus OK 206
Using the Control Panel to Set the Date-and-Time 207
Using the Control Panel for Screen Display Settings 208
Understanding the Accessibility Options 209
Understanding and Using StickyKeys 210
Understanding and Using Filter Keys 211
Understanding and Using ToggleKeys 212
Understanding and Using SoundSentry .. 213
Understanding and Using ShowSounds ... 214
Controlling Display Screen Contrast 215
Understanding and Using MouseKeys 216
Understanding and Using SerialKey Devices 217
Controlling Accessibility Option Settings 218
Understanding Fonts 219
Viewing and Printing a Font Sample 220
Understanding Font Point Sizes 221
Adding Fonts 222
Removing Fonts 223
Understanding TrueType Fonts 224
Reducing Clutter in the Font Window 225
Listing Fonts by Similarity 226
Controlling Joystick Settings 227
Controlling Your Keyboard's Responsiveness 228
Controlling the Text Cursor Blink Rate .. 229
Understanding and Using Keyboard Languages 230
Adding and Removing Keyboard Languages 231
Switching Between Keyboard Languages .. 232
Selecting Your Keyboard Type 233
Customizing Modem Settings 234
Adding and Removing a Modem 235
Controlling Modem Properties 236
Understanding Modem Speed 237

Understanding Data Connection Preferences 238
Understanding and Using Modem Call Preference Settings 239
Understanding How a Modem's UART Affects Performance 240
Controlling UART Settings 241
Understanding Advanced Modem Settings 242
Understanding Modem Dialing Properties 243
Creating a Dialing Scheme 244
Using Your Calling Card for Modem Calls 245
Customizing Your Mouse Settings 246
Switching Between a Right- and Left-Handed Mouse 247
Controlling Your Mouse Double-Click Speed 248
Customizing the Mouse Pointer 249
Using a Predefined Mouse Pointer Scheme 250
Changing a Specific Pointer 251
Controlling Mouse Pointer Motion 252
Changing Your Mouse Type 253
Understanding How Windows 95 Uses Passwords 254
Changing Your Windows Password 255
Controlling Other Passwords 256
Restricting Remote Administration 257
Understanding and Controlling User Profiles 258
Understanding Power Management 259
Controlling Your PC's Power Management Settings 260
Determining Your Notebook Computer's Battery Life 261
Understanding and Using the Start menu Suspend Command 262
Adding, Customizing, and Removing Printers 263
Adding a Printer 264
Removing a Printer Driver 265
Creating a Printer Shortcut on the Desktop 266
Viewing Printer Properties 267
Understanding and Using Separator Pages 268
Viewing and Customizing Printer Details 269

Table of Contents

Adding and Deleting Printer Ports 270
Capturing and Releasing a Printer Port 271
Sharing Your Printer Across the
  Network 272
Understanding Print Spooling 273
Understanding and Using Spool
  Settings 274
Controlling Port Settings 275
Viewing a Printer's Current Jobs 276
Pausing a Printer 277
Purging Print Jobs 278
Pausing or Canceling a Specific Job's
  Printing 279
Changing the Order of Print Jobs 280
Selecting a Default Printer 281
Viewing the Number of Jobs on
  Each Printer 282
Understanding Regional Settings 283
Controlling Numeric Formats 284
Controlling Currency Formats 285
Controlling Time Formats 286
Controlling Date Formats 287
Understanding Sounds and Windows
  Events 288
Previewing Event Sounds 289
Using Predefined Sound Schemes 290
Assigning Sounds to an Event 291
Recording Your Own Sounds for
  Windows Events 292
Understanding ODBC 293
Understanding ODBC Drivers 294
Displaying Specifics About an
  ODBC Driver 295
Adding an ODBC Driver 296
Understanding ODBC Data Sources 297
Setting Up an ODBC Data Source 298
Adding an ODBC Data Source 299
Controlling ODBC Data Source
  Options 300
Displaying General System Information .. 301
Understanding the Control Panel
  Device Manager 302
Controlling the Device Manager View 303
Locating Device Specifics 304
Printing the Device Manager Summary ... 305
Removing a Device From Your
  Device List 306
Understanding Hardware Profiles 307

Creating Your Own Hardware Profile 308
Renaming and Deleting Hardware
  Profiles 309
Displaying System Performance
  Settings 310
Understanding the Windows 95
  File System 311
Customizing the Hard-Disk File System . 312
Customizing the CD-ROM File System .. 313
Trouble Shooting the Windows 95
  File System 314
Customizing Graphics Acceleration 315
Understanding Virtual Memory 316
Understanding Swapping and Paging 317
Controlling Windows 95 Virtual
  Memory 318

USING THE WINDOWS 95 EXPLORER

Understanding the Windows Explorer 319
The Explorer Window Consists of
  Two Parts 320
Use Folders to Improve Your File
  Organization 321
Scrolling Through the Folder List and
  Opening a Folder 322
Expanding and Collapsing a Folder 323
Recognizing File Types Using Icons 324
Using the File Explorer's Toolbar 325
Using the File Explorer's Status Bar 326
Running a Program from Explorer 327
Associating a Program with a File Type ... 328
Deleting a File or Folder 329
Renaming a File or Folder 330
Selecting Two or More Successive
  Files for an Operation 331
Selecting Two or More Dispersed
  Files for an Operation 332
Selecting All the Files in a Folder 333
Inverting a File Selection 334
Displaying Properties for a File or
  Folder 335
Understanding Read-only Files 336
Understanding Hidden Files 337
Understanding System Files 338
Using a File's Archive Property 339
Creating a New Folder 340
Creating a New Shortcut 341
Using Cut-and-Paste Operations to
  Move a File 342

Using Copy and Paste Operations to
    Copy a File 343
Moving and Copying with the Mouse 344
Undoing a File Operation 345
Pasting a Shortcut 346
Using the Explorer's Large and
    Small Icon Display 347
Displaying a Folder's Contents Lists
    and Details 348
Displaying Details about a File's
    Attributes 349
Sorting a Folder's Contents 350
Refreshing an Explorer Window 351
Controlling Which Hidden Files the
    Explorer Displays 352
Understanding Complete Pathnames 353
Displaying the Complete MS-DOS
    Pathname in the Title Bar 354
Displaying File Types (Extensions) 355
Understanding and Viewing Registered
    File Types 356
Registering a New File Type 357
Removing a Registered File Type 358
Finding a File or Folder 359
Finding a File or Folder by Name 360
Using a Found File 361
Finding a File or Folder by Date 362
Finding a File or Folder by Content 363
Finding a File or Folder by Size 364
Performing Case-Sensitive Search
    Operations 365
Mapping to a Network Drive 366
Creating a Persistent Connection 367
Disconnecting from a Network Drive 368
Going to a Specific Folder or File 369
Opening Multiple Viewer Windows 370
Performing a Drag and Drop File
    Copy Operation 371
Performing a Drag and Drop File Move
    Operation 372
Performing a Drag and Drop Print
    Operation 373

USING WINDOWS 95 SYSTEM TOOLS

Understanding the Windows 95
    System Tools 374
Understanding Your Need to Backup Files 375
Invest in a Tape Drive 376
Understanding a Full-System Backup 377

Understanding Backup File Sets 378
Selecting Files for a Backup File Set 379
Saving Your File and Folder Selections to
    a Backup File Set 380
Understanding and Using File Filtering .. 381
Understanding and Performing
    Drag and Drop Backup Operations . 382
Controlling Backup's Drag and Drop
    Settings 383
Understanding Incremental Backup
    Operations 384
Understanding Backup Verification 385
Compressing Your Backup Files Saves
    Tape or Floppy Disk Space 386
Controlling Tape-Based Backups 387
Restoring Files from a Previous Backup .. 388
Restoring Files to Their Original
    Locations 389
Restoring Files to a New Location 390
Verifying a File Restore Operation 391
Controlling File Overwrite Operations
    During a Restore 392
Comparing Files to a Backup Set 393
Fragmented Disks Decrease Your
    System Performance 394
Defragment Your Disk Using Disk
    Defragmenter 395
Pausing, Resuming, or Ending Disk
    Defragmenter 396
Displaying Details of Your Disk's
    Fragmentation 397
Understanding Disk Defragmenter's
    Detailed Display 398
Understanding and Using Disk
    Defragmenter's Advanced Settings ... 399
Understanding Disk Compression 400
How Drive Compression Really Works ... 401
Compressing a Floppy Disk for Practice . 402
Always Back Up Your Disk Before
    You Compress 403
Viewing How Much Disk Space
    Compression Your Drive Gives
    You 404
Uncompressing a Drive 405
Mounting and Dismounting a
    Compressed Drive 406
Controlling Automatic Compressed
    Disk Mounting 407
Compressing Your Entire Hard
    Drive 408

Table of Contents

Compressing Part of Your Drive 409
Deleting a Compressed Drive 410
Viewing a Disk's Compression Properties 411
Adjusting the Free Space on a Compressed Drive 412
Understanding and Fine-Tuning Compression Ratios 413
Hiding or Displaying Your Host Drive 414
Formatting a Compressed Drive 415
Changing a Host Drive's Drive Letter 416
Looking Behind-the-Scenes with DriveSpace 417
Understanding and Repairing Inbox Error 418
Understanding System Resources and the Resource Meter 419
Understanding the Resource Monitor's Output 420
Understanding and Repairing Disk Errors 421
Using ScanDisk's Standard Check 422
Using ScanDisk's Thorough Check 423
Controlling ScanDisk's Thorough Check Surface Scan 424
Controlling Whether or Not ScanDisk Automatically Corrects Errors 425
Understanding and Using ScanDisk's Advanced Options 426
Using ScanDisk's Error Log 427
Fixing Lost File Fragments 428
Fixing Cross-Linked Files 429

USING WINDOWS 95 FAX AND E-MAIL CAPABILITIES

Faxing With Windows 95 430
Using the Fax Cover Page Editor 431
Using an Existing Fax Cover Sheet 432
Customizing an Existing Fax Cover Sheet 433
Creating a New Fax Cover Sheet 434
Using the Fax Cover Page Drawing Toolbar 435
Placing a Text Object on a Fax Cover Sheet 436
Using Pre-defined Text Frames 437
Controlling a Text Frame's Font 438
Aligning Text within Text Frames 439

Using Grid Lines to Align Objects 440
Placing a Graphics Object on a Fax Cover Sheet 441
Selecting and Working with Fax Cover Sheet Objects 442
Sending a Fax Cover Sheet Object to the Front or Back 443
Inserting Other Fax Cover Sheet Objects 444
Using Lines, Fills, and Colors on a Fax Cover Sheet 445
Aligning Fax Cover Sheet Objects 446
Duplicating Fax Cover Sheet Objects 447
Using the Fax Cover Sheet Paste Board 448
Sending a Fax 449
Using Fax Profiles 450
Creating a Fax Profile 451
Using a Calling Card 452
Disabling Call Waiting 453
Creating an Address Book Entry 454
Creating a Fax-based Address Book Entry 455
Creating an Internet-based Address Book Entry 456
Creating a Microsoft Network-based Address Book Entry 457
Creating a Local Area Network-based Address Book Entry 458
Creating an Address Book Entry for Other Online Services 459
Changing an Address Book Entry 460
Finding an Address Book Entry 461
Controlling Fax Options 462
Understanding Fax Security 463
Using Key Security 464
Creating and Managing Fax Security Keys 465
Attaching a File to Your Fax 466
Retrieving a Fax 467
Receiving a Fax 468
Understanding Microsoft Exchange 469
Controlling Microsoft Exchange Services 470
Working with Microsoft Exchange Messages and Folders 471
Understanding Message Icons 472
Composing a Mail Message 473

Inserting a File into a Message 474
Attaching a File to a Message 475
Inserting or Attaching an Existing
    Message Within a Message 476
Inserting an Object into a Message 477
Using the Mail Composition Toolbar 478
Customizing the Microsoft Exchange
    Toolbar 479
Working with Message Properties 480
Working with the Current Message 481
Composing a Fax within Microsoft
    Exchange 482
Reading New Mail 483
Replying to a Mail Message 484
Forwarding a Mail Message 485
Finding a Mail Message 486
Performing an Advanced Message
    Search 487
Viewing Outgoing Faxes 488
Controlling Outgoing Faxes 489
Controlling When Microsoft Exchange
    Sends a Fax 490
Controlling a Fax Format 491
Specifying Fax Redial Properties 492
Defining User Fax Properties 493
Customizing Microsoft Exchange
    Options 494
Using Microsoft Exchange Remotely 495
Retrieving Mail Remotely 496
Sending Mail from a Remote Computer . 497
Using the Remote Mail Toolbar 498
Scheduling Remote Mail Operations 499
Changing Exchange's Windows 500
Modifying Microsoft Exchange's
    Columns 501
Sorting a Folder's Contents 502
Using the Control Panel to Customize
    Microsoft Exchange 503
Using Explorer's Send To Option 504
Placing Phone Calls Using the Phone
    Dialer 505
Manually Dialing a Phone Number 506
Creating a Speed-Dial Entry 507
Specifying the Phone Dialer Device 508
Using a Phone Dialer Profile 509
Logging Calls Using Phone Dialer 510
Controlling the Phone Dialer Logs 511
Purging the Phone Dialer Log 512

USING WINDOWS 95 NOTEBOOK COMPUTER SUPPORT

Understanding Windows 95's Notebook
    Support 513
Managing Files Using Briefcase 514
Test Driving the Briefcase 515
Updating a Specific File 516
Splitting a File from an Original 517
Briefcase Uses Date and Time Stamps
    Only 518
Using Briefcase's Toolbar 519
Understanding Deferred Printing 520
Using Deferred Printing on Your
    Desktop 521
Understanding Docking 522
Windows 95 Docking Detection 523
Exchanging Files Using a Direct Cable
    Connection 524
Understanding Host and Guest
    Connections 525
Setting Up a Guest Computer 526
Setting Up a Host Computer 527
Understanding PCMCIA or PC Cards 528
Displaying the Taskbar's PC Card
    Indicator 529
Installing a PC Card Device 530
Installing a PC Card for Use 531
Removing a PC Card 532
Controlling 32-Bit PC Card Support 533
Supporting Flash Memory 533
Supporting SRAM Memory Cards 534
Supporting SRAM Memory Cards 535
Understanding PC Card Sound Effects ... 536

USING WINDOWS 95 MULTIMEDIA SUPPORT

Understanding Windows 95 Multimedia
    Support 537
Using Control Panel Multimedia
    Settings 538
Controlling Speaker Volume and the
    Taskbar Volume Icon 539
Controlling Sound Card Recording 540
Understanding Digital Audio 541
Creating a Custom Audio Setting 542
Controlling the Default Video Size 543
Understanding MIDI 544
Creating a Custom MIDI Setting 545
Understanding Audio CD 546
Customizing Advanced Multimedia

Table of Contents

Settings 547
Customizing a Multimedia Driver 548
Understanding Video and Audio Codecs . 549
Prioritizing Video and Audio odecs 550
Using the Media Player 551
Opening a Media File 552
Viewing Tracks, Time, or Frames 553
Selecting a Media Object 554
Customizing Media Player Options 555
Customizing Device Properties 556
Using the Sound Recorder 557
Recording and Saving an Audio File 558
Controlling Sound Formats 559
Editing a Recording 560
Inserting and Mixing Sound Files 561
Using Special Effects with a Recording ... 562
Using the Windows 95 Volume Control .. 563
Controlling a Device's Balance 564
Selecting Volume Control's Devices 565
Customizing Advanced Volume
    Control Settings 566
Using the CD Player 567
Understanding Audio CD Play Lists 568
Creating a Play List 569
Using the CD Player Toolbar 570
Viewing Audio CD Information 571
Controlling How Tracks Play 572
Finding a Specific Audio CD Song 573
Customizing the CD Player Preferences . 574

USING WINDOWS 95 ACCESSORY PROGRAMS

Understanding the Windows 95
    Accessories 575
Windows 3.1 Accessory Programs 576
Using the Standard Calculator 577
Performing a Simple Calculation 578
Using the Scientific Calculator 579
Accessing Calculator Buttons from the
    Keyboard 580
Performing Simple Statistics 581
Using the Clipboard Viewer 582
Changing the Clipboard Viewer's
    Display 583
Saving the Clipboard Contents 584
Understanding Windows 95 Games 585
How to Play FreeCell 586
Starting a FreeCell Game 587
FreeCell Hints 588
Controlling FreeCell Options 589
How to Play Hearts 590
Playing Network or Local Hearts 591
Getting Started With Hearts 592
Playing a Hand 593
Shooting the Moon 594
Customizing Hearts Options 595
How to Play Minesweeper 596
Marking the Mines 597
Selecting Your Minesweeper Level 598
Showing Off Your Minesweeper Scores 599
Drawing with the Paint Accessory 600
Understanding Paint's Tools 601
Drawing Straight Lines within Paint 602
Drawing Curved Lines within Paint 603
Drawing Rectangles and Squares within
    Paint 604
Selecting Paint's Foreground and
    Background Colors 605
Drawing Filled Shapes with Paint 606
Drawing Circles and Ovals within Paint . 607
Drawing a Polygon within Paint 608
Filling a Shape with a Specific Color 609
Undoing an Operation within Paint 610
Using Paint's Pencil for Detailed Drawing 611
Painting with Paint's Brush Tool 612
Using Paint's Eraser 613
Use Paint's Color Picker 614
Zooming In Using Paint's Magnifying
    Glass 615
Using Paint's Airbrush 616
Using Paint's Text Tool 617
Saving and Printing Your Image 618
Using Your Image for Wallpaper 619
Controlling Fonts 620
Selecting Objects for Cut and Paste
    Operations 621
Copying Objects to or From a File 622
Zooming In and Out Using Paint's
    Zoom Menu 623
Flipping or Rotating a Paint Image 624
Stretching and Skewing a Paint Image 625
Changing a Paint Image's Attributes 626
Editing Paint's Color Palette 627
Using the Grid to Align Objects in
    Paint 628

Using the WordPad Accessory	629
Creating, Printing, and Saving a WordPad Document	630
Only Press Enter to Separate Paragraphs	631
Controlling Paragraph Alignment	632
Controlling Paragraph Indentation	633
Using the Bold, Italics, or Underline Attribute	634
Controlling the Current Font	635
Finding Text within a Large Document	636
Replacing Text Throughout a WordPad Document	637
Inserting the Date and Time Into a WordPad Document	638
Selecting Text within a WordPad Document	639
Moving or Copying Text within a WordPad Document	640
Inserting an Object into a WordPad Document	641
Using Bullets within a WordPad Document	642
Controlling Tab Stops	643
Using WordPad's Toolbar	644
Using WordPad's Format Bar	645
Using WordPad's Ruler	646
Controlling WordPad Options	647
Using WordPad's Ruler to Set Tabs	648
Previewing a Document Before You Print It	649
Controlling Your Document's Page Attributes	650
Understanding Telecommunications	651
Configuring an Existing Connection	652
Configuring a New Connection	653
Understanding Data Communication Settings	654
Establishing Your Connections Data Communication Settings	655
Understanding Terminal Emulation	656
Controlling Your Connection's ASCII Control	657
Using File Transfer Protocols	658
Transferring a File from a Remote Computer	659
Transferring a File to a Remote Computer	660
Sending a Text File to a Remote Computer	661
Capturing Text to a File or Printer	662
Controlling the Size of HyperTerminal's Text Buffer	663
Displaying and Using HyperTerminal's Toolbar	664
Understanding the Internet	665
Online Services and the Internet	666

WINDOWS 95, THE INTERNET, AND THE WORLD WIDE WEB

Windows 95 and the Internet	667
You Still Need an Internet Provider	668
Understanding PPP and SLIP Connections	669
Use HyperTerminal to Access a Shell-Based Account	670
Understanding the World Wide Web	671
You Need a Web Browser	672
Preparing Your System to Access the Internet	673
Understanding IP Addresses	674
Understanding Domain Names	675
Configuring Your TCP/IP Connection's Domain Name Server	676
Specifying Your Computer's IP Address	677
Understanding and Configuring WINS	678
Telling Windows 95 About Your Provider	679
Installing SLIP Support Software	680
Configuring Your Provider's Properties	681
Dialing Your Provider	682
Creating a SLIP Script	683
Using Ping to Test a Site's Accessibility	684
Tracing a Connection's Route Using Tracert	685
Controlling Address Resolution Using ARP	686
Displaying TCP/IP Statistics Using Netstat	687
Control Network Routing Tables by Using Route	688
Using Telnet to Move from One Computer to Another	689
Visit These Interesting Telnet Sites	690
Understanding File Transfers Using FTP	691
Visit These Interesting FTP Sites	692

Table of Contents

Use FTP to Download a Web Browser 693
Using a Web Browser 694
Visit These Interesting Web Sites 695
Displaying TCP/IP Connections
  Using Winipcfg 696
Download a Windows-based FTP
  Program 697
Web Sites that Discuss Windows 95 698
Understanding Internet Relay Chat 699
Understanding Newsgroups 700
Visit These Newsgroups 701
Understanding Mailing Lists 702
Traversing the Internet Using Gopher 703
Visit These Gopher Sites 704
Traversing the Internet Using WAIS 705
Visit These WAIS Sites 706
Download a Windows-based Ping
  Program 707
Download a Windows-based Telnet
  Program 708
Download a Windows-based Phone
  Program 709
Download a JPEG Viewer 710
Visit Some Cool Sites for JPEG Images .. 711
Understanding Online Services 712
Introducing the Microsoft Network
  (MSN) 713
Installing the Microsoft Network
  Software 714
Microsoft Network's Requirements 715
Accessing the Microsoft Network 716
Registering with MSN for the First
  Time 717
Locating a Local Microsoft Network
  Number 718
Welcome to MSN Central 719
Traversing MSN 720
MSN's Toolbar Buttons 721
MSN's Go To Feature 722
Using Shortcuts for Quicker Access 723
MSN Today 724
The MSN Calendar of Events 725
Visiting Favorite Places 726
Adding to your Favorite Places 727
Getting an Explorer View of MSN 728
Accessing MSN News 729
Moving Around MSN News 730

Getting Member Assistance 731
Using Microsoft Network Mail 732
Using the Small Office Home Office
  (SOHO) Site 733
Accessing MSN's Categories 734
Visiting MSN Forums 735
Reading and Writing Messages 736
Participating in Chat Sessions 737
Using the Suggestion Box 738
Visit an Interesting Computer
  Information Forum 739
Visit a Windows 95 Forum 740
Check out the Home and Family Forum . 741
Play in the Sports Forum 742
Learn from the Science and Technology
  Forum 743
Get in Shape with the Health and
  Fitness Forum 744

USING WINDOWS 95 NETWORKING CAPABILITIES

Relax with the Arts and Entertainment
  Forum 745
Manage your Money in the Business and
  Finance Forum 746
Reading MSN Computing 747
Using the MSN-Internet Connection 748
Browsing the Web with MSN 749
Accessing Internet Newsgroups 750
Sending and Receiving Internet E-mail .. 751
Logging Off MSN 752
Understanding Windows 95 Network
  Support 753
Understanding Terms is Your Key
  to Mastering Networks 754
You Start With a Network Organization . 755
Next You Choose a Network Technology 756
The Network Adapter is Your PC's
  Network Card 757
Software Defines Your Network
  Interface 758
Understanding Clients and Servers 759
TCP/IP is the Language of the Internet . 760
NetBEUI is Backwards Compatible 761
Windows 95 Dial-Up Networking 762
Using Windows 95 Direct Cable
  Connect Networking 763
NFS is Sun's Unix-based Network
  File System 764

IPX/SPX is Novell-Compatible 765
SNMP is Simple Network Management
    Protocol 766
NDIS is Network Driver Interface
    Specification 767
ODI is Open Datalink Interface 768
Understanding Peer-to-Peer Networking 769
UNC Stands for Universal Naming
    Conventional 770
You Can Share Files, Folders, Printers,
    and Modems 771
Understanding Network Security 772
Understanding Remote System
    Administration 773
Viewing Current Network Components . 774
Adding a Network Component 775
Adding a Network Adapter 776
Identifying Your PC to the Network 777
Defining Your PC Share Access 778
Allowing File and Printer Sharing 779
Removing a Network Component 780
Customizing a Network Component's
    Properties 781
To Access the Network, You Must
    First Log in 782
Traversing Your Network Neighborhood . 783
Accessing a Shared Printer 784
Access a Shared Folder 785
Controlling Access to a Shared
    Folder or Printer 786
Changing a Folder or Printer's
    Password 787
Assigning a Drive Letter to a Network
    Computer or Folder 788
Specifying a Consistent Connection 789
Ending Shared Access to a Folder 790
Changing Your Network Password 791

WINDOWS 95 ADVANCED CONCEPTS AND OPERATIONS

Using Dial-Up Networking 792
Creating a Network Server 793
Monitoring Network Resources Using
    Net Watcher 794
Understanding Network Resource Use 795
Disconnecting Remote Users Using
    Net Watcher 796
Using the Net Watcher Toolbar 797
Viewing Files Opened by Network
    Users 798

Logging Off the Network 799
Using the Windows 3.1 Program
    Manager 800
Running the Windows 3.1 File Manager 801
Using the Windows 3.1 Task Manager 802
Understanding ECP and EPP 803
Providing Support for ECP and EPP
    Printers 804
Spooling EMF Files Improves Printer
    Performance 805
Understanding DOS-based Program
    Spooling 806
Understanding Windows 95 VFAT 807
Understanding VCACHE 808
Improving VCACHE Performance for
    Different CD-ROM Drive Types 809
Windows 95 Does Not Require
    MSCDEX 810
Understanding Swapping 811
Forcing a Permanent Swap File 812
Delete Windows 3.1 Permanent
    Swap File 813
Understanding Disk Partitioning 814
Still use FDISK To Partition a Disk 815
Formatting a Disk Within Windows 95 .. 816
Understanding Quick View 817
Viewing a File Using Quick View 818
Opening a Document That Has
    No Association 819
Understanding and Working with Scraps 820
Pasting a Scrap By Dragging a Document
    on to the Taskbar 821
Understanding 32-bit and 16-bit
    Programs 822
Understanding LFNBK 823
Understanding the Start Command 824
Using the Start Command to Control the
    Order in Which Windows 95 Runs
    Related Programs 825
Understanding Multitasking 826
Windows 95 Uses Preemptive
    Multitasking 827
Understanding Multithreaded
    Applications 828
How Recognize a File Copy or Move
    Operation 829
Use Esc to Cancel a Move or Copy
    Operation 830

Table of Contents

To Open a File Folder Using the Same Window, Use Ctrl-Double Click 831
Use a Lasso to Select Multiple Files and Folders 832
Rename a Selected File or Folder Easily by Pressing F2 833
All Those LNK Files Are Shortcuts 834
Viewing Recently Used Documents within a Folder 835
Using Shift-Del to Delete a File and Bypass the Recycle Bin 836
Using Command-Line Arguments to Customize Explorer 837
Use the Windows System Key to Access the Start Menu 838
Quickly Displaying a Disk's Use 839
Within Explorer, Press Backspace to Move Up One Level from an Open File 840
Shutting Down with One Keystroke 841
Closing Multiple Folders in One Step 842
Opening a Folder Branch within Explorer 843
Determining the Number of Files in a Folder 844
Quickly Selecting All But a Few Explorer Files 845
Quickly Exploring My Computer 846
Understanding Where Windows 95 Places Files 847
Viewing the Windows 95 Setup File 848
How Legacy Hardware Differs from Legacy Hardware 849
Viewing Detected Hardware 850
Viewing the Windows 95 Startup Process 851
Understanding Object Linking and Embedding 852
Using Object Embedding 853
Using Object Linking 854
When to Link or Embed an Object 855
How OLE Works 856
Creating a New Object from a File 857
Understanding VxD Device Drivers 858
Understanding 16-based Drivers 859
Determining the Device Drivers Your System is Using 860
What to Do When Windows 95 is Using 16-Bit Drivers 861
Understanding the System Monitor 862
Understanding the Windows 95 Kernel ... 863
Monitoring the Windows 95 File System 864
Improving File System Measurements 865
Monitoring Windows 95 Memory Management 866
Optimizing Memory Management Measurements 867
Changing System Monitor Graph Types 868
Changing a Measurement's Chart Options 869
Changing the System Monitor's Chart Interval 870
Monitoring a Remote Computer 871
Using the System Monitor Toolbar 872
Looking for Bottlenecks 873
Improving Paging Performance 874
Why Adding Memory Improves System Performance 875
Understanding the Windows 95 Registry 876
Windows 95 Still Updates .INI Files for Compatibility 877
When to Edit the Windows Registry 878
Starting the Windows 95 Registry Editor 879
Printing a Copy of Your Registry's Contents 880
Understanding the Basic Registry Entries 881
Taking a Close Look at HKEY_LOCAL_MACHINE 882
Editing a Registry Entry's Binary Value 883
Editing a Registry Entry's String Value 884
Taking a Close Look at HKEY_LOCAL_MACHINE \hardware 885
Taking a Close Look at HKEY_LOCAL_MACHINE \Config 886
Taking a Close Look at HKEY_LOCAL_MACHINE \Enum 887
Taking a Close Look at the

HKEY_LOCAL_MACHINE
\Network 888
Taking a Close Look at
HKEY_LOCAL_MACHINE
\Software 889
Taking a Close Look at
HKEY_LOCAL_MACHINE
\System 890
Taking a Close Look at
HKEY_LOCAL_MACHINE
\hardware 891
Taking a Close Look at
HKEY_CLASSES_ROOT 892
Taking a Close Look at
HKEY_CURRENT_USER 893
Taking a Close Look at
HKEY_USERS 894
Taking a Close Look at
HKEY_CURRENT_CONFIG 895
Taking a Close Look at
HKEY_DYN_DATA 896
Entries You May Actually Edit 897
Understanding REGEDIT
Command-Line Options..................... 898
Using the Register Editor to Remove
the Network 899
Exporting Your Registry Database 900
Viewing an Exported Registry Database . 901
Importing Your Registry Database 902
Understanding Registry Files 903
Backing Up and Restoring Your
Registry Database 904
Finding a Registry Entry or Value 905
Renaming a Registry Entry 906
Deleting a Registry Entry 907
Adding a Registry Entry 908
Not Sure About a File Type?
See HKEY_CLASSES_ROOT 909
Changing the Label Windows Uses
to Reference an Event 910
Using the Registry to Control Your
Keyboard's Responsiveness 911
Using the Registry to Control the
Cursor Blink Rate 912
Using the Registry to Control the
Screen Saver Interval 913
Using the Registry to Control
Screen Saver Password Protection 914
Using the Registry to Tile or Center
Wall Paper 915

Using the Registry to Specify the
Wall Paper You Desire 916
Using the Registry to Control
Video Resolution 917
Using the Registry to Display Installed
Device Drivers 918
Using the Registry to List the
Windows 95 32-Bit Virtual Drivers. 919
Understanding the Relationship Between
HKEY_CURRENT_CONFIG
and Others 920
Using the Registry to Change Your
Computer Name 921
Working with Accessory Program
Settings 921
Speeding Up Menu Operations 922
Turn Off Animated Window Display....... 923
Be Aware of WIN.INI 924
Updating the Registry without
Rebooting 925
Removing the Arrow From Shortcut
Icons 926
Working with Long Filenames From
the Command Line 927
Adding Printers to the Start Menu 928
Restart only Windows When You
Reboot, Not Your System 929
Isolating an Error 930
Using DETCRASH.LOG 931
Disabling 32-bit Disk Access 932
Starting Windows 95 without Network
Support... 933
Preventing Windows 95 Use of the
ROM Breakpoint 934
Insuring BIOS-based Disk
Operations 935
Preventing Windows 95
Video-Adapter Memory Use 936
Use MSD to Troubleshoot
Hardware 937
Shortcut Keys for the Microsoft
Keyboard 938
Great Resources for the Visually
Impaired 939
A Good Source for Device Driver
Files 940
Understanding the System Policy
Editor 941
Running the System Policy Editor 942
Turning Off the Network

Table of Contents

Neighborhood 943
Removing the Taskbar from the
  Settings Menu 944
Disabling the Save Settings at Exit 945
Appreciating the Impact of
  Energy-Compliant Hardware 946
Is Your Device Driver Using
  Real-Mode or 32-Bit Mode? 947
Taking a Close Look at Safe Mode
  Drivers 948
Understanding Driver Qualifiers in
  IOS.INI 949
What Drivers did Windows 95
  Load? 950
Why Some Multimedia CDs
  Automatically Run 951
Avoiding Windows Version
  Problems 952
Trouble Shooting a Slow Printer 953
Trouble Shooting Modem
  Operations 954
Editing the MSDOS.SYS File 955
Controlling the Windows 95 Boot
  Delay 956
Turning Off Boot-Key Support 957
Turning Off the Animated
  Windows 95 Logo 958
Directing Windows 95 to Double
  Buffer SCSI Devices 959
Disabling Windows 95 Graphical
  User Interface 960
Controlling the Windows 95
  Boot Menu 961
Controlling the Windows 95 Boot
  Menu Delay 962
Controlling the Boot Menu Default
  Option 963
Controlling Network Software 964
Supporting BootMulti Operations 965
Loading COMMAND.COM or
  DRVSPACE.BIN at the Top of
  640K 966
Controlling Automatic Loading of
  DBLSPACE.BIN 967
Controlling Automatic Loading of
  DRVSPACE.BIN 968
Controlling the Default Operating
  System 969
Controlling the Safe Mode Warning 970
Understanding the MSDOS.SYS
  Path Entries 971
Running Hover!, a Pretty Cool
  Game 972
Demonstrating Microsoft Products 973
Starting Explorer From the
  Command-Line Prompt 974
A Quick Way to Maximize
  DOS-based Memory Use 975
Drag and Drop a File to the
  Command-Line Prompt 976
Defining Your Own Startup Logo 977
Bypassing the Windows 95 Logo 978
Change the Shutdown Messages 979
Removing the Control Panel or
  Printers Option from the
  Start Menu 980
There's More to the Windows 95
  CD-ROM than Windows 95 981
Understanding Font Smoothing 982
Tune Your Start Menus 983
Offer a Reward for Your PC 984
Always Travel with a Startup Disk 985
Finding a Folder that Contains a
  File 986
Avoid Common Extensions 987
Need to Edit Binary Files? Try
  Write or EDIT 988
Working with AU Files 989
Obtain Internet Jump Start 990
Using Internet Jump Start 991
Viewing Wave File Specifics 992
Test Driving Some Cool Video
  Files 993
Viewing AVI File Specifics 994
Previewing an AVI, MIDI, or WAV File .. 995
Revisiting the Pentium Bug 996
Understanding Windows 95 CAB Files 997
Installing Files from CAB Files 998
Renaming Folders and Files within
  Applications 999
Lose the Tilde (~) in Short DOS
  Filenames 1000
Creating a Control Panel Folder
  on the Start Menu 1001

Starting Windows 95   1

Get ready to explore Windows 95, one of the most exciting PC products ever produced. Windows 95 makes you more productive while, at the same time, makes your PC easier to use. If you have not installed Windows 95, you can do so now by performing these steps:

1. If you are installing the CD-ROM version of Windows 95, place the Windows 95 CD into your CD-ROM drive. If you are installing Windows 95 from floppy disks, place the floppy disk labeled Disk 1 into your A: drive or B: drive.
2. Select the Program Manager File menu Run option. Windows will display the Run dialog box.
3. Within the Command line field, type SETUP preceded by the floppy disk or CD-ROM drive letter that contains Windows 95. For example, if you are installing Windows 95 from floppy disks that reside in your A: drive, type A:\SETUP.
4. Click the OK button.
5. Respond to the dialog boxes that the Setup program displays to identify the components you want to install, as well as your hardware configuration. The Windows 95 Setup program will walk you through the installation.

To start Windows 95, simply turn on your PC. After a brief pause, a beep, and some disk whirls, the initial Windows 95 screen shown in Figure 1 will appear.

Note: Your screen may differ from Figure 1 due to the options you selected when you installed Windows 95. Later in this book, you will learn how to install additional Windows 95 components.

Figure 1 *The Windows 95 opening screen.*

What You'll See   2

Now that you've started Windows 95, you may be interested in learning what the Windows 95 opening screen contains. Windows 95 often presents you with a screen that is less cluttered than those you encountered with previous versions of Windows. Figure 1 shows a typical opening screen. At the screen's center, the Welcome window displays a startup tip. The bar across the bottom of the screen is called the Taskbar. You'll learn about the Welcome window and the Taskbar as you read more of this book.

Table 2 briefly describes the purpose of the common screen elements that you'll see on your Windows 95 Desktop. Learn the icons now so that you will recognize them throughout the remainder of this book.

Icon	Element	Description
Start	Start button	Provides instant access to programs and Windows 95 activities.
	My Computer	Provides access to the My Computer window.
	Network Neighborhood	Provides access to the Network Neighborhood window.
	Inbox	Provides access to the Inbox.
	Recycle Bin	Provides access to the Recycle Bin.
	The Microsoft Network	Provides access to Microsoft's online service.

Table 2 Descriptions of the Windows 95 screen elements.

3 The Welcome Window Features

As shown in Figure 1, each time you start Windows 95, a Welcome window appears that gives you hints for using Windows 95. Although the Welcome window tips are much less exhaustive than this book's, you might like to read the tips anyway until you become better acquainted with Windows 95. In addition to reading the Welcome window's hints and definitions, you can access several Windows 95 features that you may want to explore if you are a newcomer to Windows 95. To access these features, you press the command buttons that appear at the Welcome window's right edge. Table 3 describes these Welcome window features.

Feature	Description
Windows Tour	Guides you through a short introduction to Windows 95. You may need your Windows 95 installation CD-ROM or floppy disks to see the tour.
What's New	Gives you an online overview of the new features in Windows 95.
Online Registration	Lets you register your copy of Windows 95 online with Microsoft. To use this feature, you will need a modem.
Product Catalog	Displays online advertisements for other Microsoft products. You may need your Windows 95 installation CD-ROM or floppy disks to view these advertisements.
Next Tip	Lets you read another tip inside the Welcome window.
Close	Closes the Welcome window.

Table 3 The Welcome window features.

Note: *The Online Registration button will not appear in the Welcome window if you have registered your copy of Windows 95 using online registration.*

If you don't want to see the Welcome window each time you start Windows 95, click the check box in the Welcome window's lower-left corner. Tip 38 explains how to resume the startup tips if you later decide that you want them.

4 What's New in Windows 95

Windows 95 provides a new Windows interface and many additional support programs that will change the way you work with your PC. Windows 95 not only makes it easier for you to exploit the power inside your PC more fully, but also improves upon features already available in previous versions of Windows. As soon as you start Windows 95, you will notice the new "look and feel" of the operating environment. Most notably, your Windows Desktop will be less cluttered than it probably was with Windows 3.1. Table 4 briefly describes some of the most important new features you will find in Windows 95.

Feature	Description
Taskbar	Your primary control center for Windows 95 applications.
Long filenames	Lets you use up to 255 characters (including spaces!) for your filenames.
Plug and Play	In many cases, lets Windows 95 automatically detect new hardware that you add, thus making hardware installations easy!
Explorer	Replaces the Windows 3.1 File Manager. Lets you navigate files, windows, folders, and drives. Figure 4.1 shows the Explorer window.
Right-clicking	Displays a context-sensitive, pop-up menu that lets you work with whatever object you right-clicked.
Microsoft Network	An online service, sponsored by Microsoft, that provides e-mail, forums, and Internet access.
Recycle Bin	Holds information you delete, such as files, until you empty it or it overflows. When the Recycle Bin overflows, Windows 95 permanently deletes the earliest chronologically dated files to make room for new deleted files.
My Computer	Lets you access your computer hardware and files from one central location. Figure 4.2 shows a typical My Computer window.
Network Neighborhood	Lets you control your computer's networking capabilities.
Inbox	Serves as a central repository for your online e-mail and files.

Table 4 *New features that you'll find in Windows 95.*

Figure 4.1 *The Explorer window.*

Figure 4.2 The My Computer window.

5 Where is MS-DOS?

Windows 3.1 was an operating environment that ran on top of MS-DOS. As such, you could not start Windows 3.1 without first loading MS-DOS. Windows 95 replaces the MS-DOS operating system so that Windows 95 starts when you turn on your PC. Although MS-DOS as you know it is gone, Windows 95 provides MS-DOS support if you need it—and provides better MS-DOS support than did Windows 3.1.

To start, you can open one or more MS-DOS windows while running Windows 95. All general MS-DOS commands, such as COPY and DIR, still work. The MS-DOS windows let you use long filenames while still supporting the same file system from previous versions of Windows. As a result, you can run your old MS-DOS applications and exchange files with MS-DOS and Windows 3.1 users. Also, because Windows 95 resolves many conventional memory problems that plagued Windows 3.1, most MS-DOS applications run better under Windows 95. MS-DOS windows now support an optional toolbar, as shown in Figure 5. For tips on using the new MS-DOS features, see the "MS-DOS and Windows 95" section of this book.

Figure 5 Windows 95 improves upon MS-DOS.

6 A Window is Still a Window

A *window* is a framed region on the screen that holds data, icons, and program information. Windows 95 supports the use of windows, but the windows look a little different from those in Windows 3.1. For example, most Windows 95 windows contain title bars, sizing buttons, and borders, as they did in Windows 3.1. However, these various window components appear sleek when you compare them with Windows 3.1 objects, as Figures 6.1 and 6.2 show.

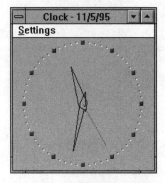

Figure 6.1 The Windows 3.1 Clock window.

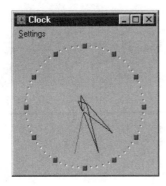

Figure 6.2 The Windows 95 Clock window.

Starting a Program — 7

Windows 95 does not need the clutter found in most Windows 3.1 Program Manager windows because the Windows 95 Start button gives you almost instant access to any program on your computer. When you click the Start button, the Start menu appears. From the Start menu, you can launch any application on your computer. As you select options from the Start menu, submenus appear that let you quickly locate the program you want to run. To practice starting programs, perform these steps to start the Windows 95 Calculator and Calendar programs:

1. Click your mouse on the Start button. The Start menu, shown in Figure 7.1, will appear.
2. Move your mouse pointer to the Start menu Programs option. The Programs menu will appear. (You do not have to click your mouse to see the menu.) The options on the Programs menu represent program groups you may have seen in Windows 3.1's Program Manager.
3. Move your mouse pointer to the Programs menu Accessories option to display the Accessories menu.
4. Click your mouse on the Accessories menu Calculator option to start the Calculator program. After a brief pause, the Calculator window will appear, as shown in Figure 7.2. Notice that the Taskbar now contains a button labeled "Calculator."
5. Click your mouse on the Start button once more to display the Start menu.
6. Select the Start menu Programs option to display the Programs menu.
7. Select the Programs menu Accessories option to display the Accessories menu.
8. Click your mouse on the Accessories menu Calendar option to start the Calendar program. Your screen should look something like the one in Figure 7.3.

Figure 7.1 The Start menu lets you access all your computer's programs.

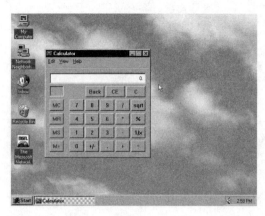

Figure 7.2 The Calculator program window.

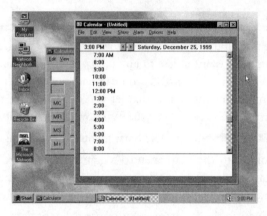

Figure 7.3 The Calendar program is now running.

8 Ending a Program

There are several ways to end a Windows 95 program. Actually, there are several ways to perform many tasks within Windows 95. Here are a few ways you can end a program:

- Select the application's File menu Exit option.
- Double-click the program window's Control menu icon.
- Click the program window's Close button (the button in the window's upper-right corner that contains an X).

To end the Calculator and Calendar programs that you started in Tip 7, perform these steps:

1. Display the Calendar program's File menu by clicking on the menu bar's File category or by pressing ALT-F.
2. Select the File menu Exit option to end the program. Windows 95 will close the Calendar's window and terminate the application.
3. Click the Calculator window's Close button to end the Calculator program.

As you will learn in Tip 15, you can also end programs using the Taskbar.

Running Multiple Programs — 9

Windows 95 is a multitasking operating system, which means you can run more than one program at one time. For example, you might want to print a spreadsheet while you wait for a database update to complete in a second program. To perform multitasking operations Windows 95 makes you think that you can run two or more programs at exactly the same time. In reality, your computer can do only one thing at a time. However, your computer is so fast and Windows 95 is so smart that Windows 95 can work on one task, then move to another, and return to the first one quickly making it appear that two or more things are happening at exactly the same time. Unlike previous versions of Windows, Windows 95 uses your computer's memory resources efficiently. Therefore, you can safely run several programs at once without encountering the memory problems that often troubled earlier versions of Windows. Figure 9 shows several programs running at the same time.

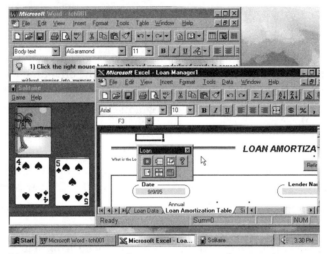

Figure 9 Windows 95 is multitasking and can run more than one program at the same time.

Switching Between Windows — 10

As you learned in Tip 9, Windows 95 can run multiple programs at the same time. When you run several programs simultaneously, you can use only one program window at any given moment. This active program window, which Windows 95 highlights and places at the front of your screen, represents the foreground task. The other programs run as background tasks. To manage two or more programs running at the same time, you need a way to switch easily between them. In short, you need a quick way to bring any background task to the foreground. Fortunately, Windows 95 provides several methods you can use to switch between running programs:

- If you can see any portion of the window to which you want to switch, click on that area to switch to that program.
- Click on the program's Taskbar button. (Each time you start a program, Windows 95 adds a button with the program's name to the Taskbar.)
- Press ALT-TAB to switch between the two programs you most recently activated.
- If you hold down ALT and press TAB more than once, you can switch to any running program. As you press TAB, you'll see a window with an icon for each running program, as shown in Figure 10. Stop pressing TAB and ALT when the highlighted box rests on the icon of the program you want to use.

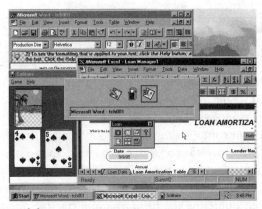

Figure 10 *A window of icons lets you switch between running programs.*

11 Minimizing a Window

Sometimes a window gets in your way. For example, when you run several programs at the same time, one window may overlap too much of another. Fortunately, you don't have to close the offending window to get it out of the way. Instead, you can *minimize* the window and thereby let its program continue to run. If the minimized program has a file open, that file stays open. Likewise, the minimized program's Taskbar button remains on your screen to remind you that the program is running even though the window isn't present. To minimize a window, perform these steps:

1. Start the Calculator program (see Tip 7's steps 1 through 4).
2. Click the Calculator window's Minimize button. Then, watch closely as Windows 95 shrinks the window into the Taskbar. The window disappears but the Taskbar button remains.
3. Start the Calendar program (see Tip 7's steps 5 through 8). The Calendar program now runs along with the Calculator.
4. Click your mouse on the Calendar window's Control menu icon. The Calendar program will display its Control menu.
5. Select the Control menu Minimize option. Windows 95 minimizes the Calendar window, as shown in Figure 11.

Note: *Windows 95 offers you two more ways to minimize a window. Right-click on the program's Taskbar button or on the program window's title bar. Windows 95 will display a pop-up menu. Then, select the pop-up menu's Minimize option.*

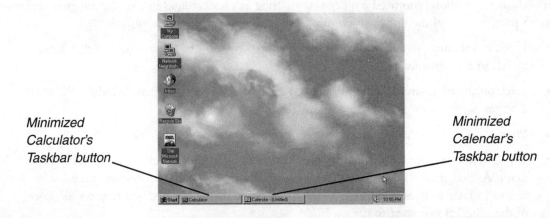

Figure 11 *The Taskbar holds buttons for all running programs.*

Minimizing All Open Windows at Once   12

Tip 11 taught you how to minimize individual windows. There may be times when you want to minimize *all* open windows at once. For example, you might want to use a Desktop icon that is hidden behind one or more open windows. Or, your screen might contain too much clutter for you to read the Start menu easily. Or, you may wish to prevent others from seeing confidential data that appears in one or more open windows. To minimize all open windows, perform these steps:

1. Move your mouse pointer to a blank spot on the Taskbar.
2. Click your right mouse button. A pop-up menu appears, as shown in Figure 12.
3. Select the pop-up menu's Minimize All Windows option. Windows 95 minimizes all open windows and displays a clean Desktop.

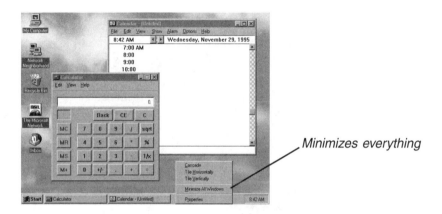

Figure 12 *The Taskbar's pop-up menu.*

Maximizing a Window   13

When you want to focus on one program among several running on your system, you can *maximize* the program's window. When you maximize a window, the window consumes the entire screen. As a result, a maximized window is easier to read than a smaller one. There are several ways you can maximize a window:

- If you've minimized the program's window, right-click over the program's Taskbar button and select the pop-up menu's Maximize option.
- If the window is visible, click the window's Maximize button. The Maximize button will then turn into a Restore button (see Tip 14).
- Select the window's Control menu Maximize option.
- Right-click the program window's title bar and select the pop-up window's Maximize option.
- Double-click the program window's title bar.

If a window contains a Maximize button or is smaller than your screen width, the window is not maximized. Figure 13.1 shows a maximized Word for Windows window. Figure 13.2 shows the same open window not maximized.

Note: *You cannot maximize all windows.*

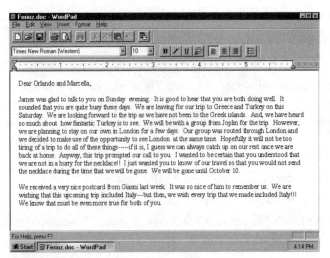

Figure 13.1 A maximized Word for Windows window.

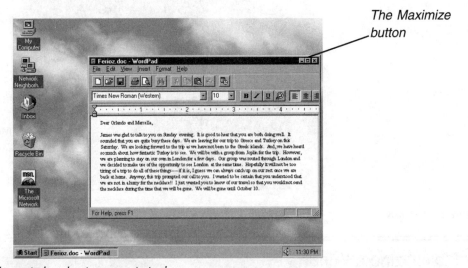

Figure 13.2 A Word for Windows window that is not maximized.

14 Restoring a Window's Original Size

The Restore button restores a window to its original size. After you click the Restore button, the window reverts to the size it was before you maximized it. Suppose that you want to focus exclusively on an open window's contents without changing the size and location of other windows on your screen. To do so, you can maximize that window. Then, after you finish using the window, you can restore it to its original size. In addition to clicking the Restore button, you can restore a window using any of these methods:

- Select the window's Control menu Restore option.
- Right-click the program's Taskbar button and select the pop-up menu's Restore option.
- Right-click the window's title bar and select the pop-up menu's Restore option.
- Double-click the window's title bar.

Using the Taskbar — 15

As you already know, the Taskbar provides access to your running programs. The Taskbar gives you a push-button command center for Windows 95. Several of the previous tips discussed ways you can use the Taskbar to maximize, minimize, and restore window sizes. Here are just a few of the things you can do with the Taskbar:

- Switch between running programs.
- Close windows.
- Adjust the volume when you play CDs and sound files on your system.
- Change the way multiple windows appear.
- Change Start menu options.

To see a sample of the Taskbar's helpful benefits, rest your mouse pointer on the clock at the Taskbar's right end. Do not click the mouse. In a few moments, Windows 95 will display the date, as shown in Figure 15.

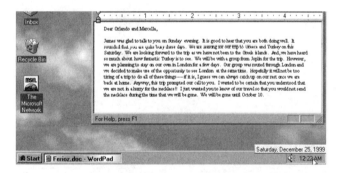

Figure 15 *The Taskbar can display the date.*

Moving a Window — 16

In Windows 95, program windows don't always appear at the screen location you desire. For example, you may want the Calculator window to reside in the lower-right portion of your screen so that, as you run other programs, the Calculator will stay out of your way but remain within reach. To move a window, perform these steps:

1. Move your mouse pointer to the window's title bar.
2. Click and hold your left mouse button and drag the window to a new location.
3. Release your left mouse button to drop the window into place.

Note: *The Control menu contains a Move option that lets you use the ARROW keys to drag a window. When you finish moving the window, press ENTER or click your left mouse button to release it.*

Figure 16.1 shows the Calculator window overlapping other program icons. Figure 16.2 shows the Calculator in a corner, out of the way of other windows.

Figure 16.1 The Calculator window's default location.

Figure 16.2 The Calculator is now out of the way.

17 Dragging the Window Frame to Size a Window

In previous tips, you learned how to stow a window on the Taskbar, enlarge a window until it occupies your entire screen, and restore a window to its default size. However, there may be times when none of these window sizes will let you perform a task effectively. For example, to copy data from one program to another, you may want to juxtapose two windows that both, by default, occupy a large portion of the screen.

Fortunately, in Windows 95, you can manually size most windows. Then, after all your windows are the height and width you desire, you can move them (see Tip 16) to create a Desktop that matches your exact specifications. To size a window, perform these steps:

1. Move your mouse pointer to the window's border. If the window permits manual sizing, your mouse pointer will change to a double-pointing arrow. (If your mouse pointer does not change, you cannot manually size the window.)
2. Click and hold your left mouse button.
3. Drag the border to the size you desire. As you drag the border, Windows 95 will expand or contract the window.
4. After the window reaches the size you desire, release your left mouse button.

Moving the Taskbar 18

No matter how good something is, it can often be better. For example, you may find the Taskbar useful but its default location obtrusive. Sitting at the bottom of your screen, the Taskbar can cover up an application's bottom line. Luckily, you can move the Taskbar to your screen's left, right, or top edge. To move the Taskbar, perform these steps:

1. Move your mouse pointer to a blank spot on the Taskbar.
2. Click and hold your left mouse button.
3. Drag your mouse pointer to the edge of the screen at which you want the Taskbar.
4. Release your left mouse button to anchor the Taskbar at its new location.

Figure 18.1 shows the Taskbar at the top of the screen. Figure 18.2 shows the Taskbar at your screen's right edge. Notice that Windows 95 shortens the Taskbar descriptions when you move the Taskbar to the right or left edge of your screen.

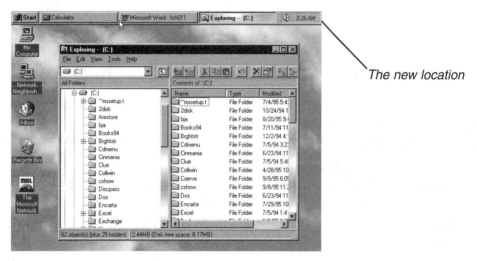

Figure 18.1 A different Taskbar location.

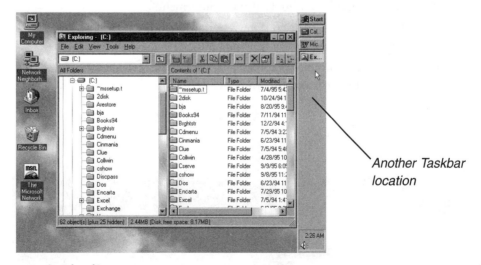

Figure 18.2 The Taskbar at your screen's right edge.

19 Getting to Your Windows 3.1 Program Groups

Windows 95 neither forgot nor erased your familiar Windows 3.1 program groups. Rather, Windows 95 keeps the program groups out of your way. However, you can access your old program groups through the Start menu. To begin, select the Start menu and choose the Programs option. Windows 95, in turn, will display a menu of options similar to that shown in Figure 19. As you examine the menu options, you will find that several correspond to your old (familar) Windows 3.1 program groups. As you highlight each option using your mouse, Windows 95 will display the programs that are contained within the group. To run a program, simply double-click on the corresponding menu entry using your mouse.

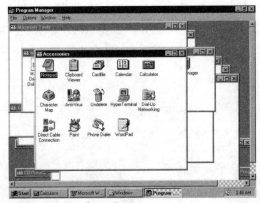

Figure 19 *You can access Windows 3.1 program groups from the Start menu.*

20 Shutting Down Your Computer

To make sure your data is safely stored away, you must shut down Windows 95 before you power off your computer. If you don't shut down properly, you may lose the work you've performed on your system. Fortunately, Windows 95 provides a safe and easy-to-use Shut Down function. Before you turn off your computer, perform these steps to shut down Windows 95:

1. Close all open programs. If you forget to close a program, Windows 95 will remind you (if you have open files you need to save) before you complete the shut down process.
2. Click the Start button to display the Start menu.
3. Select the Start menu Shut Down option. Windows 95 will display the Shut Down Windows dialog box, as shown in Figure 20.
4. Click the Yes button to shut down the computer. After shutting down, Windows 95 displays a message that tells you that you can safely turn off your computer.

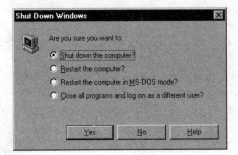

Figure 20 *The Shut Down function helps protect data.*

Rebooting Your Computer — 21

Instead of shutting down your computer, you may need to reboot it. For example, you may need to reboot Windows 95 if you've changed any startup options and want to put those options to work. Through the Shut Down Windows dialog box (see Tip 20), you can shut down and restart (reboot) your computer in one easy step.

As you saw in Figure 20, the Shut Down Windows dialog box lets you do more than just shut down your computer. Through this dialog box, you also can shut down your computer and restart it in MS-DOS mode, which is useful if you want to launch an MS-DOS program (such as a computer game) that does not run in a window. Or, if you work for businesses where two or more employees work on the same system at different times, you can shut down Windows 95 so you can log in as a different user, with different system settings (desktop colors, settings, and so on).

To restart your computer, perform these steps:
1. Click the Start button to display the Start menu.
2. Select the Start menu Shut Down option. Windows 95 will display the Shut Down Windows dialog box.
3. Select the shutdown option that you desire and choose Yes.

Taking a Look at My Computer — 22

The My Computer icon on your Desktop provides access to all your PC's components. Unlike the more limited Windows 3.1 File Manager, My Computer lets you access files, folders (formerly known as directories), drives, printers, modems, monitors, and other devices. My Computer contains icons that represent your PC's components. Table 22 explains the purpose of the icons that commonly appear inside the My Computer window.

Icon	Represents
	A floppy disk drive
	A hard disk drive
	A CD-ROM drive
	The Control Panel window
	The Printers window
	The Dial-Up Networking window

Table 22 The My Computer icons represent different areas of your PC.

Whenever you need to modify a hardware setting, manage files, or check the status of a device, you can do so within the My Computer window. To look at your system's My Computer window, double-click the My Computer icon. You will see a My Computer window that looks something like the one in Figure 22.

Figure 22 *The My Computer window lets you access files and hardware.*

23 Understanding Files and Folders

Just as your office file cabinets store paper files in manila folders, Windows 95 stores data and programs as files in electronic folders. In previous versions of Windows and MS-DOS, you stored files inside directories. A Windows 95 *folder*, for most purposes, is a directory on your disk. (See Tips 82 and 83 for a more complete discussion of folders.)

In MS-DOS and previous versions of Windows, computer users had to know filename extensions, such as DOC and TXT, to identify a file's type. To make file-type identification easier, most Windows 95 file lists display memorable, easily recognizable icons next to file or folder names. For example, Windows 95 file lists place the same icon next to the names of all Word for Windows files.

Table 23 lists several common file and folder icons that you'll see as you use Windows 95. Each application written for Windows 95 can add its own set of icons as well. Table 23 lists only the more common icons.

Icon	Represents
	A folder that contains files or other folders
	A generic file type that Windows 95 does not recognize
	An MS-DOS file
	A test file created with a text editor, such as Notepad
	A graphics file stored as a bitmap
	A font description

Table 23 *Common icons and the file types they represent.*

Traversing Drives inside My Computer   24

As you have learned, the My Computer window gives you access to your system's devices, drives, files, and folders. My Computer gives you several ways to view your system's files and folder structures. To discover My Computer's folder-viewing options and practice traversing a drive, perform these steps:

1. Double-click the My Computer icon if your My Computer window is not open.
2. Double-click your C: drive's icon. Windows 95 will display a list of icons that represent your C: drive's contents.
3. Double-click the folder icon labeled "Windows" on your C: drive. Windows 95 will display the Windows folder's contents, which will look something like those shown in Figure 24.1.
4. Select the View menu Large Icons option to increase the size of the window's icons. Figure 24.2 shows a window with large icons.
5. To look at a folder's contents, double-click the folder's icon. For example, double-click the folder icon labeled "System" to view the System folder's contents.
6. Press BACKSPACE to return to the Windows folder. BACKSPACE always lets you return to a parent folder (the folder you last opened to see the current window) if a parent folder exists.
7. Press BACKSPACE until you return to the My Computer window.

Figure 24.1 *A C: drive window with small icons.*

Figure 24.2 *A C: drive window with large icons.*

25 Getting to Know Your Network Neighborhood

Networks let you and other users share resources such as files, folders, and printers. A network keeps you from shuffling floppy disks when you transfer files between PCs. Additionally, a network lets you send electronic mail (called e-mail) to other network users. In Windows 95, the Network Neighborhood window (see Figure 25) gives you access to all of your computer's networking capabilities. To open this window, you double-click the Network Neighborhood icon. (Not all users will have a Network Neighborhood icon on their Desktop because not everybody will have a networked computer system.) You'll traverse the Network Neighborhood window in the same way that you traverse other windows that contain files and folders (see Tip 24). Later in this book, in the section entitled "Networks and Remote Access," you'll learn more about Network Neighborhood.

Figure 25 *The contents of Network Neighborhood.*

26 Retrieving Objects from the Recycle Bin

The Desktop's Recycle Bin icon is a last-chance holding area for data objects such as files, folders, and Windows 95 shortcuts that you've deleted. When you delete a file, it disappears from its original location. However, Windows 95 does not actually delete files. Instead, Windows 95 sends deleted files to the Recycle Bin. As long as an item remains in the Recycle Bin (the item remains there until you empty the Recycle Bin), you can retrieve it. When the Recycle Bin contains something, the Recycle Bin icon looks like Figure 26.1. If you retrieve everything or empty the Recycle Bin, the Recycle Bin icon will appear empty, as shown in Figure 26.2. Remember, when you delete an item, you don't recover the disk space that item occupied until you empty the Recycle Bin. If you delete an item and decide you want it back, you can retrieve the item anytime before you empty the Recycle Bin. To retrieve something from the Recycle Bin, perform these steps:

1. Double-click the Desktop's Recycle Bin icon. The Recycle Bin will display its contents in a table format, as shown in Figure 26.3.
2. Right-click the item you want to retrieve. If you want to retrieve more than one item, press **Ctrl** and right-click each item. Windows 95 will display a pop-up menu.
3. Click the pop-up menu's Restore option. After a brief pause, Windows 95 restores the item.
4. Close the Recycle Bin window.

Figure 26.1 *The Recycle Bin has something in it.*

Figure 26.2 The Recycle Bin is empty.

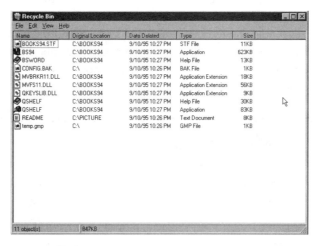

Figure 26.3 The Recycle Bin's contents in table form.

Surfing Cyberspace with Microsoft Network | 27

If you have yet to join the Information Super Highway that you hear everybody talking about, Windows 95 has just the thing to help you get on board: The Microsoft Network. The *Microsoft Network* is an online service, owned and operated by Microsoft, that competes with CompuServe, America Online, Prodigy, and others. The Microsoft Network provides you with electronic mail, news, Internet access, files you can download, business data (such as stock prices), home shopping capabilities, and more.

For Windows 95 users, one of The Microsoft Network's key benefits is that its interface, which you'll use as you *surf* (fancy computer lingo for move around) the online service, is virtually identical to Windows 95's. In fact, the link between Windows 95 and The Microsoft Network is so close that you'll sometimes wonder if it's The Microsoft Network or Windows 95 updating your screen. To learn how you can take advantage of The Microsoft Network, see the tips within this book's "Microsoft Network" section. Figure 27 shows the opening Microsoft Network screen.

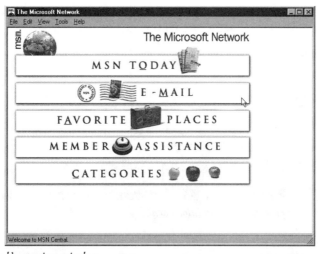

Figure 27 The Microsoft Network's opening window.

28 Using the Windows 95 Inbox

Your Desktop's Inbox icon provides access to the Inbox window (sometimes called the Microsoft Exchange Inbox window), which keeps track of data your system collects from faxes, e-mail, transferred files, network mail, and so on. In the past, if you wanted to retrieve your e-mail from CompuServe and America Online, you had to access each of those services individually and use two different sets of commands to *download* (transfer to your computer) your messages. As such, your messages would, more than likely, end up in two different directories on your disk drive. The Inbox provides one universal storage location for *all* your e-mail. The Inbox uses the services of another Windows 95 product, Microsoft Exchange, to gather the data. This book's "Networks and Remote Access" section explains how you can use the Inbox for your electronic data needs.

29 Understanding and Using Documents

As you learned in Tip 23, Windows 95 extends the concept of physical paper files and folders to your disk drives. Windows 95 often refers to files as *documents*, even if those documents contain any of the following kinds of data:

- Text
- Word-processing documents
- Graphics
- Multimedia
- Programs
- Data (such as accounting data)
- System-related files (such as Windows 95 support files)

Don't be surprised if Windows 95 sometimes refers to a program as a document. Microsoft designed Windows 95 to be as simple for newcomers as possible. Because almost everyone is familiar with paper files, Windows 95 extends the paper file concept to its own environment. As Figure 29 shows, many of the icons that appear in a window for hard-disk resemble manila folders and pieces of paper.

Figure 29 Directories and files often appear as folders and documents.

Taking Advantage of the Documents Menu — 30

Think about the way you work with your PC. Your data is much more important than the programs that process it, right? After all, an accurate tax return is much more important to you than the program that produces the return. Windows 95 is smart about the way you prefer to work. Windows 95 doesn't require you to start your word processor and *then* load the document you want to edit. To work with a document, all you must do is click its name or icon. Windows 95, in turn, will automatically load the program you use to modify the document. Windows 95 incorporates the document concept into the Start menu itself. If you move your mouse pointer to the Start menu Documents option, Windows 95 will open the Documents menu. Through the Documents menu, you can select documents you've recently edited or created. Often, you work on the same document in more than one session. Thanks to the Documents menu, you don't need to search your directories for that document. Instead, you can open the Documents menu (see Figure 30) and select the file with a single mouse click. Windows 95, in turn, will start the appropriate program and automatically load the document for you.

Figure 30 *The Documents menu.*

Running a Program Using the Run Option — 31

Although you can launch most programs from the Start menu, some applications, such as MS-DOS programs, will not appear on the Start menu or any of its submenus. Fortunately, if you know the program's name, you can choose the Start menu Run option to execute it. To start a program using the Start menu Run option, perform these steps:

1. Select the Start menu Run menu option. Windows 95 will display the Run dialog box, as shown in Figure 31.
2. Type the program's name (use either uppercase or lowercase). For example, to run the Windows 95 Calculator, type **calc**. (The full filename of the Calculator program is CALC.EXE.)

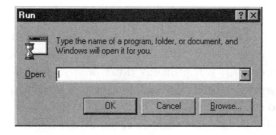

Figure 31 *The Run dialog box.*

32 Getting to an MS-DOS Prompt

Despite the visual advantages of Windows 95, some users prefer to use the MS-DOS environment when they perform certain tasks on their PC. For example, if you want a quick listing of your files, you may not want to wade through documents and folders in My Computer or use the Explorer program. (Tip 43 explains how you use Explorer). You might find it easier and faster to go the MS-DOS prompt and type **DIR.** To get to MS-DOS quickly, perform these steps:

1. Click the Start button.
2. Select the Start menu Programs option.
3. Click the Programs menu MS-DOS Prompt option. Windows 95 will open an MS-DOS window like the one in Figure 32. When you want to return to Windows 95, type **EXIT** at the MS-DOS prompt and press ENTER.

Note: You can also exit the MS-DOS window by clicking its Close button.

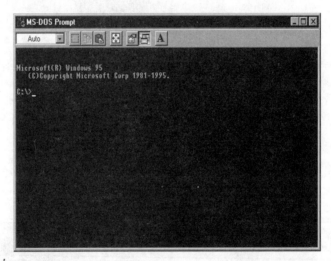

Figure 32 *The MS-DOS window.*

33 Windows 95 Doesn't Need AUTOEXEC.BAT and CONFIG.SYS

Until Windows 95 came along, two very important computer start-up files were AUTOEXEC.BAT and CONFIG.SYS. Both files were difficult for beginners to change and update. CONFIG.SYS contained configuration options that made your computer behave in certain ways and recognize certain devices, such as CD-ROM drives. The AUTOEXEC.BAT file contained commands that started programs you wanted the computer to run every time you turned on the machine.

Windows 95 does not (normally) need either of these files to operate. Thanks to the Plug and Play feature, Windows 95 recognizes most hardware devices and configures things properly without resorting to the CONFIG.SYS file. As long as you use Windows 95 programs, you probably don't need to worry about AUTOEXEC.BAT or the CONFIG.SYS files. However, if you use MS-DOS programs, especially those written before the release of Windows 95, those programs may still need entries in the AUTOEXEC.BAT or CONFIG.SYS files. Also, if you are using a hardware device for which Windows 95 does not provide a device driver, Windows 95 may use your old (real-mode) device driver that requires a CONFIG.SYS or AUTOEXEC.BAT entry. Therefore, do not delete these files from your system. If necessary, Windows 95 will use the information they contain.

34 Windows 95 and INI Files

If you tinkered with Windows 3.1, you probably had to modify one or more INI file settings. An INI file, which always has an INI filename extension, describes how Windows 3.1 will treat certain executing programs. When you install Windows 95, do not delete these files from your disk. Windows 95 uses certain settings from some of your old INI files to update the Windows 95 *Registry*.

The Windows 95 Registry is a table of program descriptions that is more organized and complete than the INI files Windows 3.1 uses. Later in this book, you will learn more about the Window 95 Registry. For now, rest easy; if you disliked (or never learned how to manage) your Windows 3.1 INI files, you don't have to worry about them when you use Windows 95.

35 Using the Taskbar to Cascade or Tile Open Windows

If you have multiple open windows on your Desktop, your screen can get quite messy. You may find that you cannot tell one window from another. To straighten things out when several windows appear on your screen at the same time, Windows 95 provides the following window-organization methods that you can use:

- Cascaded, which ensures you see each window's title bar
- Vertically-tiled, which places windows on top and next to one another instead of overlapping
- Horizontally-tiled, which places windows next to each other instead of overlapping

Note: On rare occasions, tiled windows may overlap. However, in most circumstances, tiling is an effective way to organize the program windows on your Desktop.

If you find your Desktop buried beneath a clutter of windows, perform these steps to clean things up:

1. Point to a blank spot on the Taskbar.
2. Click your right mouse button. Windows 95 will display a pop-up menu.
3. Select the pop-up menu option (Cascade, Tile Horizontally, or Tile Vertically) that you want Windows 95 to use to arrange your windows. Figures 35.1 through 35.3 show the difference a little window reorganization can make.

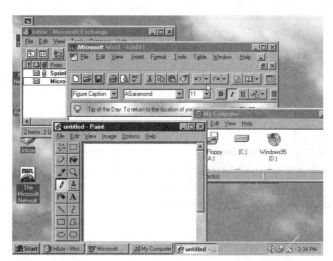

Figure 35.1 *A cluttered Desktop.*

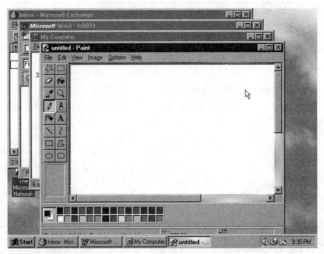

Figure 35.2 *A Desktop with cascaded windows.*

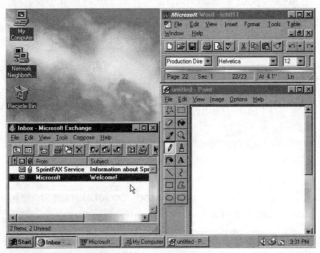

Figure 35.3 *A Desktop with vertically tiled windows.*

36 Using a Local Reboot to End an Application

There are times, albeit sad times, when your computer simply stops responding to a program. Some programs can *hang* (or crash) computers. Once your computer hangs, there is little you can do to get control back from the program. Many things can cause a program to hang. For example, the program's designer could have overlooked a program *bug* (error). Although hardware problems rarely cause a computer to hang, modem-related program crashes are not uncommon.

If a program crashes, you cannot regain control of the program. In fact, you cannot even use regular program commands to *stop* the program's execution. Luckily, Windows 95 is in control of most things inside the computer. If a program hangs, you can ask Windows 95 to stop the program for you. In effect, Windows 95 locally reboots that program but not the whole computer. When a program hangs, give it a few moments to regain control. Sometimes a program attempts to repeat a task several times and gives up after a few tries. If the program doesn't regain control on its own, you need to stop the program. To tell Windows 95 to locally reboot the program, perform these steps:

1. Hold down the CTRL key. While holding CTRL, press ALT. While you hold down those two keys, press the DELETE key. Windows 95 responds with the Close Program dialog box. The hung program's name will usually appear at the top of the dialog box's task list.
2. Move your mouse pointer to the name of the program that you want to close and click your left mouse button.
3. Click the End Task button to close the program. Do *not* press Shut Down unless the End Task button fails after you have clicked it several times.

Note: After you click the End Task button, Windows 95 may inform you that it cannot shut down the program automatically. On such occasions, Windows 95 will ask you if you wish to terminate the program. Click the Yes button.

Understanding Plug and Play — 37

Windows 95 not only attempts to make your life easier when you use the computer, but also when you add new hardware. Windows 95's *Plug and Play* feature lets you add new hardware, such as a modem or network card, by performing these simple steps:

1. Shut down Windows 95 and turn off your computer.
2. Install the new device.
3. Turn on your computer. When you see the Windows 95 Desktop, Windows 95 will have already detected the new hardware and made all adjustments for you.

Before Windows 95, you had to run installation programs and, in worst case scenarios, tinker with INI files (see Tip 34) and other settings. Now, when you install new devices, Windows 95 does all the tinkering for you. If the device is a connected to a PCMCIA card, you do not even have to turn off the computer when you plug in the new device.

Note: There is a catch to Plug and Play: the hardware you plug into your computer must have a Plug and Play BIOS chip inside before Windows 95 recognizes the new device. For Windows 95 to recognize a device made without Plug and Play BIOS technology, you must make the necessary hardware and software adjustments.

Requesting the Windows 95 Startup Tips — 38

In Tip 3, you learned that each time you start Windows 95, a Welcome window appears that displays tips and useful advice. After you work with Windows 95 for a while, you may decide that you no longer need the tips. As discussed in Tip 3, you can request that Windows 95 not display the tips. If you later decide that you want to see the tips again, perform these steps:

1. Click the Start button to display the Start menu.
2. Select the Start menu Help option. Windows 95 displays the Help Topics sheet shown in Figure 38.1.
3. Click the Help Topics sheet Index tab and type **tipv** to highlight the "tips viewing the Welcome Screen again" topic.
4. Click on the topic and press ENTER. The online Help system will open the window you see in Figure 38.2.
5. Click the Help window's jump button (the button with the curved arrow) to see a Welcome screen tip.
6. Press ALT-S to request the Window window appear at subsequent startups. Or, click the "Show this Welcome Screen next time you start Windows" check box until a check mark appears.

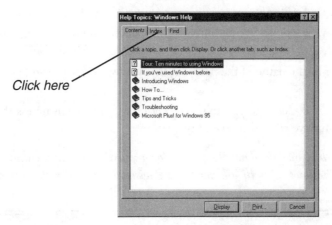

Figure 38.1 Getting ready for help.

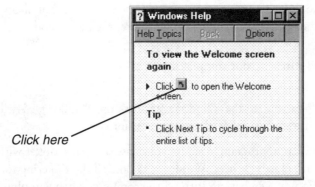

Figure 38.2 You can request the Welcome window again.

39 Understanding Windows 95 Wizards

A *wizard* is a Windows 95 program that leads you, step-by-step, through what might otherwise be a lengthy or difficult procedure. For example, when you send a fax, Windows 95 provides a wizard to walk you through the steps. Generally, a wizard will display several windows in succession. Each window will encompass one step in the procedure. To advance through a wizard's steps, you click on the Next button that appears at the bottom of most wizard windows. Figure 39 shows a wizard window. As you work with Windows 95, you will encounter several wizards. This book will describe a wizard when a tip requires you use one.

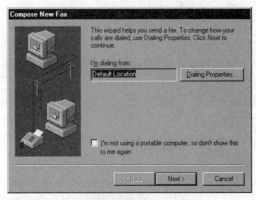

Figure 39 Wizards guide you through lengthy or difficult procedures.

Registering Windows 95 — 40

Microsoft wants to know who you are, and you want Microsoft to know that you own Windows 95. Why? Sometimes, Microsoft updates a program and corrects bugs. Although Windows 95 is a fine product, you'll certainly want to know about new features and fixes that Microsoft adds in future releases. Microsoft cannot inform you about such upgrades unless you register your copy of Windows 95. To register Windows 95, you can send the product card that came with your copy of the operating system. Or, if you have a modem, you can register Windows 95 online. To do so, perform these steps:

1. Perform Tip 38 to display the Welcome window.
2. Click the Online Registration button to start the Registration wizard shown in Figure 40.
3. Perform the wizard's instructions by clicking the Next button and filling in your personal or business information. The wizard will describe your PC hardware to Microsoft at the time of registration. Windows 95 dials a toll-free number and registers your copy of Windows 95.

Figure 40 The Registration wizard registers your copy of Windows 95.

Using AutoPlay to Play Music CDs — 41

Although you've been able to play audio CDs in your CD-ROM drive before Windows 95, Windows 95 adds a new touch: AutoPlay. AutoPlay instantly senses that you've inserted an audio CD and starts playing the CD immediately. Before Windows 95, you had to inform Windows that you wanted to play the CD. If you press SHIFT when you insert the CD, Windows 95 will not use AutoPlay to play the CD. To play a CD you've inserted without AutoPlay, you'll need to start the Media Player.

Using the Taskbar to Control Sound Card Volume — 42

When you play a CD or use a different multimedia source to produce sound through your sound card, you will want to control your system's volume and *balance* (the amount of noise that comes out of each speaker). Fortunately, the Windows 95 volume control is as close as the Taskbar. When your PC produces sound, Windows 95 displays the speaker icon on the Taskbar. Through this icon, you can access the Volume Control dialog box. To control the volume and balance of your PC's speakers, perform these steps:

Note: A slider is, as its name implies, a sliding control that you utilize by dragging it left and right or up and down.

1. Double-click the Taskbar's speaker icon. Windows 95 will display the Volume Control dialog box, as shown in Figure 42.
2. In the dialog box's Volume Control section, drag the Volume slider up or down to adjust the volume.
3. In the dialog box's Volume Control section, drag the Balance slider right or left to adjust the balance.
4. Close the Volume Control dialog box.

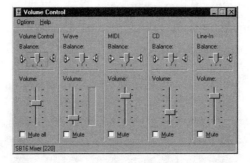

Figure 42 *Use the Volume Control dialog box to adjust volume.*

43 | File Manager is Now Explorer

If, when you were using Windows 3.1, you misnamed a file or needed to copy a file from your hard disk to a floppy so you could give the file to another user, you probably encountered the File Manager. Under Windows 95, the File Manager is gone, having been replaced by a new program called the *Explorer*. Like the File Manager, the Windows 95 Explorer lets you manage your hard, CD-ROM, network connections, and floppy disks. Explorer lets you copy, move, and manage any file within your PC. To start Explorer, simply right-click the Start button and select the pop-up menu's Explorer option. As Figure 43 shows, the Explorer window has two sections. The left section displays general items, such as disk drives and folders. The right section displays details from those items. Later in this book, in the section entitled "Using the Windows 95 Explorer," you'll encounter helpful hints for using Explorer.

Figure 43 *The Explorer window.*

Understanding and Using Long Filenames — 44

MS-DOS and previous versions of Windows limited the length of your filenames to eight characters followed by a zero (no extension) to three character extension. Under previous versions of Windows, all of the following were legal, albeit short, filenames:

- SALES.1ST
- FEB.DAT
- OLDDATA.92

In contrast, Windows 95 lets you use longer filenames (up to 255 characters) that include letters, numbers, and spaces. Under Windows 95, all of the following are valid filenames:

- Marketing sales figures from the 1st quarter
- February payroll.DAT
- Backup of 1992.BAK

Notice three things about the long filenames. 1) Windows 95 keeps upper case and lower case letters that you specify for a filename. 2) Although Windows 95 displays descriptive icons in most file listings (see Tip 23 for an explanation), you still can use extensions. And 3) Windows 95 long filenames are much more descriptive than their MS-DOS and Windows 3.1 counterparts.

Getting to the Windows 95 Control Panel — 45

The Control Panel lets you access all kinds of configuration and setup data that you'll rarely need to modify. However, if you want to add non-standard hardware, change your video settings, modify fonts, or change your PC's date-and-time, you can do so through the Control Panel. (You can also perform many of these operations from other Windows 95 locations.) To open the Control Panel, perform these steps:

1. Display the Start menu.
2. Select the Start menu Settings option.
3. Click your mouse on the Settings menu Control Panel option. Windows 95 will display the Control Panel window. Table 45 describes some of the icons in the Control Panel window.

Icon	Label	Purpose
	Accessibility Options	Lets you modify Windows 95 for those with extra needs.
	Add New Hardware	Helps install non-Plug and Play hardware.
	Add/Remove Programs	Helps you install and remove programs.

Table 45 Icons that appear in the Windows 95 Control Panel (continued on the following page).

Icon	Label	Purpose
	Display	Lets you change video display options.
	Fonts	Lets you modify font settings.
	Modems	Lets you set up and change modem parameters.
	System	Lets you modify advanced computer settings.

Table 45 *Icons that appear in the Windows 95 Control Panel (continued from previous page).*

46 Clearing the Documents Menu

As you learned in Tip 30, the Documents menu (which you access through the Start menu Documents option) displays a list of documents you've recently created or modified.

As you perform various tasks on your PC, your Documents menu may grow so large and contain so many old entries that you have trouble using it to access files. As such, you might want to clear the Documents menu regularly. For example, you might want to clear the Documents menu each day before you leave work. To clear the Documents menu, perform these steps:

1. Display the Start menu.
2. Select the Start menu Settings option.
3. Click your mouse on the Settings menu Taskbar option.
4. Click the Taskbar Properties sheet Start Menu Programs tab. Windows 95 displays the sheet shown in Figure 46.
5. Click the Clear button to clear the Documents menu.

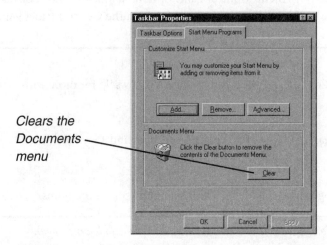

Figure 46 *You can erase the document submenu entries.*

Adding an Option to the Start Menu — 47

The Start menu is not set in stone. If you start the same program several times a day or week, you can add that program to the Start menu. Then, the next time you want to start the program, you won't need to search submenus for it. With just two mouse clicks, one on the Start button and one on the program's Start menu option, the program is up and running, saving you invaluable time. Figure 47, for example, illustrates a Start menu that contains an option for Microsoft Excel. To add a program to the Start menu, perform these steps:

1. Select the Start menu Settings option and choose Taskbar. Windows 95 will display the Taskbar Properties dialog box.
2. Select the Start Menu Programs tab.
3. Select Add. Windows 95 will display the the Create Shortcut dialog box.
4. Within the Command line field, type in the command that corresponds to the program you want to run or use the Browse button to locate the program file.
5. Click on the Next button. Windows 95 will display the Select Program Folder dialog box.
6. Click your mouse on the Start Menu folder and then click on the Next button. Windows 95 will display the Select a Title for the Program dialog box.
7. Type in the program title that you want to appear on the start menu and click on the Finish button.
8. Click on the Taskbar Properties dialog box OK button.

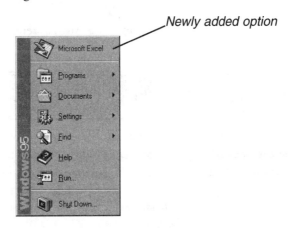

Figure 47 *A Start menu with a new option.*

Online Sources of Windows 95 Information — 48

This book will answer just about any beginning, intermediate, and advanced Windows 95 question you'll ever have. However, if you need additional information, you can use any of the services Table 48 lists. (To use these services, you must have a modem and sign up for access.)

Service	Windows 95 Location
Microsoft Network	Click on **WinNews**.
America Online	Use the keyword **winnews**.

Table 48 *Other sources of online Windows 95 information (continued on the following page).*

Service	Windows 95 Location
CompuServe	Use **go winnews**.
Prodigy	Jump to **winnews**.
GEnie	Download from **WinNews** using the Windows 95 RTC.
FTP	**ftp.microsoft.com** in the **/PerOpSys/WinNews** directory.
World Wide Web	Use address **http://www.microsoft.com**.
Internet Mail	Use address **enews@microsoft.nwnet.com** and subscribe to **winnews**.

Table 48 Other sources of online Windows 95 information (continued from the previous page).

49 Acquire the Windows 95 Resource Kit

The *Windows 95 Resource Kit* contains a wealth of information about Windows 95. If you are responsible for supporting Windows 95 within your department or company, if you are a Network Administrator who works with Windows 95, or if you just want to learn more about the inner workings of Windows 95, you should get a copy of the *Resource Kit*. Your local booksellers and software stores should have plenty of copies. Here are just a few of the items you'll find in the *Resource Kit*:

- A list of all Windows 95 files and their descriptions
- A detailed list of differences between Windows 95 and Windows 3.1
- A detailed description of how the Windows 95 MS-DOS differs from previous versions
- A list of all new Windows 95 components, such as remote access, Internet access, and peer-to-peer networking

50 Read and Print the Windows 95 Release Notes

Microsoft worked on the Windows 95 operating system as long as possible before releasing it to the public. (Microsoft continues to hone the operating system. See Tip 40 to learn how to stay on top of enhancements and bug fixes.) Long before Microsoft finished the Windows 95 software, technical writers had to complete the operating system's printed documentation. As a result, the printed documentation doesn't include last-minute changes to Windows 95. Even the comprehensive *Windows 95 Resource Kit* may leave out some of this information.

Luckily, as Tip 48 explains, you often can retrieve update information from online services. Additionally, you can learn about any last-minute software changes directly from your version of Windows 95. Windows 95 includes a text file of release notes on your disk or CD-ROM. To view or print the release notes, perform these steps:

1. Select the Start menu Programs option.
2. Select the Programs menu Accessories option.
3. Click your mouse on the Accessories menu Notepad option. Windows 95 will start Notepad, a text-editing program that works like a simple word processor.
4. Select the Notepad window's File menu Open option and type **Readme** (the file should reside in the Windows folder on your hard drive). Notepad loads the Readme text file into memory.
5. Maximize the Notepad window and use the DOWN ARROW key to scroll through the file as you read the text.
6. If you want to print the document, turn on your printer and select the File menu Print option.

Starting Windows 95 Online Help   51

Help is just a click away in Windows 95. The Start menu contains a Help option that you can explore when you want to know more about Windows 95. Additionally, most Windows 95 programs contain a Help menu category that you should select when you have specific questions about the program's operation. To access Windows 95 online Help, perform these steps:

1. Click the Start button to display the Start menu.
2. Select the Start menu Help option. Windows 95 displays the Help Topics sheet shown in Figure 51.1.

When you see a menu bar in a Windows 95 program, such as the one shown in Figure 51.2, you can click on the Help category (or press the ALT-H hot key) to get information about that particular program.

Figure 51.1 The Help Topics sheet.

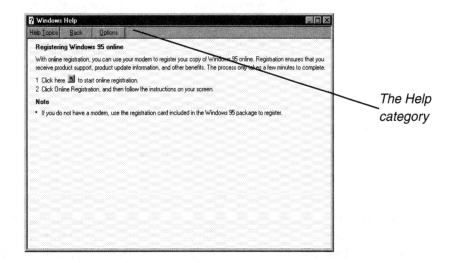

Figure 51.2 Program window menu bars usually contain a Help category.

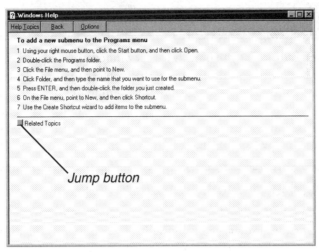

Figure 53.1 A jump button that gives you more information.

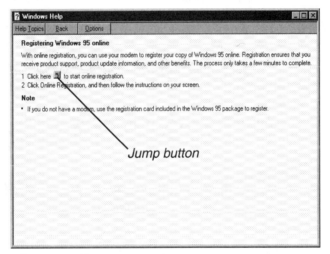

Figure 53.2 A jump button that takes you to other programs.

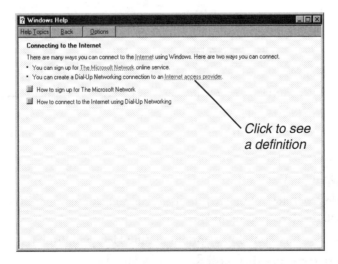

Figure 53.3 A definition link.

54 Moving Back to a Previously Displayed Help Topic

As you learned in Tip 53, jump buttons let you quickly access windows related to the current Help topic. However, just because you jump to another Help topic doesn't mean that you can't return to a Help topic you've already read. In fact, online Help makes such backtracking easy. Each time you jump to a new Help window, online Help displays a Back button just beneath the window's title bar. If you click the Back button, Help returns you to the place from which you jumped last. If you use jump buttons to travel through several different Help windows, you can backtrack through the windows by repeatedly pressing the Back button.

55 Using Browse Buttons to Traverse Help Topics

Some Help windows contain forward-browse and backward-browse buttons. The forward-browse button contains the icon >>, and the backward-browse button contains <<. The browse buttons let you search through several Help windows that are linked together sequentially. Figure 55 shows a Help window that contains browse buttons. If you click >>, the next Help window will appear. If you click <<, the previous Help window will appear.

Note: Jump buttons (see Tip 54) let you jump between related Help windows that you don't need to read in order.

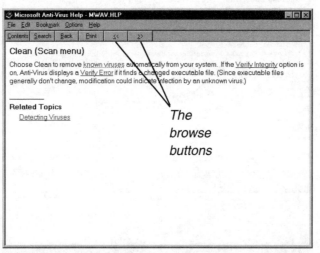

Figure 55 Some Help windows contain browse buttons.

56 Printing a Help Topic

If you find yourself looking up the same Help topic several times, you may want to print that Help topic. Perhaps you might keep a notebook of common Help topics on your desk. To print a Help topic, perform these steps:

1. Turn on your printer and make sure it has paper.
2. Display the Help topic you want to print.
3. Click on the Help window Options button (or right-click anywhere inside the window). Online Help will display a pop-up menu.
4. Select the pop-up menu's Print Topic option. Online Help will display a Print dialog box.
5. Press ENTER to start the printing process.

Using the What's This? Option   57

As you have learned, most programs written specifically for Windows 95 will contain a Help category on the menu bar. Addtionally, many such programs will include a What's This? button, which lets you request Help information about specific areas of the program window. For example, if you want to know more about the status bar at the bottom of the Microsoft Word window, you don't need to search through the comprehensive list of Word Help topics to find the information. Instead, you can perform these simple steps:

1. Click the What's This? button shown in Figure 57.1. Your mouse pointer changes to a question mark.
2. Move the question-mark mouse pointer over the item about which you want information. For this example, move your mouse pointer over Word's status bar.
3. Press your left mouse button. Online Help will provide information about that screen element, as shown in Figure 57.2.

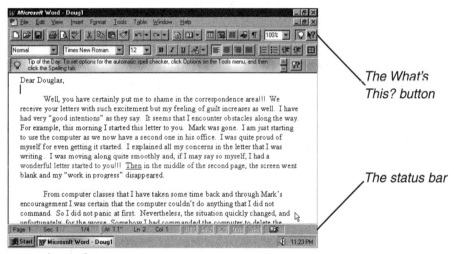

Figure 57.1 *The What's This? button and status bar.*

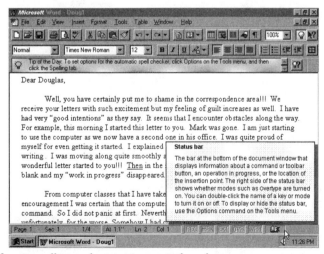

Figure 57.2 *The What's This? function tells you about program window elements.*

58 Using Help to Find Definitions

When you first use Windows 95, you must learn many new, and perhaps confusing, terms. Luckily, the online Help system helps you locate the definitions of new terms. If, while using Windows 95, you stumble across a term that you don't recognize, you can use the Help Topics sheet Index page to find the topic. (Tips 60 and 61 explain how to use the Help Topics sheet Index page to locate unfamiliar terms.) Similarly, to learn the definition of an underlined term that appears in a Help window, all you must do is click on the term. Help, in turn, will display a pop-up window that contains a definition of the term.

59 Annotating (Adding Your Own Notes to) a Help Topic

Suppose you want to add to the Help text for a particular topic. For example, suppose your office must follow a specific procedure before you can send a fax. You can add notes for that procedure to the Help topic that explains how to fax. Subsequently, everybody who seeks faxing information in online Help can read your note. Think of an annotation as a yellow reminder sticker on certain Help windows. To annotate a Help topic, perform these steps:

1. Traverse the Help topics until you find the one you want to annotate.
2. Select the Options menu Annotate option. Windows 95 displays the Annotate dialog box shown in Figure 59.1.
3. Type your annotation.
4. Click the Save button to attach that annotation to the Help topic. Figure 59.2 shows that the annotation appears as a paper clip in the Help topic's title. The annotation stays until you select the Options menu Annotate option one more time and click the Delete button.

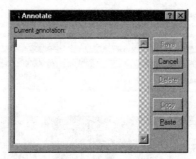

Figure 59.1 The Annotate dialog box.

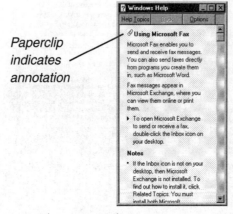

Figure 59.2 The Help topic now contains an annotation.

Locating Information Using Help's Topic Index — 60

When you want to know more about a particular Windows 95 subject or about a Windows 95 application you are running, you can use the Help Topics sheet Index page to search for that information. Although the Help topic for which you are searching might appear in several places, the Help Topics sheet Index page contains the location of the topic's primary description. For example, the term *button* might appear in several different Help topics, but online Help defines the term only once. To find that definition, you use the Help Topics sheet Index page. Figure 60 shows a typical Help Topics sheet Index page.

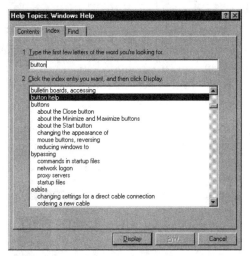

Figure 60 The Help Topics sheet Index page.

Selecting the Help Topics You Desire — 61

When you start the online Help system and click on the Help Topics sheet Index tab, Help displays a comprehensive list of Help topics from which you can choose. Tip 60 describes the index you will see. If you know the name of the Help topic you want to find, type the first few letters. Online Help, in turn, will locate that topic in the topic list. If you don't know exactly how Windows 95 refers to the topic, press PAGE UP or PAGE DOWN until you locate a topic that may contain the information you seek. Then, to view the topic, press ENTER.

Note: *You can use your mouse to scroll through the topic list and locate a topic. To do so, move your mouse pointer over the scroll bar (Tip 72 discusses scroll bars in detail) at the Index page's right edge. Then, click on the scroll bar to move forwards and backwards through the topic list. To view a topic, just double-click on it.*

Copying a Help Topic to the Clipboard — 62

The Windows 95 Clipboard holds more than just word processor text. You can copy text directly from a Help topic that you've displayed. The Help window's Options menu (which appears after you click the Option button or right-click anywhere in a Help window) contains a Copy option that you can use to copy Help text to the Clipboard. After you copy Help text to the Clipboard, you can paste it elsewhere. To copy Help text, perform these steps:

1. Display a Help topic.
2. Click the Options button to open the Options menu (shown in Figure 62).
3. Select the Options menu Copy option.

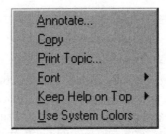

Figure 62 *The Help window's Options menu contains a Copy option.*

63 Finding Information Using Find within Help

The Help Topics sheet Index page is useful for finding specific answers, especially definitions and explanations for specific topics. But there are other ways you can view online Help. Whereas the Help Topics sheet Index page gives you the *most descriptive* Help window for your specified topic, the Help Topics sheet Find page locates *every* occurrence of that Help topic within the entire Help system.

When you first select the Help Topics sheet Find page, online Help locates every occurrence of every Help topic. To narrow your search, you can enter a term, scroll through the upper list on the Index page, or use the tools Tips 64 and 65 describe. Figure 63 shows the Help Topics sheet Find page.

Figure 63 *The Help Topics Find page.*

64 Building a Topic Index for Help

The first time you use the Help Topics sheet Find page, Windows 95 starts a wizard that requires you to build a topic index. At any time, you can rebuild this topic index to suit your needs.

Note: *The Find page's topic index is **not** the same thing as the index Tips 60 and 61 describe. The Help Topics sheet Index page finds a topic's primary definition or explanation. In contrast, the Find page's topic index contains every occurrence of a topic.*

Suppose that you have plenty of disk space, and you want to build the most comprehensive topic index possible. To build such an index, perform these steps:

1. Click your mouse on the Start menu Help option.
2. Click the Help Topics sheet Find tab.
3. Click the Rebuild button. Windows 95 will display the Setup Wizard dialog box, as shown in Figure 64.
4. Select the "Maximize search capabilities" option button.
5. Perform the wizard's instructions to build the topic index database. The next time you use the Help Topic sheet Find page, the online Help system will use the topic index you created.

As you may have noticed, the Setup Wizard dialog box in Figure 64 has three options. The first option, "Minimize database size (recommended), saves disk space and produces a compact index for fast searching. The second option, which you selected in step 4, requires about twice the disk space as the first option and takes longer to search, but produces the most comprehensive index possible. The third option, "Customize search capabilities," lets you specify more precisely how you want the wizard to build your index.

Figure 64 *You can customize the size of the Help Topics Find database.*

Fine-Tuning Help Find Options — 65

You can use the Help Topics sheet Find page to specify exactly how you want to search for information in online Help. Not only can you choose a comprehensive or speedy topic index (as Tip 64 explains), but you can specify exactly how you want online Help to search for the topics. If you display the Help Topics sheet Find page, you can click the Options button to request the Find Options dialog box shown in Figure 65.1. Through the Find Options dialog box, you can control the following options:

- The order and context that the Help system uses to search
- The way online Help matches index entries to the search characters you enter in the Help Topics sheet Find page. You can tell Help to list all entries that begin with, end with, contain, or exactly match your search characters.
- The way Help begins the search (as soon as you enter the search characters or only after you click the Find Now button)
- The specific file or files that online Help will search. To use this option, click the Files button and select Help files from the list shown in Figure 65.2.

Figure 65.1 *You can specify exactly how online Help searches.*

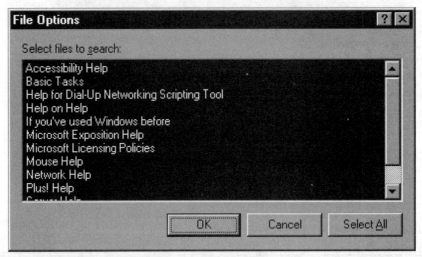

Figure 65.2 *You can specify the Help file or files the online Help system searches.*

66 Keeping your Help Windows Visible

As you use Windows 95, there may be times when you want a Help window to remain in view while you follow its instructions. Fortunately, in Windows 95, you can tell online Help to keep its windows visible even when another program is the foreground task. To do so, perform these steps:

1. Click the Help window's Options button.
2. Select the Options menu Keep Help on Top option.
3. Click your mouse on the Keep Help on Top menu option.

Note: *If you select the Not On Top option, the Help window will disappear beneath your other windows when you do something else. (You can still look at the Help window by clicking its Taskbar button.)*

Customizing the Help Window Font Size — 67

If you find your Help windows difficult to read, you may want to increase the size of the font online Help uses to display information. Conversely, if you want to see as much text as possible inside your Help windows, you may wish to decrease the font size. To change the font size of the Help window characters, perform these steps:

1. Right-click in the Help window to display the Options menu.
2. Select the Options menu Font option. Windows 95 displays three size options.
3. Select one of the three font-size options. To shrink the Help font's size, click your mouse on the Small option. To increase the Help font's size, click your mouse on the Large option. To restore the default font size, select the Normal option.

Starting an Operation From Within Help — 68

In previous versions of Windows, you could look up Help information for a particular operation. However, you couldn't use the information until you left the Help system. For example, online Help might provide you with a list of steps you couldn't perform until you exited Help and launched another program. Fortunately, online Help in Windows 95 corrects this shortcoming. From within many online Help windows, you can now perform steps and start operations. In fact, some Help topics even perform steps for you.

Note: *Tip 38 uses this feature to trigger the display of the Welcome window when you start Windows 95.*

For example, suppose that you want to change the way that your PC displays the time. To do so, perform these steps:

1. Select the Start menu Help option.
2. Click your mouse on the Help Topics sheet Index tab. Help will display the Help Topics sheet Index page.
3. Double-click the "24-hour clock, changing to" topic. Help will display a window.
4. Click the jump button (the button with the curved arrow). Help will immediately open the the Regional Settings Properties sheet shown in Figure 68.
5. Change any settings you desire and close the window. If the Help window is open, close it.

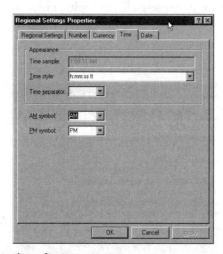

Figure 68 *Help window jump buttons open sheets for you.*

52 Selecting and Viewing a Help Topic

The online Help system takes advantage of *sheets*. A sheet is a dialog box with multiple tabbed *pages* that contain helpful information and controls. Tip 75 explains more about sheets. As you click on the tabs, different pages of the sheet appear. Figure 51.1 shows you the Contents page, one of three tabbed pages in the Help Topics sheet. To practice using the Help Topics sheet, perform these steps:

1. Perform the steps in Tip 51 to display the Help Topics sheet.
2. Double-click one of the book icons. Windows 95 will open that book and display its contents. Figure 52 shows an open "How To" book. (If you double-click an open book, Windows 95 will close it.)
3. Continue double-clicking on book icons until online Help displays topic icons, which look like dog-earred pieces of paper with question marks.
4. Double-click a topic icon. Help will display a window that contains the topic's information.
5. Click on the Help Topics button. Help will return you to the Help Topics sheet.
6. Click the Help Topics sheet Index tab to display the second of the sheet's three pages.
7. To view one of the Help topics, type the first few letters of the topic's title. Or, press the PAGE DOWN key to scroll through the topics list.
8. When you've highlighted a Help topic you want to read, press ENTER. Windows 95 will display a window that describes the topic.

Figure 52 The Help Topics sheet Contents page.

53 Understanding Help Topic Links

When you display a Help window, you often see more than just text. Online Help supports *jump buttons* that link Help windows to other windows. If you click on a jump button that appears blank, as shown in Figure 53.1, online Help will display another Help window. If you click on a jump button that contains curved arrows, such as the one in Figure 53.2, online Help runs a program or opens a properties sheet. Therefore, you'll often request information about a particular Help topic and visit two or more windows before you exit the online Help system. In addtion to jump buttons, many Help windows contain dotted, underlined terms, as shown in Figure 53.3. If you click on a dotted, underlined term, online Help will define it for you.

69 Placing and Jumping to a Bookmark within Help

When you want to remember where you are in a book, you place a bookmark. Then, when you're ready to continue reading, the bookmark lets you quickly pick up where you left off. Likewise, if you find something interesting in online Help, you can place a bookmark inside the Help text and quickly return to it at a later time. To place a bookmark in online Help, perform these steps:

Note: *Not all software supports the placement of bookmarks. You will be able to place a bookmark as long as your program's Help window contains a Bookmark option.*

1. Select the Help window in which you want to place a bookmark. Remember that the Help screen must contain a Bookmark button before you can insert a bookmark on this screen.
2. Click the Bookmark button.
3. Click the Define button and type a name and optional comment for the bookmark.
4. When you later display a bookmark menu by clicking the Help window's Bookmark button, select the bookmark name to which you want to jump and Windows 95 will display that window once again.

To remove a bookmark, select the bookmark and then click the Bookmark dialog box Delete button.

70 Finding Similar Topics within Help

Often, you may find an answer to a particular problem just by reading the first Help window you display. However, if, you click the window's jump buttons (buttons that link a Help window to sheets, dialog boxes, and other Help windows) to see other Help topics related to the one you're currently viewing, you may find a better way to accomplish your task. To locate related Help topics, you also can use a tool on the Help Topics sheet Find page. To do so, perform these steps:

1. Select the Start menu Help option.
2. Click the Help Topics sheet Find tab to display the Help Topics sheet Find page.
3. Select a topic from the list.
4. Click the Find Similar button to request a list of topics. Help, in turn, will display a Similar Topics dialog box, like the one shown in Figure 70, that lists topics related to the original topic you selected in step 3.

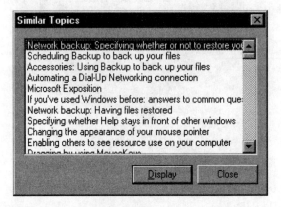

Figure 70 *The Similar Topics dialog box gathers related Help topics.*

Finding Out about Toolbar Buttons — 71

Many Windows 95 programs contain *toolbars* directly beneath their menu bars. A toolbar is a collection of buttons. Each toolbar button contain an icon that indicates its purpose. Although programmers design these icons to be easily identifiable and recognizable, there may be times when you don't recognize an icon or forget a particular button's purpose. Fortunately, to learn a button's name and purpose, all you must do is move your mouse pointer over the button. Windows 95, in turn, will display a pop-up window that contains the button's name. Addtionally, in the status bar, Windows 95 will describe the button's function (see Figure 71).

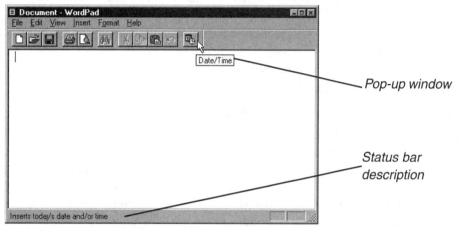

Figure 71 Windows 95 lets you learn a button's name and purpose.

Using Scroll Bars to View a Document — 72

As you work with large documents, such as a report or spreadsheet, your program windows won't always be large enough to display a document's entire contents. Even if you maximize a window, as Tip 13 describes, there may be times when you still can't see all of the data. Luckily, you can use *scroll bars* (located on the right and sometimes at the bottom of windows) to scroll your window's view up and down (vertically) and left and right (horizontally) to see additional data that was originally off your screen's edge. As you scroll, a *scroll box* inside the scroll bar moves to show relative window placement over the data. As you scroll, use the scroll box postion within the scroll bar as a guide to your relative position within the document. For example, if a scroll box in a Word window appears near the top of the vertical scroll bar, you are viewing information that appears near the start of your document. Likewise, if the scroll box appears at the bottom of the scroll bar, the program window is displaying content at the document's end. Table 72 lists the methods you can use to scroll through program windows.

Method	Description
Drag a scroll box	Scrolls the window rapidly through the document
Click on scroll bar arrows	Scrolls the window one small step (usually a column or a line of text)
Click on scroll bar	Scrolls the window one large step (almost always the window's width or height)

Table 72 Window-scrolling methods.

If a window does not contain scroll bars, the window already displays data without you needing to scroll. Figure 72 displays a window with scroll bars.

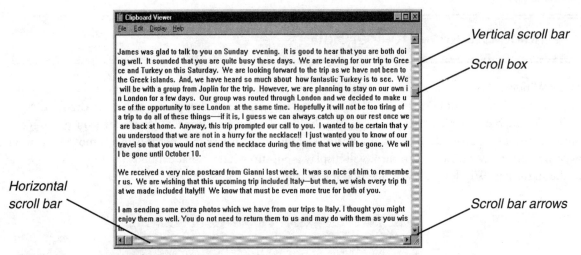

Figure 72 *Scroll bars let you see more data.*

73 Working with Pull-Down Menus

Almost all Windows 95 programs use pull-down menus to group similar commands together and thereby make them easier for you to access. For example, many of the options on Word's Edit menu let you locate, manipulate, and reshape text. To access pull-down menus, you must move your mouse pointer to the program window's *menu bar*, which typically resides just beneath the title bar, and click your mouse on the name of the menu you want to view. To access a pull-down menu from your keyboard, press ALT and the underlined letter in the menu's name (For example, on the menu bar in most in Windows programs, the letter *F* is underlined in the word *File*. Therefore, ALT-F displays the File menu).

To select an option from a pull-down menu, you can click the option with your mouse. Or, if you prefer to use your keyboard, you can press the ARROW keys to highlight the correct option and then press ENTER.

Sometimes, ellipses appear after a menu option to indicate that the program will display a dialog box if you select that option. Additionally, if you move your mouse pointer over an option with a right-pointing arrow, the program will display additional menus, as shown in Figure 73.

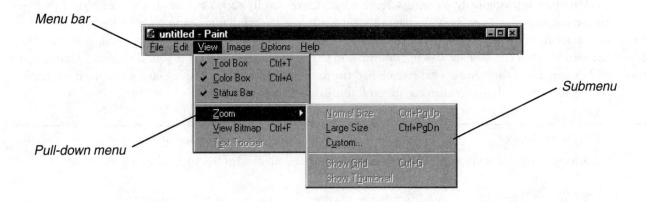

Figure 73 *Windows 95 menus let you get to commands easily.*

Understanding Menu Option Hot Keys — 74

A *hot key* is a keystroke combination you can use to immediately initiate a menu option. Often, Windows 95 menus list hot keys to the right of menu options. For example, if you see the hot key CTRL+P next to a File menu Print option, you can hold down the CTRL key and type P to select the Print option without having to display the File menu. Figure 74 shows a WordPad window displaying the File menu. To save the data in this window, you do not have to display the File menu. You only have to press the CTRL+S hot key.

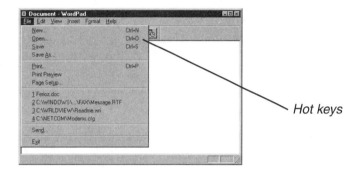

Figure 74 Hot keys save you time.

Understanding Sheets, Pages, and Tabs — 75

As Tip 73 states, when you select a menu option that contains ellipses, the program will display a *dialog box*. Dialog boxes contain controls (such as check boxes, option buttons, and pull-down lists) that you can select to respond to a program. (Tips 77 through 79 explain these controls). Dialog boxes appear when Windows 95 or a program needs information from you to complete a task. For example, if you want to open a Word document, you need to tell Word the document's name and location. Figure 75.1 shows an example of an Open dialog box. Occasionally, Windows 95 or a program will use *sheets*, advanced dialog boxes that contain multiple *pages* you access by clicking on tabs just beneath the title bar. Sheets let you access a large number of controls without opening and closing several windows. Windows 95 and other programs use sheets when they need a lot of information from you. Figure 75.2 shows an example of a sheet.

Figure 75.1 A dialog box can require several answers.

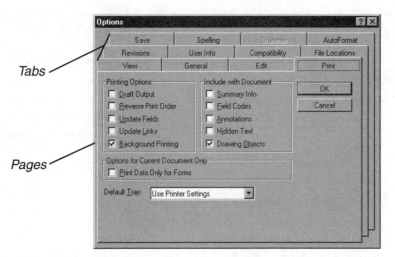

Figure 75.2 *Tabs display additional pages.*

76 | Highlighting a Dialog Box Option

As Tip 75 explains, dialog boxes can contain several controls that need your response. Rarely do you have to respond to *every* dialog box control. However, you will often need to change a particular control's setting or click a specific button control. As such, you need to know how to access dialog box controls. To select a dialog box control, you can use the following methods:

- Press TAB until the control's border appears highlighted (darkened).
- Press SHIFT-TAB until the control's border appears highlighted. (SHIFT-TAB moves the highlight backward through the order of controls.)
- Click your mouse on a control.
- Press ALT followed by the underlined letter in the control's label. To highlight a command button labeled "Open," you would press ALT-O.

Figure 76 shows a dialog box with the Properties command button highlighted.

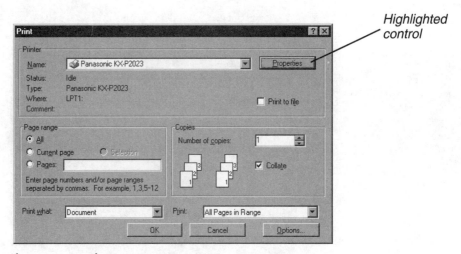

Figure 76 *The highlight shows the current control.*

Using Check boxes to Select Multiple Options — 77

Dialog boxes often require you to make choices. A program might provide a list of options and want to know which ones you want active. To obtain such information from you, many dialog boxes include *check boxes*. For example, a database program's dialog box might contain a list of check boxes that let you choose which columns of data you want printed for a report.

Check boxes are toggle controls—you perform the same actions to select and deselect them. When you select (or activate) a check box, a check mark appears in the box. When you deselect (or deactivate) a check box, the check mark disappears. To select and deselect check boxes, you can use any of the following methods:

- Move your mouse pointer to the check box and click your left mouse button.
- Press the ALT key followed by the underlined character in the check box's caption.
- Press TAB to highlight the check box and then press ENTER.

Figure 77 shows a sheet that contains a list of check boxes. Notice that only some of the check boxes have check marks.

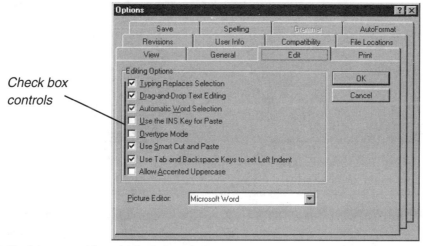

Figure 77 Check boxes provide multiple choices.

Using Option Buttons — 78

A program uses *option buttons* when it needs you to choose one and only one option from a list of options. Option button controls work like the buttons on car radios; you can select one and only one radio station at any one time. When you push a button, the previously selected button deactivates. Likewise, when you select an option button, the previously selected option button deactivates. To select an option button control, perform any of these actions:

- Move your mouse pointer to the option button and click your left mouse button.
- Press ALT followed by the underlined character in the option button's caption.

Figure 78.1 shows a dialog box with five option button controls. Often, a dialog box contains both option button and check box controls as Figure 78.2 shows.

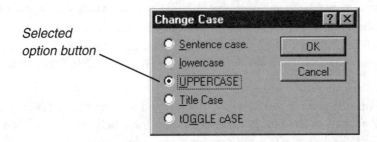

Figure 78.1 Option buttons offer single-choice selections.

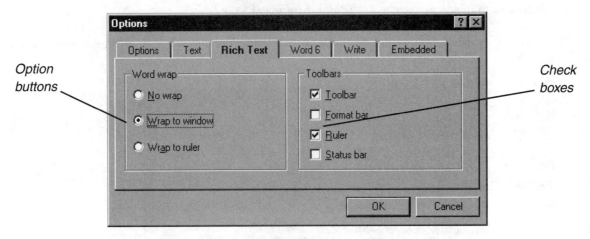

Figure 78.2 Option buttons and check boxes in the same dialog box.

79 Selecting Items from a Pull-Down List

Some dialog boxes provide option lists that are too long to display in a check box or option button controls. For example, if a dialog box needs you to choose an area code from a nationwide list of area codes, there wouldn't be enough room in the dialog box for several hundred area-code controls.

Rather than filling up an entire dialog box (or several dialog boxes) with controls, many programs will use a *pull-down list*. When you first open a dialog box, all pull-down lists are closed. Figure 79.1 shows a closed pull-down list. When you open a pull-down list, it drops downward. Figure 79.2 shows an open pull-down list. After you open a pull-down list, you can select one or more items. To select an item from a pull-down list, perform these steps:

1. Open the pull-down list. To do so, click the arrow next to the list. Or, press TAB to highlight the list and press the SHIFT-DOWN ARROW.
2. Click the item you want to select. Or, scroll to the item with the UP and DOWN ARROWS and press ENTER.
3. Select another item if the pull-down list allows for multiple choices.
4. Select a different dialog box control to close the list.

Figure 79.1 A closed pull-down list shows one item.

Figure 79.2 An open pull-down list displays several items.

Using a Text Box to Type in Data — 80

Instead of selecting from a list of options, you sometimes must enter data that a program needs. Dialog boxes often contain *text boxes* in which you can type information the program needs. Sometimes, a text box requires a numeric value. Other times, a program uses text boxes to retrieve information such as filenames, search characters, and so on. To type information in a text box, perform these steps:

1. Highlight the text box (see Tip 76).
2. Type a value into the text box. If a value is already there, you can replace or change that value (use the ARROW, DELETE, and INSERT keys to edit the text).
3. Press ENTER or highlight a different control to anchor the text in the text box.

If a text box is not big enough to display an entire value, use the LEFT and RIGHT ARROW keys to scroll through the text. Figure 80 shows the Run dialog box with its text box highlighted.

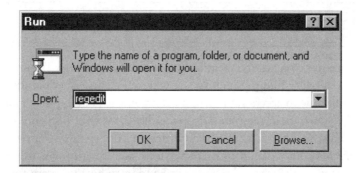

Figure 80 Text boxes let you enter dialog box text.

81 Using the OK, Cancel, and Apply Buttons

After you finish responding to a dialog box, you must tell the program that you are done. Essentially, you must command the program to do one of three things:

- Accept your control values
- Ignore any entries you made in the dialog box
- Apply your dialog box settings immediately but keep the dialog box on the screen so you can continue entering additional dialog box values.

To issue the first command, which sends all your control values to the program and closes the dialog box, select the dialog box's OK button. To send the second command, which nullifies all your control selections (everyone's entitled to change his or her mind) and closes the dialog box, click on the dialog box's Cancel button. To issue the third command, which lets you see the results of your current dialog box settings (such as screen color settings), click on the dialog box's Apply button. Figure 81 shows a dialog box with OK, Cancel, and Apply command buttons. To select one of the command buttons, you can highlight the button (by pressing the TAB) and press ENTER or click the command button with your mouse.

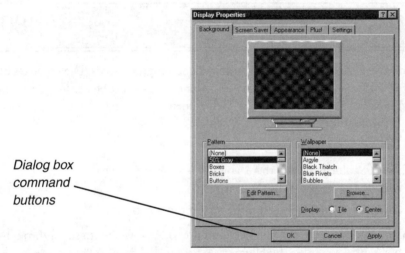

Dialog box command buttons

Figure 81 Select a command button to activate or ignore dialog box settings.

82 Organizing Your Files Using Directories

As you work with your computer, you will be creating new files. As these files accumulate, you'll need a way to organize them. As you know, a paper-filing system doesn't work efficiently if you randomly place documents in a drawer. Likewise, you won't be able to access your system's electronic files in a timely manner if you don't organize them properly. For example, your system may contain spreadsheets for your household finances, word-processing documents for your children's school projects, PowerPoint files for your spouse's business presentations, and more. To make sure no family member must spend unnecessary time searching for his or her work, you can create a separate folder (or directory) for each person's files. (See Tip 84 to learn how to create and delete folders.) That way, the next time you need to access the family's financial records, you can go directly to the appropriate folder and look for them in a list of files that doesn't include all your kids' book reports. Tip 83 explains how to access your system's folders.

Note: *Often, when you install a program, it will create folders and will use them for its own work. Additionally, the program may create folders in which you can store its data. In most cases, you don't have to use such program-created, data-storage folders. If you wish, you can create other folders and store your data in them.*

How Windows 95 Folders Relate to Directories — 83

To organize the files on your disk, you create directories within which you store specific files. Think of a directory as a drawer within a filing cabinet. You might, for example, have one directory that contains your letters, another for memos, and a third for reports. By storing your files within directories, you make the files much easier to locate at a later time. As you have learned, a Windows 95 folder icon represents a directory on your disk drive. When you double-click on a closed folder icon, Windows 95 displays the contents of the directory that icon represents.

The Windows 95 Explorer is the best place to view your disk's folder structure. Figure 83 shows an Explorer window. On the Explorer window's right side, Windows 95 displays the contents of the open folder icon on the window's left side. As you click on the folders that appear in left window, Explorer will display the folder's contents (its files) within the right window. If you talk with another user about where you have placed a file on your disk, keep in mind that a *directory* is the same thing as a Windows 95 folder.

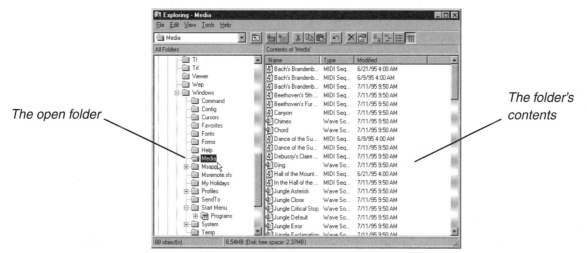

Figure 83 *Explorer lets you manage files and folders.*

Creating and Removing Folders — 84

As you have learned, many programs will create folders in which you can store data. However, you may not always want to use these folders. For example, if you work as a business executive and write fiction in your spare time, you may not want to store both your short stories and your annual reports in the Microsoft Word default folder. Instead, you might want to create two folders: one called "Stories" and the other "Reports." Similarly, if you give up story-writing, or quit you job to write full-time, you may want to delete one of these folders to help reduce the clutter on your hard disk.

To create a folder, perform these steps:

1. Start the Explorer program. (Right-click on the Start button. Then, select the pop-up menu's Explore option.)

2. Move your mouse pointer to the disk drive in which you want to create a new folder. (Look for the disk drive on the Explorer window's left side.)

3. Click your mouse to display that drive's highest level of folders and files.
4. Move your mouse pointer to the folder within which you want to create a new folder and click your mouse.
5. Select the File menu New option. Windows 95 will display the New menu.
6. Select the New menu Folder option.
7. Type the name of the new folder and press ENTER.

Note: *You can create a new folder at any level within the directory structure. If you want to create a new folder deep within the file system, click folder icons until you reach the directory within which you want the new folder to reside. If you want to create a new folder from the drive's top level (called the root directory), open no folders before you perform step 5.*

To delete a folder, perform these steps:

1. Start the Explorer program.
2. Locate the folder you want to delete.
3. Click on the folder you want to delete. Windows 95 will highlight the folder's name.
4. Select the File menu Delete option. Windows 95 displays a message box that asks you to confirm the deletion..
5. Click the Yes button to send the folder to the Recycle Bin.

85 Understanding the Open Dialog Box

If you want to modify a document you created using a Windows 95 program, such as WordPad, you must first tell the program to retrieve the document from your disk and load it into your system's *RAM* (random access memory). One way to retrieve a document is to use the File menu Open option that appears in most Windows 95 program windows. When you select this option, the program displays the Open dialog box, which gives you the power to quickly find and open any file on your system.

Using the Open dialog box, you can specify parameters for a file search. For example, if you only want to search among word-processing documents, you can tell the Open dialog box to display only files with a DOC extension. In the Open dialog box, you can view files as labeled icons or as list items that include such information as file type, size, and date last modified. Figure 85 shows the Open dialog box.

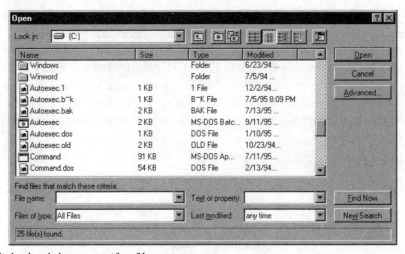

Figure 85 *The Open dialog box helps you specify a file to open.*

Using the Open Dialog Box to Locate and Open Files — 86

As you have learned, the Open dialog box lets you retrieve documents from your disk and load them into your system's memory. However, before you can actually retrieve a file, you must first locate it. Luckily, the Open dialog box makes such file searches easy. To find and access a file through the Open dialog box, perform these steps:

1. Click the Look in pull-down list button (the button with the down-pointing arrow to the right of the Look in field). The program will will display the Look in pull-down list, as shown in Figure 86.
2. In the Look in pull-down list, click the drive or network that you want to search for a particular file. The Open dialog box's work area will display that drive or network's contents.
3. In the work area, double-click on folder icons until the file you want appears.
4. Click the filename or icon and then click the Open button.

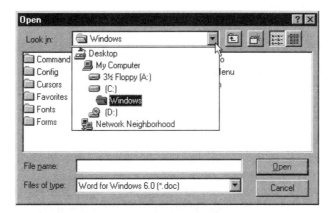

Figure 86 *The Open dialog box lets you search your system's directory structure.*

Listing Files of a Specific Type Using the Open Dialog Box — 87

The Open dialog box's Files of type field specifies the types of files that will appear in the dialog box's work area. Typically, a Windows 95 program will pre-set this field to the file type it uses the most. For example, by default, Paint pre-sets the Files of type field to "Bitmap Files." In most cases, this initial setting will serve you well. In fact, because this setting limits the types of files the dialog box will display, it actually speeds up any file searches you perform. For example, if you want to find a specific graphics file in Paint, the Files of type field's "Bitmap Files" default setting will focus your search on graphics files only. However, there may be times when you want to change the setting in the Files of type field. For example, you may want to use WordPad, which pre-sets the Files of type field to files with the DOC extension, to open an *RTF* (Rich Text Format) file. Or, you may encounter an Open dialog box in which the file type setting is too broad. (For example, if someone used WordPad immediately before you did, you may find they set the Files of type field to "All Files.") To specify a particular file type in an Open dialog box, perform these steps:

1. Click the Files of type pull-down list button. Figure 87 shows a Files of type pull-down list.
2. Select the file type you want from the Files of type pull-down list.
3. Traverse the folder and file structure as usual. The Open dialog box will display only those files that match the type you've selected.

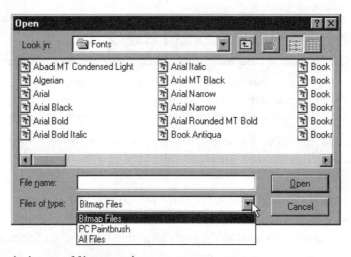

Figure 87 *You can specify exactly the type of file you need.*

88 Using the Save and Save As Options

The Open and Save As dialog boxes look very much alike. However, they perform opposite functions. Whereas the Open dialog box lets you load a file from disk into memory, the Save As dialog box lets you name and save data to a disk file. When you want to save a file, you usually have two options:

- The File menu Save option
- The File menu Save As option

Suppose you start a program and create a new document. If you select the File menu Save option or the File menu Save As option, the program will display the Save As dialog box, as shown in Figure 88. In the Save As dialog box, you specify the location at which, and the filename under which, you want the program to save your data.

After you specify a name and location in the Save As dialog box, the program will use that information each time you select the File menu Save option. (After the first time you save a new document, the program will not display the Save As dialog box when you select the File menu Save option.) If you want to change the file's location, name, or both, you must select the File menu Save As option and make your modifications in the Save As dialog box.

Note: *If you attempt to close a program without saving its data, the program will display a Save As dialog box.*

Figure 88 *The Save As dialog box helps you save files.*

Saving a File in a Specific Folder Using the Save In Field — 89

As you learned in Tip 88, the Save As dialog box lets you specify the location and name under which a program will save a file. As such, if you want to save a file in a directory, drive, or network area that is different from the selected folder, drive, and network area, all you must do is access the Save As dialog box and specify the location you desire. To change a file's location on your system, perform these steps:

1. Select the File menu Save As option.
2. Click the Save in pull-down list button. The program will display the Save in pull-down list, as shown in Figure 89.
3. Select the drive in which you want to save your file.
4. In the Save As dialog box's work area, double-click on the folder in which you want to save your file.
5. In the File name text box, enter a filename.
6. Click the Save button.

Figure 89 *The Save in pull-down list lets you specify a different location.*

Saving a File to a Specific Format — 90

Some programs let you save your data in several types of data formats. For example, Word for Windows can save a document in the native Word format, a standard text format, a WordPerfect format, and several other formats. For example, assume that you have just finished a ten-page report that you must give to your boss on disk. To create the report, you used Word for Windows. Your boss, on the other hand, uses WordPerfect. Luckily, rather than having to retype your report using WordPerfect, you can simply instruct Word to save the report in a format suitable for WordPerfect. Normally, you wll specify the format you desire, by selecting the format from a pull-down list of available options.

Most programs have a default file format. For example, if you try to save a file using the Windows 95 Paint accessory, Paint will pre-set the Save as type field to "Bitmap." If you want to override the default format, you can open the Save as type pull-down list and select a different type.

91 Quickly Move Up One Level of Folders

As you traverse folders in Windows 95, there may be times when you'll want to back up a few steps. For example, you may open a folder, find it doesn't contain the file you want, and thus need to backtrack through the directory structure to reach another folder. Fortunately, all Windows 95 Save As and Open dialog boxes, as well as all Explorer windows, provide an Up One Level button that lets you move up a folder level. For example, if you access a folder named "Silver" from a folder named "Gold" and find nothing useful, you can click on the Up One Level button or press the BACKSPACE key to return to the Gold folder. Figure 91.1 displays a Save As dialog box. If you click on the Up One Level button, Windows 95 changes the Save As dialog box to display folders and files from the next highest folder level, as shown in Figure 91.2. To use the keyboard to move up one directory level, press BACKSPACE.

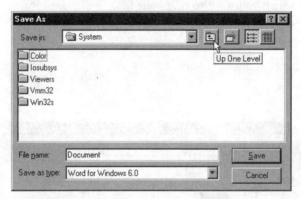

Figure 91.1 Before you select the Up One Level button.

Figure 91.2 After you select the Up One Level button or press BACKSPACE.

92 Creating Folder within a File-Related Dialog Box

As you prepare to open or save a file, there may be times when you want to create a folder. As such, you'll likely not want to use the procedure you learned in Tip 84, which would require you to close the dialog box (Open or Save As) and start Explorer. Fortunately, Windows 95 provides you with a shortcut, a way to create a folder on the spot without switching applications or even closing the dialog box. To create a new folder from within an Open or Save As dialog box, perform these steps:

1. Select the folder in which your new folder will reside.
2. Move your mouse pointer to a blank spot inside the dialog box.
3. Right-click on the blank spot. A pop-up menu appears.

4. Select the pop-up menu's New option.
5. Click your mouse on the New menu Folder option. Windows 95 creates a new folder.
6. Type a name for the new folder and press ENTER.

Note: *You can create a new folder quickly by selecting the parent folder you desire and then clicking your mouse on the New Folder button that appears to the right of the Up-One-Level toolbar button.*

93 Listing Folder Icons or Details within a File-Related Dialog Box

By default, Windows 95 file-related dialog boxes (Open and Save As dialog boxes) display files as icons. For most users, the default is acceptable. The icon format lets them view a large number of files in a single window with a minimum amount of scrolling. However, some users want more information about the files than labeled icons provide. Luckily, Windows 95 gives you several ways to view information in a file-related dialog box. For example, you can tell Windows 95 to display your files as list items rather than labeled icons. If you want to view a file-related dialog box's contents differently, click the dialog box's toolbar Details button. Figure 93.1 shows a dialog box before you click the Details button. Figure 93.1's dialog box displays its contents in the *list view*. Figure 93.2 shows the same dialog box after you press the Details button. To return to the list view from the details view, press the toolbar List button that appears just left of the Details button. As you can see, the details view displays more information about a file than the list view. In details view, the dialog box tells you a file's size, type, and the date and time it was last modified. The list view displays more items per dialog box without so much detail.

Figure 93.1 *This dialog box uses a list view.*

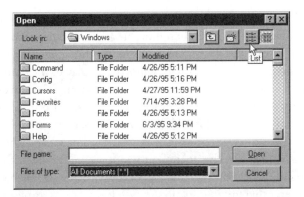

Figure 93.2 *This dialog box uses a details view.*

Note: *When you display a folder's contents using details view, you can sort your display by name, type, date, or size by clicking on the corresponding button that appears at the top of the category under which you want to perform your search.*

94 Using the Browse Dialog Box

As you use Windows 95, there will be times, such as when you use the Run option (see Tip 31), when you need to find a file but don't know its name. Luckily, several locations in Windows 95 include a Browse button that lets you maneuver through your files and folders until you come across the file you need. To use the Browse button with the Start menu Run option, perform these steps:

1. Click the Start button to display the Start menu.
2. Select the Start menu Run option.
3. Click the Browse button. Windows 95 will display the Browse dialog box shown Figure 94.
4. Select the computer (if on a network) you want to search.
5. Select the disk drive in which you want to look for the file.
6. Select the folder in which you want to look.
7. Select the program you want to run.

Note: *Without the Browse button, you would have to know every program's name and location.*

Figure 94 *This Browse button searches your system for files.*

95 Understanding Program and Document Windows

When you run a program, Windows displays the program's output within a *program window*. As you may know, many programs, such as word processors, let you open more than one document at the same time. When you open the document, the program will display the document's contents within a *document window*. When a program uses document windows, the program restricts the document window's display to the boundaries of the program window. In other words, the document window cannot be larger than the program window of the program that opened the document. Assume, for example, you have two word processing documents open. In this case, your word processor will reside within its own program window and it will display each document within its own document window. In other words, your screen will contain three windows, one for the word processor (the program window) and one for each document (two document windows). The document windows will reside within the program window. Most programs that use document windows let you tile, cascade, or individually size each document window. It is important that you distinguish between program and document windows. For example, when you maximize a program window, Windows 95 will expand the window to fill your entire screen. When you maximize a document window, on the other hand, Windows 95 only expands the document window to the size of its surrounding program window. Also, when you close a program window, Windows 95 ends the program. When you close a document window, on the other hand, the program continues to run.

Using the Control Menu — 96

In the upper-left hand corner of almost every window, Windows 95 displays a *Control menu icon*. When you click the Control menu icon, the *Control menu* shown in Figure 96 appears. The Control menu is a universal menu for all program and document windows. As Table 96 explains, the Control menu lets you control the size and placement of windows.

Note: Not every option of the Control menu will always be available. For example, depending on the window's design, you may not be able to maximize the window. Unavailable Control menu options will appear gray.

Option	Description
Restore	Restores the window to its former size.
Move	Lets you move the window with the ARROW keys.
Size	Lets you change the size of the window using the ARROW keys.
Minimize	Shrinks the window to a Taskbar icon, or if the window is a document window (a window within a parent window), shrinks the window to an icon within the parent program.
Maximize	Expands the window to consume the entire screen, or to fill the window's parent window if the window is a document window (a window within a window).
Close	Closes the window. If the window is a program, Windows 95 ends the program.

Table 96 The Control menu lets you control the size and placement of windows.

Figure 96 The Control menu appears on most windows.

Using the New, Open, Save, and Print Icons — 97

Nearly every Windows 95 program displays a toolbar or gives you the option of displaying a toolbar. Additionally, almost every Windows 95 program toolbar will contain four buttons that give you one-click access to the four most common actions (New, Open, Save, and Print) you perform. Table 97 explains the function of each of these toolbar buttons.

Icon	Name	Purpose
	New	Creates a new document.
	Open	Displays the Open dialog box.
	Save	Displays the Save As dialog box (or saves the file if the program already knows the filename).
	Print	Prints the current document.

Table 97 *The first four toolbar icons let you perform common actions.*

Figure 97 shows a running program with these four buttons at the toolbar's left edge.

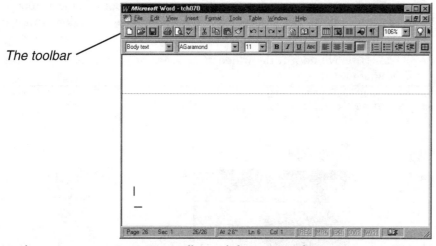

Figure 97 *Almost every program contains a toolbar with four common functions.*

98 Understanding the Windows 95 Desktop

To understand the Windows 95 Desktop, sit at your desk and examine the objects in front of you. Note the objects (pencils, sheets of paper, reference books, manila folders, and so on) that rest on your desktop. Now, sit in front of your computer and look at the objects on your screen. Note how all your system's icons, folders, and other objects don't float freely across your display (no more than your stapler and paper clips float weightless about your office). They rest against a background that users call the *Desktop*.

Like an actual desktop, the Windows 95 Desktop is always there, no matter how many objects you place on it. The Desktop never goes away, even when it lies beneath a maximized window. Additionally, you can redesign your Desktop in the following ways:

- You can alter your Desktop's appearance, just as you can paint or varnish an actual desktop. You can change your Desktop's color, specify a background pattern, assign a wallpaper, and so on.

- You can manually reposition your Desktop's objects, just as you can push aside folders and move pen holders on an actual desktop. Or, you can use Windows 95 features that automatically rearrange windows and icons for you.

- You can remove icons, windows, and other objects from your Desktop, just as you can place your actual desktop's contents into drawers.

As you read through this section's tips, you will learn how to perform all these actions and more. You will discover how to create a Desktop that is attractive and (most important) functional.

Tracking a Large Number of Programs on the Taskbar 99

As Tip 9 explains, Windows 95 lets you run several programs at the same time. Normally, the Taskbar makes it easy for you locate and switch between running programs. You simply scan its buttons and select the one that activates the program window you want to use. (Each button contains an icon and label that tells you the program it represents.)

However, if you run too many programs concurrently, your Taskbar may fill up with so many buttons that you can't quickly distinguish between them. And, if you can't easily tell which Taskbar buttons represent which running programs, you can't use your Taskbar to locate and switch between those programs efficiently.

If you find your Taskbar is getting crowded, like the one in Figure 99, you should reevaluate your need for running so many programs at one time. If you decide you do need to run so many programs concurrently, you can use the information in subsequent tips to change your Taskbar's appearance and thereby improve its effectiveness.

Figure 99 A crowded Taskbar.

100 | Making the Taskbar Wider

If you're running several programs and your Taskbar looks as cluttered as the one in Figure 99, you should consider increasing the Taskbar's width. A wider Taskbar gives the Taskbar buttons more room to display their icons and labels. To increase the Taskbar's width, perform these steps:

1. Move your mouse pointer to the Taskbar's top edge. (If your Taskbar is on your screen's left, top, or right side, move your mouse pointer to the edge closest to your screen's center.) The mouse pointer will change to a double-pointing arrow.
2. Click your left mouse button and drag your mouse pointer toward your screen's center. As you drag the mouse, the Taskbar will increase in size.
3. Release your left mouse button when the Taskbar is the size you want.

Obviously, if you expand the Taskbar size too much, you'll take away screen room from your running programs and windows. Therefore, do not make the Taskbar wider than necessary. Figure 100 shows a three-row Taskbar that holds the same buttons as the Taskbar Figure 99 displays. Note how Figure 100's Taskbar buttons are much easier to read than their counterparts in Figure 99.

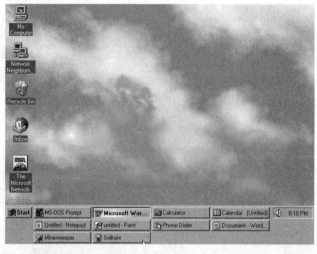

Figure 100 *This Taskbar is much less cluttered and much easier to read.*

101 | Arranging Icons on the Desktop

Just as you can move and reorder the objects on an actual desktop, you can rearrange your Desktop's icons into a configuration that you like. To rearrange your Desktop's icons, you can perform these tasks:

- Drag an icon or icons to a new location.
- Display your Desktop icons in alphabetical order. To do so, right-click on the Desktop and select the pop-up menu's Arrange Icons option. Then, select the Arrange Icons menu By Name option.
- Make Windows 95 keep Desktop icons in neat rows and columns. To do so, right-click on the Desktop and select the pop-up menu's Arrange Icons option. Then, select the Arrange Icons menu Auto Arrange option.
- Line up your Desktop icons in rows. To do so, right-click on the Desktop and select the pop-up menu's Line up Icons option.

Lining Up Icons on the Desktop   102

After you add shortcuts, remove icons, and move icons around your Desktop, you may need to straighten things up. Although you can manually move your icons until your Desktop once again appears tidy, you don't have to do all that work yourself. You can tell Windows 95 to do it for you. To tell Windows 95 to put your Desktop icons into neat rows and columns, perform these steps:

1. Close or minimize the windows on your screen until you see a clear spot on your Desktop.
2. Move your mouse pointer to the clear spot and right-click. Windows 95 will display a pop-up menu.
3. Select the pop-up menu's Line up Icons option. Windows 95 will align your icons in neat rows and columns.

Figure 102.1 shows a Desktop before you tell Windows 95 to line up the icons. Figure 102.2 shows the same Desktop after you select the pop-up menu's Line up Icons option.

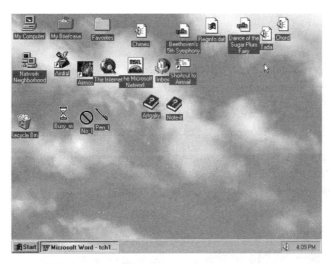

Figure 102.1 A messy Desktop.

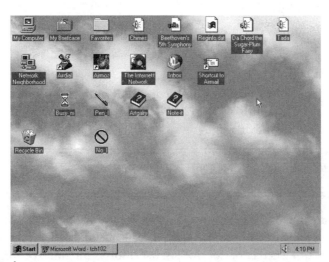

Figure 102.2 A well-ordered Desktop.

103 Insuring the Taskbar Is Always Visible

As you know, the Taskbar is integral to the operation of Windows 95. The Taskbar lets you access the programs and windows that you want when you want them. It also makes switching programs on your computer as easy as switching channels on your television. However, to use the Taskbar effectively, you must always be able access it. If a program window overlaps or covers the Taskbar, you may not be able to see or click on all or any of the Taskbar's buttons. To keep the Taskbar visible and accessible at all times, perform these steps:

1. Display the Start menu.
2. Select the Start menu Settings option.
3. Select the Settings menu Taskbar option. Windows 95 will display the Taskbar Properties sheet Taskbar Options page.
4. If the Taskbar Options page Always on top check box is unchecked, click the check box to activate the option.
5. Click the OK button.

After you select the "Always on top" check box and click the OK button, you can run maximized applications without losing the Taskbar.

Note: Maximized MS-DOS applications never display the Taskbar.

104 Hiding the Taskbar After Each Use

Although you'll want to keep the Taskbar accessible as much as possible, there may be times when you want it out of sight. For example, assume you are using a graphics program and need screen space to draw. Fortunately, Windows 95 gives you a way to hide the Taskbar without restricting your access to it. To hide the Taskbar, perform these steps:

1. Display the Start menu.
2. Select the Start menu Settings option.
3. Select the Settings menu Taskbar option. Windows 95 will display the Taskbar Properties sheet Taskbar Options page.
4. If the Taskbar Options page Auto hide check box is unchecked, click the check box to activate the option.
5. Click the OK button.

Even though you've hidden the Taskbar, you can still use it. To do so, move your mouse pointer to the lower-left corner of your screen. Windows 95, in turn, will display the Taskbar again. If you move your mouse away from the Taskbar, Windows 95 will hide the Taskbar again.

105 Displaying or Hiding the Taskbar Clock

The right side of the Taskbar contains indicators that describe events taking place in your computer. It also displays the time of day. By removing these items from the Taskbar, you free up space on the Taskbar for Windows 95 to display program icons. To control whether or not the Taskbar displays the time, perform these steps:

1. Display the Start menu.
2. Select the Start menu Settings option.

3. Select the Settings menu Taskbar option. Windows 95 will display the Taskbar Properties sheet Taskbar Options page.
4. If you want to see the clock, make sure the Show Clock check box is checked. If you don't want to see the clock, make sure the Show Clock check box is empty.
5. Click the OK button.

106. Controlling the Size of Start Menu Options

As you use Windows 95, there may be times when you want to change the size of the Start menu options. For example, if you're having difficulty reading the options, you may want to make them larger. Conversely, if your Start menu contains many options, you may want to make them smaller so you can see more of them at one time. To change the size of your Start menu options, perform these steps:

1. Display the Start menu.
2. Select the Start menu Settings option.
3. Select the Settings menu Taskbar option. Windows 95 will display the Taskbar Properties sheet Taskbar Options page.
4. If you want to make your Start menu options smaller, click on the Show small icons in Start menu check box until a check mark appears. If you want to increase the size of the Start menu icons, remove the check mark from that check box.
5. Click the OK button.

Figure 106.1 shows a Start menu with small icons. Figure 106.2 shows a Start menu with large icons.

Figure 106.1 This Start menu displays small icons and labels.

Figure 106.2 This Start menu displays large icons and labels.

107 Understanding and Creating Shortcuts

As you work with Windows 95, there may be certain programs or documents that you work with so frequently that it becomes a nuisance to go through the Start menu each time you want to open them. To save yourself time and effort, you can create a shortcut to the program (or to a document) and place that shortcut's icon on your Desktop. Then, the next time you want to access the program or document, all you must do is double-click the shortcut icon. (If you wish, you can still start the program from its location on the Start menu.)

Note: *If you delete a shortcut to a file, Windows 95 deletes only the shortcut and not the file itself. The shortcut acts like a link to the file but does not represent the actual file or a copy of the file.*

As you know, when you double-click a file icon, Windows 95 starts the program that lets you work with that file. For example, if you double-click on a WordPad document icon, WordPad starts and loads the document. Shortcuts provide that same kind of one-step program/data file loading. To create a shortcut to a file, perform these steps:

1. Find the file for which you want to create a shortcut (either in Explorer, an Open dialog box, or My Computer).
2. Right-click over the file icon. Windows 95 will display a pop-up menu.
3. Select the pop-up menu's Create Shortcut option. Windows 95 will create a shortcut icon for the file and either store the shortcut at the file's current location or on the Desktop. If Windows 95 stores the icon at the file's current location, you must move the icon to the Desktop yourself.

In some cases, you don't need to access the pop-up menu mentioned in steps 2 and 3 to create a shortcut. For example, if you can see any part of your Desktop before you create the shortcut, you can press CTRL-SHIFT and use your mouse to drag the file's icon to the Desktop. Windows 95 uses the same icon to represent the shortcut as it does to represent the original file. However, the shortcut icon has a boxed arrow in its lower-left corner. Also, Windows 95 adds the words "Shortcut to" to the shortcut icon's caption.

108 Copying Objects Using Copy and Paste

Windows 95 includes an electronic *Clipboard* that temporarily holds data and programs. If you copy an object to the Clipboard, the object remains there until you copy another object or exit Windows 95. After you copy an object to the Clipboard, you can *paste* that object to another area of your computer. Normally, users perform cut-and-paste operations to move or copy text from one document to another (within their word processor) or from one program to another. As it turns out, however, Windows 95 lets you cut and paste files, folders, and other desktop objects to move or copy the object. Using cut-and-paste or copy-and-paste operations, you can move or copy an object from one folder to another. As such, with copy-and-paste operations, you can effectively make duplicate files and program backups. To copy an object from one location to another, perform these steps:

1. Use Explorer or My Computer to find the object you want to copy.
2. Select the Edit menu Copy option. (Or, right-click on the object and select the pop-up menu's Copy option.) Windows 95 places a copy of the object on to the Clipboard.
3. Use Explorer or My Computer to find the location at which you want to paste the object.
4. Select the Edit menu Paste option.

Windows 95 lets you copy a portion of an object, such as a sentence from a word processor's document, to the Desktop. Such an object is known as a *scrap*. Windows 95 indicates scraps by putting the word "scrap" in the icon's caption.

Moving Objects Using Cut and Paste | 109

Tip 108 explains how, when you copy and paste an object, you actually create a duplicate of the object. In contrast, when you perform a *cut* operation, Windows 95 deletes the object from its original location and stores it on the Clipboard so you can paste the object somewhere else. When you cut and paste an object, such as a file, you in effect move that object from its original location to its new location. To cut and paste an object, perform these steps:

1. Use Explorer or My Computer to find the object you want to cut and paste.
2. Select the Edit menu Cut option. (Or, right-click on the object and select the pop-up menu's Cut option.) Windows 95 moves the object from its current location to the Clipboard.
3. Use Explorer or My Computer to locate where you want to move the object.
4. Select the Edit menu Paste option.

Using Drag and Drop to Move and Copy Objects | 110

Many people find it easier to use the mouse to copy or drag objects instead of using the menus described in Tips 108 and 109. When you use the mouse to drag an object, you must be able to see the object's current and target location. For example, if you want to drag a file from one folder to another folder, you must be able to see the file and the target folder before you begin dragging. If you cannot display both items at the same time, you must use the Clipboard as an intermediate holding area to copy or cut. If you want to move a file from one folder to another, simply drag the file's name or icon from its current location to the folder where you want to place the file. Release your left mouse button to complete the move operation. If you want to copy a file from one folder to another, hold down your CTRL key while you drag the file's name or icon from its current location to the folder where you want the file to reside. To anchor the object at its new location, release both the CTRL key and your left mouse button.

Using Drag and Drop Printing | 111

As you work with documents, you may need to print a document in a hurry. You may not always have time to start the program you used to create the document and select its File menu Print option. Luckily, Windows 95 provides a technique, called drag-and-drop printing, you can use to print a document quickly. To use drag-and-drop printing, perform these steps:

1. Open the My Computer window and double-click on the Printers icon. Windows 95 will display a Printers window, as shown in Figure 111, that contains an icon and description for each printer connected to your system (including fax devices).
2. In the Explorer window or through My Computer, locate the document you want to print.
3. Drag the document from its current location to the icon of the printer you want to use and release your mouse button (drop the document).

Figure 111 My Computer's Printers window.

112 Creating Your Own Folders

As you create more and more files, you'll need a way to organize and categorize them. In Windows 95, the easiest way to bring order to your files is to place them in folders. For example, if you use your computer for your personal finances, aircraft design, and recreation, you create a separate folder in which you place files for each of these activities. To create a new folder, perform these steps:

1. Open the My Computer or Explorer window.
2. Double-click the disk drive in which you want to store the new folder.
3. Select the File menu New option.
4. Select the New menu Folder option. Windows 95 will place the new folder in the window and name it "New Folder."
5. Type a new name for the folder and press ENTER.

113 Organizing Your Folders Using Subfolders

As you store more and more files on your system, you may eventually need to subdivide your folders. For example, you may want to store your insurance-related files inside a single folder named "Insurance." However, as you add files to the folder, you may see the need to further categorize your insurance files into additional folders: one folder for your home, one for your automobiles, one for your rental properties, and one for your health insurance. Luckily, Windows 95 supports a multiple-level folder structure. In the past, Windows 3.1 and MS-DOS users created subdirectories that they stored inside directories on the disk. In Windows 95, your folders hold *subfolders*. To create a new subfolder inside an existing folder, perform these steps:

1. Open the My Computer window.
2. Locate the drive on which you want to create the subfolder.
3. Locate the folder (called the *parent folder* in this case) that will contain the subfolder.
4. Double-click the parent folder.
5. Perform steps 3 through 5 in Tip 112 to create a new subfolder.

A folder can hold as many subfolders as you need. Also, a subfolder can hold additional files and subfolders.

114 Renaming a Folder

Occasionally, you will need to change a folder's name. For one reason or another, the original name may no longer be suitable. Previous versions of Windows required you to select a series of menu options to rename folders. Fortunately, Windows 95 has simplified the process. To quickly rename a folder, perform these steps:

1. Right-click on the folder.
2. Select the pop-up menu's Rename option. Windows 95 highlights the folder name so you can change it.
3. Type the folder's new name. If you want to change the existing name, use the ARROW keys, INS, or DEL, to make those changes.
4. Press ENTER.

Note: *You may rename icons and files using the same technique.*

Understanding Desktop Properties — 115

In addition to letting you move icons from one place to another, Windows 95 gives you other ways you can change your Desktop's appearance. For example, you can change your Desktop's color and background pattern. The Desktop properties that you can change include:

- The *wallpaper* (the Desktop background) color and pattern
- The size of characters
- The screen saver you want to use, if any
- The Desktop password, if you want one
- The font that Desktop icon captions use
- The color scheme that Desktop items, such as windows, use

To access these properties, move your mouse pointer over an empty spot on your Desktop and right-click. Then, select the pop-up menu's Properties option. Windows 95, in turn, will display the sheet shown in Figure 115. Using this sheet, you can change Desktop properties.

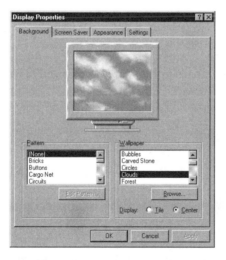

Figure 115 *The Display Properties sheet.*

Installing a Screen Saver — 116

Software engineers originally designed screen savers to keep characters from burning into the monitor when a computer was left on for a long time. Some screen savers would blank the monitor if no user touched the mouse or keyboard for a few minutes. Others would display an ever-changing pattern on the monitor so that no single location of the screen remained lit long enough for burn-in to occur. To deactivate the screen saver, users pressed a key. Today's monitors do not have the same burn-in problem. Nevertheless, users often like to put screen savers on their systems. As a result, Windows 95 includes a series of built-in screen savers. To use one of these screen savers, perform these steps:

1. Move your mouse pointer to a blank spot on your Desktop and right-click.
2. Select the pop-up menu's Properties option. Windows 95 will open the Display Properties sheet.

3. Click the Display Properties sheet Screen Saver tab to display the Screen Saver page.
4. Click on the Screen Saver pull-down list button. Windows 95 will display the Screen Saver pull-down list.
5. Select a screen saver pattern. If you want your screen to blank after a few moments of non-use, select "Blank Screen."
6. In the Wait field, enter the number of minutes you want Windows 95 to wait before starting the screen saver pattern you selected.
7. Press the OK button to save your changes.

117 Password Protecting Your Screen Saver

If you work with confidential information, you might need a way to make sure curious eyes can't view your screen's contents when you step away from your system. Luckily, Windows 95 gives you the ability to password protect your screen saver. After your screen saver pattern begins, the screen saver remains active until you or another user enters the password you specify. To add password protection to your screen saver, perform these steps:

1. Perform the first six steps of Tip 116 to select a screen saver.
2. Click the Password protected check box until a check mark appears.
3. Click the Change button. Windows 95 will display the Change Password dialog box shown in Figure 117.
4. Enter your password twice in the two text boxes. The password will appear as asterisks so nobody can see it. The double verification ensures that you've entered exactly the password you want to use. Leave the password text boxes blank if you do not want a password or if you want to remove an existing one.
5. Click the OK button. Windows 95 will display a dialog box telling you the password has been successfully changed.
6. Click the OK button.
7. Close the Display Properties sheet Screen Saver page to put your password into effect.

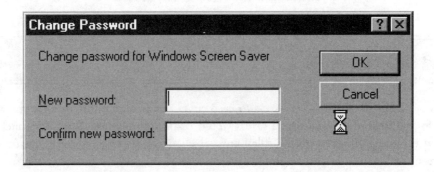

Figure 117 Changing your screen saver password.

Customizing Your Screen Saver Settings — 118

Except for the Blank Screen screen saver, you can customize each screen saver that comes with Windows 95. For example, if you choose the Starfield Simulation screen saver, you can adjust how many stars materialize on your screen, as well as the speed at which they appear. To change your screen saver settings, perform these steps:

1. Follow the first three steps of Tip 116 to display the Display Properties sheet Screen Saver page.
2. Click the Settings button. Windows 95 will display a dialog box, similar to the one in Figure 118, that contains controls you can use to adjust the particular screen saver you selected.
3. Make the modifications that you want.
4. Click the OK button.
5. Click on the Display Properties dialog box OK button.

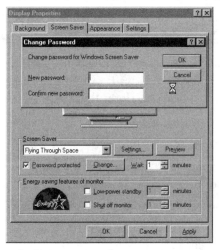

Figure 118 *Each screen saver has its own set of adjustment controls.*

Using a Color Scheme to Control Desktop Colors — 119

Although you can assign specific colors to each of your Desktop areas (see Tip 120), Windows 95 comes with several pre-defined color schemes you can use to quickly create an attractive, eye-pleasing Desktop. For example, these color schemes ensure the color of your window borders will not clash with those of your icon captions and title bars. To change your display's color scheme, perform these steps:

1. Right-click on a blank area on the Desktop.
2. Select the pop-up menu's Properties option.
3. Click on the Display Properties sheet Appearance tab. Windows 95 will display the Display Properties sheet Appearance page shown in Figure 119.
4. Click the Scheme pull-down list button. Windows 95 will open the Scheme pull-down list.
5. Select the color scheme you want to use. Windows 95 will display the scheme's colors in the sample area at the top of the screen.
6. Click the OK button.

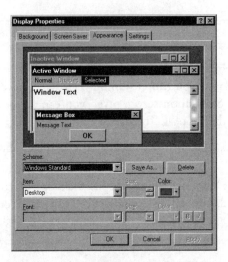

Figure 119 Changing the color scheme.

120 Assigning a Specific Color to a Desktop Item

If you want to customize your Windows 95 screens as much as possible, you may not want to use one of the Windows 95 pre-defined color schemes. You may, instead, wish to change the color of some or all of your Desktop's items. To set Desktop's items to colors you desire, perform these steps:

1. Right-click on a blank area on the Desktop.
2. Select the pop-up menu's Properties option.
3. Click on the Display Properties sheet Appearance tab. Windows 95 will display the Display Properties sheet Appearance page.
4. Click on the Item pull-down list button. Windows 95 will display the Desktop item pull-down list.
5. Select the item you want to change.
6. Click on the Color pull-down list button. Windows 95 will display the Color menu.
7. Pick a new color for the item you selected in step 5.
8. Repeat steps 4-7 until the look of your Desktop satisfies you.
9. Click the OK button.

121 Assigning a Specific Font to a Desktop Item

By default, Windows 95 assigns the MS Sans Serif font to Desktop items that contain text, such as title bars. If you want to change the font Windows 95 uses for Desktop items, perform these steps:

1. Right-click on a blank area on the Desktop.
2. Select the pop-up menu's Properties option.
3. Click on the Display Properties sheet Appearance tab. Windows 95 will display the Display Properties sheet Appearance page.
4. Click on the Item pull-down list button. Windows 95 will display the Desktop item pull-down list.

5. Select the item you want to change.
6. Click on the Font pull-down list button. Windows 95 will display the Font pull-down list.
7. Pick a new font for the item you selected in step 5. (You will only be able to open the Font pull-down list if you select an item that displays text.) As you make changes to the font information, Windows 95 will update the appearance of the sample Desktop area at the top of the screen.
8. If you want to change the size of the font, enter a new size value in the Size field. If you want to boldface or italicize the font, click the **B** or *I* button.
9. Click the OK button.

Creating a Custom Color — 122

If you do not like the colors Windows 95 provides, you can assign your own custom color to Desktop items or any other color-based Windows 95 element. By controlling the *hue*, *saturation* (purity), *luminosity* (brightness), and *RGB* (red, green, and blue) values, you can create your own colors. To create a custom color for any of your Desktop items, perform these steps:

1. Right-click on a blank area on the Desktop.
2. Select the pop-up menu's Properties option.
3. Click on the Display Properties sheet Appearance tab. Windows 95 will display the Display Properties sheet Appearance page.
4. Click on the Item pull-down list button. Windows 95 will display the Desktop item pull-down list.
5. Select the item you want to change.
6. Click on the Color pull-down list button. Windows 95 will display the Color menu.
7. Select Other at the bottom of the Color box. Windows 95 will display the Color dialog box shown in Figure 122.
8. Change the values in the hue, saturation, luminosity, and RGB fields.
9. To add your new color to the list of available custom colors, click the Add to Custom Colors button. Your new color will appear as one of the sixteen saved custom colors at the left of the screen.
10. Click the OK button.

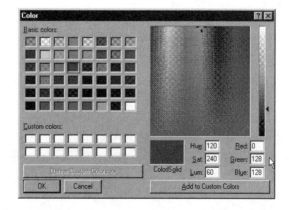

Figure 122 Creating a custom color.

123 Saving Your Color Scheme

If you spend a lot of time assigning your own colors to Desktop items and creating custom colors, you may want to save your Desktop's new look as a color scheme. That way, if you or someone else changes the Desktop's appearance, you can always retrieve that dynamic collection of colors you worked so hard to create. To save your color scheme, perform these steps:

1. Perform the steps in Tip 120 to assign colors to your Desktop's items. If you also want to create your own custom colors, perform the steps in Tip 122.
2. Click the Display Properties sheet Appearance page Save As button. Windows 95 will open the Save Scheme dialog box shown in Figure 123.
3. Enter a name for your color scheme.
4. Click the OK button.

Note: Often, Windows 95 users select a pre-defined Windows 95 color scheme they like, make modifications to that pre-defined scheme, and save the modified scheme under a different scheme name.

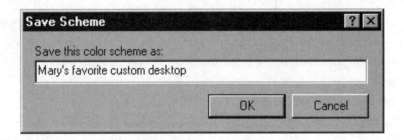

Figure 123 *Saving a custom color scheme.*

124 Assigning a Pattern to the Desktop

To decorate your Desktop, you can display a pattern of shapes on it. Windows 95 supplies several patterns you can use to make your Desktop look like a brick wall, a series of buttons, a weave, and so on. To assign a pattern to your Desktop, perform these steps:

1. Right-click on a blank area on the Desktop.
2. Select the pop-up menu's Properties option.
3. Click on the Display Properties sheet Background tab. Windows 95 will display the Display Properties sheet Background page.
4. Select a pattern in the Pattern list box. Select None in the Wallpaper list box to display the pattern on the sample screen at the top of the window.
5. Click the OK button. Windows 95 will update your Desktop to show the pattern you've selected.

Assigning a Wallpaper to the Desktop — 125

Instead of specifying a pattern (see Tip 124), you may want to specify a wallpaper design. A *wallpaper* is a bitmap graphic created using art software, such as the Paint program, or a scanner. The wallpaper Windows 95 supplies (you can supply your own, as Tip 126 explains) fills the background of the Desktop area. To change your Desktop's wallpaper, perform these steps:

1. Right-click on a blank area on the Desktop.
2. Select the pop-up menu's Properties option.
3. Click on the Display Properties sheet Background tab. Windows 95 will display the Display Properties sheet Background page.
4. Select a wallpaper from the Wallpaper scroll box.
5. Press the OK button to save your changes.

If you select a wallpaper that fills the entire screen, you'll see the wallpaper cover the sample screen at the top of the Background page, as shown in Figure 125.1. However, if you select a wallpaper that repeats a small pattern over and over, you'll see that pattern appear in the middle of the screen, as shown in Figure 125.2. If you want to repeat that pattern for the entire screen (in effect, filling the whole screen with the same wallpaper pattern), click the Tile option button in the Background page's lower-right corner. Figure 125.3 shows a tiled wallpaper.

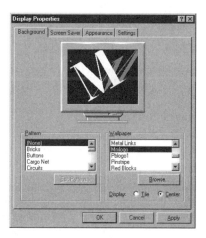

Figure 125.1 *The wallpaper fills the whole screen.*

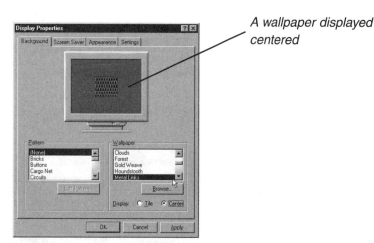

Figure 125.2 *The wallpaper takes only the screen center.*

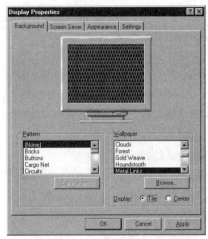

Figure 125.3 A tiled pattern fills the whole screen.

126 | Assigning a Graphic to the Desktop Using a New Bitmap

As you learned in Tip 125, Windows 95 comes with a number of wallpapers that you can use to decorate your Desktop. However, Windows 95 doesn't limit you to its wallpapers. You can purchase, create, or obtain graphic images and display them as wallpaper on your Desktop.

Note: Before you try to use an image as wallpaper, make sure it is a bitmap file. Bitmap filenames usually end with the BMP or DIB extension.

To create a wallpaper using your own bitmap graphic file, perform these steps:

1. Right-click on a blank area on the Desktop.
2. Select the pop-up menu's Properties option.
3. Click on the Display Properties sheet Background tab. Windows 95 will display the Display Properties sheet Background page.
4. Click the Browse button to display a Browsing for wallpaper dialog box.
5. Highlight the drive, folder, and file you want to use for the wallpaper and click the OK button. In the sample screen at the top of the sheet, Windows 95 will display your bitmap image (see Figure 126).
6. Click the OK button.

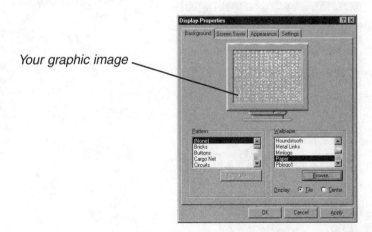

Figure 126 Using your own bitmap file for wallpaper.

Understanding and Using Energy Star Features — 127

You can save on energy bills if you purchase PC products that are Energy Star compliant. Devices with Energy Star features use less power than hardware that doesn't comply with the Energy Star standard. One of the first and most popular Energy Star features is monitor power-down, which lets Windows 95 power-off your monitor if you don't use your system for a pre-defined period of time. When you return to your PC and press a key, Windows 95 will turn on the Energy Star-standard monitor so you can get back to work.

Note: When Windows 95 powers-off your monitor, it does not turn off the device completely. Rather, Windows 95 reduces the power by as much as 90%. By keeping some power going to your monitor, Windows 95 can quickly turn the device back on when you're ready to work on your system again.

The Display Properties sheet Screen Saver page contains a section for Energy Star features, as shown in Figure 127. If you want Windows 95 to power-down your monitor after a few minutes of non-use, or power-off your monitor completely (meaning that the monitor will take a little longer to come back on when you return), check one or both of the check boxes in the Energy saving features of monitor section. Then, specify how many minutes you want Windows 95 to wait before it powers-down or turns off your monitor.

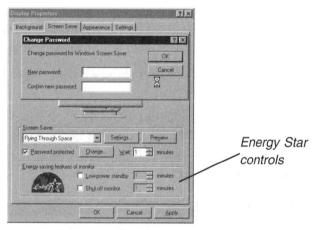

Figure 127 Save energy with Energy Star controls.

Using Drag and Drop to add a Program to the Start menu — 128

As Tip 47 explains, the Start menu is not set in stone. If you start the same program several times a day or week, you can add that program to the Start menu. That way, each time you want to access the program, you don't have to navigate through a series of submenus to reach it. If you want to add a program to your Start menu quickly, all you must do is drag and drop the program's name or icon on the Start button. To do so, perform these steps:

1. Open the My Computer or Explorer window.
2. Find the program you want to add to the Start menu.
3. Use your mouse to drag the program to the Start button.
4. Release your left mouse button to drop the program on to the Start button.
5. Close the My Computer or Explorer window and click the Start button. The program will appear among the menu items.

Note: To use a drop-and-drag operation to copy programs to the Start menu, your Taskbar must be visible. To make sure your Taskbar is always visible, perform the steps in Tip 103.

129 Using Drag and Drop to Delete a File or Folder

Windows 95's drag-and-drop capabilities let you perform a number of tasks quickly and easily. For example, as Tip 110 explains, you can use these drag-and-drop capabilities to move and copy objects. Similarly, you can use drag-and-drop to delete files from your system. To do so, perform these steps:

1. Open the My Computer or Explorer window. Do not maximize the window.
2. Adjust the window's size until you can see your Desktop's Recycle Bin icon.
3. Select the file or folder you want to delete.
4. Drag the file or folder to the Recycle Bin.
5. Release your left mouse button to drop the file or folder into the Recycle Bin.

Note: *Remember that Windows 95 sends deleted items to the Recycle Bin. Windows 95 does not erase files until you empty the Recycle Bin.*

130 Recovering Files and Folders from the Recycle Bin

When you delete an item, Windows 95 doesn't remove it entirely from your system. Instead, Windows 95 places it in a holding area called the Recycle Bin folder. As such, if you delete an item and later decide you want to work with it again, you can recover it from the Recycle Bin. To recover an item from the Recycle Bin, perform these steps:

1. Double-click the Desktop's Recycle Bin icon. The Recycle Bin will display its contents in a table format, as shown in Figure 130.
2. Right-click over the file or folder that you want to retrieve. (If you want to retrieve more than one item, press CTRL and click each item.) Windows 95 will display a pop-up menu.
3. Select the pop-up menu's Restore option. After a brief pause, Windows 95 restores the item.
4. Close the Recycle Bin window.

Note: *After you empty the Recycle Bin, any deleted files it contained are gone forever.*

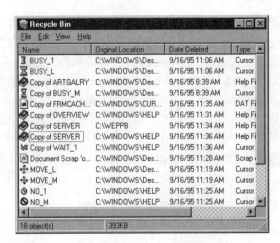

Figure 130 *Getting ready to recover an item from the Recycle Bin.*

Using Drag and Drop to Restore a Specific File or Folder — 131

When you use the steps Tip 130 provides to retrieve an item from the Recycle Bin, Windows 95 returns the item to its original location. If you don't want an item to reappear in the folder from which you originally deleted it, you can drag the file or folder from the Recycle Bin and drop it exactly where you want it to appear. To use drag and drop to restore a specific file or folder, perform these steps:

1. Open the My Computer or Explorer window.
2. Adjust the window's size until you can see your Desktop's Recycle Bin icon.
3. Double-click the Recycle Bin. Size the Recycle Bin window so that you can see both the Recycle Bin and the contents of the My Computer or Explorer window.
4. Locate the file or folder you want to retrieve from the Recycle Bin.
5. In the My Computer or Explorer window, display the disk and folder where you want to send the retrieved item.
6. Move your mouse pointer to the file or folder you want to retrieve, press your left mouse button, and drag the item to the location you displayed in step 5.
7. Release your left mouse button to drop the item at its new location. Windows 95 will remove the item from the Recycle Bin.

Removing a Specific File or Folder from the Recycle Bin — 132

As you know, you can empty the Recycle Bin's contents all at once, just as you might turn over a trash can to deposit its contents into a dumpster. However, there may be times when you don't want to delete all the items in the Recycle Bin. For example, although your Recycle Bin may contain some items that you definitely want to throw out, it may also contain a file or two whose fate you haven't decided. Fortunately, you don't have to empty the Recycle Bin's contents all at once. You can tell Windows 95 to dispose of only certain files. To remove a specific item from the Recycle Bin, perform these steps:

1. Double-click the Desktop's Recycle Bin icon. The Recycle Bin will show its contents in a table format.
2. Right-click the item you want to remove. (If you want to remove more than one item, press CTRL and click each item.) Windows 95 will display a pop-up menu.
3. Select the pop-up menu's Delete option. Windows 95 asks you to confirm the deletion.
4. Click the Yes button. Windows 95 will delete the item.
5. Close the Recycle Bin window.

All undeleted items remain in the Recycle Bin.

Note: In step 3, if you select the pop-up menu's Cut option, Windows 95 will remove the item from the Recycle Bin and send it to the Clipboard.

Emptying (Flushing) the Recycle Bin — 133

When you want to free disk space, the first place to start is often the Recycle Bin. As you delete files, Windows 95 sends them to the Recycle Bin. However, Windows 95 doesn't actually remove the items from your disk until you empty the Recycle Bin. Luckily, emptying the entire Recycle Bin is one of the easiest tasks you can perform in Windows 95. To empty the Recycle Bin, perform these steps:

1. Right-click the Recycle Bin icon. Windows 95 will display a pop-up menu.
2. Select the pop-up menu's Empty Recycle Bin option. Windows 95 will display a dialog box asking you to confirm the deletion.
3. Select Yes. Windows 95 will empty the Recycle Bin.

After you flush the Recycle Bin, Windows 95 displays an empty Recycle Bin icon on your Desktop. Trash won't appear in the Recycle Bin icon again until you delete another item.

134 Using the Properties Menu to Undo a Delete Operation

As Tips 130 and 131 explain, the Recycle Bin gives you several ways to recover files you've deleted. However, in certain circumstances, you don't need to open the Recycle Bin to retrieve a deleted file. For example, if you delete a file from the My Computer window, the Explorer window, or the Desktop, you can often recover that file immediately (before another operation overwrites the file on disk) and restore it to its original location. To do so, perform these steps:

1. Move your mouse pointer to the file icon's former position.
2. Click your right mouse button. Windows 95 will display a pop-up menu.
3. Select the pop-up menu's Undo Delete option. Windows 95 will restore the item to the folder from where you deleted it.

135 Using ALT-TAB to Select a Running Program

As Tip 9 explains, Windows 95's multitasking lets you run several programs at once. When you want to bring a particular program window to the foreground, you have several options. If the program window is visible, you can click on it to make the program the foreground task. If the program window is hidden by another window (for example, if your screen shows another window in a maximized state), you can click the window's Taskbar button to switch to the program. However, depending on the properties you've set for your Taskbar, you may not always be able to use the Taskbar buttons. For example, if you activate the Taskbar Properties sheet Auto hide check box and deactivate the Always on top check box, the Taskbar will be inaccessible each time you maximize a program window. In such cases, you need another window-switching method. Luckily, In Windows 95, you can always use the ALT-TAB keystroke combination to switch between programs. To use ALT-TAB, perform one of these operations:

- Press ALT-TAB to switch to your most recent program. Press ALT-TAB once more to switch back. ALT-TAB switches between the two programs you've most recently selected.
- Press ALT-TAB but do not let up on the ALT key. Windows 95 will display a window that contains an icon for each running program, as shown in Figure 135. Continue to press TAB until you highlight the program to which you want to switch. Release the ALT key.

Figure 135 The ALT-TAB *program switch window.*

136 Using CTRL-ESC to Access the Start Menu

If you're developing software for Windows 95, Microsoft recommends that you design your programs so that a user doesn't need a mouse to interact with them. Nobody disputes the fact that a mouse is vital to the smooth workings of Windows 95. However, mice sometimes break. Or, users misplace them (especially true for portables whose mice are not built into the PC). Additionally, some users have physical disabilities that keep them from using a mouse. As such, all program operations should be available through both the mouse and the keyboard. The Windows 95 operating system is no exception. If, for whatever reason, you want to access the Windows 95 Start menu but cannot use your mouse, press CTRL-ESC. Windows 95, in turn, will display the Start menu just as if you had clicked the Start button.

Note: Some people do not like to move their hands off the keyboard any more than necessary. Pressing CTRL-ESC to open the Start menu keeps your hands on the keyboard.

137 Changing the Number of Colors Your Monitor Displays

The Display Properties sheet Settings page lets you change the number of colors Windows 95 offers for display. If you change monitors or want to adjust the number of colors Windows 95 displays at any one time for screen captures, perform these steps:

1. Move your mouse pointer to a blank spot on your Desktop and Right-click. Windows 95 will display a pop-up menu.
2. Select the pop-up menu's Properties option.
3. Click the Settings tab to display the Display Properties sheet Settings page, as shown in Figure 137.
4. Open the Color palette pull-down list and select the number of colors you want to display.
5. Click the OK button to save your changes. Windows 95 may display a dialog box telling you that you must restart your system for the changes to take effect. If this dialog box appears, select Yes.

Some monitor and video card combinations allow for more colors than others do. Even if your monitor and video card support a high number of colors, you may want to keep the number of colors at a lower setting to ensure Windows 95 updates your screen in a timely manner. The more colors that Windows 95 has to update, the slower your Windows 95 operations may become.

Figure 137 The Display Properties sheet Settings page.

138 Changing Your Screen Resolution

Resolution refers to the crispness of your display. The higher the resolution, the more detail your screen can display. As with the number of colors (see Tip 137), not all monitors and video cards support as high a resolution as you might prefer. Resolution is measured in *pixels* (or *picture elements*). A pixel is a single dot on your screen. The more pixels on your screen, the higher the resolution. The maximum number of dots across and down your screen (the number of rows and columns of dot intersections) determine the resolution measurement. If you want to try to change your monitor to a higher screen resolution, perform these steps:

1. Right-click on a blank spot on the Desktop. Windows 95 will display a pop-up menu.
2. Select the pop-up menu's Properties option.
3. Click the Settings tab to display the Display Properties sheet Settings page.
4. Drag the Desktop area slider to the right. As you drag the control to the right, Windows 95 changes the caption beneath the control to reflect the new resolution measurement.
5. Click the OK button to save your changes. Windows 95 may display a dialog box telling you that you must restart your system for the changes to take effect. If this dialog box appears, select Yes.

Windows 95 is fairly smart about changing your resolution. If Windows 95 senses that you increased the resolution too much, Windows 95 reverts the resolution measurement back to its original value.

Note: *If you attempt to increase your computer's screen resolution but your video card and monitor combination will not support the higher resolution, you may have to reset the resolution measurement to its original value.*

139 Changing Your Screen Font Size

As you increase your screen's resolution (see Tip 138), you may also have to increase the font size of the characters your screen displays. As you increase the resolution, more windows and more text will fit in your screen. To adjust your screen's resolution, Windows 95 has to decrease the font size. Therefore, your screen's text may be too hard to read. Similarly, if you lower your screen's resolution, the font size may be too large. To change the font size that Windows 95 uses on your screen, perform these steps:

1. Right-click on a blank spot on the Desktop. Windows 95 will display a pop-up menu.
2. Select the pop-up menu's Properties option.
3. Click the Settings tab to display the Display Properties sheet Settings page.
4. Open the Font size pull-down list and select the font size that suits you.
5. Click the OK button. Windows 95 may display a dialog box telling you that you must restart your system for the changes to take effect. If this dialog box appears, select Yes.

Note: *You may have to change your screen's resolution before Windows 95 will let you change its font size. If Windows 95 displays a font dimmed in gray, you cannot select the font based on your current screen resolution.*

140 Changing Your Video Card or Monitor Type

With Plug and Play, you can often change hardware simply by shutting down and restarting Windows 95. Unfortunately, some older video cards are not Plug and Play compatible and many monitors don't support Plug and Play.

Therefore, if you change monitors or video cards and notice that your screen doesn't appear properly adjusted, you may need to tell Windows 95 about your specific video card and monitor type. To do so, perform these steps:

1. Right-click on a blank spot on the Desktop. Windows 95 will display a pop-up menu.
2. Select the pop-up menu's Properties option.
3. Click the Settings tab to display the Display Properties sheet Settings page.
4. Click the Change Display Type button. Windows 95 will open the Change Display Type dialog box shown in Figure 140.
5. Click the Adapter Type Change button and select your video card from the Adapter Type pull-down list and choose OK.
6. Click the Monitor Type Change button and select your monitor from the Models pull-down list. If your monitor is Energy Star compliant (see Tip 127), Windows 95 will check the Monitor is Energy Star compliant check box.
7. Click the OK button to return to the Change Display Type dialog box.
8. Click on the Close button to return to the Settings sheet.
9. Click on the OK button to close the Display Properties dialog box.

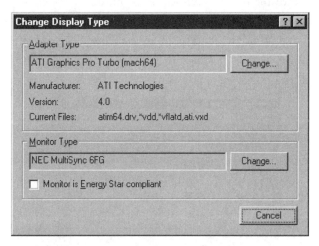

Figure 140 The Change Display Type dialog box.

Displaying the Day and Date — 141

At the Taskbar's right end, a clock appears that gives you the current time. If you want to find out the current day-and-date, all you must do is place your mouse pointer over this clock. After a brief pause, Windows 95 will display a pop-up window that contains the day-and-date, as shown in Figure 141. To keep screen clutter to a minimum, Windows 95 displays the day-and-date only when you request it.

Figure 141 See the day-and-date.

142 | Changing Your System's Date or Time

The clock and calendar inside your computer are probably more accurate than most expensive watches. Nevertheless, there may be times when you need to reset your system's day, date, and time values. For example, if you just purchased your system, its manufacturer may not have set these values properly. Or, a memory failure may make these values inaccurate. To change your system's date or time, perform these steps:

1. Double-click the Taskbar's clock to display the Date/Time Properties sheet Date & Time page, as shown in Figure 142.
2. If you want to change the month, click the Month pull-down list button, which appears just beneath the word *Date*. Then, from the pull-down list Windows 95 displays, select the current month.
3. If you want to change the year, enter a new value in the Year field, which appears immediately to the right of the Month pull-down list button. Alternatively, you can use the Year spin button to increase or decrease the year value incrementally.
4. If you want to change the day, click on the correct number in the monthly calendar, which appears directly beneath the Month pull-down list button.
5. If you want to change the time, click on the individual values (hour, minute, second, or AM/PM indicator) that Windows 95 displays in the Time field and enter new values.
6. Click the OK button.

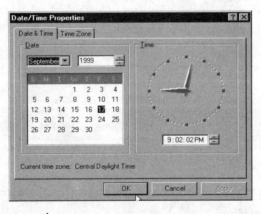

Figure 142 *You can change any date or time value.*

143 | Changing the Time Zone

If you move, you'll want to take your Windows 95 system with you! And if you move your Windows 95 system to another time zone, you'll need to inform it of the change. If you don't, your computer will operate as if it were still at its former location. Luckily, you can easily reset Windows 95's time zone value. In fact, you don't even need to know your new time zone's name to reset this value. All you must know is your new location. To change the time zone, perform these steps:

1. Double-click the Taskbar's clock to display the Date/Time Properties sheet.
2. Click the Date/Time Properties sheet Time Zone tab. Windows 95 will display the Time Zone page, as shown in Figure 143.
3. In the Time Zone page's world map, drag the highlighted time zone line over your new location.

4. Click the check box at the bottom of the Time Zone page if your time zone adjusts for Daylight Savings Time (some places do not, such as Indiana).

5. Click the OK button.

Note: *In step 3, if you don't want to use the Time Zone page's world map, you can click on the pull-down list button in the page's upper-right corner to display a list of time zone values.*

Figure 143 *Changing your time zone.*

Windows 95 Replaces MS-DOS — 144

Previous versions of Windows required you to use MS-DOS. For example, before you could start Windows 3.1, you had to load MS-DOS. Windows 3.1 was the operating environment in which you interacted with your system, but it wasn't the true operating system. Behind the scenes, MS-DOS still handled everything, and Windows 3.1 ran as just another MS-DOS program. In contrast, Windows 95 is both an operating environment and an operating system. As such, Windows 95 handles everything. Even if you start your system in MS-DOS-only mode, as Tip 150 explains, a portion of Windows 95 is still in control.

Because Windows 3.1 ran on top of MS-DOS, Windows 3.1 users often experienced memory-management problems. Fortunately, because Windows 95 doesn't have to contend with MS-DOS, you won't encounter such difficulties. Microsoft knows that many people still like to use the MS-DOS environment. Therefore, Windows 95 lets you open MS-DOS windows and run MS-DOS programs. In fact, most MS-DOS programs run better under Windows 95 than they did under its predecessors.

Opening an MS-DOS Window — 145

One way to run MS-DOS program is to open an MS-DOS window. Within the MS-DOS window you can run programs from the command prompt. To open an MS-DOS window (or several MS-DOS windows) from the Start menu, perform these steps:

1. Click the Start button. Windows 95 will display the Start menu.

2. Select the Start menu Programs option.

3. Select the Programs menu MS-DOS Prompt option. Windows 95 will open an MS-DOS window, as shown in Figure 145. (Your MS-DOS window may appear maximized or sized differently from the figure's.) From the MS-DOS window, you can execute an MS-DOS program.

4. Repeat steps 1-3 for each MS-DOS window you want to open.

Note: *If you want to run an MS-DOS program without opening an MS-DOS window, select the Start menu Run command. Then, type the path and name of the MS-DOS program and press* ENTER. *If you start MS-DOS often, you might want to create an MS-DOS shortcut (see Tip 107) to place the MS-DOS environment on the Desktop itself.*

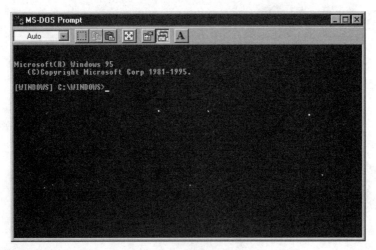

Figure 145 An open MS-DOS window.

146 Sizing an MS-DOS Window

As with any window, you can maximize, size, or minimize MS-DOS windows. As Figure 145 shows, the upper-right corner of the MS-DOS windows contain Minimize and Maximize buttons you can use to manage the window size. If you want to maximize or restore an MS-DOS window quickly, press ALT-ENTER. When you press ALT-ENTER to maximize your MS-DOS window, the title bars and window border will display as the program fills your entire screen. If you want to size an MS-DOS window, you can drag one of the window's borders or corners. However, unlike most regular Windows 95 windows, you can only drag MS-DOS windows to just a few preset sizes. As you manually size an MS-DOS window, Windows 95 adjusts the font inside the window accordingly.

Note: *The Minimize and Close buttons disappear when you maximize an MS-DOS window by pressing* ALT-ENTER.

147 Closing an MS-DOS Window

When you finish running an MS-DOS program or issuing MS-DOS commands, you can use any of these methods to close the MS-DOS window:

- Type **EXIT** at the MS-DOS prompt.
- Click the MS-DOS window's Close button.
- Double-click the MS-DOS window's Control menu icon.
- Select the Control menu Close option.

Running an MS-DOS Program — 148

As Tip 144 explains, Microsoft knows that many people still like to use the MS-DOS environment. Therefore, Windows 95 gives you many ways to run MS-DOS programs. In fact, Windows 95 lets you use many of the same methods to run both MS-DOS and Windows 95 programs. To run an MS-DOS program from Windows 95, perform any of the following operations:

- Start Explorer or open the My Computer window, find the MS-DOS program name or icon, and double-click the entry.
- Select the Start menu Run option, type the MS-DOS program name, and press ENTER.
- Create a shortcut icon for the program and then double-click the icon.
- Add the program to the Start menu and then select it from the Start menu as you do other programs.
- Open an MS-DOS window (see Tip 145), type the MS-DOS program's path and filename at the MS-DOS prompt, and press ENTER.

Some MS-DOS Programs May Not Run — 149

Some MS-DOS-based programs will not work well (or at all) under Windows 95. For example, Windows 95 may conflict with fairly old MS-DOS programs, MS-DOS utility programs that view or update memory and disk settings, and MS-DOS games that consume computer graphics, memory, and processor resources. Such MS-DOS programs often utilize memory that a multitasking operating system, such as Windows 95, needs. If you want to work with such MS-DOS programs, you must run them in a Windows 95-free mode. See Tip 150 to learn how to eliminate much of Windows 95 so you can run programs under MS-DOS.

Note: *Fortunately, many MS-DOS software providers are developing Windows 95-compatible versions of their programs.*

Starting Your Computer in MS-DOS Mode — 150

As Tip 149 explains, some MS-DOS programs are simply not compatible with Windows 95. Luckily, Windows 95 provides an MS-DOS-only mode that you can use to run such programs. While your system is in MS-DOS-only mode, you won't have access to any of the Windows 95 features, but your MS-DOS program should work. To eliminate Windows 95 from memory and run your computer in an MS-DOS-only mode, perform these steps:

1. Close any open program windows.
2. Select the Start menu Shut Down option.
3. Select the Shut Down dialog box Restart the computer in MS-DOS mode? option button and click on Yes. After a brief pause, Windows 95 will shut down and your computer will reboot itself to an MS-DOS prompt.
4. Run your program.
5. When your program ends, type **Win** to start Windows 95.

151 How Windows 95 Uses AUTOEXEC.BAT

Unlike MS-DOS, Windows 95 instantly recognizes your hardware and software drivers when you start your computer. As such, Windows 95 doesn't need to read the AUTOEXEC.BAT file to retrieve device and application information. However, Windows 95 doesn't render the AUTOEXEC.BAT file obsolete. For example, if you want to specify some settings, such as your computer's *search path* (the directory order the PC searches when looking for programs), you can do so in the AUTOEXEC.BAT file.

In addition, if you want to use the MS-DOS DOSKEY command-line editing buffer (introduced in MS-DOS 5.0), you'll need to place the DOSKEY command in AUTOEXEC.BAT. Finally, because some MS-DOS programs need information they can only get from the AUTOEXEC.BAT file, Windows 95 runs the AUTOEXEC.BAT file commands before starting an MS-DOS program. Tip 160 explains how to point such an MS-DOS program to a different batch file if you don't want to store that program's start-up commands in AUTOEXEC.BAT.

152 How Windows 95 Uses CONFIG.SYS

Previous versions of Windows used CONFIG.SYS to obtain device settings and drivers so that Windows and your computer could work with hardware that was not part of the base system. Typically, when Windows 95 starts up, it ignores the CONFIG.SYS file. Windows 95 also doesn't require HIMEM.SYS, IFSHELP.SYS, MOUSE.SYS, and MSCDEX.SYS files which were essential under Windows 3.1. To make certain hardware devices work (such as an older fax/modem or old CD-ROM drive), Windows 95 will need certain *real mode device drivers*. A real mode device driver requests that Windows 95 keep certain areas of memory free.

153 Using the MS-DOS Window Toolbar

Across the top of your MS-DOS windows, a toolbar appears that lets you control MS-DOS programs. The toolbar, which is a brand new feature of Windows 95, gives you one-button access to many MS-DOS tasks you'll perform. To display or hide the toolbar, right-click over the MS-DOS window's title bar. Windows 95, in turn, will display a pop-up menu. Select the pop-up menu's Toolbar option. Table 153 explains the different parts of the toolbar.

Toolbar Icon	Action
Auto	Describes the font the MS-DOS window uses. "Auto" specifies a default MS-DOS font that ensures you will see 25 lines of 80 column text no matter how large or small you size the MS-DOS window.
	Marks text for selection.
	Copies text you select to the Clipboard.
	Pastes text from the Clipboard to the cursor's current position.
	Maximizes the MS-DOS window.

Table 153 *The MS-DOS toolbar helps you manage MS-DOS actions (continued on the following page).*

Toolbar Icon	Action
	Displays the MS-DOS Prompt Properties sheet.
	Runs the MS-DOS window in the background.
	Changes the font the MS-DOS window uses.

Table 153 The MS-DOS toolbar helps you manage MS-DOS actions (continued from previous page).

Controlling the Font Size in an MS-DOS Window — 154

If you want to make your MS-DOS window text more readable, you can change the size of the font that the window uses for the text. If you increase the font size, you will see less text. However, that text will be larger and easier to read.

To display a list of font sizes, open the toolbar's pull-down list. Figure 154 shows the open pull-down list. From the pull-down list, you can select the dimensions (height and width) of the text characters that appear in the MS-DOS window. For example, if you select a font size of 8 x 12, each character in the MS-DOS window will be 8 dots wide by 12 dots tall. If you increase the font size too much, you will not be able to see a full 25 lines of 80 characters. Fortunately, when an MS-DOS window holds more information than it can display, Windows 95 adds scroll bars to it. These scroll bars let you view the hidden parts of the window.

Note: *Tip 138 explains more about the dots that make up screen fonts and graphics.*

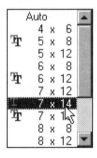

Figure 154 Increase your font size to make screens more readable.

Copying Text from an MS-DOS Window to the Clipboard — 155

The Windows 95 Clipboard is available in MS-DOS windows. When you copy text from an MS-DOS window, Windows 95 sends that text to the Clipboard. You can then paste that text at another location in the same MS-DOS window, in another MS-DOS window entirely, or in a Windows 95 window.

To copy text to the Clipboard, you must first mark it. You can mark a single character, several characters, an entire line, or several lines of text. To copy text to the Clipboard, perform these steps:

1. Find the text you want to copy.
2. Click the Mark toolbar button.

3. Move your mouse pointer to the first character you want to mark.
4. Click and hold your left mouse button.
5. Drag your mouse pointer to the right and, if you want to mark more than one line of text, downward until you fully select the area you want to copy.
6. Release your left mouse button.
7. Click the Copy toolbar button to send the marked text to the Clipboard.

156 Pasting Text into an MS-DOS Window

After you copy text to the Clipboard, Windows 95 displays the Paste button on the MS-DOS window toolbar. To paste the text elsewhere in the MS-DOS window, perform these steps:

1. Select the location where you want to paste the Clipboard contents. (If you're working in a full-screen editing program, such as the MS-DOS Editor program, you can use your mouse to select the location. If you're working at the MS-DOS prompt or in a non-editing program, you must use DOS cursor-movement commands to select the location.)
2. Click the Paste toolbar button. Windows 95 pastes the copied text from the Clipboard to the location you selected in step 1. The text remains on the Clipboard in case you want to paste it elsewhere.

Note: *If you're not able to paste from the Clipboard, you will have to use the MS-DOS Prompt Properties sheet Misc page to disable the Fast pasting feature. Tip 162 describes how to display the MS-DOS Prompt Properties sheet Misc page.*

157 The Properties Sheet Replaces the PIF Editor

Before Windows 3.1 could run a DOS-based program, the operating system needed to know a little about the program's behavior. To obtain this information, Windows 3.1 accessed a *PIF* (*Program Information File*), which described the system resources the program required. PIF filenames ended with the .PIF extension. If an MS-DOS program didn't have a corresponding PIF, Windows 3.1 used a default MS-DOS PIF, whose settings were suitable for most DOS-based programs. The PIF editor was a Windows 3.1 application that let you create and manage PIFs for MS-DOS applications. Windows 95 replaces the PIF editor with the MS-DOS Prompt Properties sheet. To display the MS-DOS Prompt Properties sheet, shown in Figure 157, click the Properties toolbar button. Or, right-click on the MS-DOS window's title bar. Then, select the pop-up menu's Properties option.

Figure 157 *The MS-DOS Prompt Properties sheet.*

Table 157 explains each page of the MS-DOS Prompt Properties sheet.

Page Name	Purpose
Program	Controls the name, icon, command, and working directory information that Windows 95 requires to run the program.
Font	Describes the MS-DOS window's font.
Memory	Describes the types and amounts of memory the MS-DOS program uses.
Screen	Controls the program's MS-DOS window size and toolbar.
Misc	Describes several MS-DOS window, mouse, and keyboard settings.

Table 157 The pages of the MS-DOS Prompt Properties sheet.

158 Controlling an MS-DOS-based Program's Command Line

When you run an MS-DOS program from the MS-DOS prompt, you must know that program's command-line requirements. (For example, the MS-DOS Editor's command line is **EDIT**.) To start the program and load a file in one step, you just specify the filename after the command. (For example, to start the MS-DOS Editor and load a file named MYFILE.TXT, type **EDIT MYFILE.TXT**.) If you execute an MS-DOS program from the Start menu Run option, Windows 95 uses the program's Properties sheet to determine how to start the program. If the command line includes more than the program name (for example, if it also includes optional MS-DOS switches or a filename), Windows 95 follows the Properties sheet's command-line instructions. To change the way that Windows 95 starts an MS-DOS program, perform these steps:

1. Use the Start menu Run option to execute the program. Or, if you've added the MS-DOS program to the Start submenus, select the program from there.
2. Click the Properties toolbar button. Windows 95 will display the MS-DOS Prompt Properties sheet for the program you selected.
3. Click the Program tab.
4. Change or add to the Cmd line field.
5. Click OK to save the changes in the MS-DOS Prompt Properties sheet.

159 Controlling an MS-DOS-Based Program's Working Directory

A *working directory* (or *working folder* in Windows 95 terminology) is the directory a program uses for data files. By default, Windows 95 will store a program and its data in the same directory. As such, the program's directory is also the working directory. As you work with MS-DOS programs, there may be times when the files you access don't reside in the program's directory. For example, you might share a system at work and create another directory to keep all your files separate from those of your colleagues. If you often load a file from a directory other than the program's default working directory, you can specify a different working directory for that program. To do so, access the MS-DOS Prompt Properties sheet Program page. Then, in the Program page's Working field, type the path to the program's new working directory. After you click the OK button, Windows 95 will, by default, store the program's data in that directory.

160 Running a Batch File Before an MS-DOS—Based Program

As Tip 151 explains, Windows 95 does not need to use AUTOEXEC.BAT files as did Windows 3.1. Windows 3.1 was an operating environment that ran on top of MS-DOS, and MS-DOS required AUTOEXEC.BAT. Therefore, AUTOEXEC.BAT played an important part in Windows 3.1. Windows 95 only needs the information in

AUTOEXEC.BAT when you run MS-DOS programs. To run properly, your MS-DOS programs still need some settings, such as a search path and environment variables, found in AUTOEXEC.BAT. Therefore, before Windows 95 runs an MS-DOS program within an MS-DOS window, Windows 95 loads the program's AUTOEXEC.BAT settings. If you have one or more MS-DOS programs that require special AUTOEXEC.BAT settings, such as a special network link or graphics card setup, you may want to activate these settings only for particular MS-DOS sessions. In other words, you don't want to place these specific program-related commands in AUTOEXEC.BAT for *all* programs; you want the settings in place for one or more MS-DOS programs only.

To place such settings before a particular MS-DOS program runs, you can tell Windows 95 to execute a batch file before it starts the program. To do so, perform these steps:

1. Create the batch file using the MS-DOS Editor program and place the needed startup commands in the file.
2. Run the DOS program before which you want Windows 95 to run a batch file. Click the Properties toolbar button. Windows 95 will display the MS-DOS Prompt Properties sheet.
3. Click the Program tab.
4. Enter the name of the program, the command line, and the working directory in the appropriate fields.
5. In the Batch file field, type the name of the batch file you created in Step 1.
6. Click the OK button. When you launch this MS-DOS program from the Start menu Run option, Windows 95 will execute the batch file before running the MS-DOS program.

161 Using a Shortcut Key to Activate an MS-DOS- Based Program

As you have learned, Windows 95 lets you run MS-DOS programs within a window. If you are running multiple programs at the same time, you can click on Taskbar buttons to select the program you desire. In addition, you can add a shortcut key that puts that MS-DOS program just one step away from activation at any time. Shortcut keystrokes begin with CTRL-ALT followed by another character that you choose. You can also use a simpler two-step shortcut key that uses either the ALT or CTRL key followed by a second key. For example, if you use the MS-DOS editor, EDIT, on a regular basis, you might use the CTRL-E shortcut key to activate EDIT. It is important to note that the program must be running for the shortcut key to take effect. The shortcut key lets you quickly activate the MS-DOS program. The shortcut does not run the program if it is not currently running. To add a shortcut key to an MS-DOS program you often run, perform these steps:

1. Start the MS-DOS program from the Start menu Run option.
2. When the MS-DOS program begins, click the Properties toolbar button. Windows 95 will display the MS-DOS Prompt Properties sheet.
3. Select the Program tab.
4. Click on the Shortcut key field.
5. Type the character you wish to use in conjunction with CTRL-ALT. If you want to use ALT (without CTRL) in the shortcut keystroke, press ALT followed by a key. If you want to use CTRL (without ALT), press CTRL followed by a key. You cannot use BACKSPACE, ENTER, ESC, PRINT SCREEN, SPACEBAR, or TAB as the last key in the shortcut keystroke.
6. Click OK.

After you create a shortcut keystroke, you can use it to activate the program (assuming the program is running as a background task). For example, if you're working in a Windows 95 spreadsheet program and want to switch to the MS-DOS program, all you must do is press the shortcut keystroke. (Note, however, you cannot use the shortcut keystroke to activate the MS-DOS program that corresponds to a shortcut key within the spreadsheet program; the spreadsheet's shortcut keystroke will take precedence.)

Controlling an MS-DOS-Based Program's Window   162

You can specify how you want Windows 95 to size an MS-DOS program window when Windows 95 runs a particular program. For example, you can tell Windows 95 to run the program in a maximized or minimized window. Likewise, you can tell Windows 95 whether or not you want its screen saver active while your system is in MS-DOS mode. To specify the way Windows 95 handles the MS-DOS window, perform these steps:

1. Start the MS-DOS program from the Start menu Run option.
2. When the MS-DOS program begins, click the Properties toolbar button. Windows 95 will display the MS-DOS Prompt Properties sheet.
3. Click the Screen tab to display the MS-DOS Prompt Properties sheet Screen page, as shown in Figure 162.1.
4. Select either the Full-screen or the Window option button. Windows 95 will start the MS-DOS window in the set mode the next time you start the program. The remaining sheet options let you control the number of lines on the screen, as well as the initial toolbar display.
5. Click the Misc tab to display the MS-DOS Prompt Properties sheet Misc page, as shown in Figure 162.2.
6. Click the Allow screen saver check box if you want your Windows 95 screen saver to remain in effect during the operation of an MS-DOS window.
7. Click the OK button.

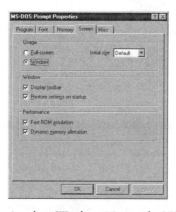

Figure 162.1 *The Screen page Usage area determines how Windows 95 sizes the MS-DOS window.*

Figure 162.2 *The Misc page Foreground area lets you request an MS-DOS window screen saver.*

163 Changing an MS-DOS-based Program's Icon

You can change the icon that Windows 95 uses to represent an MS-DOS program. If you find MS-DOS's default logo, which displays the letters *MS-DOS*, begins to bore you, you can change that icon to an umbrella, a lightning bolt, a trumpet, and more. To do so, perform these steps:

1. Start the MS-DOS program from the Start menu Run option.
2. When the MS-DOS program begins, click the Properties toolbar button. Windows 95 will display the MS-DOS Prompt Properties sheet.
3. Click the Program tab to display the MS-DOS Prompt Properties sheet Program page.
4. Click the Change Icon button. Windows 95 will display the Change Icon dialog box shown in Figure 163.
5. Click the scroll bar to view the horizontal list of icons.
6. When you see an icon you want to use for the program, click on that icon. If you do not see an icon that you like, click the Browse button to select a different icon file.
7. Click OK to save your changes. The Program page will reappear and display the new icon. After you close the sheet, Windows 95 will use the new icon to represent this MS-DOS program.

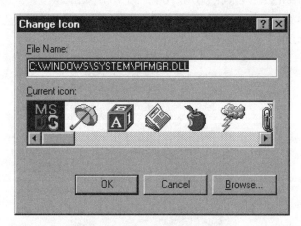

Figure 163 Selecting a new MS-DOS program icon.

164 Preventing an MS-DOS-Based Program from Knowing It's Running within Windows

In rare instances, an MS-DOS program may refuse to run if it detects that Windows 95 is also running. To prevent MS-DOS programs from detecting Windows 95, perform these steps:

1. Open Explorer or the My Computer window.
2. Locate the MS-DOS file from which you want to hide Windows 95.
3. Right-click on the program's icon. Windows 95 will display a small pop-up menu.
4. Select Properties. Windows 95 will display the program's Properties sheet.
5. Click the Properties sheet Program tab to display the Properties sheet Program page.

7. Click the Prevent MS-DOS-based programs from detecting Windows check box.
8. Click the OK button to close the dialog box.
9. Click the OK button to save your changes. The next time you run the MS-DOS program, the program will not detect Windows 95's presence.

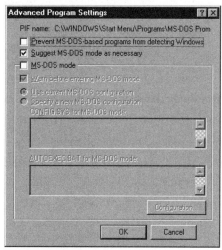

Figure 164 Keeping Windows 95 hidden from an MS-DOS program.

Suggesting an MS-DOS-Based Program Run in MS-DOS Mode 165

Certain programs (most often games) can't run within a Window and instead need to run in a special MS-DOS mode. If you try to start such a program in Windows 95, the program will run poorly or not at all. Luckily, Windows 95 contains an MS-DOS wizard that will detect if a program needs an MS-DOS operating environment. Then, if the program does need MS-DOS, the wizard will switch your system to MS-DOS mode for you. Windows 95 includes this MS-DOS wizard to help you run troublesome MS-DOS programs. To request the Windows 95 MS-DOS wizard's assistance, perform these steps:

1. Open Explorer or the My Computer window.
2. Locate the MS-DOS file for which you want to request an MS-DOS mode suggestion.
3. Right-click the program to display the MS-DOS Properties sheet.
4. Click the Properties sheet Program tab to display the MS-DOS Properties sheet Program page.
5. Click the Advanced button to display the Advanced Program Settings dialog box.
6. Check the Suggest MS-DOS as necessary check box.
7. Click the OK button to save your changes and then close the MS-DOS Properties sheet.

Note: *If you know that a program runs best in MS-DOS mode (perhaps the program's manual tells you so), click on the Advanced Program Settings dialog box MS-DOS mode check box. If you want Windows 95 to warn you that the program is entering MS-DOS mode so you can close running windows or stop communication programs (if needed), click on the "Warn before entering MS-DOS mode" check box.*

166 Controlling a Program's AUTOEXEC.BAT and CONFIG.SYS Settings

As you know, Windows 95 uses AUTOEXEC.BAT and CONFIG.SYS settings to help support MS-DOS programs that you run. For some MS-DOS programs, you may have to specify particular AUTOEXEC.BAT or CONFIG.SYS settings. To do so, you can use the program's MS-DOS Properties sheet. To specify AUTOEXEC.BAT and CONFIG.SYS settings for a program, perform these steps:

1. Open Explorer or the My Computer window and locate the program for which you want to change settings.
2. Right-click the file's icon to display the MS-DOS Properties sheet.
3. Click the Program tab to display the MS-DOS Properties sheet Program page.
4. Click the Advanced button to display the Advanced Program Settings dialog box.
5. Click on the MS-DOS mode check box until a check mark appears.
6. Select the Specify a new MS-DOS configuration option button.
7. Enter new AUTOEXEC.BAT and CONFIG.SYS values in the scrolling lists at the bottom of the Advanced Program Settings dialog box. Figure 166.1 shows the dialog box with the list of commands. If you aren't familiar with AUTOEXEC.BAT and CONFIG.SYS commands, press the Configuration button to display a dialog box, like the one shown in Figure 166.2, that will set certain MS-DOS properties for you.
8. Click the OK button to save your changes. Then, close the MS-DOS Properties sheet.

Figure 166.1 *Specify particular AUTOEXEC.BAT and CONFIG.SYS settings.*

Figure 166.2 *You can select AUTOEXEC.BAT and CONFIG.SYS settings.*

Controlling an MS-DOS-Based Program's Font — 167

You can adjust the type of font Windows 95 uses for MS-DOS programs. Tip 154 explains how to adjust the font size that Windows 95 uses to display characters in an MS-DOS window. However, depending on the MS-DOS window and font size you select, you may have to select a different font to make your MS-DOS window more readable. The MS-DOS Properties sheet Font page, shown in Figure 167, lets you select the fonts you want to use. In addition, the window displays a preview of the font as you select it. Users generally find that *True Type fonts* (those labeled "TT" in the scrolling list) display with the best resolution. Depending on the option button you select in the Font page Available types section, you can specify bitmap fonts, True Type fonts, or both.

Note: *If you select the True Type only option button and then choose "Auto" for the font size, Windows 95 shrinks or expands the font size as needed to display a full screen of text when you size the MS-DOS window.*

Figure 167 Control the font Windows 95 uses in MS-DOS.

How MS-DOS-Based Memory Management Differs from Windows 95 — 168

Before Windows 95, every program walked a memory tightrope. Both Windows 3.1 and MS-DOS programs had to measure, use, and conserve these types of memory:

- Conventional memory
- High memory
- Upper memory
- *DPMI* (DOS Protected Mode Interface) memory
- Expanded memory
- Extended memory

Windows 95, however, is a 32-bit operating environment, which uses a memory management technique called *virtual memory* that is completely different than that used by either MS-DOS or Windows 3.1. As you will learn, virtual memory lets Windows 95 use disk storage to simulate physical RAM. In other words, using virtual memory, Windows 95 can swap parts of your programs between disk and RAM as they are needed. In this way, Windows 95 can efficiently run multiple programs at the same time. Problems can arise, however, when you run MS-DOS programs under Windows 95. Windows 95 must sometimes "trick" MS-DOS programs into thinking they are running with more or less memory than is really present. Therefore, if you have problems running MS-DOS programs, you may have to adjust memory settings. Luckily, however, the following tips discuss the steps you should take to manage each memory type.

169 | Controlling an MS-DOS-Based Program's Conventional Memory

Conventional memory comprises your computer's first 640K of RAM. Figure 169.1 shows that conventional memory is the lowest memory in your system. MS-DOS programs must run in conventional memory. Therefore, the less conventional memory Windows 95 consumes, the more memory your MS-DOS programs can use and the less likely those programs will have execution problems.

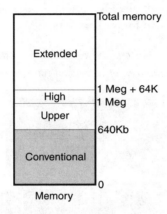

Figure 169.1 Conventional memory is low memory.

Windows 95 gives your MS-DOS programs more conventional memory than previous versions of Windows did (you can verify this using the MEM command from the command line prompt). However, if you need to control the amount of conventional memory the MS-DOS programs you run from the command prompt require, you can do so with the MS-DOS Properties sheet Memory page shown in Figure 169.2. Table 169 explains the three conventional memory settings you can adjust from the Memory page. Depending on your programs, there may be times when you will want to adjust a specific program's memory use. In such cases, select that program's Memory sheet and adjust the settings discussed in Table 169.

Setting	Purpose
Total	Specifies the highest amount of conventional memory an MS-DOS program requires. Set the total to "Auto" unless you know how much conventional memory the program requires.
Initial environment	Specifies the amount of conventional memory dedicated to the MS-DOS *command interpreter* (the program that interprets your typed and batch file MS-DOS commands). If you specify "Auto," Windows 95 uses the CONFIG.SYS SHELL= command to determine how much environment memory is required.
Protected	Specifies whether or not Windows 95 should monitor the MS-DOS program and keep the program from modifying conventional memory Windows 95 uses. Your MS-DOS program will run slower but more safely if you check the Protected check box.

Table 169 The conventional memory settings.

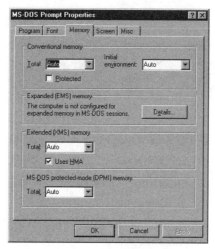

Figure 169.2 *The MS-DOS Properties sheet Memory page.*

Controlling an MS-DOS-Based Program's Expanded Memory — 170

As you have learned, MS-DOS programs were originally restricted to the PC's 640K of conventional memory. Unfortunately, as programs became more complex and the amount of data the programs required increased (such as larger spreadsheets or large databases), programs quickly outgrew the available 640K. As a solution, Lotus, Intel, and Microsoft, designed the *expanded memory specification* (also known as *EMS*)—a memory management technique that tricked the PC into thinking it had more available memory than 640K.

The EMS standard was actually designed for very old 8088-based machines (the original IBM PC). In general, the using special hardware (called an EMS card) and software, programs divided their data into 64K sections, storing all the data within the EMS memory. Next, the software would allocate a 64K memory region within conventional memory that it would use to hold pieces of data. When the program needed to access specific data, the EMS software would move the data from the EMS memory card into the 64K region (within conventional memory) the PC could access. In this way, a program could access a large (say 3Mb spreadsheet) by moving parts of the spreadsheet to and from EMS memory as needed. However, this continual swapping of data between expanded and conventional memory was time consuming. Over time, therefore, expanded memory was replaced by extended memory which is discussed in Tip 171. Today, for most of the MS-DOS programs you run, you won't need expanded memory. (Your program's manual will tell you if you need expanded memory.) If you want to run a program that requires expanded memory, you'll need to direct Windows 95 to use it. To determine if your system is currently using expanded memory and, if necessary, activate expanded memory, perform these steps:

1. Within Explorer, right click your mouse on the icon of the program you desire. Windows 95 will display a pop-up menu.
2. Select the Properties option to display program's Properties sheet.
3. Click the Memory tab to display the Memory page shown in Figure 170. The page's Expanded (EMS) memory area will let you know if you are using expanded memory.
4. If you aren't using expanded memory but want to, you may need to change an entry in your CONFIG.SYS file. You must change CONFIG.SYS itself; you cannot make this change from the MS-DOS Properties sheet. Remove the term *noems* (if it exists) from the line in CONFIG.SYS that contains the EMM386.EXE driver. To edit the file, start the Windows 95 Notepad program, load CONFIG.SYS, and make the change. Then, save CONFIG.SYS with the change and restart your computer (see Tip 21).

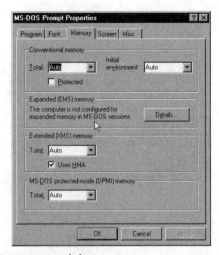

Figure 170 *MS-DOS tells you if you aren't using expanded memory.*

171 Controlling an MS-DOS-Based Program's Extended Memory

As you learned in Tip 170, expanded memory let the original IBM PC (the 8088-base system) trick programs into thinking they had memory available beyond 640K. As discussed, however, expanded memory was slow. With the advent of the 286-based PC-AT, came a new memory management technique called *extended memory*. The extended memory specification (also known as XMS) defines PC memory that resides above one megabyte. As shown in Figure 171, when you add RAM to your PC, that RAM almost always increases your amount of extended memory. If you previously used Windows 3.1, you may have noticed the HIMEM.SYS device driver in your CONFIG.SYS file. As it turns out, the HIMEM.SYS device driver let DOS (and hence Windows 3.1) use extended memory.

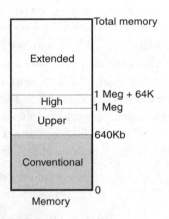

Figure 171 *Extended memory is RAM above 1 megabyte.*

As you will learn, Windows 95 does not require any special software to use extended memory. Unfortunately, MS-DOS does. If you run DOS-based programs, there may be times when you need to fine-tune the program's extended memory use. To specify a DOS-based programs extended memory use, perform these steps:

1. Within Explorer, right click your mouse on the icon of the program you desire. Windows 95 will display a pop-up menu.
2. Select the Properties option to display the program's Properties sheet.
3. Click the Memory tab to display the Memory page.

4. If the Extended (XMS) memory pull-down list contains the "Auto" value, change this value to 1024 to keep the MS-DOS window from using more than one megabyte of RAM. (1,024 kilobytes is equal to one megabyte, or one million characters, of space.) If you leave the value set to Auto, an MS-DOS program could consume your entire memory quickly.
5. Click the OK button.

Note: *High memory comprises the first 64K of extended memory. Under DOS, one program could reside within high memory, in turn, freeing up conventional memory. As such, most DOS users would .place DOS itself into the high memory area. In Windows 95, MS-DOS can utilize that 64K if you check the Uses HMA check box that appears just beneath the Extended (XMS) memory pull-down list.*

Controlling an MS-DOS-Based Program's DPMI Memory — 172

As you know, Windows 95 tricks MS-DOS into thinking it is the only task running on your PC. To make sure MS-DOS can safely use extended memory without modifying memory that other tasks use, system developers created the MS-DOS Protected Mode Interface (also known as *DPMI*). Unless your MS-DOS program documentation specifies otherwise, you can generally let an MS-DOS program take as much DPMI memory as needed so long as that DPMI memory is set to either "Auto" or is less than or equal to the amount of extended memory you've given to the MS-DOS program (see Tip 171). To specify how much DPMI memory an MS-DOS program will consume, perform these steps:

1. Within Explorer, right click your mouse on the icon of the program you desire. Windows 95 will display a pop-up menu.
2. Select Properties to display the program's Properties sheet.
3. Click the Memory tab to display the Memory page.
4. Open the MS-DOS protected-mode (DPMI) memory pull-down list and change the value as needed. Make sure that you set the value to Auto or to a value equal or less than the total extended memory available to MS-DOS.
5. Click the OK button.

Controlling an MS-DOS Program's Screen and Window Usage — 173

When you run a DOS-based program, you can run the program within a window or full-screen. A quick way to toggle between these two modes when the program is running is simply to press the ALT-ENTER keyboard combination. In addition, using the Properties sheet Screen tab, shown in Figure 173, you can control how MS-DOS screens and windows appear and behave. Table 173 describes the options in these sections.

Setting	Purpose
Full-screen	Specifies that the MS-DOS window is to open maximized.
Window	Specifies that the MS-DOS window is to open smaller than a full screen.
Initial size	Determines the number of lines the window displays.
Display toolbar	Determines whether or not the toolbar appears.
Restore settings on startup	Determines if Windows 95 restores the window settings when you quit running the MS-DOS program. If you typically run MS-DOS programs maximized, this setting is meaningless.

Table 173 Determine how you want MS-DOS windows to appear.

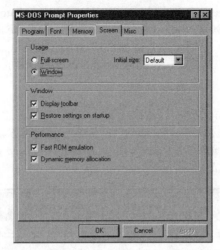

Figure 173 Control MS-DOS window and screen settings.

To control a DOS-based program's screen use, perform these steps:

1. Within Explorer, right click your mouse on the icon of the program you desire. Windows 95 will display a pop-up menu.
2. Select Properties to display the program's Properties sheet.
3. Click the Screen tab to display the Screen page.
4. Select the screen settings you desire.
5. Click the OK button.

Note: Tip 174 discusses Fast ROM Emulation and Dynamic Memory Allocation.

174 Improving an MS-DOS-Based Program's Video Output

Despite the fact that Windows 95 supports better MS-DOS program execution than previous versions of Windows, there will be times when your MS-DOS programs just don't perform the way they should. Typically, when your MS-DOS programs execute poorly, they won't write to the screen properly. The Properties sheet Screen page (shown in Tip 173) contains two settings that may help you solve MS-DOS program-output problems.

Normally, when programs perform video output, the programs use ROM-based (ROM stands for *read-only memory*) instructions to perform the video operations. Unfortunately, ROM is slow compared to your computer's RAM. The Fast ROM emulation setting specifies that the program is to use (RAM-based) instructions that emulate (replace) the slower ROM-based instructions. Using the faster RAM-based instructions, Windows 95 improves the speed of screen output. If your MS-DOS programs display too slowly, click on the Fast ROM emulation box until a check mark appears. If garbage appears when the program writes to the screen, remove the check mark from the box.

To conserve memory, Windows 95 makes assumptions about how your MS-DOS-based programs will use your computer's video memory. The Dynamic memory allocation setting maximizes the amount of memory available to other programs when you run an MS-DOS program (when this option is set, Windows 95 will allocate video memory for a MS-DOS-based program on demand. If the program never requires more video memory, Windows 95 won't allocate it.). If you have trouble running an MS-DOS program (the program might start properly but fail to continue past a certain point), remove the check mark from the Dynamic memory allocation check box.

Controlling Screen Saver Operations for MS-DOS Programs | 175

Certain MS-DOS programs will fail to operate properly if, while they run as foreground tasks, your system uses a Windows 95 screen saver. (When you switch to an MS-DOS window, that window is said to be running as a *foreground task*.) Communications programs, as well as programs that capture mouse and keystroke actions, sometimes get confused when a screen saver kicks in. If you find an MS-DOS program that conflicts with your Windows 95 screen saver, you might have to suspend the screen saver when the program is active. To suspend screen-saver capabilities, perform these steps:

1. Within Explorer, right click your mouse on the icon of the program you desire. Windows 95 will display a pop-up menu.
2. Select the Properties option to display the Properties sheet.
3. Click the Misc tab to display the Misc page.
4. Check the Allow screen saver check box if you want the Windows 95 screen saver to activate while the program is the foreground task. Do not check the box if you want to avoid any possible screen-saver conflicts.
5. Click the OK button.

Note: By following these steps you can disable or enable screen saver operations for a specific MS-DOS program. To control screen saver operations when the MS-DOS command prompt is active, you need to adjust the screen-saver settings within the Properties sheet for the MS-DOS command prompt.

Suspending or Allowing MS-DOS Programs in the Background | 176

When you switch to a program, that program runs as a *foreground task*. Programs still running, but not switched to, run as *background tasks*. Certain MS-DOS programs do not work well in the background because they utilize resources that Windows 95 might have tied up for another foreground task. If you want to prevent an MS-DOS-based program from running in the background when you switch to another task, perform these steps:

1. Within Explorer, right click your mouse on the icon of the program you desire. Windows 95 will display a pop-up menu.
2. Select the Properties option to display the Properties sheet.
3. Click the Misc tab to display the Misc page.
4. Check the Always suspend check box to freeze the MS-DOS window when you switch that window to the background.
5. Click the OK button to save your changes.

If you want to run the program in the background simultaneously while running other Windows 95 programs, remove the check from the Always suspend check box in step 4. Test both settings before you run critical MS-DOS programs in the background.

Note: The Background toolbar button lets you switch an MS-DOS program to background execution without switching to another Windows 95 or MS-DOS program.

177 Using Idle Sensitivity to Improve System or Program Responsiveness

Generally, MS-DOS programs act as if they are the only program running on a system. Therefore, an MS-DOS program might try, in some cases, to monopolize the computer processor's time. When this occurs, your Windows 95 programs running in the background can stop. The Properties sheet contains an idle sensitivity feature that lets you adjust the amount of processor time an MS-DOS program can take at any moment. For example, when an MS-DOS program is waiting for input, the program will not get as much of the processor's time as when the same MS-DOS program is calculating. To change a program's idle sensitivity, perform these steps:

1. Within Explorer, right click your mouse on the icon of the program you desire. Windows 95 will display a pop-up menu.
2. Select the Properties option to display the Properties sheet.
3. Click the Misc tab to display the Misc page.
4. Drag the Idle sensitivity slider to the right to increase the sensitivity. When you increase the idle sensitivity, MS-DOS programs will not consume as much of the processor's time.
5. Click the OK button.

178 Controlling Mouse Operations in an MS-DOS-Based Window

The check boxes in the Properties sheet Misc page control the way that MS-DOS interprets mouse movements. Normally, within a DOS-based window, when you want to select text for a cut-and-paste operation, you must click the Mark toolbar button. Tips 155 and 156 explain how to select, copy, and paste MS-DOS text. If, within the Properties dialog box Misc page, you check the QuickEdit check box, you will be able to select MS-DOS text directly with your mouse without having to first click the Mark toolbar button. Many MS-DOS programs run poorly with QuickEdit checked; therefore, Windows 95 normally leaves the QuickEdit option unchecked. If your MS-DOS programs do not respond well to mouse movements and clicks, check the Exclusive Mode check box. When you activate the Exclusive Mode setting, the MS-DOS program exclusively controls the mouse; no other program running will be able to use the mouse until you close the MS-DOS-based program's window. Due to the reliance of Windows 95 programs on the mouse, you won't want to activate the Exclusive mode setting unless a specific MS-DOS program requires exclusive use of the mouse. Set the Exclusive mode only for those MS-DOS programs that need it. Do not set the Exclusive mode for the MS-DOS Prompt option on the Start menu. (If you do, all MS-DOS programs will grab exclusive use of the mouse.) To set the exclusive mode for a specific program, perform these steps:

1. Within Explorer, right click your mouse on the icon of the program you desire. Windows 95 will display a pop-up menu.
2. Select the Properties option to display the Properties sheet.
3. Click the Misc tab to display the Misc page.
4. Choose the mouse settings you desire.
5. Click the OK button.

179 Controlling Termination of an MS-DOS-Based Program

Normally, when you close a program window, one of two things will happen:

- Windows 95 terminates the program and closes the window.
- Windows 95 displays a warning box to give you one last chance to save the data before the program terminates.

Because they were not originally designed to run within a window, MS-DOS programs cannot always recognize that you are closing the MS-DOS window. Therefore, if you have not saved data, you could close a window before the MS-DOS program writes that data to disk, and hence, lose your work. To guard against losing unsaved data, you can request that Windows 95 warn you before it honors any window-closing request. To do so, check the Warn if still active check box on the Properties sheet Misc page. Windows 95, in turn, will display a warning, like the one shown in the dialog box in Figure 179, every time you close an MS-DOS window.

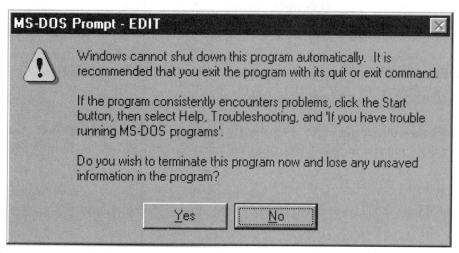

Figure 179 Windows 95 warns you before closing MS-DOS.

Controlling Shortcut Keys for an MS-DOS-Based Program — 180

Normally, Windows 95 lets you use the following shortcut keys for program-switching and printing operations:

- ALT-TAB   Displays a window of active program icons from which you can quickly select the program you desire
- ALT-ESC   Toggles through active windows
- CTRL-ESC   Selects the Start menu
- PRTSC   Copies the current screen contents to the clipboard
- ALT-PRTSC   Copies the current window contents to the clipboard
- ALT-ENTER   Toggles a program's display between a window and full screen
- ALT-SPACEBAR   Displays a program's Control menu

Occasionally, you may execute an MS-DOS program that uses one or more of these keystrokes for its operation. If so, you might want to disable the Windows 95 equivalent keystroke. For example, if the MS-DOS program uses the ALT-PRTSC keystroke to send an MS-DOS screen to a data file, you'll need to disconnect the ALT-PRTSC keystroke from Windows 95. If you don't, the Windows 95 equivalent keystroke may override the MS-DOS keystroke. To give a Windows 95 keyboard shortcut to an MS-DOS-based program for exclusive use, perform these steps:

1. Within Explorer, right click your mouse on the icon of the program you desire. Windows 95 will display a pop-up menu.
2. Select the Properties option to display the Properties sheet.
3. Click the Misc tab to display the Misc page. You will see the Windows 95 shortcut keys at the bottom of the page.

4. Remove the check from each Windows 95 shortcut key you want to *disable*. For example, if you want the MS-DOS program to have exclusive right to the ALT-PRTSC keystroke, you would remove the check for that keystroke. All keystrokes that remain checked will be available for Windows 95's exclusive use.

5. Click the OK button.

181 Windows 95 Does Not Use the Command Path

In the past, both MS-DOS and Windows used a *command path* to search for files that you wanted to execute. Typically, AUTOEXEC.BAT files specified the search path with a **PATH** command, such as the one shown below:

```
PATH C:\WINDOWS;C:\WINDOWS\SYSTEM;C:\DOS
```

The semi-colons separate directories inside the path. If you were to type a program's name from the MS-DOS prompt to execute that program, the MS-DOS command interpreter would look for the program in the following locations:

- The C: drive's WINDOWS directory
- The C: drive's SYSTEM directory located in the WINDOWS directory
- The C: drive's MS-DOS directory

Windows 95 does not need a command path to locate programs that you install. Therefore, the AUTOEXEC.BAT entry for a command path is much less critical to Windows 95 than it was to MS-DOS. However, if you run MS-DOS programs, those programs may still use the command path. Therefore, if you have trouble executing an MS-DOS program because you're not in the correct directory, you may have to use the PATH command to add the program's directory to your AUTOEXEC.BAT command path.

Note: To create a command path for a particular MS-DOS program, perform Tip 166's instructions and insert the PATH command in the Advanced Program Settings dialog box AUTOEXEC.BAT section.

182 MS-DOS-Based Windows Support Long Filenames

Windows 95 adds long filename support to MS-DOS sessions. Even when you're working at the MS-DOS command prompt, you can use long filenames.

When you issue an MS-DOS command that works with a long filename, such as a COPY command, place the long filename in quotation marks. For example, if you want to copy a file named *My office records* to a diskette in the A: drive, you could issue this command at the MS-DOS prompt:

```
COPY "My office records" A:
```

Note: *Spaces work as delimiters in MS-DOS commands. As such, they can only appear between commands, between arguments, and inside quoted long filenames.*

If you want to rename the file during the copy process, you can use either of these commands to do so:

```
COPY "My office records" A:OFFICE.DAT
COPY "My office records" A:"Old data from office"
```

Both of the above commands will copy the file to the A: drive. The first command copies the file to a regular filename. The second command copies the file to a long filename.

Note: *When you view directory listings from the MS-DOS prompt, long filenames appear to the right of the listing, as Figure 182 shows. Tip 183 explains how Windows 95 converts long filenames to the regular filenames that appear in DIR listings' first column.*

Figure 182 *DIR listings contain long filenames.*

Exchanging Files with Non-Windows 95 Users — 183

As you know, Windows 95 lets you assign long filenames to your documents. At the same time, Windows 95 lets your computer remain compatible with systems that don't use long filenames. When you specify a long filename, Windows 95 creates an entry in a long filename table. The table holds the long filename, but the file's actual name follows the same 8.3 (an 8-character filename followed by a 3-character extension file) file-naming convention that MS-DOS and Windows 3.1 used.

As shown in Figure 182, the first column in an MS-DOS directory listing contains the regular filename. The last column in the listing displays the long filenames. When you use Windows 95 to view a filename, you see the long filename. However, the file still resides on your disk under its shortened, compatible filename.

To convert a long filename to an actual filename, Windows 95 uses the first six characters of the long filename, followed by a tilde (~), followed by a number that begins at 1. For example, Windows 95 might abbreviate the long filename "Office File Accounting.DAT" to OFFICE~1.DAT.

If you copy files with long filenames to a floppy disk and use that diskette in a non-Windows 95 computer, the other computer will have no trouble reading the files because it will see only the short, valid filenames. Although the filenames look unusual to you, the other computer can use the files.

However, you do need to be cautious. If you save a Windows 95 file on a non-Windows 95 system, the long filename will be eliminated. As such, when you copy the file back to your system, you must change its filename back to a long filename. If you don't, the shorter name will overwrite the original entry on your system; from that point forward, Windows 95 will treat the file as if it's short and long filenames are short, such as OFFICE~1.DAT.

Starting Your Computer to a Non-Windows 95 Prompt — 184

If you have trouble starting Windows 95 or need to change settings in AUTOEXEC.BAT or CONFIG.SYS, you may need a pure DOS prompt. To get such a command prompt, you can request that Windows 95 start up differently from its normal routine. When you start your PC, your system will perform a self-test and memory check. After the initial hardware verification, you'll see the following message:

```
Starting Windows 95
```

As soon as you see this message, press **F8** to display the following menu:

```
Microsoft Windows 95 Startup Menu
=====================================
    1. Normal
    2. Logged (\BOOTLOG.TXT)
    3. Safe mode
    4. Safe mode with network support
    5. Step-by-step confirmation
    6. Command prompt only
    7. Safe mode command prompt only
Enter a choice:
```

If you want Windows 95 to start in its standard window-based environment, select option 1. However, if you want Windows 95 to start to a command line prompt, select option 6. Later, after you make the changes you desire from the command prompt, type WIN to start Windows 95.

185 Logging Your System Startup Using BOOTLOG.TXT

When you start your computer, you may encounter system errors. For example, you may have problems with device drivers. In addition, as your system starts, the startup messages appear and disappear so quickly on your screen that you might not be able to tell if Windows 95 loaded a particular driver properly. Although the startup is not extremely important for Windows 95, it is critical for MS-DOS operations. If you want to know exactly what is happening when you start your computer, select the Startup menu Logged option. (Tip 184 explains how to access the Startup menu.) Windows 95, in turn, will create a log of every startup detail and store it in your C: drive's root directory in the file named *BOOTLOG.TXT*. The following is a sample of BOOTLOG.TXT:

```
[001114FE]  Loading Device  = C:\WINDOWS\HIMEM.SYS
[00111501]  LoadSuccess     = C:\WINDOWS\HIMEM.SYS
[00111502]  Loading Device  = C:\WINDOWS\EMM386.EXE
[0011150E]  LoadSuccess     = C:\WINDOWS\EMM386.EXE
[00111512]  Loading Device  = C:\WINDOWS\MOUSE.SYS
[00111526]  LoadSuccess     = C:\WINDOWS\MOUSE.SYS
(Logo disabled)
[001115FD]  Loading Vxd = CONFIGMG
[001115FF]  LoadSuccess = CONFIGMG
Initializing KERNEL
LoadStart   = system.drv
LoadSuccess = system.drv
LoadStart   = keyboard.drv
LoadSuccess = keyboard.drv
LoadStart   = mouse.drv
LoadSuccess = mouse.drv
LoadStart   = gdi.exe
LoadStart   = C:\WINDOWS\SYSTEM\GDI32.DLL
LoadSuccess = C:\WINDOWS\SYSTEM\GDI32.DLL
```

As you can see, upon startup, Windows 95 loads a lot of files (this is only a partial listing). The lines in BOOTLOG.TXT indicate when Windows 95 attempts to load files and devices. Furthermore, the lines tell you if Windows 95 was successful at loading those files and devices. If you are having startup problems, scan your BOOTLOG.TXT file (you can look at it in the Notepad program) and search for a load failure. That way, you can identify the problem and research a solution.

186 Starting Your System in Safe Mode

Safe mode refers to the Windows 95 startup sequence that ignores all non-standard drivers, such as CD-ROMs, networks, and printers. When you start your computer in safe mode, Windows 95 uses default screen and mouse settings. If you are having problems accessing a device from within a Windows 95 program, you may want to start Windows 95 in the safe mode to ensure that the operating system isn't loading a conflicting driver at startup. The three ways to start Windows 95 in safe mode are:

- Press **F5** when you see the Starting Windows 95 logo appear at startup.
- Select the Startup menu Safe mode option. Tip 184 describes how to access the Startup menu.
- Select the Startup menu Safe mode with network support option. Windows 95 will load only the network drivers it needs and keep the rest of the startup sequence pure.

187 Step-by-step Confirmation of Your System Startup

When you start Windows 95, there may be times when you will want Windows 95 to walk you through the startup process (specifically the entries in CONFIG.SYS and AUTOEXEC.BAT) one line at a time. To perform a step-by-step startup, select the Startup menu "Step-by-step confirmation" option. Your system, in turn, will display each startup line, including all those in CONFIG.SYS and AUTOEXEC.BAT, followed by a prompt:

```
[Enter=Y, Esc=N]
```

This prompt lets you control the speed at which your system starts. If you press ENTER or **Y**, the computer executes that particular line and continues to the next one. If you press ESC or **N**, the computer ignores the startup line and moves on. By confirming all the steps, you customize the startup process and ensure that Windows 95 loads only the drivers and startup lines you want. As you read each startup line at your own pace, you will be able to tell which lines work and which cause problems.

188 Starting Your System to a Command Prompt

If you want to bypass Windows 95 altogether, you can request that only the MS-DOS command prompt appear at startup. Although you'll not be able to access any of the Windows 95 interface, your system will load enough of Windows 95 to support a complete MS-DOS environment. Your computer will behave as if MS-DOS is the only environment on the disk. To start at the MS-DOS command prompt, press **F8** when you see the Starting Windows 95 message on your screen. Windows 95, in turn, will display the Startup menu. Select the Startup menu option 6 to start your system in MS-DOS-only mode. If you want to start at an MS-DOS command prompt without first viewing the Startup menu, you can press SHIFT-**F5** to go directly to the command prompt.

If you display the Startup menu and press 7 to select the Safe mode command prompt only option, the MS-DOS command prompt will load but will ignore the CONFIG.SYS and AUTOEXEC.BAT files. The Safe mode with a command prompt only option starts your computer with an MS-DOS prompt but contains no support for any drivers, search paths, or special hardware. When you want to test an MS-DOS program under full resource conditions, you can use the safe mode.

189 You No Longer Need to Use SmartDrive

As you may know, to improve your system performance, MS-DOS and Windows 3.1 used *SmartDrive* program's *disk cache*. A disk cache improves your system performance by buffering extra disk data into memory with each disk read operation. In this way, when your program performs subsequent disk read operations, the data is likely to reside within the RAM-based disk cache. Your computer's electronic memory is much faster than the mechanical disk drive. As a result, your computer can retrieve cached data faster than data from disk.

Windows 95 no longer needs the SmartDrive program. SmartDrive is a 16-bit real-mode disk cache that worked well with Windows 3.1 because Windows 3.1 was a 16-bit environment. Windows 95, on the other hand, uses the new 32-bit disk cache named *VCACHE*. VCACHE takes advantage of the 32-bit processing in Windows 95. One of the biggest advantages that VCACHE offers over SmartDrive is that VCACHE caches both disk *and* CD-ROM drives. Unless you need to use MS-DOS programs that specifically require SmartDrive (probably all MS-DOS programs will work with VCACHE except disk-utility programs that may have a problem with Windows 95 anyway), you can eliminate the SmartDrive references from your AUTOEXEC.BAT file.

190 Windows 95 May Load Old TSR Programs During Startup

TSR is an acronym for *terminate-and-stay-ready*. A TSR is a program the operating system loads into memory and then sits idle until a specific event occurs. When users ran in MS-DOS-only environments, TSRs provided the means for two or more programs to reside in memory at one time. For example, if you owned a TSR text editor, you could work in your spreadsheet program and, when you wanted to write a quick note, switch to the text editor. When you closed the TSR text editor, the program remained in memory for further use. Windows 95 makes TSR virtually obsolete. On rare occasions, you may have to load a TSR when running Windows 95. For example, you may want to use a device that was built several years ago and thus won't work with a Windows 95 driver.

During your computer's startup, Windows 95 loads all *real-mode operating system* components before any other drivers or programs. TSRs are examples of real-mode operating system components. By loading these components first, Windows 95 ensures that they reside in memory where they should. The rest of the Windows 95 startup attempts to shuffle itself around any real-mode drivers that your system loaded. In fact, if Windows 95 detects an old TSR, such as the Windows 3.1 SHARE program, Windows 95 will replace that TSR with a 32-bit *virtual device driver* (provided Windows 95 has the replacement). Because a virtual device driver is not dependent on specific locations of memory, Windows 95 can move such drivers out of the way of other programs and out of conventional memory.

191 Understanding IO.SYS and MSDOS.SYS

Windows 95 requires two files named IO.SYS and MSDOS.SYS. These files are to Windows 95 what AUTOEXEC.BAT and CONFIG.SYS were to previous versions of MS-DOS and Windows. These two files form the foundation for how Windows 95 starts and operates. IO.SYS contains the actual operating system that lets your computer communicate with all the devices in your system. IO.SYS automatically incorporates several settings that CONFIG.SYS previously contained. MSDOS.SYS contains paths to files Windows 95 needs, as well as startup instructions for your computer. Unlike AUTOEXEC.BAT and CONFIG.SYS, both IO.SYS and MSDOS.SYS are hidden system files that you cannot normally see or edit. To view the files, you must use the following ATTRIB MS-DOS commands:

```
ATTRIB -H -S -R MSDOS.SYS
ATTRIB -H -S IO.SYS
```

Note: *Before you make any changes to MSDOS.SYS or IO.SYS, make a backup of the files. To do so, copy the files to a data directory on your disk.*

As Tip 193 explains, you might need to change the contents of MSDOS.SYS if you want to adjust the way your computer starts up. However, you should never change the contents of IO.SYS. As such, when you access IO.SYS, do not use the -R option. After you finish viewing the files and editing MSDOS.SYS, you can reset the attributes of MSDOS.SYS and IO.SYS by issuing the following commands:

```
ATTRIB +H +S +R MSDOS.SYS
ATTRIB +H +S IO.SYS
```

Default System Settings in IO.SYS — 192

CONFIG.SYS is less important when you run Windows 95 because IO.SYS automatically incorporates the following settings previously specified in CONFIG.SYS:

- DOS=
- HIMEM.SYS
- IFSHLP.SYS
- SETVER
- FILES=
- LASTDRIVE=
- BUFFERS=
- STACKS=
- SHELL=
- FCBS=

If you want to override the default IO.SYS settings, place the commands in CONFIG.SYS. For example, if you place the following command in CONFIG.SYS:

```
FILES=65
```

Windows 95 will ignore the default FILES= value set in IO.SYS. All the IO.SYS values that you can override in CONFIG.SYS exist to help MS-DOS. Windows 95 does not use these values.

Note: *If you need EMM386.EXE, you must add the command in CONFIG.SYS because IO.SYS cannot use EMM386.EXE. The Windows 95 installation procedure will transfer your CONFIG.SYS file's EMM386.EXE line to Windows 95's CONFIG.SYS file.*

Understanding and Using File Entries in MSDOS.SYS — 193

The MSDOS.SYS file contains startup settings that Windows 95 uses. The MSDOS.SYS file contains two sections: [Options] and [Paths]. The lines that follow the [Options] entry control the way that Windows 95 starts. Table 193.1 explains several of the common entries you may find and change in the [Options] section of MSDOS.SYS.

MSDOS.SYS [Options] Entry	Purpose
BootDelay=	Sets the wait time, in seconds, to allow the user to press **F8** (see Tip 184). If you set the boot delay to 0, Windows 95 will not give time for the user to press **F8**.
BootMenu=	Sets the display mode of the boot menu. If set to 0 (the default), the user must press **F8** at startup to see the boot menu. If set to 1, the boot menu always appears.
BootMenuDefault=	Sets the default value for the Startup menu. Windows 95 uses the default value if the user does not press **F8** to display the Startup menu and select a different option. Therefore, if you want the default menu value to be 1, set the BootMenuDefault value accordingly. The default is 3 for a non-networked com puter and 4 for a networked computer.
BootMenuDelay=	Sets the number of seconds that the computer waits for a user response to the Startup menu before the menu automatically selects the default value.
BootMulti=	Determines whether or not users can press **F8** to display the Startup menu. If set to 0, the user will not be able to press **F8** to see the startup menu.

Table 193.1 Typical MSDOS.SYS [Options] section settings.

Table 193.2 explains the entries you may find and change in the [Paths] section of MSDOS.SYS.

MSDOS.SYS [Paths] Entry	Purpose
HostWinBootDrv=	Specifies the drive used for booting Windows 95.
WinBootDir=	Specifies the path for Windows 95's startup files. Generally, the Windows 95 path is C:\WINDOWS.
WinDir=	Specifies the Windows 95 directory. Generally, the Windows 95 directory is C:\WINDOWS.

Table 193.2 Typical MSDOS.SYS [Paths] section settings.

You treat MSDOS.SYS entries very much like those within CONFIG.SYS. In other words, each entry resides on one line and you use the equal sign to specify the entry's value. For example, if you want to reduce the time that the startup sequence waits for the user to press **F8**, you could add the following line to the MSDOS.SYS file:

```
BootDelay=2
```

After you add the above line, your PC will wait only 2 seconds after it displays the Starting Windows 95 logo for the user to press **F8** to display the Startup menu. Before you edit the MSDOS.SYS file, be sure to use the ATTRIB command, explained in Tip 191, to change the file's attributes.

194 Can't Find an MS-DOS Command? Try C:\WINDOWS\COMMAND

If you are used to your system storing MS-DOS commands in a directory named DOS (generally found on your root drive), Windows 95 changes things a bit. Windows 95 replaces most of the older MS-DOS commands with newer equivalent commands that support long filenames. If you need to access the directory that contains MS-DOS commands, you'll probably find that directory on your C: drive in the path \WINDOWS\COMMAND.

Note: *You do not need to add the \WINDOWS\COMMAND path to AUTOEXEC.BAT. If you execute an MS-DOS command that resides in \WINDOWS\COMMAND, such as the EDIT command, Windows 95 will find the command.*

195 Finding Your Old System Files

When you install Windows 95, several files that were previously key system files (such as CONFIG.SYS and AUTOEXEC.BAT) are now much less important. In some cases, Windows 95 does not use these files at all. In other cases, Windows 95 will replace your previous file with its own, first making a copy of your file's contents. If you want to look at the pre-Windows 95 values in your old AUTOEXEC.BAT or CONFIG.SYS file, you can find copies of these files. The Windows 95 installation program makes backup copies of several common startup files and renames the files, as Table 195 shows.

Pre-Windows 95 name	Windows 95 renames the file to
AUTOEXEC.BAT	AUTOEXEC.DOS
COMMAND.COM	COMMAND.DOS
CONFIG.SYS	CONFIG.DOS
IO.SYS	IO.DOS
IBMBIO.COM	IO.DOS
MODE.COM	MODE_DOS.COM
MSDOS.SYS	MSDOS.DOS
IBMDOS.COM	MSDOS.DOS

Table 195 Windows 95 renames original versions of system files.

196 Moving Up Multiple Directory Levels Using the CD Command

If you're used to using the MS-DOS CD command (also called CHDIR) to change directories, you'll be happy to see how Microsoft improved the CD command for users of Windows 95 MS-DOS windows.

Before Windows 95, if you were several directory levels deep and wanted to back up three directory levels without returning to the root directory, you would issue these three MS-DOS commands:

```
CD ..

CD ..

CD ..
```

The two dots following each CD command indicate that the computer should change to the parent directory. In a Windows 95 MS-DOS window, you can still use two dots to back up one parent directory. However, Windows 95 builds on this feature—if you want to back up more than one directory, add an extra dot for each parent you want to traverse backward. The previous three MS-DOS separate CD commands would therefore become:

```
CD ....
```

The first two dots tell MS-DOS to back up one parent directory; the third dot tells MS-DOS to back up one more parent directory, and the final dot requests that MS-DOS back up to one more parent directory.

197 | Why You Need to Customize

The Control Panel contains controls that let you customize the way Windows 95 behaves. When you customize Windows 95, you configure the operating system so that it looks and acts in a way that meets your preferences and expectations. For example, you can control the way the mouse pointer moves on the screen; the method Windows 95 uses to recognize hardware devices connected to your system; the modem settings your system uses; and so on. When you need to customize your computer, the first place you should go to is the Control Panel. To access the Control Panel, you can use one of the two following methods:

- Select the Start menu Settings option. Then, click your mouse on the Settings menu Control Panel option.
- Open the My Computer window and double-click the Control Panel icon.

Figure 197 shows the Control Panel.

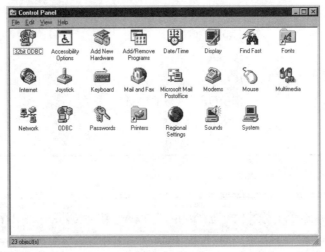

Figure 197 The Control Panel window.

198 | Understanding Control Panel Icons

Table 198 describes the icons in the Control Panel. Depending on your system's configuration, your Control Panel may contain more or fewer icons.

Icon	Purpose
32bit ODBC	Lets you configure ODBC (the *Open Database Connectivity* standard) by file name and type.
Accessibility Options	Lets you specify accessibility options for users with extra needs.
Add New Hardware	Helps you configure Windows 95 when you install new hardware.

Table 198 The Control Panel icons represent different areas of your PC (continued on the following page).

Using the Windows 95 Control Panel

Icon	Purpose
Add/Remove Programs	Provides services that let you install or remove software.
Date/Time	Displays the Date/Time Properties sheet so you can change your system's date, time, and time zone.
Display	Lets you change the way your monitor displays data.
Find Fast	Lets you find data in Microsoft Office files quickly (available only if you install Microsoft Office).
Fonts	Lets you configure, add, and remove fonts.
Internet	Provides access to the Internet.
Joystick	Lets you control joystick operations.
Keyboard	Lets you control the speed and language of your PC's keyboard.
Mail and Fax	Provides support for e-mail and fax.
Microsoft Mail Postoffice	Lets you manage the Microsoft post office located on your disk.
Modems	Provides modem-configuration support.
Mouse	Lets you control the behavior of your mouse.
Multimedia	Lets you access your computer's multimedia services.
Network	Lets you configure, display, and change your networking operations.

Table 198 *The Control Panel icons represent different areas of your PC (continued on the following page).*

Icon	Purpose
ODBC	Lets you configure ODBC by database type.
Passwords	Manages your system passwords.
Printers	Lets you manage your system's printers.
Regional Settings	Lets you adjust your computer's regional settings, such as international support.
Sounds	Controls the sounds that occur when events take place.
System	Provides advanced system configuration services.

Table 198 The Control Panel icons represent different areas of your PC (continued from the previous page).

199 Installing New Hardware

To update your computer, you will need to add and replace hardware. Windows 95 makes adding new hardware easier than previous versions of Windows. However, depending on the age and type of hardware, you may still have to configure the installation by setting switches or jumpers on the hardware card. To install new hardware, perform these steps:

1. Shut down Windows 95.
2. Turn off your computer and unplug the power cord.
3. Read your hardware manual to see if your hardware is Plug and Play compatible (see Tip 37). If it is not, you may have to change switch and jumper settings before installing the device.
4. Install the new hardware.
5. Reconnect the power cable and turn on your computer to start Windows 95.
6. Open the Control Panel and run the Add New Hardware wizard discussed in Tip 200.

200 Using the Add New Hardware Wizard

Depending on your computer type and hardware type, Installing new hardware may require more than physical installation. Often, despite Plug-and-Play capabilities, you must inform Windows 95 about your hardware. Fortunately, the Add New Hardware wizard makes hardware installations easy. The Add New Hardware wizard walks you through a series of dialog boxes that make installing hardware as painless as possible. Figure 200.1 shows the first of several windows from the Add New Hardware wizard.

Even if a device is not truly a Plug-and-Play hardware, Windows 95 can often detect the device and set up your system to use it. The second window of the Add New Hardware wizard, shown in Figure 200.2, asks if you want Windows 95 to search your computer for the new device. Although the automatic search takes a few minutes, it is the best choice because the Add New Hardware wizard might find other changes in your computer that it didn't notice before (such as a hardware setting conflict). If you select the No option button, you must specify the new device yourself.

If Windows 95 does not find the new hardware, you will have to specify the manufacturer and model of the hardware. Also, you may have to insert a driver disk, supplied by the hardware maker, to describe the new device to Windows 95. (Windows 95 supports several hundred hardware devices, so, in most cases, you won't have to use the disk that the manufacturer supplies.)

Figure 200.1 Running the Add New Hardware Wizard.

Figure 200.2 Windows 95 can search for new hardware.

Installing and Removing Software — 201

Windows 95 provides a uniform interface you can use to install and remove software. Before Windows 95, software makers supplied users with setup programs, almost all of which were different and required different kinds of keystrokes to install the programs. The setup programs often confused beginners. Windows 95's uniform software installation process should help increase beginners' confidence and make software installation easier for everybody.

One of the biggest challenges pre-Windows 95 users faced was not installing software, but *removing* it. Although you could easily delete a program's icon from the Program Manager, the program still consumed disk space. You could delete the program files, but traces of the program would still remain in one or more Windows INI files.

To be fully Windows 95 compatible, software must include a removal option that eliminates all traces of the program from your disk. To remove such software, you can double-click the Control Panel's Add/Remove Programs icon. Windows 95, in turn, will display the Add/Remove Programs Properties sheet (shown in Figure 201). Then, select the program from the list on the Install/Uninstall page and click the Add/Remove button.

Note: *Not all programs provide support for the Add/Remove Programs Properties sheet. However, over time, more and more will.*

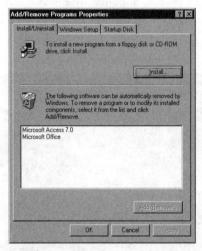

Figure 201 *The Add/Remove Programs Properties sheet.*

202 Understanding the Differences between the Windows 95 Setup Options

Four setup options are available to you when you install Windows 95. Each option will install a different Windows 95 configuration. Table 202 explains each of the four Windows 95 setup options. After you install Windows 95, you can change the Windows 95 configuration at any time by adding or removing various Windows 95 components. Tip 203 explains how to change your Windows 95 configuration after you set up Windows 95.

Setup Option	Description
Typical	Installs the Windows 95 components needed for typical desktop operation. This installation virtually runs itself. During the installation, you only need to specify the drive and directory where you want Windows 95, enter your name (and, optionally, your company name), and insert a diskette if you want the Setup program to create a setup disk.
Portable	Installs all components needed for a standard mobile computer, such as a laptop.
Compact	Installs the smallest possible Windows 95 configuration that will save disk space but let you run Windows 95.
Custom	Installs only Windows 95 components that you specify. If you are familiar with Windows 95, the Custom option lets you override default installation settings, but you must instruct the Setup program to install exactly what you want. You'll also have to inform Windows 95 of your computer's hardware devices.

Table 202 *The Windows 95 Setup Program options.*

Adding and Removing Windows 95 Components — 203

After you install Windows 95, you may still return to the Windows 95 installation program to add and remove Windows 95 options and components from your system. The Add/Remove Programs Properties sheet contains a Windows Setup page you can access by pressing the Windows Setup tab.

The four Windows 95 setup options, which Tip 201 describes, install only certain Windows 95 components. As you read through the tips in this book and learn more about Windows 95, you may require Windows 95 components that you didn't install originally. Likewise, depending on your disk space limits, you may also want to remove some Windows 95 components. To add or remove Windows 95 components, perform these steps:

1. Open the Control Panel.
2. Double-click the Add/Remove Programs icon to display the Add/Remove Programs Properties sheet.
3. Click the Windows Setup tab to open the Windows Setup page shown in Figure 203.
4. Check the Windows 95 option you want to install or remove the checkmark from the option you want to remove. To help you monitor your disk usage during the setup change, Windows 95 displays the amount of disk space each option consumes. Additionally, Windows 95 displays the total amount of free disk space on your system.
5. Click the OK button to install or remove your new Windows 95 component. The Setup program will not reinstall components already on your system. Therefore, if you already access Microsoft Exchange and want to continue to do so, leave the Microsoft Exchange option checked. Windows 95 will recognize that Microsoft Exchange already resides on your system and will not reinstall Microsoft Exchange.

Note: When you run the Windows Setup program, you will need your Windows 95 installation disks or CD-ROM so the Setup program can find components to install.

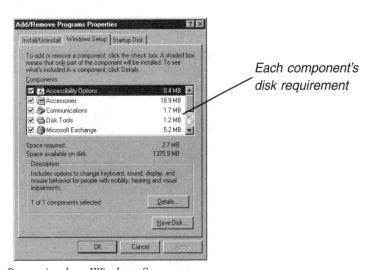

Figure 203 The Add/Remove Programs Properties sheet Windows Setup page.

204 Viewing Details about a Component

In Tip 203 you learned how to install or remove various parts of Windows 95. As it turns out, some Windows 95 setup options, such as the Communications option, install in several pieces. The Communications option is a setup category that contains four Windows 95 programs. Therefore, when you decide to set up the Communications option, you also must click the Details button to let Windows 95 know exactly which Communications components you want to install. Windows 95, in turn, will display a dialog box that shows you exactly how much disk space each detail consumes. Figure 204 shows such a dialog box.

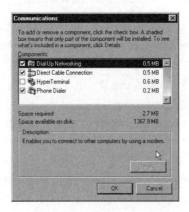

Figure 204 Some options contain several details.

205 Creating a Startup Disk

If you make changes to your system, there may be times when the changes your make introduce an error that prevents Windows 95 from starting. On such occasions, you can use the startup disk to help you start your system from floppy disk. Then, you can access your hard disk to undo the change that is preventing Windows 95 from starting. During the Windows 95 installation and setup process, the Windows 95 Setup program will ask if you want to create a *startup disk*. If you did not create a startup disk when you installed Windows 95, you can create one using the Control Panel's Add/Remove option. To create a startup disk, perform these steps:

1. Open the Control Panel.
2. Double-click the Add/Remove Programs icon to display the Add/Remove Programs Properties sheet.
3. Click the Startup Disk tab to display the Startup Disk page.
4. Click on the Create Disk button and follow the instructions that appear on your screen.

Be sure to store your startup disk in a safe place. Additionally, mark the startup disk so you can quickly find it when you need it. Without the startup disk, tracing Windows 95 startup problems can get tricky.

206 Understanding Apply Versus OK

Many of the Control Panel options and programs display sheets and dialog boxes that let you change Windows 95's configuration. Some changes require that you restart Windows 95 before they can take place. Other changes can occur immediately. When you make changes to a properties sheet and Windows 95 can activate those changes immediately, you will see three buttons at the bottom of the sheet, such as the ones shown in Figure 206. If you click

OK, the properties sheet closes and the changes take place. If you click Cancel, the properties sheet disappears and Windows 95 ignores any changes you made. If, however, you click the Apply button, Windows 95 activates those changes immediately and leaves the properties sheet on your screen in case you want to make additional changes or quickly revert back to a previous setting.

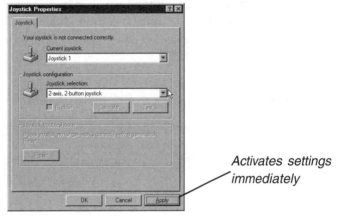

Figure 206 *The Apply button leaves the properties sheet on your screen.*

Using the Control Panel to Set the Date and Time — 207

Tip 142 explained how you can use the Taskbar clock to change your computer's date-and-time. The Control Panel's Date/Time icon also lets you change your computer's date-and-time. If you've hidden the Taskbar clock (see Tip 105), you must use the Control Panel's Date/Time option to change your system's date-and-time. Your computer's date-and-time settings are critical. For example, every time you create or modify a file, Windows 95 time-stamps the file with the date and time. Later, you may use a file's date-and-time to locate the file or to determine when you made you last changes to the file. To change your computer's date-and-time, perform these steps:

1. Double-click the Control Panel's Date/Time icon to display the Date/Time Properties sheet shown in Figure 207.
2. If you want to change the month or year, click the arrow buttons to change the values.
3. If you want to change the day, click on the correct number in the monthly calendar.
4. If you want to change the time, click on the individual portions (hour, minute, second, or AM/PM indicator) of the time display and enter new values.
5. Click the OK button to save your changes.

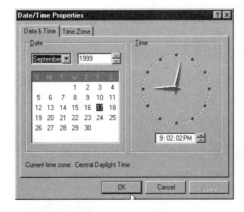

Figure 207 *Changing the date-and-time.*

208 Using the Control Panel for Screen Display Settings

In most cases, Windows 95 offers you several ways to accomplish a task. If you need a particular program such as Explorer, Windows 95 provides several places from which you can launch such a program. Likewise, the Control Panel lets you access several items that you can access from elsewhere within Windows 95. Through the Control Panel's Display icon, you can perform the same actions as you can using the Properties option on the Desktop's pop-up menu.

Through the Display icon, you can change the way your monitor looks and behaves. When you double-click the Control Panel's Display icon, Windows 95 opens the Display Properties sheet, as shown in Figure 208.

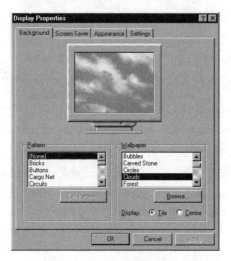

Figure 208 *The Display Properties sheet.*

209 Understanding the Accessibility Options

Microsoft created Windows 95 for a wide range of computer users. Microsoft recognized that many computer users have special needs. Ordinary computer programs and operating systems cause problems for some hearing- and sight-impaired people, as well as for people with other physical disabilities.

The Accessibility Options, available through the Control Panel, provides support for many users and helps those users access a computer more easily and comfortably than they could before. Several of the tips that follow describe how you can activate the Accessibility Options.

If you do not think you'll need the Accessibility Options, you should review them anyway just to see the great tools that Microsoft added to Windows 95. Many people who thought they wouldn't need any of the Accessibility Options have found them beneficial. To access the Accessibility Options, double-click on the Control Panel's Accessibility Options icon. Windows 95, in turn, will display the Accessibility Properties sheet, as shown in Figure 209.

Note: *As with most Control Panel options, if the Accessibility Options icon does not appear, run the Windows 95 Setup (see Tip 203) and install the Accessibility Options.*

If you are sure that you will not use the Accessibility Options after you learn what they can do, you can remove them from your system (and free up disk space) using the Add/Remove Programs sheet Windows Setup page (see Tip 203).

Using the Windows 95 Control Panel

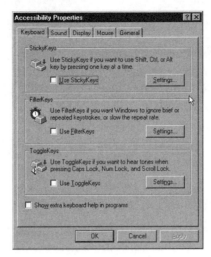

Figure 209 *The Accessibility Properties sheet.*

Understanding and Using StickyKeys | 210

Many Windows 95 programs let you use shortcut keypress combinations that involve one of three modifier keys: ALT, CTRL, and SHIFT. To make sure that all users can take advantage of these shortcuts, Microsoft designated these three keys as StickyKeys. If you are unable to press any of these keys simultaneously with another key, such as you would need to do to perform a CTRL-P keystroke, you should activate StickyKeys. After you activate StickyKeys, you can press the CTRL key, let up on CTRL, and then press another key, such as P. In effect, the CTRL key sticks (stays down) until you press a second key. If you want to activate StickyKeys, perform these steps:

1. Open the Control Panel.
2. Double-click the Accessibility Options icon to display the Accessibility Properties sheet.
3. Click the Keyboard tab if the Keyboard page does not show.
4. Click the Use StickyKeys check box.
5. Click the Settings button to display the Settings for StickyKeys dialog box shown if Figure 210. The Settings for StickyKeys dialog box determines how you want StickyKeys to act. Table 210 explains the dialog boxes values.
6. Click the OK button twice to save your StickyKeys settings.

Setting Option	Description
Use shortcut	Lets you turn StickyKeys on and off by pressing SHIFT five times.
Press modifier key twice to lock	Requires that you press a sticky key twice before the key sticks.
Turn StickyKeys off if two keys are pressed at once	If someone presses a modifier keystroke at the same time, such as CTRL-A, StickyKeys turns itself off and assumes that the current user does not need StickyKeys.
Make sounds when modifier key is pressed	Makes different sounds to indicate that you've pressed, locked down, or released a modifier key (useful for the visually impaired).
Show StickyKeys status on screen	Displays a visual indication when a StickyKeys operation is in progress (useful for the hearing impaired).

Table 210 *The Settings for StickyKeys dialog box values.*

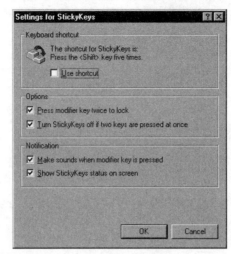

Figure 210 *The Settings for StickyKeys dialog box.*

211 Understanding and Using Filter Keys

Due to a brace or other physical disability, some users accidentally strike keys or hold down a key too long, causing the keyboard-repeating action to start. The FilterKeys option instructs Windows 95 to ignore any keystrokes that occur rapidly, as might happen if someone brushes a key or two.

FilterKeys also instructs Windows 95 to ignore repeated keystrokes and to only repeat a key if that key is struck twice or held down for an extended period of time. If you want to activate FilterKeys, check the Use FilterKeys check box on the Accessibility Properties sheet.

If you want to control the way Windows 95 interprets StickyKeys settings, click the Settings button to display the Settings for FilterKeys dialog box. Table 211 explains the values in the Settings for FilterKeys dialog box.

Setting Option	Description
Use shortcut	Lets you turn FilterKeys on and off by holding down the keyboard's RIGHT SHIFT key for eight seconds.
Ignore repeated keystrokes	Ignores keystrokes that come quickly. You can press the Settings button to determine how much time Windows 95 waits before repeating a key stroke.
Ignore quick keystrokes and slow down the repeat rate	Instructs Windows 95 to ignore briefly pressed keystrokes.
Click and type here to test FilterKeys settings	Lets you test FilterKeys settings.
Beep when keys are pressed or accepted	Sounds a beep to let you know when Windows 95 accepts a keystroke. The beep will not sound for repeated keys or quick keys that FilterKeys ignores.
Show FilterKeys status on screen	Displays a Taskbar indicator when FilterKeys are active.

Table 211 *The Settings for FilterKeys dialog box values.*

212 Understanding and Using ToggleKeys

When you activate the Windows 95 Accessibility ToggleKeys settings, Windows 95 makes a high beep sound every time you press CAPS LOCK, NUM LOCK, or SCROLL LOCK to activate those keys. When you subsequently press the keys to turn them off, Windows 95 will make a low beep sound to indicate that you deactivated the keys. For those who are visually impaired, these sounds help confirm that you actually pressed one of the keys when you activated or deactivated the key. If you want to activate ToggleKeys, check the Use ToggleKeys check box on the Accessibility Properties sheet. The Settings button in the ToggleKeys section controls the shortcut for ToggleKeys; if you select the shortcut, you can turn the ToggleKeys on and off by holding down NUM LOCK for five seconds.

213 Understanding and Using SoundSentry

When you click your mouse on the Accessibility Properties sheet Sound tab, Windows 95 displays the Sound page shown in Figure 213.1. The SoundSentry feature displays a visual screen clue whenever a sound comes through your PC's speaker. If you work in a loud environment or are hearing impaired, SoundSentry might help warn you when your PC makes a sound that you don't hear, such as a warning beep. If you click your mouse on the SoundSentry Settings button, Windows 95 displays the Settings for the SoundSentry sheet shown in Figure 213.2. This dialog box's first pull-down list lets you determine how SoundSentry visually warns you that your system has made a sound. For example, you can have SoundSentry flash the title bar, the active window, or the Desktop when your PC makes a sound. If you want SoundSentry to display during a full-screen text display, such as in MS-DOS, the second pull-down list lets you decide if you want SoundSentry to flash the screen's characters, its border, or the entire display.

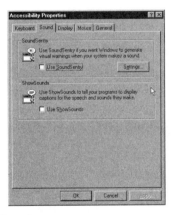

Figure 213.1 The Accessibility Properties sheet Sound page.

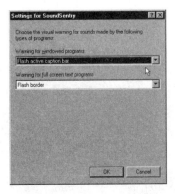

Figure 213.2 Determine how you want to see SoundSentry.

214 Understanding and Using ShowSounds

As you learned in Tip 213, if you work in a loud office or if you are hearing impaired, there may be times when you cannot hear the sounds your programs generate. In such cases, you may be able to use the Windows 95 ShowSounds option. As discussed, the ShowSounds option directs Windows 95 to display a visual indicator that a sound has occurred. For example, Windows 95 might flash a program's title bar or window border when a sound occurs. Unfortunately, the ShowSounds option is not yet available for all Windows 95 programs—but it should be eventually. When you check the ShowSounds option in the Accessibility Properties sheet Sound page, Windows 95 will display captions for the sounds that the running program normally makes.

215 Controlling Display Screen Contrast

When you click your mouse on the Accessibility Properties sheet Display tab, you'll see the Display page shown in Figure 215.1. The Display page contains the High Contrast option, which lets you view Windows 95 screens with color schemes that provide exceptional contrast between elements, such as window borders and the Desktop. The High Contrast feature lets those who have trouble distinguishing colors or reading the screen see a better contrast between the screen's elements and, thus, read the screen more easily. The Settings button on the Display page produces the Settings for High Contrast dialog box shown in Figure 215.2. If you select the dialog box's Use shortcut check box, you'll be able to turn High Contrast on or off by pressing LEFT ALT-LEFT SHIFT-PRNTSCR. In the dialog box's High Contrast color scheme section, you can choose white letters on black, black letters on white, or a custom color scheme for the high contrast-color display.

Figure 215.1 The Accessibility Properties sheet Display page.

Figure 215.2 The Accessibility Properties sheet Settings for High Contrast page.

Understanding and Using MouseKeys 216

The Accessibility Use MouseKeys option, which you set from the Accessibility Properties sheet Mouse page, lets you make mouse movements using your keyboard's 10-key numeric keypad. Some users prefer to use the keyboard exclusively, even though Windows 95 programs often work best with a mouse. Other users simply do not have room on their desks for mouse movements, or they use a laptop that does not have a mouse.

When you use MouseKeys, you can move the mouse using the keypad numbers 1, 2, 3, 4, 6, 7, 8, 9. When you press a number, your mouse pointer moves in the keypad number's direction. The number 5 simulates a mouse click, 0 locks the mouse button (for dragging operations), the decimal point (.) releases the mouse button, the slash (/) simulates a left button press, the minus sign (-) simulates a right-button click, and the asterisk (*) simulates both buttons.

When you click your mouse on the MouseKeys Settings button, Windows 95 displays the Settings for MouseKeys dialog box shown in Figure 216.1. Table 216 explains each of the dialog box's options.

Setup Option	Description
Keyboard shortcut	Lets you turn on and off MouseKeys by pressing LEFT ALT-LEFT SHIFT-NUM LOCK.
Top speed	Determines how fast the mouse pointer will move.
Acceleration	Determines how fast the mouse pointer moves from a standing position to full speed.
Hold down Ctrl to speed up and Shift to slow down	By combining the MouseKeys keypress with CTRL or SHIFT, you can accelerate or slow down individual MouseKeys mouse pointer movements.
Use MouseKeys when NumLock is	Determines if you want to use MouseKeys with NUM LOCK on or off.
Show MouseKeys status on screen	Displays the MouseKeys status on the Taskbar when MouseKeys is active. Figure 216.2 shows the Taskbar's MouseKeys status when the user clicks the left mouse button.

Table 216 *The Settings for MouseKeys dialog box.*

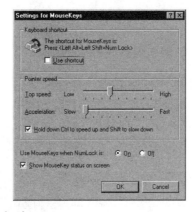

Figure 216.1 *The Settings for MouseKeys dialog box.*

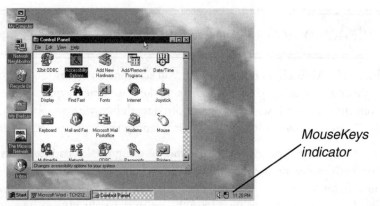

Figure 216.2 *You pressed your left MouseKeys button.*

217 Understanding and Using SerialKey Devices

A *SerialKey device* is an alternate input device that lets users with special needs operate a computer. For example, one such device lets the user perform keyboard operations by alternatively blowing and sucking through a tube. Such devices often connect to your system's serial ports, COM1 through COM4. To make Windows 95 aware that a SerialKey device is connected to your system's serial ports, you must display the Accessibility Properties sheet General page, shown in Figure 217.1, and check the Support SerialKey devices check box. Windows 95 must also know to which port you've connected the SerialKey device, so you must click your mouse on the Settings button to display the Settings for SerialKeys dialog box shown in Figure 217.2. The Settings for SerialKey dialog box lets you specify the device's serial port and speed. You may have to check the device's manual to find the correct speed setting.

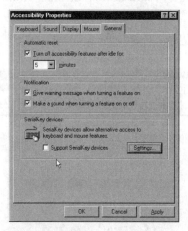

Figure 217.1 *The Accessibility Properties sheet General page.*

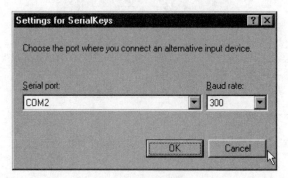

Figure 217.2 *The Settings for SerialKeys page.*

Controlling Accessibility Option Settings — 218

Through the Accessibility Properties sheet General page, you can further control the options you set from the other Accessibility Properties sheet pages. The Accessibility Properties sheet General page includes the following options:

- An automatic reset that turns off the Accessibility Options after a specified number of minutes. If a user who needs the Accessibility Options leaves the computer unattended for more than the specified number of minutes, Windows 95 turns off the Accessibility Options so the computer is ready for use by someone else.
- A warning message that alerts you when an Accessibility Options first activates
- A warning noise that audibly alerts you when an Accessibility Options activates or deactivates

Understanding Fonts — 219

A font is a specification that tells your system how to display letters, numbers, and special characters (such as # and +) on your screen and in your printouts. A font determines the shape, size, and appearance of characters. When Windows 95 displays a character on your screen, Windows 95 draws that character according to the selected font's rules. Windows 95 uses device-independent fonts so that, in most cases, you have the same selection of fonts from within every program you run. If you want to add new fonts to your PC, you can purchase them. When you need to add or remove fonts, you'll use the Fonts window shown in Figure 219. To access the Fonts window, you double-click on the Control Panel's Fonts icon. In the Fonts window, the font icons containing the letters *TT* represent TrueType fonts (Tip 224 explains TrueType fonts); the other icons represent bitmap fonts. The Fonts window works just like other windows; you can access the Fonts window options using all the window operations you know already.

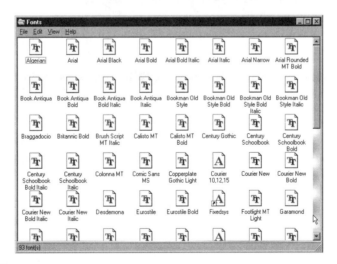

Figure 219 The Fonts window.

Viewing and Printing a Font Sample — 220

If you wish to see what a font will look like, you can view or print a font sample directly from the Fonts window. To view a font, perform these steps:

1. Open the Control Panel.

2. Double-click the Fonts icon. Windows 95 will open the Fonts window.
3. Locate the font you want to view and double-click on it. Windows 95 will display a sample of that font using a window like the one in Figure 220.
4. If you want to print the font sample, click your mouse on the Print button. When Windows 95 displays the Print dialog box, turn on your printer and press ENTER to start printing.
5. When you finish viewing or printing the font, click your mouse on the Done button.

Figure 220 Viewing a font sample.

221 Understanding Font Point Sizes

When you select a font, you must understand how Windows 95 sizes the font. Windows 95 measures all fonts in points. A point is 1/72nd of an inch, which is very small indeed. Therefore, if you want to print characters using a one-inch font size, you must set that font to 72 points. Likewise, a character printed at 36 points would appear one-half inch high. When users print text-based documents, most prefer font sizes that range from 11 to 13 points.

When you view and print documents within Windows 95, you must select a font style. (The style controls the appearance. For example, some styles generate round characters.) Additionally, you must select a font size. Tip 220 explains how to see both the style and size of various fonts.

Note: *typically, font sizes appear differently on your screen than their size measurements indicate. For example, if you have a 14-point character on the screen, Windows 95 produces the character relative to the current window size. However, the 14-point character will always appear the correct size on your printouts.*

222 Adding Fonts

To add fonts to your system, access the Fonts window. The Fonts window contains all the tools you need to add fonts to your system. To install a new font, all you need is a floppy disk or CD-ROM that contains the font. To install new fonts, perform these steps:

1. Double-click your mouse on the Control Panel's Fonts icon. Windows 95 will open the Fonts window.
2. Select the File menu Install New Font option. Figure 222 shows the Add Fonts dialog box that appears.
3. Select the drive (floppy or CD-ROM) and folder that contain the new fonts. In the list box

at the top of the window, Windows 95 will display the fonts from that drive and folder.

4. Click on the font you want to install. If you want to install more than one font, press CTRL while you click on each font to install. If you want to install all the fonts, click the Select All button. If you want Windows 95 to copy the font files to the WINDOWS\FONTS directory (recommended, unless you are short on disk space), leave the check in the Copy fonts to Fonts folder check box.

5. To install the fonts, click your mouse on the OK button.

Note: *In step 4, if you choose not to copy the font files to the WINDOWS\FONTS directory, Windows 95 will have trouble finding the files in the future, unless you keep the floppy disks or CD-ROM handy which contains the fonts.*

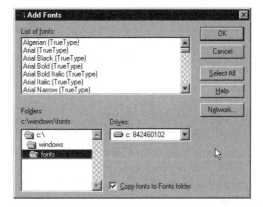

Figure 222 *The Add Fonts dialog box.*

Removing Fonts 223

If you dislike one or more of your installed fonts, or if you want to free disk space, you might want to remove fonts. To do so, perform these steps:

1. Double-click your Control Panel's Fonts icon. Windows 95 will open the Fonts window.
2. Locate the font you want to delete and right-click your mouse to display its pop-up menu.
3. Select the pop-up menu's Delete option.
4. Click your mouse on the Yes button to confirm the deletion. Windows 95 will remove the font from your WINDOWS\FONTS folder and free the disk space.

Note: *Do not delete fonts that came with Windows 95. Windows 95 uses these fonts for window and dialog box text.*

Understanding TrueType Fonts 224

When you view a list of fonts or font icons, the fonts that appear with the letters *TT* are called *TrueType* fonts. (The others are *bitmap* or *screen* fonts.) Generally, TrueType fonts look better than non-TrueType fonts. TrueType fonts look the same on the screen as they look on paper; as such, they give your programs the ability to produce what-you-see-is-what-you-get (also called WYSIWYG, pronounced *wiz-ee-wig*) documents.

Note: *You can both scale and embed TrueType fonts. Certain programs can embed TrueType fonts in your documents. As such, others can receive your documents and view fonts, even if their PCs do not contain the same fonts as yours. You can also scale TrueType fonts to enlarge or shrink them as you like.*

To see only TrueType fonts in the Fonts window and other font listings, perform these steps:

1. Double-click your Control Panel's Fonts icon. Windows 95 will open the Fonts window.
2. Select View menu Options option.
3. Click your mouse on the Options sheet TrueType tab to see the TrueType page shown in Figure 224.
4. To limit font displays to TrueType fonts only, click your mouse on the page's check box.
5. To save your changes, click your mouse on the OK button.

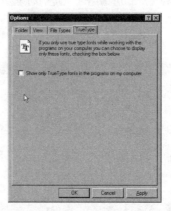

Figure 224 The Options sheet TrueType page.

225 Reducing Clutter in the Font Window

Typically, the Fonts window contains every font on your system and every font variation, such as the bold and italicized versions. Figure 225.1 contains a cluttered Fonts window. If you want to make your Fonts window more manageable, choose one of the options:

- Select the View menu Hide Variations option to display one icon for all variations of a font.
- Select the View menu List option to view lists of fonts with smaller font icons. These lists let you display more fonts at one time. Figure 225.2 shows a Fonts window that uses the List option and hides all font variations. Normally, Windows 95 displays the fonts using the View menu Large Icons option.

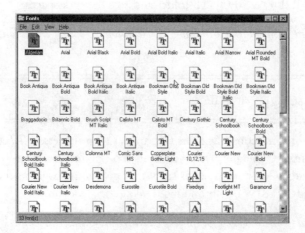

Figure 225.1 Too many fonts can be a mess.

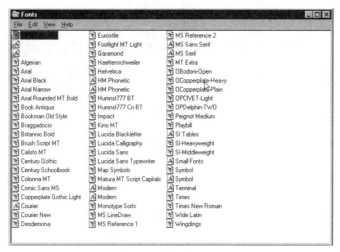

Figure 225.2 Reducing the fonts displayed.

Listing Fonts by Similarity — 226

Different fonts often look like other fonts. For example, the bitmap Courier font looks like the TrueType font called Courier New. Of course, the TrueType font offers the embedding and scaling advantages, as Tip 224 describes. Nevertheless, the two fonts are virtually identical.

Suppose that you and a friend are working on a project, but you do not have the same fonts on both your systems. If your applications do not support TrueType embedding (many do not), you may have difficulty sharing files because of the font differences. Fortunately, through the Fonts window, you can display a list of similar fonts. Therefore, if you like the Ariel font, but your friend does not have Ariel, the Fonts window can show you a list of fonts similar to Ariel. From the list, you can find a font that resides on both your systems. To display a list of similar fonts, perform these steps:

1. Double-click your mouse on the Control Panel's Fonts icon. Windows 95 will open the Fonts window.
2. Select the View menu List Fonts By Similarity option. Windows 95 will display a list of your fonts and arrange the list in the order of very similar, fairly similar, and not similar. If you and your friend each have one of the very similar fonts, you both can use the font and produce text that looks alike.
3. To close the window, select the File menu Close option.

Controlling Joystick Settings — 227

If you control games and other programs with a joystick, you need to inform Windows 95 of the joystick's type. Windows 95 supports several kinds of joysticks:

- Two-button joysticks
- Four-button joysticks
- Race car controllers
- Flight stick rudders

The Joystick Properties sheet, which you access through the Control Panel's Joystick icon, lets you make joystick settings that match your particular joystick. Figure 227.1 shows the Joystick Properties sheet. If you cannot find your exact joystick specifications in the Joystick selection pull-down list, choose the Custom option to display the Custom Joystick dialog box shown in Figure 227.2.

Figure 227.1 *The Joystick Properties sheet.*

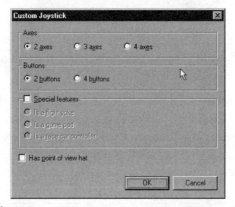

Figure 227.2 *Setting custom joystick options.*

228 Controlling Your Keyboard's Responsiveness

Through the Control Panel, you can control two important keyboard settings:

- The repeat-delay time, which determines how long you must hold down a key before Windows 95 recognizes it as a repeating key. For example, if you are typing text into a word processor and hold the **A** key down for a few moments, letter A's start appearing across your screen until you release the key.

- The repeat rate, which determines how fast Windows 95 repeats a key you hold down.

When you double-click the Control Panel's Keyboard icon, Windows 95 displays the Keyboard Properties sheet Speed page, as shown in Figure 228. The top two sliders let you set your keyboard's repeat delay time and the repeat rate. If you change one or both of these values, you can practice using them in the text box below the slider controls before you apply the values to the rest of your Windows 95 system. By practicing with the values you set, you eliminate the need to return to the Keyboard Properties sheet to make further adjustments.

Figure 228 *The Keyboard Properties sheet Speed page.*

Controlling the Text Cursor Blink Rate — 229

Several different kinds of cursors appear on your screen at various times. The two most important are the mouse and the text cursor (more accurately, but rarely, called the *insertion point*). Of the two, the text cursor is the harder to see because of its thin size. If you change the text cursor's blinking-speed rate, you can often make the text cursor easier to spot. Changing the blink rate is especially helpful if your Windows 95 system is a laptop. (Some laptops have screens that are difficult to read in certain light situations.)

The Keyboard Properties sheet Speed page contains a slider control labeled Cursor blink rate that changes the text cursor's blinking speed. As you adjust the slider control slower or faster, a sample text cursor to the left of the control changes speed accordingly. When you click your mouse on the OK or Apply button, Windows 95 records your changes and updates the true text cursor's speed.

Understanding and Using Keyboard Languages — 230

Different countries use different alphabet characters. For example, the Spanish language includes the letter *Ñ*, while English does not. If you move to a different country or want to type in another language, you can customize your keyboard to produce the other language's characters. Figure 230 shows the Keyboard Properties sheet Language page. The figure's page is currently set up for United States English only. From the Keyboard Properties sheet Language page, you can either change the keyboard language or add additional languages to those already selected.

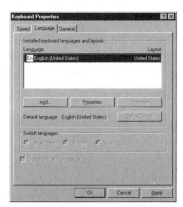

Figure 230 *The Keyboard Properties sheet Language page.*

231 Adding and Removing Keyboard Languages

It would be nice if people could learn foreign languages as easily as their keyboards can adapt to different country's character sets. To add an additional language to your keyboard, perform these steps:

1. Open the Control Panel and double-click the Keyboard icon.
2. To display the Keyboard Properties sheet Language page, click on the Language tab.
3. To display a pull-down list of available languages, click your mouse on the Add button.
4. Select the language you want to add and click your mouse on the OK button. The Keyboard Properties sheet Language page will now display the added language. Figure 231 shows a Keyboard Properties sheet Language page that supports both English and Italian keyboards.
5. Highlight the language you want Windows 95 to use as the default keyboard language. Then, click the Set as Default button.
6. To save your changes, click your mouse on the OK button.

If you want to remove a language, you only have to highlight the language in the Keyboard Properties sheet Language page and click your mouse on the Remove button.

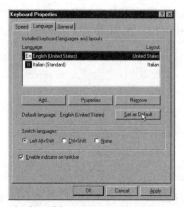

Figure 231 Your Windows 95 now supports two keyboard languages.

232 Switching Between Keyboard Languages

After you add a language, the Keyboard Properties sheet Language page displays options that let you determine how you want to switch between the different keyboard languages. If you travel to a foreign country often, you may want to keep two keyboard languages set up on your system. That way, when you visit the other country, you can switch to that country's language. To tell Windows 95 how you want to switch keyboard languages, perform these steps:

1. Open the Control Panel and double-click your mouse on the Keyboard icon.
2. To display the Keyboard Properties sheet Language page, click on the Language tab.
3. Select the method you want to use to change keyboard languages in the Language page Switch languages section. You can accept the default option, which lets you press LEFT ALT-SHIFT to change keyboard languages, or change this option to CTRL-SHIFT. You can also select the None option, which makes your system only accept keyboard language switches made through the Keyboard Properties sheet Language page.
4. If you check the Enable indicator on taskbar check box, Windows 95 will display, to the left

of the Taskbar clock, the first two letters of the keyboard language in use. If you switch to the other language, the other language's indicator will appear.

5. To save your changes, click your mouse on the OK button.

233 Selecting Your Keyboard Type

Every once in a while, you may have to replace the keyboard on your computer. For example, if your keyboard breaks, you might salvage a keyboard from an old IBM PC that has an 84-key style or, you may decide to switch to a keyboard with a built-in trackball.

If you ever change your keyboard, you should inform Windows 95 of the change. Open the Keyboard Properties sheet General page, shown in Figure 233, and click your mouse on the Change button to select the kind of keyboard to which you are changing. After you click your mouse on the OK button, Windows 95 will recognize all the replacement keyboard's features.

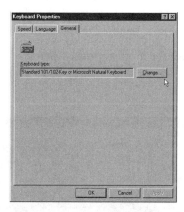

Figure 233 *You can change keyboards.*

234 Customizing Modem Settings

Windows 95 makes it very easy for you to add, customize, or remove modems. When you double-click your mouse on the Control Panel's Modems icon, the Modems Properties sheet, shown in Figure 234, appears. From the Modems Properties sheet, you can add modems, change your current modem settings, and select a default modem for your applications.

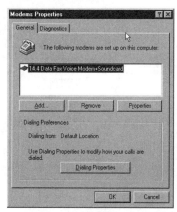

Figure 234 *The Modems Properties sheet.*

235 Adding and Removing a Modem

If you purchase and install a new modem, you can tell Windows 95 about the new modem in one of these three ways:

- Use Plug and Play if the new modem is Plug and Play compatible
- Use the Add New Hardware wizard discussed in Tip 200
- Use the Install New Modem wizard

If your modem is not Plug and Play compatible, the Install New Modem wizard is the simplest way to install a modem and inform Windows 95 of the modem's settings.

When you display the Modem Properties sheet (which you can access through the Control Panel's Modems icon) and click the Add button, Windows 95 starts the Install New Modem wizard shown in Figure 235.1. When you click the Next button, the wizard walks you through a series of screens to select your modem's manufacturer and type. Windows 95 can usually detect your modem type. However, if Windows 95 fails to detect your modem, you can select from the modem selection screen shown in Figure 235.2 (the Install New Modem wizard displays this screen).

Windows 95 does not automatically remove the modem driver when you physically remove a modem. To remove an older modem's configuration, display the Modem Properties sheet, select the old modem, and click the Remove button.

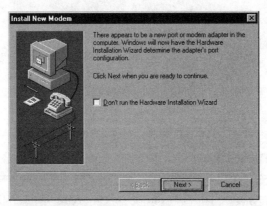

Figure 235.1 *The Install New Modem wizard's opening screen.*

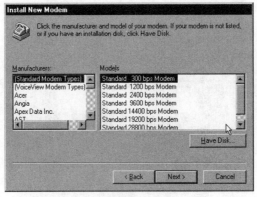

Figure 235.2 *You can select from a list of modems.*

Controlling Modem Properties — 236

After you install a modem, you may want to change the modem's properties settings. For example, you may move the modem from one serial port to another, or you may want to increase the modem's speaker volume so you can hear the calls you make. When you change modem properties, all Windows 95 programs that use modems will automatically know about the changes. In the past, you had to inform every communication and fax program of a change. To change modem properties, select your modem from the Modems Properties sheet and then click the Properties button. Windows 95, in turn, will display the properties sheet for your specific modem (see Figure 236).

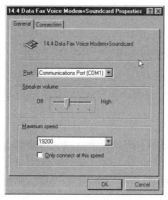

Figure 236 *You can adjust your modem properties.*

Understanding Modem Speed — 237

The term *baud rate* defines the speed of your modem. Throughout the years, PC users have been amazed and then bored by new modem speeds that appear to increase at a faster pace than processor speeds. When you replace a 2400 baud modem with a 14.4K (that's approximately 14,000 baud) modem, you can transmit and receive modem data six times faster than before.

Some people mistakenly believe that *baud* means bits-per-second. Only with early modems did baud rates indicate how many bits-per-second the modem could communicate. *Baud* refers to the number of signal changes the modem can make every second. A modem's true speed depends on several factors. In general, the higher the baud rate, the faster the modem. However, Windows 95, your computer's CPU, and your communications program all play parts in determining the final speed of your modem.

The Properties sheet General page Maximum speed setting should be higher than your modem's actual baud rate. If your computer contains a 486 or later processor, change your maximum speed setting to at least 38400. Don't worry if this setting is faster than your modem's baud rate. The maximum speed setting determines the speed at which your computer can communicate with the modem, not how fast the modem can communicate with another modem on the other end of the telephone line. If you use a 28.8K or faster modem, move the maximum speed to the highest possible setting. Drop the setting down only if you experience data problems.

The check box labeled Only connect at this speed tells the modem to process all phone connections at that speed only. Unless you connect to a single computer that has the same or faster hardware and modem than yours, leave the check box unchecked.

238 | Understanding Data Connection Preferences

When you click the Connection tab on your modem's Properties sheet, Windows 95 displays the Connection page shown in Figure 238. The page's top section, labeled Connection preferences, lets you adjust these settings:

- *Data bits* determine how many bits (the smallest pieces of data you can send over a modem) each character of data will consume. The number you use for data bits is usually 7 or 8. Modems that communicate at speeds of 14.4K and faster usually transmit best at 8 data bits.

- The *parity* determines how the modem uses error checking to help ensure accurate communications. The parity values are either none (for no parity checking), odd, even, mark, or space. Most modem communications today use no parity.

- The *stop bits* determine the value used to terminate a single data character during transmission. You can set the stop bit to either 1, 1.5, or 0. Generally, today's faster modems work with a stop bit setting of 1.

You can often leave the three settings alone. When you install your modem, Windows 95 does a good job at setting the connection preferences for you. If you must change the connection preferences, you can select them by opening the pull-down lists and choosing values from the lists. The connection preferences are the default settings that Windows 95 first uses for a phone connection. Depending on the computer to which you connect, you can change connection preferences for individual data-communication sessions. In most cases, your connection preferences must match the computer's at the other end for you to make a good connection.

Figure 238 Adjusting your connection preferences.

239 | Understanding and Using Modem Call Preference Settings

The bottom section of your modem's Properties sheet Connection page contains three check boxes you can use to specify call preference settings:

- If you select the first check box, Windows 95 requires the modem to wait for a dial tone before dialing. In most instances, you should leave this checked, unless you must manually dial the phone before connecting with the modem.

- If you select the second check box, Windows 95 requires the modem to cancel the connection attempt if the attempt fails after the specified number of seconds.

- If you select the third check box, Windows 95 requires that the modem disconnect if a call is idle (no communications) for more than the specified number of minutes.

Understanding How a Modem's UART Affects Performance — 240

When you buy a modem, make sure you get one with a 16550 UART adapter. The UART is a chip that converts the incoming analog signal into a digital signal your modem requires. Likewise, the UART converts the modem's digital signal to an analog signal for transmission over phone lines. The 16650 UART is faster than its predecessors and as such, increases your modem's speed. Even with a fast computer, if you run several Windows 95 programs at one time and want to communicate in the background while working on a different foreground task, modems without the 16550 UART adapter can fail. You should have no trouble purchasing a modem with the 16550 UART. Most of today's modems contain the adapter. Those that do proudly display the information on the box.

Controlling UART Settings — 241

The Advanced Port Settings dialog box, which appears when you click the Port Settings button on your modem's Properties sheet Connection page, controls the way your modem interacts with the 16550 UART adapter. Generally, you can leave this dialog box's settings alone unless you experience communications problems, such as loss of some data during transmission from another computer modem. Figure 241 shows the Advanced Port Settings dialog box.

If you do not have a 16550 UART adapter, make sure you uncheck the check box at the top of the dialog box. The box ensures that the modem communicates as fast as possible with the 16550 UART adapter. The two slider controls determine how fast the 16550 UART send and receive buffers can fill up. As with most modem settings, if you have a modem with a speed of 14.4K or faster, and the modem has a 16550 UART adapter, move the slider control settings to their fastest position.

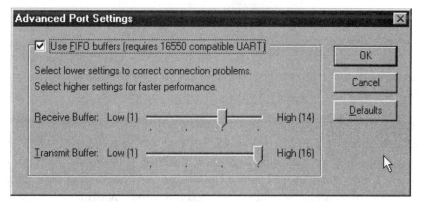

Figure 241 Adjusting your modem's 16550 UART interaction.

Understanding Advanced Modem Settings — 242

Depending on your modem type, you may enable or disable several advanced modem settings. To access these settings, click the Advanced button on your modem's Properties sheet Connection page. Windows 95, in turn, will display the Advanced Connection Settings dialog box, as shown in Figure 242. Table 242 explains each of the Advanced Connection Settings dialog box options.

Option	Purpose
Use error control	Helps eliminate errors that can occur during transmissions.
Required to connect	Only lets your computer connect to another if you enable the error control.

Table 242 The Advanced Connection Settings dialog box settings. (continued on the following page)

Option	Purpose
Compress data	Uses compressed data transmission for faster speed if your modem supports compression.
Use cellular protocol	Lets your modem communicate over cellular lines.
Use flow control	Improve data transmission if your modem cable manufacturer used RTS and CTS wires (most of today's modem cables have these wires connected). Check Software (XON/XOFF) if you cannot use hardware control.
Modulation type	Improves international call communications.
Record a log file	Creates a file named MODEMLOG.TXT that holds the text for a communications session.
Extra settings	Lets you add your own modem settings, provided you understand your modem's communications language.

Table 242 The Advanced Connection Settings dialog box settings. *(continued from previous page)*

Figure 242 The Advanced Connection Settings dialog box.

243 Understanding Modem Dialing Properties

The Dialing Properties sheet lets you specify dialing settings that will save you time when you use your modem. When you display the Modems Properties sheet and click the Dialing Properties button, you'll see the Dialing Properties sheet shown in Figure 243. The next several tips explain how you can use the Dialing Properties sheet to maximize your modem use and minimize setup time when you use your modem.

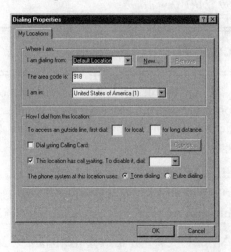

Figure 243 The Dialing Properties sheet.

Creating a Dialing Scheme   244

If you have Windows 95 and a modem on your laptop, you might want to create a different dialing scheme for each location from which you dial. Likewise, if you have more than one phone line in your office, you might want to create a new dialing scheme for each line. Through the Dialing Properties sheet, you can create a different dialing scheme for each phone you use.

Windows 95 always supplies a default location (see Figure 243) with which you to set up a dialing scheme. If you want to create another dialing scheme, click the Dialing Properties sheet New button and enter the new location's name, area code, and country. Then, make any other necessary changes to the Dialing Properties sheet's settings. For example, if you must dial a number to get an outside or long distance line, enter that number in the appropriate text boxes. When you click the OK button, Windows 95 saves your changes for the new location.

The next time you dial using a Windows 95-compatible communications program, open the I am dialing from pull-down list and select the dialing location from which you are calling. When you select a location's scheme, Windows 95 sets the modem according to that scheme's modem settings.

Using Your Calling Card for Modem Calls   245

Windows 95 makes it easy to use your calling card for modem calls. After you set up Windows 95 to use the card, you will not have to enter the calling card number again for any computer communications unless your calling card number changes. To enter calling-card instructions, perform these steps:

1. Double-click the Control Panel's Modems icon. Windows 95 will display the Modems Properties sheet.
2. Click the Dialing Properties button. Windows 95 will display the Dialing Properties sheet.
3. Click the option labeled Dial using Calling Card. Windows 95 will display the Change Calling Card dialog box shown in Figure 245.
4. Open the Calling Card to use pull-down list to see if your calling card is one of the options.
5. If you need to enter calling-card information that is not in the list, such as LifeLine, click the New button and enter a new name. If your calling card number differs for local, long distance, and international calls, click the Advanced button to enter the separate card numbers for each type of call.
6. Enter your calling card number and click the OK button to save your changes.

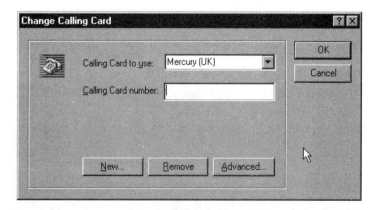

Figure 245 The Change Calling Card dialog box.

246 Customizing Your Mouse Settings

Windows 95 makes it easy to adjust your mouse settings. When you double-click the Control Panel's icon, the Mouse Properties sheet shown in Figure 246 appears. Through the Mouse Properties sheet, you can reverse mouse buttons, change the click speed, change mouse movement values, and select the icon that Windows 95 uses for your mouse pointer.

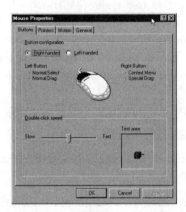

Figure 246 *The Mouse Properties sheet.*

247 Switching Between a Right- and Left-Handed Mouse

Just as many classrooms now include desks for left-handed students, Windows 95 includes a feature that lets you tailor your mouse to left-handed users. If you're left handed, you can reverse the mouse button actions so that you can more easily control the mouse with your left hand. To reverse the mouse button functions, perform these steps:

1. Click the Control Panel's Mouse icon. Windows 95 will open the Mouse Properties sheet.
2. Click the Left-handed option button.
3. Click the OK button to save your changes.

248 Controlling Your Mouse Double-Click Speed

When you double-click your mouse, you quickly press a mouse button (usually the left button, unless you've reversed the functions according to the steps in Tip 247) twice in succession. Beginning users often click too slowly and thus cause Windows 95 to think two single-clicks were made. A single-click's function differs from a double-click. Usually, you single-click to highlight or select an item, and you double-click to open icons.

If you click too slowly for Windows 95 to realize you are double-clicking, you can use the Mouse Properties sheet Double-click speed slider to adjust the time between double clicks. Move the Double-click speed slider from the fast side to the slow side. Then, use the Test area to test the double-click speed. Figure 248.1 shows the test area before you successfully double-click it. Figure 248.2 shows the test area after you successfully double-click it.

Figure 248.1 *The test area before you double-click it.*

Figure 248.2 *The Test area after you double-click it.*

Customizing the Mouse Pointer | 249

Mouse pointers come in various styles. For example, the mouse pointer usually changes to an hourglass figure while your system is processing instructions. It normally changes to a question mark when you click the Help button that appears in many windows. If you cannot see your mouse pointer easily, or you're simply tired of the "arrow" mouse pointer, you can change the icon Windows 95 uses for the mouse pointer. Through the Mouse Properties sheet Pointers page (see Figure 249), you can change any or all of your mouse pointers.

Figure 249 *The Mouse Properties sheet Pointers page.*

250 | Using a Predefined Mouse Pointer Scheme

If you get tired of the hourglass mouse pointer, you will be pleased to learn that Windows 95 provides several *mouse pointer schemes*. The mouse pointer schemes are sets of mouse pointers that Microsoft designed. To change your mouse pointers to a different scheme, perform these steps:

1. Display the Mouse Pointers sheet Pointers page.
2. Open the Scheme pull-down list and select the scheme you want to view. The list of mouse pointers in the window changes to that scheme's shapes.
3. Continue to select from the Scheme pull-down list until you find a scheme that you like.
4. When you find the mouse pointer scheme you like best, click the OK button to save your changes.

Note: Some of the mouse pointer schemes do not support all the possible pointer shapes. Therefore, if you select a scheme and Windows 95 displays an error dialog box that informs you of a missing pointer, you can press ENTER to change those pointers the scheme supports. If you want to revert to the original Windows 95 mouse pointer scheme at any time, select the scheme labeled "(None)."

251 | Changing a Specific Pointer

In Tip 250 you learned how to use a mouse pointer scheme to change the set of mouse pointers Windows 95 displays for different operations. There may be times, however, when you only want to change one or two specific mouse pointers rather than an entire pointer scheme. To change only a specific pointer, perform these steps:

1. Display the Mouse Properties sheet Pointers page.
2. Locate the mouse pointer you want to change from the pointer list at the bottom of the page.
3. Double-click the pointer to open the Browse dialog box shown in Figure 251.
4. Select the pointer you want to use.
5. Click the Open button to change to that pointer shape. Only the individual pointer you selected in Step 4 will change.
6. Click the OK button to save your changes.

If you change one or more of your pointers without using a pre-defined scheme, click the Save As button before you close the Mouse Pointers sheet Pointers page in Step 6. Then, name the scheme that you've created. If you change to a different scheme at a later time, you will be able to revert to the current scheme by selecting the scheme's name.

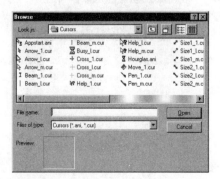

Figure 251 *You can change a specific mouse cursor.*

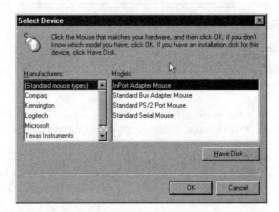

Figure 253.2 *Select a mouse manufacturer and model.*

254 Understanding How Windows 95 Uses Passwords

You can specify a Windows 95 log-on password that controls the configuration of your user profile (see Tip 258). Windows 95 uses your password to set your screen color settings, Desktop layout, and other preference items. When you log on with your password, Windows 95 checks its password files and configures its user preferences to meet yours. Similarly, if you use a network, you will have to log on to the network using a password. Your network password may be different from your user password. Through the Passwords Properties sheet (see Figure 254), you can add or change your passwords. To access this sheet, double-click on the Control Panel's Password icon.

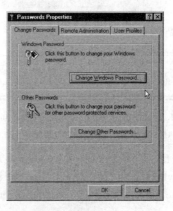

Figure 254 *The Passwords Properties sheet controls system passwords.*

Note: *Depending on the options you selected during the Windows 95 installation, the tabs that appear in your Password Properties sheet may differ from those shown here.*

255 Changing Your Windows Password

Your Windows password lets you use Windows 95 on your computer and, optionally, sets the computer and Windows 95 to your personal user profile. In addition, a password helps you prevent unauthorized persons from using your system. To add or change your Windows password, perform these steps:

1. Open the Passwords Properties sheet (see Tip 254) and click the Change Passwords tab if you do not see the Change Passwords page.

2. Click the Change Windows Password button. Windows 95 will display the Change Windows Password dialog box shown in Figure 255.
3. If you want to change an old password, enter the old password in the top text box.
4. Type your new password in the second text box and type the same password once again in the bottom text box to verify that the password is correct. As you type the password, Windows 95 displays asterisks so that nobody can look over your shoulder and read your password.
5. Click the OK button and the Close button to save your changes.

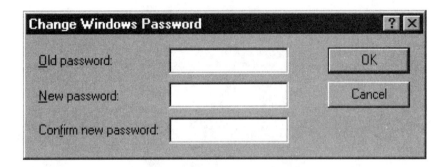

Figure 255 *You can add or change your Windows password.*

Controlling Other Passwords   256

The Passwords Properties sheet Change Other Passwords section controls the passwords for networking support. When you click the Change Other Passwords button, Windows 95 displays a Select Password dialog box that looks like the one in Figure 256. Depending on your network configuration, you may see more or fewer values in the dialog box's list. The values represent network servers to which your system may be attached. Select the server and click the Change button to change the server's password. When you first log on to Windows 95, your system will ask you for your Windows password. When you log on to your network, the server will ask you for the network password that you entered from the Select Password dialog box. Before Windows 95, you sometimes had to change your passwords using software from your network company. Windows 95 provides a uniform interface for specifying your passwords.

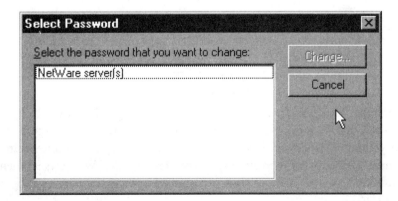

Figure 256 *You can assign passwords for networks.*

257 Restricting Remote Administration

If you use a network, you may want to let a Network Administrator control the accessibility of your folders and printers. If so, you or your Network Administrator may want to specify a remote administration password so that others without the password will not be able to change your files and printer settings or access other sensitive resources. When you click the check box at the top of the Passwords Properties sheet Remote Administration page, shown in Figure 257, you give permission to remote administration to use your computer. Like most password-setting dialog boxes, the password appears as asterisks when you type it. To verify your password before Windows 95 accepts the change, type it again.

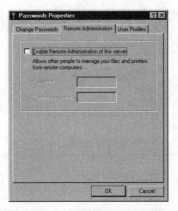

Figure 257 Enabling remote administration.

258 Understanding and Controlling User Profiles

A user profile is a Windows 95 configuration, such as Desktop settings, colors, and cursor shapes, that you create to have a comfortable Windows 95 environment. If you share a computer, each user can create his or her own profile. Then, depending on the Windows password Windows 95 receives at startup, Windows 95 changes profiles to match the current user's preferences. To set up a user profile, perform these steps:

1. Double-click the Control Panel's Passwords icon. Windows 95 will open the Passwords Properties sheet.

2. If you do not see the Change Passwords page, click on the Change Passwords tab.

3. Click the User Profiles tab to display the Passwords Properties sheet User Profiles page shown in Figure 258.

4. Click the second option to inform Windows 95 that you want users of your system to have different user profiles. If you were to leave the first option set, all users would see the same user interface when they logged on to Windows 95.

5. If you check the first check box under User Profile Settings, Windows 95 looks at your current Desktop and Network Neighborhood windows and creates a user profile from those settings. If you want Windows 95 to save the Start menu and submenu items in your user profile (some users may want more or fewer menu items in their Windows 95 menus), click the second option.

6. Click the OK button to save your passwords. Make sure that you remember your passwords. Good passwords contain special characters such as Mr#Luck and Happy&Dog.

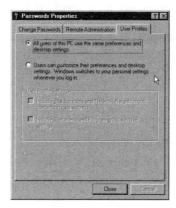

Figure 258 *User profiles are password protected. Remember your password.*

Understanding Power Management — 259

If you use a laptop, you must be concerned with battery life. Despite the fact that laptop batteries last longer today than they used to, many still cannot last through a cross-country plane ride. Windows 95 supports several power-management features that let you monitor your battery life and extend that life as long as possible between chargings. Furthermore, Windows 95 includes a suspend mode (which saves power without requiring that you turn off your computer) and Energy Star compliance (see Tip 127 for more information about Energy Star). Figure 259 shows Windows 95 power-management features.

Controlling Your PC's Power Management Settings — 260

As you learned in Tip 259, Windows 95 provides power-management support you can use to better manage your notebook computer's battery life. To access the Windows 95 power management capabilities, double click on the Control Panel's Power Management icon. Windows 95, in turn, will display the Power Properties dialog box shown in Figure 260.

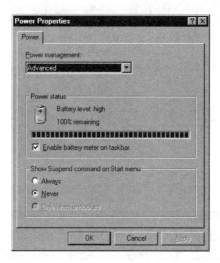

Figure 260 *The Power Properties dialog box.*

Windows 95 lets you use advanced, standard, or no power management:

Power Management	Description
Advanced	Employs power-management features that are built into Windows 95. These features maximize your computer's battery life, but may slightly decrease your system performance.
Standard	Employs only those power-management features that are built into your computer. This setting will extend your system's battery life, but not for as long as the Advanced setting.
None	Disables power-management support.

Table 260 *The Windows 95 power-management options.*

To choose your computer's power-management settings, open the Power management pull-down list and choose the option you desire.

Note: *If your Control Panel does not display the Power Management icon, your PC does not support power management.*

261 Determining Your Notebook Computer's Battery Life

When you work with a battery-powered notebook computer, you need to monitor how much power the battery contains. If you examine the Power Properties dialog box shown in Figure 260, you will see that the dialog box shows you a graph that indicates the amount of power the battery contains. In addition, if you select the dialog box's Enable battery meter on taskbar check box, Windows 95 will display a small power-plug icon on the Taskbar. When you double click your mouse on the Taskbar's power-plug icon, Windows 95 will display the Battery Meter window as shown in Figure 261.

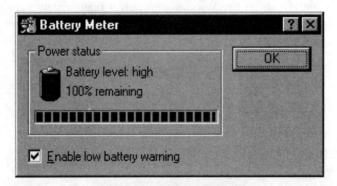

Figure 261 *The Battery Meter window.*

As you can see, using the Battery Meter, you can quickly determine how much power your battery contains.

262 Understanding and Using the Start Menu Suspend Command

As you have learned, when you are done using Windows 95, you select the Start menu Shutdown option to end your session. When you going to be away from your battery-powered notebook computer temporarily, you can direct Windows 95 to put your computer in a "suspended" mode which preserves your computer's battery power. When you return to your PC, you can resume the operations you were performing before you suspended your system.

Depending on your system type, the steps you must perform to resume normal operations will differ. If you examine the Power Properties dialog shown in Figure 260, you will find settings that let you place a Suspend option on your Start menu:

Suspend Command Setting	Description
Always	The Start menu always displays the Suspend option
Never	The Start menu never displays the Suspend option
Only when undocked	The Start menu only displays the Suspend option when the notebook computer is away from its docking station

Table 262 *Start menu Suspend option settings.*

Adding, Customizing, and Removing Printers — 263

When you add a printer to your computer, you will normally need to tell Windows 95 about the change. Unless you use true Plug and Play technology, Windows 95 cannot usually detect a printer change because the printer appears at the end of the parallel port and not on the system's end. After you inform Windows 95 about your new printer, you will need to change the printer's settings. (For further information, see Tip 264.) The Printers window, which you can reach through the My Computer window and from the Start menu Settings option, lets you specify new printers, change printer settings, and remove printers that you no longer have connected to your computer. Figure 263 shows the Printers window, which contains icons for each of your printers and fax modems.

Figure 263 *The Printers window.*

Adding a Printer — 264

After you plug a new printer into your computer, you must install the software to support that printer. Almost every printer sold today requires different printer settings, and each requires its own set of codes from the computer before the printer can properly print documents.

After you install the new printer, you can inform Windows 95 of the printer using one of two methods:

- Double-click the Control Panel's Add New Hardware icon to run the Add New Hardware wizard.

- Double-click the Printers window Add Printer icon to run the Add Printer wizard.

The Add Printer wizard is more specific for printers than the Add New Hardware wizard. If the only hardware change you made was a printer change, use the Add Printer wizard. Figures 264.1 and 264.2 show two screens from the Add Printer wizard. Before you start the Add Printer wizard, have your printer and Windows 95 installation disks (or CD-ROM) nearby. The Add Printer wizard may need them.

Note: *A Plug and Play printer can sometimes make installations even simpler than the Add Printer wizard can. If you add a Plug and Play printer to your PC and then start your system, Windows 95 recognizes the printer and automatically installs it. If your system needs the Windows 95 installation floppy disks or CD-ROM, Windows 95 prompts you for the media when it is ready.*

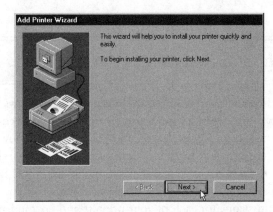

Figure 264.1 The Add Printer wizard's first screen.

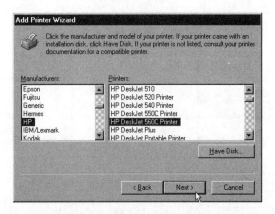

Figure 264.2 Selecting a printer.

265 Removing a Printer Driver

When you replace a printer, you should remove it from the Printers folder. Otherwise, every time you need to select a printer, you'll have to search through a Printers window filled with printers still installed on, but no longer connected to, your system. To remove a printer, perform these steps:

1. Select the Start menu Settings option.
2. Select the Settings menu Printers option. Windows 95 opens the Printers window.
3. Right-click over the printer to display its pop-up menu.

4. Select the pop-up menu's Delete option. Windows 95 will confirm that you want to remove the printer.
5. Click the Yes button to remove the printer. Windows 95 will remove the printer icon.
6. Click the next Yes button to remove the printer's related files from your disk.

Creating a Printer Shortcut on the Desktop — 266

If you access your printer often, you can create a printer shortcut on your Desktop. After you add the printer shortcut, you will be able to print files by dragging and dropping their icons from Explorer or My Computer on to the printer icon. If you've set up Windows 95 for several printers, you can create more than one shortcut. Most users create a printer shortcut only for the printer they use most. To create a printer shortcut, perform these steps:

1. Open the Printers folder from My Computer.
2. Hold down the CTRL key and drag the selected printer icon to the Desktop.
3. Release the CTRL key and your left mouse button to anchor the printer shortcut.
4. Close the Printers and My Computer windows.

Note: *If you add a fax printer icon to your Desktop, you can drag and drop a document to the icon to begin the fax process.*

Viewing Printer Properties — 267

There are a number of reasons you might want to change a printer setting. Perhaps you need to increase the printer's timeout value for those occasions when the printer does not seem to keep up with the computer. Perhaps you need to change paper trays and want to inform Windows 95 of the new paper size. Whatever the reason, if you want to change a printer setting, go to the Printers folder. To change one or more printer properties for any of your Windows 95 printers, perform these steps:

1. Open the Printers folder from My Computer.
2. Right-click the printer whose properties you want to change.
3. Select the pop-up menu's Properties option. Windows 95 will open a properties sheet much like the one shown in Figure 267. Depending on your printer's make and model, your printer's properties sheet may contain different options.
4. Click the tab that best describes the page that matches the property you want to change. For example, to change paper sizes, click the Paper tab to display the sheet's Paper page.
5. Change any property or properties you wish.
6. Click the OK button to save your changes.
7. Close the Printers folder.

Figure 267 Changing the Printer Properties sheet.

268 Understanding and Using Separator Pages

If you share a networked printer with others, you can request *separator pages* between print jobs. Subsequently, when you and an associate both send documents to the same printer, a pre-defined separator page appears before each person's output so you'll easily be able to tell when one set begins and ends. If you do not use a network printer, you still may want your printer to issue separator pages, especially if you regularly print several reports of similar-looking data. Separator pages can contain text or graphics. However, you must create separator pages as a Windows 95 metafile. Windows metafiles are special Windows 95 files that end in the .WMF filename extension. Desktop publishing and graphics programs can often create metafiles.

You may only specify separator pages for the printer or printers attached directly to your computer. If you want to produce separator pages for a printer attached to a different computer, you must issue the separator page command from that machine. To request separator pages, perform these steps:

1. Open the Printers folder from My Computer.
2. Right-click the printer whose properties you want to change.
3. Select the pop-up menu's Properties option.
4. Click the General tab.
5. Type the name of the separator page you want to use in the Separator page of the text box. If you do not remember the exact name and location of the separator page, click the Browse button to search for the file.
6. Click OK to save your changes.

269 Viewing and Customizing Printer Details

The Printer Properties sheet Details page, shown in Figure 269, contains options that let you control the printer's various port and spool settings. Generally, you will not have to change these settings routinely. However, if you change your printer port setup (see Tips 270 and 271) or want to change the way Windows 95 spools output to the disk drive (to speed up output), you may need to modify one or more of the Details page settings.

Using the Windows 95 Control Panel

Figure 269 *The Printer Properties sheet Details page.*

Adding and Deleting Printer Ports   270

If you add or remove ports on your computer, or your network System Administrator adds or removes a printer at a remote printer port, you should inform Windows 95 of the change so Windows 95 can update available port selections. Through the Printer Properties sheet Details page, you can specify such changes. To add or delete a printer port, perform these steps:

1. Open the Printers folder from My Computer.
2. Right-click the printer whose properties you want to change.
3. Select the pop-up menu's Properties option.
4. Click the Details tab.
5. Click either the Add Port button to display the Add Port dialog box shown in Figure 270.1 or the Delete Port button to display the Delete Port dialog box shown in Figure 270.2.
6. Make your port modifications and click the OK button to save your changes.
7. Select the Printer Properties sheet OK button.

Figure 270.1 *Adding a new printer port.*

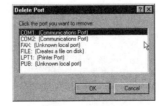

Figure 270.2 *Removing a port.*

Controlling Mouse Pointer Motion 252

If you're having difficulty pointing and selecting screen objects with your mouse, you may want to slow down your mouse pointer speed. Then, after you master using the mouse, you can increase the pointer's speed.

To change your mouse pointer speed, open the Mouse Properties sheet Motion page shown in Figure 252. Then, move the Pointer speed slider left to slow down the mouse pointer or right to speed it up.

Users with laptop computers often like to produce mouse trails on the screen to make mouse movements easier to follow. When you use mouse trails, the mouse pointer leaves tracks on the screen as you move it from one place to another. To view mouse trails, click the Show pointer trails check box. Then, use the Pointer trail slider to adjust the length of the mouse trails.

Figure 252 You can control the mouse pointer speed and activate a pointer trail.

Changing Your Mouse Type 253

If you change from a mouse to a trackball, or change from a three-button mouse to a two-button mouse, you must inform Windows 95 of the change using the Mouse Properties sheet General page shown in Figure 253.1.

After you display the General page, click the Change button to select your new mouse from the list. Figure 253.2 shows the Select Device dialog box from which you can select a different mouse. To change your mouse device type, select the appropriate device type from the Models pull-down list and then click on the OK button.

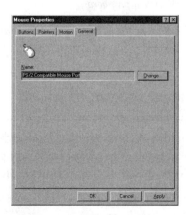

Figure 253.1 The Mouse Properties sheet General page.

271 Capturing and Releasing a Printer Port

If you use a network printer, you must specify the network (port) path to the network printer when you set up the printer on your computer. As you will learn, it is often easier to "trick" your computer into thinking that the network printer is connected directly to your machine. If you *capture* a printer port, you re-map a printer port to a port on your computer. Afterward, you can send printed output to one of your local printer ports such as LPT1 or LPT2 and Windows 95 will route the output to a remote printer port. When you click the Capture Printer Port button on the Printer Properties sheet Details page, Windows 95 displays the Capture Printer Port dialog box shown in Figure 271. Select a local port you want to use from the Device option on the pull-down list and enter a remote network port on the Path in the text box. You do not actually have to have the local port you specify; for example, if your computer does not contain a third printer port, you can still specify LPT3 as the remote printer port.

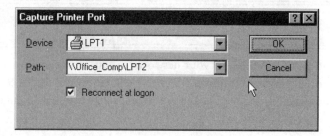

Figure 271 Capturing a printer port.

272 Sharing Your Printer Across the Network

If the printer attached to your computer is a fast one, others on your network may want to use the printer to print from their remote computers. To share your printer, you must specify three items:

- A printer name others will use for your printer
- A description others may see that describes the printer
- An optional password others must use before the network will let them print to your printer

To specify these values, open the Printer Properties sheet Sharing page, shown in Figure 272, and enter the values. If you do not specify a password, everyone on the network will be able to use your printer. If you specify a password, only those users who enter the password will have access.

Figure 272 You can let others share your printer.

Understanding Print Spooling 273

The printer is slow relative to your computer's processor and disk drives. Even the slowest computers must often wait for the fastest printers to print. If, every time you printed a document, your system would send printed output directly to your printer, there would be long idle times during which you could not use your computer. In short, your computer would do little more than wait for the printer to complete its task. Fortunately, Windows 95 does not send printed output directly to the printer. Instead, Windows 95 sends the output to a *spool file*. Windows 95 can send data to a spool file much faster than it can to a printer directly. After Windows 95 finishes sending the output to the spool file, you can continue working on your computer. While you work, Windows 95 sends the spool file to the printer. Windows 95 places all spool files in the SYSTEM\SPOOL\PRINTERS directory. The spool files appear and disappear when printing starts and when it ends. All spool files end with the SPL filename extension.

Note: *Windows 95 corrects the spooling contention problems users found when trying to print both from a Windows 3.1 and MS-DOS session simultaneously. Windows 95 also supports* EMF, *or **Enhanced metafile** spooling, which releases the computer much more quickly than Windows 3.1 did when printing.*

Understanding and Using Spool Settings 274

If you want to modify the way your computer spools output, open the Printer Properties sheet Details page and click the Spool Settings button. Windows 95, in turn, will display the Spool Settings dialog box shown in Figure 274. You can set different spool settings for each printer you use. Table 274 explains the spool settings.

Option	Purpose
Spool print jobs so program finishes printing faster	Turns spooled printing on and off. Always spool your output unless you are having trouble printing.
Start printing after last page is spooled	After you issue a print command, Windows 95 does not release itself back to you until the entire print output arrives in the spool file.
Start printing after first page is spooled	After you issue a print command, Windows 95 releases itself back to you as soon as the first page of the output arrives in the spool file. The printing may take a little longer, but you will regain control of your computer faster if you set this option.
Print directly to the printer	Turns spooling off. Print directly only if you cannot print with spooling capabilities. Shared network printer users cannot set this option.
Spool data format	If you select EMF, the spooling will be faster. However, if you are experiencing spooling problems, change this option to RAW to create a printer-specific spool file.
Enable bi-directional support for this printer	Enables two-way, PC-to-printer communication if your parallel port supports bi-directional communications.
Disable bi-directional support for this printer	Disables two-way, PC-to-printer communication if your parallel port supports bi-directional communications.

Table 274 The Spool Settings options.

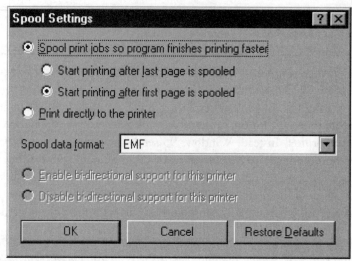

Figure 274 Changing the spool settings.

275 Controlling Port Settings

The Configure LPT Port dialog box, shown in Figure 275, lets you change your printer port settings. Some users experience MS-DOS printing problems when using the Windows 95 spool file. The Configure LPT Port dialog box, available from the Printer Properties sheet Details page when you click the Port Settings button, lets you turn off spooled printing when you print from inside MS-DOS windows. The dialog box also contains an option that requires the Windows 95 printing system to check the port's state before sending any printed output to the port to eliminate possible port conflicts with other background printing tasks.

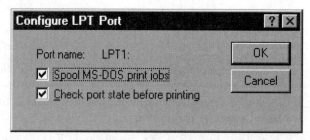

Figure 275 Modifying the printer port settings.

276 Viewing a Printer's Current Jobs

If you want to manage all the print jobs (possibly changing the order in which the jobs print, or even canceling a job) your system is spooling to your printer, you can open a window that gives you access to every document waiting in line to print. When you first begin printing, Windows 95 displays a printer icon at the right of the Taskbar. If you double-click this icon, Windows 95 will display a window (see Figure 276.1) that lists the documents in line to print. (You can also double-click a printer icon inside the Printers window to see jobs for that particular printer.) If you forget to turn on your printer, or if the printer has a problem, Windows 95 displays the message box shown in Figure 276.2. If you can fix the problem, click Retry. If the problem persists, you may have to click the Cancel button to terminate the printing and take corrective measures. Table 276 explains each of the print job window's columns.

Note: If you right-click the Taskbar printer icon, you can then select a printer whose jobs you want to view.

Column	Purpose
Document Name	Displays the name of the document waiting to print.
Status	Displays "Printing" if the job is going to the printer at the time you view the window.
Owner	Shows the name of the printer that started the output.
Progress	Displays the status of the printing.
Started At	Contains the time and day the user issued the print command for each job in line to print.

Table 276 Columns in the print job window.

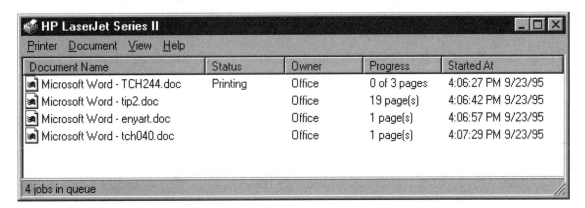

Figure 276.1 A list of documents waiting to print.

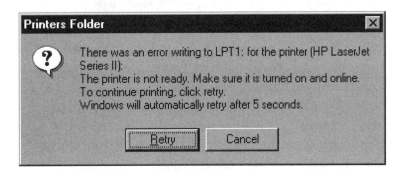

Figure 276.2 Windows 95 detected a print problem.

Pausing a Printer

As you work with Windows 95, there will be times when you need to pause a print job. For example, you may start a large print job just as you realize it is quitting time. Or, someone else may need to print something more urgent. On such occasions, Windows 95 lets you pause a printer if you meet these conditions:

- You use print spooling.

- The printer you want to pause is connected to your own computer and is not a remote network printer.

To pause a printer, perform these steps:

1. Open the Printers folder.
2. Double-click the print icon that represents the printer you want to pause.
3. Select the Printer menu Pause Printing option.
4. Select the Printer menu Close option to close the Printer window.

Repeat these steps when you want to resume printing again.

278 Purging Print Jobs

In Tip 277 you learned how to pause a print job. In some cases, however, there may be times when instead of pausing a print job, you want to cancel it completely. For example, you might start printing a report before you realize the wrong paper is in the printer. To *purge* (cancel) the jobs waiting to print, perform these steps:

1. Open the Printers folder.
2. Double-click the print icon that represents the printer you want to pause.
3. Select the Printer menu Purge Print Jobs option.
4. Select the Printer menu Close option to close the Printer window.

279 Pausing or Canceling a Specific Job's Printing

In Tips 277 and 278, you learned how to pause and cancel all print jobs spooled to a particular printer. However, you won't always want to pause or cancel an entire series of print jobs. For example, you send a collection of important documents to your printer and then realize that one, and only one, of them needs more work. Fortunately, Windows 95 lets you pause or cancel a specific print job. To do so, perform these steps:

1. Open the Printers folder.
2. Double-click the print icon that represents the printer holding the job you want to pause or cancel.
3. Highlight the document you want to pause or cancel.
4. If you want to pause a print job, select the Document menu Pause Printing option. To cancel a print job, select the Document menu Cancel Printing option. Windows 95 pauses or cancels only the highlighted print job, not all the printer's jobs (see Tips 277 and 278).
5. Select the Printer menu Close option to close the Printer window.

280 Changing the Order of Print Jobs

After you spool several print jobs to the printer, you may decide that one of your print jobs is more important than another. For example, the report that your boss needs immediately may be fifth in line to print. Fortunately, Windows 95 lets you change the order of your print jobs. To do so, perform the following steps:

1. Open the Printers folder.
2. Double-click the print icon of the printer holding the jobs you want to rearrange.
3. Drag the document whose order you want to change to another location in the list.
4. Release your left mouse button to insert the document into the list.
5. Select the Printer menu Close option to close the Printer window.

281 Selecting a Default Printer

If you connect several printers to your computer, as is often the case for networked PCs, you need to designate one of the printers as your system's default printer. All Windows 95 applications will use the default printer automatically unless you specify a different printer to print. To select a default printer, perform these steps:

1. Open the Printers folder.
2. Right click your mouse on the printer you desire to display the pop-up menu shown in Figure 281.
3. Select the pop-up menu's Set As Default option. Windows 95 will display a check mark next to the option.
4. Close the Printers folder. The next time you print, the application will automatically route the output to the default printer unless you override the default printer setting.

Figure 281 *You should select a default printer.*

282 Viewing the Number of Jobs on Each Printer

To determine the printer to which they want to print (often the least busiest), networked users often need to determine the number of jobs listed on each printer. In other words, if you need to print a document quickly, you'll want to know which network printer is least busy. To look at the number of jobs on each printer, perform these steps:

1. Open the Printers folder.
2. Select the View menu Details option. Windows 95 displays a table that shows the number of print jobs listed on each printer.
3. Close the Printers folder.

283 Understanding Regional Settings

Not every country uses the same format to represent numbers, times, and dates for countries. For example, some countries, such as Italy, use commas to separate whole money amounts from fractional amounts while other countries, such as the United States, use periods. The number *1,234.56* in the United States is written as *1.234,56* in Italy.

Through the Control Panel's Regional Settings icon, you can tell Windows 95 which formats you want Windows 95 applications to use. By locating the regional settings in one place, Windows 95 eliminates the need for you to specify the settings in every program that you use. To select settings for a region, perform these steps:

1. Open the Control Panel.
2. Double-click the Regional Settings icon to open the Regional Settings sheet shown in Figure 283.
3. Make your changes. Each time you go to a new country, you will need to change to that country's regional settings. After you select the correct country, Windows 95 will update the remaining settings according to the standards of that country.
4. Click OK.
5. Restart your computer as directed by the Regional Settings sheet.

As you can see, the Regional Settings Properties sheet looks similar to the Time Zone sheet described in Tip 143.

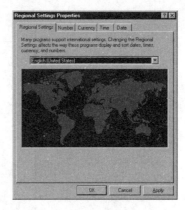

Figure 283 *The Regional Settings Properties sheet.*

284 Controlling Numeric Formats

The Regional Settings Properties sheet Number page, shown in Figure 284, lets you change the way Windows 95 applications display numbers. You can control every aspect of the number, from the decimal separator to the number of digits that appear to the right of that decimal separator. By specifying your number preferences, you ensure that all Windows 95 applications display numeric data in the format you desire.

Figure 284 *The Regional Settings Properties sheet Number page.*

Controlling Currency Formats — 285

The Regional Settings Properties sheet Currency page, shown in Figure 285, lets you change the way Windows 95 applications display money amounts. You can control every aspect of currency display, including the sign applications use for the currency character (for example, the dollar sign or lira symbol). By specifying your currency preferences, you ensure that all Windows 95 applications display currency data in the format you desire.

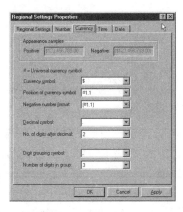

Figure 285 *The Regional Settings Properties sheet Currency page.*

Controlling Time Formats — 286

The Regional Settings Properties sheet Time page, shown in Figure 286, lets you change the way Windows 95 applications display time values. You can control every aspect of the time display, including the symbol that applications use to represent morning and afternoon hours (such as A.M. and P.M.). By specifying your time preferences, you ensure that all Windows 95 applications display time data in the format you desire.

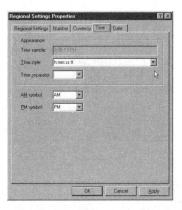

Figure 286 *The Regional Settings Properties sheet Time page.*

Controlling Date Formats — 287

The Regional Settings Properties sheet Date page, shown in Figure 287, lets you change the way Windows 95 applications display date values. You can control every aspect of the date display, including the date separator symbol. For example, you can tell Windows 95 to display dates spelled out, such as "Sunday, September 24, 1995," or abbreviated, such as "9/24/95." By specifying your date preferences, you ensure that all Windows 95 applications display dates in the format you desire.

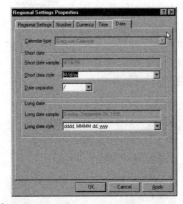

Figure 287 *The Regional Settings Properties sheet Date page.*

288 Understanding Sounds and Windows Events

As you work with Windows 95, you may realize quickly that your computer makes different sounds as Windows 95 performs different operations. As you will learn, Windows 95 gives you the option to have a visual (one field with menus and icons) and audible (one with different sounds) computer environment by allowing you to integrate sounds. One of the most common ways Windows 95 supports the use of sound is through *sound events*. An event is any common Windows 95 action, such as a window opening or closing. You can assign sounds to most Windows 95 events. You can access event sounds through the Control Panel's Sounds icon. When you double-click on the Sounds icon, Windows 95 displays the Sounds Properties sheet shown in Figure 288.

Figure 288 *The Sounds Properties sheet.*

289 Previewing Event Sounds

The best way to learn about sound events is to hear them. You can use the Sounds Properties sheet to preview sound events that are set up on your computer. To preview a sound, perform these steps:

1. Double-click on the Control Panel's Sounds icon. Windows 95 will open the Sounds Properties sheet.

2. In the Events list box, click on an event with a speaker icon next to it. The speaker icon indicates that a sound is attached to that event.
3. Click the button to the right of the Preview speaker icon (at the right side of the sheet). Windows 95 will play the event's sound through your sound card.

Using Predefined Sound Schemes · 290

Windows 95 comes predefined with sets of event sounds called *sound schemes*. Microsoft developers put together a series of sound schemes that harmonize. Although you can assign your own sound to any event, you may want to try one of the predefined sound schemes first. To see a list of Windows 95 sound schemes, like the one shown in Figure 290, click the Schemes pull-down list button. If you do not see any sound schemes, you'll have to run the Windows 95 Setup program to add the sounds.

Note: If you do not want any event sounds, select the sound scheme labeled "No Sounds."

Figure 290 *You can use a predefined sound scheme.*

Assigning Sounds to an Event · 291

Windows 95 stores event sounds in *wave files*. A wave file ends with the WAV filename extension and contains a short digitized sound. If you want to connect a sound to an event, you must assign a wave file to that event. (Tip 292 explains how you can record your own wave sound files.) To assign your own sound to an event, perform these steps:

1. Use the Events list box to select the event to which you want to assign a sound. For example, if you want to hear a sound when you maximize a window, select the Maximize event.
2. Open the Name pull-down list to display a list of wave files. Select the sound file that you want to assign to the event you selected in Step 1.
3. Click the Preview's play button (see Tip 289) to preview the event's sound.
4. Click the OK button to save your changes. The next time the event occurs, you will hear the sound that you assigned to that event.

If you assign several sounds to several events, you can save that set of event sounds in your own sound scheme file. To do so, click the Save As button and name your sound scheme.

292 Recording Your Own Sounds for Windows Events

If you have a multimedia computer and a microphone attached to your sound card, you can record your own sounds and store them in wave files. The Sound Recorder, a Windows 95 program, controls the recording and saving of sound files.

Note: If you want additional sound files but do not want to record your own, most on-line services, such as CompuServe and the Internet, contain scores of sound files you can download to your computer and use for event sounds. You can also purchase sound files from your software retailer.

The Sound Recorder, shown in Figure 292, contains all the recording and playback tools you need to create sound files. The Sound Recorder works just like simple cassette recorders and displays the same record, play, pause, fast forward, rewind, and stop buttons. To start the Sound Recorder, perform these steps:

1. Click the Start button to display the Start menu.
2. Select the Start menu Programs option.
3. Select the Programs menu Accessories option.
4. Select the Accessories menu Multimedia option.
5. Select the Multimedia menu Sound Recorder option. Windows will 95 run the Sound Recorder program.

Figure 292 *The Sound Recorder window.*

293 Understanding ODBC

If you write database programs, check out the Control Panel's ODBC icon. ODBC, the Open Database Connectivity standard, helps you write database applications that access external data. You do not have to know a lot about ODBC to incorporate it in your programs. The Microsoft SQL. Server is one of the most popular ODBC database systems that Windows 95 database developers use. ODBC helps provide data to networked *client/server* environments. A client (such as the computer on which you work) can use data from a networked remote server that resides in another room or even another state. You can specify ODBC data sources (see Tips 297 and 298) to access that remote data. The remote server actually supplies the data, whereas in a regular non-client/server network, your computer must know how to manage the data directly.

Windows 95 gives you high-level support so that you can access ODBC data. If you double-click your mouse on the Control Panel's ODBC icon, Windows 95 opens the Data Sources dialog box shown in Figure 293. You then use that dialog box to connect to ODBC data sources.

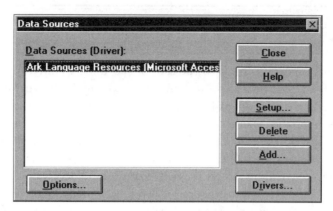

Figure 293 *The ODBC Data Sources dialog box.*

Understanding ODBC Drivers 294

Windows 95 installs on your system with these pre-defined ODBC drivers:

- Microsoft Access
- dBASE
- Microsoft FoxPro
- Borland Paradox

Each of these drivers describes a different Windows 95 database to applications. The drivers, in effect, teach Windows 95 how to access those kinds of database data files. By supplying such a system-level database access driver, Windows 95 gives across-the-board database support for database programs you may write or use. Instead of each program having to include proper drivers, Windows 95 includes the drivers. As with modem and other hardware configurations, Windows 95 integrates data access into the operating system to speed up data access while making your database programs more robust. To view your installed drivers, perform these steps:

1. Double-click your mouse on the Control Panel's ODBC icon to open the Data Sources dialog box.
2. Click your mouse on the Drivers button to display the drivers currently installed on your system. Figure 294 shows a sample Drivers dialog box.
3. Click your mouse on the Close button to close the Drivers dialog box.
4. Click your mouse on the Close button to close the Data Sources dialog box.

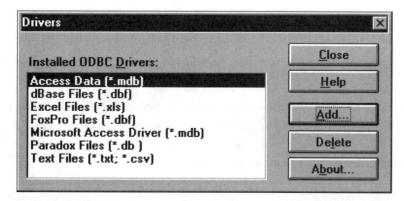

Figure 294 *The ODBC Drivers dialog box.*

295 | Displaying Specifics About an ODBC Driver

When you purchase additional database software so you can connect to data sources, the software will install its own set of drivers into Windows 95. If you want to see information about any ODBC driver (such as the company that supplied the driver), open the Drivers dialog box (see Tip 294), click on a driver, and click your mouse on the About button. Figure 295 shows the specifics for the Microsoft FoxPro database driver. The About button produces the driver's version number, the driver's size, and the originating company that created the driver. The drivers come supplied to you as *DLLs* (or *Dynamic Link Libraries*). DLLs are small routines that your database applications can use to access data. If you write a Microsoft Access program that needs to access FoxPro data, the Microsoft Access program can use the FoxPro DLL's internal instructions to work with the foreign FoxPro data; without the driver, Access would not be able to access FoxPro unless you added special programming code. When you finish viewing the driver's specifics, click your mouse on the OK button.

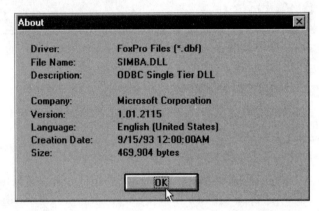

Figure 295 Viewing a driver's specifics.

296 | Adding an ODBC Driver

If you purchase additional ODBC drivers, add them to your current ODBC driver list by performing these steps:

1. Double-click the Control Panel's ODBC icon to open the Data Sources dialog box.
2. Click your mouse on the Drivers button.
3. Click your mouse on the Add button to open the Add Driver dialog box.
4. Type the disk or CD-ROM drive's name that contains the driver file you want to add. You can specify a directory to search in as well.
5. Click your mouse on the OK button to begin the add procedure.
6. Close the Add Drivers dialog box. Then, click the Data Sources dialog box Close button.

297 | Understanding ODBC Data Sources

A *data source* is simply a collection of data that your database program (or whatever kind of program you use that needs external database data) can access. The data source always includes the data, as well as the path to that data. The data source can reside on a separate computer. You can define data sources for the ODBC drivers you install.

Therefore, if you want to use Microsoft Access data sources, you must ensure that you have a Microsoft Access driver loaded (as Tip 296 explains). To view the currently defined data sources on your computer, double-click the Control Panel's ODBC icon to open the Data Sources dialog box. Figure 297 shows a sample Data Sources dialog box with three data sources listed.

Note: *The Data Sources dialog box specifies occurrences of data you want to access. The Drivers dialog box (see Tip 294) lists general database types that you can access.*

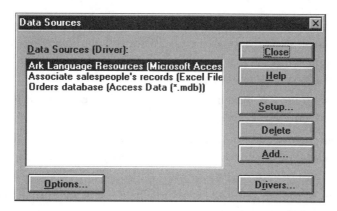

Figure 297 You can display your defined data sources.

Setting Up an ODBC Data Source   298

In Tip 297 you learned that an ODBC data source is simply a collection of data values, such as records, recognized by a database driver. Before you can access an ODBC database using a data source you specified in the Data Sources dialog box, you must set up ODBC sources. After you add a data source (see Tip 299), you can set up that data source and configure it for use.

From the Data Sources dialog box, click your mouse on the Setup button to display the ODBC Setup dialog box shown in Figure 298. You will not always need to configure the data source. However, there may be times when you want to do so. For example, you might want to limit the number of rows from the source that a Windows 95 application can access. To accomplish such configuration tasks, click your mouse on the Options button.

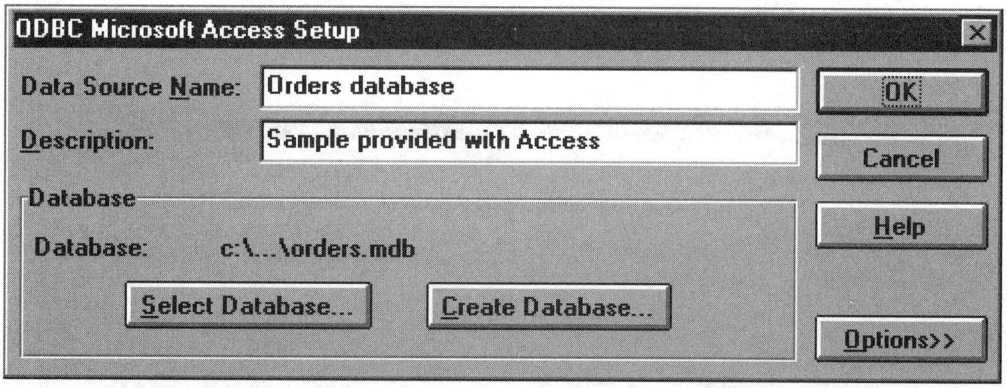

Figure 298 Configure your data source from this Setup dialog box.

299 Adding an ODBC Data Source

If you want to define additional data sources for your Windows 95 applications, use the Data Sources dialog box. To add data sources, perform these steps:

1. Double-click the Control Panel's ODBC icon to open the Data Sources dialog box.
2. Click your mouse on the Add button. Windows 95 displays the Add Data Source dialog box shown in Figure 299.1.
3. Select the driver needed for the data source you want to add. For example, if you want to add a text-file data source, select the Text Files ODBC driver. You *must* already have installed a correct driver before you can add a data source. The driver internally tells Windows 95 how to access the data source you now specify.
4. Click your mouse on the OK button. An ODBC Data Source Setup dialog box, similar to the one shown in Figure 299.2, will appear.
5. Type the data source name and a description. If you want to browse your disk or network for the data source, click your mouse on the Select Directory button and choose the directory where the data source resides.
6. Click your mouse on the OK button to save your changes and add the data source to the list of available Windows 95 data sources.
7. Click on the OK button to close the Data Sources dialog box.

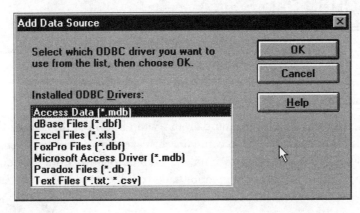

Figure 299.1 Adding a new data source.

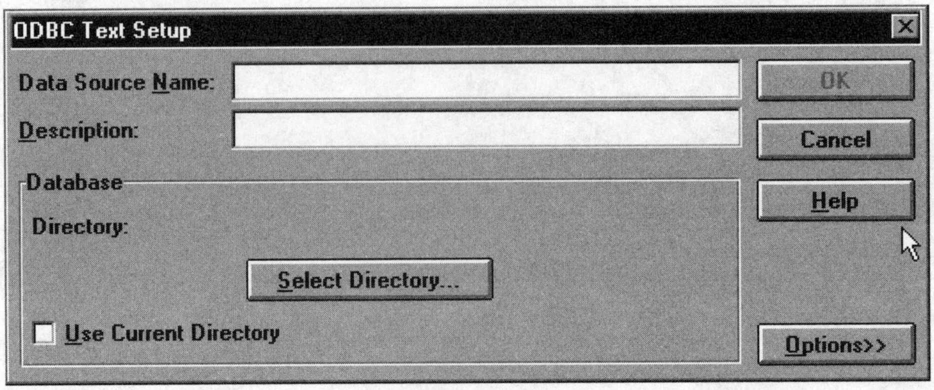

Figure 299.2 Defining your new data source.

Controlling ODBC Data Source Options   300

The Options button, located on the ODBC Data Sources dialog box, lets you control the way your applications trace ODBC resources. When you click your mouse on the Options button, Windows 95 displays the ODBC Options dialog box shown in Figure 300. From this dialog box, you can have Windows 95 make a trace of your ODBC database accesses. Furthermore, you can use this dialog box to control the way that Windows 95 makes the trace. If you experience data problems, you can check the generated trace file to locate the problem.

If you remove the charkmark from the Trace ODBC Calls check box, the ODBC system stops tracing ODBC database access. However, if you check the Trace ODBC Calls check box, the ODBC manager traces all access to the ODBC data source.

To ensure that the device manager stops tracing ODBC calls, check the Stop Tracing Automatically check box. If you leave this check box unselected, the ODBC manager will continue to add to the ODBC trace file. To begin a new trace, you must open the ODBC Options dialog box once again to start the trace. The default name for the trace file is SQL.LOG. To change the name, click the Select File button.

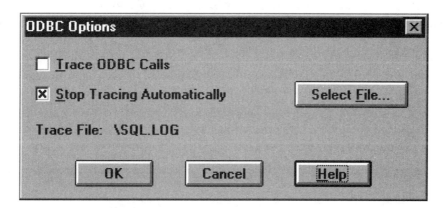

Figure 300 *Requesting a trace from the ODBC manager.*

Displaying General System Information   301

When you want to display general system information, open and double-click the Control Panel's System icon. Windows 95, in turn, will display the System Properties sheet General page shown in Figure 301. The System Properties sheet General page is the first of several pages that contain system information about your hardware and device drivers.

The General page contains two helpful pieces of information: the total amount of RAM installed in your system and your exact Windows 95 version number. If you call Microsoft's support line for help, the support staff will want to know your Windows 95 version number.

Note: *If you purchased a computer pre-installed with Windows 95, your computer manufacturer may have added support information to the General page. If you see a button labeled "Support Information," click your mouse on the button to find support phone numbers for your computer.*

Figure 301 *The System Properties sheet General page.*

302 Understanding the Control Panel Device Manager

With new features such as plug-and-play and hardware wizards, most Windows 95 users will never have to worry about low-level hardware settings. However, for those times when you need to change or view your system's hardware configuration, the System Properties sheet Device Manager page gives you one location from which you can see your hardware settings. Through the Device Manager page, you can locate information about each piece of equipment installed on your system. The System Properties sheet Device Manager page contains all known hardware connected to your computer. You can use the device listing to find out whether devices conflict with one another and track down problems if you experience hardware troubles. The following tips discuss ways you can use the Device Manager page to control your computer's hardware settings. Figure 303.1 shows a hardware device listing by type. Figure 303.2 shows the same listing by connection.

303 Controlling the Device Manager View

Using the System Properties sheet Device Manager page, you can see two views of your system's devices. If you display the devices by type, Windows 95 lists each device by hardware category, such as modems and CD-ROM drives. If you instead view the devices by their hardware connection, Windows 95 lists devices as they connect to your computer. As such, all the devices connected to your parallel ports will list together, and so on.

Note: *You cannot check network resources from the System Properties sheet Device Manager page. Although you can look at network adapter cards, you cannot see the network resource properties. To view network resources, you must double-click the Control Panel's Network icon.*

Figure 303.1 *Listing the hardware by type.*

Figure 303.2 Listing the devices by connection.

Locating Device Specifics — 304

The System Properties sheet Device Manager page displays an overview of your hardware settings, just as Explorer displays an overview of your directory folders. If you want more detail about a particular device, you can click your mouse on the plus sign next to the device in the list box. For example, if you click your mouse on the plus sign next to the Sound device (assuming you have a sound card), the device list expands to show your sound card and the sound card options. Additionally, the plus sign changes to a minus sign to indicate the detail. After you locate and highlight a specific device, click on the Properties button to display that device's properties. Windows 95 shows the interrupt setting and memory the device uses, if applicable. Users can often trace hardware problems to interrupt conflicts. If two devices use the same interrupt, change the interrupt for one of the devices to an unused interrupt. To return the list box to a general view of hardware devices, click your mouse on the minus sign next to an expanded list. Windows 95, in turn, will collapse the detail list back into its general category. Figure 304 shows an expanded listing that displays all the system devices.

Figure 304 Expanding the System detail.

Printing the Device Manager Summary — 305

If you experience hardware trouble, especially after you install a new board such as a memory expansion card or a sound card, you may want to print a device settings list to locate potential conflicts that might arise. To do so, access the System Properties sheet Device Manager page. Then, click your mouse on the Print button. Windows 95, in turn, will display the Print dialog box. Select OK and Windows 95 will print a hardware summary, a list of the resources each device uses, and the names of the device driver file the device uses.

Note: *If you click your mouse on the Print to file button (which appears after you click your mouse on the Device Manager Print button), Windows 95 sends the device summary to a file which you can edit and search for information. Some users like to store these hardware summaries in disk files for reference later.*

306 Removing a Device From Your Device List

If you remove a hardware device, you have to remove the device driver from within the System Properties sheet Device Manager page. When you remove a device, Windows 95 collects the system resources that device used and makes those resources available for other devices. However, if the device is a true Plug and Play device, you will not have to remove the device driver from the Device Manager page. After you physically remove the device, Windows 95 updates your device listing accordingly.

307 Understanding Hardware Profiles

As you work with your computer, you may need to use different hardware configurations (or *hardware profiles*). For example, your portable computer may have a docking station at work. As such, you want to use one hardware profile (the docking station might have two printers and a modem) at work and another (one that does not include the printers and modem) on the road. Similarly, network users do not always want to use the network. In such cases, network users can create a network and a non-network profile. When the user does not need the network drivers, he or she can select the non-network profile and utilize the extra memory freed up by not having network drivers. The hardware profiles keep you from having to select a new set of hardware device drivers every time you change your hardware. Instead of adjusting hardware settings each time you change hardware, you only have to select a different profile. The System Properties sheet Hardware Profiles page, shown in Figure 307, lets you create and select hardware profiles.

Figure 307 *The System Properties sheet Hardware Profiles page.*

308 Creating Your Own Hardware Profile

After you set up your computer's hardware configuration for one profile, you must name that profile. You can have as many named profiles as you have hardware configurations. When you begin to work on the computer and need a particular profile, display the System Properties sheet Hardware Profiles page to select the profile.

The best way to create a new hardware profile is to start with one that already exists. When you installed Windows 95, Windows 95 added a hardware profile named Original Configuration to your Hardware Profiles page. To create a new profile, perform these steps:

1. Double-click the Control Panel's System icon. Windows 95 will display the System Properties sheet.
2. Click on the Hardware Profiles page.
3. Select the hardware profile that most closely matches the hardware profile you want to create. If you see only one hardware profile listed, click your mouse on that single profile.
4. Click your mouse on the Copy button to copy the selected profile. Windows 95 will display the Copy Profile dialog box, which you can use to enter a new profile name.
5. Type the new profile name. Figure 308 shows the creation of a profile named Non-networked computer copied from a profile named Original Configuration.
6. Click your mouse on the OK button to save the new profile.
7. Make changes to the profile as needed. When you exit the System Properties sheet, Windows 95 updates the new hardware profile with the new settings.

Figure 308 Creating a new hardware profile.

Renaming and Deleting Hardware Profiles — 309

The remaining buttons on the Hardware Profiles page, Rename and Delete, rename and remove your hardware profiles. When you rename a profile, the profile settings remain the same. Only the name changes.

If you decide that you no longer need a particular hardware setting, select the hardware profile and click your mouse on the Delete button. After you confirm the deletion, Windows 95 removes the profile. You cannot remove the profile named Original Configuration. Likewise, if you renamed the Original Configuration profile, you cannot delete that renamed version. Windows 95 always requires the original profile to be present.

Displaying System Performance Settings — 310

The System Properties sheet Performance page, shown in Figure 310, contains information about your current system resources and describes your memory and file system's high-level attributes. If Windows 95 begins to act sluggish after you open several programs, display the Performance page to check the System Resources value. The System Resources value describes the percentage of free system resources. If the percentage of used system resources drops below 35%, your system will begin to slow down noticeably. To recapture resources, you can close program windows.

Figure 310 *Check your resources if your system slows down.*

311 Understanding the Windows 95 File System

A you know, when you store information on your disk, the operating system places that information within a file. Specifically, the part of the operating system that performs file operations (such as opening, reading, writing, and closing a file is called the file system). As you will learn, Windows 95 has a new file system that improves your system performance. In general, the Windows 95 file system differs from the Windows 3.1 file system in the following ways:

- Windows 95 uses a 32-bit virtual File Allocation Table (VFAT).
- Windows 95 supports simultaneous network redirectors for quick network file access.
- Windows 95 supports an improved caching mechanism.
- Windows 95 includes CD-ROM support that caches and optimizes CD-ROM access.
- Windows 95 supports long filenames while maintaining DOS-based compatibility .

312 Customizing the Hard-Disk File System

Different computer users require different kinds of hard disk access. For example, if you regularly use a network, you may want Windows 95 to make better use of network access at the expense of your own disk access. On the other hand, if you use your computer as a stand-alone desktop system, you will want Windows 95 to improve the efficiency of your own disk access as much as possible. If you click your mouse on the File System button on the System Properties sheet Performance page, Windows 95 displays the File System Properties sheet shown in Figure 312. To improve your disk performance, select the typical role of your machine from the Typical role of this machine pull-down list. Drag the Read-ahead optimization slider to the right as far as possible to maximize the amount of caching your system performs. If you experience disk-access trouble, you may need to reduce caching.

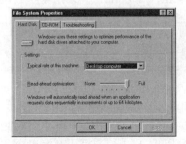

Figure 312 *You can maximize your hard disk usage.*

Customizing the CD-ROM File System — 313

As you learned in Tip 312, Windows 95 lets you customize your hard disk's file system for optimal use. Additionally, through the File System Properties sheet CD-ROM page (see Figure 313), you can customize and enhance the performance of your CD-ROM drive. To maximize CD-ROM access speed, you can drag the page's Supplemental cache size slider to the largest value possible. If you begin to experience intermittent CD-ROM problems, you can lower this value. In addition, the CD-ROM page provides a pull-down list that lets you specify the type of CD-ROM drive your system uses. For example, if you use a quad-speed CD-ROM drive, make sure you select the Quad speed or higher setting from the list.

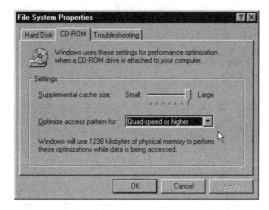

Figure 313 *You can maximize your CD-ROM performance.*

Trouble Shooting the Windows 95 File System — 314

If you experience disk problems, such as file-sharing violations or intermittent data loss, you may need to modify your file system properties. The File Systems Properties sheet Troubleshooting page, shown in Figure 314, provides several file systems options you can use to modify your file system. Make sure you fully understand a setting's purpose before you change the setting. If you use a setting incorrectly, you may destroy the information stored on your disk. Table 314 explains each of the options.

Option	Purpose
Disable new file sharing and locking semantics	Helps your MS-DOS applications share files properly.
Disable long name working preservation for old programs.	Helps your non-Windows 95 applications that have trouble with Windows 95 filenames.
Disable protect-mode hard disk interrupt handling.	Improves disk access; however, if you add a hard disk drive that Windows 95 cannot access properly, this option will slow disk performance.
Disable synchronous buffer commits.	Lets Windows 95 write a buffer's contents to disk, as needed, asynchronously.
Disable all 32 bit protect-mode disk drivers.	Disables all 32-bit protected disk drivers and routes all I/O through real-mode drivers.
Disable write-behind caching for all drives.	Disables disk caching. Windows 95 writes all disk output immediately, instead of first buffering the data in memory.

Table 314 *The trouble shooting file system options.*

Note: *Be sure you know what you are doing before you change any of the options Table 314 lists. If you use any of these options without understanding how they work, you may damage disk data.*

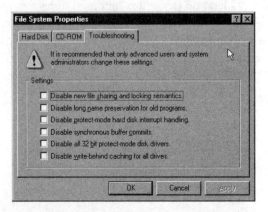

Figure 314 *The File System Properties sheet Troubleshooting page.*

315 Customizing Graphics Acceleration

One of the easiest ways to improve your system performance is to add a graphics-accelerator card that actually performs screen output operations. To make the best use of your graphics accelerator card, Windows 95 lets you customize various card characteristics. When you click your mouse on the Graphics button in the System Properties sheet Performance page, Windows 95 displays the Advanced Graphics Settings dialog box shown in Figure 315. Thorough this dialog box, you can troubleshoot display problems. For example, if you notice screen glitches when you view program output, your graphics card may have compatibility problems with Windows 95. If the problem is crucial, your system can even crash.

However, if you disable the hardware acceleration feature, Windows 95 will let you use your computer despite the display problems, though the display may be somewhat distorted. If you drag the Hardware acceleration slider to "None," and your system stops crashing and the glitches cease, you know that the graphics problem is in your display card. In such cases, you should change your card to a Windows 95-compatible graphics card.

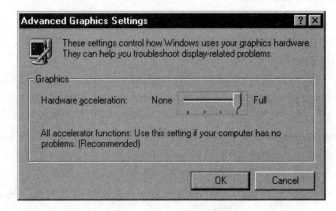

Figure 315 *Controlling graphics acceleration.*

Understanding Virtual Memory — 316

When you run several programs at the same time, those programs can consume a lot of memory. Actually, it is possible for a multitasking session to require more memory than your computer actually contains. Windows 95 uses *virtual memory* to handle memory overload. As it turns out, Windows 95 sets aside a portion of your disk drive to simulate (behave like) your computer's RAM memory. When Windows 95 needs more RAM than is available, Windows 95 uses the virtual memory (the space on the disk) for program memory. In other words, Windows 95 moves parts of programs out of memory to disk as they are not needed.

As it turns out, Windows 95 does not just use virtual memory when you are running multiple programs. In some cases, a single program may require more memory than your computer contains. For example, assume that your computer contains 4Mb of RAM. However, you are using a spreadsheet that requires 8Mb. In such cases, Windows 95 will load part of your spreadsheet into your computer's RAM and part into virtual memory on disk. The more RAM your system has, the less Windows 95 needs to use virtual memory. Using RAM memory is faster than physically accessing the slow, mechanical disk. As a result, the less that Windows 95 has to use virtual memory, the faster your system performs.

Understanding Swapping and Paging — 317

When you run multiple programs at the same time (multitask), there may be times when the programs require more memory than your computer actually contains. In such cases, Windows 95 may swap one program out of memory to disk (into a special file called a *swap file*) to make room for another program. When you later select the program that Windows 95 previously swapped to disk, Windows 95 will swap a different program from memory to disk and the program you desire back into memory. By *swapping* programs between RAM and disk as needed, Windows 95 is able to let multiple programs run at the same time.

To reduce the amount of memory a program consumes, Windows 95 divides a program into fixed-sized pieces called *pages*. When you run a program, Windows 95 keeps only those parts of the program you are using (the corresponding pages) within RAM. Windows 95 can leave the unused parts of the program (the other pages) on disk. For example, assume you are running an accounting program that lets you manage payroll, accounts receivable, accounts payable, and other account information. When you use the program to perform payroll operations, Windows 95 will load the parts of the program (the pages) that correspond to the payroll operations into memory while leaving the other parts of the program on disk. By bringing (*paging*) into RAM, only those pages (parts of a program) that the program really needs, Windows 95 leaves more memory available for use by other programs.

Controlling Windows 95 Virtual Memory — 318

Most of the time, you can forget all about the paging and swapping Windows 95 performs behind the scenes. The typical Windows 95 user does not and should not care about such issues. However if you want to gain extra PC performance, you may want to try adjusting the virtual memory settings. When you click your mouse on the Virtual Memory button on the System Properties sheet Performance page, Windows 95 displays the Virtual Memory dialog box shown in Figure 318.

If you begin to run out of disk space, the best thing to do is add more physical disk space to your system. Disk drives are relatively inexpensive these days. However, to get by a little longer at the expense of system speed degradation, you can specify your own virtual memory swap file size. To do so, click the option labeled "Let me specify my own virtual memory settings" and enter a smaller swap file size. Or, specify a minimum and maximum size range.

However, after you add hard drive space, click your mouse on the option labeled "Let Windows manage my virtual memory settings" because Windows 95 does a good job of swapping when you have plenty of disk space.

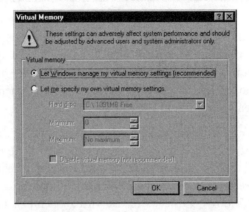

Figure 318 You can control virtual memory settings.

319 Understanding the Windows Explorer

The Windows 95 Explorer is an integral part of the Windows 95 operating system. The Explorer lets you navigate and manage files across your entire computer system. If you want to copy a file from a networked computer to yours, you can use Explorer to make the copy as painlessly as dragging an icon. To open the Explorer window, right-click on the Start button and select the pop-up menu's Explore option. Windows 95, in turn, will open the Explorer window shown in Figure 319.

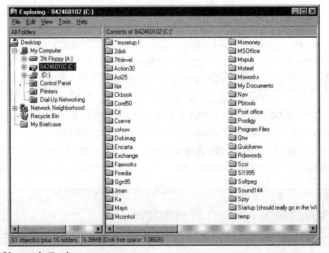

Figure 319 Manage disks and files with Explorer.

320 The Explorer Window Consists of Two Parts

If you examine Figure 319, you will see that the Explorer displays its data in two sections. The left section displays a higher-level overview of your computer system's files and folders than the right section. The right section displays the details of selected items in the left section. If you double-click on a folder in the left section, Explorer displays the folder's contents in the right section.

Explorer's two-section design lets you easily transfer files back and forth among disk drives and network drives. For example, to move a file from one disk drive to another, display the file in the right section and drag that file to the target disk drive in the left section. The following tips discuss ways you can use folders to organize your files and the Windows 95 Explorer to simplify file operations (such as copying, moving, renaming, or deleting files).

Use Folders to Improve Your File Organization — 321

Tip 83 explains why the Windows 95 concept of *folders* makes using the computer for novices more intuitive. Nowhere does Windows 95 use the folder concept more thoroughly than inside Explorer. Explorer makes it easy for you to create, manage, and remove folders from your computer system. You can organize your disk files in electronic folders just as you organize your physical records in file folders. Explorer supports the following folder tasks:

- Creating folders when you need to create a holder for related files
- Viewing folders and their contents
- Deleting folders when you no longer need them
- Copying and moving files between folders
- Copying and moving folders and all the folder contents from one location to another

Scrolling Through the Folder List and Opening a Folder — 322

As you have learned, Windows 95 lets you collect and organize your disk file inside folders. If you want to open a folder to view the folder's contents, perform these steps:

1. Start Explorer (see Tip 319).
2. In Explorer's left section, double-click the disk drive that holds the folder you want to open. (You may have to scroll the left section if your computer contains a lot of disk drives, CD-ROM drives, and network drives.) Windows 95 displays the drive's contents in the right section and changes the left section's closed folder icon to an open folder icon. Additionally, Windows 95 increases the detail in the left section to show any files that might reside in the open folder.
3. If you want to see additional detail, such as one of the sub-folder's contents displayed in the left section, double-click that sub-folder to see its contents.

Expanding and Collapsing a Folder — 323

As you work with Explorer, you'll notice that Explorer places plus and minus signs next to folders and drives in the left section, as shown in Figure 323.1. The plus sign indicates that the folder is collapsed. You can click your mouse on the plus sign next to a folder to expand it. The right section does not change when you expand a folder by clicking its plus sign. The right section changes only when you double-click on a closed folder.

Figure 323.1 shows an Explorer window with the Windows folder collapsed. Figure 323.2 shows the same Explorer window after the user expands the Windows folder. Notice the right section did not change. In both figures, the right section displayed the Excel folder's contents. Therefore, you can locate a file to move or copy in the right section's detail and then locate the target folder location in the left section by expanding folders. If you click on a folder's minus sign in the left section, Explorer collapses the folder and returns the left section to a more generalized state, showing the folder's name but not its contents.

Note: *Expanding and collapsing folders is not the same thing as opening and closing folders. When you double-click a folder in Explorer's left section to open or close the folder, Explorer always updates the right section to display the results. When you expand or collapse by clicking a folder's plus or minus sign, Explorer only changes the left section.*

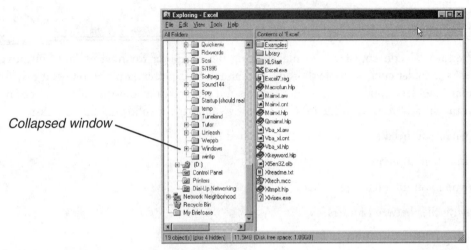

Figure 323.1 Before you expand the Windows folder.

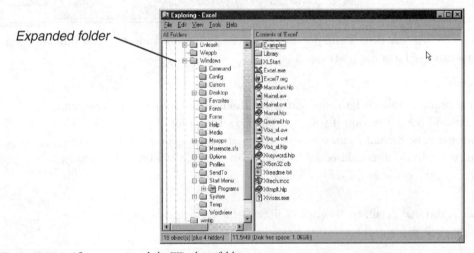

Figure 323.2 After you expand the Windows folder.

324 Recognizing File Types Using Icons

To recognize a file's type in the Windows 3.1 File Manager, you had to know the file's three-letter extension. In contrast, the Windows 95 Explorer makes things easier for you. Explorer displays an icon next to files that indicate the files' types. After you familiarize yourself with common file icons and their types, you will recognize files quickly and easily. Table 324 describes the common file icons and their associated file types.

Using the Windows 95 Explorer

Icon	Represents
📁	A folder that contains files
	A generic file type that Windows 95 does not recognize
	An MS-DOS system program
	An MS-DOS application program
	A text file, such as one you create with a text editor like Notepad
	A graphics file stored as a bitmap
	A bitmap font file description
	A TrueType font file description
	A Microsoft Excel spreadsheet
	A Microsoft Word for Windows document
	A Microsoft Access database

Table 324 A file's icon represents the file's type.

Using the File Explorer's Toolbar — 325

The Explorer toolbar, shown in Figure 325, gives you one-button control over many of Explorer's features. Instead of selecting from a menu or remembering a shortcut keystroke, you can click on toolbar buttons to perform many of Explorer's functions. To view the Explorer's toolbar, select the View menu Toolbar option, placing a checkmark next to the option. If you want to eliminate the toolbar to give more screen space to your Explorer window, select the View menu Toolbar option once again. Table 325 explains each of the toolbar's functions.

Toolbar Button	Purpose
842460102 (C:)	Accesses a different folder or drive
	Backs up one folder level
	Maps a network drive to a local drive letter
	Disconnects a network drive from a local drive letter
	Cuts selected information to the Clipboard
	Copies selected information to the Clipboard
	Pastes selected information to the Clipboard
	Undoes a previous change
	Deletes selected information to the Recycle Bin
	Displays the selected item's properties sheet
	Displays large icons in the Explorer window
	Displays small icons in the Explorer window
	Displays the Explorer window contents in list form
	Displays the Explorer window contents in detail form

Table 325 The Explorer toolbar functions.

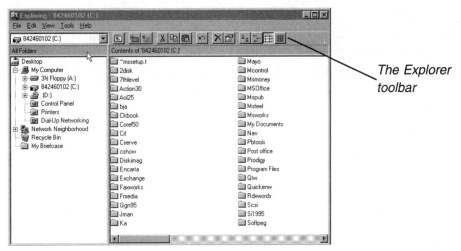

Figure 325 Use the Explorer toolbar for common tasks.

Using the File Explorer's Status Bar 326

The Explorer status bar, shown in Figure 326, provides information about your Explorer window activities. If you cannot see the status bar, you need to hide your Taskbar. If you hide your Taskbar but still cannot see the Explorer status bar, select the View menu Status Bar option to view the status bar. Explorer constantly updates the status bar to display various messages:

- Explanations for toolbar buttons as you move the mouse over the various buttons
- The number of items the Explorer window's left section displays
- The amount of free and used disk space in the Explorer window's right section

Before you move or copy files and folders, check the status bar to ensure adequate free space exists.

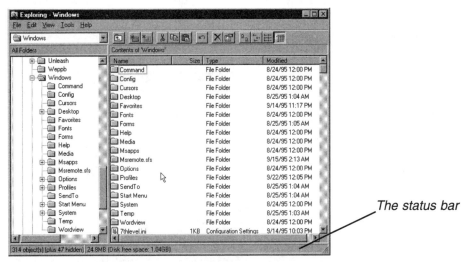

Figure 326 The Explorer status bar displays helpful messages.

327 Running a Program from Explorer

Explorer lets you do more than just view and manage drives, folders, and files. You can execute programs that the Explorer window displays. When you see a program you want to run, you can execute that program in the following four ways:

- Double-click the program name to run the program.
- Double-click on a data file to run the program associated with the data file.
- Right-click over the file and select the Open option.
- Click your mouse on the program file your desire and select the File menu Open option.

After you run a program from within Explorer, the Explorer window remains open so you can return to it and work within Explorer some more.

328 Associating a Program with a File Type

Every file is associated with a file type. In previous Windows versions, a three-letter extension, such as .DOC and .TXT, described the file type. Windows 95 associates file types with programs that can run and manage those files. For example, the Windows 95 Paint program is associated with all bitmap files, or the extension .BMP. Files that Windows 95 cannot recognize by type are identified as "unrecognized file types." After a program is associated with a file type, you can double-click a data file from within Explorer or My Computer to have Windows 95 run the associated program and automatically load the data file.

If you right-click a file in the Explorer window and Windows 95 recognizes the file's type, Windows 95 displays a pop-up menu with an Open option. However, if Windows 95 does not recognize a file type, the right-click menu displays an Open With option. When you select the Open With option, the Open With dialog box shown in Figure 328 will appear. In this dialog box, you select the program you want Windows 95 to use to open files of that type and give a description of the file type. After you identify a new file type, Windows 95 displays the Open option each time you right-click over a file of that type.

Figure 328 Associating a file type with a program.

Deleting a File or Folder — 329

Explorer makes it easy to delete a file or folder. Windows 95 sends all deleted files and folders to the Recycle Bin, where they remain until you empty the Recycle Bin or restore the Recycle Bin's contents. If you want to delete a file or folder, perform these steps:

1. Locate the file or folder in the Explorer window.
2. Move your mouse pointer over the file or folder and right-click your mouse.
3. Select the pop-up menu's Delete option. Windows 95 will ask you to confirm the deletion.
4. Click the Yes button to confirm that you want to delete the item and send it to the Recycle Bin.

If you delete a folder, the entire folder and its contents go to the Recycle Bin.

Renaming a File or Folder — 330

As you perform file operations within Windows 95, there will be times when you may need to rename a file that you previously stored on your disk. As you will learn, Explorer provides two ways you can rename files and folders:

- Right-click over the file or folder and select the pop-up menu's Rename option. Then, type the new name and press ENTER.
- Click over the file or folder name, pause, and click once again. The pause cancels the double-click action that would occur if you quickly clicked twice over the file or folder. Type the new name and press ENTER.

Note: *Only rename files or folders whose contents you know. If you rename an unfamiliar file or folder, you may keep a program from running successfully later.*

Selecting Two or More Successive Files for an Operation — 331

If you want to copy or delete a group of files, Explorer offers several time-saving ways to select more than one file for the operation. If Explorer did not let you select a group of files, you would have to copy, move, or delete every file individually, which could get tedious for a large file set. If Explorer sequentially lists the files or folders you want to move, copy, rename, or delete, you can highlight the entire group of files. To do so, perform these steps:

1. Click over the first file in the group (the file at the top of the group).
2. Press and hold the SHIFT key.
3. Click over the last file in the group. Explorer selects the entire group of files, as shown in Figure 331. You can move, copy, or rename the entire selected group just as you do with individually-selected files.

The files do not have to appear in the same column for you to select a group. If the Explorer window contains a columnar list of several files, you can select groups of files residing in columns next to each other by holding down a Shift key and clicking your mouse on the first and last file in the group.

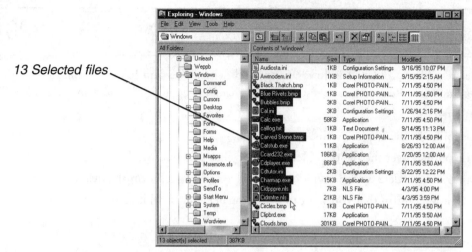

Figure 331 *After selecting a group of files.*

332 | Selecting Two or More Dispersed Files for an Operation

The group of files that you need to copy, move, or delete does not always appear consecutively in Explorer listings. Fortunately, the Explorer window also lets you select a group of non-consecutive, or *dispersed*, files. To select a group of dispersed files, hold down the CTRL key as you click your left mouse button on each file. Windows 95, in turn, will select each file, as shown in Figure 332. When you've selected the files you desire, let up on the CTRL key and the left mouse button. You can now copy, move, or delete the entire group of dispersed files.

Figure 332 *After selecting a group of dispersed files.*

333 | Selecting All the Files in a Folder

When you perform file operations, there may be times when you want to perform an operation for all the files in a folder. For example, you might want to copy a folder's contents to another disk. To work with all the files in a folder, you simply select all the files in a folder (including any subfolders the folder may contain) and then perform the operation you desire. To select all the items in a folder, you can use the following methods:

- Press CTRL-A (the *A* stands for *All*) to select all the folder's files.

- Select the Edit menu Select All option.

If you try to select a folder that contains hidden files (see Tip 337), Explorer displays a message box that tells you that these files will not be selected until you unhide them.

334 Inverting a File Selection

As you work with Explorer, there may be times you need to copy, move, or delete most of the files from a folder. If the files you want to keep are scattered throughout the folder, you may find it easier to first select those files you *do not* want to move, copy, or delete and then invert your selection. For example, if you wanted to copy, move, or delete all but three files in a folder, select those three files and choose the Edit menu Invert Selection option. Explorer, in turn, will invert the selection and highlight all files *except* the three you originally selected.

335 Displaying Properties for a File or Folder

Files and folders have properties that describe file types and attributes. To view a file or folder's property settings, right-click over the file or folder and select the pop-up menu's Properties option. Explorer opens the file's (or folder's) Properties sheet, as shown in Figure 335. (If the file is a program, the Properties sheet may contain additional pages that describe the program's author and source.) The file's Properties sheet displays information about the file or folder, including the full name, the last date modified, the last date accessed, the creation date (if known), and the file's four *attribute* property settings (Read only, Archive, Hidden, and System). Although you can use the MS-DOS ATTRIB command to change file attribute settings, you can change the settings more easily if you use the Properties sheet. The next few tips more fully explain the file-attribute property settings.

Note: *If you select several files before you display the Properties sheet, an attribute check box will be empty if none of the files contain that attribute, gray if some of the files contain that attribute, and check marked if all the files contain that attribute.*

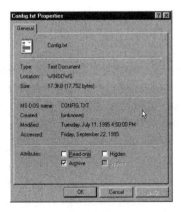

Figure 335 *Displaying file properties.*

336 Understanding Read-only Files

Neither Windows 95 nor MS-DOS will let you change or delete a file whose attribute is read-only. Read-only files are protected from change—you cannot change them until you remove the read-only attribute. If you create a file that you want to protect and not overwrite, such as a critical backup file or a program file, you can turn on that file's read-only attribute. After that, another program cannot overwrite or change that file. To apply a read-only attribute to a file, click your mouse on the Read-only check box in the file's Properties sheet. To remove a read-only attribute from a file, click your mouse on the Read-only check box once again.

337 Understanding Hidden Files

A hidden file usually doesn't appear in Explorer and MS-DOS listings. Sometimes, hidden files are system files and critical driver files that only computer experts should access. Other times, hidden files may contain sensitive data that you want to keep out of plain sight. Although hiding the file does not prevent access to the file, it will not appear in normal file listings. To hide a file, access its Properties sheet and click the Hidden check box in the sheet's Attributes section until a check mark appears. After you hide a file, you must know the filename to display it again.

338 Understanding System Files

System files are hidden, read-only files that Windows 95 uses for its own operations. You should never delete a system file—doing so may prevent your program from running. However, you may change a system file's attribute from a system file to a non-system file long enough to view the file, or if you are an experienced user, to make edits to it. For example, as Tip 191 explains, you can make changes to your system's MSDOS.SYS file.

To change a file back to a system file, access the file's Properties sheet. Then, in the Properties sheet Attributes section, click the System check box until a check mark appears. To change the file back to a non-system file, click your mouse on the System check box again.

339 Using a File's Archive Property

When you backup your files, you create a copy of the file you can safely store away on a different disk or tape. File backups are sometimes called *archive files*. As it turns out, Windows 95 assigns every file an archive property that lets Windows 95 determine when the file needs to be backed up. For example, each time you back up your files using a Windows 95 backup program, Windows 95 turns off the file's archive property. (The file no longer needs the Archive attribute set because the file has been archived.) Later, when you change the file in any way, Windows 95 sets the file's archive property. When you later perform a backup operation, the backup software can determine which files it needs to backup simply by examining their archive properties. In short, the backup software will backup those files with their archive property set (and will then clear the archive property) and will ignore those files whose archive property is clear (because the file has been backed up previously).

Backup operations that only backup those files whose archive property is set are called *incremental backups*. Because such backup operations only backup files that have changed since the last backup operation, the backup operations complete much faster than those that backup every file on your disk. You can change a file's Archive property by clicking the Archive check box in the file's Properties sheet. You might, for example, change set the Archive property for a file that you want to insure gets backed up, or you might want to clear the Archive property for a large file whose contents you don't want to backup today.

340 Creating a New Folder

As you create new documents, there will be times when you need a new folder to hold a related set of files. Luckily, you can create a new folder from the Explorer window. To create a new folder, perform these steps:

1. Locate the place on your disk where you want the new folder to reside. For example, if you want to create a new folder inside your MSOFFICE folder, double-click the MSOFFICE folder to open it.
2. Select the File menu New option.
3. Select the New menu Folder option. Windows 95 adds the new folder to the Explorer window's right section and names the folder "New Folder."
4. Type a new name for the folder.
5. Press ENTER to save the new folder's name. The folder is now part of your system; you can open or store files in it.

Note: If you create a new folder inside another folder, the new folder is known as a *subfolder*.

Creating a New Shortcut — 341

A *shortcut* is a link to a file or folder that you can place on your Desktop or inside folders. Shortcuts offer you two advantages. One, shortcuts let you get to items quickly. Two, shortcuts use less disk space than complete copies of files and folders. To create a shortcut to a file or folder using Explorer, perform these steps:

1. Select the File menu New option.
2. Select the New menu Shortcut option. Windows 95 will start the Create Shortcut wizard, shown in Figure 341.
3. Enter the name and location of the file or folder for which you want to create a shortcut. If you don't know the file or folder's name, click your mouse on the Browse button to locate the file or folder.
4. Click your mouse on the Next button and enter a name for the shortcut.
5. Click the Finish button. Windows 95 will create the shortcut in the current folder. To move the shortcut to the Desktop, drag the shortcut from its folder location to the Desktop.

Note: If you inadvertently delete a shortcut, the original file remains intact.

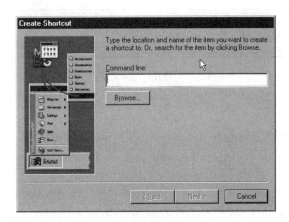

Figure 341 Creating a shortcut.

342 Using Cut-and-Paste Operations to Move a File

If you want to move a file from one drive or folder to another, you can *cut* the file to the Clipboard. Then, after you find where you want to store the file, you *paste* it from the Clipboard. The Clipboard acts as an intermediary. You can paste a file in multiple locations if you want to scatter several copies across your disk. However, as explained in Tip 341, you can accomplish the same goal with shortcuts and use less disk space. To move a file, perform these steps:

1. Use Explorer to locate the file you want to move.
2. Move your mouse pointer over the file and right-click.
3. To cut the file from its current location to the Clipboard, select the pop-up menu's Cut option. Windows 95 lightens the file's icon to show that the file resides on the Clipboard. To reverse a cut operation, click your mouse on the Undo toolbar button.
4. Find the location where you want to move the file in the Explorer's left section.
5. Right-click over a blank area in Explorer's right section.
6. To send the file from the Clipboard to its new location, select the pop-up menu's Paste option. The file is now completely moved from its original location.

343 Using Copy and Paste Operations to Copy a File

When you copy a file, Windows 95 creates a replica of the file and stores that replica at a target location you designate. Like the file-moving process, the file-copy process uses the Clipboard as an intermediary. To copy a file, perform these steps:

1. Use Explorer to locate the file you want to copy.
2. Move the mouse pointer over the file and right-click.
3. To put a copy on to the Clipboard, select the pop-up menu's Copy option.
4. Find the location where you want to move the file in the Explorer window's left section.
5. Right-click over a blank area in the Explorer window's right section.
6. To send the file from the Clipboard to its new location, select the pop-up menu's Paste option. The file now resides in two different places.

344 Moving and Copying with the Mouse

Tips 342 and 343 explain how to use the Clipboard to move and copy files. In this tip, you'll see how Explorer's two-section format lets you use your mouse to move and copy between drives and folders. To move or copy a file or folder with the mouse, perform these steps:

1. Double-click on the file or folder that contains the file or folder you want to copy or move.
2. Scroll the Explorer window's left section until you see the drive and folder to which you want to copy. If you need to expand a folder or two to locate the target folder, click on the appropriate plus signs to open the target folder that will receive the copied or moved file.
3. If you want to *copy* a file from Explorer's right section to a drive or folder in the left section, hold down the CTRL key while you drag the file from the right section to its new location. If you want to *move* a file from Explorer's right section to a drive or folder in the left section, drag the file or folder without pressing CTRL.
4. Release the file or folder to anchor the item at its new location.

Undoing a File Operation | 345

As you copy and move files, there may be times when you inadvertently drop a file at the wrong location. Luckily, you can reverse a copy or move with an *undo* operation. When you undo a copy or a move, Windows 95 puts the file or folder back where it was before you copied or moved it. If you copy or move a file, the Undo option appears on the Explorer's pop-up menu. When you select Undo Copy or Undo Move, Windows 95 reverses the previous copy or move operation. However, undo reverses only the most recent copy or move operation. If you copy three files, you cannot use Undo to reverse the first two file copies.

Pasting a Shortcut | 346

In Tip 343 you learned how to copy a file or document using cut-and-paste operations. When you perform such cut-and-paste operations, you can make an actual copy of an object, or you can paste a shortcut to the object. By creating a shortcut, you provide a quick way to access the object, but you don't actually create a duplicate of the object. To create a shortcut using cut-and-paste operations, perform these steps:

1. Use Explorer to locate the file you want to copy.
2. Move the mouse pointer over the file and right-click.
3. To put a copy on to the Clipboard, select the pop-up menu's Copy option.
4. Find the location where you want to move the file in the Explorer window's left section.
5. Right-click over a blank area in the Explorer window's right section.
6. To send the file from the Clipboard to its new location, select the pop-up menu's Paste Shortcut option.

Using the Explorer's Large and Small Icon Display | 347

The Explorer window can use large or small icons to represent your system's files. When you view the Explorer window using small icons, as shown in Figure 347.1, you can see more files and folders. However, when you view the Explorer window using large icons, as shown in Figure 347.2, the icons are easier to read. To switch between the two kinds of views, select the View menu Large Icons option or the View menu Small Icons option.

Figure 347.1 Viewing the small icons.

Figure 347.2 Viewing the large icons.

348 | Displaying a Folder's Contents Lists and Details

In addition to changing the size of the icons that Explorer uses to represent your files (see Tip 347), you can also have Explorer display its contents in a List or Detail view. When you look at the Explorer window in the List view, as shown in Figure 348.1, you see many Explorer items. In contrast, if you display the Detail view, as shown in Figure 348.2, Explorer shows fewer items but more information about each file, such as the file size, type description, and last date modified.

Note: *The Explorer window's Type column contains a file description if Windows 95 recognizes the file's extension. Normally, Explorer displays an icon for recognized files as well as the type of file, such as* **Icon**.

To switch between the two views, select the View menu Details or List options.

Figure 348.1 Viewing the Explorer window in List view.

Using the Windows 95 Explorer

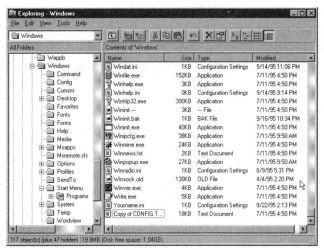

Figure 348.2 Viewing the Explorer window in Detail view.

Displaying Details about a File's Attributes   349

In Tip 335, you learned just how easy it is to view a file's attributes. All you must do is select the Properties option from the file's pop-up menu. Windows 95, in turn, displays a Properties sheet that contains all the file's information, such as the date and time created (if known), last modified date, last accessed date, size, and attributes. Figure 349 shows a file's Properties sheet. Since a file's Properties sheet is only a right-click away at any time, you might want to use the Explorer window's List view so that you can see more files at any one time in the window's right section. If you want to know the specifics about a file, right-click the file and select the pop-up menu's Properties option.

Figure 349 A file's Properties sheet.

Sorting a Folder's Contents   350

As you have learned, the Explorer Detail view lets you display a file's name, size, type, and date-and-time stamp. To sort the Explorer window Detail view by column, filename, size, type, or date last modified, click your mouse on the heading of the corresponding column. For example, to view your files in size order, from smallest to largest, click once over the column labeled "Size." Explorer, in turn, will instantly sort the right section's files into a size order from smallest to largest. To reverse the sort (the files in order from largest to smallest), click the Size column heading again.

The Detail-view sorting feature helps you locate files quickly and easily. For example, suppose you are looking for a particular accounting file inside a large folder and can't remember if the name is ACCT.DAT or ACCTG.DAT. To find the file, you can click your mouse on the Name column to alphabetize the file listing by name. Then, you can see whether the filename is ACCT.DAT or ACCTG.DAT without having to scroll through a lengthy list of random names looking for a match.

351 Refreshing an Explorer Window

Many users keep the Explorer window open at all times while working in Windows 95. If you run Explorer in the background, you can always switch to Explorer (using the Taskbar buttons or by pressing CTRL-TAB) to copy or move a file. Windows 95 does not constantly update your Explorer window if you run Explorer in the background. For example, if you display a folder's contents in Explorer and then start your word processor and create a new file, the file will *not* be in Explorer's window when you switch back to Explorer. However, at any time, you can request that Explorer re-read the disk drive to update its view. If you've added or deleted files from other running programs, the Explorer window will reflect those changes when you select the View menu Refresh option. The Refresh option tells Explorer to re-read the disk and refresh its list of files and folders.

352 Controlling the Display of Hidden Files within the Explorer

As you have learned, Explorer normally doesn't display hidden files. In addition, Explorer normally does not display any file of the following file types:

- Dynamic link library files with the DLL extension
- System files with the SYS extension
- Virtual device drivers with the VXD, 386, or DRV extensions

As you work with Windows 95, there may be times when you want to work with files that use these extensions. For example, you might want to change some system files around or write your own device drivers using a programming language, such as C++. To view files that Explorer normally hides, perform these steps:

1. Select Explorer's View menu Options option. Windows 95 displays the Options page shown in Figure 352.
2. To tell Explorer to show all files no matter what the file type or attribute says, click the Show all files option button.
3. To save your changes, click your mouse on the OK button.

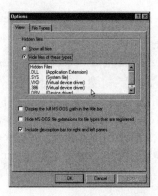

Figure 352 *Selecting files to show or hide.*

Understanding Complete Pathnames   353

Just as every house has an address that describes its exact location in a city, every file on your system has a *pathname* that describes its unique location. As you know, two houses on two different streets may share the same house number but not the same address. Similarly, files in two separate directories (or folders) might have the same filename but different pathnames. The pathname describes a file's exact location, including the disk drive, directory, and subdirectories in which it resides.

For example, the following pathname refers to a file named MIKE.TXT that resides in the A: drive's *root directory* (when you don't specify a directory for a file, Windows 95 stores it in the disk's root directory):

A:\MIKE.TXT

The backslash (\) separates the disk drive from the filename. In a pathname, the filename always appears last (to the right) of everything else. If a file resides in a directory, the directory name goes between the disk drive and the filename. The following pathname refers to a file named JUDY.TXT that resides in a directory named DEPT on the C: drive:

C:\DEPT\JUDY.TXT

Even if a file has no extension, a file has a pathname that describes how to reach the file. The following pathname describes a file named FRANK (there is no filename extension) located three subdirectories beneath the root directory on the D: drive:

D:\DEPT\COMPANY\SALES\FRANK

FRANK is the filename and not a directory because FRANK appears last in the pathname. Although you can specify a pathname without specifying a file, such as when you specify the path to several files grouped into one directory, a pathname usually describes both a file and its exact location.

Displaying the Complete MS-DOS Pathname in the Title Bar   354

MS-DOS users relied heavily on file pathnames. Similarly, Windows 3.1 users had to be familiar with pathnames. Although understanding pathnames was more important in previous versions of MS-DOS and Windows, Windows 95 users can benefit from understanding how their system stores files on the disk. The folder concept makes understanding pathnames less important for many end-users, but the more you know about pathnames, the more efficiently you can navigate through your system's files and folders.

As you work with Windows 95, there may be times when you want to view pathnames to your files. For example, you may want to rearrange your disk drive and eliminate files you no longer need. Or, you may be an old MS-DOS die-hard who feels most comfortable when you see pathnames. Luckily, you can tell Explorer to display pathnames in its file listings.

Explorer's *title bar*, the bar directly between the toolbar buttons and the window's right section, displays the complete MS-DOS path to the window's files if you perform these steps:

1. Select the Explorer View menu Options option. Windows 95 will display the Options sheet.
2. Select the Display the full MS-DOS path in the title bar check box.
3. Click your mouse on the OK button to save your changes.

As Figure 354 shows, the Explorer title bar now displays the MS-DOS path to your files listed in the Explorer window's right section.

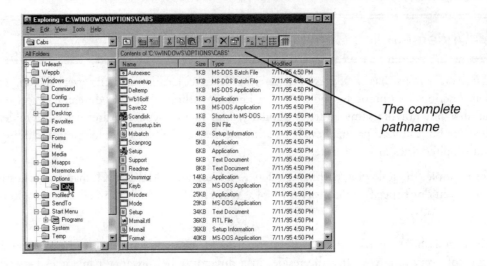

Figure 354 You can display a window's MS-DOS pathname.

355 Displaying File Types (Extensions)

As Tips 324 and 328 explain, the Explorer window displays file icons to indicate the type of file you are viewing. Windows 95 determines the file's type by the filename extension. Therefore, the filename extension is important in Windows 95. To make Explorer display both file extensions and icons, perform these steps:

1. Select the Explorer View menu Options option. Windows 95 will display the Options sheet.
2. Uncheck the Hide MS-DOS file extensions for file types that are registered check box.
3. Click your mouse on the OK button to save your changes.

Figure 355 shows an Explorer window that includes the filename extensions. If you leave the extension option checked, Explorer only displays filename extensions for those file types (extensions) it does not recognize.

Figure 355 Displaying the file extensions.

Understanding and Viewing Registered File Types — 356

When you install Windows 95, the operating system already recognizes several file types. For example, Windows 95 knows that a file ending with the TXT extension is a text file that you can display using the Notepad application. Additionally, Windows 95 knows exactly which icon represents files with the TXT extension. Windows 95 knows this information because Microsoft registered the TXT extension, and many other common file types, with your copy of the operating system.

As you install additional Windows 95 applications on your hard disk, those applications may register additional file types. For example, if you install CorelDRAW, a popular graphics program, CorelDRAW registers files that end in the CDR extension as CorelDRAW files. Therefore, if you display an Explorer window that contains CorelDRAW files, Explorer knows to use the CorelDRAW icon for CorelDRAW file types.

However, until you or an application registers a file type, Windows 95 will not be able to associate a file with an icon or file type. To view the file types registered with your system, select the View menu Options option and display the File Types page. Figure 356 shows the File Types page.

Figure 356 *The File Types page contains registration details.*

Registering a New File Type — 357

As you work with Windows 95, there may be times when you need to register a new file type and thereby teach Windows 95 how to display files of that type in future listings. In addition, the registration tells Windows 95 which program to start automatically when you double-click a file of that type. To register a file type, perform these steps:

1. Select Explorer's View menu Options option. Windows 95 will display the Options sheet.
2. To display the File Types page, click your mouse on the File Types tab.
3. Click your mouse on the New Type button. Explorer displays the Add New File Type dialog box shown in Figure 357.
4. To select a new icon, click your mouse on the Change Icon button.
5. Enter the new file type's information in the Add New File Type dialog box. Table 357 explains each the dialog box's entries.
6. Click your mouse on the OK button to save your changes and add the new file registration to Windows 95.

Option	Purpose
Description of type	A description that appears in Explorer's Type column when you display Detail view
Associated extension	The filename extension that you want Explorer to recognize for this file type
Content Type (MIME)	The MIME type that informs Windows 95 how to read the file if you use Explorer to search the Internet (using the Internet tools such as those supplied with Windows 95)
Default Extension for Content Type	The MIME (Multipurpose Internet Mail Extensions) filename extension that your Internet search tools can recognize when files of this type appear on the Internet
Actions	The pop-up menu actions that appear whenever the user right-clicks over these files or their shortcuts. When you click your mouse on the New button, Windows 95 displays an Action window and you can type the action name (the pop-up menu option) and the associated command for that action.
Enable Quick View	Lets you specify whether or not you want the type to support the Windows 95 Quick Viewers
Always show extension	Lets you specify whether or not Explorer is to display the extension when displaying files of this type

Table 357 *The Add New File Type dialog box entries.*

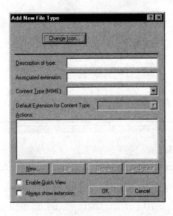

Figure 357 *Registering a new file type.*

358 Removing a Registered File Type

If you remove an application from your system, that application's de-installation procedure should erase the file associations for that application. However, not all applications have de-installation procedures. If you need to disassociate a file from its registered file type, perform these steps:

1. Select Explorer's View menu Options option. Windows 95 will display the Options sheet.
2. Click your mouse on the Options sheet File Types tab.
3. In the Registered file types list box, click to highlight the file type you want to remove.
4. Click your mouse on the Remove button. After confirming the deletion, Windows 95 will remove the registration.

5. Click your mouse on the OK button.

After you remove a file type from the Registered file types list box, you will not be able to run associated programs that manage those types of files by simply double clicking on the file.

Finding a File or Folder — 359

If you forget where you stored a file, or if you cannot remember a file's exact name, you can ask Explorer to locate the file for you. The Tools menu includes a Find submenu that contains the following options:

- Files or Folders: Locates files and folders.
- Computer: Locates a networked computer.
- On the Microsoft Network: Locates a file on the online Microsoft Network.

When searching for files and folders, you can use the MS-DOS wildcard characters * and ?. The asterisk stands for zero or more characters. The question mark stands for a single character. Therefore, the name CON*.* would represent all the following files:

- CONFIG.SYS
- CONFIG.TXT
- CONSERVE.EXE
- CONA.A
- CON.12

The name CON?.? might represent these files:

- CONA.A
- CON4.Q

The wildcard searches give you the ability to locate groups of files that match a filename pattern. Explorer's Find command is similar to the Start menu's Find command. The following tips discuss the Explorer's Find feature.

Finding a File or Folder by Name — 360

If you know the name of a file or folder but forgot where you put the file or folder, use the Explorer's Tools menu Find option to locate the lost item. To find a file or folder by name, perform these steps:

1. Select Explorer's Tools menu Find option. Explorer will display the Find menu.
2. Select the Find menu Files or Folders option. Explorer will display the Find dialog box shown in Figure 360.1.
3. Type the filename or a wildcard specification in the Named text box.
4. Open the Look in pull-down list and specify the initial search path. You can request that Explorer search your entire computer, a single disk drive, a folder, or a network.
5. Check the Include subfolders check box if you want the search to include every level of folders and subfolders in the search path.
6. To start the search, click your mouse on the Find Now button. Explorer will search for a file match.

As Explorer finds files that meet your filename specification, Explorer lists those files at the bottom of the Find dialog box. Explorer does not stop searching at the first occurrence found. Therefore, if Explorer does find the file you want, you can click your mouse on the Stop button to stop the search. If you do not click Stop, Explorer will continue to search until it exhausts all search locations on your selected search path. When the search completes, you'll see a list of all found file matches at the bottom of the dialog box, as shown in Figure 360.2.

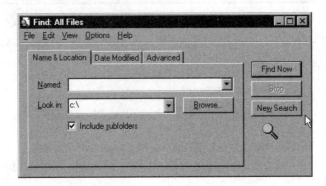

Figure 360.1 Getting ready to search.

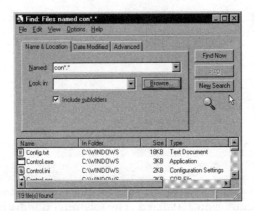

Figure 360.2 Explorer found several matches.

361 Using a Found File

When Explorer finishes locating all occurrences of a file, as shown in Figure 360.2, Explorer displays a list of those files, their locations, sizes, types, and last modified dates at the bottom of the Find dialog box. If you want to use one of the files in the list, you can double-click your mouse on the file to open it. In addition, you can right-click over the file to display the file's pop-up menu, which lets you cut, rename, copy, delete, or create a shortcut for the file. As such, you do not have to exit the Find dialog box to work with a found file.

362 Finding a File or Folder by Date

As you work with Windows 95, there may be times when you don't recall the name of a file you want, but you do remember the approximate date you last worked with it. For example, perhaps you want to locate last year's tax records, and all you know is that you worked with the file sometime last April. In this situation, you can use Explorer's Find sheet Date Modified page, shown in Figure 362, to search for a file by a date or date range. Specifying a date range, you can search for a file modified within a span of days, weeks, months, or even years. If you use the Date Modified page in tandem with the Name & Location page, you can create a search with very narrow parameters. For example, if you specify a file name or wildcard on the Name & Location page and then specify a date range on the Date Modified page, Explorer will list only files that meet both your naming and date-search criteria.

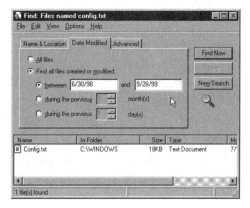

Figure 362 *You can limit file searches to date ranges.*

Finding a File or Folder by Content — 363

Perhaps the most powerful search capability Explorer offers is the ability to search across files, folders, and computers for files that contain certain text. For example, if you wrote a letter to your broker recently but have no idea where the document resides on your computer, you can ask Explorer to search your computer for a file or files that contain your broker's name. In addition, you can limit the search to files that meet a certain registered type, such as a Microsoft Word document. To search for a file by content and type, perform these steps:

1. Select Explorer's Tools menu Find option. Explorer will display the Find menu.
2. Select the Find menu Files or Folders option.
3. To display the Find sheet Advanced page shown in Figure 363, click your mouse on the Find sheet Advanced tab.
4. Open the Of type pull-down list if you remember the file's type. Otherwise, leave the value set to All Files and Folders.
5. Type the text for which you want to search in the Containing text field.
6. To start the search, click your mouse on the Find Now button.

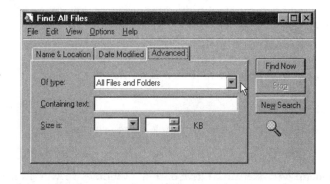

Figure 363 *You may search for a file by type and content.*

364 | Finding a File or Folder by Size

When you misplace a file on your disk, there may be times when you can't remember the file's name, but you have you a pretty good idea about the file's size. In such cases, you can use Explorer to search for a file by specifying a minimum or maximum size. For example, if you are running low on disk space, you can request a list of all data files over one megabyte. Then, you can purge your computer of those files, if you like. To search for files by size, perform these steps:

1. Select Explorer's Tools menu Find option. Explorer will display the Find menu.
2. Select the Find menu Files or Folders option.
3. Click your mouse on the Advanced tab to display the Find sheet Advanced page.
4. Select either At least or At most from the Size pull-down list.
5. Next to the KB label, specify the size amount to which you want to limit the search size. The amount is the number of kilobytes (a kilobyte is approximately 1,000 characters) to which you want to limit your search.
6. To start the search, click your mouse on the Find Now button.

365 | Performing Case-Sensitive Search Operations

Tip 363 explains how to search your hard disk or your entire computer system (across several hard disks) for files that contain specific text. Unless you specify otherwise, Explorer performs a *case-insensitive search*, which means you can search for the word *Car* and Explorer returns all files that contain *Car*, *car*, and *CAR*. Explorer ignores upper case and lower case when making matches.

However, you can make the search case-sensitive so that Explorer locates files that contain your text in exactly the same upper-case and lower-case pattern. To do so, simply select the Options menu Case Sensitive option on the Find sheet. After you select the Case Sensitive option, Explorer will locate files containing text that matches both the case and content of your search characters.

366 | Mapping to a Network Drive

Windows 95 makes accessing a network disk drive as easy as reaching a drive on your own computer. When you *map* a network drive, you specify a disk-drive letter, such as E:, that you want to assign to a remote networked computer's disk drive. Then, every time you access the mapped drive name, your computer goes out over the network to retrieve the information. The mapped drive does not have to be an entire disk drive on the network. You can map a drive letter to a specific folder on the remote computer (in this way, a remote user can limit the files other users can access to only those contained in the folder as opposed to all the files on their disk). If you want to map an entire network drive to a local drive letter, you can map that drive's root directory to a local drive name.

Note: *Before you map a network drive or folder to a local drive name, you must first ensure that the network drive or folder is sharable.*

To map a network path to a local drive name, perform these steps:

1. Start Explorer.
2. Select the Tools menu Map Network Drive option. Windows 95 will display the dialog box shown in Figure 366.

3. To select a drive letter to use as the network mapped drive, open the Drive pull-down list. Explorer will use your computer's next available drive letter as the default mapped drive name. Therefore, if your computer contains an A: drive, a B: drive, and a C: drive, Explorer will display D: for the mapped-drive name. You can choose another unused drive letter if you prefer.

4. Type the full network path in the Path text box. For example, if you want to map a folder named "MRKTG" on a networked computer named "Office Computer" to a local drive letter, you would type **\\Office Computer\MRKTG** for the path. If you don't know the exact name of your network drive or shared folder, open the Path pull-down list and select from the computer and paths displayed.

5. Click your mouse on the OK button to save your changes.

You can now access the mapped drive as if it were a local disk drive. Every time you use the mapped drive letter, your computer goes to the networked drive and folder to retrieve information.

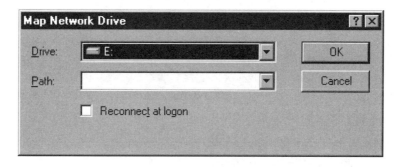

Figure 366 Mapping a network drive to a local drive name.

Creating a Persistent Connection 367

If you work with the same network drives on a regular basis, you can eliminate the time you spend establishing the network connection each time you start by telling Windows to connect to the disk automatically, each time you start Windows 95. Tip 366 explains how you can map a network drive to your computer so that the networked drive acts like a local disk drive. If you want to create a *persistent connection* (a mapped-drive connection that establishes itself automatically every time you start Windows 95), follow Tip 366's instructions for mapping a network drive and check the Reconnect at logon check box. Until you change or delete this connection (see Tip 368), your computer will start up with the mapped drive every time you start Windows 95.

Disconnecting from a Network Drive 368

As you work with remote devices, there may be times when you no longer need to use a specific network drive. To disconnect a mapped network drive from your computer, perform these steps:

1. Start Explorer.
2. Select the Tools menu Disconnect Network Drive option. Explorer will display a dialog box that shows any mapped drives currently in effect.
3. Select a mapped drive from the dialog box and click OK.

369 Going to a Specific Folder or File

Despite Explorer's powerful searching features, you will not always want to wade through a series of folders and subfolders to display a file list. Luckily, Explorer provides a shortcut feature that lets you go directly to a specific folder or file without first traversing the entire Explorer tree of computers, drives, and folders. When you open Explorer and select the Tools menu Go To option, Explorer displays the dialog box shown in Figure 369. To use the Go To Folder dialog box, type the pathname of the folder or file you want to access. Or, display the pull-down list to select from the most recent folders you've opened. Then, click the OK button. Explorer, in turn, will update its windows to display the files that reside in the folder you specified.

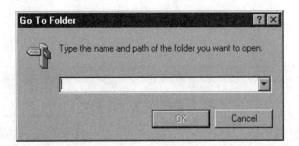

Figure 369 *You can go directly to a drive, folder, or file.*

370 Opening Multiple Viewer Windows

As you know, Explorer typically uses a two-section format to display the files on your system. Normally, if you double-click your mouse on a folder that appears in Explorer's left section, Explorer uses its right section to display the folder's contents. Occasionally, you'll want to open additional Explorer windows so you can drag-and-drop files from one folder window to another. For example, you may want to move files between Explorer's right section and a separate Explorer window that displays the contents of another folder. Or, you may want to open windows for three or four folders and shuffle files between them.

To open a second Explorer window, highlight the folder whose contents you want to display. Then, select the File menu Open option. Explorer, in turn, will open a new window. For example, in Figure 370.1, the Explorer window's right section displays the C: drive's contents. If you click on the Windows folder and select the File menu Open option, Explorer will open a window that displays the Windows folder's contents, as shown in Figure 370.2. The two windows can now act as source and target windows. From the source window, you can select and drag a file or folder to the target window.

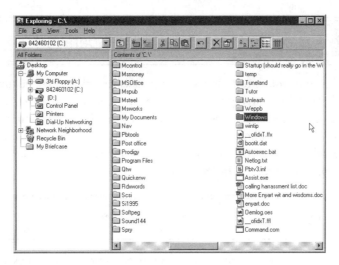

Figure 370.1 Before you open another window.

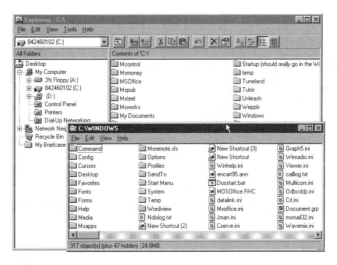

Figure 370.2 After you select the File menu Open option.

Performing a Drag and Drop File Copy Operation   371

In Tip 370, you learned how to open multiple Explorer windows. An advantage of using multiple windows is the ease with which you can then move or copy files. For example, after you use Tip 370 to open an additional Explorer window, you can easily copy a file using a drag-and-drop operation. To perform a drag-and-drop copy operation, hold down the CTRL key as you drag the file or group of files from one window to the next. The CTRL key makes the drag-and-drop operation copy (rather than move) your files. Using such drag-and-drop operations, you can copy folders as well as files. When you copy a folder, Windows 95 copies the folders contents and the contents of any subfolders the folder contains.

372 Performing a Drag and Drop File Move Operation

As you work with programs such as your word processor or spreadsheet, there may be times when you inadvertently store a file in the wrong folder. Luckily, moving files between open Explorer windows is extremely easy. Use the steps Tip 370 presents as your guide to open the window that contains the document you want to move and a window that contains the folder into which you want to move the document. Next, use your mouse to drag-and-drop a file or group of files from one window to the next. As you might guess, you can move folders as well as files. When you move a folder, Windows 95 moves subfolders the folder contains.

373 Performing a Drag and Drop Print Operation

As you work with Windows 95, there may be times when you need to print a file quickly. In fact, in some cases, you may not have time to even open the file's associated program. Luckily, using a drag-and-drop operation in Explorer, you can get a file printout in a hurry. To print a file using a drop-and-drag operation, perform these steps:

1. Select the folder that contains the file you want to print and, using Tip 370 as a guide, open a separate window for that folder's contents.
2. Scroll to the Printers folder in the Explorer window's left section.
3. To open the folder and display your computer's printer and fax capabilities, double-click your mouse on the Printers folder.
4. Press ALT-TAB to display once again the window that contains the (icon of the) file you want to print.
5. Drag the file from the window you opened in step 1 to the printer on which you want to print the file. The Windows 95 print spooler takes over and prints the file.

374 Understanding the Windows 95 System Tools

Depending on the installation options you selected when you installed Windows 95, your Accessories submenu may contain a System Tools submenu. (To display the Accessories submenu, select the Start menu Programs option and choose Accessories.) The system programs, known as the *system tools*, help you protect, monitor, and manage your Windows 95 software and hardware. Table 374 describes several common programs that appear in the System Tools menu. To display your System Tools menu, perform these steps:

1. Click your mouse on the Start button.
2. Select the Start menu Programs option.
3. Select the Programs menu Accessories option.
4. Select the Accessories menu System Tools option. Windows 95 will display the System Tools menu.

Menu Icon	Title	Purpose
	Backup	Creates backup files from your disks.
	Create System Disks	Creates a set of backup Windows 95 disks.

Table 374 The System Tools menu. (continued on the following page)

Menu Icon	Title	Purpose
	Defragmenter	Eliminates gaps between files and file blocks.
	DriveSpace	Squeezes more space from your disk drive.
	Inbox Repair Tool	Repairs your Microsoft Exchange Inbox.
	Net Watcher	Monitors network activity.
	Resource Meter	Displays the status of your system performance.
	ScanDisk	Monitors disk activity to ensure that the disk is working well.
	System Monitor	Lets you analyze various aspects of your system.

Table 374 The System Tools menu. (continued from the previous page)

375 Understanding Your Need to Backup Files

When you make a *backup*, you copy your disk files on to floppy disks or tape. The backup is insurance; if something happens to your hard disk, such as a disk *crash* (the hard disk breaks), or you inadvertently erase an important file, you can use the backup disk to restore data you've lost. Nobody ever regretted making a backup, but many people have regretted *not* making one! If you ever lose important information and must recreate the files and reenter data to get the information back on your disk, you'll appreciate how much time and effort making a backup can save you.

Many people and businesses make backup files every day. How often you make backup files will depend on how much critical data you enter into your computer. Keep your backup files off-site so if a fire or other disaster destroys your computer, your data will be safe elsewhere. You'll then be able to restore that data once you get to a working computer. Similarly, if your computer's hard disk fails (everything mechanical, like disk drives, fails eventually), you can use the backup copy to restore the data as soon as you get the hardware problem resolved.

376 Invest in a Tape Drive

Hard disks are getting bigger and less expensive every day. A hard disk holds a tremendous amount of data, much more than a floppy disk holds. If you make backup files on floppy disks, you will need several (or several hundred) floppy disks, depending on the amount of information you want to stow for safekeeping. As such, using floppy disks to store backup files may not be a workable option for you.

If it takes too may floppy disks to hold your backup files, you should use a tape backup system. Tapes can hold as much data as most disk drives. Although it takes longer to write to tapes than to disks, you can schedule your backups so they run automatically day or night when you are not using your computer. As long as you invest in a large enough tape drive, you will not need to sit in front of your system during the backup, which you would have to do if you backed your files up to floppy disks.

377 | Understanding a Full-System Backup

A *full-system backup* is a backup of your entire computer system, including your hard disk (or hard disks, if your computer has more than one). A full-system backup not only copies your document files and programs, the backup operation also copies key, hidden Windows 95 system files. (The only way to restore your entire Windows 95 system and all your files in one step is to perform a full-system backup.) Normally, you only need to make a full-system backup one time (often the first time you perform a backup). After you make one full-system backup, you then make *incremental backups* that contain only the files that are new or have changed since the previous backup. (See Tip 384 for more information on incremental backups.)

Some people choose never to make a full-system backup; instead of backing up programs that they can install from the original floppy disks or CD-ROMs, these users backup only their data files. However, restoring an entire system is *much easier* if you have a full-system backup. If you choose not to make a full-system backup, be sure to keep your original installation disks and CD-ROMs off-site. That way, you can reinstall the programs if something happens to your hardware.

Note: Every month or two, you might want to make another full-system backup so that you don't have to keep as many incremental tapes around. After you make a full-system backup, you won't need the incremental tapes you've made since the previous full-system backup.

To make a full-system backup, perform these steps:

1. To run the Backup program, select the System Tools menu Backup option. Windows 95, in turn, will display the Backup sheet Backup page, as shown in Figure 377.
2. Select the File menu Open File Set option.
3. Select the Full System Backup.
4. Click your mouse on the Open button.
5. Click your mouse on the Next Step button.
6. Select the destination hardware, such as your tape drive, where you want Windows 95 to store the full-system backup. Windows 95 will then write a backup of your system.

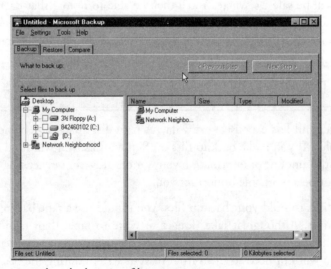

Figure 377 The Backup program is ready to backup your files.

Understanding Backup File Sets — 378

Tip 377 explained how to create a full-system backup file set. The full-system backup file set contains a list and location of every file on your computer, including system files Windows 95 needs to restore the machine in case of a total data loss.

After you create a full-system backup file set, you can safely store that full-system backup file set away. Subsequently, you should make more limited backups for the small portion of your computer files that change in any given day or week. For example, suppose you share a computer with two co-workers in an office. At the end of each day, you may want to backup only the files that appear in your folder, which might contain additional subfolders that hold your accounting files, word processing documents, and other work. To safeguard your work, you can create a backup file set that contains only the files and folders located in your folder. When you then backup, you can insert enough floppy disks or tape to backup only the files in your folder. Then, if you later encounter system problems and your company has to replace your computer with a new one, you can use your backup file set to restore your files.

Note: *A single tape can hold several backup file sets; therefore, you must assign a unique name to each backup file set so you can restore a specific backup file set later.*

Selecting Files for a Backup File Set — 379

To create a backup file set that contains a selected number of files and folders, you must tell the Backup program exactly where to look for the selected files. You must also tell the Backup program exactly which files to select. To select files for a backup file set, perform these steps:

1. Display the Backup sheet Backup page.
2. Expand the drive on which your files reside by clicking the plus sign next to the disk that holds your files.
3. Continue to expand folders until you get to the highest level of folder or file you want to backup in this backup file set.
4. If you want to open a folder to select specific files, click your mouse on the folder. The files will appear in the Backup page's right section.
5. As you display files and expand folders, click your mouse on the box next to the files and folders you want to save in this backup file set.

Note: In step 5, if you click a folder name, the backup file set you create here will backup every file in that folder. If you accidentally select a file or folder that you don't want to include in this backup file set, click your mouse on the file or folder again to remove the checkmark.

Saving Your File and Folder Selections to a Backup File Set — 380

After you select every file and folder you want in the current backup file set (see Tip 379), you need to specify a destination disk or tape drive and name for the file set. To specify a destination disk or tape drive, click your mouse on the Next Step button and enter the destination drive.

To name your backup file set, click your mouse on the Start Backup button. The Backup program, in turn, will display the Backup Set Label dialog box shown in Figure 380. In this dialog box, type a name, such as **Martha's backup files**, for your backup file set. Then, click the OK button. The Backup program, in turn, will create the backup file set.

After the Backup program creates the backup file set, you only have to select the File menu Open option to open a backup file set and begin the backup of just that file set's files. In other words, each time you perform a backup operation, you simply need to select your backup file set and begin. You will not have to change that backup file set again, or specify a new backup file set, unless you want to add or remove files and folders from the set.

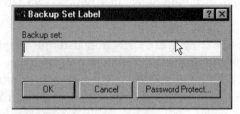

Figure 380 *Entering a name for the new backup file set.*

381 Understanding and Using File Filtering

To save time (reduce the amount of time a backup operation requires) users normally only backup their documents and other key data files. Users normally will not backup program files that they could later reinstall should a disk error occur. As you will learn, Windows 95 makes it easy for you to exclude (not backup) specific file types (such as executable programs). When you use *file filtering*, you limit the kinds of files that the Backup program includes in a backup file set. The Backup program includes a Settings menu File Filtering option that displays the dialog box shown in Figure 381. The settings in the File Filtering dialog box specify details about files you do *not* want to backup. In other words, you can specify the file patterns that you want your backup file sets to skip. You can exclude files last modified before or between certain dates. In addition, you can exclude certain registered file types.

As you highlight file types from the File types list box, you can click your mouse on the Exclude button to send those types to the list of files excluded from the next backup. If you accidentally select a file type that you do not want to exclude, highlight that file type in the File Filtering dialog box's bottom list and click your mouse on the Delete button. When you click your mouse on the OK button, Backup excludes all those files that meet your filtering conditions from the next backup file set it creates. If you are in the process of creating a backup file set when you specify file-filtering options, your backup file set will always filter those files from the backup copy.

Figure 381 *You can specify types of files not to backup.*

Understanding and Performing Drag and Drop Backup Operations 382

When you create backup file sets, the Backup program creates a file that includes all specifications necessary (including filenames, locations, and destinations) to backup the files in that set. If you used file filtering, the backup file set filters out unwanted files during the process as well. Due to Windows 95's ability to perform powerful, but easy, drag-and-drop operations, you can use drag and drop to create a backup of any backup file set without having to start the Backup program first. There are three ways to take advantage of drag and drop when making backup files:

- Use Explorer to locate the backup file set. Then, drag the backup file set to the Desktop to create the shortcut. Then, to start the backup at any time, double-click your mouse on the shortcut.

- Open the My Computer window and locate the Backup program icon. Drag the program's icon to your Desktop. You can now drag any backup file set to the Backup icon shortcut to start the backup.

- Drag a backup file set icon, found in the My Computer window, to the Backup program icon which is also in the My Computer window. Windows 95, in turn, will start the backup operation using the file set you specified.

Note: *You can also double-click a backup file set inside Explorer or My Computer to begin a backup that meets the backup file set specifications.*

Controlling Backup's Drag and Drop Settings 383

Figure 383 shows the Drag and Drop dialog box that appears when you select Backup's Settings menu Drag and Drop option. The dialog box controls the way all subsequent drag-and-drop, backup operations work. The Drag and Drop dialog box contains the following options:

- *Run Backup minimized*: Specifies that the backup program remains minimized on the Taskbar when you drag and drop a backup file set from the My Computer window to the Backup program icon.

- *Confirm operation before beginning*: Requires that you confirm the files in the backup file set before a backup begins when you drag and drop a backup file set onto the Backup icon.

- *Quit Backup after operation is finished*: Specifies that the Backup program closes when a drag-and-drop backup operation finishes.

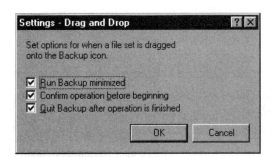

Figure 383 *Controlling the drag-and-drop Backup options.*

384 Understanding Incremental Backup Operations

There is no reason to perform a lengthy full-system backup every time you want to backup files. After you make a full-system backup, you should thereafter make *incremental backups*. An incremental backup is a backup of only those files you changed or modified since your last backup. If you have a disk crash, you should restore your full-system backup and then all incremental backups, in order, since the most recent full-system backup.

When the Backup program backs up a file, Backup turns off the file's archive attribute (see Tip 339). The next time you perform an incremental backup, Backup knows not to backup any file without the archive attribute. If you modify a file in any way, Windows 95 sets the archive attribute, so the next incremental backup that you make will backup the file. To perform an incremental backup, perform these steps :

1. Select the Backup program's Settings menu Options option.
2. Click your mouse on the Backup tab to display the Backup page shown in Figure 384.
3. Click your mouse on the Incremental backup option button.
4. Click your mouse on the OK button.
5. Select the files you want to backup. Backup then scans your computer and flags only those files with set archive attributes.
6. Click your mouse on the Next Step button and select a destination for the backup.
7. To start the backup, click Start Backup, provide a name for your backup set, and then click OK.

Subsequent incremental backups of this file set will continue to backup those files you selected, but only if those files' archive properties are turned on (indicating the file is new or has been changed since the last backup operation).

Figure 384 Specify incremental backups on the Backup page.

385 Understanding Backup Verification

Backup systems are not perfect. The tape you use may be flawed or a write operation may not have worked properly during the backup. However, don't be alarmed; the chance of a backup being bad is slim. Nevertheless, it is a good idea to verify full-system backups and incremental backups of critical data.

When you request a verification, Backup rereads the backup files it stored on the destination drive and compares those files, character-by-character, to the files on your computer. If the complete backup is good, the verification will be successful. However, if Backup cannot properly verify the backup you just made, the verification procedure will fail. In this instance, you can try the backup again using a different tape or backup media.

A verification takes a while. However, if you backup to tape and start the backup and verification procedure before you go to lunch or leave work for the day, the procedure should be completed before you return to your desk. To request a verification, select the Backup program's Settings menu Options option. Then, on the Settings Options sheet Backup page, check the option labeled Verify backup data by automatically comparing files after backup is finished.

Note: The Backup program's Compare page also lets you select individual files and folders and compare the selection against one or more backup file sets. Tip 393 explains how to use the Compare page.

Compressing Your Backup Files Saves Tape or Floppy Disk Space — 386

If your disk contains a large number of files, your backup operations can quickly consume many floppy disks or even multiple magnetic tapes. If you want to squeeze as large a backup as you can on to the destination floppy disks or backup tape, you can *compress* the backup. When you compress the backup, the Backup program uses compression algorithm to reduce the size of all files in the backup file set. As a result, file compression lets you fit much more data (sometimes twice as much) on to a single disk or tape.

To request that Backup compress data during the backup, check the option Use data compression on the Settings Options sheet Backup page. Compression makes the backup process take longer to complete. However, if you need to save space because you are backing up on to floppy disks or on to a small tape, you may not mind the wait.

Controlling Tape-Based Backups — 387

Like floppy disks, tapes require special formatting and occasional erasure. The Backup program Tools menu provides the following tape-maintenance options:

- *Format Tape*: Writes magnetic grooves into tapes that hold your backup data. After you format a tape, you do not have to format the tape again unless you experience tape verification problems. If, after you reformat a tape, you receive verification errors, discard the tape.

- *Erase Tape*: Erases without reformatting tapes. Erasing a tape takes much less time than reformatting it. If you've just made a full-system backup, you can erase your incremental backup tapes and use them for new backup file sets.

- *Redetect Tape Drive*: If you change tape drives and the new tape drive is not fully Plug and Play compatible, you may have to select the Tools menu Redetect Tape Drive option so that Backup recognizes your tape drive.

Restoring Files from a Previous Backup — 388

If your disk crashes and you must restore a backup, use the Backup program's Restore page to restore your lost files. To restore your entire system, perform these steps:

1. Click your mouse on the Backup program's Restore tab to display the Restore page.
2. In the Restore page's left section, click your mouse on the drive letter or tape drive that contains your backup file set.
3. In the Restore page's right section, click your mouse on the full-system backup file set.
4. Click your mouse on the Next Step button.

5. Select the full-system backup file set.
6. Click Start Restore. Backup restores your entire computer system as it was when you first backed up the system. For the restore to take effect, you must restart Windows 95.

389 Restoring Files to Their Original Locations

Tip 389 explains how to restore your entire system should your disk crash or some other catastrophic event occur. In this tip, you will learn how to restore selected files and folders to their original locations (the locations where the files and folders resided when you made the backup). To restore selected files and folders, perform these steps:

1. Select the Settings menu Options page Restore tab and click your mouse on the Original locations option.
2. Click your mouse on the OK button.
3. Click your mouse on the Backup program's Restore tab to display the Restore page.
4. In the Restore page's left section, click your mouse on the drive letter or tape drive that contains the files you want to restore.
5. Select the backup file set that contains the files you want to restore.
6. Click your mouse on the Next Step button to display a path structure.
7. Click your mouse on the box to the left of each folder you want to restore. If you want to restore selected files from a folder, click on the folder to display its files. Then, click each file you want to restore.
8. Click your mouse on the Start Restore button to restore the files and folders you selected.

390 Restoring Files to a New Location

You do not have to restore files in their original disk locations. For example, suppose that you use the same computer configuration both at home and at work. Also, suppose that, while you are sick for a week at home, you type a few business letters, store them in your home computer's My Letters folder, and back up the folder to a tape. When you return to work, you'll certainly want to restore every file from the tape's backup file set. But you may not want to place them in a folder named "My Letters." Instead, you may want to restore the files to a folder named Office Memos. To restore files to an alternate location, perform these steps:

1. Select the Settings menu Options page Restore tab and click your mouse on the Alternate location, single directory option.
2. Click your mouse on the OK button.
3. To display the Restore page, click your mouse on the Restore tab.
4. In the Restore page's left section, click your mouse on the drive letter or tape drive that contains the files you want to restore.
5. Select the backup file set that contains the files you want to restore.
6. Click your mouse on the Next Step button to display a path structure.
7. Click your mouse on the box to the left of each folder you want to restore. If you want to restore selected files from a folder, click on the folder to display its files. Then, click each file you want to restore.
8. Select the location where you want the restored files to go.
9. Click your mouse on the Start Restore button to restore the files and folders you selected to the destination folder.

Verifying a File Restore Operation — 391

When you perform backup operations, you may want Backup to verify that it correctly copied files to the floppy disk or magnetic tape. Periodically, when Backup writes data to a disk or tape, a disk or tape error will prevent the data from being stored correctly. In such cases, the only way you become aware of such errors is to have Backup read its stored information, comparing the backup copy to the original file. Unfortunately, because Backup must read and compare each backup file to its original, verify operations consume a significant amount of time. If you want Backup to verify the accuracy of a restore, check the Settings menu Options Restore page advanced option labeled Verify restored data by automatically comparing files after the restore has finished. Although the verification makes the Backup program take longer to restore files and folders, the verification will assure you that the restore worked properly.

Controlling File Overwrite Operations During a Restore — 392

As Figure 392 shows, you can choose from three overwrite options when you restore a backup. The overwrite options determine what the Backup program does when you attempt to use it to restore a file or folder in place of another with the same name. Table 392 explains each option.

Option	Purpose
Never overwrite files	If Backup attempts to restore a file or folder, but the file or folder already exists on the destination drive, Backup does not restore the file.
Overwrite older files only	If Backup attempts to restore a file or folder, but the file or folder already exists on the destination drive, Backup overwrites it only if the destination file or folder is older than the one you want to restore.
Overwrite files	Backup restores all files and folders it finds.

Table 392 *The overwrite options.*

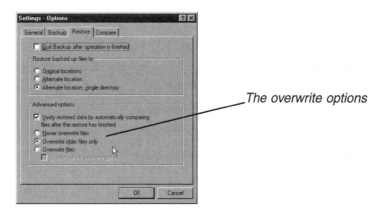

Figure 392 *The overwrite options control how restore operates.*

Comparing Files to a Backup Set — 393

When you want to make sure that the files on your disk are the same as the backup file set you have on tape, use the Backup program's Compare feature. The Compare feature neither backs up nor restores; Compare simply compares a backup file set with your disk files and reports differences in file versions. To compare a backup file set to its counterpart on your disk, perform these steps:

1. Display the Backup program's Compare page.
2. In the Compare page's left section, select the tape or disk drive that holds the backup file set.
3. In the Compare page's right section, select the backup file set from the backup that you want to compare. A tape can hold several backup file sets, so you must tell Backup which backup file set to use for the comparison.
4. Click your mouse on the Next Step button.
5. Click all or some of the folders and files you want to compare. For example, if you want to make sure your entire C: drive is backed up, click your mouse on the entire C: drive. However, if you only want to make sure a folder or specific set of files are properly backed up, you select only that folder or set of files.
6. To begin the comparison, click your mouse on the Start Compare button. The Compare process informs you of any differences it finds between the disk files and the backup file set.

394 Fragmented Disks Decrease Your System Performance

As you create, delete, add to, and edit files, your disk drives become cluttered with empty sections. Such a disk is *fragmented*. A badly fragmented disk drive slows down your computer's overall performance because file-searching routines must skip the empty spots when reading data. A single file can be fragmented, or spread in blocks, all over a disk. An unfragmented file is a file that occupies a single sequential section of a disk drive. Your programs can locate, load, and manage unfragmented files much faster than fragmented files.

If you notice your disk drive access slowing down (file operations take longer to complete), you may have to defragment your disk. When you defragment your disk, you remove the empty spots between and inside files. Additionally, you place each file in a single sequential section of the disk. You don't actually gain free disk space when you defragment, but you do make your disk access more efficient. Even if you do not notice a decrease in disk performance, you should run the Disk Defragmenter program regularly to check the disk's fragmentation and correct any fragmentation problems. Tip 395 explains how to access the Disk Defragmenter.

Note: *Before you run Disk Defragmenter, close all windows and programs except for Windows 95 to make the Disk Defragmenter program run as quickly as possible.*

395 Defragment Your Disk Using Disk Defragmenter

When you want to run the Disk Defragmenter program to defragment your disk drive, perform these steps:

1. Select the Start menu Programs option.
2. Select the Programs menu Accessories option.
3. Select the Accessories menu System Tools option.
4. Select the System Tools menu Disk Defragmenter option. Windows 95 will display the dialog box shown in Figure 395.1.
5. Select the disk drive you want to defragment. Then, click your mouse on the OK button.

The Disk Defragmenter checks the disk drive and uses the dialog box shown in Figure 395.2 to report how much, if any, of the disk is fragmented. Depending on the amount of fragmentation, you may or may not want to defragment. Disk Defragmenter will give you an evaluation and recommendation.

6. Click your mouse on either the Start button to defragment the disk drive, the Select Drive button to check another disk drive, the Advanced button to adjust Disk Defragmenter settings (see Tip 399), or the Exit button to terminate the program. If you choose to defragment the disk drive, the Disk Defragmenter program displays a window showing its progress.

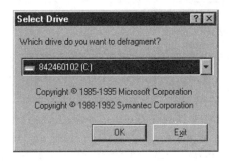

Figure 395.1 *Getting ready to defragment a disk.*

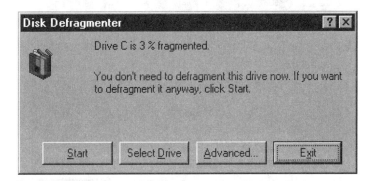

Figure 395.2 *This disk is slightly defragmented.*

Pausing, Resuming, or Ending Disk Defragmenter | 396

The defragmentation can take a while. Fortunately, if you start the Disk Defragmenter program and someone else comes along who needs to use your computer, you can pause or end the disk defragmentation process. If you pause the Disk Defragmenter program, you can run another program and resume the Disk Defragmenter when you are finished. If you end the Disk Defragmenter, you will have to restart the Disk Defragmenter all over again to defragment your disk drive.

During the defragmentation, Disk Defragmenter displays the Defragmenting status dialog box shown in Figure 396. If you click your mouse on the Stop button, Disk Defragmenter terminates. If you click your mouse on the Pause button, the Disk Defragmenter halts until you click your mouse on the Resume button (the Pause button becomes the Resume button during the pause).

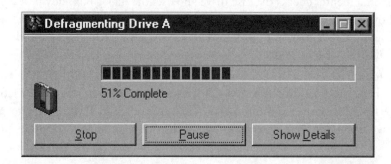

Figure 396 *You can pause, end, and resume the defragmenting.*

397 Displaying Details of Your Disk's Fragmentation

If you click your mouse on the Show Details button during a disk's defragmentation process, the Disk Defragmenter program displays a disk drive map that shows the drive's fragmented and unfragmented areas, as shown in Figure 397. The map shows you the disk's fragmented and non-fragmented areas, as well as the areas the Disk Defragmenter program will move to recollect continuous disk space.

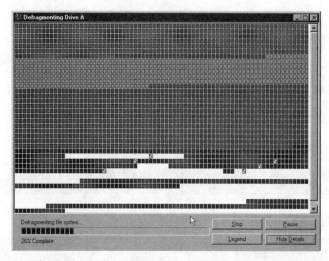

Figure 397 *The detailed defragmentation map.*

398 Understanding Disk Defragmenter's Detailed Display

If you click your mouse on the Legend button at the bottom of the Disk Defragmenter map's window, the Disk Defragmenter program displays a legend that explains what function each colored block performs. Figure 398 shows the legend. Table 398 explains the legend's details.

Legend Entry	Purpose
Optimized data	Disk data that is not fragmented
Belongs at beginning of drive	Any disk data belonging at the beginning sectors of a disk drive, such as critical-system information
Belongs in middle of drive	Data that can appear in the middle of the disk drive

Table 398 *The Disk Defragmenter legend's details. (continued on the following page)*

Legend Entry	Purpose
Belongs at end of drive	Data that belongs at the end sectors of a disk drive
Free space	Disk space that contains no data
Data that will not be moved	Rare kinds of advanced system data that Disk Defragmenter cannot move from the data's current location, even if it means that you cannot fully defragment the disk
Bad (damaged) area of the disk	A damaged part of the disk that Windows 95 marks as unusable
Data that is currently being read	The area of the disk that Disk Defragmenter is currently analyzing for fragmentation
Data that's currently being written	The area of the disk that Disk Defragmenter just analyzed and is writing to a new location

Table 398 *The Disk Defragmenter legend's details. (continued from the previous page)*

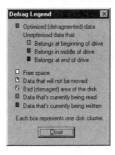

Figure 398 *Displaying a legend of the map.*

399 Understanding and Using Disk Defragmenter's Advanced Settings

When you start the Disk Defragmenter, click your mouse on the Advanced button to display the Advanced Options dialog box shown in Figure 399. Generally, the advanced options are set for a general defragmentation, and you will not need to change the settings. Nevertheless, you can customize the way that Disk Defragmenter defragments your disk drive if you wish. Table 399 explains each of the Advanced Options dialog box's settings.

Option	Purpose
Full defragmentation	Puts all file areas together in a continuous space on your disk. Also, puts the free space in a continuous block at the end of the disk. A full defragmentation ensures the best and fastest disk access in the future.
Defragment files only	Ensures that every file resides on the disk in a single, continuous block, but does not consolidate the disk's free space.
Consolidate free space only	Ensures that the free space resides in a continuous block on the disk, but does not ensure that your files will not be fragmented.
Check drive for errors	Checks your drive for errors before the defragmentation begins (strongly recommended so your errors do not get worse during the defragmentation).
This time only	Keeps changes in effect only for the current defragmentation session.
Save these options	Keeps option changes in effect for all future defragmentation sessions until you change the settings.

Table 399 *Advanced Options dialog box settings.*

Figure 399 *The Advanced Options dialog box.*

400 Understanding Disk Compression

You can use disk compression to free extra storage space on your disk drives. When Windows 95 compresses a disk, it squeezes the disk's data and thereby reduces the amount of disk space the data consumes. Windows 95 compresses the data before physically writing it on to the disk. Then, when a program requests the compressed data, Windows 95 decompresses the data and releases it to the program. Although disk compression saves disk space, some computer users will experience slight delays when reading and writing to disk because of the compression and decompression routines that Windows 95 performs. However, some computer users actually notice an *increase* in disk I/O (*input/output*) speed because the computer has to perform less mechanical disk I/O than would be required without disk compression. Windows 95 offers *DriveSpace*, a disk-compression system that you can use to gain additional disk space. Depending on the content and format of your computer files, you may be able to double the amount of free space on your disk drive when you use DriveSpace.

Note: DriveSpace supports compressed disks that you may have created with Windows 3.1 DoubleSpace and MS-DOS 6.22 DriveSpace. However, unlike DoubleSpace or MS-DOS 6.22 DriveSpace, the Windows 95 DriveSpace also protects long filenames.

401 How Drive Compression Really Works

When you use DriveSpace to increase the amount of free space on a disk drive, DriveSpace doesn't actually compress the disk. Instead, DriveSpace creates a compressed file, called the *compressed volume file* (or *CVF* for short), for the drive. Windows 95, in turn, places the CVF on an uncompressed drive called the *host drive*. The host drive is not necessarily a physical drive, but it's often a logical one. (A physical drive actually exists on your system, such as drive A or drive C. A logical drive, on the other, is a portion of the physical drive that Windows 95 allocates and uses as if it were its one drive, with its own drive letter).

For example, suppose you have only a single hard disk (your C: drive). After you compress your C: drive, your applications will think your system has two disks—the compressed C: drive and an uncompressed H: drive (host drive), which holds the CVF. Because the uncompressed host drive probably won't contain much free space, you should continue using the C: drive for your programs and data.

Note: You will not see the host drive in Explorer or the My Computer window unless the host drive has more than 2 megabytes free.

You can completely compress an existing drive or you compress only the drive's free space (that part of the drive that is not currently storing files). For example, if you have a C: drive with 100 megabytes of free space, you can run DriveSpace to turn 75 megabytes of that free space into a compressed drive named D: that holds as much as 150 megabytes. DriveSpace can compress a disk drive as large as 512 megabytes. If you have a larger hard disk, you'll have to partition the disk into multiple logical drives and compress each logical drive individually. Microsoft offers a Windows 95 add-on product called *Microsoft Plus!*, which compresses drives as large as two gigabytes (2 billion characters of storage).

Compressing a Floppy Disk for Practice | 402

Before you compress a hard disk, you may want to compress a floppy just for the practice. To start, find a floppy disk whose contents you do not need. That way, if something goes wrong during your DriveSpace practice session, you won't lose any valuable data. To practice disk compression, perform these steps:

1. Insert the floppy disk in your floppy disk drive.
2. Select the System Tools menu DriveSpace option. Windows 95 will display the DriveSpace window shown in Figure 402.1.
3. Double-click your mouse on your floppy disk drive. DriveSpace will open a Compression Properties sheet that displays your floppy disk's free and used space, as shown in Figure 402.2.
4. Click your mouse on the OK button to close the Compression Properties sheet.
5. Click your mouse on the Drive menu Compress option. DriveSpace will display the Compress a Drive window (see Figure 402.3), which shows the compression's result. Depending on the floppy disk's contents, you may gain a little or a lot of space after the compression (see Tip 404).
6. Click your mouse on the Start button.
7. Click your mouse on the Compress Now button to start the compression. After compressing the drive, DriveSpace displays a summary window that shows you the compression results.

Note: Tip 403 explains why you should always make a backup before you compress a disk.

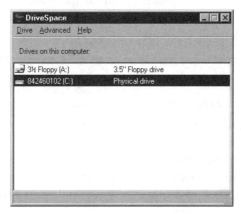

Figure 402.1 The opening DriveSpace window.

Figure 402.2 DriveSpace displays your disk space.

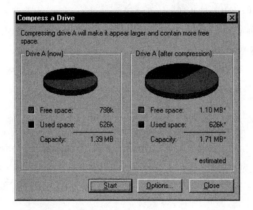

Figure 402.3 See an advanced compression status.

403 Always Back Up Your Disk Before You Compress

Generally, Windows 95's DriveSpace program works well. As such, the likelihood that the compression process will damage your disk is small. Nevertheless, if a power failure or hardware failure occurs during the compression, DriveSpace could damage your files. To be safe, make a backup of your disk before you use DriveSpace to compress it. To learn more about making backups in Windows 95, read Tips 375-393.

404 Viewing How Much Disk Space Compression Your Drive Gives You

Some files, such as word-processing documents and text files, compress better than others. Other files, such as ZIP files and optimized graphic images (such as GIF images), do not compress well because those files already contain highly compressed data. As a result, depending on the types of files that reside on them, two equal-size drives may not yield the same amount of disk space after compression. For example, if you and a friend both compress your 100Mb hard drives, you may gain 200Mb of compressed space while your friend only gains 110Mb.

Fortunately, you don't have to wait until the compression process completes to learn how much disk space you'll gain from it. When you start the compression, DriveSpace displays a window, much like the one shown in Figure 404, that tells you how much free disk space the compression will create. At that point, if you decide you don't want to continue the compression process, click your mouse on the Close button.

Note: *DriveSpace requires that the drive you want to compress contain some free space. During the compression process, DriveSpace uses the free space for a work area. If DriveSpace cannot find enough free space to compress the drive, DriveSpace informs you that you need to free space before the compression process can continue.*

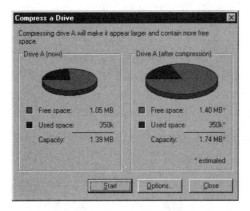

Figure 404 *Preview how much DriveSpace can free.*

Uncompressing a Drive — 405

As you work with Windows 95, there may be times when you want to uncompress a drive or floppy disk's data. For example, you may have compressed all your floppy disks but need to give one of them to a friend who does not use DriveSpace (perhaps your friend still uses Windows 3.1). If you need to uncompress a drive or floppy disk, perform these steps:

1. Select the System Tools menu DriveSpace option. Windows 95 will start DriveSpace.
2. Highlight the drive you want to uncompress.
3. Select the Drive menu Uncompress option. DriveSpace requires a certain amount of free space for a work area before the uncompress will work. If you see the Error message box shown in Figure 405, you must delete files from the compressed drive before the uncompression process will begin.
4. To uncompress the drive, click your mouse on the Start button. DriveSpace will display a dialog box asking you to confirm the operation.
5. Select Uncompress Now.

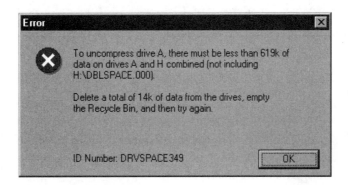

Figure 405 *The drive may not have enough room for uncompression.*

406 Mounting and Dismounting a Compressed Drive

When you start Windows 95, the operating system checks all drives to see which are compressed and uncompressed. If you use a compressed hard disk, Windows 95 recognizes that the disk is compressed upon startup. After Windows 95 starts, you can access the compressed drive normally. You'll have no visible indication that the compression process is occurring, save the extra disk space you gain from it. However, if you insert a compressed floppy disk into a disk drive, Windows 95 cannot know in advance that the floppy disk is compressed. As such, you must tell Windows 95 that you've inserted a compressed floppy disk. In DriveSpace terminology, you must *mount* the disk. To do so, select the Advanced menu Mount option. When you remove the diskette, select the Advanced menu Unmount option so you can insert additional compressed and uncompressed floppy disks.

Note: *If you use compressed floppy disks regularly, follow Tip 407's instructions to have DriveSpace automatically mount compressed disks when you insert them.*

407 Controlling Automatic Compressed Disk Mounting

To simplify floppy disk operations, you can direct DriveSpace to automatically mount and unmount compressed floppy disks that you insert into your floppy disk drive. To direct DriveSpace to automatically mount compressed floppies for you, select the DriveSpace's Advanced menu Settings option to display the DriveSpace Compression Settings dialog box shown in Figure 407. Then, check the Automatically mount new compressed devices check box.

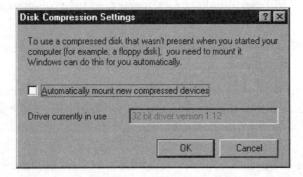

Figure 407 *DriveSpace can automatically mount floppy disk.*

408 Compressing Your Entire Hard Drive

As Tip 400 explains, disk compression lets you utilize more space on your system's hard drive. To compress your entire hard disk at once, perform these steps:

1. Click your mouse on the System Tools menu DriveSpace option.
2. Click your mouse over the hard disk you want to compress.
3. Select the Drive menu Compress option. DriveSpace will display a window that shows you the compression result. If your hard disk is more than 500 Mb, DriveSpace cannot compress the drive and will display an error message.
4. Click your mouse on the Start button.

5. Click your mouse on the Back Up Files button to make a backup of your hard disk. If you've recently used DriveSpace to create a full-system backup, you don't have to backup your hard disk before you compress it.

6. Click your mouse on the Compress Now button. DriveSpace begins to compress the drive you selected in step 2. Depending on the size of your hard disk, the compression process may take up to an hour. When DriveSpace completes the compression, DriveSpace will display a status window that shows how much your disk compressed and how much free space it now contains.

7. Click your mouse on the Yes button to restart the computer.

After you restart your system, Windows 95 will recognize the compressed drive and let you resume your work. You probably won't observe any change in the way your disk performs. The only difference you'll notice is the additional free space your disk contains. Also, if the host drive contains more than 2 Mb of free space, you will be able to use both the host drive and compressed drive for storage.

Compressing Part of Your Drive   409

If you have a disk drive with lots of free space, you can compress part of that disk drive to gain even more space. For example, if you have a one gigabyte C: drive with 250 Mb of free space, you might want to compress 100 Mb of the free space. After the compression, you will have a C: drive with 150 Mb free, a D: drive (the compressed portion of the C: drive) with up to 200 Mb of compressed free space, and a host drive (drive H:). In this case, the disk compression process adds up to 100 Mb of free space to your disk. To compress part of your drive, select the Advanced menu Create Empty option. DriveSpace displays the Create New Compressed Drive dialog box shown in Figure 409. This dialog box lets you tell DriveSpace how much of your existing drive's free space you want to use as the new compressed drive.

Note: *You may find the compressed portion of your drive useful for storing temporary files.*

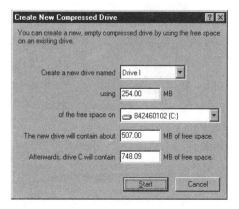

Figure 409 *Creating a compressed drive from your hard disk's free space.*

Deleting a Compressed Drive   410

As you work with Drive Space, there may be times when you want to delete a compressed drive. For example, you may have created the compressed drive to store temporary files, and you no longer need those files. When you delete a compressed drive, DriveSpace uncompresses the drive and deletes *all* its data. (If you want to uncompress a drive without deleting its contents, see Tip 405.) To delete a compressed drive, perform these steps:

1. Click on the System Tools menu DriveSpace option. Windows 95 will start DriveSpace.
2. Click your mouse on the compressed drive you want to delete. Do not click on the compressed drive's host drive.
3. Select the Advanced menu Delete option. DriveSpace will display a dialog box that tells you the data will not be available after DriveSpace deletes the drive.
4. Click your mouse on the Yes button if you want to continue with the drive deletion. After DriveSpace deletes the drive, DriveSpace will display a dialog box that informs you it has completed the deletion.
5. Click the Yes button in response to the dialog box that asks if you want to remove the compression driver. (If you had not mounted the compressed drive, you will not have to perform this step.)
6. Close the DriveSpace program.

411 Viewing a Disk's Compression Properties

Before you install a program on to a compressed drive, you may want to find out how much free space the drive contains. To find out such vital information, you can tell DriveSpace to display a properties sheet that contains all the drive's compression statistics. To do so, start DriveSpace. Then, in the DriveSpace window, select the drive whose properties you want to view. Finally, select DriveSpace's Drive menu Properties option. If the drive you selected is not compressed, DriveSpace displays a properties sheet much like the one shown in Figure 411.1. If the drive is compressed, DriveSpace displays a properties sheet like the one shown in Figure 411.2.

Figure 411.1 This drive is not compressed.

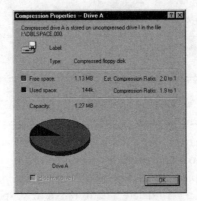

Figure 411.2 This drive is compressed.

Adjusting the Free Space on a Compressed Drive 412

Normally, DriveSpace puts as much free space as possible on a compressed drive and reserves the host drive for the compression's system information. As such, if you want to store uncompressed data on a host drive (perhaps to get slightly better performance when you access the file), you will need to transfer free space from the compressed drive to the host drive. To adjust the free space on the compressed drive, perform these steps:

1. Click your mouse on the System Tools menu DriveSpace option. Windows 95 will start DriveSpace.
2. Select the drive whose free space you want to adjust.
3. Select the Drive menu Adjust Free Space option. DriveSpace will display the Adjust Free Space dialog box shown in Figure 412.
4. To transfer free space from the compressed drive to the host drive, use your mouse to drag the dialog box's slider toward the right.
5. Click your mouse on the OK button.

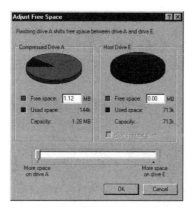

Figure 412 Adjusting the compressed drive's free space.

Understanding and Fine-Tuning Compression Ratios 413

As you use DriveSpace, you will sometimes want to change the compression ratio DriveSpace uses to compress your drive. For example, if you plan to store highly compressible files, such as text files, you may want to increase the compression ratio. To change your compressed drive's compression ratio, perform these steps:

1. Click your mouse on the System Tools menu DriveSpace option. Windows 95 will start DriveSpace.
2. Select the drive whose compression ratio you want to adjust.
3. Select the Advanced menu Change Ratio option. DriveSpace will display the Compression Ratio dialog box shown in Figure 413.
4. To increase the compression ratio, use your mouse to drag the dialog box's slider to the right.
5. Click your mouse on the OK button.

Note: *DriveSpace may not always be able to honor your compression ratio request, but DriveSpace will probably be more accurate in its compression ratio estimates once you adjust the ratio to fit the data you are about to store on the drive.*

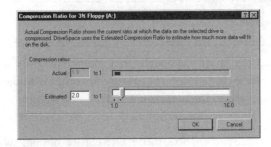

Figure 413 Adjusting the compressed drive's compression ratio.

414 Hiding or Displaying Your Host Drive

Because the host drive exists just to provide compression information for Windows 95, the operating system typically hides the host drive from view. However, if you adjust your host drive's free space (see Tip 412) so the drive contains more than 2 Mb of free space, Windows 95 automatically displays the host drive in the Explorer window, the My Computer window, and dialog boxes that contain drive information. Through DriveSpace, you can tell Windows 95 to hide or display a host drive. However, you can do so only when you compress a disk drive. When you compress a drive, click the Drive menu Compression option to display the Compress a Drive dialog box. Next, click on the Options button to display the Compression Option dialog box. Then, if you want the host drive to remain hidden no matter how much free space appears on the drive, check the Hide host drive option. If you want Windows 95 to display the host drive when the drive's free space surpasses 2 Mb, leave the Hide host drive option unchecked.

415 Formatting a Compressed Drive

If you want to erase all the information on a compressed drive, a faster way than deleting all the drive's files is to format the drive. Neither the MS-DOS FORMAT command nor the My Computer window's Format option can format compressed drives. To format a compressed drive, you must perform these steps:

1. Click your mouse on the System Tools menu DriveSpace option. Windows 95 will start DriveSpace.
2. Select the compressed drive you want to format.
3. Select the Drive menu Format option. DriveSpace will check the drive to make sure it is compressed and request that you confirm the format command. Remember that formatting erases *everything* on your disk.
4. To confirm the format command, select the Yes button.

Note: DriveSpace cannot format uncompressed disks. Use the Control Panel to format uncompressed drives.

416 Changing a Host Drive's Drive Letter

If you only have a single hard disk named C: and you compress the entire hard disk, Windows 95 will partition your disk into two logical drives—a compressed C: drive and an H: drive (or host drive). The new C: drive will hold all your data while the H: drive will contain only the compression system files. Although you cannot change a compressed drive's letter, you can change a host drive's letter. Depending on your disk, CD-ROM, and network drive configuration, there may be times when you want to assign your host drive a specific drive letter.

To change a host drive's letter, select the Advanced menu Change Letter option. DriveSpace, in turn, will display the dialog box shown in Figure 416. Using this dialog box, you can select a new name for your host drive.

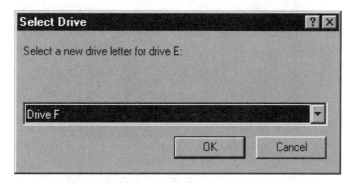

Figure 416 You can change your host drive's letter.

Looking Behind-the-Scenes with DriveSpace — 417

When you compress a disk drive, DriveSpace makes you think you've gained almost twice as much disk space as you previously had. In reality, DriveSpace compresses data on your disk so the data takes up to half as much space as before. To achieve this compression magic, DriveSpace compresses every byte of data from your disk drive and stores that compressed data on the host drive in a single file named DRVSPACE.000. DRVSPACE.000 is the compressed volume file, or CVF for short.

When you access a compressed drive, Windows 95 actually searches the huge compressed volume file on the host drive and returns the file's compressed information as if it were uncompressed. The reason you must mount a floppy disk before you can use it in your system (Windows 95 mounts compressed hard disks automatically) is that Windows 95 must know that your floppy drive contains compressed data. If you don't mount the disk, Windows 95 will view the huge CVF file as if it were just another file on the floppy and not realize that the CVF is actually a compressed image of the floppy's original contents.

Understanding and Repairing Inbox Error — 418

In previous versions of Windows, you had to navigate to different areas of your system to access your e-mail, fax, and external files. In Windows 95, the Microsoft Exchange program collects all these files for you in one convenient, easily accessible location—the Inbox. Windows 95 stores all your Inbox files as personal folder files, all of which have the PST filename extension.

Normally, your Inbox will function without a glitch. However, you will occasionally need help recovering data if some unfortunate event occurs, such as a power failure, as you try to create or access a personal file folder. Luckily, when you have trouble accessing an Inbox personal file folder, you can use the Inbox Repair Tool to help correct the problem. The Inbox Repair Tool scans your personal file folders and retrieves any recoverable data.

To start the Inbox Repair Tool, select the System Tools menu Inbox Repair Tool option. Windows 95, in turn, will display the Inbox Repair Tool window shown in Figure 418. Next, enter the name of the personal folder file that is giving you trouble. (You can click your mouse over the Browse button to search for the file.) After you select a file, click on the Start button to search for and repair errors. The Options button lets you specify whether or not you want a log file to record the error and repair session.

Note: *The Inbox Repair Tool will not appear on your menu unless you have installed Microsoft Exchange.*

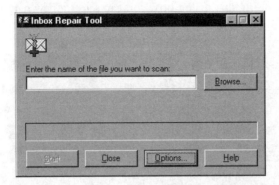

Figure 418 *The Inbox Repair Tool window.*

419 | Understanding System Resources and the Resource Meter

Your system has a number of hardware resources that play critical roles in the way your system functions. For example, your system's CPU executes all your programs, your PC's RAM holds all currently running programs (including Windows 95), and your computer's drive contain your programs' data. How efficiently Windows 95 allocates and consumes such hardware resources will often determine how well your system performs.

Note: *Generally, the more RAM your computer has, the faster Windows 95 performs. However, depending on your computer's CPU and disk drive speed, extra RAM may or may not improve performance.*

To measure its own use of RAM, Windows 95 uses three special resource values: System resources, User resources, and GDI resources (see Tip 420 for an explanation of each resource). These values tell you how much RAM memory Windows 95 is using and how much remains for additional processing.

To see the Windows 95 special resource values, click the System Tools menu Resource Meter option. Windows 95, in turn, will start the Resource Meter and display it as a green icon next to your Taskbar clock. To display the Resource Meter window shown in Figure 419, double-click the green icon.

When you click your mouse on the OK button, the Resource Meter window disappears, but the Taskbar icon remains. To eliminate the Taskbar icon, right-click the icon and select the pop-up menu's Exit option.

If your System Tools menu does not contain the Resource Meter option, you can use the Control Panel's Add/Remove Programs icon to install the Resource Meter from your Windows 95 installation CD-ROM or floppy disks.

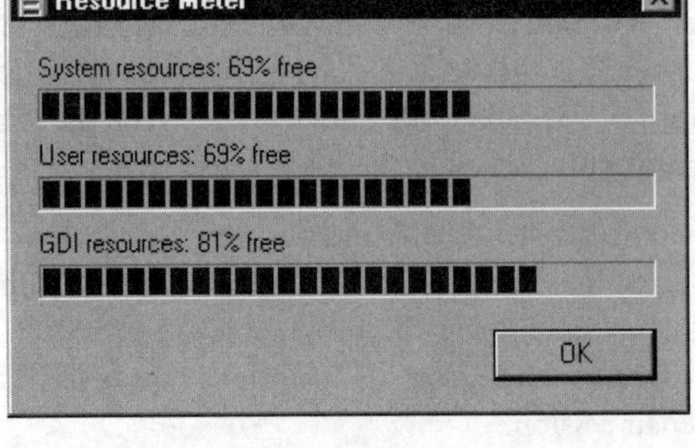

Figure 419 *The Resource Meter window.*

Understanding the Resource Monitor's Output | 420

As Tip 419 explains, the Resource Meter lets you monitor these system resources:

- *System resource*: A combination percentage of the User and GDI resources consumed. Generally, your System resource value will match the User resource value unless you are running graphically intensive Windows 95 programs.

- *User resources*: The percentage of resources devoted to user system components, such as open windows, running programs, menus, and dialog boxes.

- *GDI (Graphics Device Interface) resources*: The percentage of resources devoted to graphics, such as icons and figures.

Windows 95 manages these system resources more effectively than Windows 3.1 did. Windows 95 can move its 32-bit resources to upper memory regions, whereas Windows 3.1 could not move its 16-bit system resources. As such, you normally do not have to worry about your system resources. However, when you multitask several large programs, you should check the Resource Meter periodically to ensure that you have enough available system resources to keep your system stable. If any of your resources fall below 35%, you may not be able to load another program or continue running a program currently in memory without exiting.

Understanding and Repairing Disk Errors | 421

As you use Windows 95, your disk may acquire errors that prevent you from accessing certain files. For example, your disk might acquire an error if your system experiences a power failure as it tries to write a data file. Or, you might run a program that contains an error (called a *bug*) that corrupts a disk file. Fortunately, Windows 95 includes the *ScanDisk,* a program that can test for, and often repair, disk errors. When ScanDisk detects an error in a certain area of your disk, Scandisk moves the area's data to another disk location. Additionally, ScanDisk marks the area where the error occurred so no future programs use it. Of course, depending on the nature of the problem, ScanDisk may not be able to recover all your data. If a bad area occurs in a program file, the program is almost always unusable, and you'll have to reinstall the program. To start ScanDisk, click your mouse on the System Tools menu ScanDisk option. Windows 95, in turn, will display the opening ScanDisk window, as shown in Figure 421. Depending on your computer usage, you should run ScanDisk every week or so to make sure your disks contain no errors that could lead to data loss.

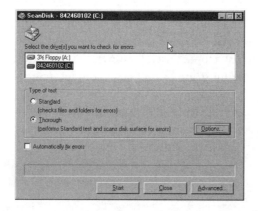

Figure 421 *ScanDisk's initial window.*

422 Using ScanDisk's Standard Check

As Tip 421 explains, ScanDisk is a Windows 95 program that tests for, and often repairs, disk errors. In its opening window, ScanDisk presents you with two test-type options—Standard and Thorough. If you select the ScanDisk Standard option, ScanDisk detects and usually fixes the following problems:

- Directory errors
- DriveSpace compressed drive errors
- FAT (*File Allocation Table*) errors
- File system errors, such as lost file fragments clusters and cross-linked files
- Long filename errors

The Standard test takes less time than the Thorough test (see Tip 423). Furthermore, Standard tests detect and correct most problems. However, the Standard test may not catch every error, especially physical problems with the disk's surface, such as weak magnetic signals.

423 Using ScanDisk's Thorough Check

Like ScanDisk's Standard test, the Thorough test scans and usually fixes the problems that Tip 422 lists. In addition, the Thorough test checks your disk's surface for bad locations and marks such locations so no future programs will use them. As such, if you experience any disk reading or writing problems, you should run ScanDisk's Thorough test.

Note: *The Thorough test requires more time to complete than the Standard test, but the Thorough test is more exhaustive.*

You should run ScanDisk about once a week, depending on your computer usage, to make sure your disks contain no errors that could cause data loss. Additionally, you should select ScanDisk's Thorough option about every third or fourth time you run ScanDisk (select the Standard option the other times).

424 Controlling ScanDisk's Thorough Check Surface Scan

As Tip 421 explains, ScanDisk is a Windows 95 program that tests for, and often repairs, disk errors. However, using ScanDisk often involves a tradeoff between speed and thoroughness. If you choose ScanDisk's Standard test, ScanDisk will detect and usually fix the errors that Tip 422 lists. However, the Standard test will not detect every problem. To run a more comprehensive check, you must use ScanDisk's Thorough test, which requires more time to complete than the Standard test. Fortunately, ScanDisk gives you a solution to this problem. To minimize the amount of extra time a Thorough test requires, you can tell ScanDisk how to conduct the test. To do so, select the Thorough option button on ScanDisk's initial window. Then, click the Options button to display the Surface Scan Options dialog box shown in Figure 424. Table 424 explains each of the ScanDisk options.

Option	Purpose
System and data areas	Scans both the system areas and the non-system areas of your disk.
System area only	Scans only the system areas of your disk, including the FAT and directory areas.
Data area only	Scans the non-system areas of your disk, including your disk's data and program file areas.
Do not perform write-testing	To detect write errors, a Thorough test must write to each location on your disk and then immediately read that location to see if the write worked or failed. If you check this option, ScanDisk will disable the write-testing, and the Thorough test will complete faster. However, the test will not be as reliable as it would be if you performed write-testing.
Do not repair bad sectors in hidden and system files	Keeps ScanDisk from repairing certain bad disk locations. In rare instances, programs write bad sectors to specific hidden and system locations on your disk to create a copy-protection algorithm. Although such programs are rare these days, they do still exist. If the program manual describes such a copy protection scheme, check this option to ensure that ScanDisk does not confuse the copy protection scheme.

Table 424 The ScanDisk Thorough test options.

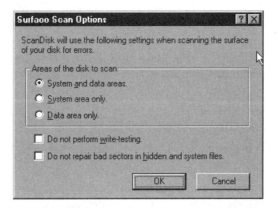

Figure 424 Modifying the thorough scanning options.

Controlling Whether or Not ScanDisk Automatically Corrects Errors | 425

If you check the ScanDisk option labeled Automatically fix errors, which appears in ScanDisk's initial window, ScanDisk makes every attempt to fix errors as it scans your disk. ScanDisk follows a set of pre-defined guidelines for fixing errors (see Tip 426). If you do not know a lot about the technicalities of disk storage, check the Automatically fix errors option to let ScanDisk use conventional repair methods to fix errors it encounters. After you check this box, ScanDisk will detect and fix most of the problems it finds. However, there may be times when you need to adjust ScanDisk's error-fixing guidelines to make the program more effective. Tip 426 discusses some of the adjustments you can make.

Note: *If you are an inexperienced user, you may want to stick with the Automatically fix error option until you understand more about how Windows 95 and ScanDisk function.*

426 Understanding and Using ScanDisk's Advanced Options

As Tip 425 explains, ScanDisk's conventional repair methods will detect and fix most disk problems. However, there may be times when you need to adjust ScanDisk's error-fixing guidelines to increase the program's effectiveness. To do so, click your mouse on ScanDisk's Advanced button, which appears in the initial ScanDisk window. ScanDisk, in turn, will display the Advanced Options dialog box shown in Figure 426. This dialog box's options control the way that ScanDisk displays its findings and attempts to correct errors. Table 426 explains each of these options.

Option	Purpose
Display summary	You can direct ScanDisk to display a summary always, never, or only if errors occur. If you set up ScanDisk to run automatically upon Windows 95 startup (by copying the ScanDisk program to the Startup folder) or if you schedule ScanDisk to run in the middle of the night (using the Microsoft Plus! program), you probably will not want ScanDisk to display a summary unless ScanDisk encounters errors.
Log File	You can tell ScanDisk to replace, add to, or ignore the ScanDisk log file (see Tip 427) during each scan.
Lost file fragments	Occasionally, due to a disk error, parts of a file, called fragments, are essential broken away from the file. If you check the Free option, ScanDisk deletes such *lost file fragments*, leaving you with extra disk space. If you request that ScanDisk convert the fragments to files, ScanDisk creates a sequential file for each fragment and names such files FILE0000.CHK, FILE0001.CHK, and so on. ScanDisk stores the fragment files in the computer's root directory.
Cross-linked files	If you click on Make copies, each cross-linked file receives its own copy of the cross-linked cluster. Next, determine which file contains the correct information and then delete the second file.
Check files for	You can tell ScanDisk to check files for invalid filenames and date-and-time stamps.
Check host drive first	If you use a compressed disk drive (see Tips 400 through 417), you can request that ScanDisk check the host drive for errors before checking the compressed drive. This option is useful because compressed drive errors often relate to host drive errors.

Table 426 The purpose of ScanDisk's Advanced Options.

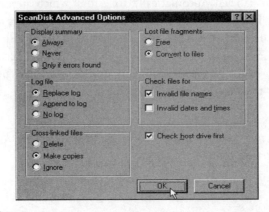

Figure 426 The ScanDisk Advanced Options settings.

Using ScanDisk's Error Log

When you run ScanDisk and request a log file, ScanDisk creates or adds to SCANDISK.LOG, a file that contains the details of the most recent scan. ScanDisk stores the file in the root directory of your C: drive. If ScanDisk finds errors during the scanning process, ScanDisk writes those errors to the log file. If you choose not to fix errors during the scanning process, you can use the log file to fix the errors later. Here is a sample of an error log file:

```
*******************
Microsoft ScanDisk for Windows

NOTE: If you use an MS-DOS program to view this file, some of the
characters may appear incorrectly. Use a Windows program such as
Notepad instead.

Log file generated at 16:28 on 9/29/1999.

ScanDisk used the following options:
  Thorough test
  Check dates and times

Drive 842460102 (C:) contained the following errors:

The C:\WINDOWS\TEMP

folder contained incorrect information about Copy of ~DF2B1.TMP
(MS-DOS name COPYOF~1.TMP):

The file or folder's long name was stored incorrectly on your disk.

  Resolution: Repair the error
  Results: Error was corrected as specified above.

The C:\PBTOOLS\WINTEMP
folder contained incorrect information about ~WRD0003.doc (MS-DOS
name ~WRD0003.DOC):

The last-modified date or time for the file or folder was invalid.

The date or time on which the file or folder was created was in-
valid.
  Resolution: Repair the error
  Results: Error was corrected as specified above.

ScanDisk found errors on this drive and fixed them all.
```

428 Fixing Lost File Fragments

A *lost file fragment* generally occurs when you delete a file and, because of power losses or program errors, Windows 95 does not delete all the file's fragments from the disk. ScanDisk cannot completely fix lost file fragments. However, ScanDisk can store any lost file fragments it finds.

If you click the Free option button, which appears in the Scandisk Advanced Options dialog box (see Tip 426), ScanDisk deletes all lost file fragments from your disk drive. If you click the Convert to files option button, ScanDisk stores each fragment in files named FILE0000.CHK, FILE0001.CHK, and so on.

If you request that ScanDisk save these lost file fragments, you can later use Notepad to look at the fragment files. Often, you will not recognize the information in the files, and you can safely delete the files. Other times, you will recognize data as being data you deleted long ago and no longer need. You might see information in the files that you recognize, but you know that the information is safely stored away elsewhere. You can usually delete the ScanDisk lost file fragments once you've reviewed those files. If you run across data that you've been looking for, you may be able to use Notepad's cut and paste features to salvage some of the data, especially if the data is textual data.

429 Fixing Cross-Linked Files

A *cross-linked file* is a file that occurs when two or more filenames incorrectly point to the same location on your disk drive. You can direct ScanDisk to delete cross-linked files or make copies of them, which you can use Notepad to review. Cross-linked files are much rarer than lost file fragments. As with lost file fragments, if you do not recognize cross-linked file contents, you can generally delete the saved cross-linked files that ScanDisk creates. If ScanDisk reports cross-linked files, check your ScanDisk log to determine the names ScanDisk used to store copies of those cross-linked files. Once ScanDisk makes copies of the cross-linked files (assuming you did not check the Advanced window's Delete option), ScanDisk removes the cross-links from your disk.

430 Faxing With Windows 95

Microsoft Fax, the Windows 95 fax program, lets you use your PC to send and receive faxes. You can access Microsoft Fax in one of three ways: from the Accessories menu (which you access through the Start menu), from your Windows 95 word processor, or from a shortcut icon on your Desktop (Tip 107 explains how to create a shortcut icon).

When you create a document in a Windows 95 word processor, such as Word for Windows, you can fax that document as easily as you can print it. When you print a document, use the Print dialog box to select your regular Windows 95 printer. When you fax, use the Print dialog box to select your fax printer driver.

Microsoft Fax includes a fax Cover Page Editor that lets you create your own cover pages. Using the Cover Page Editor, you can create your cover pages from scratch or modify the sample cover pages that Microsoft Fax provides.

431 Using the Fax Cover Page Editor

As you may know, a fax cover page gives the recipient of your fax several vital pieces of information. Typically, the fax cover page tells who sent the fax, who should receive the fax, how many pages the fax contains, where the recipient can reach the fax sender, and so on. Without such information, your fax may not reach its final destination. For example, in a large organization, dozens of people may receive faxes from the same fax machine. For your fax to land on the correct desk, it must have a cover sheet that provides proper routing information in an easily accessible format.

Fortunately, the Windows 95 Cover Page Editor lets you manage, create, and edit cover pages to send with your faxes. Every time you send a fax from within Windows 95, Microsoft Fax lets you access the Cover Page Editor to add a cover page to your fax. To start the Cover Page Editor, perform these steps:

1. Click on the Start button.
2. Select the Start menu Programs option.
3. Select the Programs menu Accessories option.
4. Select the Accessories menu Fax option.
5. Select the Fax menu Cover Page Editor option. Windows 95 opens the Cover Page Editor window and shows you a Cover Page Editor startup tip, as shown in Figure 431.1.
6. Click your mouse on the OK button to access the Cover Page Editor window shown in Figure 431.2.

Note: *The Cover Page Editor window shows only a portion of the cover page. Use the scroll bars to display additional portions of the page.*

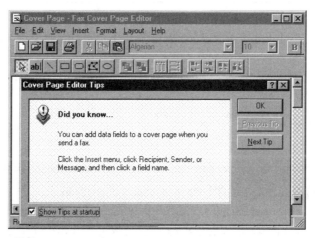

Figure 431.1 *The Cover Page Editor startup tip.*

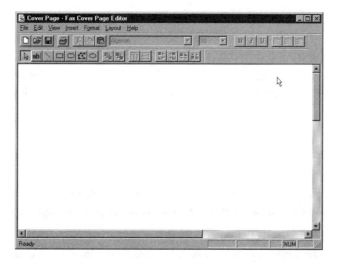

Figure 431.2 *The Cover Page Editor window.*

432 Using an Existing Fax Cover Sheet

All the cover page samples that come with the Cover Page Editor have a CPE filename extension. Windows 95 uses the extension to determine cover page file types. As such, any cover pages you create using the Cover Page Editor will also have the CPE extension. To open an existing fax cover sheet file (there are several in the Windows directory), perform these steps:

1. Use the steps in Tip 431 to start the Cover Page Editor.
2. Select the File menu Open option. The Cover Page Editor will display an Open dialog box that shows only folders and cover page files that have the CPE extension.
3. Select a cover page.
4. Click your mouse on the Open button.

Table 432 describes the sample cover sheet files you'll find with the Cover Page Editor.

Cover sheet file	Purpose
CONFIDENTIAL!	Informs the fax recipient that the fax contents are confidential.
FOR YOUR INFORMATION	Informs the fax recipient that the fax contents are informational and not necessarily confidential or urgent.
GENERIC	Displays only a simple fax banner with the recipient's name, address, and fax number.
URGENT!	Informs the fax recipient that the fax contents are timely.

Table 432 Sample cover sheets that come with the Cover Page Editor.

433 Customizing an Existing Fax Cover Sheet

One of the best ways to create your own fax cover sheet is to change an existing cover sheet and save the file under your own fax cover sheet filename. For example, you can start with an existing cover sheet and alter the text it contains. Additionally, you can add your own graphics or text to the cover sheet. The Cover Page Editor contains tools you can use to add and edit both text and art. Many of the Cover Page Editor's tools work like those you'll find in the Windows 95 Paint program. If you want to create a new cover sheet from an existing one, perform these steps:

1. Use the steps in Tip 432 to open an existing fax cover sheet. If you maximize the Cover Page Editor window, the editing is easier.
2. Click on the object you want to change. The Cover Page Editor will display *sizing handles* around the object. As Figure 433 shows, the handles appear as eight black boxes; these boxes let you size the object.
3. Press the DEL key if you want to delete the object.
4. Click your mouse on the Drawing toolbar Text button (the button labeled ab|) if you want to add your own text. (Tip 435 explains how to use the toolbar.)
5. After you click your mouse on the text tool, drag your mouse to the area where you want to add text and release the mouse when the text area that appears is large enough to hold text.
6. Type your text in the text area and press ENTER.
7. When you've finished making your edits, select the File menu Print command to make a cover sheet printout.

8. Select the File menu Save As option to save your changes under a new name. Remember to use the CPE file extension.

Subsequent tips more fully explain how you use the Cover Page Editor.

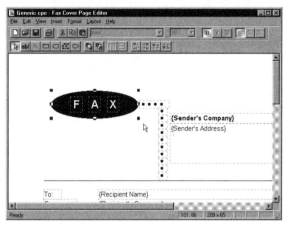

Figure 433 *Sizing handles appear around the objects you select.*

Creating a New Fax Cover Sheet — 434

If you can't (or don't wish to) use or modify the sample fax cover sheets that come with Windows 95, you can use the Cover Page Editor to create your own fax cover sheet from scratch. To create a fax cover sheet, perform these steps:

1. Use the steps in Tip 431 to start the Cover Page Editor.
2. Select the File menu New command. The Cover Page Editor will open a blank fax cover page.
3. Use the Drawing toolbar to select and place text and graphics on the new cover sheet, which appears in the Cover Page Editor window's work area. If you have a graphics file that contains your company's logo, you might want to put the logo at the top of the fax sheet.
4. When you've completed the fax cover sheet, select the File menu Save As option.

Using the Fax Cover Page Drawing Toolbar — 435

The Drawing toolbar, which appears directly above the Cover Page Editor window's work area, gives you one-button access to many cover-sheet drawing and styling tools. If you cannot see the toolbar when you start the Cover Page Editor, select the View menu Drawing Toolbar option. If you see the Drawing toolbar and want to turn it off, select the View menu Drawing Toolbar option once again to hide the Drawing toolbar. Table 435 explains the function of each of the Drawing toolbar's buttons.

Toolbar Icon	Purpose
	Selects the mouse pointer and deselects any other toolbar button.

Table 435 *The Cover Page Editor Drawing toolbar lets you perform common tasks. (continued on the following page)*

Toolbar Icon	Purpose
ab|	Lets you add text to the cover page.
\	Draws lines.
▭	Draws rectangles.
▢	Draws rounded rectangles.
⬠	Draws polygons.
⬭	Draws ellipses.
⬚	Brings graphics to the front of text.
⬚	Sends graphics to the back of text.
|||	Equally spaces selected items across the cover page.
≡	Equally spaces selected items down the cover page.
⊣	Left-aligns selected items.
⊢	Right-aligns selected items.
⊤	Top-aligns selected items.
⊥	Bottom-aligns selected items.

Table 435 The Cover Page Editor Drawing toolbar lets you perform common tasks. (continued from the previous page)

Placing a Text Object on a Fax Cover Sheet   436

To place text on a fax cover page, you use the Drawing toolbar Text button. To add text to a cover page, perform these steps:

1. Click your mouse on the Drawing toolbar Text button (the second toolbar button). The Cover Page Editor mouse pointer will change to a plus sign.
2. Move your mouse pointer to the location where you want to add text.
3. Hold your left mouse button at the upper-right position of the text you want to add to the cover sheet. Drag the mouse to create a text frame in which the text will appear.
4. Release the mouse button to anchor the text frame. Figure 436.1 shows a text frame.
5. Open the Font pull-down list and select a font style.
6. Open the Font Size pull-down list and select a font size.
7. Type the text that you want to appear in the text frame. Figure 436.2 shows text that appears in the text frame.
8. After you type the text, you can continue to move, size, and format the text.

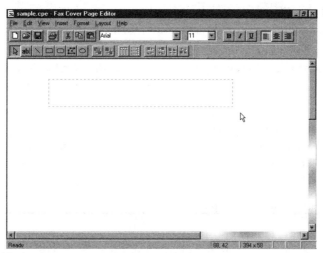

Figure 436.1 *The text frame holds the text you type.*

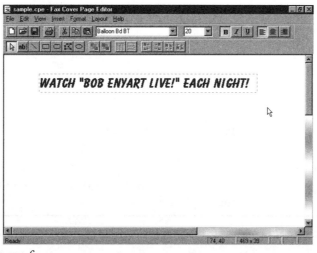

Figure 436.2 *Text appears in the text frame.*

437 Using Pre-defined Text Frames

To simplify your fax cover page creation, you can insert pre-defined text frames. The Cover Page Editor includes common text elements usually included on fax cover pages. The pre-defined text frames keep you from having to change a cover page for each fax recipient. As long as Microsoft Fax has the text frame's information, Microsoft Fax inserts the proper name, address, or other piece of data into the correct location when you send the fax. When you select the Insert menu Recipient, Sender, or Message options, you can insert the following pre-defined text frames:

Name	Fax number	Company
Street address	City	State
Zip Code	Title	Department
Office location	Home telephone number	Office telephone number
To: List	Note	Subject
Time start	Number of pages	Number of attachments

438 Controlling a Text Frame's Font

After you've typed text into a text frame, you can add other objects to the fax cover sheet, such as graphics and pre-defined objects. If you later need to change an object, you can select that text by clicking your mouse over the object's text. The Cover Page Editor, in turn, will display sizing handles around the text to indicate that you've selected the text.

On the Style toolbar, which appears directly beneath the Cover Page Editor window's menu bar, you will find tools you can use to format the characters you type into text frames. If you do not see the Style toolbar, select the View menu Style Toolbar option. Table 438 explains the purpose of each Style toolbar button. The eight rightmost Style toolbar buttons let you control text formatting.

Style Toolbar Button	Purpose
[new page icon]	Creates a new cover page.
[open folder icon]	Opens an existing cover page.
[save disk icon]	Saves the current cover page.
[printer icon]	Prints the current cover page.
[scissors icon]	Cuts selected items from the cover page and sends those items to the Clipboard.

Table 438 The Cover Page Editor Style toolbar lets you format text. (continued on the following page)

Style Toolbar Button	Purpose
📋	Copies selected items from the cover page to the Clipboard.
📋	Pastes the Clipboard contents onto the cover page.
Courier ▼	Pulls down to display font names.
20 ▼	Pulls down to display font sizes.
B	Boldfaces selected text.
I	Italicizes selected text.
U	Underlines selected text.
≡	Left-justifies text inside a selected text frame.
≡	Centers text inside the selected text frame.
≡	Right-justifies text inside a selected text frame.

Table 438 *The Cover Page Editor Style toolbar lets you format text. (continued from the previous page)*

Aligning Text within Text Frames — 439

You can use the three rightmost Style toolbar buttons to align text within text frames. Figure 439 shows the result of using left-, center-, and right-alignment on three text frames. If you drag a text frame's edges and thus change the frame's size, the Cover Page Editor changes the alignment to keep the text properly aligned within the frame's borders.

Note: *The Cover Page Editor views all the text within a text frame as one object. As such, you cannot change the format, size, or alignment of only a few characters inside a text frame. For example, you can not italicize a few characters inside a text frame; you must italicize the text frame's entire contents.*

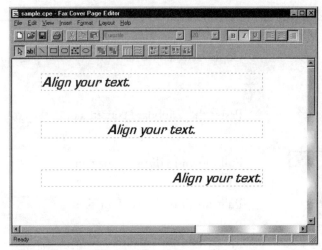

Figure 439 *Three ways you can align your text in text frames.*

440 Using Grid Lines to Align Objects

If you move and size text and graphic objects by dragging them with your mouse, you will want to align those objects so they appear neatly spaced on your cover page. To help you align objects in neater rows and columns and to help you space fax cover sheet objects evenly, the Cover Page Editor lets you turn on *grid lines*, as shown in Figure 440.1 (use the View menu Grid Lines option).

The grid lines will not show in the final cover page; they serve only as guides for your cover page design. Figure 440.2 shows a badly aligned fax cover page. Figure 440.3 shows the same cover page after the designer used grid lines to align the page's objects.

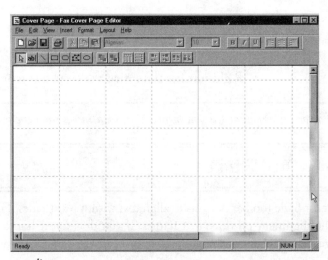

Figure 440.1 *Use grid lines for even alignment.*

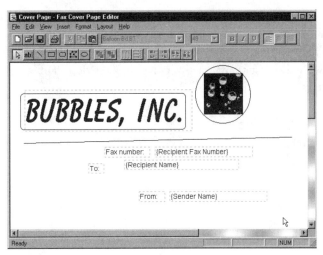

Figure 440.2 *A badly-aligned cover sheet.*

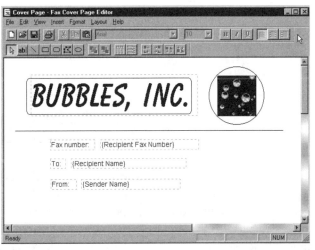

Figure 440.3 *A well-aligned cover sheet.*

Placing a Graphics Object on a Fax Cover Sheet | 441

In previous tips, you learned that the Cover Page Editor lets you add graphic elements (such as dividing lines, circled objects, and borders) to your cover sheets. As Tip 435 explains, the Drawing toolbar contains several tools you can use to select and draw various graphic elements. To add a circle, rectangle, or ellipse, perform these steps:

1. Click the Drawing toolbar button that activates the Drawing tool you want to use.
2. Move your mouse pointer to the location at which you want the object's upper-left corner to reside.
3. Click and hold your left mouse button to start drawing the object.
4. Drag the mouse pointer down and to the right until you've sized the object properly.
5. Release your left mouse button to anchor the object.

Note: *When you draw graphic elements, you should size them at the time you initially place them in the Cover Page Editor window's work area. However, if you later need to adjust the size or shape, you can click your mouse on the object to display the sizing handles.*

To draw a polygon (a figure with three or more sides), click the Drawing toolbar Polygon button. After you draw one side, click your left mouse button to anchor that side. When you finish drawing the polygon, double-click your left mouse button to anchor the figure. If you do not completely enclose each side of the polygon, the Cover Page Editor will connect your last line with the first point on the polygon to enclose it. Figure 441 shows a cover page that contains several graphic objects.

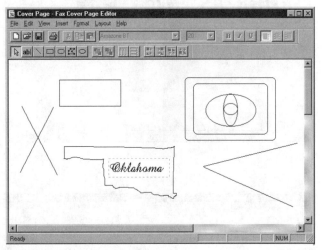

Figure 441 *A cover page can hold several graphic objects.*

442 Selecting and Working with Fax Cover Sheet Objects

When you select an object, the sizing handles that appear around the object determine how you can size and shape it. Eight sizing handles appear when you select an ellipse. Ten or more sizing handles can appear around polygons, depending on how many polygon sides you drew. When you click your left mouse button over a handle and drag your mouse, that handle's edge follows the mouse pointer movement and expands or contracts the object's size and shape. You can also use your mouse to perform a number of other common operations with cover page objects. For example, you can use your mouse to move an object to a new location. To do so, click your mouse over the object. Then, move your mouse pointer to any of the object's sides. The Cover Page Editor, in turn, will transform your mouse pointer into a plus sign with four arrows on each end. You can use this reshaped mouse pointer to move the object. Additionally, you can use your mouse to delete an object, as well as copy or send an object to the Clipboard. To delete an object, click on the object and press the DEL key. To copy an object to the Clipboard, select the object and then select the Edit menu Copy option. To cut an object to the Clipboard, select the Edit menu Cut option.

Note: *To select multiple objects, hold down the CTRL key as you move your mouse pointer over each object and click your left mouse button. You can then copy, cut, or move all the objects as a group.*

If you don't want to use your mouse to select objects, you can press the TAB and SHIFT-TAB keys to move the highlighted selection back and forth across the cover page's objects.

443 Sending a Fax Cover Sheet Object to the Front or Back

The objects that you place on a cover sheet may overlap one another. For example, Figure 443.1 shows a dark ellipse covering a text frame. Notice how you can't read the text frame's contents. In this situation, the cover page designer has two options. He or she can select the text frame and then click the Drawing toolbar Bring to Front button. Or, the cover page designer can select the ellipse and click the Drawing toolbar Send to Back buttons. Either way, Cover

Page Editor will bring the text frame to the front, as shown in Figure 443.2. Using these two toolbar buttons, you can make sure that the correct objects are always in the foreground on your fax cover sheets.

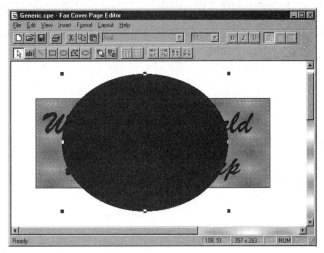

Figure 443.1 *The ellipse hides the text.*

Figure 443.2 *The text now appears on top of the ellipse.*

Inserting Other Fax Cover Sheet Objects — 444

As you have learned, Cover Page Editor lets you insert pre-defined text frames into your cover sheets. Additionally, you can also insert special graphics and other objects from outside the Cover Page Editor. For example, if you use CorelDRAW! to create a bitmap company logo, you can place that CorelDRAW! logo on your cover page. You can even insert Excel worksheets and Word documents if you wish. To insert an object into your cover sheet, perform these steps:

1. Select the Insert menu Object option. The Cover Page Editor will display the Insert Object dialog box shown in Figure 444.

2. Click your mouse on the Create from File option button. Only select the Create New option button if you wanted to insert a new object and create the object from scratch, and then select OK.

3. Type the pathname and filename for the object. You can click your mouse on the Browse button to search your computer for the object you want to insert.
4. Select OK. The Cover Page Editor will insert the object into your cover sheet.

Note: *The object you insert in step 4 is **OLE-compatible**. As such, when you double click your mouse on the object, the object's parent program menus appear so you can edit and modify the object using its native program. When you click your mouse over a different cover page object, the Cover Page Editor's regular menus appear once again.*

If you want to create new objects from scratch, such as a CorelDRAW! image, click your mouse on the Insert Object dialog box Create New option and select the proper parent program from the Object Type pull-down list. When you click your mouse on the OK button, the Cover Page Editor's menus change to those of the object's parent program. You can then use the parent program to create the object before you return (use a File menu exit option) to the Cover Page Editor to complete the cover page.

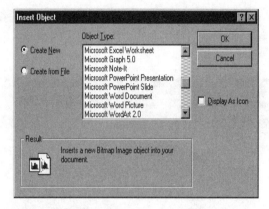

Figure 444 *There are several kinds of objects you can insert.*

445 Using Lines, Fills, and Colors on a Fax Cover Sheet

After you add text and graphic objects to your cover sheets, you can change the style of those objects in the following ways:
- Change the line thickness to create wider lines and shape outlines
- Change the object's line and internal colors
- Change the text color

When you select a text frame or graphic object and then select the Format menu Line, Fill and Color option, a Line, Fill and Color dialog box appears, as shown in Figure 445. If you want a border around the object, check the Draw border/line option. Then, use the Thickness and Color controls to specify the border's width and color. The width appears in points and defaults to 1.

The Fill Color options let you change the background color of an object. If you want an object to display a background color, select the Color option button, open the Color pull-down list, and choose a color. To change the color of an object's text, open the Text color pull-down list and choose a color. When you finish selecting object borders and colors, click the OK button to have Cover Page Editor implement your changes.

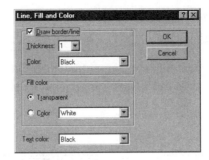

Figure 445 Change an object's line sizes, fill colors, and text colors.

Aligning Fax Cover Sheet Objects | 446

As Tip 439 explains, Cover Page Editor lets you align text inside a text frame's boundaries. Additionally, you can make page-alignments for your cover sheet's graphic objects and text frames. The Cover Page Editor window's Layout menu contains three options that let you align one or more selected cover page objects:

- *Align Objects*: Left-, right-, top-, and bottom-aligns objects with one another. When you select multiple objects, the Align Objects option aligns those objects with the rightmost-, leftmost-, uppermost-, or lowermost-object in the selection. For example, if you wanted to align a series of text frames in a single margin down your cover sheet's left side, you would select the Align Objects menu Left option. The Align Objects menu Horizontal Center and Vertical Center options center selected objects along an imaginary center line.

- *Space Evenly*: Uniformly spaces selected objects horizontally or vertically on the cover page.

- *Center on Page*: Centers one or more objects vertically or horizontally on the cover page.

Duplicating Fax Cover Sheet Objects | 447

As you create your fax cover pages, there may be times when you may want to use the same image at several locations on the page. Rather than recreate or reinsert that object at each location, you can copy the object to the Clipboard and then paste it wherever you like, as many times as you like. To make copies of cover page objects, perform these steps:

1. Select the object or objects you want to copy to the Clipboard.
2. Select the Edit menu Copy option. Windows 95 will copy the selected object or objects to the Clipboard.
3. Select the Edit menu Paste command. The Cover Page Editor will paste the Clipboard object or objects on to the cover page.
4. Move the pasted objects to their final destination.

Using the Fax Cover Sheet Paste Board | 448

If you've ever moved furniture, you know how useful it is to have an empty room in which you can store some of your chairs, nightstands, and book shelves while you figure out where the larger items go. With most of the furniture out of the way, you can easily move around and rearrange the couch, coffee table, entertainment center, and whatever else remains. Cover Page Editor's paste board, which is the gray area on the Cover Page Editor window's right side, is like that empty room—you can use it to store objects you've created but aren't ready to place on the cover sheet. When you drag objects to the paste board, they remain within reach but don't appear on the cover sheet. If you decide to add the objects later, you can drag them back from the paste board to the cover sheet.

Note: *If you cannot see the paste board, use the horizontal scroll bar to scroll to the right to bring the paste board into view.*

449 Sending a Fax

One of the truly revolutionary features of Windows 95 is the numerous ways it lets you send faxes from your computer. From within your Windows 95 word-processing applications, as well as from multiple points in the operating system, you can access your computer's fax/modem. To send a fax in Windows 95, you can use the following methods:

- Print from your Windows 95 application. When you do send a fax from within an application, select your fax printer driver.

- Open the Printers window and drag your system's fax printer driver to the Desktop. Then, when you want to fax a document, you can drag the document's icon from My Computer or Explorer to the Desktop fax icon.

- Use Microsoft Exchange to send a message as a fax.

- Start the Compose New Fax application from the Accessories menu Fax option, which you can access through the Start menu.

Each method starts Windows 95's Compose New Fax wizard, whose opening screen appears in Figure 449.1. After the Compose New Fax wizard starts, complete the fax by performing these steps:

1. Using the I'm dialing from pull-down list, select the location from where you are sending the fax. Most people send only from a single location, so their I'm dialing from pull-down list contains only a single location.

2. Click your mouse on the Next button.

3. Enter the recipient's name and fax number. Or, click your mouse on the Address Book button and select the recipient if he or she appears in your address book file. If you want to send the fax to multiple recipients, click your mouse over the Add to List button after you type in each recipient's name and fax number. Figure 449.2 shows a fax recipient list that contains two recipients.

4. Click your mouse on the Next button.

5. Select a cover page and click your mouse on the Next button.

6. Enter a subject and note. If you selected a cover page in step 5, the note and subject will appear on that cover page. If you didn't, the subject and note will appear on a separate piece of paper.

7. Click your mouse on the Next button.

8. If you started the Compose New Fax wizard from the Start menu, select the file you want to send for the fax.

9. Click your mouse on the Next button.

10. Click your mouse on the Finish button to send the fax.

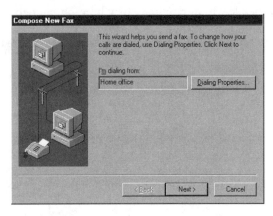

Figure 449.1 The Compose New Fax wizard.

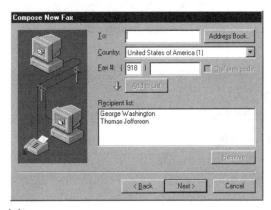

Figure 449.2 Sending a fax to two recipients.

Using Fax Profiles   450

A *fax profile* contains dialing instructions for a specific location. Microsoft Fax lets you set up fax profiles for multiple locations, such as your home, your office, and your hotel room when you're on the road. For example, you may need to disable call waiting from your home phone. Or, your office switchboard may require you to dial 9 to reach an outside line. Or, when you're traveling on business, you might want to use a special calling card from your hotel room. Whenever you regularly send faxes from a certain location, create a new fax profile for that location. That way, you can save yourself the trouble of re-entering dialing instructions the next time you want to send a fax from that location.

Creating a Fax Profile   451

As Tip 450 explains, a fax profile contains dialing instructions for a specific location. If you take the time to create fax profiles for all the locations from which you regularly send faxes, you can save yourself considerable time and effort. To create a fax profile, perform these steps:

1. Start the Compose New Fax wizard. (Tip 449 discusses how to start this wizard.)
2. Click your mouse on the Dialing Properties button. The Compose New Fax wizard will open the Dialing Properties dialog box shown in Figure 451.

3. Click your mouse on the New button, enter a new location, and enter all the dialing information for the new location.
4. Click your mouse on the OK button to add the new location to the fax profile list.

Figure 451 *Creating a new fax profile.*

452 Using a Calling Card

Calling card information can be difficult to remember. Fortunately, you can have Microsoft Fax remember it for you. To request that Microsoft Fax enter a calling card number before dialing a fax, perform these steps:

1. Click your mouse on the Dialing Properties sheet (shown in Figure 451) Dial using Calling Card option when you create a new fax profile. Microsoft Fax displays the Change Calling Card dialog box shown in Figure 452.
2. Select a calling card type from the Calling Card to use pull-down list. Or, click your mouse on the New button to add your own calling card type.
3. Enter the calling card number in the Calling Card number text box. If you have a different calling card for local, national, and international locations, click your mouse on the Advanced button to enter those numbers.
4. Click your mouse on the OK button to save your changes. Microsoft Fax will now dial the calling card number before it starts a fax transmission from this location.

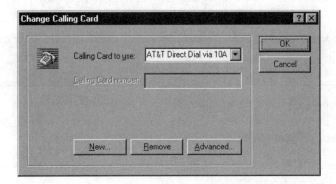

Figure 452 *Enter your calling card information.*

Disabling Call Waiting — 453

Call waiting lets you hear the ring of an incoming call while you talk with someone else. Call waiting eliminates the busy signals that people calling you would otherwise receive. As such, call waiting is a useful feature for phone lines that handle only voice calls. However, the call waiting ring damages fax communications and may render a fax transmission unusable.

To deactivate your phone line's call waiting, check the Dialog Properties sheet This location has call waiting. To disable it, dial: option. Then, from the pull-down list next to the check box, select the code that disables call waiting in your area. (Generally, though not always, the code is #70.) If your call waiting disable code does not appear in the list, enter your disable code in the text box next to the pull-down list button. Microsoft Fax, in turn, will disable call waiting before it starts a fax transmission from this location.

Creating an Address Book Entry — 454

The Windows 95 address book supplies all Windows 95 programs with a universal phone and address book. When you fax with Microsoft Fax, dial with the Phone Dialer, insert an address entry from Word for Windows 95, or use any application that requires phone and address information, you can use the Windows 95 Address Book for the dialing information.

Note: Before the Windows 95 Address Book, every communication and fax program had to include its own address book. Therefore, you would have to update every application's address book when a phone number or address changed.

You must install Microsoft Exchange before you can work with the Windows 95 Address Book. To create an address book, perform these steps:

1. Select the Start menu Programs option.
2. Select the Programs menu Microsoft Exchange option. Windows 95 will start Microsoft Exchange.
3. Select the Tools menu Address Book option to open the Address Book window shown in Figure 454.1.
4. Select the File menu New Entry option to display the New Entry dialog box shown in Figure 454.2.
5. Select Other Address from the New Entry dialog box's list box.
6. Click your mouse on the OK button. Address Book will display the New Other Address Properties sheet shown in Figure 454.3.
7. Enter all the information for the Address Book entry and click your mouse on the OK button when done. (Due to a minor bug in the Address Book program, all entries must have e-mail addresses. You cannot leave the E-mail text boxes blank. If your entry does not use e-mail, type **None** in the E-mail address and E-mail type text boxes.

If you run Windows 95 from multiple locations or use the computer to dial for several different purposes, you may have different lists of users you fax for different reasons. For such cases, the Address Book application lets you create multiple address books. When you first install Microsoft Exchange, the Address Book contains a Personal Address Book file and, if you've also installed the Microsoft Network, the Microsoft Network file as well. By using multiple address books, you can better organize the entries you fax on a regular basis.

Figure 454.1 The Address Book window.

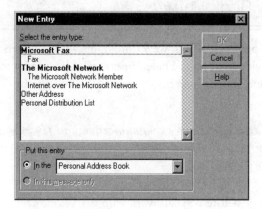

Figure 454.2 The New Entry dialog box.

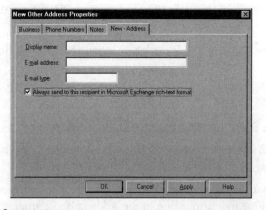

Figure 454.3 Ready for the address information.

455 Creating a Fax-based Address Book Entry

As you work with Windows 95, there may be persons or companies with whom you communicate only through faxes. For example, for legal purposes, you may want to keep certain correspondence in writing. However, you may not want to wait for the postal service to deliver letters to and from other parties. Fortunately, you no longer have to wait to get things in writing. Faxing combines the speed of telecommunication with the legal security of a written document.

If you communicate with someone only through faxes, there is no point to having anything in your Address Book except for their fax information. To enter an exclusively fax-based address into your Address Book, select Fax from the New Entry dialog box and click the OK button. Address Book, in turn, will display the New Fax Properties sheet, as shown in Figure 455. The fax properties work better for fax recipients than the Other Address entries because you do not have to enter e-mail information for fax recipients.

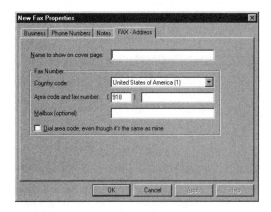

Figure 455 Entering a fax recipient.

Creating an Internet-based Address Book Entry — 456

If your Address Book recipient resides on the Internet, select Internet over the Microsoft Network from the New Entry dialog box when you add a new entry to the Address Book. To send e-mail across the Internet using Microsoft Network, you must already be set up to use the Microsoft Network.

The Address Book displays a different set of New Internet over The Microsoft Network Properties page as shown in Figure 456. To access the Internet, the Address Book requires more technical information, such as the domain name (such as microsoft.com), to send and receive messages.

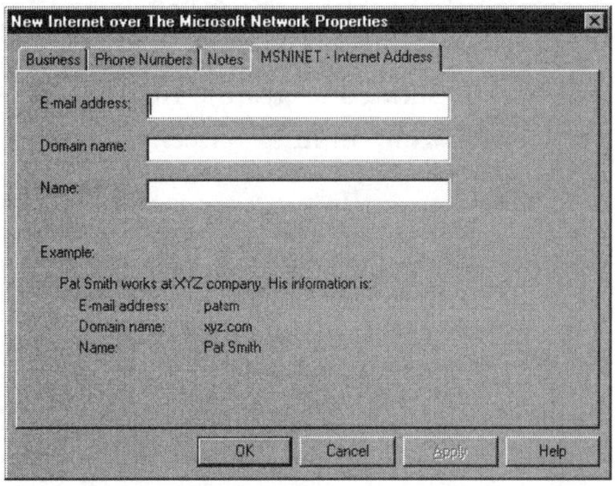

Figure 456 Entering an Internet recipient.

457 Creating a Microsoft Network-based Address Book Entry

If your Address Book recipient uses the Microsoft Network, select The Microsoft Network Member from the New Entry dialog box when you add a new entry to the Address Book. To send e-mail or a fax across the Microsoft Network using Microsoft Network, you must already be set up to use the Microsoft Network.

The Address Book displays a different set of New The Microsoft Network Member Properties page as shown in Figure 457. To access the Microsoft network recipient, the Address Book requires Microsoft Network information, such as the user's Member ID.

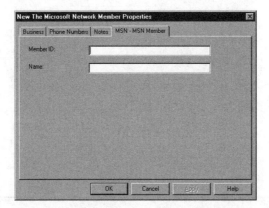

Figure 457 *Entering a Microsoft Network recipient.*

458 Creating a Local Area Network-based Address Book Entry

If you use Microsoft Mail, you can use your Address Book to keep track of network addresses for individuals with whom you exchange electronic mail. To do so, select The Microsoft Mail (which only appears if you work with Microsoft Mail) from the New Entry dialog box when you add a new entry to the Address Book.

459 Creating an Address Book Entry for Other On-line Services

Within your Address Book entries, you are not limited to just the Internet and the Microsoft Network. In fact, you can also add Address Book entries for the following on-line services:

- CompuServe
- America Online
- Prodigy

However, before you can add Address Book entries from most on-line services, you must get an Exchange driver disk from the services (call the on-line service's technical support and request the Exchange driver). (Windows 95 comes with the CompuServe driver only.) After you get the driver disk from the on-line service, start the Microsoft Exchange from the Start menu and select the Tools menu Services option. The Add button walks you through the driver's installation steps. After you install the driver, you'll be able to add Address Book entries for individuals on those services.

Changing an Address Book Entry — 460

After you add Address Book entries, you'll need to update them to keep the names, addresses, phone numbers, and e-mail addresses they contain as current as possible. Remember that all Windows 95 applications utilize your central Address Book. As a result, after you update the Address Book, all applications that use the Address Book will also know about the changes. To change an Address Book entry, perform these steps:

1. Select the Microsoft Exchange Tools menu Address Book option to start the Address Book program.
2. Right-click your mouse button over the entry you want to change.
3. Select the pop-up menu's Properties option. Address Book will display the properties sheet for the entry you selected in step 2. Figure 460 shows such a properties sheet.
4. After you have finished your changes, click your mouse on the OK button to save them.

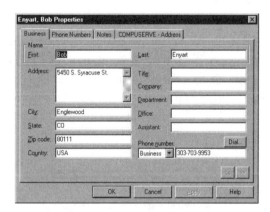

Figure 460 *Changing an Address Book entry.*

Finding an Address Book Entry — 461

When your Address Book has few entries, it's no trouble to scroll through the entry list to find a particular entry. However, as your Address Book becomes more crowded, scrolling to find an entry requires far too much time and effort. Fortunately, Address Book gives you several alternative ways to locate entries. For example, to quickly locate an entry, you can type the entry's last name in the Type Name or Select from List field, which appears directly beneath the Address Book toolbar. Address Book, in turn, will highlight the first entry whose initial characters match those you type in the field.

When Address Book highlights the name you want, press ENTER. Address Book, in turn, will display the rest of the address information for that name. If Address Book doesn't highlight the name you want but the name appears in the entry list, double-click your mouse over the name to select it.

Address Book also contains a Find feature that searches through the entries for you. When you select the Tools menu Find option, Address Book displays the Find dialog box shown in Figure 461. To use the Find dialog box, type enough letters to distinguish the name you want from other names in the entry list. (The characters you type don't have to reside at the beginning of the search name.) Address Book, in turn, will return a list of all names that contain the letters you type in the Find dialog box.

Figure 461 *The Address Book Find dialog box.*

462 Controlling Fax Options

Microsoft Fax includes many options that let you control fax operations. The options let you control fax times, message formats, dialing properties, and security controls. When you start the Compose New Fax wizard, click your mouse on the Compose New Fax page Option button. In turn, Microsoft Fax will display the Send Options for this Message dialog box shown in Figure 462. The following tips explain how you can set the options that appear in this dialog box and thereby change the way your system sends faxes.

Figure 462 *Microsoft Fax's Send Options for this Message dialog box.*

463 Understanding Fax Security

When you send a fax, several people may see the fax before it reaches your intended recipient. For example, you may send a fax to a Windows 95 system that your intended recipient shares with several co-workers. If you send the fax when your recipient is out of the office, his or her co-workers may read the fax's contents before your recipient returns. To make sure unauthorized persons can't read your confidential faxes, you may want to use Microsoft Fax's security feature. When you use the Microsoft Fax security feature, you encrypt fax messages using one of the following two methods:

- *Password-protected encryption*: You specify a password when you send the fax, and the recipient must enter the same password to receive the fax.

- *Key-encryption*: Your entire fax is encrypted, and only a person with the key (a password) can decipher the fax. After the recipient deciphers the fax, anyone can view the fax's contents.

Note: *You can only encrypt faxes you send as editable files to Windows 95 systems. You cannot encrypt faxes that you send to a fax machine or to a computer not running Windows 95. The recipient's Windows 95 controls the password protection on the recipient's end.*

To encrypt your fax, display the Message Security Options dialog box, shown in Figure 463. The easiest kind of fax to send is the password-protected encryption fax. To add the password, click your mouse on the Password-protected option. Then, click your mouse on the OK button. Microsoft Fax, in turn, will request a password—the same password the recipient must type to read the fax. The password is case-sensitive, so both you and the recipient must use the same set of upper-case and lower-case letters in the password.

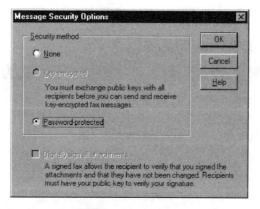

Figure 463 *You can password-protect a fax.*

Using Key Security 464

As you have learned, Microsoft Fax lets you encrypt your faxes to protect them from unwanted access as they travel over phone lines, Microsoft Network, or the Internet. One of the most common encryption schemes is public-key encryption. A *public key* is a password that the recipient needs to decode your encrypted fax. You cannot use Microsoft Fax to create a public key. Rather, you must use Microsoft Exchange (see Tip 465). When you create the public key, Microsoft Exchange creates a *private key*, which tells receivers that you sent the fax rather than another user who knows the public key. To send a fax using the public key, select the Key-encrypted option button in the Microsoft Fax Message Security Options dialog box.

Note: *You can store other people's public keys in your Address Book if you want to keep track of them.*

Creating and Managing Fax Security Keys 465

As Tip 464 explains, a public key is a password that the recipient needs to decode your encrypted fax. When you create a public key, Microsoft Exchange creates a private key, which tells the fax recipient that you sent the fax rather than another user who knows the public key. To create a public and private key (your key set), perform these steps:

1. Start Microsoft Exchange.
2. Select the Tools menu Microsoft Fax Tools option.

3. Select the Microsoft Fax Tools menu Advanced Security option. Exchange will display the Advanced Fax Security dialog box shown in Figure 465.
4. Click your mouse on the New Key Set button to open the New Key Set dialog box.
5. Type your public key. Windows 95 will display asterisks as you type so that nobody can see your password. You must type the password twice to verify its accuracy.
6. Click your mouse on the Save the password in your password list option if you want Windows 95 to remember your key set. Otherwise, the current key set remains in effect only for the current fax session.
7. Click your mouse on the OK button. After a brief pause, Exchange will display the Advanced Fax Security dialog box once again. You can now send your fax.

The buttons that appear in the Advanced Fax Security dialog box manage your key set. The Public Keys button lets you create a backup of your public key in a file that you can distribute to others. You can open the file and add the public keys it contains to the addresses your Address Book stores. The Your Keys button lets you replace, restore, or delete your key set. The Change Password button lets you change your public key. The New Key Set lets you replace your key set with a new one.

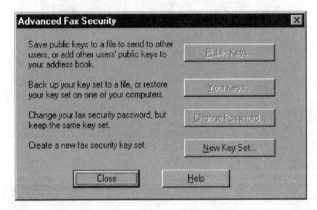

Figure 465 *The Advanced Fax Security dialog box.*

466 Attaching a File to Your Fax

As long as you use a file type Windows 95 recognizes, such as a text or Word for Windows file, you can attach a file to a fax. If a user running Windows 95 receives the fax, the recipient can view and edit the file in the file's native format (using Word for Windows and so on). However, if you send the fax with a file attachment to a fax machine or to a non-Windows 95 computer, the recipient will receive the file as a printout or an on-screen graphic image.

To attach a file to your fax, click your mouse on the Add File button that appears in the Compose New Fax Wizard window. The wizard, in turn, will display a File Open dialog box from which you can browse and select a file to attach to the fax. Microsoft Fax then sends your fax cover sheet (if you specify one), fax page or pages, and the attached file to the recipient.

467 Retrieving a Fax

You can send and retrieve faxes from several fax-information services. Windows 95 can receive any fax that conforms to the Group 3 polling standard (most do). You can also request faxes from specific fax machines and fax-on-demand systems, which send faxes when you use your fax/modem to dial them. To retrieve a fax, start the Request a Fax wizard. (You can reach the Request a Fax wizard through the Accessories menu Fax option.) The wizard's opening screen, shown in Figure 467, lets you request one or more faxes. If you know of one specific document waiting to be faxed to you, enter the document title and password (if the document is password-protected). After you enter a fax number to dial (you can select the number from your Address Book), Microsoft Fax dials the number and retrieves the waiting fax or faxes. If the fax comes in a Microsoft At Work (Windows 95) format, Microsoft Fax receives the file in its native format.

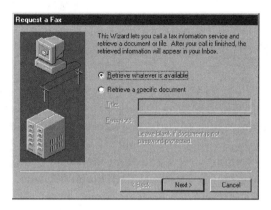

Figure 467 *The Request a Fax wizard.*

Receiving a Fax — 468

When you get a fax, you can print it, view it, edit it, or store it in a file. If the fax comes to you in a Windows 95 standard format (called *Microsoft At Work* format), you don't get a typical fax graphic image; instead, you get an editable file. If you used a regular fax machine to retrieve the fax, the fax would appear as a graphic image. Microsoft Exchange works as your system agent to receive faxes that come to your computer. The next several tips discuss Microsoft Exchange and explain how you can use Microsoft Exchange to manage all your messages, including faxes, e-mail, and files.

Understanding Microsoft Exchange — 469

Microsoft Exchange works like a universal in- and out-box. Microsoft Exchange sends and receives all kinds of messages—e-mail messages, faxes, and files. If you use Microsoft Mail, you can also exchange e-mail messages, faxes, and files with others on your network. To start Microsoft Exchange, select the Start menu's Programs submenu Microsoft Exchange option. After a brief startup pause, you'll see the Microsoft Exchange window, as shown in Figure 469.

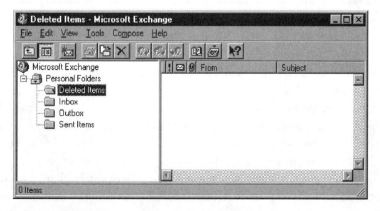

Figure 469 *The Microsoft Exchange window.*

470 Controlling Microsoft Exchange Services

If you purchased Windows 95 on installation floppy disks, you can access the following services with Microsoft Exchange:

- The on-line Microsoft Network
- The Internet via the Microsoft Network
- Microsoft Fax

If you purchased Windows 95 on a CD-ROM, you can also access the CompuServe on-line service. Unlike most stand-alone communications programs (such as WinCIM), Microsoft Exchange is a single-source exchanger for all data you send and receive through the Internet and CompuServe. As such, you can use Microsoft Exchange as a universal inbox for messages, faxes, and files you receive from nearly any source. To add or remove a service from Microsoft Exchange, select the Tools menu Services option. Microsoft Exchange, in turn, will display a sheet similar to the one shown in Figure 470. To add a service, click your mouse on the sheet's Add button and select the Have Disk button to install a new service.

Figure 470 *A list of Microsoft Exchange services.*

Note: *If you want to connect to an additional service, such as America Online or Prodigy, you must obtain the proper Microsoft Exchange driver files from those services. To obtain these driver files, contact the service's technical support staff.*

471 Working with Microsoft Exchange Messages and Folders

Microsoft Exchange uses an Explorer-like folder system to hold your Exchange messages, faxes, and files. (When you start Exchange, if the Microsoft Exchange window doesn't have a left section that displays folder icons, select the View menu Folder option.) To open a folder, double-click your mouse on its name or icon. Microsoft Exchange, in turn, will display the folder's messages in Microsoft Exchange window's right section. You can drag and drop messages from one folder to another. Additionally, you can use the Edit menu's Copy, Cut, and Paste options to move and copy items. Microsoft Exchange stores all mail, faxes, and files you receive within the Inbox folder. After you finish reading your Inbox messages, you can leave the messages in your Inbox, move them to another location, delete them, or reply to their original author. In a similar way, you can store messages and faxes you want to send at a later time within the Outbox folder. You can also route those items to different locations, such as three Microsoft Network users and one CompuServe user. When you request that Microsoft Exchange send all Outbox messages, Microsoft Exchange connects to every service it needs to fulfill your Outbox sending requirements. Figure 471 shows an Outbox folder that contains two messages.

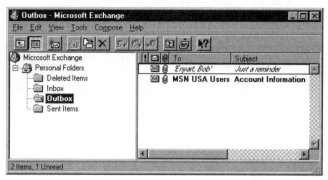

Figure 471 *The Outbox has two messages.*

Understanding Message Icons — 472

In its window, Microsoft Exchange displays icons that tell you the status of each message inside Exchange's folders. The icons appear next to messages in the Exchange window's right section. Table 472 describes the appearance and purpose of these icons.

Appearance	Purpose
Sealed envelope	Indicates that you have a message composed by WordMail (use Tip 473's instructions).
Paper clip	Indicates that the message contains an attachment.
Circle with a red arrow	Indicates that Exchange could not deliver a message for you.
Down arrow	Indicates that the message is low priority.
Exclamation mark	Indicates the message is high priority and needs your attention quickly.

Table 472 *Microsoft Exchange's message icons.*

To indicate a message's read status, Microsoft Exchange changes the style of the message header (the To and Subject columns in the Exchange window's right section). If the message header appears in boldface letters, you have yet to read the message. If the message header appears in italics, you created the message. If the message header appears as regular text, you have read the message. In Figure 471, you can see the user created the first message because the message's header appears in italics. Likewise, you can tell the user has not read the second message because its header appears in boldface letters.

Composing a Mail Message — 473

When you want to compose and send a message, select Microsoft Exchange's Compose menu New Message option. Exchange, in turn, will open the New Message window shown in Figure 473. Next, click your mouse on the To button to select one or more primary recipients from your Address Book. Then, click your mouse on the Cc button if you want to select one or more secondary recipients to receive copies of the message. (The secondary recipients will read that you sent them messages using the Cc, or *carbon copy*, option.) Next, enter a Subject heading. Finally, type your message in the window's work area.

If you wish, you can select a new font style and size for the message. If the recipient uses a fax machine to receive your message or uses a computer that is not running Windows 95, he or she will receive a rendered graphic image of your message with the same fonts you selected. If the recipient uses Windows 95, the recipient will receive a Word for Windows file that he or she can use WordMail to view.

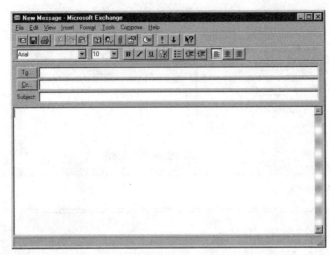

Figure 473 Composing a new message.

474 Inserting a File into a Message

As you work with Microsoft Exchange, you can insert a file, such as a text file, directly into the text of your message. In this way, you don't have to retype information you already have saved in a different file. For example, if you store a list of people's names in a file and want to include that list directly inside your message, perform these steps:

1. Select the File menu Insert File option.
2. Select the file you want to insert.
3. Check the Insert as Text Only option.
4. Type the path and filename at the File name text box and press ENTER. WordMail will insert the contents of the file at the text cursor's current location.

When you insert a file, the text appears inside your message as if you had typed the text within the message.

475 Attaching a File to a Message

In Tip 474 you learned how to insert a file within a message using Microsoft Exchange. In some cases, however, rather than inserting a file within your message, you may want to attach the message instead. For example, assume you have just completed your company budget as a spreadsheet. To send the spreadsheet to your boss, you might create a simple message that states "Here's the budget" and then attach the budget to your message. When your boss receives the message, he or she can simply detach the spreadsheet. To attach a file to a message, perform these steps:

1. Use Exchange's Compose menu New Message option to open a New Message window.
2. Select the recipient and copy recipients as usual.
3. Enter a subject heading.
4. Select the Insert menu File option.
5. Check the Insert as an Attachment option.
6. Enter the path and filename of the file you want to attach. WordMail will attach the file to your message. The attachment appears as an icon inside the message.

If your message recipient is running Windows 95, the file's contents do not appear inside the message. Instead, next to the message header in the recipient's Exchange Inbox, Exchange places a paper clip icon to indicate that an attachment file accompanied the message. The recipient can edit and work with the attached file. If your message recipient uses a fax machine that's incompatible with Windows 95, the received fax will contain both the message and the contents of the inserted file as if the file were text that you typed directly in the fax.

Inserting or Attaching an Existing Message Within a Message — 476

As you compose new messages, there may be times when you want your recipient to refer to a message you or someone else sent some time ago. For example, you may want to send an e-mail message to a colleague to remind him or her of something you mentioned in a past message. Rather than type the previous message's contents into your new message, you can simply insert it within, or attach it to, your new message. To insert or attach another message to the message you are composing, select the Insert menu Message option. WordMail, in turn, will display the Insert Message dialog box, as shown in Figure 476. From this dialog box, you can select a message to insert. Depending on whether you select the Insert as Text Only option or the Insert as an Attachment option, WordMail inserts or attaches the past message into your current one.

Figure 476 Inserting an existing message into a new one.

Inserting an Object into a Message — 477

The objects you insert into your messages do not have to be text files. Using the Insert menu Object option, you can insert files of virtually any type, including video clips, sound files, graphics files, worksheet files, and formatted word-processor documents. If your message's recipient is a Windows 95 user, he or she will see an icon that represents the attached object file. To open the icon's parent program, the recipient only has to double-click the icon. Additionally, if the recipient right-clicks the icon and selects the pop-up menu's QuickViewer option, he or she can see, hear, or play the attached file's contents.

Using the Mail Composition Toolbar — 478

When you compose an e-mail message, you can save time and mouse operations by using the WordMail Drawing toolbar. To display the WordMail Drawing toolbar, select the toolbar from the View menu Toolbars submenu. As you will learn, the toolbar gives you one-button access to many mail composition tasks. Table 478 explains each toolbar button.

Toolbar Icon	Purpose
	Sends the message to the recipient.
	Saves the message page.
	Prints the message.
	Cuts selected text to the Clipboard.
	Copies selected text to the Clipboard.
	Pastes items from the Clipboard into the message.
	Opens the Address Book.
	Checks the recipient names against the Address Book and reports unfound names.
	Inserts a file.
	Displays the Message Properties sheet.
	Requests or cancels a Read Receipt requirement.
	Increases the message importance.
	Decreases the message importance.
	Offers roving help on selected items.

Table 478 The WordMail toolbar lets you perform common tasks.

Customizing the Microsoft Exchange Toolbar — 479

Within Microsoft Exchange, you can use the toolbar to simplify many tasks. As it turns out, you can change the Microsoft Exchange toolbar to suit the way you work. When you select the Tools menu Customize Toolbar option, Exchange displays the Customize Toolbar dialog box shown in Figure 479. The Available buttons list box determines which toolbar buttons you want Exchange to display. To delete a toolbar button, select the button in the list box and click the Remove button. If you want to add a button to the toolbar, select the button in the Toolbar buttons list box and click on the Add button. To eliminate the pop-up window that appears when you move your mouse pointer over a toolbar button, remove the check from the Tools menu Options page Show ToolTips on toolbars option.

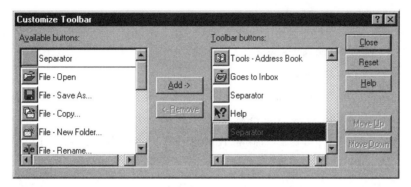

Figure 479 *Customizing the Microsoft Exchange toolbar.*

Working with Message Properties — 480

Before you send a message, you may want to view or change its properties. To do so, highlight the message and select the File menu Properties option. Microsoft Exchange, in turn, will display the message's properties sheet, as shown in Figure 480. The properties sheet displays information about the message, such as the date and time you created the message and tells when you sent or received the message. The properties sheet also lets you change some of a message's characteristics. For example, you can also change the message's importance by clicking your mouse on the High, Normal, or Low importance option buttons. Likewise, through the properties sheet, you can tell Microsoft Exchange to track the message and inform you of its progress. If you want Microsoft Exchange to tell you when your message recipient reads your message, just set the Read Receipt requested option to Yes. Similarly, if you want Microsoft Exchange to tell you when your message reaches its recipient's Inbox, set the Delivery Receipt requested option to Yes. You must set both options at the time you compose a message.

Figure 480 *A message's properties sheet.*

481 Working with the Current Message

When you receive a message in your Inbox folder, you can use the File menu's option to perform most actions with the message. Table 481 lists and describes the File menu's options.

Option	Description
Open	Displays the selected message.
Save As	Saves the message in a separate file.
Move	Moves the message to a different folder on your computer (use the File menu New Folder option to create a new folder).
Copy	Copies the message to a different folder on your computer (use the File menu New Folder option to create a new folder).
Print	Prints the message on your printer.
New Folder	Creates a new folder.
Delete	Deletes the message.
Rename	Renames the message or folder.
Import	Imports a Personal Address Book or a Microsoft Mail file.
Exit	Closes Microsoft Exchange.
Exit and Log Off	Closes all messaging programs.

Table 481 Options on the Microsoft Exchange File menu.

482 Composing a Fax within Microsoft Exchange

If you are working in Microsoft Exchange and want to send a fax, you don't need to start Microsoft Fax. Instead, you can just select the Compose menu New Fax option. Microsoft Exchange, in turn, will run the Compose New Fax wizard, which will lead you step-by-step through the fax composition and transmission process.

483 Reading New Mail

To read new mail (i.e., mail whose message header is boldfaced), select the File menu Open option. Or, right-click the message header and select the pop-up menu's Open option. Or, double-click your left mouse button over the message header. Microsoft Exchange, in turn, will start WordMail so that you can read the message's text. If your message has an object attached to it, double-click your left mouse button over the object's icon to start the object's parent program.

484 Replying to a Mail Message

When you receive a message, you can compose a reply and tell Microsoft Exchange to route that reply back to the original message's sender. For example, if someone sends you a message with a question, you can use options on WordMail's Compose menu to reply with the answer. If you select the Compose menu Reply to Sender option, WordMail transmits your reply message to the original sender. If you select the Compose menu Reply to All option, WordMail transmits your reply message to the sender and the original message's other recipients.

When you send reply messages, there may be times when you may want to restate, or copy, some of the original message in your reply. Such restatement is a good way to remind the sender about the original subject. Fortunately, WordMail gives you a number of ways to incorporate the original message text into your reply. To view your options, select the Tools menu Options option. Then, click your mouse on the Read tab. WordMail, in turn, will display a page that contains the options Table 484 describes:

Option	Description
Include the original text when replying	Includes the entire sender's message at the top of your reply.
Indent the original text when replying	Indents the original text that WordMail includes at the top of your reply. As a result, the receiver can easily distinguish the original text from your reply.
Close the original item	Closes the message to which you are replying.

Table 484 *Your options when you use original message text in a reply.*

When you finish your reply message and click the Send button, Exchange sends your reply.

Forwarding a Mail Message — 485

Some people confuse a message's *reply* action with a message's *forward* action. When you reply to a message, as Tip 484 explains, you send a message back to the original sender. When you forward a message, you simply send the message to another user in your Address Book. The forward action is useful in a number of situations. For example, if someone sends a message to you by mistake, you can forward the message to its correct destination. Likewise, if you receive a message you think someone else should read, you can forward it to that person or persons. To forward a message to another user, perform these steps:

1. Select the message you want to forward.
2. Click your mouse on the Compose menu Forward option. WordMail will open with the original sender's message inside the editing area.
3. Select a new recipient and, optionally, select a recipient (or recipients) to whom you want to send a copy of the forwarded message.
4. Click your mouse on the Send button to forward the message.

Note: *The reply options that Tip 484 describes are available to you when you forward a message to another address. As such, you can add your own comments to a message and then forward it to other users.*

Finding a Mail Message — 486

If your mail box folders fill up before you get a chance to delete some of your messages they contain, you may want to take advantage of Microsoft Exchange's Find command to search for particular messages that you've read before but can no longer locate.

To use the Find command, select the Tools menu Find option to open the Find dialog box shown in Figure 486. Then, enter one or more values into any field in the dialog box. To search your Address Book too, click your mouse on the From or Sent To buttons.

After you specify the search information, click your mouse on the Find Now button to begin the search. Microsoft Exchange, in turn, will display a list of every message in your mail box folders that meets the criteria you specified.

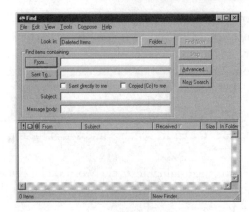

Figure 486 *The Microsoft Exchange Find dialog box.*

487 Performing an Advanced Message Search

When you specify criteria for a message search, Microsoft Exchange does not limit you to the parameters the Find dialog box displays. To specify additional criteria, click your mouse on the Find dialog box Advanced button. Microsoft Exchange, in turn, will display the Advanced dialog box shown in Figure 487. Using this dialog box, you can search for a message based on its size, date delivered, and importance level.

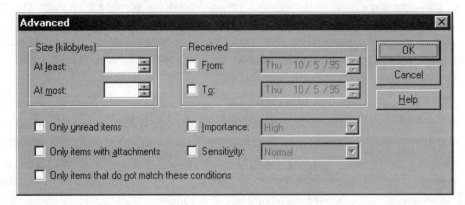

Figure 487 *Using Find's Advanced dialog box.*

488 Viewing Outgoing Faxes

When you open or double-click your mouse over a fax that you have sent or are about to send, Microsoft Exchange starts the WordMail program to display the fax. If the fax contains attached objects, WordMail displays an icon for those objects. Sometimes, the entire fax will be the object.

A problem occurs when a fax contains objects for which you don't have a parent program. For example, if a friend sends you a fax of a photo stored in a Photo-CD format and you don't have a graphics program that can read Photo-CD formatted graphics, WordMail cannot open a parent program that lets you edit the image. On such occasions, WordMail starts the Microsoft Fax Viewer program to display the fax graphically. When you use Microsoft Fax Viewer to view a fax, the fax is said to be *rendered* and not editable. Figure 488 shows the Microsoft Fax Viewer.

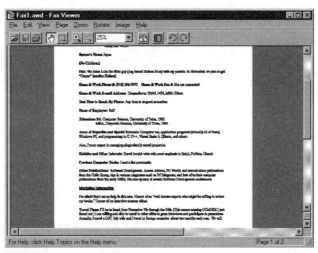

Figure 488 *Viewing a rendered fax.*

Controlling Outgoing Faxes   489

As you use your system to send faxes, there may be times when you'll want to adjust Microsoft Exchange's fax priorities. For example, if have a number of faxes ready to send, you may decide that you want to reshuffle the order in which your system will transmit them. Fortunately, Microsoft Exchange provides a tool you can use to manage outgoing faxes. To change fax priorities, perform these steps:

1. Select Microsoft Exchange's Tools menu Microsoft Fax Tools option.
2. Select the Microsoft Fax Tools menu Show Outgoing Faxes option. Exchange will open an Outgoing Fax dialog box with a list of faxes.
3. Drag the fax you want to send first to the top of the list. If you want to cancel a fax, click your mouse on the fax and select the right-click menu Cancel option.
4. When you've arranged your faxes, select File menu Exit option to return to Microsoft Exchange.

Controlling When Microsoft Exchange Sends a Fax   490

If you want to send your faxes at night when long-distance rates are lower, or if you want to send a fax at a time when you know the recipient will be at his or her system, select the Tools menu Microsoft Fax Tools option. Then, click your mouse on the Options option to display the Microsoft Fax Properties sheet shown in Figure 490.

If you want your computer to send faxes at a particular time, click the sheet's Specific time option button. Then, in the field next to the option button, enter the time at which you want your system to send faxes. If you send faxes at night when rates are lower, you can set up a discount rate time that Microsoft Fax will remember and use. To set up a discount rate time, click your mouse on the Discount rates option button, click on the Set button, and enter the time you want to send subsequent faxes.

Figure 490 You can specify a time for faxing.

491 Controlling a Fax Format

As Tip 490 explains, the Microsoft Fax Properties sheet lets you control when your system sends faxes. Additionally, you can use this sheet to select how you want to send a fax. Specifically, the Microsoft Fax Properties sheet offers you three message formats:

- *Editable, if possible*: Transfers the fax as a regular file if the recipient has Windows 95.
- *Editable only*: Transfers the fax only if the recipient uses Windows 95.
- *Not editable*: Always renders a fax to its graphical image before sending it.

Through the Microsoft Fax Properties sheet, you can also specify the size of paper you want the receiving fax to use if your fax will not be editable. (Not all fax machines can respect your paper size request.) Select the option that best suits your needs from the Microsoft Fax Tools menu Options option. The message format options appear on the Options sheet Message page.

492 Specifying Fax Redial Properties

When the receiving phone line is busy, Microsoft Fax can retry the fax at time intervals that you specify. Through the Microsoft Fax Properties sheet Dialing page, shown in Figure 492, you can set the following redial options:

- *Number of retries*: Specifies the number of times that Microsoft Fax will dial (retry) the recipient's fax if the line is busy or recipient's fax does not answer.
- *Time between retries*: Specifies the amount of time (in minutes) that Microsoft Fax will wait before it dials the recipient's fax again.

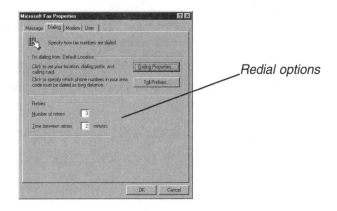

Figure 492 Specify redial options.

Defining User Fax Properties — 493

You can specify user options that appear on the faxes that you send by clicking your mouse over the User tab on the Microsoft Fax Properties sheet. Thus, if you don't send a cover page, the recipient will know who you are. Figure 493 illustrates the Microsoft Fax Properties sheet User page. Microsoft Fax gets the information when you set up your modem. If you don't want to send user information with every fax, you need to blank out each option on the page. You can change the information for one or more faxes and then change the information back once again if you dial using different properties.

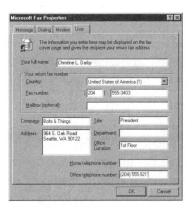

Figure 493 The Microsoft Fax Properties sheet User page.

Customizing Microsoft Exchange Options — 494

The Microsoft Exchange Options sheet, which you can access through the Exchange's Tools menu Options option, contains several pages of options you can set to control the way Exchange works. Table 494 explains the common Microsoft Exchange options you may want to change.

Page	Option	Purpose
General	When mail arrives	Specifies the action Exchange takes when you receive mail of any kind.
General	Deleting items	Makes message deletions more cautious.
General	When starting Microsoft Exchange	Lets you specify a default profile to use.
Read	Determines message reading actions	See Tip 480.
Send	Font	Describes the default font WordMail uses.
Send	Save a copy	Saves a copy of your sent messages.
Spelling	General options	Determines how WordMail handles the message spell-checking.
Spelling	When checking	Determines if the WordMail spell-checker should ignore certain kinds of words.
Services	Services	Lets you add or remove services that Exchange uses.
Delivery	Deliver new mail	Specifies the location where Exchange stores your new messages.
Delivery	Secondary location	Selects an alternate location for mail delivery (useful if you normally set the delivery to a folder on a remote networked computer and the network happens to be down when Exchange delivers your mail).
Addressing	Show this address list first	Specifies the default address book file the Address Book program displays when you access it.

Table 494 Options you can set through the Microsoft Exchange Options sheet.

495 Using Microsoft Exchange Remotely

You don't have to be at your computer (for example, the computer in your office) to retrieve your messages from a remote computer's Exchange folders. Instead, if you use dial-up networking to the remote computer, you can remotely access Exchange and retrieve your messages. Likewise, when you send messages, you can place the messages into your Outbox folder for Microsoft Exchange to send at a later time. After you select the Tools menu Remote Mail option, you must select a server to which you want to send or retrieve remote mail. Not all online services support remote mail, but the Microsoft Network and CompuServe services do. Before you can work with remote mail, you must prepare your computer for remote access. To prepare for remote access, perform these steps:

1. Start Microsoft Exchange.
2. Create a folder on your remote computer for your received mail.
3. Copy your personal Address Book files, as well as other files you need to use for mailing messages, to the remote computer.
4. Before you disconnect from the remote computer, disconnect from Microsoft Network. To do so, select the Remote Mail window's Tools menu Disconnect option.

496 Retrieving Mail Remotely

As Tip 495 explains, you can receive your remote mail through a dial-up phone connection. After you prepare your computer for remote mail access, use dial-up networking to connect to the server. To retrieve your mail, perform these steps:

Using Windows 95 Fax and E-Mail Capabilities

1. Connect to server computer and update the mail headers from your Remote Mail Tools menu.
2. Mark the items you want to retrieve.
3. Download those marked items to your own portable computer. You can also mark items for deletion without reading or downloading those items.
4. When you've finished marking all the mail you wish to transfer or delete, select the Tools menu Connect and Transfer Mail option to retrieve mail from the remote site.

Sending Mail from a Remote Computer — 497

If you want to send mail to a remote site, perform these steps:

1. Create all the mail you want to send to others.
2. Click your mouse on the Send button to store the outgoing mail in your portable computer's folder.
3. Start Exchange.
4. Open your Remote Mail window for the server you want to access.
5. Select the Tools menu Connect and Update Mail Headers option.
6. Select the Tools menu Connect and Transfer Mail option to send your outgoing mail to the remote computer.

Using the Remote Mail Toolbar — 498

As you perform remote-mail operations, you can save considerable time and effort by taking advantage of the Remote Mail toolbar. Table 498 explains each button on the Remote Mail toolbar.

Toolbar Button	Purpose
	Connects to the remote server.
	Disconnects from the remote server.
	Updates your remote headers.
	Transfers remote mail.
	Marks remote mail to receive.
	Marks remote mail so you receive a copy of the mail but the mail remains on the remote server.

Table 498 The Remote Mail toolbar lets you perform common tasks. (continued on the following page)

Toolbar Button	Purpose
	Marks remote mail you want to delete.
	Clears all remote mail marks.
	Displays help on selected items.

Table 498 *The Remote Mail toolbar lets you perform common tasks. (continued from the previous page)*

499 Scheduling Remote Mail Operations

When you send electronic mail, you may want to schedule your remote mail access at certain times of the day, such as when long distance rates are lowest. To schedule your remote-mail operations, perform these steps:

1. From the Remote Mail window, select the Tools menu Options option.
2. Click your mouse on the Advanced tab to display the Mail Settings dialog box.
3. Click your mouse on the Schedule Connect Times button. Exchange will display the Connection Times dialog box shown in Figure 499.
4. Select an option to schedule your remote mail operations. You can automatically receive mail when you start Microsoft Exchange, receive mail at regular time intervals, or receive mail at the same time each day.
5. Click your mouse on the OK button to save your changes.

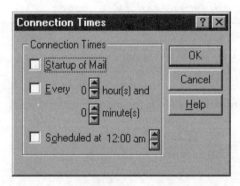

Figure 499 *The Connection Times dialog box.*

500 Changing Exchange's Windows

You can customize the Microsoft Exchange window so that it better serves your needs. For example, if you want to work exclusively with your Inbox mail, you can select the View menu folders option to hide Exchange's display of folders from view. To customize the Exchange window, you can use the following methods:

- Move your mouse over the dividing line between Exchange's two sections and drag the line left or right to display more of one window.

- Select the View menu Folders option to hide or display the folders window. Figure 500.1 shows an Exchange window that does not show the folders.

- Select the View menu New Window option when you want to create another Microsoft Exchange window. For example, if you want to view your Inbox and Outbox folders at the same time, you can open a second Exchange window and display the Inbox folder in one window and the Outbox folder in the other, as shown in Figure 500.2.

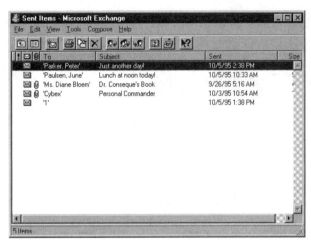

Figure 500.1 *You may not want to see folders.*

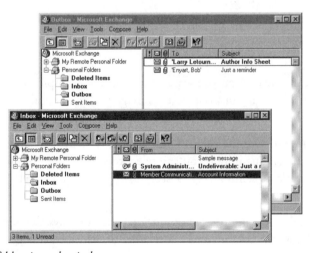

Figure 500.2 *Viewing different folders in each windows.*

Modifying Microsoft Exchange's Columns | 501

As you manage your Microsoft Exchange mail, there may be times when you want to change the information Exchange displays about your messages. For example, you may want to know the number of lines your messages contain before you read them. That way, when you have a few minutes to kill, you can review short messages and save the longer ones for when you have more time. As you know, Microsoft Exchange displays information about your messages in columns. By default, Exchange displays two columns of information for the messages you send (To and Subject) and two columns for the messages you receive (From and Subject). To change the columns of information Exchange displays, select the View menu Columns option. Microsoft Exchange, in turn, will display the Columns dialog box shown in Figure 501.

In the Columns dialog box, the Available Columns list box contains every kind of column you can display, such as message comments and number of pages. The Show the following columns list box contains columns you want to display in the Microsoft Exchange window. To add a new column to the Microsoft Exchange window, click on the column item you want in the Available columns list box. Then, click on the Add button. For example, if you want to view the number of lines in a message, click your mouse on the Available columns list box Number of Lines item and then click your mouse on the Add button. If you want to change the new column's position in the list, click your mouse on the Move Up or Move Down button.

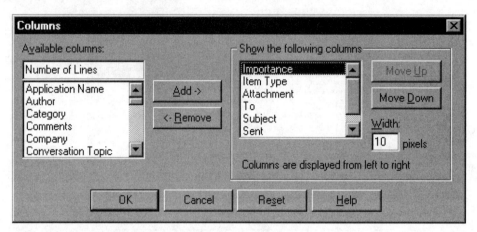

Figure 501 *Customize your message columns.*

502 Sorting a Folder's Contents

If you want to sort a Microsoft Exchange folder's messages so they appear in the order you prefer, you can use the following three methods:

- Click your mouse on the column you want to sort by. For example, if you click your mouse on the To column, Exchange displays your message in alphabetical order based on the To column's contents.

- Right-click your mouse over the column you want to sort by. Exchange displays a pop-up menu with a Sort Ascending option you can select to sort the column in alphabetical order. The pop-up menu also contains a Sort Descending option you can select to reverse the sort order.

- Select the View menu Sort option. Microsoft Exchange displays the Sort dialog box, from which you can choose the column and a sort order on which Exchange will base the sort.

503 Using the Control Panel to Customize Microsoft Exchange

The Control Panel contains a Mail and Fax icon you can select to customize Microsoft Exchange's behavior. When you double-click your mouse on the Mail and Fax icon, Windows 95 opens the MS Exchange Settings Properties sheet. From this sheet, you can change your system's setup of information services, change the properties for a given service, specify new message-delivery locations, and set Address Book options.

Note: *You can access these same properties from Microsoft Exchange's Tools menu Options option.*

Using Explorer's Send To Option   504

If you are a Windows 95 user who works a lot with Explorer (some users prefer to keep Explorer open at all times), you can fax, mail messages, copy files to diskette, and update your laptop's Briefcase by right-clicking your mouse over a file or group of files. When you right-click your mouse on a file or group of files, Explorer displays a pop-up menu that contains a Send To option. If you select the Send To option, Explorer displays the Send To menu, which shows you where you can send the file or group of files upon which you right-clicked. For example, if you select the Send To menu Fax option, Explorer starts the Microsoft Fax wizard and sends the file to your fax. If you select the Send To menu 3-1/2 Floppy option, Explorer sends the file to your A: drive. Although you can use other methods (such as drag and drop) to send files, the Send To menu is sometimes easier to use, especially if your Desktop does not have a Microsoft Fax printer-driver icon to which you can drag files.

Note: *When you send an item some place, Explorer sends a copy of the item. Explorer never moves a file when you select an option from the Send To menu.*

Placing Phone Calls Using the Phone Dialer   505

If you have a modem connected to your PC, you can use the Phone Dialer program, to place phone calls for you from your PC's keyboard. When hear your the speaker sound the ring of the remote phone, you simply pick up your phone's handset and prepare to talk. To access the Phone Dialer, select the Start menu Programs option. Next, choose the Accessories menu and choose the Phone Dialer option. When you start the Phone Dialer, Windows 95 displays the Phone Dialer window shown in Figure 505. Although rather primitive, the Phone Dialer is a good base program for add-on products that you'll find in the Windows 95 software market. The Phone Dialer integrates your modem properties and the *TAPI* (Telephone Applications Programming Interface) routines to give you speed-dial capabilities, call logging, and a handler to select from multiple phone lines.

Figure 505 *The Phone Dialer window.*

Manually Dialing a Phone Number   506

As Tip 505 explains, the Phone Dialer program lets you dial phone numbers directly from your PC's keyboard. To dial a number with Phone Dialer, perform these steps:

1. Select the Accessories menu Phone Dialer option to start the Phone Dialer program.
2. Type the number you want to dial. Or, click your mouse over the Phone Dialer window's number buttons.

3. Click your mouse on the Dial button or press ENTER. Phone Dialer will dial the number and display the Call Status dialog box shown in Figure 506.1.
4. When the person answers at the other end, lift your phone receiver and click your mouse on the Talk button to complete the call. If you hear a busy signal or no answer, click your mouse on the Hang Up button.

Normally, each time you use Phone Dialer, the program adds an entry to your phone log. However, Phone Dialer can add an entry to your phone log only if the program recognizes the number you dial. If Phone Dialer does not recognize the number, the program will display the Dialing dialog box shown in Figure 506.2, which you can use to let Phone Dialer know the calling location's name. (Tips 510 through 512 discuss the phone log.)

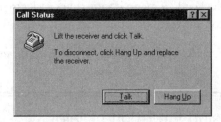

Figure 506.1 Talk when the call-recipient answers.

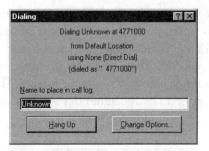

Figure 506.2 Update your phone log when necessary.

507 Creating a Speed-Dial Entry

Phone Dialer supports ten speed-dial buttons that you can use to dial quickly. For example, you might create a speed-dial button that dials your best friend's phone number. Similarly, you might create speed-dial buttons for your local fire and police numbers. To create a speed-dial button, perform these steps:

1. Select the Edit menu Speed Dial option to display the Edit Speed Dial dialog box shown in Figure 507.1.
2. Click your mouse on the speed-dial button you want to modify or add. If you click over a used speed-dial button, you can replace its current name and number with new ones. If you click over an unused speed-dial button, you can add a name and number for that button.
3. Click your mouse on the Save button to save your speed-dial changes.

If you click your mouse over one of the Phone Dialer window's unused speed-dial buttons, Phone Dialer displays the Program Speed Dial dialog box (shown in Figure 507.2), which you can use to add a name and number for that button.

Using Windows 95 Fax and E-Mail Capabilities

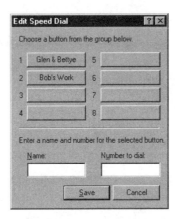

Figure 507.1 Adding speed dial button information.

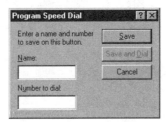

Figure 507.2 Instantly program speed dial numbers.

Specifying the Phone Dialer Device — 508

If you connect more than one modem to your computer, you can specify which modem Phone Dialer should use. When you select the Tools menu Connect Using option, Phone Dialer displays the Connect Using dialog box shown in Figure 508. From the dialog box's Line pull-down list, you can select your system's modems. If you use a second phone line, you can select the line from the Address pull-down list.

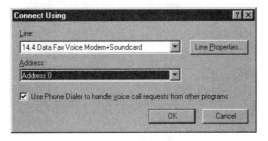

Figure 508 Selecting a Phone Dialer modem.

Using a Phone Dialer Profile — 509

If you use Phone Dialer on a laptop computer, each location from which you dial might require different dialing properties. For example, when you use your laptop at work, you might have to dial 9 to get an outside line. Fortunately, you can set up different Phone Dialer profiles so that Phone Dialer dials differently depending on your location. To set up a Phone Dialer profile, perform these steps:

1. Select the Tools menu Dialing Properties option. Phone Dialer will display the Dialing Properties sheet shown in Figure 509.
2. Click your mouse on the New button to create a new location.
3. Enter the new Phone Dialer profile's location name and press ENTER.
4. Set the various dialing properties on the Dialing Properties sheet.
5. Click your mouse on the OK button to save your new profile.

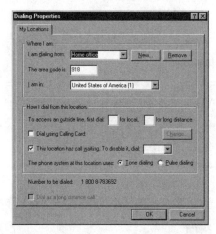

Figure 509 *Specifying a new Phone Dialer profile.*

510 Logging Calls Using Phone Dialer

Phone Dialer can log the location, number, date, time, and duration of calls you place. (Some applications can use Phone Dialer to monitor both incoming and outgoing calls, so your phone log might contain incoming calls as well.) Every time you use Phone Dialer to place a call, Phone Dialer adds to the log.

To view the log, select the Tools menu Show Log option. After you display the log, you can copy, cut, or delete information from it. However, Phone Dialer does not let you change specific log information, such as the number or person you called.

511 Controlling the Phone Dialer Logs

As Tip 510 mentions, you can copy or cut information from, as well as paste information to, a phone log, such as the one shown in Figure 511. For example, to copy call information from the phone log, click your mouse on a call (or press CTRL and click your mouse over several calls). Then, use the File menu to copy that information to the Windows 95 Clipboard.

If your Phone Dialer and related calling software supports incoming calls (including Caller ID, if available in your area), you can select whether you want to view incoming, outgoing, or both kinds of calls in the call log. To do so, click your mouse on the Log menu Options option.

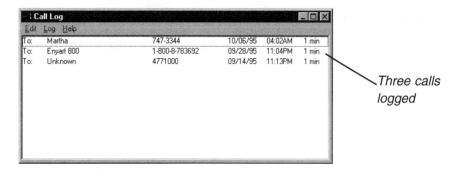

Figure 511 A sample call log.

Purging the Phone Dialer Log — 512

The Phone Dialer log fills up quickly if you use it to place many calls. As such, you may periodically need to remove old log entries to make room for new ones. To remove an entry, click your mouse on it and then select the File menu Cut option. Phone Dialer, in turn, will move the entry to the Windows 95 Clipboard.

Note: To select multiple items for removal, hold down the CTRL key and click on each entry you want to send to the Clipboard.

Understanding Windows 95's Notebook Support — 513

Windows 95 integrates notebook support into most Windows 95 applications, such as Explorer and the My Computer window. Microsoft calls the Windows 95 notebook support *Mobile Computing Services*. You can work more easily with your notebook computer, both at home and on the road, using the following mobile computing services:

- *Power management*: Tips 259 through 262 explain Windows 95 power management features.
- *Briefcase*: Lets you keep portable and desktop computers' files in sync with each other.
- *Direct connect*: Lets you connect two computers with a parallel or serial cable to simulate simple network access.
- *Deferred printing*: Lets you print documents when you do not have a printer attached to your computer. Windows 95 completes the printing when you attach a printer.
- *Docking station detection*: Supports notebook docking stations, which turn notebook computers into desktop computers at work or at home.

Managing Files Using Briefcase — 514

If you work with a desktop computer in the office and a notebook on the road, you've faced the challenge of trying to keep your files in sync with each other. Before you leave on a trip, you copy your desktop data files to your notebook. As you travel, you make changes to one or more of those files. Then, when you return from your trip, you must copy the files you changed back to your desktop computer. As you know, this file-shuffling process is not only time-consuming, but also somewhat dangerous. For example, after a long, tiring trip, you might inadvertently copy an old file on your desktop system over a file you modified during the trip.

Luckily, Windows 95 includes the Briefcase program to help you keep files in sync more easily. The files you store in the Briefcase program (you drag files to the Briefcase icon to store files in Briefcase) stay up-to-date. Additionally, when you return from a trip and reconnect your notebook and Desktop computers, these files can copy themselves from one computer to the other. Briefcase checks files on both your desktop computer and notebook and, at your command, updates both computers with the latest versions.

Note: *If you installed Windows 95 without the Briefcase program, run the My Computer's Add/Remove Programs option to add the briefcase program to your computer.*

The easiest way to work with Briefcase is to copy a Briefcase shortcut to your Desktop. To do so, perform these steps:

1. Start Explorer.
2. Locate the Briefcase folder.
3. Drag the Briefcase folder to your Desktop.
4. Double-click your mouse on the Briefcase icon to display the Briefcase window shown in Figure 514. Your Briefcase window will be empty when you first display it.

Figure 514 The Briefcase program.

515 Test Driving the Briefcase

The best way to learn the Briefcase program is to try it. As such, this tip walks you through a Briefcase-based scenario so you can see how Briefcase works. This tip uses your floppy disk drive to simulate a remote notebook computer. You can use a floppy disk as a Briefcase go-between storage medium, a network if your notebook contains a network card, or a direct connect parallel or serial connection. To test-drive Briefcase, perform these steps:

1. Start WordPad or any other word processor to create and save a simple one-line file.
2. Close the word-processor program.
3. Hold the CTRL key and drag the file from Explorer to the Briefcase window. The CTRL key ensures that Explorer copies and does not move the file. The file now resides in both your desktop computer's Briefcase window and at your desktop hard disk's regular word-processor location.
4. Open the My Computer window.
5. Hold the CTRL key and drag the Briefcase icon to your floppy disk icon inside the My Computer window. Notice how the Briefcase icon is the storage device for all your portable files. You are, in effect, taking a briefcase full of files to your notebook. However, in this example, don't copy the files to your notebook. Your floppy disk drive will act like an external computer.
6. Start your word processor again.

7. Add a line to the *floppy disk's* Briefcase file. When you save the file and close the word processor, your floppy disk's file will be different from the desktop computer's. This mirrors your notebook work. Instead of changing the Briefcase file on your notebook and copying the Briefcase back to your floppy to transfer it to your desktop again, you skip the copying to and from your notebook stage.

8. Open your desktop computer's My Computer window and double-click your floppy disk drive. Notice that the Status column shows the file needs updating. Briefcase realizes that the floppy disk's file differs from the desktop's version.

9. Select the Briefcase menu Update All option. Briefcase displays the Update Briefcase window, as shown in Figure 515. The Update Briefcase window displays the differences between the two file versions, including the files' size and date-and-time stamps. The arrow indicates the update's direction. If there are several files to update, the window will display similar information for all of them.

10. Click your mouse on the Update button to put the latest file version on both computers.

Again, the basic process is to copy your needed notebook files to your Briefcase icon, copy the Briefcase icon to your floppy disk (or to the notebook over a network or direct cable connection), and then copy the floppy disk to your notebook. (Be sure to work on only those files in the notebook's Briefcase folder.) When you return from your trip, you copy your notebook's Briefcase to your floppy disk (or to the desktop computer over a network or direct connect cable), use My Computer to open your desktop computer's floppy disk window, and select the Briefcase menu Update All option. Your desktop files will now be identical to your notebook's.

Note: Briefcase eliminates the drudgery of having to check every file by hand, on both your notebook and desktop, to make sure both computers contain the latest versions.

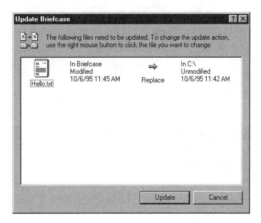

Figure 515 Briefcase keeps you informed.

Updating a Specific File — 516

When you return from a trip, you may decide that you don't like the changes you made to some of your Briefcase files. Or, someone at your office may have changed a desktop file, and you want to keep their changes and not your notebook's. In either case, when you use Briefcase to synchronize the files on your desktop and portable computers, you will want Briefcase to update some files and leave others alone. To update only one particular file, click your mouse on that file in the Briefcase window. Then, select the Briefcase menu Update Selection option. Briefcase, in turn, will update that file (by transferring the latest version into the Briefcase window) and mark the file's Status column "Up-to-date." To update several files, hold down the CTRL key, click your mouse on the files, and select the Briefcase menu Update Selection option.

517 Splitting a File from an Original

As you work with Briefcase, there may be times when you want to sever the link between an original file and a Briefcase file. For example, if you take a file on the road and, while you're away, a co-worker makes changes to the same file on your desktop system, you may want to preserve your and your co-workers's changes as separate files.

Luckily, Briefcase lets you separate the link between a Briefcase file and the original file. The Briefcase version becomes an *orphan*. As such, you can no longer update that orphaned Briefcase file with another file. However, you can leave the orphaned file inside Briefcase if you want to keep the archival file copy around for a while. To split a Briefcase file from the desktop computer's version, open the Briefcase window. Then, in the Briefcase window, select the file you want to split. Finally, select the Briefcase menu Split From Original option.

518 Briefcase Uses Date and Time Stamps Only

Your computer files always carry date-and-time stamps that tell when you last modified the files. When Briefcase updates a file, Briefcase compares the date-and-time stamps of both file versions (desktop and notebook) to decide which one is the most current. As such, you'll want to make sure that the date-and-time on both your desktop and notebook computers is correct before you use Briefcase. If you don't, Briefcase may replace the latest version of a file with an earlier one and thus cost you hours or even days of work.

519 Using Briefcase's Toolbar

The Briefcase window has a toolbar that provides you with one-button access to many important Briefcase program functions. To turn this toolbar on and off, select the View menu Toolbar option. Table 519 explains the purpose of each Briefcase toolbar button.

Toolbar Icon	Purpose
New Briefcase	Lets you move to a different folder in case you've stored multiple Briefcase folders on your computer or network.
⬆	Moves up one subfolder level.
⇄	Updates all the Briefcase files.
⇄	Updates only the selected Briefcase file or files.
🖧	Maps a network drive to a local drive letter.
✕	Disconnects a mapped drive from its local drive letter.
✂	Cuts Briefcase files to the Clipboard.
📋	Copies Briefcase files to the Clipboard.
📋	Pastes Briefcase files from the Clipboard.

Table 519 The Briefcase toolbar.

Understanding Deferred Printing — 520

In the early days of PCs, if you tried to print something without a turned-on printer attached to your system, your computer would freeze up until you attached and turned on a printer (or, worse, rebooted your PC and possibly lost some data). Then came Windows 3.1, which didn't freeze the computer but did issue an error message if your printer was not turned on or plugged in.

Unlike its Windows predecessors, Windows 95 offers seamless and transparent *deferred printing* for notebook users. If you print documents on your notebook but do not have a printer attached, Windows 95 spools those documents and prints them automatically when you plug in a printer or dock the notebook into a docking station (see Tip 522).

Using Deferred Printing on Your Desktop — 521

If you want to use deferred printing on your desktop or network computer, you can; but, you must tell Windows 95 that you want the deferred printing. Otherwise, Windows 95 will issue an error message, such as the one in Figure 521, that says your printer is not hooked up.

When you want to use deferred printing on a network computer, select your Printers folder Work Offline option. If your desktop is not networked and you want to defer printing from your stand-alone desktop computer, select the Pause Printing command inside your printer's window.

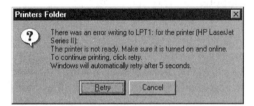

Figure 521 *Your computer does not defer printing automatically.*

Understanding Docking — 522

Notebook users generally do not have the same peripheral equipment as desktop computer users. For example, people do not often carry around large monitors when they work on a notebook. No notebooks exist that have 20-inch color monitors, although desktop computers can use such monitors. Fortunately, to enjoy the benefits of full-size and full-capacity peripheral equipment, you don't need to purchase a notebook and a desktop computer. Instead, you can buy a notebook with a *docking station*.

A docking station, which remains at your home or office, is a chassis into which you slide your notebook. You connect all the external devices to the docking station, such as a printer and a large monitor, that are too big to travel with you. As such, when you're at home or in the office, a docking station lets you use your notebook as if it were a desktop computer. Then, when you go on a trip, you can remove your notebook from the docking station and use your notebook on the road.

If you use a docking station, create two configuration profiles—one for the docked notebook and one for the undocked one. To do so, double-click the Control Panel's System icon. Windows 95, in turn, will display the System Properties sheet. Use the sheet's Hardware Profiles page to create your profiles. Windows 95, in turn, will change to the correct profile when you make a docking change.

523 Windows 95 Docking Detection

If you use a notebook and a docking station, the configurations your system uses while you're in the office may differ greatly from those it uses while you travel. For example, your notebook by itself may not have a CD-ROM drive, but your notebook's docking station may have one. When you dock your notebook, Windows 95 automatically detects the docking. As such, you don't need to reboot, log on to Windows as a different user, or even power off your notebook when you slide it into the docking station. Windows 95 updates your notebook's configuration automatically and instantly. When you undock your notebook, you must only select the Start menu's Eject PC command (non-docking notebooks will not offer this command). Windows 95, in turn, will reconfigure itself for notebook use. You do not have to turn off your computer to undock it.

524 Exchanging Files Using a Direct Cable Connection

Before Windows 95, users transferred files between computers by one of these methods:

- *Sneaker ware*: Users store files on floppy disks and travel to the other computer (hence the name *sneaker*).
- *Network control*: Users transfer files between computers over network wires.
- *Third-party direct cable connection*: Users purchase and run special software that lets them transfer files from one computer to the other, using a parallel or serial cable that plugged the two computers together.

Windows 95 includes its own cabling-connection feature, called *Direct Cable Connection*. Using this feature, you can hook a null-modem cable to the two computers' serial ports, or a bi-directional printer cable to the two computers' parallel ports, and transfer files almost as easily as if the two computers were networked together. Windows 95's Direct Cable Connection feature eliminates the need to buy third-party direct cable connection software.

525 Understanding Host and Guest Connections

When you use the Windows 95's Direct Cable Connection feature, you must designate one computer as the host and one as the guest. The *guest* computer pulls files from the host system. Therefore, you designate the computer that has the files to transfer as the *host* and the other, the target computer, as the guest. The Direct Cable Connection uses the host and guest information to transfer files.

526 Setting Up a Guest Computer

As Tip 525 explains, to use Windows 95's Direct Cable Connection feature, you first designate the computer that you want to receive files as the guest. You must set up the guest computer before you set up the host. As such, after you physically connect the host and guest computers, perform these steps:

1. Display the guest computer's Start menu.
2. Select the Start menu Programs option.
3. Select the Programs menu Accessories option.
4. Select the Accessories menu Direct Cable Connection option. Windows 95 will display the Direct Cable Connection wizard, as shown in Figure 526.

5. Click your mouse on the Change button if you need to change from a parallel connection to a serial connection.

6. Click your mouse on the Connect button. Windows 95 will poll the parallel port looking for a host computer.

Note: *The Direct Cable Connection program is not very patient. If you do not set up the host computer in a few seconds, Windows 95 displays a reminder window that informs you the host is not ready. Click your mouse on the OK button to restart the guest connection. When you set up the host (see Tip 527), the Direct Cable Connection will sense the connection.*

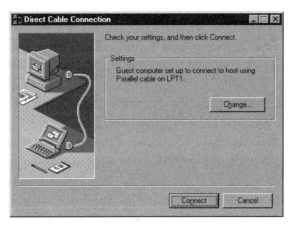

Figure 526 *Setting up the guest computer.*

Setting Up a Host Computer 527

After you designate one computer as a guest computer, you must setup the second or host computer. After you designate a host and guest, you transfer files back and forth between computers. You can even gain access to the host computer's network if you connect the host to a network. However, the files must reside in shared folders (you can specify the folder to be shared from Explorer's File menu). To set up a host, perform these steps:

1. Display the guest computer's Start menu.
2. Select the Start menu Programs option.
3. Select the Programs menu Accessories option.
4. Select the Accessories menu Direct Cable Connection option. Windows 95 will display the Direct Cable Connection wizard.
5. Select the Host option button.
6. Click your mouse on the Next button.
7. Select the port that holds the direct cable connects. You must connect a parallel port to the other computer's parallel port, or a serial port to the same serial port (COM1 or COM2), on the other computer.
8. Click your mouse on the Next button.
9. If you want to require the guest computer to use a password before it connects to the host computer, check the Use password protection option. Then, click your mouse on the Set Password button to enter the password.
10. Click your mouse on the Finish button to initiate the connection. After a brief pause, the Direct Cable Connection window will display the successful connection.

528 Understanding PCMCIA or PC Cards

A PCMCIA card (which stands for Personal Computer Memory Card Interface Association), or PC card as the industry more commonly calls it today, lets you easily swap port devices on your notebook computer. If you want to add an extra hard disk to your notebook, you can get a hard disk connected to a PC card and plug the card into your notebook. PC cards exist for CD-ROM drives, tape backup drives, and memory. The PC cards are credit-card shape and size, so they consume little weight or space.

PC cards have been anything but standard over the past few years. However, with the emergence of Windows 95 Plug and Play, PC card manufacturers now follow a de facto standard: the Windows 95 standard. As such, all PC cards sold today should be compatible with one another and with Windows 95.

Note: *The PC card is so popular that even some desktop computers support the PC card interfaces.*

529 Displaying the Taskbar's PC Card Indicator

You can add a PC card Taskbar indicator, shown in Figure 529, to display the status of your PC card. The PC Card might be active, inactive, or indicating I/O throughput with blinking lights. If you cannot activate a device attached to your PC card, you might want to display the PC card icon on the Taskbar, so you can see if Windows 95 sends any activity to the PC card. To display the Taskbar's PC card indicator, perform these steps:

1. Select the Start menu Help option.
2. Click your mouse on the Index tab.
3. Type **PC card**. The index displays all the PC card Help features on the list.
4. Double-click your left mouse button on the item labeled displaying the status indicator. The Help system will display Help information for the PC card indicator.
5. Click your mouse on the jump button (the button with the curved arrow) inside the Help window. The Windows 95 Help system will take you to the PC Card (PCMCIA) Properties sheet.
6. Click your mouse on the Show control on taskbar option to display the Taskbar indicator.
7. Click your mouse on the OK button to save your changes.

Figure 529 *The PC card Taskbar indicator.*

530 Installing a PC Card Device

When you install a PC card into your computer, you must make Windows 95 aware of the card's presence and let the operating system know the card's type. Luckily, Windows 95 provides a wizard that helps you easily accomplish both these tasks. To run this wizard, perform these steps:

1. Open the Control Panel.
2. Double-click your left mouse button on the Add New Hardware icon. Windows 95 will start the Add New Hardware wizard.
3. Click your mouse on the Next button.

4. Select the No option.
5. Click your mouse on the Next button.
6. From the list of hardware devices, click your mouse on PCMCIA socket. Figure 530.1 shows the list.
7. Click your mouse on the Next button. The Add New Hardware wizard will display the list boxes shown in Figure 530.2.
8. Select your PC card's manufacturer from the Manufacturers list box. Then, select your PC card's model from the Models list box.
9. Click the Next button twice. Windows 95 may ask for your Windows 95 installation CD-ROM or floppy disks. Windows 95 will copy the PC card driver from the installation disk to your Windows 95 system.
10. Click your mouse on the Finish button to complete the PC card setup.

Figure 530.1 Installing a PC card.

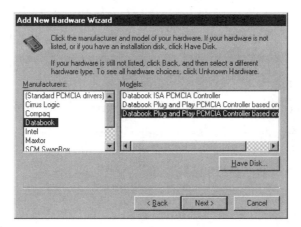

Figure 530.2 Selecting a PC card.

Installing a PC Card for Use   531

After you've set up your PC card's driver (following Tip 530's steps), you only have to plug your PC card into your computer for Windows 95 to recognize the card and update every needed driver. For example, if you insert a modem PC card, Windows 95 will automatically load the proper modem driver. Before Windows 95, users had to power off their computers to install PC cards and use the new device.

532 Removing a PC Card

When you want to remove a PC card, simply do so and let Windows 95 reconfigure its drivers for your missing card. If, the PC card has a network adapter on it and you remove the card, you can direct Windows 95 to automatically remove all network traces from your configuration. In this way, Windows 95 makes removing hardware from your system as easy as installing hardware that supports plug and play.

533 Controlling 32-Bit PC Card Support

Windows cannot detect some non-plug and play, 32-bit PC cards when you install them. Therefore, you may have to enable, and in rare instances disable, the PC card if Windows 95 does not recognize the card's presence or absence. To enable the 32-bit PC card support, click your mouse on the Start menu Help option. Then, on the Help Topic sheet Index page, select the 32-bit PC cards enabling support for Help topic. Finally, click your mouse on the jump button that appears in the Help window. Online Help, in turn, will display one of two windows:

- A wizard (Tip 530 describes the wizard) that you can follow to enable the PC card support
- The PC card Properties sheet, which you can close because Windows 95 already recognizes your PC card

To disable the 32-bit PC card support, perform these steps:

1. Select the Help topic called 32-bit PC card disabling support for to display a Help window.
2. Click on the Help window's jump button to display the Device Manager window.
3. Double-click your left mouse button on both the plus signs to the left of the "PCMCIA socket" and "PCMCIA controller" entries.
4. Click your mouse on the OK and Close buttons.
5. Click your mouse on the Cancel button.
6. Start the Windows 95 Notepad editor and remove the following line from CONFIG.SYS, AUTOEXEC.BAT, and SYSTEM.INI:

```
REM - by PC Card (PCMCIA) wizard
```

7. After you save your changes to the three files, shut down Windows 95 and restart the system.

These steps do not remove the actual driver from your computer. However, they do disable the driver that you have. Running through these steps every time you add or remove a PC card is tedious. Fortunately, you will not have to perform these steps for the majority of cards you use.

534 Supporting Flash Memory

To improve the battery life of notebook computers, hardware manufacturers now provide ways to reduce the computer's battery consumption. For example, when you are not actively using your notebook, many computer's now "spin down" the hard disk. In the future, many notebook computers will take advantage of *flash memory* to hold common operating system elements. Flash memory is similar to read-only memory (ROM) in that it retains its contents when the computer is not powered on. Unlike ROM, whose contents cannot be changed, you can change the contents of flash memory (although it is not something you would do on a regular basis). Using flash memory, notebook computers will reduce their long boot times during which the operating system must load itself into memory. Because the operating system will already reside in flash memory, your computer will be able to perform "instant on" operations.

Using PCMCIA Memory Card | 535

As you learned in Tip 528, you can purchase PCMCIA cards that contain modems, network adapters, SCSI connectors, and more. As the size and complexity of Windows-based applications continues to grow, many notebook computers will feel a "memory crunch" because they simply cannot hold enough RAM. Because notebook computers are more difficult to open up and work within, users are often less likely to install RAM themselves. As an easy solution, watch for PCMCIA cards that containing 8 to 16Mb of RAM to become very popular in the near future.

Understanding PC Card Sound Effects | 536

As Tips 288 through 292 explain, you can add sounds to various Windows 95 events. Because Windows 95 supports sound and multimedia far better than previous versions of Windows and MS-DOS did, these "event" sounds give you audible feedback that goes far beyond the quality of the little PC speaker that beeps when you boot your computer. To take advantage of Windows 95's sound effects, you need a sound card, such as a SoundBlaster-compatible card, and an amplified set of speakers.

Before sound cards became so popular and inexpensive, game and multimedia software developers had to rely on the one-voice, poor-quality PC speaker, which reproduces most sounds as a series of buzzes. The next several tips introduce various Windows 95 sound capabilities and teach you a little about how your PC reproduces sound.

Understanding Windows 95 Multimedia Support | 537

As you know, sound is not the only multimedia feature. A computer with multimedia capabilities supports sound recording and playback, video playback of video files, CD music playback, and CD-ROM video/audio playback. Windows 95 is an excellent operating system for multimedia users for many reasons:

- Windows 95 Plug and Play makes multimedia-hardware installation easy.
- The Windows 95 32-bit, local-bus video support increases graphics speed.
- Windows 95 contains a new technology called *Polymessaging MIDI*, which lets programs play MIDI (see Tip 544) sounds without sacrificing CPU performance.
- The CD-ROM AutoPlay feature lets you insert CD-ROMs in your CD-ROM drive and start using them without requiring startup commands.
- Windows 95 supports multi-speed CD-ROM drives, as well as video CDs and the Kodak PhotoCD standard.
- Windows 95 includes a programmable audio CD player that lets you manage a CD collection of song titles and artists.

Using Control Panel Multimedia Settings | 538

Almost every PC sold today includes a CD-ROM and sound card. As such, Windows 95 makes it very easy for you customize such hardware. The Control Panel includes a Multimedia icon you can double-click to open the Multimedia Properties sheet shown in Figure 538. This Multimedia Properties sheet lets you customize your multimedia devices and change the way your audio, video, MIDI sound, and CD-ROM works.

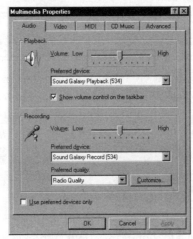

Figure 538 *The Multimedia Properties sheet.*

539 Controlling Speaker Volume and the Taskbar Volume Icon

When you want to change the volume of your PC's sounds or those sounds you record from your PC, you have three options:

- Use the Multimedia Properties sheet Audio page to adjust the global system volume.
- Click on the Taskbar speaker icon and use the slider to set the volume.
- Double-click your Taskbar speaker icon to adjust the volume settings.

To raise or lower your computer's sound output volume, open the Multimedia Properties sheet Audio page. Then, slide the Playback volume control left or right to suit your needs. If your sound card respects the Audio page's interface, all your computer's sounds will reflect the change in volume when you close the Audio page. (If you cannot use the Multimedia Properties sheet to change your sound card's volume, your Audio page's volume controls will appear gray.) The Taskbar's volume control lets you adjust one of several volume levels, such as your sound card and your CD-ROM. Tips 563 through 566 explain how to use the Taskbar's volume control.

Note: As you slide the global volume lever, Windows 95 sounds a beep to let you know the current volume.

540 Controlling Sound Card Recording

The Windows 95 Sound Recorder program lets you record, playback, and edit sound files. (Tip 557 explains how to start the Sound Recorder.) The Multimedia Properties sheet Audio page contains a volume control you use to set your sound card's recording volume. If you want to adjust your sound card's recording volume control, drag the Recording Volume slider.

541 Understanding Digital Audio

All noise you hear is *analog-based*. If you were to view the breakdown of a sound, such as a spoken word, you would see hundreds of up and down signals. Figure 541.1 shows a visual presentation of an analog wave. Note how the up and down points of analog wave lines are connected. A digital signal, on the other hand, is *discrete*—the up and down points cannot connect. Digital can track only a fixed number of ups and downs, something like the series in Figure 541.2's chart. Therefore, a digital signal cannot sound as good as an analog signal if the digital signal contains a small sample of the analog signal's up and down points.

Because computers are *digital* devices, the quality of any sound that comes out of your sound card depends on the sample of digital up and down signals Windows 95 creates from the original sound's analog signal. Therefore, the larger the *sampling rate*, the better the sound becomes. However, quality sound has one drawback. The larger a sound's sampling rate, the more disk space the sound file consumes. Your computer can sample at either an 8-bit rate or a 16-bit rate. The 16-bit sampling rate sounds better but consumes much more disk space.

Note: Your computer can produce sounds in two-channel stereo or in one-channel mono. Just as two stereo speakers sound better than a single-speaker mono radio (because a stereo's sound adds spatial separation), a stereo computerized sound file sounds better than a mono sound file. However, stereo sound requires more disk space than mono sound.

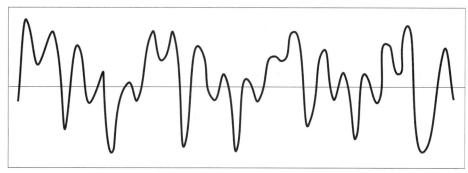

Figure 541.1 *An analog sound signal.*

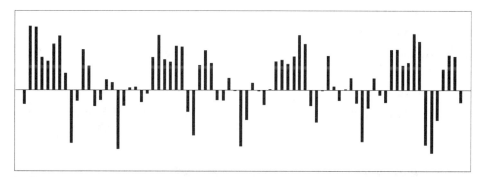

Figure 541.2 *A digital sound signal.*

Creating a Custom Audio Setting 542

The Multimedia Properties sheet Audio page contains a Preferred quality pull-down list from which you can change your sound's sampling rate (see Tip 541). From this pull-down list, you can select the following settings:

- *CD Quality*: Gives you the highest sampling rate and requires the most disk space for the sound files you create.

- *Radio Quality*: Gives you an acceptable, but limited, sampling rate that consumes less disk space than CD Quality.

- *Telephone Quality*: Gives you a poor sampling rate that works well for voice, but not music. If you have limited disk space, Telephone Quality might be your best option.

If you click your mouse on the Customize button, Windows 95 will display the Customize dialog box, as shown in Figure 542. The Customize dialog box lets you add your own customized Preferred quality settings. To create your own customized setting, first type a title for the setting in the Name field and click your mouse on the Save As button. Then, from the Attributes pull-down list, select an item that shows the attributes you want your custom Preferred quality setting to have. You can select your setting's Hz value. (Generally, the higher the Hz value, the higher the tones that your sound card can produce.) Additionally, you can specify whether sound files you record at this setting are mono or stereo, 8- or 16-bit sound files. Windows 95 tells you the number of kilobytes of disk space a second of music you record at each setting will consume.

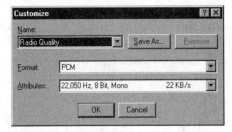

Figure 542 *Create your own sampling qualities.*

543 Controlling the Default Video Size

The Windows 95 installation CD-ROM provides several sample videos you can view with the Media Player (see Tips 551 through 556). Generally, the size of the video picture determines the quality of the video playback. The larger the video picture, the slower and choppier the picture becomes. If the videos you play are choppy, you may need to shrink the size of the playback picture. To do so, perform these steps:

1. Open the Control Panel.
2. Double-click your mouse on the Multimedia icon.
3. Click the Multimedia Properties sheet Video page. Windows 95 will display the Video page, as shown in Figure 543.
4. Click your mouse on the Window option button
5. From the Window pull-down list, select the size picture you want Windows 95 to use for your videos. In the sample monitor at the top of the page, Windows 95 will show you the amount of screen space your selection will consume.
6. Click your mouse on the OK button to save your changes.

Note: *The playback picture's size is not the only factor that determines the quality of video playback. Your computer's speed and memory, as well as your CD-ROM drive and video card, can also affect playback quality.*

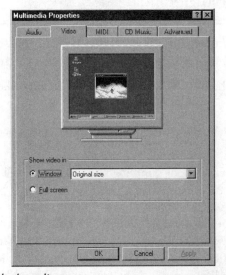

Figure 543 *The video size affects the playback quality.*

Understanding MIDI 544

MIDI (Musical Instrument Digital Interface) is a standard set of audio routines that your computer's sound card uses to simulate musical instruments. The *Polymessage MIDI support* offered in Windows 95 lets your computer play several MIDI instructions and consume very little processor resources. The end result is a better-sounding MIDI playback that uses fewer computer resources than previous MIDI implementations. The Multimedia Properties sheet MIDI page, shown in Figure 544, lets you control the way MIDI works on your computer. The Single Instrument option uses an industry standard scheme whereby a MIDI channel 4, for example, represents the same musical instrument as MIDI channel 4 on other computers. The Custom configuration option lets you assign musical instruments to any MIDI channel you choose. Therefore, if you assign various instruments to one or more channels and then use the Media Player to play a MIDI song file (all MIDI files have the MID filename extension), your computer will play the MIDI song differently than another system would.

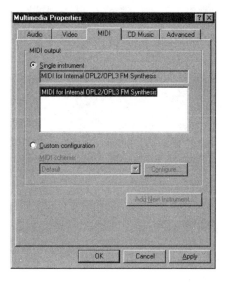

Figure 544 *You can adjust MIDI settings.*

Creating a Custom MIDI Setting 545

Advanced users who combine computers and musical instruments to produce music and sound effects may want to change certain MIDI channels. As Tip 544 explains, Windows 95 assigns a musical instrument sound to each MIDI channel (there are 16 channels). If you want to change your system's MIDI channel assignments, perform these steps:

1. Open the Multimedia Properties sheet MIDI page.
2. Click your mouse on the Custom configuration option button.
3. Click your mouse on the Configure button. Windows 95 will display the MIDI configuration window, which you can use to assign an instrument sound to each MIDI channel.
4. Click your mouse on the Save As button and enter a new name for your MIDI configuration.
5. Click your mouse over each MIDI channel and select an instrument you want your sound card to play for that channel.
6. Click your mouse on the OK button to save your changes.

In step 4, if you substitute one instrument for another, the Media Player will use the sound of the new instrument for all notes assigned to that channel. For example, if you change channel 1's setting from piano to trombone, the Media

Player will play a trombone instead of a piano for the notes assigned to channel 1. However, to successfully change your MIDI settings, you must have some understanding of music composition. If you don't understand music composition, you'll likely spend much time experimenting before you find a group of harmonious MIDI settings.

546 Understanding Audio CD

As you know, you can play audio CDs in your CD-ROM drive. Windows 95's AutoPlay feature starts the CD Player program as soon as you insert a CD into your CD-ROM. Additionally, CD-ROM drives contain headphone jacks you can use to listen to the audio CD privately. (Many computer users also run their CD output through their sound cards.) The Multimedia Properties sheet CD Audio page, shown in Figure 546, lets you change the headphone volume level directly from your PC's keyboard. If you have multiple CD-ROM drives, you can set a different volume level for each drive.

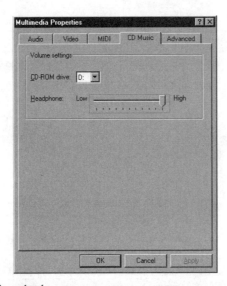

Figure 546 Adjusting audio CD's headphone levels.

547 Customizing Advanced Multimedia Settings

The Multimedia Properties sheet Advanced page contains a list of every multimedia device driver installed in your computer. These device drivers are programs that control the multimedia sounds and videos your computer reproduces. Additionally, the Advanced page is the only location in Windows 95 that lets you adjust *all* of your system's multimedia capabilities. Depending on your system's hardware and software, you may see fewer or more device-driver categories than Figure 547 shows. To view the components inside a driver category, click your mouse on the plus sign next to the category name. You can assign a *friendly name* to many of the listed drivers, but keep a record of the original name in case you need to refer to that name later. To assign a friendly name to a device driver, perform these steps:

1. Click your mouse on the plus sign of the device's general category you want to change. You cannot change general category names, only the specific driver names.
2. Right-click your mouse over the driver to display a pop-up menu.
3. Select the pop-up menu's Friendly Name option to change the name. If the pop-up menu's Friendly Name option appears gray, you will not be able to assign a friendly name to that particular device.

4. Click your mouse on the Yes button to confirm the name change.
5. Type the new name and press ENTER.
6. Click your mouse on the Yes button to save the name change.

The friendly name will subsequently appear for that particular device in the list.

Figure 547 *The Multimedia Properties sheet Advanced page.*

Customizing a Multimedia Driver | 548

To change one of the multimedia device drivers that the Multimedia Properties sheet Advanced page lists, click your mouse on the device and then click the Properties button. (You can also select the pop-up menu's Properties option.) Windows 95, in turn, will display the properties sheet for that driver. Typically, the properties sheet will contain the name of the company that authored the device driver file (generally, the same company that created the device the driver controls) and settings for the device driver. After you change a device driver's properties, click your mouse on the OK button to save your changes.

Note: *The drivers appear on the Multimedia Properties sheet Advanced page because their settings require advanced knowledge of the multimedia driver and its related hardware. As such, before you change a device driver setting, be sure you know exactly what you are doing. If you make an error, you could confuse the driver and accidentally shut down a portion of your multimedia capabilities.*

Understanding Video and Audio Codecs | 549

Video and audio files require huge amounts of disk space. A simple one-minute video file can consume a hundred megabytes of disk space. To reduce the amount of disk space such files require, hardware and software manufacturers have developed a series of compression schemes, called *audio* and *video codecs*.

The Multimedia Properties sheet Advanced page contains two general categories of codecs: Video Compression Codecs and Audio Compression Codecs. If you click on these general categories, Windows 95 will display a list of the specific compression schemes you can use for your video and audio files. Because different applications use different codecs (compression descriptions), the list will grow as you add multimedia software to your computer.

550 Prioritizing Video and Audio Codecs

Each audio and video codec has an assigned number. The number may or may not be unique. For example, when a program is about to play video, that program must ensure that your computer uses the proper compression driver to read the video file and expand the file for playback. (Codecs describe the compression description to your computer so your computer can read and decompress the compressed files.) Some codec schemes compress better than others others. The codec number, however, determines which codec driver (software) Windows 95 will use. The driver's codec number determines the driver's priority. For example, if an audio codec is lower than another's, Windows 95 selects the low audio codec first. If, however, a program requests that Windows 95 use a specific codec driver, Windows 95 respects the application's wishes and uses that driver in spite of the driver's priority.

551 Using the Media Player

The Media Player is a Windows 95 program that lets you play virtually any multimedia file. The Media Player plays MIDI sound files, wave sound files (sample sounds recorded and sampled into digital sounds), audio CD music, and video files. The Media Player contains controls that let you adjust the way the audio or video operates. Table 551 describes each Media Player button. The buttons look and act just like VCR buttons. To start the Media Player, perform these steps:

1. Click your mouse on the Start menu Programs option.
2. Click your mouse on the Programs menu Accessories option.
3. Click your mouse on the Accessories menu Multimedia option.
4. Click your mouse on the Multimedia menu Media Player option. Windows 95 will load the Media Player window, as shown in Figure 551.

Media Player Button	Purpose
▶	Plays the current sound.
❚❚	Pauses the playback (the Play button turns into the Pause button after you start playing a video or sound).
■	Stops the CD.
▲	Ejects the CD.
⏮	Returns the sound to a previous mark.
⏪	Rewinds the sound.
⏩	Fast forwards the sound.
⏭	Moves the sound to the next mark.
⤓	Starts selecting part of the sound.
⤒	Stops selecting part of the sound.

Table 551 *The Media Player's buttons.*

Figure 551 The Media Player.

Opening a Media File — 552

As Tip 551 explains, the Media Player plays a variety of sounds and videos. However, before you load a sound or video file, you must tell Media Player the type of device you want to use with the file. For example, if you want to listen to an audio CD that's in your CD-ROM drive, you must select the audio CD device. To select a device, click your mouse on the Device menu and choose the option that best suits the file you want to play. For example, for sound files, select the Sound option. Likewise, for audio CDs, select the CD Audio option. If you want Media Player to play a file's sound or video clip, select the File menu Open option to open the file. Then, click your mouse on the play button.

Viewing Tracks, Time, or Frames — 553

As you know, when you play a tape in a cassette deck, the cassette deck uses a meter to keep track of the tape's progress. Similarly, Media Player can use meters to show you a sound or video's progress. Media Player can display three kinds of progress meters:

- *Tracks*: For audio CDs
- *Time*: For MIDI, audio CDs, and sound files
- *Frames*: For video files

You can access these three meters through the Media Player window's Scale menu. Some devices, such as video devices, let you display specific frames from the current video. When you specify the scale, Media Player updates the numbers below the status bar to track numbers, times, or frame numbers. You can drag the playing scale left and right to position the device to a specific track, time, or frame.

Selecting a Media Object — 554

You can place Media Player objects (sound files or video clips) on to the Clipboard. Then, you can paste that selection into another file. (You can even paste the clip within a word-processing document if your word processor is OLE compliant, as almost all are. For example, if you want to copy a sound, such as a song on an audio CD, to the Clipboard, you must first mark the beginning and end of the selection. To mark the beginning of a clip, click your mouse on the Start Selection button. To terminate the clip, click your mouse on the End Selection button. Then, select the Edit menu Copy option to copy your file to the Clipboard.

If you want to select a clip based on more precise measurements, you can save a copy of a specific time, track, or set of frames to the Clipboard. To do so, select the Edit menu Selection option and enter the specific values in the Set Selection dialog box.

Note: *If you select the Edit menu Copy object option immediately after loading a sound or video file, Media Player selects and sends the entire file to the Clipboard.*

555 | Customizing Media Player Options

Media Player lets you customize the playback of several options. When you select the Edit menu Options option, Media Player displays the Options dialog box. This dialog box includes the following options:

- *Auto Rewind*: Automatically rewinds (resets actually) a sound or video clip when the clip finishes.

- *Auto Repeat*: Automatically repeats the sound or video when the playback reaches the end.

- *OLE Object*: Determines if the control bar (the buttons) and caption appear when you copy a clip to an OLE-compatible program.

- *Border around object*: When you copy an object from the Clipboard to another application, Windows 95 will display a thin border around an object's icon.

- *Play in client document*: Starts playing the selected object when you double-click an embedded sound or video object's icon into another program. If you uncheck this option, Media Player will load and plays the clip from the double-clicked icon.

- *Dither picture to VGA color*: Sometimes, if you play a video clip that you did not create, the video image plays back poorly due to the quality of the originating system's video capabilities. If you click th Media Player will adjust video clips to your monitor's resolution.

556 | Customizing Device Properties

If you want to change a device's properties, select the Device menu Properties option. The device you select for playback (audio CD, video, or whatever) determines what the properties sheet contains. For example, if your selected device is an audio CD, your properties sheet will look like the one shown in Figure 556.1. If your selected device is a MIDI sound file, your properties sheet will look like the one shown in Figure 556.2. If your selected device is a Video for Windows file, your properties sheet will look like Figure 556.3. You can also access these properties sheets through the Multimedia Properties sheet (see Tips 538 through 550).

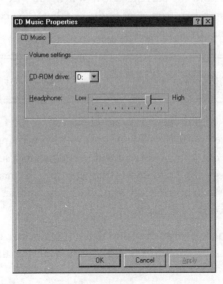

Figure 556.1 The Audio CD Properties sheet.

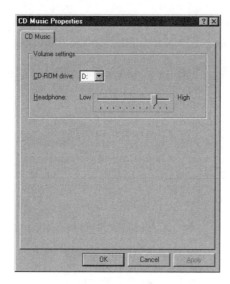

Figure 556.2 The MIDI Properties sheet.

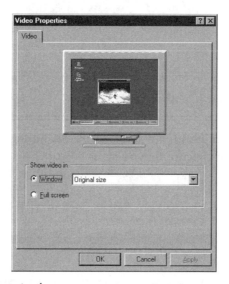

Figure 556.3 The Video for Windows Properties sheet.

Using the Sound Recorder | 557

The Sound Recorder program lets you record your own sound files as long as your sound card supports a microphone input (all sound cards approved for Windows 95 support recording). Table 557 explains the function of each Sound Recorder button. The buttons look and act just like a cassette recorder's buttons. To start the Sound Recorder, perform these steps:

1. Select the Start menu Programs option.
2. Select the Programs menu Accessories option.
3. Select the Accessories menu Multimedia option.
4. Click your mouse on the Multimedia menu Sound Recorder option. Windows 95 will load the Sound Recorder window, as shown in Figure 557.

Sound Recorder Button	Purpose
◀◀	Resets the sound to the sound's beginning.
▶▶	Sets the sound to the sound's endpoint.
▶	Plays the sound.
■	Stops the sound in progress.
●	Starts recording of a sound.

Table 557 The Sound Recorder's buttons.

Figure 557 The Sound Recorder window.

558 Recording and Saving an Audio File

After you plug a microphone into your sound card and start the Sound Recorder program, you're ready to record your own sounds. To record a sound file, perform these steps:

1. Click your mouse on the Record button.
2. Record the sound into your microphone. As you record, you'll see the sound's wave signal (see Tip 541) in the Sound Recorder's window.
3. Click the Stop button to stop recording.
4. Select the File menu Save As option.
5. Enter a sound filename. Sound Recorder automatically adds the WAV extension to the filename so that Windows 95 recognizes the sound file's type.

559 Controlling Sound Formats

Tip 541 explains how your computer converts analog sounds into digital files that represent those sounds. If you do not like the quality of the sounds you record, you can increase the digital sound quality, as well as increase the disk space your sounds will consume, through options on the Sound Recorder's File menu and Edit menu.

If you click on the File menu Properties option, Sound Recorder will display the properties sheet shown in Figure 559.1. To change a sound's recording quality, playback quality, or both (the "All formats" option), click your mouse on the Convert Now button and change the sound's sampling rate quality.

If you click on the Edit menu Audio Properties option, you will see the Audio Properties sheet shown in Figure 559.2. Using this sheet, you can select specific sampling rates or create your own.

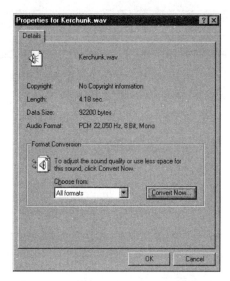

Figure 559.1 *The sound quality's Properties sheet.*

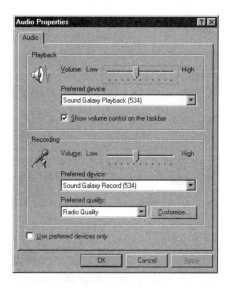

Figure 559.2 *The Audio Properties sheet.*

Editing a Recording   560

After you record a sound, you can delete some portion of that sound. The moving position indicator (the slider control that moves forward when you play a sound) keeps track of the sound's current position. If you want to delete part of a recording, you can use these two Edit menu options:

- *Delete Before Current Position*: Deletes all the sound up to the current position.
- *Delete After Current Position*: Deletes all the sound from the current position to the end of the sound.

To move the sound to its editing point, listen to the sound and pause it when you hear the location at which you want to delete. Or, drag the moving position indicator to the editing point.

Note: *Unlike the Media Player, the Sound Recorder does not let you enter a specific time point value for editing.*

561 Inserting and Mixing Sound Files

When you *insert* a sound into a sound clip, the new sound expands the current sound file. For example, if you insert the sound of a barking dog in the middle of a flute solo, the flute solo will play until the barking dog's insertion point. Then, the barking dog will play. Then, the flute solo will continue. When you *mix* one sound with another, the new sound overlays the old one. Therefore, if you mix the flute solo with a dog's barking, you will hear *both* sounds at the same time when you play the clip. The Edit menu Insert File option and Mix with File options let you insert and mix sounds at the loaded sound's current position.

Note: *If you've stored a sound clip on the Clipboard, you can insert and mix from the Clipboard using the Edit menu Paste Insert and Paste Mix options.*

562 Using Special Effects with a Recording

The Sound Recorder offers some special-effects capabilities that let you change the way the current clip sounds. Specifically, the Sound Recorder's Effects menu contains the following options:

- *Increase Volume (by 25%)*: Increases the sound file's volume level by 25%.
- *Decrease Volume*: Decreases the sound file's volume level by 25%.
- *Increase Speed (by 100%)*: Doubles the sound file's play speed.
- *Decrease Speed*: Halves the sound file's play speed.
- *Add Echo*: Adds an echo effect to the sound file.
- *Reverse*: Reverses the sound file so the sound plays backward.

As Tip 541 explains, digital sounds do not always sound as good as their analog equivalents. However, after you record a digital sound, you can insert clips, add special effects, and edit the sound without any degradation in sound quality. In contrast, you cannot cut and paste analog tape and re-record different parts of the tape several times without losing quality.

563 Using the Windows 95 Volume Control

The Windows 95 Volume Control program lets you adjust the volume for all these sound devices:

- The global sound from all sound sources
- Wave sound files
- MIDI sound files
- Microphone input
- Line-In connections
- Audio CDs

You can start the Volume Control program through the Start menu. (Select the Accessories menu Multimedia option. Then, select the Multimedia menu Volume Control option to reach the Volume Control program.) Additionally, you can use the Taskbar to open the Volume Control program. When you begin to play any multimedia file or CD-ROM, the speaker icon appears on the Taskbar. When you double-click your mouse on the speaker icon, the Volume Control program loads. Figure 563 shows the Volume Control program's window. Your Volume Control window might contain more or fewer volume control levers (see Tip 565).

Figure 563 *The Volume Control window.*

Controlling a Device's Balance 564

Most multimedia systems contain two speakers for stereo reproduction. *Balance* refers to the equality in loudness between those two speakers. When you set one speaker (or channel, to a higher volume than the other, the balance is out of alignment. If you want to hear a particular effect that comes out of only one of the two stereo channels, you can shift the balance to that channel—an action that simultaneously raises the volume in the selected channel and lowers the volume in the other. However, most of the time, you'll want to keep the volume equally balanced between your speakers.

Each section of the Volume Control window contains a Balance control you can slide left or right. Below each balance control is the volume control for that particular sound device.

Note: If you click your mouse on a volume control's Mute check box, the corresponding device stops outputting sound until you once again click your mouse on the Mute check box. During the muted time period, the sound keeps playing even though you cannot hear it. The Mute All option instantly mutes every sound playing.

Selecting Volume Control's Devices 565

You can decide which of your system's multimedia devices have volume controls in the Volume Control window. For example, if you use a microphone to record sounds, you can add the microphone's volume control to the Volume Control window. Likewise, if you never play audio CDs in your CD-ROM drive, you can hide the audio CD volume control from view. To select volume controls, perform these steps:

1. Select the Options menu Properties option. The Volume Control program displays the Volume Control Properties sheet shown in Figure 565.

2. Click your mouse on a device to change its volume control setting. To add a device's volume control to the Volume Control window, check the check box next to the device's name. To remove a device's volume control, remove the check from the check box next to the device's name.

3. Click your mouse on the OK button.

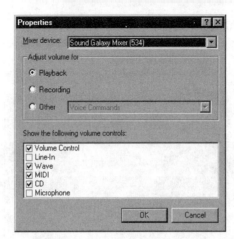

Figure 565 *Selecting volume controls.*

566 Be Aware of Sound Card Volume Controls

Depending on your sound card type, there may be times when your sound card has its own volume control knob. If you examine your sound ports (at the back of your system chassis) you may see a small volume control knob. Use this knob to set your computer's volume to the level you desire. Later, you can use the Windows 95 Volume Control to fine-tune your sound card's setting. If, when you use the Volume Control, your PC sound does not change, look first to determine if your sound card has such a volume control knob.

567 Using the CD Player

To play an audio CD, just insert the audio CD into your CD-ROM drive. In response, the CD Player, shown in Figure 567, will automatically play the CD. To stop playing an audio CD, close the CD Player window. If you want to play the audio CD once again after you've closed the window, click your mouse on the Multimedia menu CD Player option. (To reach the Multimedia menu, select the Accessories menu Multimedia option.) Table 567 explains each button on the CD Player window.

CD Player Button	Purpose
▶	Plays the CD.
❚❚	Pauses the CD.
■	Stops the CD.
◄◄	Starts the current CD track over.
◄◄	Skips backward a few seconds.
►►	Skips forward a few seconds.
►►❙	Starts the next CD track.
▲	Ejects the CD from the CD-ROM drive.

Table 567 *The CD Player's buttons.*

Figure 567 *The CD Player.*

Understanding Audio CD Play Lists — 568

The contents of an audio CD reside in one or more *tracks*. A track might contain a song, a symphony, background sounds, a comedy routine, and so on. As you use your system to play your audio CDs, there may be times when you don't like every track that resides on a particular audio CD. One of your favorite CDs might have eight or ten tracks you enjoy. Conversely, another CD might include only two or three tracks you want to hear. Luckily, for each of your audio CDs, you can set up a *play list* that tells the CD Player program exactly which tracks to play.

Creating a Play List — 569

As Tip 568 explains, the CD Player program lets you create a play list for each of your audio CDs. After you create a play list for a particular audio CD, the CD Player program will play only those tracks you specified in the list. To create a play list, perform these steps:

1. Insert a CD. The CD Player program starts automatically.
2. Select the Disc menu Edit Play List. The CD Player displays the Disc Settings dialog box shown in Figure 569.1. All ten tracks on the CD will play because all ten available tracks, although unnamed in the figure, appear in the play list at the left of the window until you delete one or more of them.
3. Type the artist name and CD title in the Artist and Title text boxes. Then, fill in the contents of the CD by entering the name of each song or section of each track. The back of the CD usually contains this information.
4. Click your mouse on the Track text box at the *bottom* of the dialog box.
5. Enter the name for the first track item, such as the first song.
6. Click your mouse on the Set Name button to add the name to the Available Tracks list box. The song title now appears as Track's name.
7. Click your mouse on the Track text box, enter the next track item's name, and click your mouse on the Set Name button. Continue this process until you've specified the name for all tracks on the CD.
8. If you want all the CDs tracks to appear in your play list, hold down the CTRL key and click your mouse on each track title that appears in the Available Tracks list box. If you want fewer tracks in the play list, hold down CTRL and click your mouse over the tracks you want to hear the next time you play the CD.
9. Click your mouse on the Add button to add the tracks you selected to the play list. Should you want to start over and create a new play list, click your mouse on the Clear All button.
10. Click your mouse on the OK button to return to the CD Player window. The CD Player now plays only those tracks in your play list.

When you complete the above steps for a CD, the CD Player remembers the CD's title, artist, track list, and play list the next time you insert that CD. You do not have to save anything for the CD Player to remember the CD.

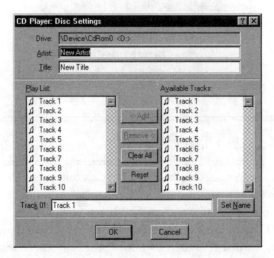

Figure 569.1 The Disc Settings dialog box.

570 Using the CD Player Toolbar

The CD Player's toolbar gives you one-button access to many of the CD Player program's functions. To display or hide the toolbar, select the View menu Toolbar option. Table 570 explains each toolbar button.

CD Player Button	Purpose
	Displays the Play List window.
	Displays the current track's elapsed playing time (see Tip 571).
	Displays the current track's remaining playing time (see Tip 571).
	Displays the CD's remaining playing time (see Tip 571).
	Plays CD tracks randomly (see Tip 572).
	Repeats the CD play continuously (see Tip 572).
	Plays only the first few seconds of each track (see Tip 573).

Table 570 The CD Player's toolbar buttons.

571 Viewing Audio CD Information

To let you view information about the current CD, the CD Player window's View menu contains these three options:

- *Track Time Elapsed*: Changes the display to show the amount of play time elapsed since the current track began playing.

- *Track Time Remaining*: Changes the display to show the amount of play time remaining on the current track.
- *Disc Time Remaining*: Changes the display to show the amount of play time remaining on the current CD.

As Tip 570 explains, the CD Player's toolbar also holds three buttons that let you view this information.

Controlling How Tracks Play   572

Like a CD player that you might purchase in a stereo store, the Windows 95 CD Player program lets you change the order in which it plays a CD's tracks. For example, if you play a CD at a party, you'll probably want to select the Continuous Play option so that the music doesn't stop when the play list finishes. To control the track-playing order, you can select these Options menu options:

- *Random Order*: Plays your play list's tracks randomly instead of sequentially.
- *Continuous Play*: Repeats the play list automatically.
- *Intro Play*: Plays the first ten seconds of each song remaining in the song list to help you locate the file you desire.

Finding a Specific Audio CD Song   573

The CD Player offers a sampling feature that lets you search for a specific track. After you insert a CD, you can tell the CD Player to play only the first ten seconds of each track. To search for a specific song, perform these steps:

1. Select the Options menu Intro Play option.
2. Play the CD to hear only the first ten seconds of each track in the play list. Tip 574 explains how to change the amount of time each track plays.
3. When you hear a song you like, click your mouse on the Stop button and note the track number.
4. Select the Options menu Intro Play option once again to turn off the sampling.
5. Open the Track pull-down list and select the track you want to hear.
6. Click your mouse on the Play button to hear the song.

Customizing the CD Player Preferences   574

When you select the Options menu Preferences option, the CD Player displays the Preferences dialog box shown in Figure 574. Table 574 explains each of the dialog box's options. You can change the preferences so that the CD Player performs the way you want.

Preferences	Purpose
Stop CD Playing on exit	Stops the CD's play when you close the CD Player program. If you unselect this option, the CD continues to play after you've closed the CD Player program.
Save settings on exit	Saves any preferences and viewing selections so that the CD Player program uses those settings the next time you start it.

Table 574 The CD Player's Preference options. (continued on the following page)

Show tool tips	Shows or hides the pop-up windows that appear when you move your mouse pointer over a toolbar button.
Intro play length	Changes the duration of the samples CD Player plays when you're searching for a specific track. (See Tip 573.)
Display font	Changes the digital readout to large or small displayed values.

Table 574 *The CD Player's Preference options. (continued from the previous page)*

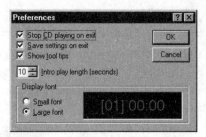

Figure 574 *The CD Player Preferences dialog box.*

575 Understanding the Windows 95 Accessories

Windows 95 provides accessory programs you can use to manage your Desktop and eliminate physical accessories, such as desk calculators and calendars. Since the first Windows version, nearly every Windows user has used some accessory program. Windows 95's accessory programs appear in the Accessories menu, which you access through the Start menu. Depending on your installation, your Accessories menu might display a few or many accessory programs. If you upgraded to Windows 95 from Windows 3.1 or Windows for Workgroups, the Windows 95 installation program transferred your previous version's Program Manager Accessories group to the Windows 95 Accessories menu and added other programs to the menu.

In addition to accessory programs, the Windows 95 Accessories menu contains a Games submenu with several games you can play between computing tasks. The rest of this section describes many of your accessory programs and provides tips on how to use them.

576 Windows 3.1 Accessory Programs

If you upgraded from Windows 3.1 or Windows for Workgroups, Windows 95 probably, depending on your previous version's configuration, transferred the following programs to your Accessories menu:

- *Calendar*: A simple calendar-scheduling program that lets you keep track of appointments and set alarms
- *Card File*: A database program that records data in an index file-like format
- *Character Map*: A utility program that lets you access special Windows 95 characters, such as foreign characters and math symbols
- *Clipboard Viewer*: A program that lets you see and change the Windows Clipboard
- *Notepad*: A simple text editor you can use to create and edit small text files

In addition, Windows 95 updates several other accessory programs and adds many of its own.

Using the Standard Calculator 577

As you use Windows 95, there may be times when you need to quickly calculate some numbers. For example, you may need to multiply some figures that you're including in a memo to your boss. In such cases, you don't need to search your desk drawers for a hand-held calculator or an adding machine. Instead, you can start the Windows 95 Calculator program. Then, after you use Calculator to crunch numbers, you can paste the result into your document. To start the Calculator program, perform these steps:

1. Display the Start menu.
2. Select the Start menu Programs option.
3. Select the Programs menu Accessories option.
4. Select the Accessories menu Calculator option. Windows 95 will open the Calculator program, as shown in Figure 577. If the Calculator that appears on your screen looks much more advanced than the one in Figure 577, select the View menu Standard option to change to the Standard Calculator.

Figure 577 *The Calculator program.*

Performing a Simple Calculation 578

Most of the time, people use the Calculator program for simple computations. For example, as you draft a memo for your boss, you might run the Calculator program to multiply a few numbers. To use the Calculator program for a simple calculation, perform these steps:

1. Start the Calculator program.
2. Press NUM LOCK, if your NUM LOCK light is off.
3. Use your numeric keypad to enter a number, such as **123**.
4. To add a number to the first one, press the + (plus) key. To subtract, press the - (minus) key. To multiply, press the * (asterisk) key. And, to divide, press the / (frontslash) key.
5. Enter the next number, such as **456**.
6. Press the ENTER key, the equal sign, or click your mouse on the = button to see the result.
7. Select the Edit menu Copy option if you want to copy the result to the Windows 95 Clipboard.

Note: *Although you can click your mouse over any of Calculator's buttons to enter numbers or specify mathematical operations, most users use the keyboard to enter their calculations. See Tip 580 for more information on using the keyboard and mouse with Calculator.*

579 Using the Scientific Calculator

The Scientific Calculator, shown in Figure 579, is much more advanced than most of us need on a daily basis. However, if you want the answer to a scientific calculation, the Scientific Calculator probably contains the appropriate statistical, trigonometric, logarithmic, or Boolean operation. To display the Scientific Calculator, select the Calculator window's View menu Scientific option. Calculator, in turn, will switch from Standard to Scientific mode.

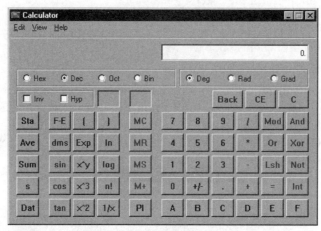

Figure 579 *The Scientific Calculator.*

580 Accessing Calculator Buttons from the Keyboard

If you use the calculator on a regular basis, you may find the mouse interface a little slow. However, the problem with using the keyboard is that not all the keyboard combinations work as you might expect. For example, to clear the Calculator's result window using your mouse, you click over the "C" button. Conversely, to clear the window using your keyboard, you press the Esc key (not the C key). Table 580.1 contains the Standard Calculator's keyboard combinations, and Table 580.2 contains the Scientific Calculator's keyboard combinations.

Button	Keyboard	Button Function
C	Esc	Clears the current calculation.
CE	Del	Clears the current value.
Back	Backspace	Clears the current value's rightmost digit.
MC	Ctrl-L	Clears the Calculator's memory.
MR	Ctrl-R	Recalls the Calculator's memory.
M+	Ctrl-P	Adds the current value to the Calculator's memory and stores the result in memory.
MS	Ctrl-M	Stores the current value in the Calculator's memory.
+/−	F9	Changes the current value's sign.
1/x	R	Calculates the current value's reciprocal.
sqrt	@	Calculates the current value's square root.
%	%	Treats the current value as a percentage.

Table 580.1 *The Standard Calculator's buttons and keyboard combinations.*

Button	Keyboard	Button Function
C	Esc	Clears the current calculation.
CE	Del	Clears the current value.
Back	Backspace	Clears the current value's rightmost digit.
MC	Ctrl-L	Clears the Calculator's memory contents.
MR	Ctrl-R	Recalls the Calculator's memory contents.
M+	Ctrl-P	Adds the current value to the Calculator's memory and stores the result in memory.
MS	Ctrl-M	Stores the current value in the Calculator's memory.
+/-	F9	Changes the current value's sign.
Mod	%	Calculates the remainder from division.
Or	|	Performs a bitwise OR.
Lsh	<	Performs a bitwise shift to the left. Inv+Lsh performs a bitwise shift to the right
And	&	Performs a bitwise exclusive AND.
Xor	^	Performs a bitwise exclusive OR.
Not	~	Performs a bitwise inverse.
Int	;	Displays the current value's integer portion.
A-F	A-F	Enters a hexadecimal digit.
PI	P	Displays the value of PI. Inv+PI displays 2 times PI.
Sta	Ctrl-S	Activates the Statistics Box.
Ave	Ctrl-A	Displays the average of the Statistics box values.
Sum	Ctrl-T	Displays the sum of the Statistics box values.
s	Ctrl-D	Calculates the standard deviation of the Statistics box values.
Dat	Ins	Places the current value into the Statistics box.
F-E	v	Toggles scientific notation on and off.
dms	M	Converts the current value into the degrees-minutes-seconds format. Inv+dms converts the value back.
sin	s	Displays the current value's sine. Inv+sin displays the arc sine.
cos	o	Displays the current value's cosine. Inv+cos displays the arc cosine.
tan	T	Displays the current value's tangent. Inv+tan displays the arc tangent.
()	()	Groups expressions.
Exp	X	Enables the entry of exponential numbers.
x^y	Y	Displays the value of X raised to the power of Y. Inv+x^y displays the result of X to the Y root.
x^3	#	Displays the value of X cubed. Inv+x^3 displays the cube root of X.

Table 580.2 The Scientific Calculator's buttons and keyboard combinations. (continued on the follownig page)

Button	Keyboard	Button Function
x^2	@	Displays the value of X squared. Inv+x^2 displays the square root of X.
ln	N	Displays the current value's natural logarithm.
log	L	Displays the current value's base 10 log.
n!	!	Calculates the current value's factorial.

Table 580.2 The Scientific Calculator's buttons and keyboard combinations. (continued from the previous page)

581 Performing Simple Statistics

Statistical calculations compute statistics on a series of numbers (such as the average, standard deviation, and so on), whereas regular math operations such as add and subtract work on two values at a time. The Scientific Calculator can calculate statistics based on values you enter into the Statistics Box. To place values in the Statistics Box, perform these steps:

1. Display the Scientific Calculator.
2. Click your mouse on the Sta button. The Scientific Calculator will open the Statistics Box shown in Figure 581.
3. Enter a value from your statistical series and click the DAT button. Repeat this step until you've entered all the series' values. If you enter an incorrect value, select it and click your mouse on the CD button to delete the entry from the list.
4. To calculate the sum, average, or standard deviation of the values you entered in the Statistics box, click your mouse on the Sum, Ave, or s button. The statistical result appears in the result window.

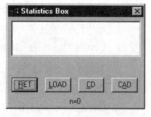

Figure 581 The Statistics Box.

582 Using the Clipboard Viewer

The Clipboard Viewer program displays the contents of the Windows 95 Clipboard. As such, if a cut, copy, or paste operation fails and you cannot figure out why, you can start the Clipboard Viewer program and further investigate the problem. To start the Clipboard Viewer, select the Accessories menu Clipboard Viewer option.

Figure 582 shows the Clipboard Viewer window. In this case, the Clipboard Viewer contains a paragraph of copied text. However, the Clipboard Viewer can also store graphics, worksheets, videos, and sounds.

Note: *If you upgraded from Windows for Workgroups, your Accessories menu will contain the **Clipbook Viewer** and not the Clipboard Viewer program. The Clipbook Viewer lets you cut and paste between networked computers.*

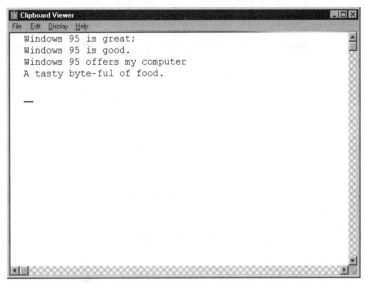

Figure 582 *The Clipboard Viewer window.*

Changing the Clipboard Viewer's Display — 583

As you know, the Clipboard stores clipboard contents in many different formats. If you are copying data between two programs that support different data formats, you can change the display of the Clipboard's contents from one format to the other to make sure that once you paste that data into the next program, the data will appear in the format you prefer. When you change the Clipboard's display type, the actual Clipboard data does not change but the data's display changes.

When you open the Clipboard Viewer's Display menu, the menu shows different formats to which the Clipboard can convert its data. For example, if you copy a graphic image to the Clipboard, the Display menu will show several graphic formats. If you select one of the formats, the graphic image could change slightly to reflect the new data format. If you want to return the Clipboard's data to its original format, select the Display menu Auto option.

Saving the Clipboard Contents — 584

As you cut and copy objects to the Windows 95 Clipboard, there may be times when you'll want to store the object to a file for pasting later. As you know, when you cut or copy an object to the Clipboard, Windows 95 replaces the Clipboard's current contents with the new object. As such, you can't paste more than one object to the Clipboard at a time. However, using the Clipboard viewer's File menu Save As option, you can store the Clipboard's contents in a data file. As such, you can save as a separate file each object you send to the Clipboard. Then, when you're ready to paste the object, you can select the File menu Open option to load it back into the Clipboard.

Understanding Windows 95 Games — 585

Windows 95 offers a few, easy-to-learn games that you can play between computing tasks. Table 585 describes some of the games you can access through the Accessories menu Games submenu.

Note: *If you do not see the Games submenu or one or more of Table 585's games, select the Control Panel Add/Remove Programs icon and choose the Setup tab. Next, install the missing games that you want to play.*

Icon	Name	Description
	FreeCell	A challenging solitaire card game
	Hearts	The classic card game
	MineSweeper	A mine searching game with some booms
	Solitaire	The classic solo card game

Table 585 The games on the Games menu.

586 How to Play FreeCell

The goal of FreeCell is to transfer every card from the bottom of the window to the *home cells*, which appear in the window's upper-right corner. The first card you place in a home cell must be an Ace. The second card can be another Ace next to the first one, or a 2 on top of the Ace if the 2 is the same suit as the Ace. In other words, you build the home cells up from Aces to Kings, and each of the four home cells holds a suit. If you are able to place all 52 cards in the four home cell stacks, you win. If you give up early or make selections that leave you with no legal moves, you lose. When you have no moves left, FreeCell tells you that the game is over. To move a card, click your mouse over the card's initial position and then click your mouse over the final destination. If you accidentally try to move a card illegally, FreeCell displays an error message window and does not complete the illegal move. If you need a card that another card is covering, you can move the top card to one of the four free cells that appear in the window's upper-left corner. A *free cell* is a temporary storage area for cards you move from the bottom of the window. You can place no more than one card in each free cell. And, after you place a card in a free cell, you can only move it to a home cell (provided the home cell can accept it), to an empty free cell, to an empty column between the card stacks, or to a card stack with a cover card that is the opposite color and one number higher. For example, if you want to move a 7 of Hearts from a free cell, you must find an empty column or a card stack with an 8 of Spades or Clubs cover card. You can also move a card from one card stack to another if the destination card stack has a cover card that is the opposite color of, and one number higher than, the card you want to move. Figure 586 shows a FreeCell game in progress. If you were to finish the game in Figure 586, you could make the following moves:

- You can drag the 3 of Diamonds to its home cell location on top of the 2 of Diamonds.
- You can uncover the 3 of Clubs by moving the 10 of Diamonds to one of the two free cells.
- You can then move the 3 of Clubs to its home cell location on top of the 2 of Clubs.
- You can open another free cell by moving the 4 of Spades to sit on the 5 of Hearts.

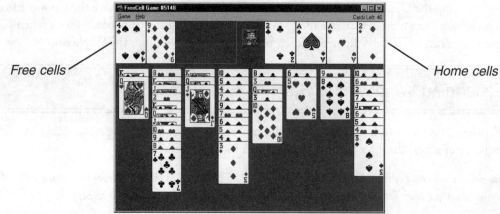

Figure 586 A FreeCell game.

Starting a FreeCell Game — 587

To run FreeCell, select the Games menu FreeCell option. (You can reach the Games menu through the Accessories menu.) To start a FreeCell game, click your mouse on the Game menu New Game option. FreeCell, in turn, will shuffle the deck and randomly deal 52 cards at the bottom of the window. You'll begin with four free cells and four home cells. If there's an Ace showing, you can move the Ace directly to a home cell. If not, move cards to free cells and on top of opposite-color cards one higher in value to locate your first Ace.

FreeCell Hints — 588

When you can place a card in a home cell, from either the bottom work area or from a free cell, move that card to the home cell. You win by filling up the home cells. However, don't put too many cards on to just one or two home cell stacks. If you do, there won't be enough cards of those colors left below to hold other cards that you arrange.

Look ahead. If two cards cover an Ace in one stack, and only one card covers an Ace in another stack, the best Ace to choose is probably the one beneath the single card. Be careful not to fill all four free cells without leaving legal moves available, or you'll lose the game.

Controlling FreeCell Options — 589

As you know, you can customize many aspects of Windows 95, including the operating system's accessory programs. When you click your mouse on the Game menu Options option, FreeCell displays the FreeCell Options dialog box. Within this dialog box, you will find the following options:

- *Display messages on illegal moves*: Displays an error dialog box when you attempt to make an illegal move. When you uncheck this option, FreeCell refuses to let you make illegal moves but does not display the message dialog box.

- *Quick Play (no animation)*: When you uncheck this option, Free Cell shows the quick card movement from one location to another. When you check the option, FreeCell does not show any card's movement. If you play FreeCell on a slow computer, check this option only.

- *Double-click moves card to free cell*: After you check this option, you can double-click any card to move it to an empty free cell. If you don't check this option, you must click over the card and then the destination free cell to move the card there.

How to Play Hearts — 590

Hearts is fairly easy to learn and hard to master. This tip teaches you enough to get started. The object of Hearts is to achieve the *lowest* score in a game. A game consists of several hands, and the first person to achieve a score of 100 or more loses, and the game ends.

Note: *You can play Windows 95 Hearts against others in a networked computer environment.*

In Hearts, scoring directly correlates to the number of Hearts cards you have when a hand ends (a hand ends when all cards have been played). At scoring time, you get one point for each Heart you hold, as well as thirteen points if you hold the Queen of Spades. No other card counts against you. As such, you want to avoid taking Hearts and the Queen of Spades.

Figure 590 shows a hand in progress. You're always the player at the bottom of the window. When the game begins, the person with the 2 of Clubs clicks the mouse button over the card to throw the card in the middle of the window (to start the *trick*) and waits for others to throw out cards of that suit. The person who throws out the highest card in the suit loses and must take all the cards. If any Hearts, or the Queen of Spades, exist in that set, the person who loses the hand will get points scored against him or her. In clockwise order, each person begins a new trick by throwing out a card. When it's your turn to start a trick, throw out a low card if you only have Hearts because you do not want to acquire any Hearts. (See Tip 594 for an exception.)

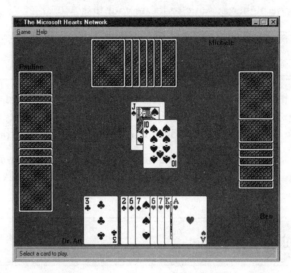

Figure 590 *Playing a game of Hearts.*

591 | Playing Network or Local Hearts

When you play Hearts on a network, you are playing against none, one, two, or three other networked humans. Because Hearts requires four players, the Hearts program supplies the missing player or players and plays their game automatically.

One of the networked players is called the *dealer,* even though that player does not really deal cards. Rather, the dealer is more like the game server—the dealer must start a game before others can join in. If you want to play a networked game of Hearts, perform these steps:

1. The dealer loads and begins the game by clicking the mouse on the Games menu Hearts option.
2. The dealer enters a name and selects the I want to be dealer option.
3. Others on the network then start Hearts, enter their own names, and click their mice on the I want to connect to another game option. The dealer sees when each player joins the game.
4. When all players are at the card table (on the network), the dealer presses **F2** to start the game. If fewer than four people are playing, the computer adds its own player or players so the game can begin.
5. The players begin the first hand.

If you do not use a network or prefer to play a solo game of Hearts, start the game, enter your name, and click your mouse on the I want to be dealer option as if you were playing on a network. The Hearts program, in turn, will generate three computer opponents for you.

Getting Started With Hearts — 592

As you begin each hand in a game of Hearts, you'll select three cards and pass those cards to the player on your left. The Hearts program walks you through this process. Usually, you'll want to send your highest cards to the person at your left. Of course, you'll get three from the player on your right as well, and you can bet they will be that player's worst (that is, highest) cards.

Note: Advanced players do not always send their highest cards to the next player; they like to keep a few high Hearts if they see a good chance of shooting the moon (see Tip 594).

Remember that you play a series of hands until someone reaches 100 points. At that time, the player with the lowest score wins the game. During these hands, you only pass cards to your left every three hands. No one passes cards on the fourth hand.

Playing a Hand — 593

After you pass three cards to the left, the player with the 2 of Clubs starts the game by tossing out the 2 of Clubs. (If you have the 2 of Clubs, click your mouse over the card to toss it out.) Then, all players with a Club throws out a Club, and the highest "Club thrower" gets the trick (the four cards). If a player doesn't have a Club, he or she can throw out anything (most likely a high Heart to get rid of it) and won't have to take the trick.

To begin the next trick, the person clockwise from the player who threw out the 2 of Clubs throws out an initial card. When it's your turn, you most likely will want to throw out small Hearts or large cards from the other suits.

Note: You cannot throw out Hearts anytime you want. You can only throw out a Heart if you have no cards in the trick's current suit or another player has led a Heart.

The hand ends when all cards have been played. At the end of each hand, the Hearts program displays a scoreboard much like the one that appears in Figure 593.

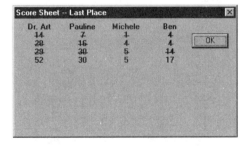

Figure 593 Scoring after four hands.

Shooting the Moon — 594

Typically, you *don't* want to collect tricks with Hearts or with the Queen of Spades in them because those cards count against you at scoring time. However, if two other players throw out hearts and the third player throws out the Queen of Spades, you can win the hand by throwing out the highest heart. When you win a hand in this fashion, you have *shot the moon,* and the Hearts program gives you a score of 0 and penalizes every other player *26 points*!

595 Customizing Hearts Options

Hearts offers only a few options to customize. When you click your mouse on the Game menu Options option, the Hearts Options dialog box lets you change the animation speed and the computerized player's names. If the game updates tricks and passes left too quickly for you, you can slow the game down to the Slow or Normal speed option.

596 How to Play Minesweeper

The Minesweeper game combines lots of luck with a little skill. Your overall mission is to locate all the mines in a mine field without getting blown up in the process. The computer randomly generates each mine field every time you start a new game. To run Minesweeper, click your mouse on the Games menu Minesweeper option. (You can reach the Games menu through the Accessories menu Games option.) Windows 95, in turn, will start the Minesweeper program. To start a new game, click your mouse on the happy face or select the Minesweeper window's Game menu New Game option.

Figure 596.1 shows the Minesweeper window before you start a game. Each square in the game area represents an empty spot or a mine. To hunt for mines, you click your mouse over a square. The square will contain one of three values:

- *An empty spot*: No mine resides in the square nor in any of the eight surrounding squares.

- *A number*: The number represents how many mines reside in the surrounding squares. Therefore, if you click over a square and a "4" appears in the square, four of the eight surrounding squares contain mines. The number is the only clue you get as to a mine's location.

- *A boom*: If a flash appears, the game ends. Figure 596.2 shows the tragic end to a Minesweeper game.

If you're used to fancy multimedia sound effects and graphics, Minesweeper may disappoint you. Minesweeper is a simple game of luck, a little strategy, and ultra-simple graphics. However, despite Minesweeper's simple nature, may users find the game both fun and addictive.

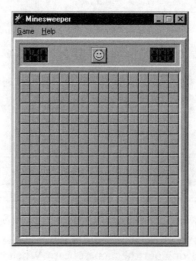

Figure 596.1 *The start of a Minesweeper game.*

Figure 596.2 *The tragic end to a Minesweeper game.*

Marking the Mines — 597

As you hunt for mines, you'll uncover many squares. As long as the squares contain numbers or spaces, you can keep hunting. As you gain more experience with Minesweeper, you'll begin to learn when a mine definitely exists under an uncovered square and when a mine might *possibly* exist under a square. In either case, you can mark such suspicious squares. To mark a square, right-click on it. Minesweeper, in turn, will place a red flag in the square to indicate the mine. If you right-click your mouse over the square again, Minesweeper will place a question mark in the square. You can leave a question mark over a suspicious square until you can determine, either by viewing numbers that appear around the square or clicking your left mouse button over the square, that a mine does or does not reside there.

Note: *If you don't know where to start searching for mines, click on a corner square first. If a 3 appears, you can mark the three mines that surround the square. If a 1 or 2 appears, try an adjacent square; if you don't blow up, you'll know the location of at least one mine.*

Selecting Your Minesweeper Level — 598

The Minesweeper level that you select (beginning, intermediate, or advanced) determines the size of the playing field (or game area). The beginning level displays an 8 x 8 playing field with 10 hidden mines. The intermediate level displays a 16 x 16 playing field with 40 hidden mines. And the advanced level displays a 16 x 30 playing field with 99 hidden mines. As you can see, the larger the playing field, the more mines you must locate and thus the harder the game. To change the Minesweeper level, display the Minesweeper window's Game menu and select the Beginner, Intermediate, or Advanced option.

Showing Off Your Minesweeper Scores — 599

Minesweeper keeps track of the fastest successful mine-field hunt for each level of play. When you win a game, Minesweeper asks for your name if your time at that level beat the previous best score. To see the high scores, such as the ones shown in Figure 599, click your mouse on the Game menu Best Times option. If you want to reset the scores, click your mouse on the Reset Scores button.

Figure 599 *The best Minesweeper scores.*

600 Drawing with the Paint Accessory

The Paint accessory is a drawing program you can use to create pictures, drawings, and Desktop wallpaper bitmaps. Just as an artist uses several different brushes, pencils, pens, and colors to create a painting, you can use Paint's many drawing and coloring tools to create startling images. To start Windows 95 Paint, click your mouse on the Accessories menu Paint option. Windows 95, in turn, will open the Paint program's window. Figure 600 shows the Paint window with a sample image.

Figure 600 *A Windows Paint image.*

601 Understanding Paint's Tools

When you start Paint, Paint displays a set of drawing and coloring tools along the Paint window's left side. These tools make up Paint's *tool box*. To select a tool from the tool box, all you do is click on the tool. Table 601 explains each of the tool box tools.

Icon	Tool name	Purpose
	Free-Form Selection	Selects any shape.
	Select	Selects a rectangular shape.

Table 601 *Paint's tool box tools. (continued on the following page)*

Icon	Tool name	Purpose
	Eraser	Erases lines and colors.
	Fill with Color	Colors drawn shapes.
	Pick Color	Selects a color from the color palette.
	Magnifier	Magnifies an object's editing area.
	Pencil	Draws free-form.
	Brush	Paints free-form.
	Airbrush	Spray paints color on to the drawing area.
	Text	Inserts text.
	Line	Draws lines.
	Curve	Draws curves.
	Rectangle	Draws rectangles.
	Polygon	Draws polygons (multi-sided enclosed shapes).
	Ellipse	Draws ellipses.
	Rounded Rectangle	Draws rectangles with rounded corners.

Table 601 Paint's tool box tools. (continued from the previous page)

Drawing Straight Lines within Paint — 602

To draw a straight line on an actual sheet of paper, you have to use a pencil or pen and a ruler. To draw a straight line in Paint, all you need to do is use the Line tool to designate a beginning and an end point. Paint takes care of the rest. To draw straight lines on Paint's editing area, perform these steps:

1. Click your mouse over the Line tool. The pointer will change to a cross-hair pattern. Below the tool box, Paint will display five line thicknesses from which you can choose a line width.
2. Click your mouse on the line width you want to use.
3. Move your mouse pointer to the location at which you want to begin the line. Then, click and hold down your left mouse button.
4. Drag your mouse pointer to the location at which you want to end the line.
5. Release your left mouse button.

603 Drawing Curved Lines within Paint

As you use Paint, there may be times when you want to draw a smooth curved line. For example, you may want your drawing to include a happy face with a huge smile or a sad face with teardrops. To draw a smooth curved line, perform these steps:

1. Click your mouse on the Curve line tool. The mouse pointer changes to a cross-hair pattern.
2. Anchor the curved line's end point by clicking and holding down your mouse button over Paint's editing area where you want to begin the curved line.
3. Drag the mouse to the end point and release the mouse to draw a straight line.
4. Hold down your left mouse button and drag the mouse. As you drag the mouse, Paint bends the line in response to your mouse movements.
5. Release your left mouse button to position the curved line.

604 Drawing Rectangles and Squares within Paint

Rectangles and squares are defined by two points: the upper-left corner and the lower-left corner (or the two other opposite corner points). As long as you position these points correctly, Paint will draw the rectangle or square for you. To draw a rectangle or square, perform these steps:

1. Click your mouse on the Rectangle tool. Paint will display three icons immediately below the toolbox.
2. Select the type of rectangle you want to draw from the list of three icons below the tool box. If you select the top icon, Paint draws an outline of a box. The background color or picture appears in the box because the box is transparent. If you select the second icon, Paint draws the box and fills it with the selected *background* color. (See Tip 605 for an explanation of foreground and background colors.) If you select the third icon, Paint draws a box, fills it with the background color, and displays its border in the background color.
3. Move your mouse pointer to the location at which you want the box's beginning point. Then, click and hold down your left mouse button.
4. If you want to draw a square, hold down the SHIFT key.
5. Drag your mouse pointer to the location at which you want the box's end point.
6. Release your left mouse button.

605 Selecting Paint's Foreground and Background Colors

Each shape you create in Paint has a *foreground color* and a *background color*. The foreground color is a shape's outline color, and the background color is the color inside the shape. For example, if you drew a red box with a green outline, the green color would represent the foreground and the red color would represent the background. In the two diagonal boxes that appear to the left of the color palette, Paint displays the current foreground and background colors. The top box represents the foreground color and the lower, partially-hidden box represents the background color. To change the foreground color, click your mouse on a color in the color palette. To change the background color, right-click your mouse on a color in the color palette. Paint, in turn, will assign those colors to the next shape you draw.

Drawing Filled Shapes with Paint — 606

When you click on a shape tool, such as the Rectangle tool, three *fill* options appear below the tool box. As shown in Figure 606, the options indicate how color fills the shape you're drawing.

The first fill option uses the foreground color for the shape's outline and leaves the shape's interior transparent. The second fill option uses the foreground color for the shape's outline and the background color for the shape's interior. The third fill option uses the background color for both the shape's outline and interior.

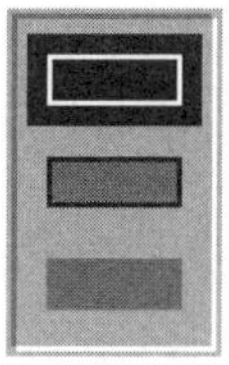

Figure 606 *The fill color box choices.*

Drawing Circles and Ovals within Paint — 607

If you've ever tried to draw a circle on an actual piece of paper, you know how difficult it can be to get it just right. In fact, because drawing circles is so difficult, many people simply find circular objects, such as the bottom of a glass or coffee can, that they can trace a pencil or pen around. Fortunately, when you use Paint, you won't need to hold the bottom of a glass up to your monitor to draw a perfect circle. Instead, you can use Paint's Ellipse tool to draw filled and unfilled circles and ellipses. To draw circles and ellipses, perform these steps:

1. Click your mouse on the Ellipse tool.
2. Click your mouse on the shape's foreground and background colors. See Tip 605 for more information on foreground and background colors.
3. Move your mouse pointer to the location at which you want to place one of the ellipse's edges.
4. If you want to draw a perfect circle, press and hold your SHIFT key.
5. Hold down your left mouse button and drag your mouse pointer to draw the ellipsis or circle size you want.
6. Release your left mouse button to position the shape.

Drawing a Polygon within Paint — 608

In previous tips you have learned to draw circles, ovals, and squares. As your drawings become more complex, you will need to draw polygons. A *polygon* is a multi-sided shape. Figure 608 shows you a few examples of polygons. Paint draws both filled and unfilled polygons. To draw a polygon, perform these steps:

1. Click your mouse on the Polygon tool.
2. Select a polygon fill option.
3. Move your mouse pointer to one of the polygon's corner points and click your left mouse button to begin the polygon.

4. Move your mouse pointer to the next corner location and click your left mouse button. Paint will connect the two corner locations.
5. Repeat Steps 3 and 4 until you've drawn the polygon you need.
6. Click your mouse on the polygon's beginning point to position the polygon.

Figure 608 Polygons.

609 Filling a Shape with a Specific Color

You can fill any closed shape with any color. For example, if you draw a rectangle and want to make its interior red, such as that shown in Figure 609.1, you can do so as long as the rectangle contains an outline that differs from the editing window's color. To fill a shape, perform these steps:

1. Click your left mouse button on one of the color palette's colors.
2. Click your mouse on the Fill tool. The mouse pointer changes to the Fill tool icon.
3. Move your mouse pointer to the interior of the shape you want to fill. Be sure that the shape is completely enclosed or the color will spill out and fill the entire editing window.
4. Click your left mouse button. Paint will fill the shape with the color you selected in step 1.

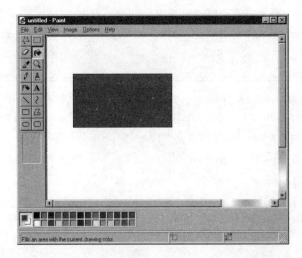

Figure 609 A filled rectangle.

610

Whatever you do in Paint, you can undo. You can use Paint's Undo feature to reverse your three most recent edits. For example, if you fill a shape with the incorrect color, you can select the Edit menu Undo option to restore the image back to its original color. Likewise, if you draw a red oval and then realize you meant to draw a green circle, you can select the Edit menu Undo option twice to reverse both the color red and the oval. Then, you can draw a green circle in the red oval's place.

611 Using Paint's Pencil for Detailed Drawing

Paint's Pencil tool lets you make detailed edits for fine-point and critical shapes. To use the Pencil tool, select a foreground color and then click your mouse on the tool box Pencil tool button. To draw lines with the Pencil tool, hold down your left mouse button and drag your mouse pointer to another location in the editing area. Paint, in turn, will draw a line that follows the mouse pointer's path. To end the line, release your left mouse button.

612 Painting with Paint's Brush Tool

Paint's Brush tool paints colors in the editing area. The Brush tool uses the current foreground color to paint. When you paint with the Brush tool, the colors appear stroked instead of drawn. Paint provides twelve different brush-style options, which appear directly below the tool box when you select the tool box Brush button. Some of the brush styles paint broad strokes, and some paint thin strokes. Several of the slanted-brush options produce calligraphy-like drawings. Figure 612 shows the 12 brush-style options. Be sure to select the proper brush-style option before you use the Brush tool.

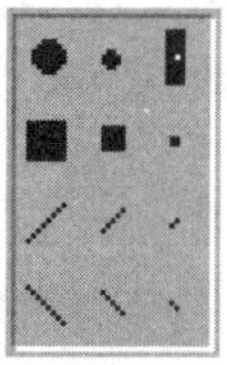

Figure 612 Selecting a brush style.

613 Using Paint's Eraser

Just as you can use Paint's Pencil and Brush tools to add to drawings, you can use Paint's Eraser tool to erase parts of drawings. As you drag your mouse across the screen, the Eraser tool erases by coloring everything in its path with background color. For example, if the current background color is black, the Eraser tool paints black as you hold down your left mouse button and move your mouse pointer across the editing area. Therefore, before you use the Eraser tool, choose your background color carefully so the eraser leaves only the color you want to appear. The four Eraser size options let you erase large and small areas.

614 Use Paint's Color Picker

As you draw within Pain, there will be times when you want to use a color that corresponds to an object you have already drawn. As it turns out, Paint's Pick Color tool copies color from one object to another. To use the Pick Color tool, perform these steps:

1. Click your mouse on the tool box Pick Color button.
2. Click your mouse on the object whose color you want to copy.
3. Move your mouse pointer over the object whose color you want to change.
4. Click your mouse button to copy the color.

615 Zooming In Using Paint's Magnifying Glass

If you want to edit an image's fine points, you can change the image's *pixels* (the individual dots that make up images on your screen). However, before you can change pixels, you must be able to see them up close. Luckily, you can use Paint's Magnifier tool to get a closer look at a drawing. The Magnifier tool magnifies a selected image area several times. To edit an image, one pixel at a time, perform these steps:

1. Click on the tool box Magnifier button. Paint will display a rectangle in the editing area.
2. Move the rectangle over the image area you want to zoom.
3. Click your left mouse button. Paint will display the image area so large that you can edit individual pixels. All of Paint's tools work on the newly magnified image.
4. Click your mouse on the View menu Zoom option.
5. Click your mouse on the Zoom menu Show Thumbnail option. Paint will display the zoomed portion of your picture at its regular size in a small window, called the *thumbnail*, as shown in Figure 615. Tip 623 explains more of the Zoom menu's options.
6. Click on the Zoom menu Normal Size option to reduce the image back to its original size.

Figure 615 *Editing a magnified drawing.*

616 Using Paint's Airbrush

Paint's Airbrush tool works just like a can of spray paint. When you select the Airbrush and drag the mouse pointer across your editing area, a trail of paint follows. The longer you hold the Airbrush in one spot, the darker and more complete the coverage becomes. The quicker you drag the mouse pointer, the more mist-like the spray looks. Paint offers three Airbrush sizes (which appear just beneath the tool box) for an extra-wide, medium, or smaller spray. Figure 616 shows the result of spraying graffiti over a photo.

Figure 616 Use the Airbrush tool to spray paint your pictures.

Using Paint's Text Tool   617

Paint's Text tool lets you add text to pictures. When you add text, you can select a font style and size (see Tip 620). To add text to an image, perform these steps:

1. Click your mouse on the tool box Text button.
2. Click your mouse on the Text tool's second style (the two Text styles appear just below the tool box). The second style lets the picture's background show behind each letter. The first style places text on a solid background that obscures the picture underneath.
3. Move your mouse pointer to the editing-area location at which you want to place text.
4. Hold down your left mouse button and drag your mouse pointer down and to the right to create a *text frame*. (Text frames hold text that you add to pictures.) After you release your mouse button to anchor the text frame, Paint will display the Fonts dialog box. Figure 617.1 shows the Paint window right after a user adds a text frame.
5. Select a font name, size, and style from the Fonts dialog box.
6. Select a font color.
7. Click your mouse on the text frame and type the text. If the text takes more room than the text frame, press ENTER to expand the text frame. Or, drag one of the text frame's sizing handles to change the text frame size.

Figure 617.2 shows the result of placing text on a bitmap image. After you've placed text in a text frame, you can change the text's font name, size, style, or color attribute. To do so, simply click your mouse over the text frame and make any attribute adjustments you wish.

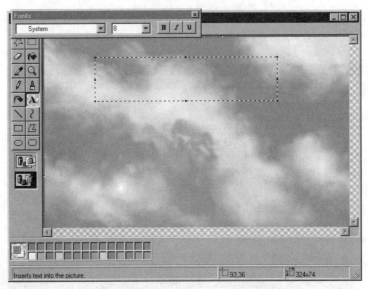

Figure 617.1 A text frame holds text.

Figure 617.2 Text appears on the image.

618 Saving and Printing Your Image

Paint's File menu contains Save, Save As, and Print options you can use to save and print your images. Paint uses the standard Windows 95 Save, Save As, and Print dialog boxes to perform these tasks. Paint lets you load both bitmaps (with the BMP extension) and Windows 3.1 Paintbrush files (with the PCX extension). However, you can only save in the bitmap format. As such, if you load and modify a PCX file in Paint, you must save that file in the bitmap file format.

Before you print an image, click your mouse on the File menu Page Setup option. Paint, in turn, will display the Page Setup dialog box, which lets you select paper size, orientation, and margins to use for the printing.

Using Your Image for Wallpaper 619

Wallpaper is your Windows 95 Desktop's graphic background. You can use any bitmap file (files with BMP extensions) for Desktop wallpaper. Additionally, you can make the bitmap image cover your entire Desktop or sit at the center of your Desktop. Paint provides a View menu View Bitmap option that lets you see how your bitmap image will look if you use it for wallpaper. Figure 619.1 shows a small bitmap image inside Paint's editing area. Figure 619.2 shows how that image will appear when you use it for wallpaper. When Paint displays the image as wallpaper, Paint shows you what the image will look like at the center of your Desktop.

Note: To change your Desktop's wallpaper to the bitmap file, right-click your mouse on the Desktop and select the pop-up menu's Properties option. Then, use the Display Properties sheet Background page to locate and select your bitmap file.

Figure 619.1 A bitmap image.

Figure 619.2 After you select the View Bitmap option.

620 Controlling Fonts

When you use the Text tool to create a text frame, Paint displays a small dialog box from which you select a font name, size, and style. This dialog box contains a list of all the fonts available to your Windows 95 programs. If you select a font, type text into the text frame, and then if you decide you do not like the font's appearance, you can select another font from the list. Paint, in turn, will change the text inside the text frame to the font style and size you select. When you place the text on your drawing, make sure you format your text as accurately as possible and use the font, style, and size that looks best. After you select another tool, you cannot edit the text again. To fix the text, you must completely erase it and start over.

621 Selecting Objects for Cut and Paste Operations

As you use Paint, you can copy and cut data to, as well as paste data from, the Windows 95 Clipboard. The data can consist of text or graphics, so you can transfer graphic images between Paint and other programs. Paint lets you select graphic images to copy or cut to the Clipboard in two ways:

- *The Edit menu Select All option*: Selects the entire Paint image so you can copy and cut the image to the Clipboard.

- *The Free-Form Select and Select tools*: These tools let you drag your mouse to select graphic objects inside the editing area. The Free-Form Select tool drags a selection line around odd-shaped graphic images. The Select tool drags a selection rectangle around graphic images. After you select part of an image using either selection tool, you can copy or cut that selection to the Clipboard.

If you click your mouse on the Edit menu Clear Selection option, Paint will erase the area you've selected. Additionally, Paint will fill the erased area with the current background color. After you've selected an item, you can cancel the selection by clicking your mouse on the Edit menu Cancel Selection option.

Note: *You can also drag a selection to a different part of Paint's editing area.*

622 Copying Objects to or From a File

When you click your mouse on Paint's File menu Open option, Paint erases the editing area's contents and loads a new image into the area. (If you have not saved the editing area's current image, Paint gives you a chance to do so before it erases the image.) As you use Paint, there may be times when you want to copy a picture into your current image. For example, if you use Paint to create a banner for your Dalmatian club's monthly newsletter, you can pull a Dalmatian image from another file and place that image anywhere within your editing area.

Paint can also store selected images to files as well. To copy and paste images, use the Edit menu Copy To and Paste From options. After you select either option, Paint displays a dialog box (either a File Open or Save As dialog box) you can use to specify the filename. In a way, Paint lets you go beyond the single Clipboard because you can copy and paste to and from files as well as the Clipboard.

Zooming In and Out Using Paint's Zoom Menu 623

Tip 615 explains how the Magnifier tool increases an image's detail. After you increase the detail, you can edit the image pixel by pixel. When you select the View menu Zoom option, Paint displays the Zoom menu. To let you customize the way you magnify the editing area's image, the Zoom menu contains the following options:

- *Normal Size*: Displays the editing area's image at its normal size.
- *Large Size*: Zooms into the image and increases the editing detail, just as the Magnifier tool does.
- *Custom*: Displays the Custom Zoom dialog box, shown in Figure 623, which you can use to select a zoom percentage factor.

Depending on an image's original size, the Custom Zoom dialog box lets you increase the editing detail by as much as 800% so that you can more easily edit individual pixels.

Figure 623 *The Custom Zoom dialog box.*

Flipping or Rotating a Paint Image 624

After you select an image using the Free-Form Select or the Select tool, you can flip or rotate the image. To do so, select the Image menu Flip/Rotate option. Paint, in turn, will open the Flip and Rotate dialog box, as shown in Figure 624.1. Using this dialog box, you can flip images vertically (for mirror images), horizontally (for upside-down images), and by a factor of 90, 180, and 270 degrees (to rotate images left, upside down, and right).

When you click your mouse on the Flip and Rotate dialog box's OK button, Paint flips or rotates the selected image. Figure 624.2 shows a Paint window with a house image that I flipped and rotated a few times.

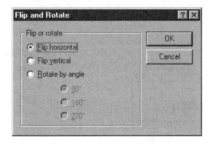

Figure 624.1 *The Flip and Rotate dialog box.*

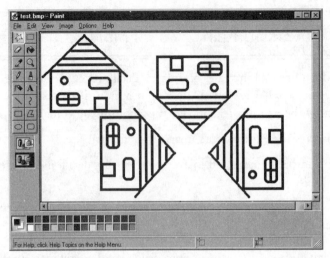

Figure 624.2 *An image rotated 3 times.*

625 Stretching and Skewing a Paint Image

You can expand or shrink a selected image on its horizontal or vertical axis, as well as skew the image on its x or y axis. To do so, select the Image menu Stretch/Skew option. Paint, in turn, will open the Stretch and Skew dialog box shown in Figure 625.1. The numbers next to the dialog box's options determine how much stretching and skewing you want Paint to perform. Figure 625.2 shows the before and after effects of stretching and skewing an image.

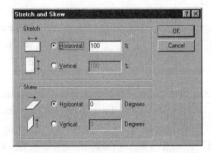

Figure 625.1 *The Stretch and Skew dialog box.*

Figure 625.2 *Before and after you stretch and skew an image.*

Changing a Paint Image's Attributes | 626

The Attributes dialog box, shown in Figure 626, lets you enter exact inch, centimeter, or pixel measurements for your image's editing area. As such, if you use the Attributes dialog box to crop an image, the overall image will consume less space in the editing area and on your disk. The Attributes dialog box does *not* expand or shrink the size of items *in* the editing area. Rather, the Attributes dialog box changes the amount of room in the editing area. As such, if a picture contains several images that fill up the entire editing area and you can use the Attributes dialog box to decrease the editing area's size, Paint will crop off some of the images in the original picture. To open the Attributes dialog box, select the Image menu Attributes option.

Figure 626 *The Attributes dialog box.*

Editing Paint's Color Palette | 627

The Edit Colors dialog box, shown in Figure 627.1, lets you edit Paint's color palette. You can use this dialog box to create your own colors and add up to 16 of your own defined colors to Paint's color palette. To create your own color, perform these steps:

1. Select the Options menu Edit Colors option. Paint will display the Edit Colors dialog box.
2. Click your mouse on the color that most closely matches your desired color.
3. Click your mouse on the Define Custom Colors button. Paint will expand the Edit Colors dialog box to let you enter specific hue, saturation, luminosity, and red/green/blue values as shown in Figure 627.2.
4. Drag the arrow pointing to the vertical color bar up and down to change the values to reflect your desired color. As you drag past different color combinations, the Color|Solid box changes to show your new color.
5. Click on the Add to Custom Colors button to add your color to the set of 16 custom colors.
6. Click your mouse on the OK button to close the dialog box and save your changes. Paint's color palette now includes your custom color.

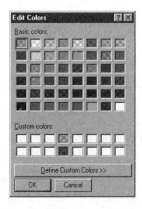

Figure 627.1 *The Edit Colors dialog box.*

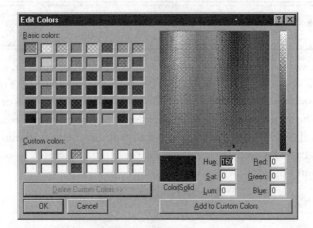

Figure 627.2 Creating a custom color.

628 Using the Grid to Align Objects in Paint

As you place images in the editing area, you may want to align images horizontally or vertically so the picture looks neater. Paint's grid lines help you position images more accurately and align them with each other. To turn on editing grid lines, perform these steps:

Note: The grid lines will not appear in saved or printed images.

1. Click your mouse on the View menu Zoom option. If the resulting Zoom menu does not display an active Show Grid option (if the option appears gray), select the Zoom menu Large Size option to magnify your picture. The grid lines only show for zoomed pictures. If you change the magnification, click your mouse on the View menu Zoom option once again.
2. Click your mouse on the Zoom menu Show Grid option. Paint will display grid lines in the editing area.
3. Select and align objects to the grid lines.
4. Click your mouse on the Zoom menu Show Grid option once again to turn off the grid lines.

629 Using the WordPad Accessory

Windows 95 includes the WordPad word processor. WordPad lets you create and edit documents, as well as take advantage of special fonts and embedded graphics. WordPad lets you edit Word for Windows-compatible documents and supports bulleted and numbered lists. Just a few years ago, WordPad would have been considered a powerful word processor. Even today, many people are able to use WordPad for much of their writing.

Note: WordPad does not contain a spell or grammar checker. For those features, use a more complete word processor, such as Word for Windows.

To start WordPad, click your mouse on the Accessories menu WordPad option. Figure 629 shows the WordPad program window.

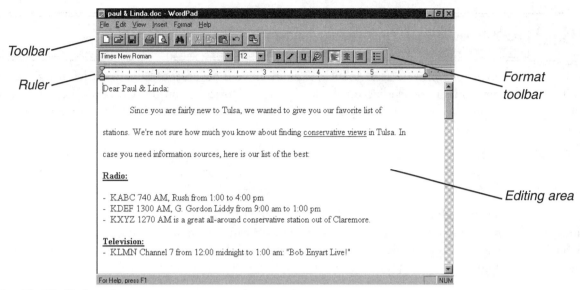

Figure 629 *The WordPad word processor.*

Creating, Printing, and Saving a WordPad Document   630

As Tip 629 explains, WordPad makes creating, printing, and saving documents easy. To see for yourself how easy WordPad makes such operations, perform these steps:

1. Select the Accessories menu WordPad option. Windows 95 will start WordPad.
2. Type your document's text. As you type, WordPad automatically wraps text to successive lines.
3. Click your mouse on the File menu Print option. WordPad displays the Print dialog box.
4. Click your mouse on the OK button to print the document.
5. To save the document, click your mouse on the File menu Save As option. WordPad displays the Save As dialog box.
6. Type a filename. WordPad automatically adds the DOC extension to your document.
7. Click your mouse on the OK button.
8. To exit WordPad, select the File menu Exit option.

Note: *WordPad's default data type is Word for Windows (with the DOC extension). However, you can load ASCII text or Rich Text Format (RTF) documents into WordPad. Similarly, you can save a file as a Word for Windows, ASCII text, or RTF document. Tip 647 explains how to change the behavior of WordPad for the various document types that you edit.*

Only Press Enter to Separate Paragraphs   631

WordPad *word wraps* text. In other words, as you type close to the edge of the right margin, WordPad automatically sends the text cursor to the beginning of the next line. Additionally, WordPad pulls down any word you've started that the word wrap would otherwise chop in half. As a result, when you type a WordPad document, the only time you need to press ENTER is when you reach the end of a paragraph.

632 | Controlling Paragraph Alignment

WordPad normally *left-justifies* your text. As such, each line in your document begins at the left margin and ends in a different column position, depending on the line's length. However, you don't need to stick with WordPad's default paragraph alignment. You can *right-justify* your WordPad text and thus make all lines begin in a different left-hand column and end flush at the right margin. You can also center text, such as titles at the top of documents.

In WordPad, you can change the alignment of one paragraph, several paragraphs, or your entire document. To select a single paragraph for realignment, click your mouse over the paragraph to put the text cursor somewhere within the paragraph's borders.

If you want to justify multiple paragraphs, you must select all the paragraphs. To do so, click and hold your left mouse button over the first paragraph. Then, holding down your left mouse button, drag your mouse pointer to highlight preceding or subsequent paragraphs. When you've highlighted the paragraphs you want to realign, release your left mouse button. To control the justification of any and all your document's paragraphs, perform these steps:

1. Select the paragraph or paragraphs you want to justify.
2. Click your mouse on the Format menu Paragraph option. WordPad will display the Paragraph dialog box shown in Figure 632.
3. Open the Alignment pull-down list and click your mouse on the Left, Right, or Center option.
4. Click your mouse on the OK button. WordPad justifies all selected paragraphs.

Note: *If you select a justification before you write, all paragraphs will take on that justification until you change the alignment settings.*

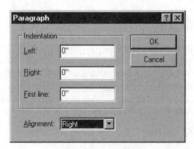

Figure 632 Formatting a paragraph.

633 | Controlling Paragraph Indentation

Tip 632 explains how you use the Paragraph dialog box to control justification. The Paragraph dialog box also controls *indentation*. You can select from three kinds of paragraph indents by entering a value into one or more of the Paragraph dialog box's Indentation options:

- *Left*: Determines how far from the left margin the selected paragraph or paragraphs begin.
- *Right*: Determines how far from the right margin the selected paragraph or paragraphs end.
- *First Line*: Determines how much WordPad indents the first line of the selected paragraph or paragraphs.

Using the Bold, Italics, or Underline Attribute — 634

As you create documents, you will want to assign different font style attributes, such as bold, italics, or underline. If you can select a style attribute before you type, subsequent text appears with that attribute. If you select a character, word, paragraph, or several paragraphs, and then select a style attribute, WordPad changes all the selected text to that attribute. After you select the text whose style attribute you want to change, click your mouse on the Format menu Font option to display the Font dialog box, as shown in Figure 634. Then, in the Font style list box, select the attribute you want the text to have. If you want to underline your text, check the Effects area Underline option. If you want to strikeout (draw a line through) your text, check the Strikeout option. When you finish changing the Font dialog box's settings, click the OK button. WordPad, in turn, will implement your changes.

Note: Tip 645 explains how to use the Format Toolbar to change font style attributes and more.

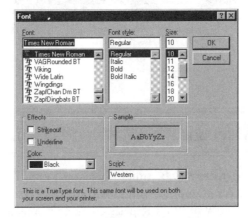

Figure 634 Formatting text with special attributes.

Controlling the Current Font — 635

As Tip 634 explains, you can select text and use the Font dialog box to change its font style attributes. However, you can use the Font dialog box to do much more than just italicizing, boldfacing, or underlining your text. Through the Font dialog box, you can also select a new font, font size, and font color. When you select a new font, font size, font style, or font color, the Sample box (which appears just beneath the Font style list box) will show you how your selection will change the font's appearance. When you click your mouse on the OK button, WordPad updates the text's font. If you haven't yet entered text in the WordPad window, the text you subsequently type will use the font information you specify in the Font dialog box.

Finding Text within a Large Document — 636

When you edit large documents, you may have difficulty locating certain words, phrases, or sentences that you need to find. Luckily, WordPad provides a Find command you can use to locate text. To find text within a document, perform these steps:

1. Click your mouse on the Edit menu Find option. WordPad displays the Find dialog box shown in Figure 636.
2. Type the text you want WordPad to locate.

3. If you want WordPad to distinguish between full and partial words (WordPad would not, therefore, match *Rose* with *Rosey*), click your mouse on the Match whole words only check box.
4. If you want WordPad to distinguish between upper case and lower case letters, click your mouse on the Match case check box.
5. Click your mouse on the Find Next button to start the search.
6. After WordPad finds a match, you can continue the search by selecting Find Next.
7. After WordPad finds the text you want, click your mouse on the Cancel button to end the search.

Note: *WordPad lets you quickly search for the next occurrence of the text by clicking your mouse on the Edit menu Find Next option or by simply pressing F3.*

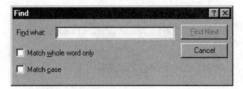

Figure 636 *The Find dialog box.*

637 Replacing Text Throughout a WordPad Document

As you revise documents in WordPad, there may be times when you'll want to replace all occurrences of a word or phrase with another word or phrase. For example, if you use WordPad to create party invitations that mention the invitee's name several times, you can use WordPad's Replace command to search for and replace names before you print each invitation. To use WordPad's Replace command, perform these steps:

1. Click your mouse on the Edit menu Replace option. WordPad will display the Replace dialog box, as shown in Figure 637.
2. Type the text you want WordPad to replace.
3. Press TAB to move the text cursor to the Replace with text box. Type in your replacement text.
4. If you want WordPad to distinguish between full and partial words (WordPad would not, therefore, match *Rose* with *Rosey*), click your mouse on the Match whole words only check box.
5. If you want WordPad to distinguish between upper case and lower case letters, click your mouse on the Match case check box.
6. If you want WordPad to replace all occurrences of the text, click your mouse on the Replace All button. WordPad will replace all occurrences.
7. If you want to review the text before you replace it, click your mouse on the Find Next button. WordPad will locate the next occurrence of the text, and you can then decide if you want WordPad to replace it.
8. If you want to replace the text, click your mouse on the Replace button. If you want to continue searching for another occurrence to replace, click your mouse on the Find Next button.
9. To end the replacement operation, click your mouse on the Cancel button.

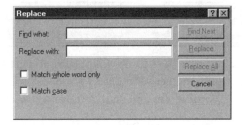

Figure 637 *The Replace dialog box.*

Inserting the Date and Time Into a WordPad Document   638

As you use WordPad, there will be times when you want to insert the date or time into a document. For example, if you use WordPad as a billing or telephone log tool, you may want to insert a date and time next to each log entry. To insert the date or time at the current text cursor's position, click your mouse on the Insert menu Date and Time option. WordPad, in turn, will display the Date and Time dialog box shown in Figure 638. In this dialog box, choose the date or time format that best suits your needs. WordPad, in turn, will insert a date or time value that matches the format you selected.

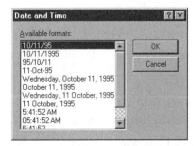

Figure 638 *The Date and Time dialog box.*

Selecting Text within a WordPad Document   639

Many WordPad operations require you to select text. For example, before you can cut or copy text to the Windows 95 Clipboard, you must first select the text. To select text, you can use either of the following methods:

- Move your mouse pointer over the first character you want to select. Then, hold down your left mouse button and drag your mouse pointer until WordPad highlights all the text you want to select. Finally, release your left mouse button.

- Press your ARROW keys until the text cursor appears directly in front of the first character you want to select. Then, hold down your SHIFT key and press your RIGHT ARROW to move the selection to the right and your LEFT ARROW to move the selection to the left. If you need to increase the selected area, press your UP ARROW and DOWN ARROW keys. As you press the ARROW keys, WordPad highlights text to indicate the selection. Release your SHIFT key when you've completed the selection.

Note: *Tip 647 explains how to use the Automatic word selection option, which selects complete words at a time instead of characters. The Automatic word selection speeds up the selection process.*

640 Moving or Copying Text within a WordPad Document

When you use WordPad, you can copy or cut text to the Clipboard and paste that text elsewhere in the current document, into another document, or into another Windows 95 application. The Clipboard makes it easy to rearrange sentences and copy text in your WordPad documents. To move text in a document, perform these steps:

1. Select the text you want to move (see Tip 639).
2. Click your mouse on the Edit menu Cut option. WordPad will remove the text from the document and store the text on the Clipboard.
3. Click your mouse at the location where you want to insert the Clipboard's contents.
4. Click your mouse on the Edit menu Paste option to insert the text at the location you selected in step 3.

To copy text in a WordPad document, perform these steps:

1. Select the text you want to copy (see Tip 639).
2. Click your mouse on the Edit menu Copy option. WordPad leaves the text at its original location and also stores the text on the Clipboard.
3. Click your mouse at the location text where you want to insert the Clipboard's contents.
4. Click your mouse on the Edit menu Paste option to insert the text at the location you selected in step 3.
5. If you want to copy the text elsewhere in the document, repeat steps 3 and 4.

641 Inserting an Object into a WordPad Document

Like most Windows 95 programs, WordPad lets you insert an object of virtually any data type directly into your document. You can insert worksheets, graphics, video clips, sound clips, and more.

The inserted object appears as text, a graphic, or an icon inside the WordPad document. Most non-text and non-graphical objects appear as icons. You can request that a graphic image or inserted text object appear as an icon as well when you insert that object. When you right-click your mouse over the icon, you can select the appropriate open, play, or edit menu option that appears. WordPad lets you create an object or insert an object from a file. WordPad uses the object's type to determine which program to load for you to create or view the object. To insert an object, perform these steps:

1. Click your mouse on the Insert menu Object option. WordPad will display the Insert Object dialog box shown in Figure 641.
2. If you want the object to appear as an icon in the document, click your mouse on the Display As Icon option. (Some objects always enter the document as icons.)
3. If you want to create an object, click your mouse on the object's type in the Object Type list box. WordPad will start the parent program for that object's type (such as Excel or Paint). When you close the parent program, WordPad will insert the object at the text cursor's position.
4. If you want to load an object from a file, click your mouse on the Create from file option button. Then, type the path and name of the object you want to insert. For example, if you want to insert a bitmap, type that bitmap's full path and filename in the File text box. When you click your mouse on the OK button, WordPad will insert the object.

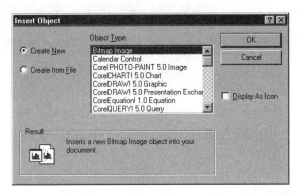

Figure 641 The Insert Object dialog box.

Using Bullets within a WordPad Document   642

You can easily create bulleted lists inside WordPad documents. Figure 642 shows a document with a bulleted list of four items. To create a bulleted list, perform these steps:

1. Move your text cursor to the location at which you want the bulleted list to begin.
2. Click your mouse on the Format menu Bullet Style option. WordPad will insert a bullet at the beginning of the line.
3. Type the first item in the list.
4. Press ENTER to complete the first item. WordPad will automatically insert a bullet for the next item.
5. Repeat steps 3 and 4 for the remaining items.
6. Click your mouse on the Format menu Bullet Style option to turn off the bullets. WordPad will remove the last bullet that it placed in the document and let you continue to type the document's regular text.

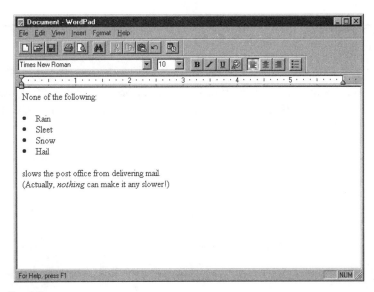

Figure 642 A WordPad bulleted list.

643 Controlling Tab Stops

If you use WordPad to create tables, tab stops come in very handy. Tab stops keep your table columns aligned. In addition, you can use tab stops in your regular writing to indent certain kinds of text. To specify tab stop locations, perform these steps:

1. Click your mouse on the Format menu Tabs option. WordPad will display the Tabs dialog box shown in Figure 643.
2. Type a tab stop location. Type the location in inches (type **1"** or **1 inch** to enter a one-inch tab stop) or centimeters (type **1 cm** to enter a one-centimeter tab stop).
3. Press ENTER or click your mouse on the Set button. WordPad will add the tab stop to the Tab stop position list box.
4. Continue to add tab stop locations until you've defined every tab stop you need.
5. Click your mouse on the OK button to save your changes. If you display the ruler, you will see it contains an angled bracket for each tab stop.

If you want to remove a tab stop, display the Tabs dialog box, select a tab stop in the Tab stop position list box, and click your mouse on the Clear button. The Clear All button erases all tab stops. (Tip 646 explains how to use the ruler to set and remove tab stops.)

Figure 643 *The Tabs dialog box.*

644 Using WordPad's Toolbar

WordPad's toolbar gives you one-button access to WordPad's more common features. To display or hide the toolbar, click your mouse on the View menu Toolbar option. The toolbar appears directly beneath WordPad's menu bar. Table 644 describes each toolbar button.

Icon	Purpose
	Opens a new document.
	Displays the Open dialog box.
	Saves the current document.
	Prints the current document.
	Displays in page preview mode.

Table 644 *WordPad's toolbar buttons. (continued on the following page)*

🔍	Opens the Find dialog box.
🔍	Cuts selected text to the Clipboard.
📋	Copies selected text to the Clipboard.
📋	Pastes selected text from the Clipboard.
↶	Undoes the most recent edit.
🕔	Displays the Date and Time dialog box.

Table 644 WordPad's toolbar buttons. (continued from the previous page)

Using WordPad's Format Bar — 645

WordPad's format bar is a second toolbar (see Tip 644) that gives you one-button access to the word-processing program's formatting capabilities. To display or hide the format bar, click your mouse on the View menu Format Bar. Table 645 explains each of the format bar's items.

Item	Purpose
Times New Roman (Western) ▼	Selects a font name.
10 ▼	Selects a font size.
B	Selects the bold attribute.
I	Selects the italics attribute.
U	Selects the underline attribute.
🎨	Selects a font color.
≡	Left-justifies selected paragraphs.
≡	Centers selected paragraphs.
≡	Right-justifies selected paragraphs.
≔	Creates a bulleted list.

Table 645 WordPad's format bar items.

Using WordPad's Ruler — 646

The WordPad ruler displays tab stops, margins, and the cursor's current position. (To display or hide the ruler, click your mouse on the View menu Ruler option.) Additionally, the ruler updates itself each time you move the text cursor to a different paragraph. If you move the text cursor to a paragraph with narrow margins, the ruler updates its markings to reflect that paragraph's settings. If you move the text cursor to a paragraph with a set indentation, the ruler changes to reflect that paragraph's indentation settings. As such, the ruler lets you quickly see the style of the paragraph in which you're currently working.

WordPad's ruler also lets you adjust a selected paragraph's (or paragraphs') margin and indentation settings. To increase or decrease margin and indentation settings, move either the left or right margin mark or the indentation mark. Figure 646 describes the ruler's markings so you'll be able to read the ruler. Tip 648 describes how you can use the ruler to set and clear tab stops.

Figure 646 *The ruler and its markings.*

647 Controlling WordPad Options

One of the most interesting WordPad features is its ability to change behavior and appearance when you edit or save a file using different data types. When you click your mouse on the View menu Options option, WordPad displays the tabbed Options sheet shown in Figure 647. You can use the Options sheet's pages to change the behavior of WordPad to match the document type you're editing. For example, Word for Windows uses the DOC document extension. If you load or save a WordPad document and use the default DOC extension, the Options sheet Word 6 page determines how WordPad displays toolbars and controls word wrap. However, if you load or save a text document using the TXT extension, the Options sheet Text page's options take over. The Text page's default settings tell WordPad not to word wrap because many text documents are computer controlling files and program codes. As you can see, the document's data type determines how WordPad looks and behaves. The Options sheet contains the following pages:

- *Options*: Controls the default unit of measurement for tab stops and margins and determines whether WordPad uses character or word selection.
- *Text*: Controls word wrap and toolbar display for text files.
- *Rich Text*: Controls word wrap and toolbar display for Rich Text Format (RTF) files.
- *Word 6*: Controls word wrap and toolbar display for Word for Windows version 6 and later.
- *Write*: Controls word wrap and toolbar display for Windows Write files.
- *Embedded*: Controls word wrap and toolbar display for embedded objects.

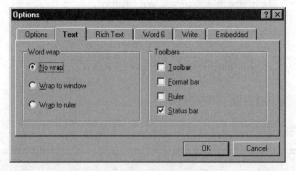

Figure 647 *The WordPad Options sheet.*

648 Using WordPad's Ruler to Set Tabs

As you work with WordPad, you may not always have time to add and remove tab stops using the steps in Tip 643. You may not have time to select a menu option, specify exact tab stop measurements, and click on several buttons.

Fortunately, WordPad provides you with a faster way to accomplish tab stop tasks. To quickly add tab stops, click your mouse over the ruler locations at which you want them to reside. To quickly remove a tab stop, click your mouse on the tab stop. Then, holding down your left mouse button, drag the tab stop off the ruler.

Previewing a Document Before You Print It — 649

Before you print a WordPad document, you can *preview* the document to see how it will look on paper. WordPad is a *WYSIWYG* (which stands for *What You See is What You Get*) word processor in which the text you see on the screen looks like the text that appears on paper. However, in a WordPad window, you cannot see an entire page at once.

When you select WordPad's File menu Print Preview option, WordPad displays a full-page representation of your document. As Figure 649 shows, the print preview shows how your document will look when you print it. If your margins are set incorrectly, print preview lets you discover this fact without wasting paper.

You cannot make edits to your document while WordPad is in print preview mode. However, you can zoom in and out of the document to make the text more readable. To look at the print preview close up, click your mouse on the Zoom In button. To see the full page again, click your mouse on the Zoom Out button. To get a close-up of a particular location, move your mouse pointer (which becomes a magnifying glass when WordPad is in print preview mode) to the place you want to examine and click your left mouse button. WordPad, in turn, will zoom in on the exact spot at which your mouse pointer resides.

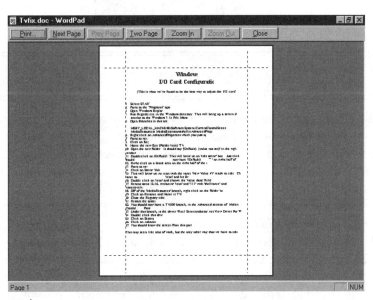

Figure 649 Getting a print preview.

Controlling Your Document's Page Attributes — 650

A document's page attributes control the overall placement of the document on the page. When you click your mouse on the File menu Page Setup option, WordPad displays the Page Setup dialog box shown in Figure 650. This dialog box lets you control the following page attributes:

- *Paper*: If your printer can hold multiple paper types, such as laser printers, you can inform WordPad which tray to use when it prints your document. You can also tell WordPad what size paper the tray contains. WordPad will use this information to layout and paginate your document.

- *Orientation*: These option buttons let you change the orientation of the document on the page. In Portrait mode, the document prints up and down on the paper. Most paperback novels contain pages printed in a portrait orientation. In Landscape mode, the document prints sideways on the paper, just as a landscape painting is often wider than it is tall.

- *Margins*: In these text boxes, you can specify the paper margins. WordPad will not print outside the margins. Enter margin values in inches or in whatever setting you specified for the "Measurement units" value in WordPad's Options sheet Options page.

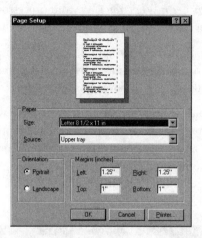

Figure 650 *Specifying page attributes.*

651 Understanding Telecommunications

Telecommunications is the process your computer uses to communicate with other computers over telephone lines. Telecommunications has many practical uses. For example, through your PC and a modem, you can contact university computers and gather valuable information. Likewise, you can collect files and data from the thousands of *BBS* (electronic Bulletin Board Systems). Additionally, you can use telecommunications to dial up a software or hardware vendor's computer and download new driver updates and product information. Windows 95 contains the HyperTerminal accessory program you can use to connect your computer to a phone, as long as you have the remote computer's phone number. To start HyperTerminal, click your mouse on the Accessories menu HyperTerminal option. HyperTerminal, in turn, will display a window that looks much like the one in Figure 651. As you can see from the window, HyperTerminal comes predefined with several communications profiles that connect your system to online services, such as CompuServe. The profiles contain phone numbers and communications settings. For computers you regularly dial that the window doesn't list, you can create your own profiles (see Tip 653). You must register to use most online services. Luckily, many online services let you register (and pay a month's dues with your credit card, perhaps) the first time HyperTerminal connects you to them. When you double-click your mouse on one of the HyperTerminal profile icons, HyperTerminal loads the profile and begins the connection process.

Figure 651 *The HyperTerminal window.*

Configuring an Existing Connection 652

If you want to connect to an existing service, such as CompuServe, open the HyperTerminal window (see Tip 651) and double-click that service's icon. HyperTerminal, in turn, will load the service's profile and use all necessary parameters to connect to that service. However, you must verify phone numbers. For example, when you first start the CompuServe HyperTerminal option, HyperTerminal displays the Phone Number dialog box in the middle of a HyperTerminal window, as shown in Figure 652. Verify the access number to the online service. Generally, the access number is a toll-free number you can use to register with the online service. If you've already registered to use the service, and know your local access number, enter that number and click your mouse on the OK button. HyperTerminal then displays a Connect dialog box, in which you either change or dial access numbers.

Note: *You can use the File menu Properties option to change the online service's access number or related settings.*

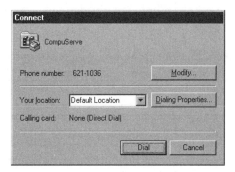

Figure 652 *HyperTerminal needs an access number.*

Configuring a New Connection 653

Before you can use HyperTerminal to call a service for the first time, you need the remote computer's phone number. Then, you must connect to the computer and create a new profile. To create a new profile, perform these steps:

1. Click your mouse on the Accessories menu HyperTerminal option.
2. Double-click your mouse on the icon labeled Hypertrm. When you click on the Hypertrm icon, HyperTerminal knows that you want to define a new connection.
3. Enter a name for the connection. For example, if you were dialing a university computer, you might call the connection "University Connection." When you subsequently click your mouse on the Accessories menu HyperTerminal option, this name will appear in HyperTerminal window with the other online services' icons.
4. Select an icon for the connection you want to establish. For example, a good university connection icon might be the telephone with an open book behind it.
5. Click your mouse on the OK button.
6. Enter the remote site's phone number and the modem you want to use (if you have more than one modem defined for Windows 95).
7. To display the Connect window, click your mouse on the OK button. HyperTerminal dials the number and connects to the remote computer as soon as you click your mouse on the Dial button.

When you finish communicating, be sure to save the settings in a new HyperTerminal profile file by selecting the File menu Save As option.

654 Understanding Data Communication Settings

In the past, to connect to a remote computer, you had to know several of the computer's technical settings, such as baud rates and stop bits. Fortunately, when you use HyperTerminal, you usually don't need to know such settings. Most of the time, HyperTerminal can sense the remote computer's technical settings and take care of the connection process for you. However, if you have trouble connecting to a remote computer, you may have to inform HyperTerminal of specific settings. Table 654 explains the common communication settings you should know and understand.

Setting	Purpose
Baud Rate	Determines the communications speed. Generally, the baud rate is 9600, 14400 (14.4K), or 28800 (28.8K).
Data Bits	Specifies the amount of information transferred at one time. Generally, the data bits are 5, 6, 7, or 8 bits.
Stop Bits	Indicates the number of bits that follow a data packet. Generally, the stop bits are 1, 1.5, and 2.
Parity	Determines the communication error-correction method. Generally, the parity value is None, Odd, or Even.

Table 654 Common communication settings.

655 Establishing Your Connections Data Communication Settings

As Tip 654 explains, HyperTerminal normally senses all communication settings from the remote computer. As such, you usually don't have to specify such settings. However, if you experience connection problems, you may have to specify the remote computer's setting to HyperTerminal. To learn the remote computer's settings, contact a representative at the remote computer and ask for the computer's connect baud rate, data bits, stop bits, and parity.

Normally, the remote computer's communications documentation or personnel will tell you that the settings are "9600 8N1" or "14.4 7E1." The first number is the baud rate; the second is the data bit value; the letter indicates odd, even, or no parity; and the final digit represents the stop bit value.

To change HyperTerminal's settings, use one of the HyperTerminal profiles to start the HyperTerminal program. Or, click your mouse on the Hypertrm icon and create a new profile. When HyperTerminal displays the Connect dialog box shown in Figure 655.1, perform these steps:

1. Click your mouse on the Modify button to display the profile's Properties sheet.
2. Click your mouse on the Configure button to display Properties sheet as shown in Figure 655.2.
3. Set the maximum speed to at least the remote computer's baud rate. (Generally, you should set the maximum speed to a higher value than your modem's own speed. This value indicates how fast Windows 95 can respond to your modem.)
4. Click your mouse on the Connection tab to display the Connection page.
5. Change the page's settings to the remote computer's data bit, parity, and stop bit requirements.

Using Windows 95 Accessory Programs

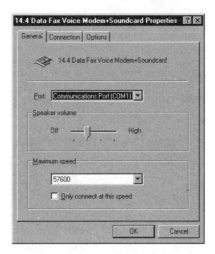

Figure 655.1 *The Connect dialog box.*

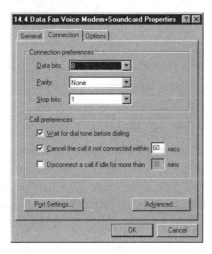

Figure 655.2 *The HyperTerminal Properties sheet.*

Understanding Terminal Emulation — 656

When you dial into a remote mainframe computer, such as a large university computer, that computer treats your PC as if it were a *terminal*. A terminal is a screen and keyboard connected directly to the computer. The remote computer views your PC as just one of the many screen and keyboard terminal combinations attached to it directly with wires. If you've performed the steps in Tip 655 and still have trouble communicating with such a computer, you may need to set your profile to use a different terminal-emulation method. After you set the terminal emulation method, your PC behaves (emulates) the same signals and actions as an attached terminal of that type. To specify your connection's terminal emulation, perform these steps:

1. After you start HyperTerminal with the remote computer's profile (see Tip 653), click your mouse on the Connect dialog box Modify button. HyperTerminal will display the profile's Properties sheet.

2. Click your mouse on the Settings tab to display Figure 656's Settings page.

3. Open the Emulation pull-down list and select the remote computer's preferred terminal type.
4. Click your mouse on the OK button. HyperTerminal will save your changes and return you to the Connect dialog box, from where you can dial the remote computer.

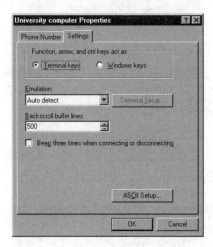

Figure 656 *The Settings page.*

657 Controlling Your Connection's ASCII Control

Characters are represented by *ASCII* symbols. ASCII stands for the *American Standard Code for Information Interchange*. Some computer systems use 8-bit (extended) ASCII; others use 7-bit; and still others treat ASCII characters differently, such as when some UNIX systems convert carriage-return characters into carriage-return and linefeed characters. If you experience communications problems, you may need to specify ASCII control settings, especially if you communicate with a mainframe or a UNIX system. To specify ASCII settings, perform these steps:

1. After you start HyperTerminal with the remote computer's profile (see Tip 653), click your mouse on the Connect dialog box Modify button. HyperTerminal will display the profile's Properties sheet.
2. Click your mouse on the Settings tab.
3. Click your mouse on the ASCII Setup button. HyperTerminal will display the ASCII Setup dialog box, as shown in Figure 657.

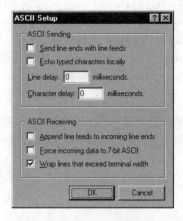

Figure 657 *The ASCII Setup dialog box.*

Using File Transfer Protocols 658

A *protocol* is a set of rules that specifies how the participants in an operation must behave. When two systems exchange files, they must agree on which file transfer protocol they will use to send, receive, and reconcile the data transmission. When you transfer a file to or from a remote computer, you normally tell the remote computer which protocol you want to use. Then, you tell HyperTerminal to use that protocol. Both the Send File and Receive File dialog boxes contain Protocol pull-down lists from which you can select a protocol before starting the file transfer. HyperTerminal lets you select from the following protocols:

- 1K Xmodem
- Xmodem
- Ymodem
- Ymodem-G
- Zmodem
- Kermit

Some protocols are faster than others. Generally, Zmodem is the quickest protocol.

Transferring a File from a Remote Computer 659

When you transfer a file from a remote computer to your PC, you *download* the file. After you establish a connection with the remote computer, you must enter commands that start the download process. These commands will differ for virtually every remote computer you use, so you must read through that computer's instructions (and Help messages, if the remote computer uses online Help) to start the download process. Additionally, you must select a download protocol that both the remote computer and your PC will use (see Tip 658). Finally, you must know the name and location of the file you want to download. (The remote computer may have its own file-naming and file storage conventions.) After you initiate the remote computer's download process, perform these steps to receive the file inside HyperTerminal:

1. Click your mouse on the Transfer menu Receive File option. HyperTerminal will display the Receive File dialog box shown in Figure 659.
2. Enter the path and filename HyperTerminal will use to store the received file on your computer.
3. Select the protocol HyperTerminal and the remote computer will use for the file transfer.
4. Click your mouse on the Receive button. HyperTerminal will display a Download status dialog box, which shows you the progress of the download and estimated time for completion. When the dialog box disappears, the file will reside on your computer.

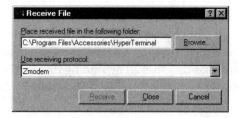

Figure 659 *The Receive File dialog box.*

660 Transferring a File to a Remote Computer

When you transfer a file to a remote computer from your PC, you *upload* the file. After you establish a connection with the remote computer, you must enter commands that start the upload process. These commands will differ for virtually every remote computer you use, so you must read through that computer's instructions (and Help messages, if the remote computer uses online Help) to start the upload process. Additionally, you must select an upload protocol for both the remote computer and your PC to use (see Tip 658).

Note: Be sure you have permission to upload to the remote computer. Some mainframe systems let you download files, but not upload files. This practice ensures system integrity and security.

After you initiate the remote computer's upload process, perform these steps to send the file from HyperTerminal:

1. Click your mouse on the Transfer menu Send File option. HyperTerminal will display the Send File dialog box shown in Figure 660.
2. Enter the path and filename for the file you want HyperTerminal to send to the remote computer.
3. Select the protocol HyperTerminal and the remote computer will use for the file transfer.
4. Click your mouse on the Send button. HyperTerminal will display an Upload status dialog box, which shows you the progress of the upload and estimated time for completion. When the dialog box disappears, the file will reside on the remote computer.

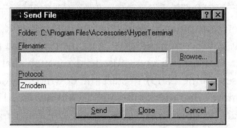

Figure 660 The Send File dialog box.

661 Sending a Text File to a Remote Computer

Tips 659 and 660 explain how to send and receive files between your computer and the remote computer to which you are connected. You can upload and download text files, binary files (programs and compressed data files), graphic files, and any other kind of file that can reside on both computers.

However, sometimes you will *not* want to upload a text file to the remote computer using the normal upload procedure. For example, suppose you're working on a remote computer from your home PC inside a HyperTerminal window, using the computer's text editor, and you want to include the contents of a PC file in the text you're writing. You can stay in the text editor, and initiate HyperTerminal's Transfer menu Send Text File option. HyperTerminal does not wait for the remote computer's receive protocol. Instead, HyperTerminal sends the text file (you can only send text files this way) directly to the remote computer. The remote computer's text editor receives the data from your PC's text file as if you were typing that data instead of sending it. After HyperTerminal sends all the data, you can issue the remote computer text editor's saving commands to save the text file that you created partially by typing and partially by text-file transfer.

Capturing Text to a File or Printer — 662

An online session with a remote computer can last several hours if you maintain the connection. As such, there may be times when you have trouble remembering everything you encountered during an online session. Luckily, you can direct HyperTerminal to record a log of an online session. To do so, all you must do is select the Transfer menu Capture Text option and enter a filename. HyperTerminal, in turn, will store in a file every character that appears on its window. After you break the remote connection, you can access the file to see a log of your online session. If you want a printed copy of an online session, click your mouse on the Transfer menu Capture to Printer option. HyperTerminal, in turn, will print a hard copy of the entire online session.

Controlling the Size of HyperTerminal's Text Buffer — 663

When you use Tip 662 to capture your online session to a text file, your whole session goes to that file. Instead of capturing your *entire* online session, however, you may want to be able to scroll the HyperTerminal window backwards to see what happened earlier in the session. The scrolling buffer is easier to use than having to look in a log file once the session ends. You can control the number of lines HyperTerminal uses for the scrolling buffer. If, for example, you set up the text buffer to hold 250 lines, you'll be able to scroll at any time to see the most recent 250 lines of your online session. Use the vertical scroll bar to the right of HyperTerminal's window to scroll backward. To change the scrolling text buffer size, perform these steps:

1. Click your mouse on the File menu Properties option.
2. Click your mouse on the Settings tab to display the Properties sheet Settings page.
3. Enter a new value in the Backscroll buffer lines text box. The value determines the number of lines HyperTerminal starts recording, and you'll be able to scroll back that many lines during the session to see what happened earlier.
4. Click your mouse on the OK button to save your changes.

Displaying and Using HyperTerminal's Toolbar — 664

The HyperTerminal toolbar gives you one-button access to many of the program's most common commands. To display (or hide) the toolbar, click your mouse on the View menu Toolbar option. Table 664 explains the purpose of each HyperTerminal toolbar button.

Icon	Purpose
	Creates a new communications profile.
	Opens a new communications profile.
	Connects to the current profile's remote computer.
	Disconnects from the remote computer.
	Sends a file to the remote computer.
	Receives a file from the remote computer.
	Displays the HyperTerminal Properties sheet.

Table 664 The buttons on the HyperTerminal toolbar.

665 Understanding the Internet

The *Internet* is not one gigantic computer in Washington, D.C., or anywhere else, as some people think. Rather, the Internet consists of many computer networks linked together by phone lines, direct wires, satellites, and cellular communications. In essence, the Internet is really just a huge computer network. The *World Wide Web* (*WWW*), in turn, is a subset of the Internet. Computers on the Web communicate using a graphical interface standard. After you use Windows 95 or other tools to connect to the Internet, you can send and receive e-mail and files to other Internet users across the country and around the world. Additionally, you can search the pages of the Wide World Web for files, information, and entertainment. Why, you can even use the Web to order a pizza delivered hot at your doorstep.

Note: *To access a file or Web page, you must know its location. Millions of computers connect to the Internet, so finding exactly what you need is not always easy. Luckily, the Internet offers search tools you can use to find some things. Also, many great computer magazines and books publish various Internet locations (see Tip 695).*

666 Online Services and the Internet

Many of today's online services (such as CompuServe, Prodigy, America Online, and The Microsoft Network) provide partial or full access to the Internet and usually provide full support for Internet e-mail. If you use one or more of these services, you can access many of the Internet's features, usually in a cost-effective manner. In fact, most of the online services will let you "try out" their service and the Internet for a month for free! If your PC has a modem, take the online services up on their free offers and test drive the Internet.

667 Windows 95 and the Internet

To access the Internet from within Windows 3.1, you had to have special software called *Winsock* (for *Windows Sockets*). Additionally, you had to purchase third-party Internet access tools that supported Winsock. In contrast, Windows 95 provides built-in software that supports Microsoft's *TCP/IP*, the primary protocol used on the Internet. (TCP/IP stands for *Transmission Control Protocol/Internet Protocol*.) When you use TCP/IP, your computer links-up to the Internet and becomes another node on the vast Internet system. If you want to access the Internet, check to see if you have Dial-Up Networking access installed in your version of Windows 95. To do so, open the My Computer window and look for the Dial-Up Networking icon. If you don't see the icon, open the Control Panel and double-click on the Add/Remove Programs icon. Then, use the Add/Remove Programs Properties sheet Windows Setup page to install Dial-Up Networking.

Note: *To access the World Wide Web, you need the Windows 95 add-on product called* **Microsoft Plus!** *or another company's Web software. Tip 672 explains more about Web software.*

668 You Still Need an Internet Provider

The Internet was originally used by government and research organizations, as well as universities. As a result, the only way you could access the Internet was through government and research institutions. Fortunately, as the Internet grew, businesses began providing Internet connections. These companies are called *Internet providers*. To access the Internet, you need an Internet provider. Contact a company with which you can register to dial up their Internet-connected computer and access the Internet.

To find an Internet provider, look in the back of computer magazines and in the business section of your local newspaper. You'll likely find advertisements for scores of local and remote provider companies. Typically, an Internet connection will cost you $10 to $30 per month.

Understanding PPP and SLIP Connections 669

Two of the most popular dial-in connections you can use for Internet access are the *SLIP*-based connection (*Serial Line Internet Protocol*) and *PPP*-based connection (*Point-to-Point Protocol*). PPP-based connections provide the fastest access for the typical computer user connecting to the Internet with a modem. Windows 95 provides built-in support for PPP-based access.

If you use a SLIP-based access connection, you must either load special software available only on the Windows 95 CD-ROM (see Tip 680) or get third-party software (usually available from your Internet provider) that you use with Windows 95 to access the provider's Internet connection. One of your best resources to which you can turn to for answers is your provider's technical support.

Use HyperTerminal to Access a Shell-Based Account 670

Many colleges and business provide a UNIX *shell* (a shell is an operating environment similar to the DOS command line where you issue commands at a system prompt) connection the Internet. If you work at such a business or attend such a school and you go home at night and want to access the UNIX computer's Internet account, you can use HyperTerminal to access your UNIX computer first.

After you've established a UNIX connection (you'll be controlling the UNIX computer from home just as if you were in front of your UNIX terminal at work), issue your UNIX shell's commands to get on the Internet. HyperTerminal, in turn, will route the Internet's messages from the remote UNIX computer to your own home computer.

Understanding the World Wide Web 671

The *World Wide Web* (also known as the *Web*, *WWW*, or just *W3*) provides you with graphical, hypertext-based access to the information stored on the Internet. The Web's hypertext feature (which connects related documents) lets you jump from subject to subject by just clicking your mouse on highlighted keywords that appear in each document. You can think a of hypertext Web document much like the Windows 95 Help system which lets you move from subject to subject by clicking on jump buttons and underlined text.

Using the Web's graphical interface, you can visually tour the Louvre in Paris, see the inside of a running motor, browse collections of classical literature, and download virtually every graphic, video clip, and sound file that you see (and watch and hear) along the way. After you are connected to the Internet, all you need to use the Web is browsing software.

You Need a Web Browser 672

To access (or surf) the World Wide Web, you need a *web browser*, a program that links to the World Wide Web through your Internet provider. Companies such as Spry and Netscape offer Web browsers. In addition, your local computer software store should have ample supplies. Tip 693 describes how to get a free web-browser.

Microsoft offers a web browser, called *Internet Explorer*, that works great with Windows 95. Internet Explorer is one of the tools you get in the Microsoft Plus! Windows 95 add-on product. Internet Explorer provides access to a full-featured Internet Web browser and to a new Microsoft Network software interface that connects to the Internet better than the pure Windows 95 Microsoft Network driver. (Without the Microsoft Plus! product, The Microsoft Network offers only line-oriented and limited Internet access.)

673 Preparing Your System to Access the Internet

In the past few tips, you have learned a little about the Internet and how it functions. Now it's time to learn how to connect to the Internet. To access the Internet from within Windows 95, perform these steps:

1. Locate an Internet provider that supplies PPP-based access. Use SLIP-based access only if you can't obtain PPP-based access.
2. Install Windows 95 Dial-Up Networking support if your My Computer window does not show a Dial-Up Networking icon.
3. Install the TCP/IP Internet protocol so Windows 95 can access the Internet. To determine if your Windows 95 is setup for TCP/IP, double-click your Control Panel's Network icon. Then, scroll through the installed components to see if any contain the letters *TCP/IP*. If no components contain these letters, click your mouse on the Add button, double-click your mouse on the Protocol option, and select Microsoft's TCP/IP option.
4. Use the following few tips to configure your TCP/IP protocol.

674 Understanding IP Addresses

The *Internet Protocol*, or *IP*, is the part of the TCP/IP protocol that keeps track of Internet address nodes (locations) and tracks data going back and forth between them. When you access the Internet, the data that you send to others, and that which they send to you, has to arrive at the correct destination computers. No central Internet tracking system exists that keeps track of every computer's address. Instead, each computer that connects to the Internet has a node location that, given the proper protocol (such as TCP/IP), other computers can locate.

IP address consist of four numbers separated by periods, such as 111.222.112.213. Each computer on Internet has its own unique IP address. Information on the Internet moves in the form of small messages. Each message (or packet) specifies its destination using an Internet address. Luckily, as you will learn in Tip 675, users don't have work with numeric Internet addresses. Instead, users specify domain names such as microsoft.com.

675 Understanding Domain Names

Across the Internet, each computer has its own unique Internet address. Internet addresses consist of four numbers separated by periods, such as 111.222.101.123. Before two computers can communicate across the Internet, each computer's software must know the other computer's Internet address. As you can imagine, however, having to use and remember each computer's numeric address could become quite difficult.

Luckily, neither you nor your software has to work the IP address of *every* computer to which you connect. Instead of using a technical IP address value, you can often specify a *domain name*. Network designers developed the Internet's *Domain Name System (DNS)* to let users refer to Internet computers by alphabetical names, such as jamsa.com or microsoft.com instead of an IP addresses, such as 192.102.249.3.

Domain names contain several parts called *labels*. Therefore, *ftp.microsoft.com* consists of three labels: *ftp*, *microsoft*, and *com*. The last label specifies an organizational group type. For example, if you contact a computer whose domain name ends in *.edu*, that name indicates that an educational institution houses the computer. Table 675 describes the common organizational labels.

Domain	Description
com	Commercial organizations
edu	Educational institutions
gov	U.S. governmental organizations
int	International governmental organizations
mil	U.S. military organizations
net	A network that does not fit into another organizational domain category
org	An organization that does not fit into one of the other organizational domain categories

Table 675 Common 3-letter organizational domains.

676 Configuring Your TCP/IP Connection's Domain Name Server

As you have learned, Internet users get to address systems using domain names, such as microsoft.com, while the underlying software must use numeric IP addresses. As you might imagine, Internet programs need a way to convert a domain name into an IP address. To perform such conversions, programs ask for help from a special computer called a domain name server. In genernal, a domain name server is simply a computer on the Internet that knows the domain name and IP address for a large number of Internet sites. A program sends a message to the domain name server asking it for the IP address that corresponds to a given domain name. If the domain name servers knows the IP address, it immediately sends an answer back to the program. Otherwise, the domain name server asks a different server for help.

After you register with an Internet provider, the provider will tell you the domain name server they want you to use. To configure your TCP/IP connection to use the correct domain name server, perform these steps:

1. Double-click your left mouse button on the Control Panel's Network icon. Windows 95 opens the Network Properties sheet shown in Figure 676.1.
2. Scroll the installed components list until you see the TCP/IP option.
3. Click your mouse on the TCP/IP option to highlight it.
4. Click your mouse on the Properties button. Windows 95 will display the TCP/IP Properties sheet.
5. Click your mouse on the DNS Configuration tab to display the DNS Configuration page shown in Figure 676.2.
6. Click your mouse on the Enable DNS option button.
7. Type the name of your Internet provider's host computer in the Host text box.
8. Type your Internet provider's domain name in the Domain text box.
9. Type the 4-part DNS server address of the domain name server you want to use. Windows 95 separates each part with a period. When you type a part, press RIGHT ARROW to move to the next part number.
10. Click your mouse on the Add button and then click on OK.

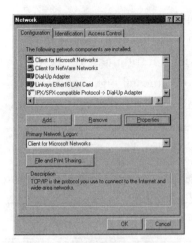

Figure 676.1 *The Network Properties sheet.*

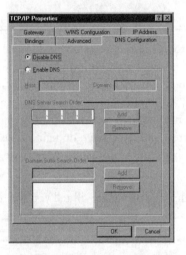

Figure 676.2 *The TCP/IP Properties sheet.*

677 | Specifying Your Computer's IP Address

When you use an Internet provider to connect to the Internet, your provider must give you an IP address that uniquely identifies your system. Your provider can specify your address in one of two ways: the provider can give you a fixed IP address or, more often, send to your computer an address that changes each time you dial in to specify your IP address. If your Internet provider sends you a dynamically changing address each time you dial in, you don't have to set any TCP/IP default IP settings. (Sometimes, your provider will specify your IP address as "0.0.0.0," which indicates a dynamic IP address.) If your Internet provider gives you a fixed IP address, your provider will also give you a *subnet mask* needed for TCP/IP access as well. To enter your provider's IP address, perform these steps:

1. After you set up the DNS information (see Tip 676), click on the TCP/IP Properties sheet IP Address tab. Windows 95 will display the IP Address page, as shown in Figure 677.

2. Click your mouse on the "Specify an IP address" option button.

3. Type the 4-part IP address of your Internet provider's server. Windows 95 separates each part with a period. When you type a part, press RIGHT ARROW to move to the next part number.

4. Type the 4-part subnet mask of your Internet provider's server. Again, use the RIGHT ARROW key to move to the next part number.

5. Click your mouse on the OK button to save your changes.

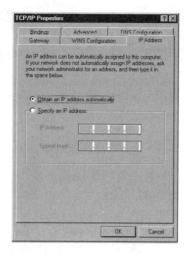

Figure 677 *The IP Address page.*

678 Understanding and Configuring WINS

Although most Internet users will not need *WINS* (the *Windows Internet Naming Service*), the TCP/IP Properties sheet contains a WINS Configuration page, shown in Figure 678, where you can specify WINS settings. Some programs that require the *NetBIOS Protocol* also require a WINS setting. If you need to make WINS settings, your Internet provider (or network administrator) can supply you with the details. To configure WINS information, perform these steps:

1. After you set up the DNS and IP address information (see Tips 676 and 677), click your mouse on the TCP/IP Properties sheet WINS Configuration tab. Windows 95 will display the WINS Configuration page, as shown in Figure 678.

2. Click your mouse on the Enable WINS Resolution option button and enter the WINS information in the space provided.

3. Click your mouse on the Use DHCP for WINS Resolution option button (*DHCP* stands for *Dynamic Host Configuration Protocol*) if your server provides you with access to a dynamic WINS server.

4. Click your mouse on the OK button to save your changes.

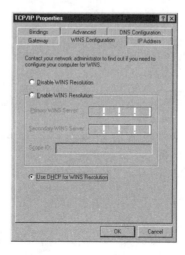

Figure 678 *The WINS Configuration page.*

679 | Telling Windows 95 About Your Provider

As you have learned, using a modem and standard phone lines, you connect your computer to your Internet provider, which in turn, gives you access to the Internet. Obviously, to connect to the Internet, Windows 95 must know your Internet provider's phone number. Windows 95 provides a wizard you run to inform the operating system of your provider's phone number, protocol (such as PPP or SLIP), and other pertinent details that your provider gives you. Before you dial your provider for the first time, perform these steps:

1. Double-click your My Computer window's Dial-Up Networking icon. Windows 95 will display the Dial-Up Networking Make New Connection icon, indicating that you've yet to set up the Dial-Up Networking details.
2. Double-click your mouse on the Make New Connection icon to start the Dial-Up Networking wizard. Figure 679.1 shows the wizard's opening window.
3. Click your button on the Next button to start the wizard.
4. Type a name for your provider's computer. The name can be whatever you want to call the computer, such as "My Internet Provider."
5. Select the modem you want to use for Internet access. If you've got only one modem set up for Windows 95, use that modem.
6. Click your mouse on the Next button.
7. Enter your Internet provider's phone number.
8. Click on the Next button. Windows 95 will display the Make New Connection dialog box.
9. Click on the Finish button to complete the Internet provider configuration. After Windows 95 completes the configuration, your Dial-Up Networking folder will contain your Internet provider's connection, labeled with the name you entered in Step 3.

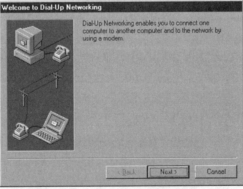

Figure 679.1 The Dial-Up Networking wizard.

680 | Installing SLIP Support Software

Windows 95 offers built-in PPP support. However, if your provider offers only SLIP-based Internet access, you need to install SLIP software found on the Windows 95 CD-ROM. To install the SLIP software, perform these steps:

1. Double-click your Control Panel's Add/Remove Programs icon to open the Add/Remove Programs Properties sheet.
2. Click your mouse on the Windows Setup tab to display the Windows Setup page.

3. Click your mouse on the Have Disk button.
4. Click your mouse on the Install From Disk dialog box Browse button. Then, select or type this pathname: D:\ADMIN\APPTOOLS\DSCRIPT\RNAPLUS.INF. If your CD-ROM drive name is not D:, use your CD-ROM drive's name at the start of the path.
5. Click your mouse on the "SLIP and Scripting for Dial-Up Networking" option.
6. Click your mouse on the Install button to install the SLIP software.
7. Click your mouse on the OK button to save your changes.

Configuring Your Provider's Properties 681

Although you've created a Dial-Up Networking configuration for your Internet provider (if you followed Tip 679), Windows 95 needs additional information about your provider, such as the provider's server type (PPP or SLIP). To configure your provider's properties, perform these steps:

1. Open your Dial-Up Networking folder. You'll see your Internet provider's configuration icon.
2. Right-click the configuration icon and select the pop-up menu's Properties option. Windows 95 displays your Internet computer's Properties sheet General page.
3. Click your mouse on the Server Type button. Windows 95 displays the Server Types dialog box shown in Figure 681.
4. Select your server type (probably either PPP or SLIP).
5. Do *not* check the "Log on to network" option. If the option is checked, uncheck the option by clicking your mouse over it. Your service provider will give you log-on instructions that you'll enter by hand when you log on to the Internet provider's computer.
6. To speed up Internet access, leave the NetBEUI and IPX/SPC Compatible options *unchecked*.
7. Click your mouse on the OK button to save your changes.
8. To complete the Internet provider configuration, click your mouse on the General page's OK button.

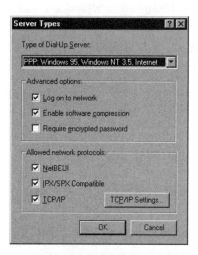

Figure 681 *The Server Type dialog box.*

682 Dialing Your Provider

To dial your provider, double-click your mouse on the Dial-Up Networking folder's provider icon. Windows 95, in turn, will display the Connect To window. The Connect To User Name and Password contains your Windows 95 username and password, which, probably, will not be the same as the ones that you set up on the Internet when you registered with your provider. Type your Internet username and password. If you click your mouse on the Save password option, Windows 95 remembers the password the next time you log on. If you leave the option unmarked, you'll have to type your password each time you log on to the Internet.

If the Internet provider's phone number is correct, click your mouse on the Connect button to dial the number. Then, follow your provider's log-on procedure. Depending on your provider, you may need to type **SLIP**, **PPP**, or possibly **TIA** (*The Internet Adapter,* which lets you switch to a SLIP account after you log on) when the provider's computer prompts you. Also, if you are using a SLIP account, write down the IP address your provider displays; to complete the log-on procedure, you will need to type this IP address in the dialog box that appears next.

683 Creating a SLIP Script

SLIP users need to check with their service providers to see if they have to write down an IP address as soon as they log on to the provider's computer (the provider will display the IP address on the user's screen). These users must enter that IP address when Windows 95 prompts for the IP address. (This SLIP IP address is not fixed, and can change with each log-on.)

If you must use such a SLIP account, you can simplify the log-on process. Create a script file that interacts with your Internet provider to capture the IP address and automatically use it, instead of requiring that you write down the address. Windows 95 provides a SLIP script utility that Windows Setup automatically installed when you installed the SLIP software.

The script you write must conform to your service provider's log on requirements. Your service provider may be able to help you code the script so that the script contains the proper log-on commands. The script, which becomes your automatic SLIP log-on assistant, simulates the entering of your username, password, and captures, and uses the IP address automatically. It is not easy getting a script just right, so expect to work on it a while and use Window 95's online Help a lot. (Hopefully, your provider already wrote one you can use.)

You'll create SLIP scripts using a text editor, such as Notepad. To access the SLIP script program, which uses the script and offers online Help, perform these steps:

1. Double-click your left mouse button over your My Computer window's C: drive icon.
2. Double-click your left mouse button over the Program Files folder.
3. Double-click your left mouse button over the Accessories folder.
4. Double-click your left mouse button over the Scripter program. The Scripter program reads the text script files you create in Notepad and connects those files to your next SLIP session. Be sure to read through Scripter's Help menus for guidance. You'll find sample scripts from which you can copy and paste into your own scripts.

684 Using Ping to Test a Site's Accessibility

As you run different programs to connect to or to retrieve files from a computer across the Internet, there may be times when the program fails and displays an error message that states the program cannot connect to the remote computer. If you cannot access a specific computer, you can use the PING command to determine if the computer is available.

To use the PING command, select the Start menu Run option and type **PING** followed by the name of the computer you are trying to access. For example, to "ping" jamsa.com, you would type **PING jamsa.com**. If Ping reports no problems, the remote computer is up and operational. On the other hand, if PING displays an error message, the remote computer may be down. Should PING display such an error message, try to connect to the remote computer at a later time.

Tracing a Connection's Route Using Tracert

Windows 95 includes the *Tracert* program, which traces the route your Internet connection follows to get to its destination. For example, when you connect to a computer in Italy, your provider does not send a signal straight to the Italian computer. Instead, the Internet sends the signal (called a *packet*) to a more local computer, who in turn, sends the packet to a third computer. In this way, your packet might go through several computers on the vast Internet network before arriving in Italy.

To trace a connection's route, click your mouse on the Start menu Run command and type **TRACERT** followed by the domain name of the remote computer to which you want to trace a connection. Figure 685 shows a trace made from a computer in Tulsa, Oklahoma to a computer in Las Vegas, Nevada.

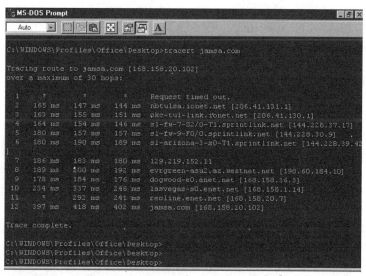

Figure 685 Use the Tracert program to track Internet inter-connections.

Controlling Address Resolution Using ARP

Use *ARP* if you are an advanced Internet user who needs to display or modify IP-to-Ethernet or IP-to-Token Ring address translation tables that the Address Resolution Protocol uses. You can run ARP from the MS-DOS command prompt or from the Start menu Run option. The ARP command has three formats:

    ARP -a [inet_addr][-N [if_addr]]

    ARP -d inet_addr [if_addr]

    ARP -s inet_addr ether_addr [if_addr]

Table 686 explains each of the ARP command-line arguments.

Argument	Purpose
-a	Queries TCP/IP and displays current ARP entries.
-d	Deletes the ARP cache table's entry specified by *inet_addr*.
-s	Associates the *inet_addr* with the *ether_addr*'s physical address in the ARP cache.
-N	Displays the *if_addr* network interface's ARP entries.
ether_addr	Specifies a physical address to use.
if_addr	Specifies the IP address whose address translation tables need modifying (the default is the first applicable interface).
inet_addr	Specifies a dotted IP address.

Table 686 ARP's command-line arguments.

687 Displaying TCP/IP Statistics Using Netstat

If your network connection seems slow, you may want to use the Netstat utility provided with Windows 95 to take a closer look at your connection. The *Netstat* program provides networking statistics and information on TCP/IP network connections. You can run Netstat from an MS-DOS prompt or from the Start menu Run option. To run NETSTAT, type the following command:

```
NETSTAT [-a] [-ens] [-p protocol] [-r] [interval]
```

Table 687 explains each of Netstat's command-line arguments.

Argument	Purpose
-a	Produces statistical information on all connections, including server connections that Netstat typically does not show.
-e	Produces Ethernet statistics.
-n	Displays both addresses and port numbers in numerical form instead of by name lookup, as is the default.
-s	Often used along with the -e command-line option to produce a per-protocol statistical table.
-p	Shows protocol connections.
-r	Displays the routing table.

Table 687 Netstat's command-line arguments.

If you use no command-line arguments, the default Netstat output produces the following statistical network information values in the following order:

- *Proto*: The name of the connection's protocol
- *Local Address*: The local computer's IP address, as well as the port number
- *Foreign Address*: The remote computer's IP address and connection socket
- *State*: Displays the TCP connection state

Note: *You can increase the amount of information by using the arguments.*

688 Control Network Routing Tables by Using Route

The Internet is a collection of so many different network technologies that a *router* is one of the most important elements of successful Internet maneuvering. A router transfers data between networks. Routers have their own network addresses and act as intermediate destinations between computers. As such, the networked computers do not have to use the same networking technologies.

Windows 95's Route program diagnoses and manipulates network router tables. Obviously, only technically-advanced Internet users will have a need for Route. To start Route, open an MS-DOS window and type **ROUTE** followed by one or more arguments. Here is the format of the ROUTE command:

```
ROUTE [-f][command[destination][MASK  netmask][gateway]]
```

Table 688 explains each of ROUTE's arguments.

Argument	Purpose
-f	Clears all gateway entry routing tables.
command	Specifies either PRINT, ADD, DELETE, or CHANGE, to display, add, delete, or change a route.
destination	Specifies the host-to-send command.
MASK	Indicates that the next argument is a *netmask* argument.
netmask	Specifies this route's subnet mask value (the default is 255.255.255.255).
gateway	Specifies the gateway.

Table 688 Route's command-line arguments.

689 Using Telnet to Move from One Computer to Another

Across the Internet, there are thousands of computers to which you can connect and run programs. The *Telnet* program opens a window on your computer and turns it into a terminal session on a remote Internet computer. In other words, the remote computer treats your computer as if your computer was a terminal connected to the computer. In other words, the programs you run (within the Telnet window) are actually running on the remote computer.

Your computer simply displays the program's output. You must be authorized to use the computer to which you connect with Telnet, although many public Telnet sites are available (see Tip 690). When you connect to a remote computer, Windows must behave like (emulate) a terminal (which connects directly to the computer). Telnet supports the following terminal emulations:

- DEC VT 100
- DEC VT 52
- TTY

To run Telnet, select the Start menu Run option and type **TELNET** (followed by an optional host and port name for the remote computer, if you have that information when you start Telnet). Windows 95, in turn, will load Telnet's terminal window (shown in Figure 689) and let you work on that remote computer as if you were a local user.

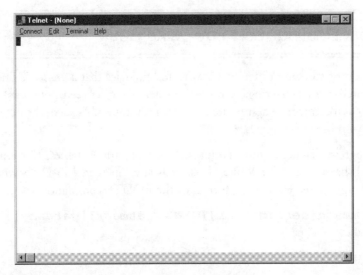

Figure 689 *Telnet provides terminal emulation.*

690 Visit These Interesting Telnet Sites

As you have learned, using Telnet, you can connect to computers across the Internet. When you "Telnet" across the Internet, you do so for free. In other words, it does not cost you any more to connect to a computer across the world than it does to connect to a computer across town. You can visit several public Telnet sites to get information, such as those listed in Table 690.

To access a Telnet site, start Telnet (see Tip 689) and click your mouse on the Connect menu Remote System option. Some sites require a port number; others do not. Use "Telnet" as your Windows 95 port value for those sites that do not require port numbers.

Some Telnet sites request that you log in using your own Internet member name, such as gwashington@govt.com; however, if that login does not work, try typing **guest** or **new**. Many sites describe the log-in procedure on the initial banner that welcomes you to the system.

Name	Port	Description
debra.dgbt.doc.ca	3000	Natural-language (English) database on various current affairs and health issues
india.colorado.edu	13	The exact time of day
library.cmu.edu	Telnet	Carnegie Mellon University's Library
locis.loc.gov	Telnet	Library of Congress records
ukanaix.cc.ukans.edu	Telnet	Interactive historical database
spacelink.msfc.nasa.gov	Telnet	NASA information

Table 690 *Interesting public Telnet Sites.*

691 Understanding File Transfers Using FTP

Across the Internet, there are millions of files. In fact, each day, over 75,000 new files are added to the Internet. These files can be research reports, pictures, and even electronic books. One way to access these files is to use the FTP program provided with Windows 95. *FTP* stands for *File-Transfer Protocol*. With FTP, you can access other Internet computers and download files from those computers. The downloads are free and available on those FTP sites that support *anonymous* logon (you don't need your username or a password to access files available to the public). The anonymous logon limits FTP access to file downloading and thus maintains the remote site's security.

You may transfer both text and binary files to your computer. (Many Internet users use *FTP* as a verb as in "I'll FTP that file to my computer.") Some sites also let you use FTP to upload files, so read the instructions you find at each site. To access an FTP site, perform these steps:

1. Access the Internet through your Internet Dial-Up Connection.
2. Click your mouse on the Start menu Run option.
3. Type **FTP** and press ENTER.
4. After you find an FTP site, type **OPEN** followed by the site name, such as **OPEN ftp.microsoft.com**.
5. When the site asks you for a username, type **anonymous**.
6. To get FTP access, type your Internet user ID as your password.

Visit These Interesting FTP Sites — 692

Table 692 lists several FTP sites you may want to access. To access an FTP site, start FTP (see Tip 691) and open any of the sites listed in Table 692. Type **anonymous** for the log-on ID and type your Internet ID (such as **gwashington@gov.com**) as the password. When you complete the log-on procedure, type **cd /pub** to change to the public directories. After you find a file you want to download, follow the steps in Tip 693 to get the file to your computer.

FTP

Name	Description
ftp.books.com	The complete text from thousands of books in the public domain, including many classics in literature
ftp.microsoft.com	Microsoft support and news files
ftp.ncsa.uiuc.edu	Free World Wide Web tools (see Tip 693)
wiretap.spies.com	Government publications and information
madlab.sprl.umich.edu	Kid's weather service software and files
ftp.cs.vu.nl	German/French/Dutch/Italian dictionaries

Table 692 Interesting FTP sites.

Use FTP to Download a Web Browser — 693

To practice downloading a file with FTP, you can download a sample *web browser* program named *Mosaic*, which you can use to surf the World Wide Web. To download Mosaic, perform these steps:

1. Use Dial-Up Networking to connect to the Internet.
2. Click your mouse on the Start menu Run option.
3. Type **FTP**.
4. Type **open ftp.ncsa.uiuc.edu** and wait to connect to the Mosaic computer.
5. Type **anonymous** as your username.

6. Type your username as your password.
7. Type **cd Web** to change to the Web-browser directory on the remote computer. Be sure to type the **cd** command using the same upper-case and lower-case combination shown here.
8. Type **cd Mosaic/Windows/Win95/Disk** to change to the Windows 95 Mosaic directory. Be sure to type *forward slashes* between the words and not the PC-based backslash.
9. Type **type binary** to permit downloading of compressed binary files. Until you type this command, you can only download ASCII files.
10. Type **get disk1.exe** and wait while FTP downloads the file to your PC. By default, FTP downloads the file to your WINDOWS\Profiles\Office\Desktop directory.
11. Type **get disk2.exe** when the prompt returns.
12. Type **disc** to disconnect from the remote computer.
13. Disconnect from your Internet provider. To do so, click your mouse on the Disconnect button on the Taskbar's Connected to Internet computer dialog box.

The two files, DISK1.EXE and DISK2.EXE, are high-density floppy-disk images that contain Windows 95 Mosaic Web browsers. To create a Windows 95 Mosaic Web browser, perform these steps:

1. Open an MS-DOS window.
2. Insert a high-density formatted floppy disk into your floppy disk drive.
3. Change to your WINDOWS\Profiles\Office\Desktop directory by typing **CD WINDOWS\Profiles\Office\Desktop** and pressing ENTER.
4. Type **DISK1 A:** to create the first Mosaic installation diskette.
5. Write "NCSA Mosaic v2.0 Disk 1 of 2" on the floppy disk's label.
6. Replace the floppy diskette with a second high-density formatted floppy disk.
7. Type **DISK2 A:** to create the second Mosaic installation diskette.
8. Write "NCSA Mosaic v2.0 Disk 2 of 2" on the floppy disk's label.
9. Reinsert the first of the two diskettes and type **SETUP** to begin the Mosaic installation. Follow the instructions that appear on your screen to complete the process.

Note: *If you have Microsoft Plus!, you already have a Web browser. To access this browser, click your mouse on the Accessories menu Internet Tools option. Then, click your mouse on the Internet Explorer option. The Microsoft home Web page appears.*

694 Using a Web Browser

To help you surf the Web, a Web browser must know where to find Web pages that you want to see. Web browsers require a *URL (Uniform Resource Locator)* for each Web page. A URL provides a unique address for a particular Web page. To access a Web page, find the Web page's URL address and type that address in your Web browser's URL list box. When you press ENTER, your Web browser displays that Web site's *homepage*. (The first page of a Web site is always called the site's homepage.)

A Web page can contain text and graphics, as well as hyperlinks on which you can click your mouse to jump to related sites. Web pages also offer special features. For example, if you click your mouse over most Web page graphics, the Web browser automatically downloads those graphics to your computer. Figures 694.1, 694.2, and 694.3 show three different Web pages.

Windows 95, the Internet, and the World Wide Web

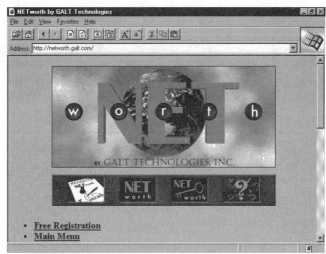

Figure 694.1 Analyze mutual fund options.

Figure 694.2 Visit Italy online!

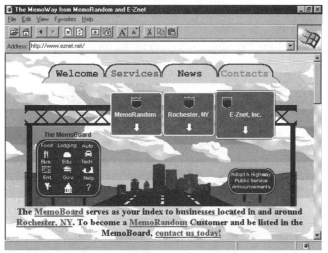

Figure 694.3 Take the Information Super Highway literally.

695 Visit These Interesting Web Sites

Table 695 lists just a few of the thousands of Web sites you can visit. To access a Web site, start your Web browser and type the site's complete URL address.

URL Address	Description
www.jamsa.com	The Jamsa Press Homepage
www.bbcnc.org.uk/	The British Broadcasting Corporation (BBC) Network
www.usa.net/home/daily.html	News, entertainment, and online literature classics
mmnewsstand.com/index.html	Multimedia magazines, entertainment news, and products
www.ampas.org/ampas/	Academy Awards news
sunsite.unc.edu/wm/	Tour of the Louvre and other Paris museums
www.dtic.dla.mil/defenselink/	Department of Defense information
www.cts.com/~vrman/	Virtual reality games and information
home.mcom.com/fishcam/fishcam.html	Watch a tropical fish tank
www.tvnet.com/UTVL/utvl.html	The ultimate television list!

Table 695 Interesting Web sites.

Note: Check out thousands of Web sites in Jamsa Press *1001 Really Cool Web Sites* and *World Wide Web Directory.*

696 Displaying TCP/IP Connections Using Winipcfg

If you experience trouble connecting to (or staying *connected* to) the Internet, you can run the *Winipcfg* (*WINdows IP-address ConFiGuration*) program to obtain information about your Internet connection. After you start your Internet connection, click your mouse on the Start menu Run option and type **WINIPCFG**. Windows 95, in turn, will display the IP Configuration window shown in Figure 696.1.

To see additional IP information, click your mouse on the More Info button. The advanced IP Configuration information window will be displayed, as shown in Figure 696.2. Record the information the dialog boxes display and contact your Internet provider. In many cases, by knowing the setting values, your provider can quickly identify your problem and can then help you correct the cause.

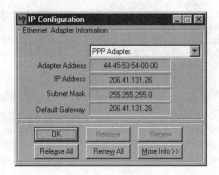

Figure 696.1 The Winipcfg information window.

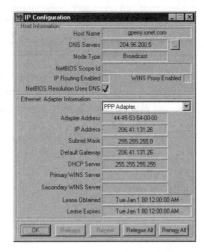

Figure 696.2 Advanced Winipcfg information.

Download a Windows-based FTP Program | 697

As you have learned, Windows 95 provides an FTP program you can use retrieve (download) or put (upload) files across the Internet. To use this FTP program, you opened a DOS window and issued FTP commands from the DOS prompt. As it turns out, across the Internet, there are several "Windows-based" FTP programs you download. The advantage of the Windows-based FTP programs is that rather than issuing commands from a system prompt, you can use work within a window that contains file lists, icons, and so on. For more information on how you can download a Windows-based ftp program and other Windows-based Internet utilities, connect to the following Web site:

> http://sage.cc.purdue.edu/~xniu/winsock/ws-ftp.htm

The site provides a listing of software programs for Windows 95 (and Windows 3.1) that you can download and install.

Web Sites that Discuss Windows 95 | 698

If you want information on Windows 95 and related products, refer to the sites that Table 698 lists.

URL Address	Description
198.105.232.5:80/windows/	Microsoft's Windows 95 Web page
198.105.232.5/windows/software/drivers/drivers.htm	Updated Windows 95 driver files
www2.pcy.mci.net/marketplace/mzone/	Windows 95 products for sale
www.austin.ibm.com/pspinfo/os2vschg.html	Windows 95 versus OS/2 comparisons
www.xmission.com/~eheintz/Win95/	Windows 95 solutions
oeonline.com/~frankc/fjcw95.html	Incredible free source of Windows 95 solutions, tricks, and drivers

Table 698 Interesting Windows 95 Web sites.

699 Understanding Internet Relay Chat

The *Internet Relay Chat* (*IRC*) lets Internet users "talk" when they log on to the same chat area. IRC works a lot like a computerized CB radio system—at any one time, you can chat with many users. To participate in an IRC session, you can run a *client* program that connects to the IRC network *server* connection program. The client program must be Windows 95 compatible. The following FTP sites often contain good IRC programs that you can FTP to your computer:

- ftp.funet.fi
- ftp.informatik.tu-muenchen.de
- coombs.anu.edu.au

Although some chat sessions require IRC software, others do not. If you access the following Web site, you'll be able to connect to the current session's chat or select from a different topic at the bottom of the Web page:

    http://alamak.bchem.washington.edu/~sjohn/chat/chat.cgi

The advantage of chatting from within a Web browser is that you don't have to start a second chat program. Figure 699 shows a chat session in progress. The session looks busy and hectic, but that's what makes it fun.

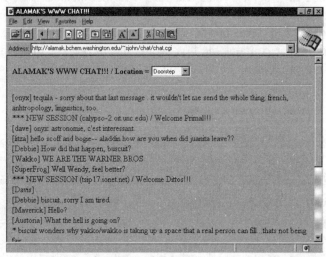

Figure 699 A busy chat session.

700 Understanding Newsgroups

One of the tremendous features the Internet offers to you is a wealth of knowledge from its huge user base. As you have learned, by connecting to a chat session, you can talk (type) with other Internet users in real time. In addition to chat sessions, you may find answers to many of your questions (on an unending number of topics) within newsgroups. A *newsgroup* is a meeting place for messages and files that relate to particular topics. For example, there are newsgroups for many popular television shows. In those newsgroups, you'll find files and messages related to the shows. You can read those messages and download the files.

*Note: If you use a **newsreader**, a special newsgroup program, you can respond to messages and upload your own files to newsgroups.*

If you've accessed online services, such as CompuServe, or electronic bulletin board systems (BBSs), you've probably used *forums* before. An Internet newsgroup is just like a forum. Windows 95's Microsoft Network supports both Microsoft Network forums (see Tip 735) and Internet newsgroups. However, Microsoft Network provides read-only access to Internet newsgroups. Just as Web sites have URL addresses and Telnet sites have locations, newsgroups have names that you use to locate and address newsgroups. Newsgroup names contain several parts, separated by periods. All of the following are newsgroup names:

- rec.aviation.stories
- comp.databases.ms-access
- talk.politics.theory
- alt.binaries.tv.seinfeld
- alt.tv.muppets

Newsgroup names are hierarchical. From left to right, each component in the name further defines the newsgroup's topic. For example, many computer-related newsgroup names begin with "comp." Many computer programming-related newsgroup names, in turn, begin with "comp.programming." Often, you'll see a series of newsgroups with a wildcard. For example, "sci.physics.*" means every newsgroup whose name begins with "sci.physics." Table 700 contains common *top-level* (the first part of a newsgroup's name) names and their category descriptions. Every newsgroup whose names begin with these top-level names relate to Table 700's descriptions in some way.

Top-level Name	Description
biz	Business newsgroups
clari	Commercial newsgroups
comp	Computer newsgroups
news	Newsgroup newsgroups
rec	Recreational newsgroups
talk	Discussion newsgroups
misc	Miscellaneous newsgroups

Table 700 Interesting top-level newsgroup descriptions.

If you want to download newsgroup software that you can use to both read and write to newsgroups, you can do so from these FTP locations:

>ftp://scss3.cl.msu.edu/pub/pc/newsreaders
>
>ftp://ftp.ibm.net/pub

Visit These Newsgroups — 701

After you FTP a newsreader and install the software, you can visit a wide variety of interesting newsgroups, including those Table 701 lists.

Newsgroup Name	Topic
alt.binaries.pictures.fine-art.graphics	Computer art (moderated)
alt.tv.talkshows.late	Late night talk shows
clari.biz.market.dow	New York Stock Exchange reports

Table 701 Interesting newsgroups you can visit. (continued on the following page)

Newsgroup Name	Topic
clari.biz.urgent	Late-breaking business news (moderated)
misc.jobs.offered	Job offers
misc.legal.moderated	Legal information (moderated)
news.newusers.questions	Newsgroup information
rec.arts.cinema	Cinema information (moderated)
soc.religion.christian	Christian topics (moderated)

Table 701 Interesting newsgroups you can visit. (continued from the previous page)

If a newsgroup is *moderated*, a newsgroup administrator maintains it. To make sure the newsgroup stays focused on its target topic, the administrator reviews all messages and files before posting them.

Note: Before you post messages or files to a newsgroup, spend some time in the newsgroup to get acquainted with what goes on there. After you learn the message and file styles, you can begin posting your own messages and files. Most newsgroups contain a file named FAQ.TXT that introduces the newsgroup and its policies. This file also answers common questions about the newsgroup.

702 Understanding Mailing Lists

A *mailing list* is another source of information available to you from the Internet. Unlike other kinds of Internet information, mailing list information comes to you automatically when you *subscribe* (or *join*) a particular mailing list. After you subscribe to a mailing list, you simply wait for that list's information to arrive in your Inbox. When you want to receive mail from a mailing list, you usually send an e-mail message to the mailing-list administrator. In this message, you simply ask to receive mail. Table 702 lists a few mailing lists you may want to check out. To subscribe to a mailing list, you normally simply send an e-mail message to the list that contains the keyword SUBSCRIBE followed by your e-mail address.

Mailing list	Contact & Description
mystery	mystery-request@csd4.csd.uwm.edu
	A mystery-lover's dream list
new-orleans	elendil@mintir.new-orleans.la.us
	New Orleans culture, food, people, and life
sf-lovers	sf-lovers-request@rutgers.edu
	Science-fiction books, movies, and art

Table 702 A few mailing lists to which you can subscribe.

To find additional mailing lists (thousands of mailing lists exist), search the following Web sites:

    http://www.oai.org/External/ActiveMailLists.html

    http://www.lantz.com/mailinglists.html

The following FTP site contains additional mailing lists in a file named LISTSERV.LISTS:

    ftp.nic.surfnet.nl (in the /surfnet/net-management/earn/services directory)

To join some mailing lists, you must use special commands, called *listserv* commands. Typically, mailing-list sites that don't have administrators require you to use listserv commands. When you obtain the list of mailing-list sites, the list will tell you which sites require listservs. Additionally, the list will tell you how to use the listserv commands.

703 Traversing the Internet Using Gopher

The Internet resources are so vast that finding information can often be difficult. Fortunately, you can use *Gopher* to search (go for) Internet areas and files. Gopher sites provide menus whose options will lead you to the information you desire and sometimes to other locations on the Internet. Using Gopher menus, you can track down specific Internet resources. Assume, for example, you are looking for information about Michael Jordan. To start, you might select a Gopher menu option entitled Sports. Next, you might choose a Basketball menu option. Lastly, you might find the information you desire by selecting an option entitled Players. By letting you track down information in a step-by-step fashion, Gopher makes it very easy for you to locate the information you need. In many cases, the Gopher screen will contain the information you desire. At other times, Gopher may point you in other directions, such as an FTP or Telnet site. For example, suppose you want to use FTP to transfer a specific gardening program to your computer. Before you can FTP the file, you need to know if and where it exists on the Internet. Luckily, you can have Gopher look for the file on the Internet. After Gopher locates the file, you can FTP the file to your computer. To access a Gopher site (that is, to read Gopher menus that describe data on the Internet), you need to obtain Gopher software called the *Gopher client*. At the following FTP site, you will find Gopher software that you can download and install:

boombox.micro.umn.edu (use CD to change to the "/pub/gopher" directory).

Most Internet providers also offer Gopher programs that you can use. If you want to find Gopher client software on the World Wide Web, use your Web browser to access the following URL:

http://www.tahperd.sfasu.edu/sites.html.

704 Visit These Gopher Sites

If you don't have your own Gopher software, you can instead use Telnet (see Tip 689) to connect to one of the following sites:

consultant.micro.umn.edu   gopher.ora.com   gopher.msu.edu

After you connect to the site, type **gopher** for the log-on ID and use your Internet ID as the password. The remote computer, in turn, will run the Gopher command letting you search for the information you need.

705 Traversing the Internet Using WAIS

WAIS (the *Wide Area Information Server*) servers help you find data in huge databases and retrieve that information. Whereas Gopher offers menus for a variety of data, WAIS actually finds specific information for you. For example, if you're writing a thesis on the banking industry's margin requirements, your WAIS server software will find and retrieve journal articles on the subject. Just as the Internet contains Telnet, FTP, Web, and Gopher sites, the Internet also has WAIS sites. To access those sites, download WAIS software from the following anonymous FTP location:

quake.think.com (look in the /pub/wais/ directory for the software)

Instead of using a WAIS server software from your own computer, visit Tip 706's WAIS server sites to request WAIS information from other computers.

706 Visit These WAIS Sites

As you have learned, the WAIS program helps you locate information across the Internet. To help you get started, use Telnet to connect to the following WAIS sites. After you log into the site, you can use WAIS to search for the information you need.

    kudzu.cnidr.org (use wais for your log on name)

    quake.think.com (use wais for your log on name)

    sunsite.enc.edu (use swais for your log on name)

    swais.cwis.uci.edu (use swais for your log on name)

707 Understanding Java—the Web's New Programming Language

Although the World Wide Web has become one of computing's hottest topics, the Web is about to experience a major "change of face." Today, sites on the World Wide World are static, much like advertisements that appear within a magazine. In other words, Web sites don't benefit from animation. In the near future, however, Web content will migrate toward television-like commercials. To improve Web-site presentation, Sun Microsystems recently released Java, a new programming language that lets programmers create animated Web sites. Using Java, programmers create small "applets" which browsers download and execute automatically when the user connects to a Web site. For example, using a Java applet, a Web site might spin a company's logo, play MIDI music or audio clips, or perform other animations. Java is a programming language that closely resembles C++. In the near future, Java will become a household word. To learn more about Java and to see examples of Java's use, connect to Sun's Web site at http://java.sun.com.

708 Understanding VRML

In Tip 707 you learned that Java is the Web's newest programming language. Using Java, programmers can create animated Web sites. In addition to Java, Web programmers are also taking VRML, the Virtual Reality Modeling Language. Using VRML, programmers create Web sites that display 3-D graphics that mimic real-world objects. For example, using VRML, a programmer might create an image of a hotel or restaurant the user can enter, walk around, and view! One of the best ways to understand VRML is to check out some VRML sites. Depending on the site's contents, you may need a special browser. However, in such cases, the site should provide you with an easy way to download the browser you require. Check out the following sites to better understand VRML:

    http://www.artificia.com/html/vrml.htm

    http://www.wired.com/vrml.tech/vrml.art

    http://www.oz.is/OZ/Misc/VRML.html

    http://www.paperinc.com/vrml.html

709 Download a Windows-based Phone Program

Due to its interconnecting network of computers, the Internet is capable of transmitting huge amounts of data over long distances. Therefore, with the right software and hardware (a sound card and microphone is all you need), you can talk, literally *speak*, to another Internet user on the other side of the world without paying a long distance charge. Your only charge will be the normal fee you already pay to your Internet service provider. Internet phone programs are *full-duplex,* which means you can speak and hear at the same time (although you won't communicate very much if *one* of you does not listen sometimes!). Typically, an Internet phone program compresses your spoken voice and transmits it using voice-activation technology. If you want to download a free Internet phone program, use your Web browser to find this URL:

>   www.vocaltec.com/dnload.htm

The Internet phone program at www.vocaltec.com/dnload.htm is *freeware*—a program you can use free for 30 days. If you like the program, you can pay for it and get full support and subsequent use. When you connect to the site, click your mouse on the Download Evaluation Copy button. Next, click your mouse on the "ftp.vocaltec.com" hot topic. (You can also FTP directly to "ftp.vocaltec.com" anonymously and download the "IPHONE17.EXE" software.) After you download and start the free Internet phone program, you will see the Internet Phone window, as shown in Figure 709. To use the program, you and the Internet user at the other end of the phone must both have a copy of the program and must connect a microphone to your sound cards.

Figure 709 Talk with your friends on the Internet.

Download a JPEG Viewer — 710

JPEG images are graphic files with a JPG filename extension. JPEG lets you compress images into relatively small files. As such, JPEG images don't require as much time to download, or as much disk space to store, as other kinds of images. However, before you can look at JPEG images, you must have a JPEG viewing program. The following FTP site can supply you with a JPEG viewing program (use upper-case letters):

>   FTP.UU.NET

To find a JPEG viewer, change to the graphics/jpeg directory.

Visit Some Cool Sites for JPEG Images — 711

Across the Internet, there are many sites that provide you with JPEG (graphics) images you can download using FTP or with your Web browser. In fact, Table 711 lists some great sites from which you can view or download images.

Site	Description of JPEG images
www.execpc.com/~jeffo/webpage/gallery.html	Photo gallery
www.is.kochi-u.ac.jp/FTP/images/JPEG6/	Progressive JPEG images
www.electriciti.com/~dwhite/	3-dimensional art
www.goldcanyon.com/htm/images.htm	Dessert pictures
www.islandtel.com/newsbytes/	Pacific rim sights

Table 711 Interesting sites for JPEG images.

712 | Understanding Online Services

Although the world buzzes with Internet hype, the Internet is problematic, often unfriendly, and simply does not offer a sealed environment in which many people prefer to work. The Internet offers too many cumbersome ways of doing simple things and too many overlapped, outdated, and yet-to-be-released Internet locations. Fortunately, the Internet is not the only online option available to Windows 95 users. For example, for a monthly fee of $7 to $30, you can connect to a non-Internet online service. Through an online service, you can find a date, download files, get the latest news, look up recipes, locate Windows 95 driver files, discuss deep-rooted philosophical issues, read magazine columns, request news clips, get stock quotes, buy automobiles, order plane tickets, send flowers, learn higher math, chat with your favorite stars, chart your favorite stars, find a pet, sell rare books, complain about Windows 95, praise Windows 95, speak a foreign language, and play a few games along the way. Whew! Online services offer a lot! Non-Internet online services generally fall into these two categories:

- *Electronic Bulletin Board Systems (BBSs)*, often local to your area, with local events, shareware files, and message centers. Generally, your e-mail is limited to others signed up with the BBS. Some BBS systems charge monthly fees and others do not. Your local library should be able to provide you with a list of local BBS numbers.

- *Commercial online services*, such as America Online (AOL), CompuServe, and Prodigy provide national and international e-mail, topic forums (similar to Internet newsgroups), files, world news and information, and online reference sources, such as encyclopedias and zip code directories. Most online services also provide limited Internet access.

713 | Introducing the Microsoft Network (MSN)

The Microsoft Network (MSN) is a graphical online service that works well with the Windows 95 environment. MSN includes national and international news, weather, events, forums, shopping, file downloading, and some Internet access. Microsoft's online services equal those of CompuServe and AOL. However, MSN offers a key advantage to Windows 95 users—it integrates seamlessly with the Windows 95 operating system. Your Windows 95 Desktop includes a shortcut icon to the Microsoft Network (if you did not install the MSN, see Tip 714). When you click your mouse on the MSN icon, it's sometimes hard to tell when MSN takes over. As Figures 713.1 and 713.2 show, the Microsoft Network windows look like Windows 95 windows. Additionally, much of MSN's information comes to you in an Explorer-like window. Finally, if you see something you like in MSN, you can create your own Desktop shortcut to that MSN item. One of MSN's most interesting features is its tight multimedia integration. If you see a video or sound clip in an MSN window, you can download the clip by dragging it to your Desktop. The only evidence you'll have that an online service, rather than a multimedia program, is running on your computer is the slow speed at which MSN transfers files and data.

Figure 713.1 User categories within the Microsoft Network.

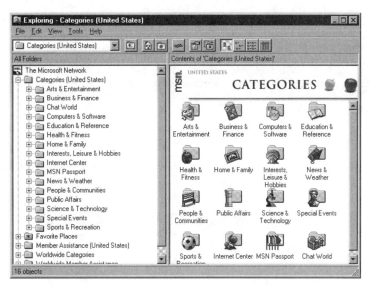

Figure 713.2 MSN's Explorer-like windows.

Installing the Microsoft Network Software   714

If you do not see the Microsoft Network icon on your Desktop, you need to install MSN. To install MSN, perform these steps:

1. Open your Control Panel.
2. Double-click your mouse on the Add/Remove Programs icon.
3. Click your mouse on the Windows Setup tab.
4. Scroll the Components list box until you see The Microsoft Network.
5. Click your mouse on the check box at the left of The Microsoft Network.
6. Click your mouse on the OK button to install the MSN software. You'll need your Windows installation CD-ROM or installation diskettes.
7. Follow the on-screen instructions. The Windows Setup program will not change, replace, or add software other than the Microsoft Network software.

When the installation completes, you'll see the Microsoft Network icon on your Desktop.

Microsoft Network's Requirements   715

To use the Microsoft Network, you'll need the following items:

- A modem that's at least 9600 baud and preferably 14.4K or 28.8K baud
- A phone line
- The installed Windows 95 Microsoft Network software (see Tip 714)
- A credit card for payment
- A username, called a *member ID*, that you create. You'll log on under that member ID and be known to other MSN users by that member ID. (This name acts a lot like a CB radio user's handle.) Don't use your real name unless you have good reason to be known to the

world. Some people use their first initial and last name, such as *gperry*, but others prefer a more colorful member ID, such as *BlueJeans*, *SnappleLover*, or *Happy*.

- A password that you must protect from others and that you must remember

716 Accessing the Microsoft Network

Accessing the Microsoft Network is as easy as starting any Windows 95 program on your system. To start MSN, double-click your mouse on the Microsoft Network icon. Windows 95, in turn, will load the MSN start-up program and display the Microsoft Network window, as shown in Figure 716.

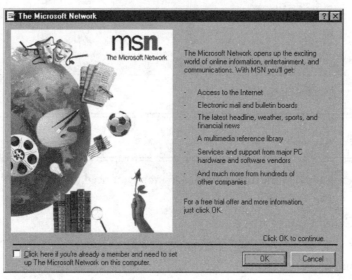

Figure 716 The introductory Microsoft Network window.

717 Registering with MSN for the First Time

The first time you use MSN, you will need to give MSN your member ID and password. Then, MSN will dial a toll-free number to Microsoft's central computer system and will look up a local phone number that it will use for your future connections. To register the first time, perform these steps:

1. Perform Tip 716 to start MSN.
2. Click your mouse on the opening MSN window's OK button. MSN will display the window shown in Figure 717.
3. Type your area code and three-number phone prefix. (If MSN already displays these numbers, MSN retrieved the information from your default modem properties file.) MSN will later use this information to locate a local MSN phone number.
4. Click your mouse on the OK button. MSN will inform you that it's about to call a toll-free number to continue the registration. Make sure that your modem is turned on and your phone is plugged into your modem.
5. Click your mouse on the Connect button. MSN will dial the toll-free number to begin your initial registration. During the call, MSN will download a list of local MSN phone numbers.
6. Enter your registration information, including your preferred member ID and a password. If someone else already has your member ID, MSN will request another one. You must also

enter your name, address, and payment information, including a credit card number. Even if you sign up for a free trial period, Microsoft requires the credit card.

7. When you complete the full registration process, click your mouse on the Join Now button.

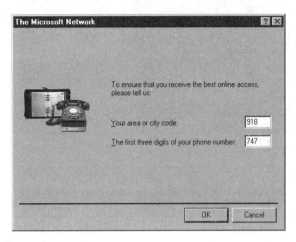

Figure 717 Microsoft needs your calling area.

Locating a Local Microsoft Network Number — 718

Microsoft does not give toll-free, long-distance access to every MSN user. Instead, Microsoft provides a local phone number you can call to connect to MSN. These local phone numbers, which Microsoft has installed across the country, are less expensive for both Microsoft and you. When you dial a local number, Microsoft does not have to supply many expensive toll-free lines.

When you first register with MSN (see Tip 717), MSN dials the toll-free number once to download a database of your country's local MSN phone numbers to your computer. If you relocate, the database of local phone numbers stays in your computer. This database lets you find another local MSN phone number in the area where you move. As such, when you relocate, you don't have to go through the MSN registration process again.

Welcome to MSN Central — 719

After you register with Microsoft Network, double-click your Desktop's Microsoft Network icon to display the MSN Sign In window shown in Figure 719.1. Then, enter the member ID and password that you created when you registered. If you want MSN to remember your password the next time you log on (which MSN calls "signing in"), click your mouse on the Remember my password check box. If you share your computer with other users, you may want to type your password every time you sign in so that others who know your member ID will not be able to use your account.

After you sign in, MSN will display the MSN Central window shown in Figure 719.2. From this window, you can access all areas of MSN. The MSN Central window always stays on your Desktop (or stays minimized) until you close it. Immediately after the MSN Central window appears, MSN begins to download the MSN Today window. Figure 719.3 shows an example of the MSN Today window.

Figure 719.1 MSN's Sign In window.

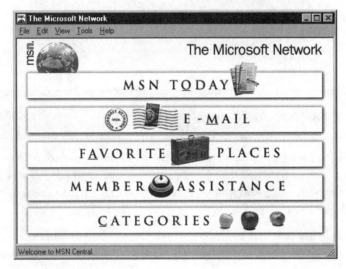

Figure 719.2 The MSN Central window.

Figure 719.3 The MSN Today window.

Traversing MSN 720

MSN and Windows 95 use remarkably similar interfaces. For example, in both MSN and Windows 95 windows, you can view list items or icons (see Figures 720.1, 720.2, and 720.3). Likewise, in both MSN and Windows 95, you can double-click a window item to open additional windows. In addition, both programs display a pop-up menu when you right-click a Window item. Finally, to navigate through MSN's windows, you can use the Windows 95 Explorer. Tip 728 explains how to get an Explorer view of MSN. As you view MSN graphics and windows, you'll find several hypertext cross-links that act as hot spots on which you can click your mouse for further details. For example, if you read one of MSN's news pages and move your mouse over an article, your mouse pointer will change to a pointing-hand icon (indicating you are pointing to a hot spot). Click your mouse on the hot spot to get additional information on that topic. To return to your previous location, click your mouse on the File menu Up One Level option. When you access MSN, an MSN icon appears next to your Taskbar's clock. When you right-click the MSN icon, MSN displays a pop-up menu that you can use to travel to one of several popular MSN areas, including MSN Central, the Favorite Places window, and the Microsoft Network's e-mail center.

Figure 720.1 View a list of MSN topics.

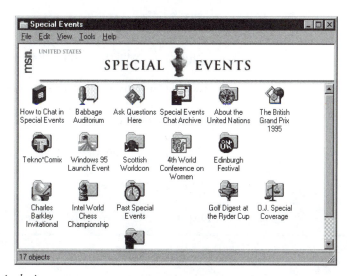

Figure 720.2 View MSN topics by icons.

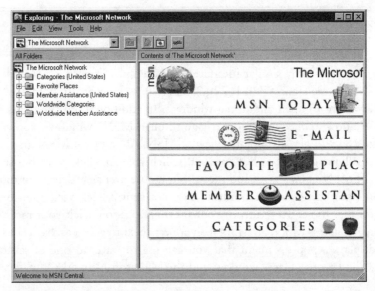

Figure 720.3 An Explorer view of MSN.

721 MSN's Toolbar Buttons

The MSN toolbar gives you one-button access to some of MSN's most important features. To turn the MSN toolbar on and off, click your mouse on the View menu Toolbar option. Table 721 explains the function of each of the toolbar's buttons.

Icon	Purpose
Microsoft Word 95 Forum	Displays a list of MSN locations.
	Transfers you up one MSN level.
	Transfers you to MSN Central.
	Transfers you to your favorite places.
	Disconnects you from MSN.
	Displays the window's Properties sheet.
	Adds the current location to your favorite places area.
	Displays large icon views of MSN sites.
	Displays small icon views of MSN sites.
	Displays list views of MSN sites.
	Displays detail views of MSN sites.

Table 721 MSN's toolbar buttons.

MSN's Go To Feature — 722

Although you'll often traverse MSN by opening and closing folders, MSN contains many levels and sublevels with topics on virtually any subject. As such, you sometimes may find it tedious and time-consuming to follow the folder and subfolder paths. Fortunately, MSN gives you an easier way to move from one location to another. After you visit a location, you can click your mouse on that location's File menu Properties option to learn that location's *Go word*. (Every site has a Go word assigned to it.) Later, when you want to go directly to that site from another MSN location, click your mouse on the Edit menu Go to option, select Other Location, and type the site's Go word.

Note: *If you go to a location frequently, add the location to your Favorite Places list (see Tip 726).*

Using Shortcuts for Quicker Access — 723

If you frequently access a site, or if you find a site you want to return to while working on a project (such as a research paper), add a Desktop shortcut for that location. To do so, click your mouse button over the site's icon, hold down your left mouse button, and drag the icon to your Desktop from the MSN window. Windows 95, in turn, will create a shortcut to that location. (Each window's File menu also contains a Create Shortcut option you can use.) The next day, instead of logging on to MSN and going to that particular location, you can turn on your modem and double-click the location's Desktop icon to go directly to that MSN location.

Note: *You can also add shortcuts to any folder on your computer. If the Explorer or My Computer window is open, and a disk drive or folder is showing in one of the windows, you can drag the MSN icon to the folder to add the shortcut to that folder instead of to your Desktop.*

MSN Today — 724

The MSN Today window changes each day. Microsoft updates the window with late-breaking news from around the globe. Microsoft also places human interest categories in the MSN Today window. Figure 724 shows one such MSN Today window. Each of the icons provides a hot spot from which you can click for more information. For example, if you click on the Special Places hot spot, as shown in Figure 724, MSN will transport you to a Special Places window that shows you around-the-world retreat locations. The MSN Today window always contains a list of categories down its left side. This category list includes a calendar of events (see Tip 725) and other common topics. To reach the area of MSN a category represents, just click your mouse on the category.

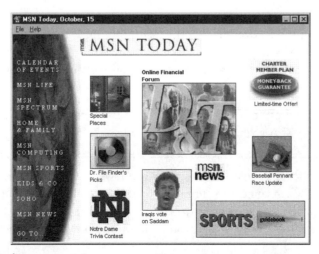

Figure 724 *The MSN Today window.*

725 The MSN Calendar of Events

When you click your mouse over the MSN Today's Calendar of Events category, MSN displays an MSN Calendar of Events, such as the one shown in Figure 725. The Calendar lists upcoming events on the Microsoft Network. If special guests will be attending live chat sessions (see Tip 737) or if special online events will take place, such as the announcement of a new product or MSN service, the Calendar of Events will tell you well ahead of time.

Note: *If a particular Calendar of Events date interests you, click your mouse over that date to read more information about the day's event.*

Figure 725 The MSN Calendar of Events window.

726 Visiting Favorite Places

When you find an interesting MSN location to which you'll want to return, you can add it to a special MSN area called "Favorite Places" (see Tip 721 for the MSN toolbar button that adds to Favorite Places). Then, no matter where you are inside MSN, you can access your Favorite Places list and quickly return to the location. Tip 727 explains how to add an MSN location to your Favorite Place list.

To select a location from the Favorite Places list, return to the MSN Central window (the first window MSN opens when you log on) and click your mouse over the Favorite Places button. Or, select the Edit menu Go To option that appears on most MSN windows. MSN, in turn, will display a menu option you can select to reach the Favorite Places list. When you first begin to use MSN, your Favorite Places window will be empty. However, as you add your favorite MSN sites, the window will become your second home on the Microsoft Network.

727 Adding to Your Favorite Places

Virtually every MSN window (forums, chat sessions, news windows, game areas, and so on) contains a File menu Add To Favorite Places option. When you click your mouse on this option, MSN will update your Favorite Places list with the window's location. When you subsequently open your Favorite Places window, that site appears in your Favorite Places list. To remove an item from your Favorite Places window, perform these steps:

1. Display your Favorite Places window.
2. Click your mouse once over the item you want to remove.
3. Click your mouse on the File menu Delete option. MSN will remove the item from your Favorite Places window.

Getting an Explorer View of MSN — 728

The Explorer window displays not only your computer's disk drives, CD-ROM drives, and network access, but also Microsoft Network information. As such, if you get lost in MSN's categories and sub-categories of topics, open Explorer for a hierarchical overview of MSN's structure.

Figure 728 shows an Explorer view of MSN. Notice that general information appears in Explorer's left section while details appear to the right. If you want to expand or collapse an MSN location you see in Explorer's left section, click your mouse over a plus or minus sign.

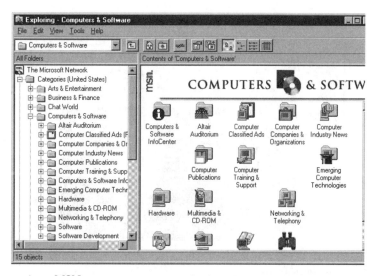

Figure 728 Use Explorer to navigate MSN.

Accessing MSN News — 729

The Microsoft Network doesn't just bring you the news; the Microsoft Network brings you the news in a full-color, text and graphics (and sometimes video and sound), multimedia presentation. As such, you can print MSN news, save it in your own files, or read it from your computer.

The MSN Today window, the second window that Microsoft Network always displays when you log on to MSN, contains an entry called *MSN News*. The name can be misleading. Instead of news about Microsoft Network, you'll see a window, such as the one in Figure 729.1, that contains news as well as weather and sports links. If you click on the News Browser button and select Arts and Entertainment, you'll move to a multimedia Arts and Entertainment window, such as the one in Figure 729.2. If you click your mouse on the News Browser menu Today's Weather option, MSN will display a weather forecast for your selected city, such as the one in Figure 729.3.

Figure 729.1 The MSN News window.

Figure 729.2 View Arts and Entertainment News.

Figure 729.3 Weather is a keypress away.

Moving Around MSN News — 730

To move to an area of MSN News quickly, click your mouse on the News Browser pull-down list to display a list of news-related topics, such as "Business" or "Arts and Entertainment." Figure 730 shows the News Browser pull-down list. When you read the news, you can use the MSN News window Backtrack button to revisit news items you've previously read. The Next Story button takes you to the next story in the multimedia newspaper. If you want to print the current news story, click your mouse on the Printer toolbar button.

To copy story text to the Windows 95 Clipboard, hold down your left mouse button and drag you mouse pointer until you've selected all the text you want to copy. Then, click your mouse over the Copy toolbar button (the button to the right of the Printer button) to send the selected text to the Clipboard. If your mouse pointer becomes a pointing hand when you move it over a picture, click your mouse select button to read the picture's detailed caption.

Figure 730 Browse through a list of news topics.

Getting Member Assistance — 731

When you need help with the Microsoft Network, access the Member Assistance area. Although MSN includes a fairly comprehensive online Help system, the Member Assistance window can help you with billing questions, problems, and MSN-related services.

When you click your mouse on MSN Central's Member Assistance button, MSN displays the Member Assistance window, shown in Figure 731. To open a folder in this window, double-click the folder's icon. Perhaps the most helpful Member Assistance folder is the Maps and Information folder. From this folder, you can learn MSN's detailed structure, display a complete Go word directory (see Tip 722), and ask technical questions.

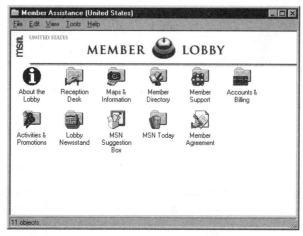

Figure 731 The Member Assistance window.

732 Using Microsoft Network Mail

As you know, the Inbox is your Windows 95 central repository for incoming and outgoing mail, faxes, and files. When you log on to MSN, if you have mail, MSN will ask if you want to read it. If you do, MSN downloads the mail to your Microsoft Exchange Inbox so you can retrieve it. When you click your mouse on MSN Central's E-Mail button, MSN starts your Microsoft Exchange Inbox so you can select a recipient from your Address Book and send e-mail, a file, or a fax to that person on the Microsoft Network.

Note: *You don't have to be signed on to MSN to create mail. Click the Deliver Now Using button to create all your Outbox mail offline (before you log on to MSN) and send all the mail at the same time. Then, select the Microsoft Network option. Exchange, in turn, will start MSN, log you on, and send the mail.*

To send e-mail to other MSN users, simply type their MSN member ID in Exchange's To text box. (If you use the Microsoft Exchange Address Book program, and you've set up other MSN users in the Address Book, the Address Book program knows to use the member ID when sending e-mail to MSN members.)

733 Using the Small Office Home Office (SOHO) Site

The *Small Office Home Office* (*SOHO*) MSN site gives help to users who work in small offices or who run businesses from home. You'll find the SOHO category on your MSN Today window. When you click on the SOHO category, MSN takes you to the current SOHO window, one of which you'll see in Figure 733. The SOHO window caters to home-based users, giving them helpful tricks and tips, as well as occasional home-based business tax advice.

Figure 733 The SOHO window helps home businesses.

734 Accessing MSN's Categories

The Categories window gives you a launching point for all of MSN's services and folders. To display the Categories window shown in Figure 734, click on MSN Central's Categories button. Whereas the MSN Central and MSN Today windows give you access to the most popular and timely services, the Categories window gives you access to the *bulk* of MSN's services. The highest level of MSN's forums (see Tip 735) all start from the Categories window.

Figure 734 *The Categories window.*

Visiting MSN Forums — 735

An MSN *forum* is a location on the Microsoft Network where you can exchange e-mail with other users, read and leave messages related to the forum topic, and upload and download files and programs related to the forum topic. Often, popular forums will schedule events, such as visits by famous authors, actors, and politicians. The MSN Calendar of Events (see Tip 725) keeps you informed about various forum events.

The Categories window, described in Tip 734, contains general topic categories. When you open one of the Categories folders, you'll see additional folders that further subdivide the general category. As you keep opening folders, you'll eventually find folders listed with the word "Forum" after their name, such as "Astronomy & Space Forum." (Figure 735 shows this forum.)

In the forum folder, the About icon describes the forum, its purpose, and what you'll find there. You'll also find icons for all the forums you can access from the folder, as well as icons that describe upcoming forum chat sessions (see Tip 737), file libraries where you can find files to download, and message areas (see Tip 736).

Table 735 lists Go words for several popular MSN forums you might want to visit.

Go word	Forum
Movies	Movies
TV	Television & Radio
CareerConnect	Career opportunities
SOHO	Small Office/Home Office
csGames	Games and Casino
MSNComputing	Microsoft Network Guidebook
Reference	Reference materials
Parents	Parenting issues
Kids	For Kids
Travel	Travel
msnnews	MSN News

Table 735 *Locate these forums quickly with Go words.*

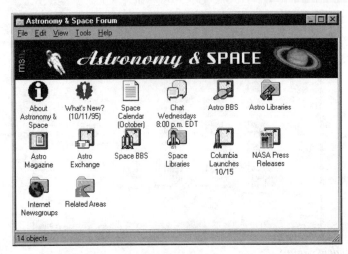

Figure 735 A forum window.

736 | Reading and Writing Messages

When you enter a forum folder and start searching through its subfolders, you will run across a message window that resembles the one shown in Figure 736.1. These windows contain messages and files you can read and download. In addition, you can send messages of your own or upload your own files to the forum. To read a message, double-click on it. MSN, in turn, will open a WordMail window to show the message. If the message has an attached file, that file will appear as an icon in the WordMail window (see Figure 736.2.) To open the file, double-click your mouse on the icon. To save the message and the attachment to your disk, click your mouse on the File menu Save As option.

If you read a message that does not contain an attached file, click your mouse on the File menu Close option to close the WordMail window and return to the list of forum messages. You can reply to the message by clicking your mouse on the Compose menu Reply to BBS option. MSN will post your reply to the forum; your reply will directly follow the original message. If you want to add your own message without replying to another, click your mouse on the forum window's Compose menu New Mail option to create a new message and, optionally, insert an attached object in the message. When you click your mouse on the File menu Post option, your message and attached file (if any) appear on the board after a brief time lapse.

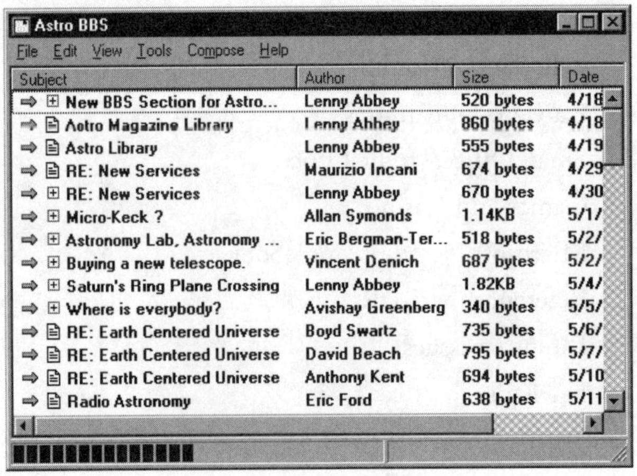

Figure 736.1 A forum message window.

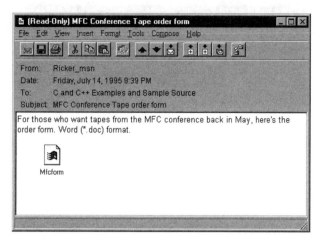

Figure 736.2 *A message with an attachment.*

Participating in Chat Sessions — 737

Using your keyboard, you can participate in online group discussions (*chat sessions*) about the forum's topic. To locate such discussions, look for chat session icons. Usually, the icon's title will include the word "chat." Also, chat icons often appear as comic-strip word balloons. After you double-click your mouse button over a chat icon, you'll enter a *chat room* where you can converse with other MSN members.

When you enter a chat session, you can join right in. However, you'll probably enjoy the session more if you first read the messages from others. Observing for a while will give you some insight about the current discussion. If your member ID is the only one that shows up at the right of the chat session window, you're the only user in the chat session. You can wait for someone else, or you can click your mouse over the File menu Up One Level option to find a livelier chat room.

Using the Suggestion Box — 738

The *suggestion box*, shown in Figure 738, is a place for you to leave suggestions or complaints directed to Microsoft. Every suggestion will be read, but you rarely will receive a response. Keep in mind that the suggestion box is an area where users can voice their MSN concerns and wants. (If you have specific billing problems or technical questions, use the Member Assistance folder's Member Support subfolder to leave questions that Microsoft will answer.) To send Microsoft an MSN suggestion, perform these steps:

1. Log on to MSN.
2. From the MSN Central window, click your mouse on the Member Assistance button.
3. Double-click your mouse on the MSN Suggestion Box icon. After a brief pause, MSN will display the MSN Suggestions sheet.
4. Read the Welcome page. Then, click your mouse on the Suggestion tab.
5. Type your suggestion.
6. Click your mouse on the Transmit button to send your suggestion to Microsoft.

Figure 738 *Leaving a suggestion in the box.*

739 Visit an Interesting Computer Information Forum

The best place for MSN newcomers to begin is MSN's forums. The next few tips will explain the purpose of several popular MSN forums. When you visit the forums, you will pick up helpful information, have access to multi-megabyte files, learn what others have to say about topics that interest you, and participate in a world-wide discussion of events happening on the Microsoft Network. Visit a few forums before you participate in one; that way, you'll get a good feel for the nature of the forum and its members.

740 Visit a Windows 95 Forum

The Microsoft Network online service offers a tremendous wealth of advice for Windows 95 users. In MSN's Windows 95 forum, you'll find hardware compatibility lists, software compatibility lists, online Help, multimedia support files, cursor bitmaps, Desktop bitmaps, games, network services, tips, tracks, new driver files, future release notes, Microsoft Windows 95 application support, and more. To visit the Windows 95 forum, click on MSN Central's Edit menu Go to option and type the Go word **Windows**. MSN, in turn, will display the Windows 95 forum window, as shown in Figure 740.

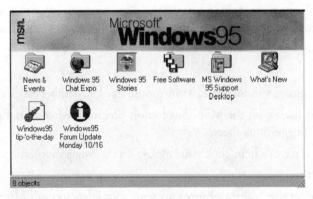

Figure 740 *The MSN Windows 95 Forum.*

Check Out the Home and Family Forum 741

The Home and Family forum, shown in Figure 741, (contains genealogy, home improvement, children's resources, family-based Web homepage addresses, home remedies, and a colorful BBS-like forum for kids) lets the whole family join in thoughtful chat discussions, file downloading, and messaging around the world. In short, this forum has something for everyone in your household. To enter the Home and Family forum, type the Go word **Home**.

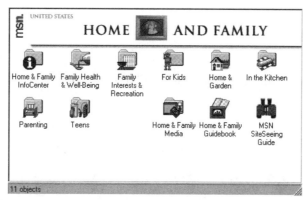

Figure 741 *The MSN Home and Family Forum.*

Play in the Sports Forum 742

If you've just spent all Sunday afternoon watching football and your family want's their turn at the TV, don't fret, you can turn to the MSN Sports forum. In short, sports fans will get a treat in the Sports forum. Learn the scores around the world from all events and get tips from the pros. To enter the Sports forum, which Figure 742 shows, type the Go word **Sports**.

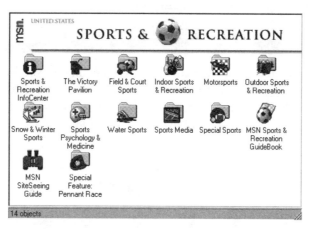

Figure 742 *The MSN Sports Forum.*

Learn from the Science and Technology Forum 743

MSN forums are not just fun and games. In the Science and Technology forum you will find exciting and late-breaking science and technology news, as well as information for home-based and collegiate researchers. Some of the subjects this forum covers include:

- Biology
- Computers
- Electronics
- Engineering
- Math
- Physical sciences
- Physics
- Space

To visit the Science and Technology forum, type the Go word **Science**. Figure 743 shows the Science and Technology forum's opening window.

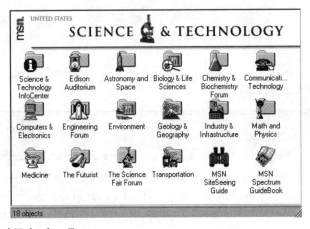

Figure 743 *The MSN Science and Technology Forum.*

744 Get in Shape with the Health and Fitness Forum

If you want to lose weight, gain weight, or just eat better, there's something for you in the Health and Fitness forum. With information for health professionals as well as Monday-morning athletes, Health and Fitness is one of the most comprehensive forums on the MSN. Learn about nutrition, download heart-smart recipes, and get the latest healthcare news. Figure 744 shows the Health and Fitness forum's opening window. To access the forum, type the Go word **Health**.

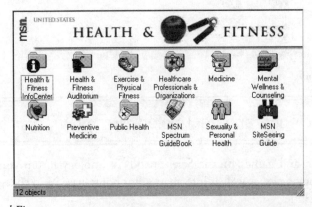

Figure 744 *The MSN Health and Fitness.*

Relax with the Arts and Entertainment Forum — 745

In the Arts and Entertainment forum, you'll find information on your favorite book, movies, theater groups, musical artists, radio shows, and more. Before you spend your hard-earned money on a movie, read what others have to say about it. If you want a good novel for a getaway vacation, download the top ten bestsellers. To access the Arts and Entertainment forum, type the Go word **Entertainment**.

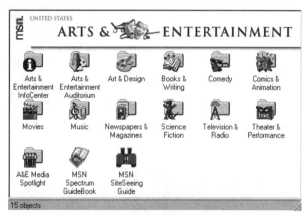

Figure 745 MSN's Arts and Entertainment forum.

Manage Your Money in the Business and Finance Forum — 746

The Business and Finance forum contains information for both amateur and professional investors. Technical stock market investors will find enough graphs to fulfill their investor desires while fundamentalists will love the company earnings reports. The Business and Finance forum provides stock market, mutual fund, Federal reserve, and precious metal reports. In addition, the forum offers helpful information and advice for small business owners, commercial marketers, and job seekers. To access the Business and Finance forum, type the Go word **Business**.

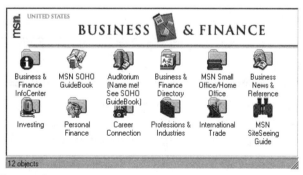

Figure 746 MSN's Business and Finance forum.

Reading MSN Computing — 747

The Microsoft Network offers its own interactive, multimedia, online magazine called *MSN Computing*. Figures 747.1 and 747.2 show sample windows from *MSN Computing*. *MSN Computing* contains articles about computers and the people who use them. You'll learn new ways to use your computer and, of course, new ways to use Windows 95 and the Microsoft Network. You'll also find online articles on computing lifestyles and computer buying tips. To access *MSN Computing* magazine, type the Go word **MSN Computing**.

Figure 747.1 The MSN Computing online magazine.

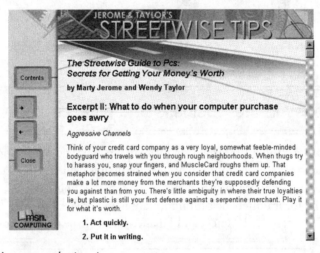

Figure 747.2 MSN Computing's computer buying tips.

748 Using the MSN-Internet Connection

The Microsoft Network includes an Internet-based connection that you can use for limited and, sometimes, full Internet access. The standard Windows 95 environment comes with limited Internet access: a read-only newsreader (you cannot leave your own files or respond to messages) and an Internet e-mail client that lets you exchange mail with other Internet users.

Note: When you register with MSN and select a local phone number, your phone number may or may not allow for full Internet access. MSN's registration program will let you know if you have full Internet access in your area. If you do not have access, register with an Internet provider (see Tip 672) for a local access number. Eventually, Microsoft will make full Internet access available to all local calling areas.

If you have an Internet provider or a local MSN number that supports full Internet access, you can access the World Wide Web from Windows 95 as long as you purchase the Microsoft Plus! software. In addition to a Web browser, Microsoft Plus! provides some Windows 95 utilities and a pinball game.

Browsing the Web with MSN — 749

To access the World Wide Web through your MSN account (assuming you use an Internet access number, as described in Tip 748), you must have a Web browser. You can download a browser (see Tip 693), obtain a browser from your Internet provider, or use Microsoft Plus!'s Web browser—Internet Explorer. If you have full MSN/Internet access and you have Microsoft Plus!, click your mouse on the Internet Tools menu Internet Explorer option to start the Internet Explorer. Or, double-click the World Wide Web icon in MSN's Internet Center folder. MSN, in turn, will display an Internet Web page, as shown in Figure 749. To go to or search for other Internet locations, click your mouse on the Web page hot spots. To display additional Web pages, enter URL addresses in the URL text box. Many of MSN's forums contain Web hot spots you can access. However, be careful when you click on these hot spots. Some of them take you to Web sites from which you can't return to MSN without restarting MSN's software and logging in again.

Figure 749 *The Internet Explorer is a full-featured Web browser.*

Accessing Internet Newsgroups — 750

Many of MSN's forums offer newsgroup access. For example, the Home Interests forum contains a Home Interests Internet Picks folder that, when you open it, contains numerous newsgroup sites you can access with a mouse double-click. If you want to access newsgroups by their top-level part names (such as comp or rec), perform these steps:

1. Display the MSN Categories window.
2. Double-click your mouse on the Internet Center folder. MSN will open the folder shown in Figure 750.1. (Owners of Microsoft Plus! should see the World Wide Web icon.)
3. Double-click your mouse over the Internet Newsgroups folder. MSN will open the folder shown in Figure 750.2.
4. Double-click over any of the newsgroup folder icons. The newsgroup folders contain subfolders for each of the newsgroup top-level names, such as comp and talk.
5. Open folders and subfolders until you access the newsgroup you want. For example, access the top-level talk folder, then the talk.politics folder, then the talk.politics.european-union folder to read the contents of that newsgroup folder. Figure 750.3 shows that MSN displays the newsgroup contents in the familiar Windows 95 window and folder format.

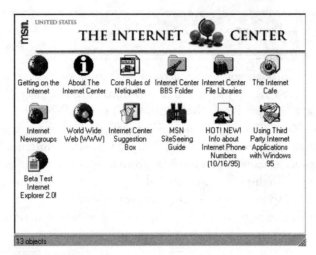

Figure 750.1 The Internet Center offers newsgroup access.

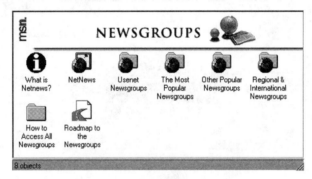

Figure 750.2 The Internet newsgroups.

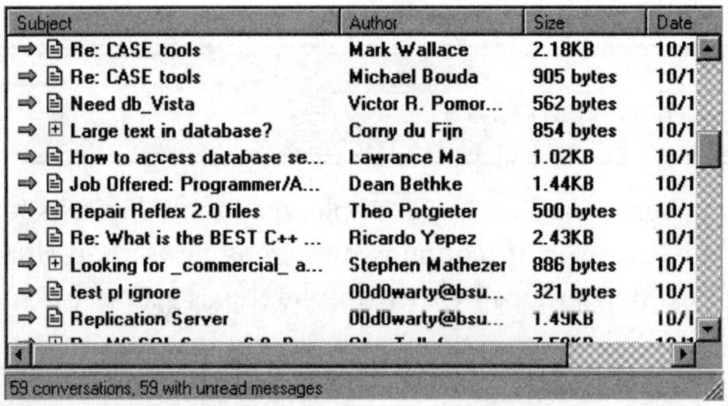

Figure 750.3 Reading newsgroup news.

751 Sending and Receiving Internet E-mail

Due to Microsoft Exchange's universal Inbox, sending and receiving Internet e-mail is as simple as sending and receiving other electronic mail in Windows 95. If you've used cumbersome Internet e-mail programs in the past, you'll appreciate the Internet e-mail ease Exchange provides. To send Internet e-mail, perform these steps:

1. Start MSN.
2. Display the MSN Central window.

3. Click your mouse on the E-Mail button.
4. Click your mouse on the Compose menu New Message option. MSN will start your WordMail program.
5. Type an Internet e-mail address in the To text box. Or, select the message recipient from your Exchange Address Book if you've set up Internet recipients.
6. Type your message.
7. Click your mouse on the Send toolbar button to send the message.

When you receive e-mail over the Internet, MSN places the mail in your Inbox. MSN lets you know that you have Internet mail as soon as you log on.

Note: Be sure to give your e-mail address to Internet users in this format: memberID@msn.com (use your memberID in place of the format's **memberID** area).

Logging Off MSN — 752

If you close all MSN windows or click your mouse on MSN's File menu Sign Out option, MSN displays the Sign Out window shown in Figure 752. To leave MSN, click your mouse on the Yes button. To remain logged on to the Microsoft Network, click on the No button.

Note: If you ever close all MSN windows without logging off and you want to return to an MSN window (such as MSN Today), right-click your mouse on the Taskbar's MSN icon.

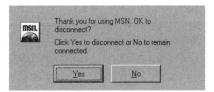

Figure 752 The Sign Out window.

Understanding Windows 95 Network Support — 753

Unlike DOS and Windows 3.1, Windows 95 includes low-level support for networked systems. As such, when you want to connect two or more computers running Windows 95, all you must do is run a null-modem or parallel cable between them. If you want a full-fledged networking system, all you must do is run cables and install network cards. Windows 95 includes driver files for virtually every network card and configuration that exists today.

You can access your system's network settings through the Network Neighborhood icon. When you double-click the Network Neighborhood icon, Windows 95 will display the Network Neighborhood window, which lists all the networked computers and network workgroups your computer can access. The Windows 95 Explorer includes extensive network support. Using the Explorer, you can use drag-and-drop operations within Explorer to copy files from your computer to a remote network computer, and vice versa.

Note: Unlike previous versions of Windows, Windows 95 requires no conventional memory for networks.

754 Understanding Terms Is Your Key to Mastering Networks

To understand networks, you must know some of the terms technicians use to describe networks. At its lowest level, a *network* is little more than wires connecting computers together so the computers can exchange information. Data and programs travel along these wires so you don't have to transfer files on floppy disks. To help you get started, the next few tips explain network terminology.

In addition to knowing network terminology, you need to understand the protocol (data transfer language) and hardware your system will use for network operations. To get maximum use of your system's networking capabilities, you must make sure that the network hardware and protocol work effectively with your operating system and application software.

755 You Start with a Network Organization

A *topology* specifies the network's shape or geometric arrangement of computers. The topology determines how signals travel between the computers. To connect your Windows 95 system to other computers, you can use the following topologies:

- *Star*: Star networks require a central *hub*, or connecting site, to route signals to the proper computers. If the central hub crashes, the network will not function. However, a breakdown on one network computer will not disable the network. Figure 755.1 shows a star network topology.

- *Ring*: Ring networks don't require hubs. Instead, to create a ring network, you must run wires to and from each network computer, which doubles the amount of cable you need. In a ring network, data travels through each network computer that resides between the sending and receiving computers. As such, if one computer malfunctions, the entire network crashes until you route the wire past the broken computer. Figure 755.2 shows a ring network topology.

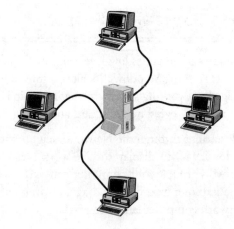

Figure 755.1 The star topology.

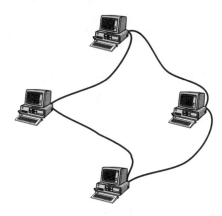

Figure 755.2 *The ring topology.*

756 Next You Choose a Network Technology

A network technology specifies the type of cables and network cards you use to connect computers. In most cases, you'll need to choose between one of the following networking technologies:

- *Ethernet*: Ethernet is one of the most popular (and best supported) networking standards today. Ethernet cards are inexpensive and offer fast networking speeds. PCI- and MCA-bus Ethernet cards are available for computer users with special bus requirements.

- *Token ring*: Developed by IBM and Texas Instruments, the token ring is used primarily by IBM-only computer sites. The token ring architecture is the fastest of the three technologies but one of the most expensive. If you work in a small network environment (2 to 10 networked computers), the Ethernet typically offers more efficient networking speeds. If you work on a larger network, the token ring becomes more efficient than the Ethernet.

- *ArcNet*: The ArcNet technology has been around a long time. However, its cards are expensive, and the ArcNet technology does not work well in today's networked microcomputer environment. Technically, ArcNet is the fastest of the three technologies, but most of today's networked environments already have ample speed.

757 The Network Adapter is Your PC's Network Card

As you explore Windows 95's networking capabilities, you'll often encounter the term *network adapter* or *network card*. The network adapter is simply the card inside your PC into which you plug the network cable. Although different kinds (different brands of the same network technology, such as two different brands of Ethernet cards) of network cards can communicate with one another, your network will function most efficiently if all the systems you connect to it use the same type of card (such as Ethernet).

758 Software Defines Your Network Interface

You can run many different networked programs using different vendors' network software interfaces. Windows 95 supports networking and talks to computers running Novell networking software, Windows 95 networking software, client/server environments, peer-to-peer environments, and other networking configurations. (However, the *protocol*, or communication software standard, must be the same or compatible for each computer.) Windows for Workgroups and Windows NT also support networking software that can communicate with other computers. Some networks run multiple software. The software you run determines how your network interface communicates with another networked computer.

759 Understanding Clients and Servers

Generally, *network administrators* (people who manage and monitor network configurations) designate the network's fastest computer, or the computer with the most disk space, as the *file server*. This computer serves files (either data files, program files, or both) to *client* computers (other computers on the network). The client computers, in turn, use those files. Additionally, the network administrator may designate another computer as the network's *printer server*; through the printer server, all clients can route their output to paper.

When you set up your network, you can designate one computer as the file server, one (perhaps the same computer) as the printer server, and the rest as network clients (computers on which users generate work). Generally, nobody uses the file server for routine computing tasks. The network administrator works on the server to set up file sharing and file access for other network users. Tip 769 defines the alternative to client/server networking—*peer-to-peer networking*. The client/server network setup decreases network traffic and generally makes the network faster than peer-to-peer network configuration. However, this speed has a price: you must dedicate one or more computers exclusively to server functions.

760 TCP/IP is the Language of the Internet

As Tip 667 explains, *TCP/IP* is the primary protocol used on the Internet. TCP/IP stands for *Transmission Control Protocol/Internet Protocol*. When you use TCP/IP, your computer becomes another node on the vast Internet system. If you want Internet access, you'll need some kind of TCP/IP network driver on your system. Luckily, Windows 95 and most network adapters come with TCP/IP driver files.

Note: *Windows 95 supports both* WINS *(the Windows NT Internet Naming Service) and the DNS (Domain Naming Service) TCP/IP communications.*

761 NetBEUI is Backward Compatible

NetBEUI stands for *Networking BIOS Extended User Interface* protocol. The NetBEUI protocol, for which Microsoft included a driver in Windows 95, lets Windows 95 clients and servers communicate with network computers running Windows for Workgroups, Windows NT, and Microsoft LAN Manager.

762 Windows 95 Dial-Up Networking

When you take your laptop computer on the road, dial-up networking lets you dial into and use your office-based network as if you were directly connected to it. In addition, if you use an Internet provider, dial-up networking lets you dial into your provider's computer and access the Internet as if you were at your provider's site.

To run the Dial-Up Networking wizard and create a new dial-up networking service, open the My Computer window and double-click your mouse on the Make New Connection icon. After you create a new Dial-Up Networking service icon, right-click on the icon to set up dial-in properties, such as the phone number and target network. From a remote phone, dial-up networking users can access the following services:

- Printing
- File sharing with other users
- Network access of any network device
- Central database access
- Network Mail and scheduling

763 Using Windows 95 Direct Cable Connect Networking

If you need to move a large block of files from one system to another, you could save all the files on desk, physically carry them to the second system, and load them in. However, this file-transfer process may be time-consuming, especially if the files you want to transfer are very large and require compression and decompression. Fortunately, you don't need to transport files on floppy disk if both your source and destination systems run Windows 95. Instead, you can establish a direct cable connection. Known by some as a "poor man's network," a direct cable connection lets you quickly and easily connect two computers together using a null-modem or parallel cable. One computer must always be the "host" and one the "client," but you can reverse that designation at any time.

Note: *The direct cable connection comes in especially handy if your laptop does not have a network card and you need to use Briefcase to synchronize a laptop's and desktop's files.*

764 NFS is Sun's Unix-based Network File System

If you work within a UNIX-based environment, you may hear the term NFS when users discuss files. The NFS, or *Network File System*, is a file system protocol that UNIX-based computers use. Windows 95 does not directly support NFS. However, you can, using dial-up networking, access a UNIX computer as a terminal from your computer or from your networked computer. If you obtain proper NFS protocol driver files from your network or UNIX vendor, you'll be able to network to NFS-based UNIX networks.

765 IPX/SPX is Novell-Compatible

Novell Corporation, a leader in networking software, often runs on top of networked computers that Windows 95 users will use or connect to. Although Windows 95 includes networking support, Novell's software goes far beyond the network management capabilities of Windows 95. Windows 95 includes the IPX/SPX-compatible protocol which stands for *Internetwork Packet Exchange/Sequential Packet Exchange* protocol. With the protocol, a Windows 95 computer can communicate with Novell-based client or server computers.

766 SNMP is Simple Network Management Protocol

SNMP, or *Simple Network Management Protocol*, helps a network administrator manage and configure a network. Windows 95 includes an *SNMP agent* (which conforms to the SNMP version 1 specification) that will let a network administrator monitor and manage remote network computers and TCP/IP and IPX/SPX protocol connections. If you want to use SNMP, insert your Windows 95 installation CD-ROM and perform these steps:

1. Double-click the Control Panel's Network icon. Windows 95 will open the Network sheet.
2. Click your mouse on the Add button.
3. Double-click your mouse on the Network Service dialog box's Service entry.

4. Click your mouse on the Have Disk button.
5. Type the pathname **D:\ADMIN\NETTOOLS\SNMP** in the Install From Disk dialog box (if your CD-ROM drive is not the D: drive, use the CD-ROM's drive letter).
6. Click your mouse on the OK button. You can now create custom SNMP scripts. For additional information, read the Microsoft Windows 95 Resource Kit (see Tip 49).

767 NDIS is Network Driver Interface Specification

Windows 95 supports *NDIS*, the *Network Driver Interface Specification*, versions 2 and 3.1. NDIS is a general specification that, when followed, lets computer operating systems support a wide range of network hardware and protocols. With the NDIS drivers, Windows 95 supports Ethernet, token ring, and the ArcNet network architectures (see Tip 756). To minimize your downtime during network installation, NDIS's version 3.1 supports Windows 95 Plug and Play features.

768 ODI is Open Datalink Interface

Novell and Apple Computer developed the *ODI*, the *Open Datalink Interface*, to support a general range of network architectures and protocols. ODI is not as robust as NDIS. For example, ODI does not support Windows 95 Plug and Play features. If you have used ODI drivers in the past, try NDIS first when you install your Windows 95 network (provided you use Microsoft's Client for NetWare file and printer sharing client). However, if you use a Novell-supplied client, use ODI-based client software.

769 Understanding Peer-to-Peer Networking

In a client/server network model, a small number (usually one or two) of computers act exclusively as servers while the rest function as clients. In a peer-to-peer network, all computers on the network act as both clients and servers. As such, one computer on the network can access another computer's resources (as long as those resources are sharable). In peer-to-peer networks, network traffic is generally high. As a result, peer-to-peer networking typically works best in small computing environments (2 to 10 systems) where speed is not crucial for most computing tasks.

770 UNC Stands for Universal Naming Convention

UNC, or Universal Naming Convention, is a naming standard for networks. Each computer in a network has a name, such as Office-133 or AcctgJim. The UNC standard lets different network protocols route files back and forth between computers as long as each computer's protocol supports UNC, as most do. UNC file-location specification follows this format:

*server**volume*

Some examples of UNC names that network protocols might route back and forth include:

\\Office-133\Payroll\Weekly

\\Office-133\Payroll\Monthly

\\RemoteSite\Data

The double backslash, \\, precedes the computer name. The volume name typically refers to a shared Windows 95 folder available to others in the network workgroup.

771 You Can Share Files, Folders, Printers, and Modems

A computer *resource* might be a file, folder, printer, or modem. Before two or more computers can use the same resource, you must declare that resource to be *sharable*. By default, a file is not sharable. As such, only the computer on which the file resides can read or write to that file. When you make a file sharable, all authorized network computers can access it. The network administrator can give read-only or full sharable access to a network user.

772 Understanding Network Security

You can implement two basic kinds of Windows 95 network security: *share-level access control* and *user-level access control*. Share-level access control lets you specify a password for each file, folder, disk drive, CD-ROM drive, printer, or modem resource that you want to share. The network user who wants to use that resource must supply the password. For example, if you worked in a payroll department, you certainly wouldn't want just anyone to have access to your check printer. As such, you might assign a share-level password to the printer.

User-level access control lets you create users and workgroups who have access to particular shared resources. For example, you might create a workgroup named DevTeam for a group of programmer computers. The DevTeam workgroup, in turn, might offer sharable access to programming files and folders but not to accounting files. Similarly, for an Accounting department, you might create a workgroup named AcctDept that gives department employees access to accounting files but not programming files.

Tip 778 explains how to define access controls for your network.

773 Understanding Remote System Administration

A network administrator has the authority (and the responsibility) to give and revoke network access, manage the network, and configure the network. Networks come in all sizes. Some networks encompass only a few systems on one floor of a building. Other networks, such as *WANs* (*Wide Area Networks*), can link thousands of computers around the globe. Of course, the larger the system, the more difficult the Network administrator's job becomes. Fortunately, the network administrator has a valuable tool—*remote system administration*. Remote administration lets the network administrator perform all his or her network maintenance tasks from one location. Without remote administration, the network administrator would have to attend to each computer to make configuration changes to that machine's network settings. Windows 95 includes the following remote administration tools:

- *Net Watcher*: Lets the administrator manage remote-computer file and printer sharing services.
- *Registry Editor*: Lets the administrator edit remote-computer Registry entries.
- *System Policy Editor*: Lets the administrator edit remote-computer policies, such as access rights.
- *System Monitor*: Lets the administrator troubleshoot network performance problems and monitor individual computer network device drivers to search for efficiency leaks and breakdowns.

Note: *Do not enable remote administration if you do not need remote administration. Remote administration adds overhead that slows down your network and makes administering it more difficult.*

774 Viewing Current Network Components

When you install Windows 95, the Setup program installs your correct network software. If someone else installed Windows 95 for you, your network is probably ready to use. To view your current Network components, perform these steps:

1. Open your Control Panel window.
2. Double-click your mouse on the Network icon. Windows 95 will display the Network Properties sheet, as shown in Figure 774.
3. Click your mouse on the Configuration, Identification, and Access Control tabs to see those pages.

If you have any network components installed in the Network Properties sheet, you can move on to Tip 783 to traverse your network.

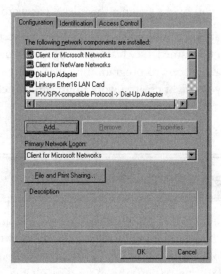

Figure 774 *The Network Properties sheet.*

775 Adding a Network Component

If network components are not currently installed on your system (see Tip 774), use the Network Properties sheet to add network components. To add network components, perform these steps:

1. Click your mouse on the Add button and select a component to install from Windows 95's available list. Table 775 describes the components you can install.
2. Set that component's properties by clicking your mouse over the Properties button and changing the settings.
3. Use the Network Properties sheet Access Control page to set up initial network security. Tip 778 explains how to define your PC's share access level.
4. Restart Windows 95 when prompted to do so.

Component	Description
Client	Describes the client software your computer needs to respond to the network. You can install as many clients as you want, but you can have only one *real-mode* (16-bit) client at any one time.
Adapter	Describes the driver files that your computer's network adapters use.
Protocol	Describes the network protocol or protocols you want to be able to use.
Service	Describes peer-to-peer file and printer sharing services.

Table 775 Network components you should install.

Adding a Network Adapter 776

When you install a network, you must tell Windows 95 what kind of network adapter your computer uses. Your network adapter is the card inside your computer that connects your system to other networked computers. To install a network adapter, perform these steps:

1. Double-click the Control Panel's Network icon. Windows 95 will open the Network Properties sheet.
2. Click your mouse on the Add button.
3. Select Adapter from the list of components.
4. Click your mouse on the Add button. Windows 95 will display the Select Network Component Type dialog box.
5. In the Manufacturers list box, click your mouse on your network adapter card's manufacturer. The Network Adapters list box will list every adapter that your manufacturer makes and Windows 95 supports.
6. In the Network Adapters list box, click your mouse on your network adapter card. If you do not see your adapter, click your mouse on the Have Disk button and insert your network adapter's Windows 95 driver diskette.
7. Click your mouse on the OK button. Windows 95 will install your adapter driver software.

Note: *If you buy a true Plug and Play network adapter card, Windows 95 will probably recognize and install the card without your intervention when you start your system.*

Identifying Your PC to the Network 777

Each computer in a network must have a unique name so the network can properly route messages, data, and files to the correct target machines. When you install a network and connect your computer to the network, you'll have to create a name for your computer that the network will use for all network maintenance. (The UNC (see Tip 770) requires a computer name for reconciling computer locations.)

To name your computer, use the Network Properties sheet Identification page, shown in Figure 777. The name can include up to 15 characters but cannot include blanks. (Use a dash to separate name parts, such as OFFICE-133.) To identify the workgroup to which your computer belongs, type a workgroup name (up to 15 characters) in the Workgroup text box. (The workgroup identifies all computers within an area that will communicate with each other.) The Computer Description field is optional and describes your computer and, possibly, its capabilities.

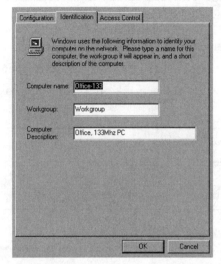

Figure 777 Identifying your computer's network name.

778 Defining Your PC Share Access

As shown in Figure 778, the Network Properties sheet Access Control page describes your computer's share access levels. As Tip 772 explains, the two kinds of access, share-level and user-level, determine whether an individual computer resource requires a password or whether groups of users have access to certain hardware based on their group restrictions.

If you click your mouse on the Share-level access control option button, you will be able to specify a password for your computer's shared resources. Only someone with the password can use your system's shared resources. On the other hand, if you click your mouse on the User-level access control option button, you can specify a list of users and groups who have automatic access to each of your computer's resources.

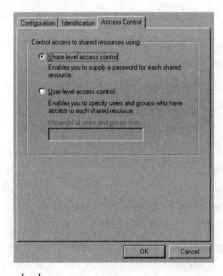

Figure 778 Identifying your computer's access level.

Allowing File and Printer Sharing   779

File and printer sharing allows other users on your network to share your computer's files and printer. For example, suppose your computer, which has the only laser printer in the office, is three peer-to-peer networked with six other systems that only have dot matrix printers. For most tasks, your colleagues will likely be content to use their dot matrix printers. However, to print final company reports and other important documents, they'll probably want to use your laser printer. For your colleagues to use your laser printer, you must enable print sharing on your computer. If you want to give others on your network access to your files, you must also enable file sharing. To enable (or disable) your computer's file and printer sharing, perform these steps:

1. Click your mouse on the File and Print Sharing button. Windows 95 will display the File and Print Sharing dialog box, as shown in Figure 779.
2. Click your mouse on one or both options to enable or disable file and printer sharing.
3. Click your mouse on the OK button to implement your changes.

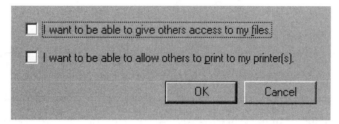

Figure 779 Enabling file and printer sharing.

Removing a Network Component   780

If you do not use fully compliant Plug and Play hardware, you will need to remove drivers from your Network Properties sheet when you remove network adapter boards from your system. To remove a driver, perform these steps:

1. Open your Control Panel window.
2. Double-click your mouse on the Network icon to open the Network Properties sheet.
3. Click your mouse on the component that you want to remove.
4. Click your mouse on the Remove button. Windows 95 will remove the component you selected in step 3.
5. Click your mouse on the OK button to save your changes.
6. Restart Windows 95 to implement your driver change.

Customizing a Network Component's Properties   781

If you need to make special configuration changes to a network component, such as specifying the slot number in which a Micro Channel Adapter (MCA) card resides, you will have to customize the component's properties. To customize a particular network component, perform these steps:

1. Open the Control Panel window.
2. Double-click the Network icon to open the Network Properties sheet.
3. Click your mouse on the component that you want to configure.

4. Click your mouse on the Properties button. Windows 95 will display the component's Properties sheet, as shown in Figure 781. (The Properties sheet that appears on your screen may appear different depending on your network component's options.)
5. Click on each of the tabs and set the page values to your hardware's special settings.
6. Click your mouse on the OK button. Windows 95 will save your changes.

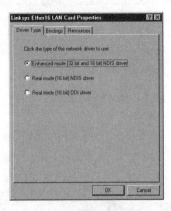

Figure 781 *A component's Properties sheet.*

782 To Access the Network, You Must First Log In

To use the network, you must log in to it. Generally, your system administrator will set up a username and password for you. You can specify or change your password if you use the Passwords Properties sheet, as shown in Figure 782. When you start Windows 95, it will display the log-in window. As you know, network and non-network users have to log in to Windows 95 and specify a user profile. If your network log in and Windows 95 passwords are the same, you'll only need to log in one time and specify a combined profile and network password.

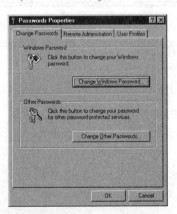

Figure 782 *The Passwords Properties sheet.*

783 Traversing Your Network Neighborhood

The Network Neighborhood offers a graphical folder-like window from which you can traverse your network. When you traverse your network, you span the network looking at workgroups (those to which you have access), other computers' shared disk drive resources, and the network's shared folders. If you double-click your Desktop's Network Neighborhood icon, Windows 95 will open a Network Neighborhood window, like the one shown in Figure 783. What you see in the window will depend on your network's capacity; sometimes you will see several items, sometimes very few.

Note: *If you double-click your mouse on a Network Neighborhood workgroup name, you will see a list of all resources available to that workgroup.*

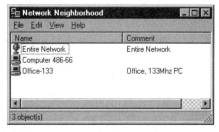

Figure 783 *The Network Neighborhood window.*

Accessing a Shared Printer — 784

After you've enabled printer sharing (see Tip 779) for a printer attached to your computer, you must make that printer available to other network users. To share your printer, perform these steps :

1. Open the Printers window from My Computer.
2. Right-click on the icon that represents the printer you want to share. Windows 95 will display a pop-up menu.
3. Select the pop-up menu's Shared option. Windows 95 will display the printer's Properties sheet Sharing page, as shown in Figure 784.
4. Click your mouse on the Shared As option.
5. Enter a printer name that other users on the network will select to use the shared printer.
6. Enter an optional printer description in the Comment text box.
7. Enter an optional password that other users will need to enter to use the shared printer.
8. Click your mouse on the OK button. Windows 95 will save your changes.

After you click the OK button, your shared printer will appear in the printer selection lists and Network Neighborhood windows of other computers on the network. When another computer's application displays a Print dialog box, the user will be able to select your shared printer. Additionally, other users will be able to drag-and-drop files to your shared printer.

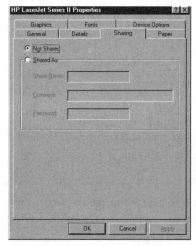

Figure 784 *A printer's Properties sheet Sharing page.*

785 Access a Shared Folder

After you enable file sharing (see Tip 779), you need to specify which of your folders other network users can access. To share a specific folder, perform these steps:

1. Open your My Computer window.
2. Double-click your mouse on the disk drive that contains the folder you want to share.
3. Right-click your mouse over the folder you want to share.
4. Select the pop-up menu's Sharing option. Windows 95 will display a Properties sheet like the one shown in Figure 785.
5. Click your mouse on the Shared As option.
6. Enter a name and optional comment that other network users will see as the name for this folder.
7. To specify how others will use the folder, select the Full, Read-Only, or Depends on Password option button.
8. If you want to password-protect your folder, enter passwords in the sheet's Passwords section. You can specify a read-only password, a full-access password, or both.
9. Click your mouse on the OK button. Windows 95 will save your changes.

After you click the OK button, your shared folder will appear in the folder selection lists and Network Neighborhood windows of other computers on the network. When another network computer's application displays an Open dialog box, the user will be able to select your computer's shared folder.

Note: You can share complete disk drives by selecting a disk drive name instead of a folder from within My Computer.

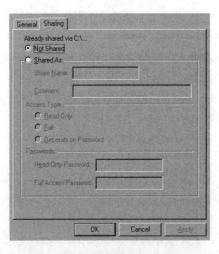

Figure 785 *The Sharing page.*

786 Controlling Access to a Shared Folder or Printer

Windows 95 lets your network administrator specify a list of usernames on an attached Windows NT or Novell NetWare server that Windows 95 can later use to determine who has access to certain network resources. The name list contains users who have access to certain shared devices that other users do not have. By providing such user-level access (see Tip 772 for an explanation), the network users will not have to type a resource's password every time that user uses the resource.

To specify a user-level access control list of usernames, perform these steps:

1. Open your Control Panel's Network Properties sheet.
2. Click your mouse on the Access Control tab. Windows 95 will display the Access Control page.
3. Click your mouse on the User-Level Access Control option.
4. Type the name of the computer that holds the list of usernames. The computer must be a Windows NT or NetWare server. (User-level access is not available on peer-to-peer networks.)
5. Click your mouse on the OK button. Windows 95 will save your changes. As soon as the network administrator adds a name to the username list, that user has access to all resources that recognize the user list.

Changing a Folder or Printer's Password — 787

After you share a folder or printer, the network administrator (or you, if the folder or printer is on your computer) can change the password assigned to the resource. To change a password, open the My Computer window and click your mouse on the folder whose password you want to change. If you want to change a shared printer's password, open the Printers window (which you access through My Computer) and click your mouse on that printer's icon.

To change the password, click your mouse on the File menu Properties option. Then, click your mouse on the OK button. Windows 95, in turn, will change the password for that folder or printer.

Assigning a Drive Letter to a Network Computer or Folder — 788

You don't have to specify a full pathname every time you want to reach a shared drive or folder on a network. Instead, you can map a local drive to the drive or folder. If your last disk and CD-ROM drive name is E:, you can assign any letter from F: through Z: to shared folders and drives that reside on other network computers.

After you map a local drive to a shared folder, the resource will appear as just another disk drive in Explorer, My Computer, and your Windows 95 applications' Open and Save As dialog boxes. To map a local drive letter to a remote resource, perform these steps:

1. Start Explorer.
2. Open toolbar's pull-down list of computer resources.
3. Click your mouse on the Network Neighborhood list item. Windows 95 will display the network resources available to you.
4. After you locate the remote computer or click your mouse on the folder you want to map, click your mouse on Explorer's Map Network Drive toolbar button (or select the Tools menu Map Network Drive option). Windows 95 will display the Map Network Drive dialog box, as shown in Figure 788.
5. Select a drive letter from the pull-down list.
6. Click your mouse on the OK button. Windows 95 will save your changes.

If you want to disconnect a mapped local drive name from a remote resource, select Explorer's Tools menu Disconnect Network Drive option. Then, in the drive-mapping list, select the drive you want to disconnect.

Figure 788 Mapping a local drive to a remote resource.

789 Specifying a Consistent Connection

In Tip 788, you learned how to map a local drive to a network resource, such as a file or folder. By default, Windows 95 eliminates all mapped drives each time you reboot your system. As such, if you want Windows 95 to remember the mapped drive when you subsequently start Windows 95, you need to specify that folder's mapped network drive as a consistent connection. A *consistent connection* is one that automatically reestablishes itself each time you login. To establish a consistent connection, click your mouse on Explorer's Reconnect at logon option.

790 Ending Shared Access to a Folder

As you use Windows 95, there will be times when you'll want to remove shared access from a folder. For example, a remote user may no longer require access to the folder. Or, you may have just added sensitive information to the folder. To remove shared access from a folder, perform these steps:

1. Double-click My Computer's Printers icon. Windows 95 will open the Printers window.
2. Right-click on the icon for the printer that you want to end sharing.
3. Select the pop-up menu's Shared option. Windows 95 will display the printer's Properties sheet Shared page.
4. Click on the Not Shared option. Windows 95 will remove the folder's shared access.
5. Click your mouse on the OK button. Windows 95 will save your changes.
6. If Windows 95 asks you to restart your computer, click your mouse on the Yes button to restart your system.

791 Changing Your Network Password

Good security standards require that users change their passwords routinely. Likewise, if you let someone else use your password for a special project, change your password when the project ends. To change your network password, perform these steps:

1. Open your Control Panel window.
2. Double-click on the Passwords icon. Windows 95 will open the Passwords Properties sheet.
3. If you use the Novell NetWare client protocol, click your mouse on the Change Other Password button. Otherwise, click your mouse on the Change Windows Password button.
4. Enter both your old and new passwords. Enter your new password again to verify it.
5. Click your mouse on the OK button. Windows 95 will save your changes.

Note: *If you use a small, home-based network computer, you may want to omit the password. To do so, leave your new password text boxes empty in step 4.*

Using Dial-Up Networking 792

Tip 679 explained how to use Windows 95's Dial-Up Networking feature to dial into an Internet provider's computer and access that computer's Internet features. Laptop computer users can also use Windows 95's Dial-Up Networking to dial into their office or home networks and work from the remote site as if they were connected directly to the network.

However, dial-up networking does have one serious limitation—you can only dial up, and use the shared resources of, a server computer. You cannot dial a peer-to-peer-based network computer and expect to use the network capabilities or any of its shared resources.

To use Windows 95's Dial-Up Networking feature, locate your laptop's Dial-Up Networking icon in the Control Panel. (Run Windows Setup if you do not see the Dial-Up Networking icon.) The first time you use the Dial-Up Networking feature, Windows 95 will walk you through the Dial-Up Networking wizard so you can describe the remote site to which you want to connect. Then, Windows 95 will place an icon for the remote site inside the Dial-Up Networking window. You can connect to that site when you double-click the new icon.

Creating a Network Server 793

Generally, your network's server is the most powerful computer on the network. Because the server acts as a central repository of data and programs, the server should have ample disk space. Also, because the server must *serve* the networked computers data and programs quickly, the server should be a fast computer.

You usually designate a server computer when you first install Windows 95. To be a server, the server computer must run one of the following networks:

- Banyan VINES 5.52
- Microsoft Windows NT Server
- Novell NetWare 3.x or 4.x

To install Windows 95 on the server, you need to run the NETSETUP program. Use the server's existing network software to log on to the network server with full system-administrator privileges. The NETSETUP program prompts you for the server information needed to install Windows 95's server version.

Note: *If you purchase the Microsoft Plus! add-on product, you'll be able to configure a remote computer to act as a dial-up server even if that computer is not set up for a true server/client environment.*

Monitoring Network Resources Using Net Watcher 794

If you are a system administrator, you can use *Net Watcher* to perform remote network administration from your computer. The Net Watcher program will let you view network resources and determine who is using them. Net Watcher also lets you add shared files and folders, as well as disconnect users from specific files or computers on the network. As long as you have installed the Client for Microsoft Networks client software and have enabled file and printer sharing, you can use Net Watcher to monitor your network.

To start Net Watcher, click the System Tools menu Net Watcher option. (To access the System Tools, select the Accessories menu System Tools option). Figure 794 shows the opening Net Watcher window. Click the first toolbar button, the Select Server button, to select the server computer (or computer on the peer-to-peer network) you want to monitor.

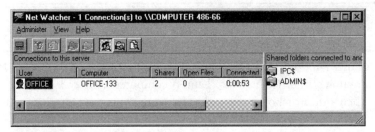

Figure 794 The Net Watcher program.

795 Take Advantage of the Net Watcher Toolbar

Table 795 lists Net Watcher toolbar buttons you can use to monitor with Net Watcher (see Tip 797 for a complete list of Net Watcher toolbar buttons and their descriptions).

Button	Description
By Connections	Lets you see who is connected to your computer.
By Shared Folders	Lets you see all the shared folders on your computer that others are currently using.
By Open Files	Lets you see files on your computer that others are currently using.

Table 795 Toolbar buttons you can use to monitor with Net Watcher.

796 Disconnecting Remote Users Using Net Watcher

Depending on the operations you are performing, there may be times when you will want to disconnect other users from your system. For example, assume you need to make changes to your network configuration. Before you do so, you can disconnect the users who are currently connected to your system. In such cases, you can use the New Watcher to disconnect users. To disconnect a user from the network, perform these steps:

1. Start Net Watcher.
2. Click your mouse on the By Connections toolbar button. Windows 95 will show you who is connected to the computer network.
3. Click your mouse on the user you will disconnect next.
4. Click your mouse on the Administer menu Disconnect User option. Windows 95 will disconnect the user.

Note: Before you disconnect users from a network, you should notify them. For example, you can send an e-mail message to each user and advise what time you will shut down the network. The users will still be able to use their own computer files.

797 Using the Net Watcher Toolbar

The Net Watcher toolbar provides you with one-button access to all of Net Watcher's most important functions. To display or hide the Net Watcher toolbar, click your mouse on the View menu Toolbar option. Table 797 explains each of Net Watcher's toolbar buttons.

Toolbar Icon	Purpose
	Selects a different server to monitor.
	Disconnects users from the network.
	Closes open files.
	Adds sharing capabilities to folders.
	Stops the sharing of folders.
	Shows the network users.
	Shows the shared folders on the network.
	Shows the open files on the network.

Table 797 The Net Watcher toolbar.

Viewing Files Opened by Network Users 798

As long as your computer is set up for user-level security, and as long as other network computers are set up for file and printer sharing, you can view names of files that other network users open.

Additionally, you can actually force a user's open file closed. If a user is working with a file whose security you need to remove or update, you can close that user's file. However, be sure to let the user know that you're going to close the file. If the file's user is away from his or her computer when you need to close the file, send the user an e-mail message that says you had to close the file for maintenance. To close a file, select Net Watcher's Administer menu Close File option

Logging Off the Network 799

When you want to leave the network, even if you still want to use your computer for something else (a non-network task), be sure to log off the network. By logging off, you'll improve the network speed for other users because you'll lower the network traffic and computer polling that the network regularly performs. To log off the network, perform these steps:

1. Close all open programs.
2. Click your mouse on the Start menu Shut Down option.
3. Click your mouse on the Close All Programs and Log On As A Different User option. Windows 95 will log off the network and restart Windows 95.
4. Click your mouse on the Yes button. Windows 95 will let you reuse your computer.
5. To use your computer without logging into the network, click your mouse on the Cancel button when the login program requests the network password. Windows 95 will start without logging you on to the network.

800 Using the Windows 3.1 Program Manager

If you like Windows 3.1's Program Manager more than Windows 95's Start menu, or if you need to run Program Manager for someone who only knows Windows 3.1, Windows 95 contains Program Manager. To run Program Manager, click your mouse on the Start menu Run option and type **PROGMAN** and press ENTER. You'll see the familiar Windows 3.1 Program Manager shown in Figure 800.

Figure 800 *You can run Windows 3.1's Program Manager.*

801 Running the Windows 3.1 File Manager

If you like Windows 3.1's File Manager more than Windows 95's Explorer, or if you need to run File Manager for someone who knows only Windows 3.1, Windows 95 contains File Manager. To run File Manager, click your mouse on the Start menu Run option and type **WINFILE** and press ENTER. You'll see the familiar Windows 3.1 File Manager shown in Figure 801.

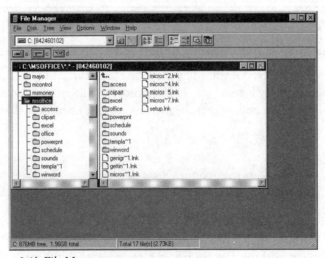

Figure 801 *You can run Windows 3.1's File Manager.*

Using the Windows 3.1 Task Manager | 802

The Windows Task Manager pre-dated the Taskbar by giving Windows for Workgroups users one-click access to their open program windows. Unlike the Taskbar, the Task Manager remains in a window that you can minimize or keep on top of your other windows. Due to Windows 95's ability to alter Taskbar settings, you have little reason to use the Task Manager. Nevertheless, if you want to use the Task Manager, type **TASKMAN** at the Start menu Run option and press ENTER. The Task Manager window appears like the one shown in Figure 802.

Figure 802 Running Task Manager.

Understanding ECP and EPP | 803

In the past, printer ports were one-directional (or omni-directional). That is, your computer sent data to the printer, but the printer could not send data back to the computer. Omni-directional printer ports were not considered limited; it never occurred to anyone that the printer would ever need to send data *back* to the computer because printers are output devices, unlike disk drives that your computer both writes to and reads from. With the introduction of *ECP* (*Extended Capability Ports*) and *EPP* (*Enhanced Parallel Ports*), however, your printer ports became bi-directional. Your parallel ports can support Plug and Play because they send sensing information to Windows 95. For example, when you install printers, the printer port informs Windows 95 of your printer's type. Make sure that you buy printers that support bi-directional ports if you want ECP or EPP to function. Such bi-directional ports also allow the printer to send status messages to the computer, such as out of paper and off-line information.

Providing Support for ECP and EPP Printers | 804

In Tip 803 you learned that ECP and EPP printers communicate with Windows 95 to exchange status information. As you will find, Enabling ECP and EPP support is very straightforward. You'll only need to enable them once, however. To enable bi-directional printer support, perform these steps:

1. Locate your computer or bi-directional port's manual to determine required IRQ and DMA settings.
2. Open your Control Panel's System window.
3. Click on the Device Manager tab to display Figure 804.1's Device Manager page.
4. Click your mouse on the Ports (COM & LPT) entry and select the ECP/EPP device you've attached to your computer.
5. Click your mouse on the Properties button.
6. Display Figure 804.2's Resource page by clicking your mouse on the Resources tab.
7. Select Basic Configuration 2 in the Settings based on list box.
8. Click your mouse on the Resource Settings' Interrupt request option.

9. Click your mouse on the Change Setting button and type your port's IRQ value.
10. To save your changes, click your mouse on the OK button.
11. Click your mouse on the Direct Memory Access button and type your port's DMA settings.
12. To save your changes, click your mouse on the OK button.
13. Restart Windows 95 to implement the bi-directional port settings.

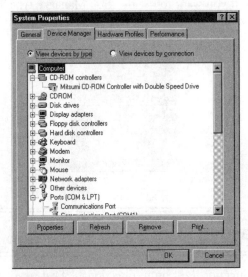

Figure 804.1 The System Properties screen Device Manager page.

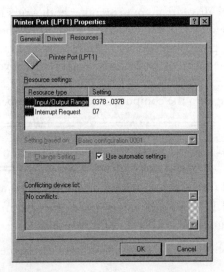

Figure 804.2 The Printer Port Properties' Resource page.

805 Spooling EMF Files Improves Printer Performance

Windows 95 uses *EMF* (*Enhanced Metafile*) printing for all printed output except output that you route to PostScript printers. Using EMF, Windows 95 can print as much at as two times the printing speed of Windows 3.1's print spooler. Instead of sending raw printed data to your printer or spooler, Windows 95 first turns your output into a graphical EMF representation, releases it to your computer, and then sends the EMF data to your spooler for printing.

Understanding DOS-based Program Spooling — 806

When you print from a Windows 3.1 MS-DOS window, Windows 3.1 bypasses the spooler. Therefore, MS-DOS releases the system much more slowly after you print from MS-DOS than after you print from within a Windows 3.1 window. MS-DOS can also conflict with Windows 3.1 if the user starts two simultaneous print jobs, one from Windows 3.1 and one from an MS-DOS window.

Windows 95 spools MS-DOS output using the 32-bit Windows 95 spooler. Therefore, your MS-DOS print jobs will release the system much more quickly under Windows 95. In addition, Windows 95 users will not get print device conflict problems when they print both from an MS-DOS window and from a Windows 95 program.

Note: MS-DOS users cannot take advantage of EMF print spooling, but the regular Windows 95 spooler does accept MS-DOS's printed output.

Understanding Windows 95 VFAT — 807

The *VFAT (Virtual File Allocation Table)* handles all Windows 95's file I/O. VFAT uses a 32-bit virtual driver. VFAT supports long filenames, as well as the read-ahead VCACHE (see Tip 808). The VFAT contains hooks that other operating systems, such as UNIX, can use to access your Windows 95 computer's disk files. VFAT also supports the multitasking disk I/O so that two or more applications can read and write to the disk simultaneously. To maintain compatibility with files from older Windows and MS-DOS versions, Windows 95's VFAT also supports the Windows 3.1 12-bit and 16-bit file allocation tables.

Understanding VCACHE — 808

Whereas Windows 3.1 used SmartDrive to speed disk I/O by caching disk data, Windows 95 replaces SmartDrive with *VCACHE*, the 32-bit virtual caching driver that provides more efficient disk I/O than did SmartDrive. VCACHE handles not only system disk I/O, but also networking disk I/O and CD-ROM access. A disk cache improves your system performance by reducing slow disk read and write operations. Instead of physically reading and writing data each time a Windows 95 program performs a read or write operations, VCACHE bunches reads and writes. Therefore, not every read or write has to access the physical disk. For example, when your program reads data from a file, VCACHE will not just read the requested data, but it will also read and buffer (cache) extra data (the information that immediately follows that data the program has requested). Should the program later need this extra data, VCACHE can eliminate a slow disk read operation because it already has the data in memory.

When programs (such as database) write information to disk, VCACHE may not immediately write the information to disk. Instead, VCACHE may wait until it has more data to write to disk. Then, VCACHE will write all the information in one operation, hence reducing several smaller (and slow) disk operations. Unlike SmartDrive, you do not have to initiate VCACHE, change VCACHE settings, or install VCACHE. However, if you use a CD-ROM drive, you may want to check the VCACHE CD-ROM settings, as explained in Tip 809, to improve CD-ROM performance.

Improving VCACHE Performance for Different CD-ROM Drive Types — 809

Depending on your CD-ROM drive type, you may be able to improve CD-ROM performance by changing CD-ROM VCACHE options. Perform these steps to make the CD-ROM performance change:

1. Open the Control Panel.
2. To open the System Properties sheet, double-click your mouse on the System icon.
3. Display Figure 809.1's System Properties sheet Performance page by clicking your mouse on the Performance tab.
4. Display Figure 809.2's File System Properties sheet by clicking your mouse on the File System button.
5. Display Figure 809.3's File System Properties sheet CD-ROM page by clicking your mouse on the CD-ROM tab.
6. Slide the Supplemental cache size slide control to the right to increase the amount of VCACHE resources Windows 95 devotes to your CD-ROM drive. Use the following settings: If your computer contains less than 8Mb of RAM, slide the cache size setting to 64K. If your computer contains 8 to 12 Mb of RAM, slide the cache size to 626K. If your computer contains more than 12 Mb of RAM, select 1238K for the cache size.
7. Display the Optimize access pattern for pull-down list and select your CD-ROM drive's speed. For example, if you use a single-speed CD-ROM, select Single-speed drives from the list.
8. To implement your changes, click your mouse on the OK button and restart Windows 95.

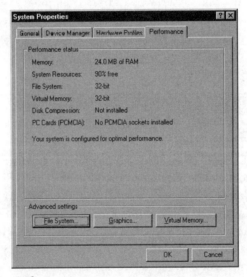

Figure 809.1 *The System Properties sheet Performance page.*

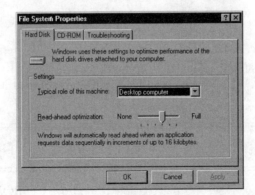

Figure 809.2 *The File System Properties sheet.*

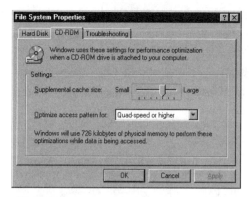

Figure 809.3 *File System Properties sheet CD-ROM page.*

Windows 95 Does Not Require MSCDEX — 810

Previous MS-DOS and Windows users had to load the *MSCDEX* (*Microsoft CD Extension*) device driver to use a CD-ROM. Windows 95, however, includes a 32-bit virtual CD-ROM driver that eliminates the need for MSCDEX. Windows 95 provides the *CDFS* (the *CD-ROM File System*) that loads automatically when you start Windows 95. In addition to Read-only devices, CDFS supports recordable CD media if you use a recordable CD drive. When you open an MS-DOS window, the CDFS provides MS-DOS support without requiring additional MS-DOS drivers. When you install Windows 95, the Windows 95 Setup program removes MSCDEX from AUTOEXEC.BAT.

Understanding Swapping — 811

When you run several programs at the same time, Windows 95 uses a *swap file* to move programs in and out of memory to disk. Before you can run a program, that program must reside in RAM. When you run multiple programs at the same time, you can easily run out of RAM. In such cases, Windows 95 swaps sections of memory to and from the hard disk. In other words, Windows 95 moves one program out of memory temporarily to make room for a second program. Therefore, the more programs you run simultaneously, the more Windows 95 swaps programs between RAM and your swap file. The more RAM your computer has, the less Windows 95 has to swap to and from the disk. Windows 95 reserves space on your hard disk, called a swap file, to hold the information it swaps to and from memory. In previous versions of Windows, you had to configure your Windows swap file settings yourself. Windows 95 uses a dynamic swap file that automatically configures itself as needed.

Forcing a Permanent Swap File — 812

Although Windows 95 configures its own swap file settings, you can take control and configure your own swap file. Perhaps the only time you'd need to set your own swap file size is when you are running out of disk space and you must install a fairly large program that would normally not have room on your system due to the swap file. In this case, you could permanently set your swap file to a low size, but doing so will greatly decrease your system performance and could result in your running out of memory resources when multitasking programs. To force a permanent swap file size, perform these steps:

1. Open the Control Panel.
2. To open the System Properties sheet, double-click your mouse on the System icon.
3. To display the System Properties sheet Performance page, click on the Performance tab.

4. Display Figure 812's Virtual Memory page by clicking on the Virtual Memory button.
5. Click your mouse on the Let me specify my own virtual settings and enter a minimum and maximum size value for your swap file.
6. To save your changes, click your mouse on the OK button.
7. Restart Windows 95 to implement your swap file settings.

If you later add additional disk space, be sure to set the first option on the Virtual Memory page so that Windows 95 can resume managing its own swap file settings.

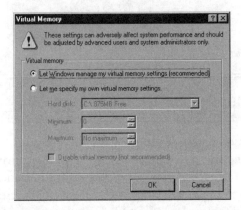

Figure 812 The Virtual Memory page.

813 Delete Windows 3.1 Permanent Swap File

If you no longer use Windows 3.1, or if you use a dual-boot setup and only rarely use Windows 3.1, delete your Windows 3.1 permanent swap file to free disk space that Windows 95 can use. To delete your Windows 3.1 swap file, perform these steps:

1. Open your Windows 3.1 Program Manager's Control Panel window.
2. Double-click your mouse over the 386 Enhanced icon. Windows 95 will display the 386 Enhanced dialog box showing your Windows 3.1 swap file setting. If the Size value is zero, you do not use a Windows 3.1 swap file, and you can click your mouse on the Cancel button to terminate this tip's operation.
3. To display the Virtual Memory Settings page, click your mouse on the Change button.
4. Click your mouse on the New Size option and enter **0** for the swap file size.
5. To save your changes and remove the swap file, click your mouse on the OK button.

814 Understanding Disk Partitioning

If your hard disk drive is large, you may want to *partition* your disk drive into two or more logical disk drives. Once you partition a single physical disk drive into multiple logical drives, Windows 95 views the logical drives as if they were separate physical disk drives. When you issue a read or write command from or to the logical disk drive, Windows 95 reads or writes the data to the proper partitioned logical drive and keeps the two drives separated in directory and Explorer listings. You can repartition a disk by changing its logical drives back into a single large disk drive; the disk's physical and logical size then matches once again. When you install a new disk drive, you must partition the disk using the FDISK command (see Tip 815) and format the disk drive. Your system's disk drive structure must contain a *Primary DOS partition* that contains the boot-up information (usually your C: drive).

Still use FDISK To Partition a Disk   815

FDISK is an MS-DOS program that you can run inside an MS-DOS window to partition a disk drive into multiple logical drives or repartition a drive back into a single drive. Windows 95 does not provide a Windows 95 FDISK replacement; you must use the MS-DOS FDISK program to partition your disk. To start FDISK and partition or repartition a drive, perform these steps:

1. Open an MS-DOS window.
2. Type **FDISK**.
3. Select whether you want to create a new partition, set an active partition to use, delete a partition, or display partition size information.
4. Follow the instructions on your screen.

If you use a non-DOS partition, such as a partition used by another operating system on your computer, FDISK will not be able to delete that partition. You must use your operating system's software to remove the non-DOS partition.

Note: Be warned: Back up your disk completely before you repartition an existing disk drive. FDISK erases all data on the disk drive.

Formatting a Disk Within Windows 95   816

To format a disk drive, use Windows 95's Explorer. When you right-click over the disk drive name and click on the Format option, Windows 95 displays the Format dialog box shown in Figure 816. You'll have to select the proper disk size from the Capacity pull-down list. Use the following options to decide the type of format you want.

- *Quick format*: Erases previously-formatted diskettes but does no error checking
- *Full*: Completely formats new and old diskettes by writing new tracks to the disk and marking bad sectors on the disk so they won't be used again
- *Copy system files only*: Creates a boot-up hard disk or floppy disk, but does not reformat the disk or check for errors.

If you want to specify a disk *label* (more accurately a *volume label*) that Explorer and directory listings can display, enter a label name in the Label text box. The Format program will display a summary, if you opt for one, that displays the details of the formatting and explains how much free and bad disk space the formatting process uncovered.

Note: You cannot format a Windows 95 system disk or a disk with open files.

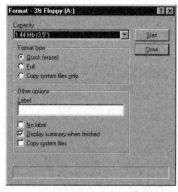

Figure 816 The Format dialog box.

817 Understanding Quick View

Quick View is a Windows 95 utility program that lets you quickly view data files without requiring that you start the file's associated program. For example, Quick View quickly displays Microsoft Excel worksheets, and lets you scroll through the worksheet contents, without starting Excel. Excel takes a few moments to load and a large amount of system resources. The Quick Viewer, on the other hand, loads quickly and consumes very few resources. Quick View supports most file formats, and can display graphics, text, worksheets, and word processor documents. Quick View uses the file's extension to determine which associated program format to use so you can view the file. Before you can use Quick View, you must install it using the Control Panel's Add/Remove Programs windows Setup option in order to install Quick View.

818 Viewing a File Using Quick View

Explorer contains Quick View support once you install Quick View. To use Quick View to display data file contents, right-click your mouse over a filename and select the right-click menu Quick View option. Windows 95 displays the contents of the file in a window, such as the one in Figure 818.1. You can change the font size by clicking toolbar buttons and if you want to edit the file, select the File menu Open File for Editing option to start the associated program with which you can edit the file. Windows 95 includes a special Word for Windows viewer, named *Word Viewer*, that uses the powerful Word for Windows quick viewer shown in Figure 818.2 with which you can zoom in and out or print documents. If you use Quick View to display an executable file or a *.DLL (dynamic link library)* file, Quick View displays information *about* the file instead of displaying the contents of the file which would make little sense. Figure 818.3 shows a Quick View .DLL file information window.

Figure 818.1 Using Quick View on a text file.

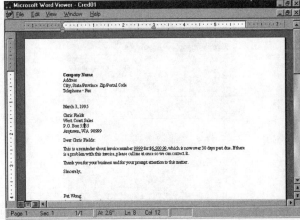

Figure 818.2 Using Word Viewer.

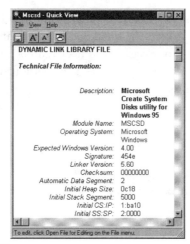

Figure 818.3 *Using Quick View on a .DLL file.*

Opening a Document That Has No Association | 819

Quick View looks at a file's filename extension to determine the best way to display the file. For example, if the file's extension is .TXT, Quick View displays the file in a text format. If the file's extension is .BMP, Quick View uses a bitmap viewer to show you the file's graphic. If you right-click over a file whose filename extension Quick View does not recognize, the right-click menu will contain an Open With option instead of Quick View. If you select Open With, Windows 95 displays the Open With dialog box shown in Figure 819. Select a program you want to associate with that file's extension. Subsequently, when you right-click that program's filename, Windows 95 opens the file using the associated program. Although Quick View will not be able to display the file, you will be able to see the file and edit its contents.

Note: *As software developers write new programs for Windows 95, they will include Quick View add-on products so that Quick View will be able to display the new programs' data files.*

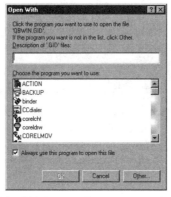

Figure 819 *The Open With (file association) dialog box.*

Understanding and Working with Scraps | 820

You already know that you can drag and drop programs and files to your Desktop. However, you can also drag and drop selected clipboard contents to the Desktop. Such contents become *scraps* on your Desktop. For example, if you start your word processor and select a sentence by highlighting that sentence with your mouse, you then can move you mouse pointer over the selected text, click and hold your mouse button, and drag that selected sentence to the

Desktop. Windows 95 places the scrap on the Desktop and names the icon Document Scrap followed by the first few words of the selected text. If you want to rename the scrap document, right-click your mouse and select the Rename option. A scrap is one of the quickest ways to select text from a document and send that text to its own separate file. By dragging the selected scrap to your Desktop, you create a file without having to select File Save As commands, entering a file name, and returning to your primary document. If you drag a scrap to the Start button, Windows 95 adds the scrap to your Start menu. When you subsequently click your mouse over the Start menu scrap, Windows 95 starts the associated program with which you can edit, copy, and print that scrap.

821 Pasting a Scrap By Dragging a Document on to the Taskbar

If you've started and minimized your word processor, or Paint, or any other Windows 95 program that supports *OLE (Object Linking and Embedding)* drag and drop operations (most programs written for Windows 95 do support OLE), you can drag a Desktop scrap to that program's Taskbar button. Do *not* release your mouse button to drop the scrap or file on the Taskbar button, but let the scrap or file hover over the taskbar button without dropping it. When Windows 95 senses that you have moved the scrap over a Taskbar button, Windows 95 maximizes that Taskbar button's program window, and then you can release your mouse button to drop that item into the open document or data file.

822 Understanding 32-bit and 16-bit Programs

As you know, Windows 95 is a *32-bit operating system*. Window 3.1 and Windows for Workgroups were 16-bit operating environments. A 32-bit operating system, when running programs written for 32-bit operating systems, runs those programs faster than a 16-bit operating system running 16-bit programs. The difference is something like the difference between a 2-lane and a 4-lane highway. The traffic flows much faster down the 4-lane highway due to the wider path. Windows 95 provides backwards compatibility by supporting the 16-bit Windows 3.1 and MS-DOS programs. The 32-bit Windows 95 operating system uses *Win32*, an *Applications Programming Interface (API)*, that programmers use to create 32-bit programs. All Windows NT programs run smoothly on Windows 95 because of this 32-bit architecture. Microsoft really outdid themselves when they created Windows 95 to support both 16- and 32-bit applications for past and future compatibility.

823 Understanding LFNBK

If you use a hard disk utility program written before the release of Windows 95, that program will have a problem with Windows 95's long filenames. Some people still use older backup tape drives and do not have Windows 95 driver files for those tape drives. Such users must continue to back up with the older legacy hardware and software until they update their tape drive's driver software or hardware. If you back up your Windows 95 hard disk with an older backup program, the backup will not contain long filenames. Even if you limit your data files to the older Windows 3.1's and MS-DOS's 8.3 short format, Windows 95 contains system files that have long filenames. Your backup will appear to work but if you have to restore that backup, you'll find that the restore erased all your long filenames. Windows 95 will then have problems when you try to run a option that uses a file that's supposed to have a long filename. Windows 95's LFNBK program lets you remove, and more importantly later restore, long filenames from your system. Therefore, you can run LFNBK before your older utility program and you won't have filename problems. To turn off long filenames temporarily while you run an older program, perform these steps:

1. Select the Control Panel's System Properties sheet Performance page.
2. Click your mouse on the File System button to display the File System page.

3. Click your mouse on the Troubleshooting tab to display the Troubleshooting page.
4. Click on the Disable Long Name Preservation for Old Programs option to check the option.
5. To save your changes, click your mouse button on the OK button.
6. Close all open applications.
7. Open an MS-DOS window.
8. Type **LFNBK /B C:** (substitute the drive to disable if you want to disable long filenames on a drive other than C:). LFNBK renames all long filenames to shorter 8.3-length names and stores the list of long and short filenames, for later restoration, in a file named LFNBK.DAT.
9. Press the ENTER key.
10. Restart Windows 95 to an MS-DOS prompt if the utility program is an MS-DOS program, or to Windows 95 if the utility program is a Windows program.
11. When the program finishes, repeat Steps 1 through 4. Step 4 now unchecks the Disable Long Name Preservation for Old Programs option.
12. Click your mouse on the OK button.
13. Restart your computer once again.
14. Open an MS-DOS window and type **LFNBK /R C:** to restore the long filenames.
15. To start the restoration, press ENTER.

Understanding the Start Command — 824

The MS-DOS START command starts Windows 95 programs from the MS-DOS-based Start menu Run option. Once those programs finish executing, control returns to the MS-DOS environment to search for additional commands. If no additional commands are found, control returns to Windows 95. The START command is useful for executing several Window 95 programs in a specific order, automatically as Tip 825 explains.

Using the Start Command to Control the Order in Which Programs Run — 825

Suppose that you want to run three Windows 95-compatible programs, in a specific order, every time you start Windows 95. If you place those three programs in the Windows 95 Startup folder, Windows 95 will execute those three programs, but not in a pre-defined order.

You can put those three programs' start up commands in an MS-DOS batch file using Notepad or a similar text editor. Instead of starting the programs by their executable file names, use the START command to start the batch file. For example, the batch file might contain the following three lines:

```
START BACKMON.EXE

START DISKLITE.EXE

START CALC.EXE
```

Place the batch file in the Windows 95 startup group. Windows 95 will then run the batch file every time you start Windows 95. The three programs will then execute, in the order you listed them, every time you start Windows 95. If you placed those three commands in the batch file without using START to initiate each batch file command, Windows 95 would execute only the first program named BACKMON.EXE.

826 Understanding Multitasking

Multitasking is the process of running two or more programs at the same time, or at least what appears to be at the same time. A single processor-based computer can actually perform only one task at any one time, but today's computers can switch between two or more running tasks so quickly that they appear to be able to run two or more tasks simultaneously. Windows 95 rapidly exchanges CPU control among the active programs. Each application takes a small piece of processor time, called a *time slice*. The more programs you run simultaneously, the slower each program becomes, because more have to share smaller slices of the CPU's time.

827 Windows 95 Uses Preemptive Multitasking

Due to its *preemptive multitasking* ability, Windows 95 multitasks several programs more smoothly and efficiently than did previous versions of Windows. Preemptive multitasking refers to the ability of the CPU to give or take away time to or from programs running in memory. For example, if a worksheet calculation requires more of the CPU's time than a word processor, the CPU gives a larger time slice to the worksheet for that calculation. When the calculation completes, the CPU can even out the two tasks' time requirements. Windows 3.1 used *cooperative multitasking*, which required that programmers write applications to check for other tasks that might need the CPU and to release it for the other tasks if needed. The problem is, not all cooperative multitasking programs cooperated! If a programmer did not write a program to respect the cooperative multitasking rules, then that program could consume all the CPU's time slices and not release any time to other programs, making multitasking jumpy and unpredictable. Communications programs run poorly in cooperative multitasking environments, because accurate data communications require a steady flow of the CPU's time. If another task did not cooperate well, the communications program would fail.

828 Understanding Multithreaded Applications

Multithreaded applications take advantage of preemptive multitasking operating systems, such as Windows 95, to provide smoother multitasking and more efficient CPU use. A programmer writes a multithreaded application so that it contains one or more *threads*. A thread is a section of code that can run concurrently with other processes. Windows 3.1's 16-bit architecture cannot run multithreaded applications, but programs written for Windows 95 (using 32-bit architecture) can be multithreaded. For example, if a word processor contains multithreaded code, it can use one thread to check spelling and another to print in the background, while you type in the foreground with yet another thread. The multitasking operating system gives each of these threads equal time slices so that they seem to run concurrently. Without the multithreaded code, these three functions will compete with each other instead of working in parallel, and you will not work in a smooth environment. For example, you may have to finish typing a word after another paragraph's spell-checking ends.

829 How to Recognize a File Copy or Move Operation

As you know, the Windows 95 environment lets you move and copy files by dragging filenames with your mouse. If you drag a file from one location to another by clicking and holding your mouse on the filename, then you move the file to its new location. If you hold the CTRL key down while dragging the mouse, Windows 95 copies the file to the destination. Two ways to remember the difference between a copy or move operation:

- Hold CTRL when you want to *copy* (both CTRL and Copy begin with the letter C).
- When you drag to copy a file, Windows 95 drags the filename along with the mouse pointer,

but places a small plus sign under the filename (see Figure 829.1). When you see the plus sign, Windows 95 copies the file, but if you drag the file and do not see the plus sign (see Figure 829.2), Windows 95 moves the file.

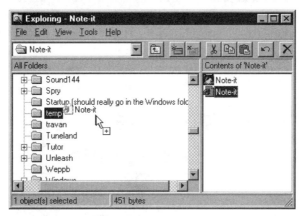

Figure 829.1 *The plus sign indicates a copy.*

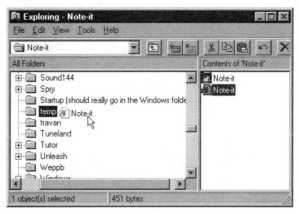

Figure 829.2 *No plus sign indicates a move.*

Use Esc to Cancel a Move or Copy Operation | 830

If you begin to copy or move a file by dragging the file with your mouse, then you decide that you want to cancel the move or copy operation, press Esc before releasing your mouse button. Windows 95 cancels the operation and neither moves nor copies the file to the destination.

To Open a File Folder Using the Same Window, Use Ctrl-Double Click | 831

Normally, when you double-click your mouse over a folder in the My Computer or Network Neighborhood window, Windows 95 opens the folder and displays its contents in a second window. Therefore, you can open a folder and its subfolders to find a file from the My Computer window and end up with several open windows before you find the file. You'll eventually need to close those windows. You can save a little effort by pressing the Ctrl key when you double-click a disk drive or folder in the My Computer or Network Neighborhood window. Instead of opening another window to display the opened folder's contents, Windows 95 replaces the current window with the opened folder's contents. Each time you hold Ctrl when you double-click a folder, Windows 95 suppresses the opening of a new window, but displays the open folder's contents in the current window.

832 Use a Lasso to Select Multiple Files and Folders

As you already know, you can select multiple files listed together within Explorer's or My Computer's windows by holding CTRL as you click over each filename. Windows 95 provides an easier way to select a group of files, however. Instead of clicking over each file, you can *lasso* the files just as a cowboy lassos cattle rustlers. Hold your mouse button down while you loop the mouse pointer around the files you want to select. As you surround the files with your mouse pointer, Explorer or My Computer creates a square lasso highlight (as Figure 832 shows). When you finish circling the files, release your mouse button to complete the multiple file selection.

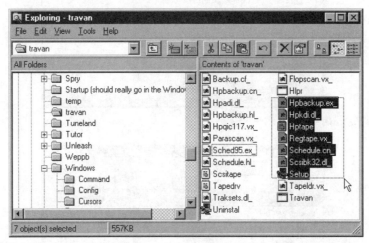

Figure 832 Lasso multiple files with your mouse.

833 Rename a Selected File or Folder Easily by Pressing F2

In the Explorer, Network Neighborhood, and My Computer windows (as in most Windows 95 File Open and File Save As dialog boxes) you can rename a file or folder by clicking your mouse on the file two times. The problem is that you can easily double-click your mouse and open the folder or start the file's associated program. Instead of double-clicking your mouse over the name, you must click once, wait a moment, and click a second time to enter the rename mode. Instead of risking a double-click, you can rename a file or folder by clicking your mouse once on the name to highlight it, and then press F2. The text cursor automatically appears over the name. Press the HOME key to edit the front of the name, END to edit the end of the name, or press the LEFT ARROW or RIGHT ARROW key to edit within the name.

834 All Those LNK Files Are Shortcuts

As Tip 723 explains, a shortcut is a link to a file, not a copy of one. When you create a file shortcut on your Desktop or in a folder, Windows 95 places a link or pointer to the file on your Desktop or in the folder, and creates an icon for the link labeled "Shortcut to . . .".

To keep track of shortcuts, Windows 95 creates a link file with the .LNK filename extension. The link file is a link to the original file. If you delete a shortcut, you do not have to worry about deleting the original file, because the shortcut is only a linked pointer to the file and not the file itself. If you see several files with the .LNK extension, you'll now know that those are shortcuts to other files.

Viewing Recently Used Documents within a Folder 835

As you know, the Start menu's Documents option displays a list of documents you've recently opened. People often work on the same document or data over a period of a few days, and the Documents option lets you select from a list of recent documents by name. When you select a document, Windows 95 starts that document's associated program. The Start menu's Documents option is rather limited due to space. If you want a more complete list of documents you've last worked with, start Explorer and open the Windows/Recent folder. As Figure 835 shows, the Recent folder contains a large list of documents that you've recently edited or created. The small arrow on each document's icon lets you know that the item is a shortcut link to the actual document. You can rearrange, rename, or delete documents from the Recent folder, something you cannot do with the Start menu Documents option. Therefore, the Recent folder gives you more control over your recent documents than you get from the Start menu.

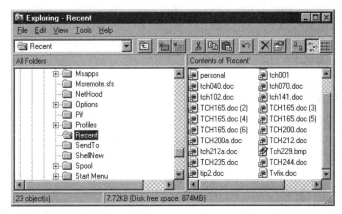

Figure 835 *Viewing recently edited document names.*

Using SHIFT-DEL to Delete a File and Bypass the Recycle Bin 836

The Recycle Bin holds your deleted files until you either delete its contents or restore them back to their original, undeleted location. Although it adds safety to file deletions by giving you a second chance to delete files you really no longer want, the Recycle Bin can get in the way at times. If you want to delete a huge file to reclaim needed disk space, the file does not really go away when you delete the file from Explorer or My Computer. The file will not go away until you open the Recycle Bin's window and issue the command to delete the file from there. If you hold your SHIFT key while you press DEL to delete a selected file from within an Explorer or My Computer window, Windows 95 bypasses the Recycle Bin and truly deletes the file from your computer. Therefore, you will not have a second chance to reclaim that file because it will disappear as soon as you delete it.

Using Command-Line Arguments to Customize Explorer 837

If you start Explorer from a batch file or from the Start menu Run option, you can limit Explorer's initial computer, disk drive, folder, or file selection by adding a *command-line argument* to Explorer's startup command. The command-line arguments determine how Explorer begins. If you simply type **EXPLORER** from MS-DOS, from a batch file, or from the Start menu Run option, Explorer starts as usual, showing you the contents of your computer's desktop. If, however, you add one of the command-line arguments from Table 837, Explorer displays information based on those command-line arguments. Here is the general format of Explorer's start-up command:

```
EXPLORER [/n] [/e] [,/root,object] [[,/select], subobject]
```

Command-line argument	Description
/n	Opens a new window even if the specified folder is already open
/e	Uses the Explorer view as opposed to the default Open view
/root,object	Specifies a new Explorer root. Therefore, instead of displaying Explorer using your Desktop as the root, Explorer could open displaying a particular folder or network computer as the root
/select	Overrides the *subobject* option and specifies a parent folder that should be opened, and an object that should be selected
subobject	Specifies the folder that receives the initial open focus

Table 837 Explorer's command-line arguments.

The following Start menu Run option command starts Explorer and requests that Explorer select a Word for Windows document named MYDOC.DOC:

```
EXPLORER /select.c:\WINWORD\MYDOC.DOC
```

The following Start menu Run option command starts Explorer and requests that Explorer use a networked computer for the root of Explorer's display:

```
EXPLORER /e,/root,\\Actg-PC
```

838 Use the Windows System Key to Access the Start Menu

The Start menu is only a mouse click away when you click your mouse on your Taskbar's Start button. You can also press CTRL-ESC to display the Start menu. New keyboards are now on the market that provide yet another way to access Windows 95. If your computer's keyboard has a key marked with the Windows 95 logo, press that key to display the Start menu.

839 Quickly Displaying a Disk's Use

Disk drives fill up with data very quickly in today's world of large programs and online database access. You can determine the available disk space, as well as other disk statistics, by performing these steps:

1. Open the My Computer window.
2. To see that disk drive's statistics, right-click your mouse over that disk drive.
3. Select the Properties option. Windows 95 will display the disk drive's Properties sheet shown in Figure 839.
4. To display additional information about the disk drive, click your mouse on the Properties sheet's other page tabs.
5. To close the Properties sheet, click your mouse on the OK button.

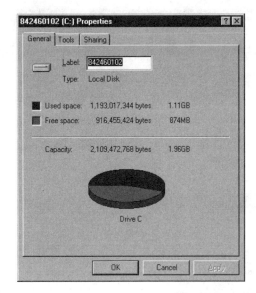

Figure 839 *Viewing disk drive statistics.*

Within Explorer, Press Backspace to Move Up One Level | 840

Explorer gives several different views of your computer, disk drives, folders, and files. If you know some of Explorer's tricks, you can maneuver through Explorer's display of your computer's data quite easily. For example, when you double-click your mouse over a folder, Explorer opens that folder and displays the folder's contents in the Explorer right-hand window.

To move up a level, that is, to close the folder and replace the window views with the previous closed folder's display, press the BACKSPACE key. This works as a shortcut to the Up One Level toolbar button. When you press BACKSPACE, Explorer restores the display back to its original level.

For example, Figure 840.1 shows Explorer before the user clicks the mouse button over the Corel50 folder to open it. When the user clicks the mouse over the Corel50 folder, its contents appear in the right-hand window, as shown in Figure 840.2. If the user then presses BACKSPACE, the Explorer window returns the display to the level it was in Figure 840.1, with the closed Corel50 folder.

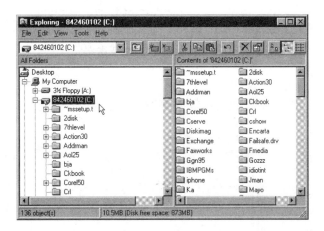

Figure 840.1 *About to open Corel50.*

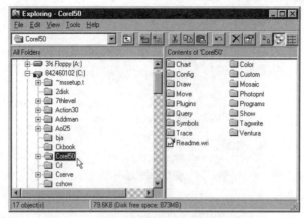

Figure 840.2 After opening Corel50.

841 Shutting Down with One Keystroke

Instead of clicking your mouse on the Start menu Shutdown option when you want to shut down Windows 95 and your computer, press ALT-F4 from Windows 95's Desktop. ALT-F4 displays the Shutdown menu and starts the process even if you have other program windows open. (As always, Shutdown gives you a chance to save any unsaved data before the shutdown occurs.)

842 Closing Multiple Folders in One Step

Within My Computer, you can open multiple folders and subfolders searching for files that you want to access. If you want to close every open folder, you can close them in one step by pressing your SHIFT key and clicking the subfolder window's Close button. Without the SHIFT keypress, only the current My Computer subfolder window closes.

843 Opening a Folder Branch within Explorer

If your right-hand Explorer window contains folders that contain other subfolders, a plus sign appears next to the folder to let you know this. If you want to see all of the current folder's subfolders, open its *branch*. To display the subfolder branch, Click your mouse on the plus sign to display the branch of subfolders, and click once again on the minus sign to close the branch. Figure 843.1 shows a closed Msapps subfolder branch and Figure 843.2 shows an open Msapps subfolder branch opened with one of the methods described in this tip.

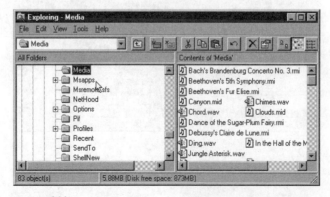

Figure 843.1 About to open the Msapps folder.

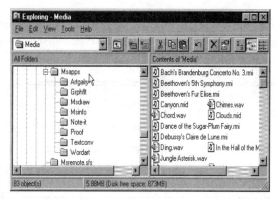

Figure 843.2 After opening Msapps.

Determining the Number of Files in a Folder   844

If you want to get a count of the number of files in a folder, click on the folder in your Explorer window and right-click your mouse. When you click your mouse on the Properties option, Windows 95 displays a Properties sheet such as the one shown in Figure 844. The Properties sheet tells the number of files and folders located in that folder.

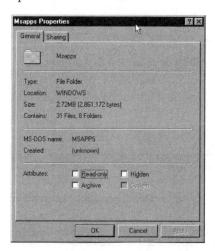

Figure 844 Describing the folder.

Quickly Selecting All But a Few Explorer Files   845

Within Explorer, there may be times when you want to perform an operation on all but a few specific files. In such cases, you can more easily *deselect* a few files than select a large number of them. First, select all the files in the right-hand window by pressing CTRL-A (for *All*). Explorer highlights every file and folder in the right-hand window. After you select every file, deselect the few files you do *not* want to include by holding your CTRL key and clicking your mouse on them. As you CTRL-click individual files and folders, Explorer deselects those files, leaving the remaining files selected. After you select the specific files you want, you then can start the delete, move, or copy command.

Quickly Exploring My Computer   846

If you prefer the Explorer's viewpoint instead of the My Computer's icon window, display an Explorer view of any folder in your My Computer window by pressing SHIFT and double-clicking your mouse on the My Computer folder's icon. If you select more than one folder by holding CTRL and clicking your mouse on two or more of them in the My Computer window, when you press SHIFT and CTRL, and double-click your mouse on the final folder, My Computer opens a different Explorer window for *each* of your selected folders.

847 Understanding Where Windows 95 Places Files

Table 847 describes where Windows 95 places its important files. Although the general Windows 95 end-user will not need to know where they are stored, many users will want to know this.

File	Directory
Application shortcuts	Windows\Start menu\Programs
Drivers	Windows\System
Font files	Windows\Fonts
Help files	Windows\Help
I/O subsystems	Windows\System\Iosubsys
MS-DOS commands	Windows\Command
PIF Files	Windows\Pif
Printer drivers	Windows\Spool\Printers
Setup and device files	Windows\Inf
Viewers	Windows\System\Viewers
VxDs uninstalled	Windows\System
VxDs installed	Windows\System\Vmm32
Windows 95 files	Windows

Table 847 Important Windows 95 file locations.

848 Viewing the Windows 95 Setup File

When you install Windows 95, its Setup installation program creates an installation log file named SETUPLOG.TXT. SETUPLOG.TXT contains setup information that describes the installation procedure, the files written to your disk, and errors that occurred during the setup (if any occurred). If an error does occur, Setup uses SETUPLOG.TXT to determine where the installation failed, then attempts to recover from that error. Here are a few of the items SETUPLOG.TXT contains:

- The beginning of the installation process
- The copying of installed files
- Directory used for Windows 95
- Options selected at Setup
- System restart commands
- System startup parameters

Note: *SETUPLOG.TXT contains the hidden-file attribute, so you will not see the file in MS-DOS directory listings.*

How Legacy Hardware Differs from Plug-And-Play | 849

As you have learned plug-and-play hardware makes it easy for you install and use new hardware. When you install a plug-and-play device, for example, the device communicates with other plug-and-play devices in your system to determine its proper settings. Because the plug-and-play devices communicate in this way, they eliminate your need to change jumpers or switches on the device that let you specify the device settings. Unfortunately, not all hardware devices support plug-and-play. When you install a non-plug-and-play device (Windows 95 documentation calls such devices legacy hardware), Windows 95 will perform a series of different tests on the device in an attempt to determine the device type and its manufacturer. By testing legacy hardware in this way, Windows 95 can determine which device drivers it needs to install. Unfortunately, with legacy devices, Windows 95 does not have any easy way to determine memory buffer addresses or interrupt request settings (IRQs). Instead, you must examine each card's switches to determine such settings. When you install Windows 95, the installation procedure performs legacy-hardware tests to determine your system's current hardware. As Windows 95 recognizes a legacy device, Windows 95 will install the corresponding device drivers.

Viewing Detected Hardware | 850

Windows 95 creates a file named DETLOG.TXT that detects your hardware and identifies the properties for it. Windows 95 updates DETLOG.TXT when you install Windows 95 and when you select from your Control Panel's Add New Hardware option. Windows 95 saves DETLOG.TXT in a file named DETLOG.OLD when you once again add new hardware. Therefore, if a crash occurs during the hardware's installation, Windows 95 can restore the system to its previous state. If you use Explorer and Quick View to look at DETLOG.TXT (found in the root directory on your Windows 95 disk), you'll find hardware settings and error messages that might be able to help you track advanced hardware device problems. To use DETLOG.TXT for troubleshooting, however, you must understand how advanced hardware settings (such as IRQs and DMAs) work with your system.

Note: DETLOG.TXT contains the hidden file attribute, so you will not see the file in MS-DOS directory listings.

Viewing the Windows 95 Startup Process | 851

Your Windows 95's disk drive contains a file named BOOTLOG.TXT (in its root directory) that contains a record of your most recent Windows 95 start up procedure. Setup first creates BOOTLOG.TXT, then Windows 95 updates the file every time you subsequently start Windows 95. BOOTLOG.TXT contains drivers and programs loaded during the startup process, as well as any errors that the Windows 95 start up process may have found.

Note: BOOTLOG.TXT contains the hidden file attribute, so you will not see the file in MS-DOS directory listings.

Here is a sample of BOOTLOG.TXT:

```
[000C0FB7]  Loading Device  = C:\WINDOWS\HIMEM.SYS
[000C0FB7]  LoadSuccess     = C:\WINDOWS\HIMEM.SYS
[000C0FB7]  Loading Device  = C:\WINDOWS\DBLBUFF.SYS
[000C0FB9]  LoadSuccess     = C:\WINDOWS\DBLBUFF.SYS
[000C0FB9]  Loading Device  = C:\WINDOWS\IFSHLP.SYS
[000C0FB9]  LoadSuccess     = C:\WINDOWS\IFSHLP.SYS
[000C0FB9]  Loading Device  = C:\WINDOWS\SETVER.EXE
[000C0FBA]  LoadSuccess     = C:\WINDOWS\SETVER.EXE
[000C0FE4]  Loading Vxd = VMM
```

```
[000C0FE5]  LoadSuccess  =  VMM
[000C0FE5]  Loading Vxd  =  C:\DBLSPACE.BIN
[000C0FE6]  LoadSuccess  =  C:\DBLSPACE.BIN
[000C0FE6]  Loading Vxd  =  IOS
[000C0FE7]  LoadSuccess  =  IOS
```

852 Understanding Object Linking and Embedding

OLE, or *Object Linking and Embedding*, lets you combine *objects* (any kind of data you can create with a program) to create a final document file. For example, you can embed a Paint picture and a wave sound file in a WordPad document. When you embed an object, Windows 95 places a copy of that object in your document. If you then double-click your mouse on the object, Windows 95 opens the object's associated application so you can edit the object. When you link an object, its associated application can change that object at any time. The changes to the object immediately appear in any document to which the object is linked. For example, if you embed an object, such as an Excel worksheet, into ten WordPad documents, then decide you want to change that object, you must edit all ten occurrences. If, however, you *link* an object to ten documents, then change the original object, all ten occurrences automatically update to reflect those changes. How you want to manage the object dictates whether you link or embed it. While not all Windows programs support OLE, many do, including most programs written specifically for Windows 95.

853 Using Object Embedding

Windows 95 applications normally contain an Insert menu Object option that displays an Insert Object dialog box (see Figure 853.1). When you click your mouse on the Create from File option, the dialog box changes to look like Figure 853.2. If you're working in a word processor, the Create from File option lets you embed an existing object to the word document. To embed an object into your current document, click your mouse on the dialog box's Browse button and locate the object you want to embed from the Browse dialog box. When you click your mouse on the object and then click on the OK button, Windows 95 embeds that object at the text cursor's current location in the original document. Once you embed an object into a document, you can later double-click your mouse on the object to edit it. For non-visual embedded objects, such as sound and video files, Windows 95 normally displays an icon at the object's location. When you double-click your mouse over the icon, Windows 95 plays the sound or video file. The Insert Object gives you a choice to see an icon, or the actual object if the program using the embedded object can display it.

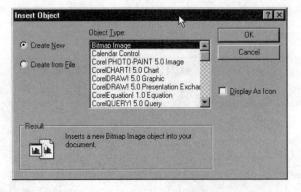

Figure 853.1 *The Insert Object dialog box.*

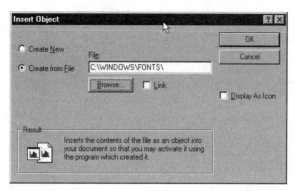

Figure 853.2 Selecting an object to embed.

Using Object Linking   854

To link the object (as opposed to embedding the object, as discussed in Tip 855), click your mouse on the Link option so a check appears in the Link's checkbox. Locate the object to link to your document, click your mouse on the dialog box's Browse button, and locate the object you want to link from the Browse dialog box. When you click your mouse on the object and then click on the OK button, Windows 95 links that object to the text cursor's current location in the original document.

After you link an object into a document, you can later double-click your mouse on that object to edit it. For non-visual embedded objects such as sound and video files, Windows 95 normally displays an icon at the object's location. When you double-click your mouse over the icon, Windows 95 plays the sound or video file. The Insert Object gives you a choice to see an icon or the actual object if the program using the embedded object can display the object. As you will learn in Tip 855, there are times when you will want to link objects while other times you want to embed objects.

When to Link or Embed an Object   855

Linked objects appear and behave just like embedded objects, except that linked objects consume less disk space. When you embed an object, Windows 95 places a copy of the object into the target document; when you link the object, Windows 95 places only a link to that object. Linked objects not only consume less disk space, but they also remain more current. If you link a graphic image to three documents, then use Paint to change that image, those three documents will contain the updated Paint image. If, however, you embed the Paint image into the three documents, changing one image will not affect the other ones.

How OLE Works   856

Windows 95 lets you embed or link objects from one document or program to another. Although not all applications support OLE, most Windows 95 applications do. The applications that support OLE are typically classified as *client* or *server* applications. This use of *client* and *server* differs from the network use of the terms (see Tip 759). A client is an application that can accept embedded or linked objects. WordPad, for example, is a client program.

A server is an application whose objects can be embedded or linked into another document. The Sound Recorder, which plays back .WAV sound files, is an example of a server. Some applications, such as Paint, are both a client and a server application because Paint can hold inserted objects as well as create objects that you can insert into other applications.

857 Creating a New Object from a File

If you want to insert a new object (one that does not yet exist) into a document file you are creating, you can start that object's associated program (such as Paint), create the object, save it, then insert it into the client application (such as WordPad). Such steps make inserting new objects a chore. Windows 95 gives you a shortcut method for creating and inserting new objects in one step. When you first select Insert Object, Figure 853.1's dialog box appears. If you select an object type from the list and click your mouse on the OK button, Windows 95 automatically starts that object's associated program, and you can create the object. When you click outside the object's editing area (do not select File Exit or File Save As), Windows 95 inserts that object into the client application. Therefore, if you're writing a letter in WordPad and want to embed a graphic image in your document, click your mouse on the Insert menu Object option and select a Paintbrush picture. WordPad starts Paint, and you can create the image. When you click outside the image's editing area, WordPad returns with the graphic image embedded (or linked) to your document.

858 Understanding VxD Device Drivers

A *VxD (Virtual Device Driver)* is a 32-bit *protected mode driver*, which manages a system resource such as a disk drive or a CD-ROM. Protected drivers often have fewer conflicts (with other device drivers) than the older 16-bit real device drivers used in MS-DOS and Windows 3.1. The *x* in *VxD* refers to a type of device driver. VDD is a virtual device display (video) driver, VTD is a virtual device timer driver, and VPD is a virtual device printer driver. Windows 95 is able to make each multitasking application, which is virtual and not *real*, think that it has its own printer, display, and so on, without affecting other running tasks. Here are the things that Windows 95's VxDs control:

- Caching of disks
- CD-ROM drives
- Disk drives
- DriveSpace (and DoubleSpace) compressions
- File systems
- Mice
- Network activities

859 Understanding 16-Bit based Drivers

If Windows 95 supported only VxDs, then none of your pre-Windows 95 MS-DOS or Windows 3.1 programs would run under Windows 95. Therefore, Windows 95 also supports 16-bit based drivers. 16-bit device drivers run in the Windows 3.1 cooperative multitasking environment (see tips 826 and 827). In order of importance, Microsoft wanted to achieve the following three 16-bit driver goals:

- Maintain compatibility
- Keep driver size reasonable
- Keep speed reasonable

Due to its third-place importance, if Microsoft needed to sacrifice speed to make a 16-bit driver work fully under Windows 95, Microsoft kept the compatibility and wasted execution speed to do so. Therefore, the 32-bit VxD drivers can run significantly faster than 16-bit driver-based programs, not just due to the wider data path, but also because Windows 95 must perform more compatibility conversions to make the 16-bit drivers work consistently.

Determining the Device Drivers Your System is Using — 860

If a device runs slower than you think it should, Windows 95 might be using a 16-bit driver for that device. If you want to see whether Windows 95 uses a 32- or 16-bit driver for a particular hardware device, perform these steps:

1. Open your Control Panel window.
2. To open the Systems Properties sheet, double-click your mouse on the System icon and choose the Device Manager tab.
3. Click your mouse on the plus sign next to the type of hardware you want to check.
4. Double-click the hardware whose driver you are curious about.
5. To display Figure 860's Driver page, click your mouse on the Driver tab. The Driver page lists every device driver used for that device. If the driver uses the .VxD filename extension, the driver is a 32-bit driver. If, however, the driver contains the .DRV filename extension, that drive is a 16-bit driver. Some devices, such as many display adapters, use both 16-bit and 32-bit drivers.

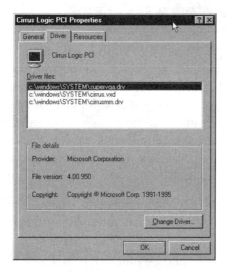

Figure 860 *Viewing device drivers.*

What to Do When Windows 95 is Using 16-Bit Drivers — 861

If a device experiences sluggishness, that device may use a 16-bit device driver. Sometimes you have no choice but to use the 16-bit driver because, perhaps due to your hardware's age, the hardware vendor just has not written a 32-bit driver yet. Therefore, you're forced to use the 16-bit driver. If you find 16-bit drivers, you may want to contact that driver's manufacturer to see if you can get a 32-bit Windows 95 driver. Check online services, such as CompuServe or the Microsoft Network because those online services often distribute updated driver files.

Understanding the System Monitor — 862

Windows 95 includes the *System Monitor* program that lets you monitor your system's network or disk access. Start the System Monitor program, shown in Figure 862, by clicking your mouse on the System Tools menu System Monitor option. When you first start System Monitor, the System Monitor window will be empty. Use the next few tips to activate System Monitor's services for particular resources.

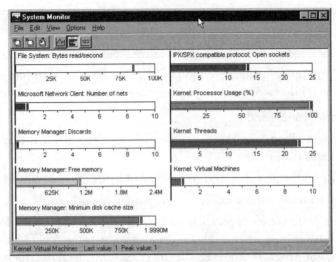

Figure 862 Running the System Monitor.

863 | Understanding the Windows 95 Kernel

The Windows 95 *kernel* is the heart of the Windows 95 operating system. The kernel is one of three core operating system components (the other two are the User component and the *GDI*, or *Graphical Device Interface* components). The kernel handles all the low-level operating system tasks such as threading management (see Tip 828), memory management, file I/O, and keyboard input. The kernel is responsible for loading programs and starting their execution when the user requests a program. To maintain compatibility, the kernel supports both 16-bit and 32-bit applications. Use the System Monitor program to monitor kernel activities if your system begins to slow down. Starting too many multitasking programs at once, for instance, can strain your system and slow down processing. When you start System Monitor, perform the following steps to monitor your kernel's usage:

1. Click on the Edit menu Add Item option to display Figure 863.1's Add Item dialog box.
2. Click your mouse on Kernel in the Category list to display three items: Processor usage (%), Threads, and Virtual Machines in the right-hand window's Item list.
3. Press and hold your CTRL key and click your mouse over each item to monitor each kernel item in the list.
4. To display Figure 863.2's System Monitor graphs, click your mouse on the OK button. (Your graphs may appear as line charts instead of bar charts. See Tip 872 to learn toolbar buttons that change the graph's appearance.)

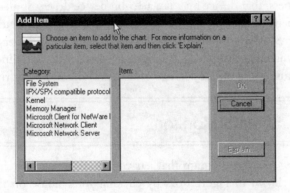

Figure 863.1 The Add Item dialog box.

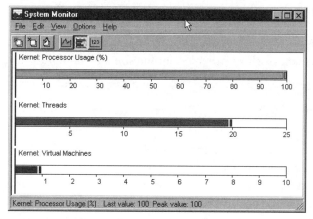

Figure 863.2 Monitoring three kernel items.

Monitoring the Windows 95 File System | 864

Use System Monitor to monitor your disk I/O activity to learn where speed and efficiency bottlenecks occur as you work with your computer. When you open the Add Item dialog box (see Tip 863) and Click your mouse on the File System category, you'll be able to select one or more of the following file system items to monitor in graph form:

- *Bytes read/second*: The number of bytes read per second
- *Bytes written/second*: The number of bytes written per second
- *Dirty data*: The amount of data still in the system cache that needs to be written to the disk
- *Reads/second*: The number of read requests the file system receives per second
- *Writes/second*: The number of write requests the file system receives per second

Improving File System Measurements | 865

If System Monitor indicates that your system is running slowly (when graph values lean towards the high end), try these suggestions to improve file system performance:

- Use Tip 394 to defragment your disk drives
- Click your mouse on the File System button on the Control Panel's System Properties sheet Performance page to adjust disk drive system properties
- Use ScanDisk (see Tip 421) to check for disk problems

Monitoring Windows 95 Memory Management | 866

Use System Monitor to track your computer's memory usage. When you click your mouse on System Manager's Add Item dialog box's Memory Manager Category list, System Monitor displays a list of several memory-related measurements for which you can request a graph-based analysis. Listed below are a few of the measurements you can track with System Monitor:

- Total allocated memory in your system
- The current value of your disk cache

- Amount of memory not currently used
- Minimum and maximum disk cache size
- Swap file measurements such as current swap file size and amount of usage

867 Optimizing Memory Management Measurements

The best way to gain memory manager improvements is to add more physical RAM (Random Access Memory) to your computer. Windows 95 requires only 4Mb of RAM; however, if you add more RAM, you'll notice tremendous speed improvements. If you add more than 16Mb of RAM, these speed improvements will continue, but at a smaller pace than they did between 4Mb and 16Mb. If you get poor system performance despite added RAM, you might be multitasking too many programs at one time. Although Windows 95 processes multitasking more efficiently and at greater volumes than did Windows 3.1, running too many graphics-intensive and processor-intensive programs at the same time will reduce memory management and performance speed.

868 Changing System Monitor Graph Types

System Monitor provides different graph views of your system's measurements. The default view is a bar chart, as shown in Figure 868.1. If you click your mouse on the View menu Line Charts option, System Monitor changes to a line graph display, as shown in Figure 868.2. The View menu Numeric Charts option produces a numeric display for each system resource as Figure 868.3 shows.

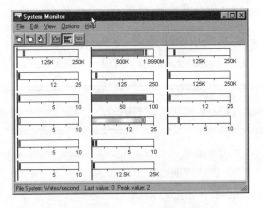

Figure 868.1 Viewing bar charts.

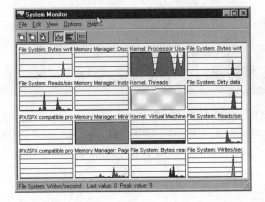

Figure 868.2 Viewing line charts.

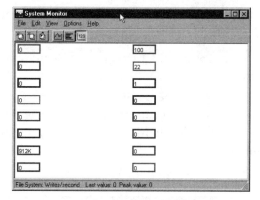

Figure 868.3 Viewing numeric charts.

Changing a Measurement's Chart Options — 869

Use the Edit menu to add, remove, or edit the chart's monitored values. The Edit menu Add Item option adds additional measurements to the monitoring windows. The Edit menu Remove Item option removes measurements you no longer want to track. The Edit menu Edit Item option produces Figure 869.1's Edit Item dialog box. When you click over an Edit Item's value, System Monitor displays Figure 869.2's Chart Options dialog box in which you can change a measurement's display color and scale value.

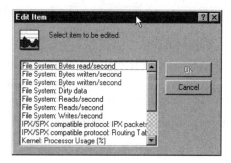

Figure 869.1 Selecting a value to edit.

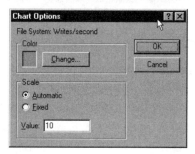

Figure 869.2 Editing a measurement value's display.

Changing the System Monitor's Chart Interval — 870

System Monitor continually updates its charts to reflect your system's performance. Every three seconds, System Monitor checks the measurement values that you've chosen for the graph's display. If you want to reduce this interval for better performance monitoring, or increase the interval so that System Monitor consumes fewer system resources, perform these steps:

1. Click your mouse on the Options menu Chart option. System Monitor will display Figure 870's Options dialog box.
2. Drag the slider control left to reduce the update interval so that System Monitor monitor's your system resources as often as every quarter of a second. Drag the slider control right to increase the update interval so that System Monitor monitor's your system resources as infrequently as every ten minutes.
3. To save your changes, click your mouse on the OK button.

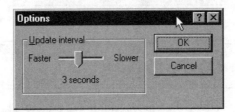

Figure 870 Change interval settings with the Options dialog box.

871 Monitoring a Remote Computer

Network system administrators can use System Monitor to monitor another computer's resources. To monitor other computers to which you have system administration access, open the File menu Connect dialog box and type the remote computer's name. (If, for some odd reason, the dialog box does not let you browse your network to select another computer on the network, you must type the remote computer's name.) When you click your mouse on the OK button, the system resources that you monitor will belong to the remote computer and not to your own.

872 Using the System Monitor Toolbar

The System Monitor View menu Toolbar option hides and displays System Monitor's toolbar. Table 872 explains each of the toolbar buttons.

Button	Purpose
	Adds a system resource for monitoring
	Removes a system resource from monitoring
	Edits a system resource's monitoring display
	Displays line charts
	Displays bar charts
	Displays numeric charts

Table 872 System Monitor's toolbar buttons.

873 Looking for Bottlenecks

System Monitor is not a tool for fine-tuning a system that works fairly efficiently. Use System Monitor to find major bottlenecks in your system. If you run System Monitor continuously every time you use your computer, you will not be utilizing your computer as efficiently as you could. System Monitor is a check-up tool that might be good to use after you make each full-system backup. Once you make the full backup, you'll have safely stored your complete file system on tape so that you can make file system changes and restore the system if something goes wrong.

After you run System Monitor a few times, you'll gain a good understanding of your system's normal performance. You will notice if a measurement varies from its normal value, and thus, spot problems as they occur. A few items to look for when using System Monitor are listed below:

- Monitor the kernel to check for application memory leaks. If a program, such as Word for Windows 2.0, consumes additional memory the longer you use the program, you should shut down the program and restart the program every hour or two of use. Even better (although time-consuming), you can restart Windows 95 every hour or two to ensure that your memory is as uncluttered as possible.

- Add RAM if your Memory Manager statistics consistently look full.

- If your Memory Manager Page Faults value stays high, you may be running a program that consumes more memory than your computer is capable of handling, even with disk swapping in place.

- You may have to change or update network protocol drivers if the IPX/SPX values remain too high.

- If the NetWare statistics run high, check your network server to make sure the server is not running unnecessary drivers.

874 Improving Paging Performance

Windows 95 uses a *demand-paging virtual memory system*. Basically, this fancy term means that Windows 95 moves pages (sections) of memory to and from the disk during multitasking so that each multitasking program thinks that it has access to as much as 2 gigabytes (2 billion bytes) of RAM when you don't really have anywhere near that much.

System Monitor's listed Page Faults, Page-Ins, and Page-Outs performance items values become high when you begin to experience paging strains. You have only two choices to make if paging starts slowing down your computer: Add more RAM or multitask fewer programs at one time.

875 Why Adding Memory Improves System Performance

Added RAM gives Windows 95 more breathing room to manage multitasking programs and files. Windows 95 uses RAM for a tremendous number of separate and distinct storage areas. For example, Windows 95 uses RAM to hold running programs, program data, VCACHE information, device drivers, video memory blocks, boot-up instructions, messages routed to and from multitasking tasks, OLE messages between OLE clients and servers, and network messages routed from the network.

As your RAM fills up, Windows 95 begins to page RAM to disk drive memory in order to make additional room for critical memory requirements. As you multitask programs, Windows 95 uses memory more and more. The most active task must be in memory and not on the disk's paged swap file; therefore, Windows 95 loads and saves pages of the swap file as you work inside Windows 95 and run various programs.

When you add RAM, Windows 95 reduces swapping to the disk drive, which reduces paging to the disk drive. This allows Windows 95 to process more data in RAM which is quicker than disk storage. The added RAM greatly improves your overall system performance speeds.

876 Understanding the Windows 95 Registry

The Windows 95 *registry* is a database that contains computer settings. The registry contains your hardware setup information, installed application information, default file names, user settings, and current Plug and Play specifications. Whereas Window 3.1 used .INI files to hold system and program settings, Windows 95 uses the single registry to hold such information so that neither you, nor an installation program, needs to modify files when updating your system's hardware or software. Even when you change your computer's settings inside the Control Panel window, Control Panel updates the registry to ensure that all your changes are recorded and that other applications can read the registry to find the current settings.

877 Windows 95 Still Updates .INI Files for Compatibility

As you know, Windows 95 makes every effort to support older 16-bit Windows 3.1 and MS-DOS-based programs. To do so, Windows 95 must keep .INI files in order, even though the registry is a better central repository for hardware and software information. Therefore, if you know that a Windows 3.1 program uses an .INI file, as most do, you can safely run and install that program under Windows 95. Windows 95 updates the registry and the necessary .INI files so that 32-bit Windows 95 programs, as well as older programs, can access the information.

878 When to Edit the Windows Registry

The registry, a central repository of system-wide data, is not a beginner's playing field. If a user messes up the registry, Windows 95 will not work well at best, and will probably cause several problems, including automatic and unexpected shutdowns, depending on the user's actions.

Windows 95 includes a registry editing program named REGEDIT.EXE that you can use to make direct modifications to the registry. Do not use REGEDIT unless you know what you are doing, or you could damage your system beyond repair. The REGEDIT program includes a Registry menu Export option that you can use to make a copy of your current registry file, and if needed, import that file to restore the registry. Such a backup will be invaluable if something goes wrong with your registry.

879 Starting the Windows 95 Registry Editor

REGEDIT is a Windows 95 program, but you must use the Start menu Run option to start the program. To discourage users from running the program and accidentally destroying their registry's integrity, Windows 95 does not install REGEDIT on the start menu. To start REGEDIT to modify or view your registry, perform these steps:

1. Click your mouse on the Taskbar's Start button.
2. Display the Run dialog box by clicking your mouse on the Start menu Run option.
3. Type **REGEDIT** and press ENTER. Windows 95 starts REGEDIT and will display the initial REGEDIT window shown in Figure 879.

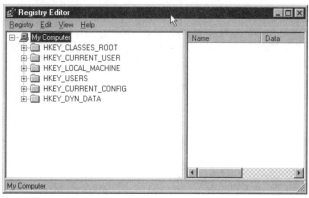

Figure 879 *The Registry editor's opening window.*

Printing a Copy of Your Registry's Contents 880

Your registry is extremely large, and you have little reason to print the entire registry although you can if you want. However, users more often print portions of their registry, especially before making changes to those portions of the registry. The printout gives the users a chance to restore that part of the registry if something goes wrong. To make a printout of your registry, perform these steps:

1. Start the registry editor (see Tip 879).
2. If you want to print only a selected portion of your registry (strongly recommended), locate the registry branch you want to print by clicking your mouse over registry folders and subfolders until you find what you want to print.
3. Select the Registry menu Print option to display the Print dialog box.
4. In the dialog box's Print Range section, click your mouse on the Selected branch option to print a portion of the registry, or leave the setting on the All option to print the entire registry. (If you leave the option set to All, you'll be printing for a while because of the registry's great length.)
5. Type the registry branch name you want to print. Branch names are typically very long and you must type the exact branch. If, however, you selected a branch before beginning to print, the registry editor already stored your selected branch's full name in the Selected branch text box so that you do not have to type the long branch name.
6. To start printing, click your mouse on the OK button.

Understanding the Basic Registry Entries 881

The registry isn't extremely complicated once you understand its main entries. Table 881 explains each of the registry's main entries, which you'll see in your registry's left-hand window when you start REGEDIT. The main entries make up the highest level in the hierarchical registry database.

Entry	Description
HKEY_CLASSES_ROOT	Points to the registry's HKEY_LOCAL_MACHINE branch that describes current software settings such as OLE mappings, shortcuts, and user interface settings.
HKEY_CURRENT_USER	Points to the branch that describes the current user.

Table 881 *The registry's main entries. (continued on the following page)*

Entry	Description
HKEY_LOCAL_MACHINE	Points to the registry branch that contains information about the current computer's hardware and software settings.
HKEY_USERS	Points to the registry branch that describes all users who log onto the computer and their profile settings.
HKEY_CURRENT_CONFIG	Points to the registry branch that contains information about hardware currently attached to the computer.
HKEY_DYN_DATA	Points to the registry branch that contains dynamic Plug and Play information which updates, as needed, to reflect Plug and Play devices you attach or remove from your system.

Table 881 The registry's main entries. (continued from the previous page)

882 Taking a Close Look at HKEY_LOCAL_MACHINE

HKEY_LOCAL_MACHINE contains your computer's settings information such as a list of your installed hardware and software. The registry makes this information available when you log into Windows 95, either in a stand-alone mode or on a network. Your device drivers, software, and Windows 95 use HKEY_LOCAL_MACHINE information to adjust settings that match the computer's hardware and software. The registry's HKEY_LOCAL_MACHINE entry is a general category that contains the following subkey, or more specific, pieces of information:

- Config
- Enum
- hardware
- Network
- Security
- SOFTWARE
- System

As Figure 882 shows, when you open the HKEY_LOCAL_MACHINE registry branch, these subkey values appear. Tips 885 through 891 explain these subkey details.

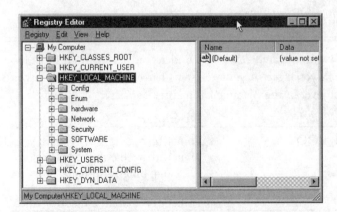

Figure 882 The registry's HKEY_LOCAL_MACHINE category.

Editing a Registry Entry's Binary Value   883

Although it's best and safest to let Windows 95 change your registry, the REGEDIT program lets you make specific changes. Some programs do not update the registry properly (the software's installation instructions should explain if this is the case) due to the program's esoteric nature. Generally, such programs are hardware-specific, non Plug and Play compatible, device drivers that require your intervention to install properly.

The registry is a hierarchical database with many layers of categories and subcategories just as your disk drive is a collection of folders and subfolders. Each value in the registry contains a key that labels that value. To access a value, search down the registry or enter the key name directly and let the registry locate the data value for you. Keys are high-level value names. Subkeys, like subfolders, describe more specific values.

The registry's values appear when you view the registry's lowest levels. The registry's right-hand window displays those details. The registry is a database, and at its lowest levels, contains three kinds of data: Binary values, string values, and DWORD values. Each kind of value refers to the value's stored data type. When you change a value, you must retain the value's data type. For example, Figure 883.1 shows a registry's details in the right-hand window for a registry subkey entry named 01. Most of this entry's values are string values because the right-hand window displays the values as strings enclosed in quotation marks with "ab" icons that indicate the string data type. The single binary value, named ConfigFlags, holds 00 00 00 00, and you must use that format when changing that binary value.

To change a binary value such as the ConfigFlags value (don't make this change, just follow along), perform these steps:

1. Right-click your mouse over the binary value's name (in this case, the name is ConfigFlags) to display the right-click menu.
2. Click your mouse on the right-click menu's Modify option to change the value. The registry displays Figure 883.2's Edit Binary Value dialog box from which you can change the binary value. Binary values appear in a two-character *hexadecimal* (base 16) notation. Your software or hardware's installation instructions should give you the proper values to enter. The hexadecimal numbers make entering binary values easier than if you entered those values using a strict binary (base-2) notation.
3. Enter the two-character values to change the binary entry until you've made the required changes.
4. Click your mouse on the OK button to implement your changes.

Again, be warned that you can only change these binary values when you know exactly which hexadecimal values to enter.

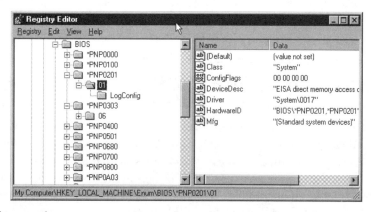

Figure 883.1 String and binary values.

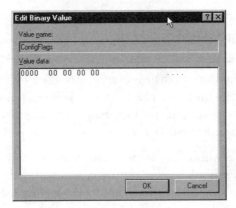

Figure 883.2 Editing a binary value.

884 Editing a Registry Entry's String Value

When you right-click over a registry's string value and select the right-click menu Modify option, the registry displays an Edit String Value dialog box such as the one shown in Figure 884. The dialog box contains the name of the value you want to change and displays the current value in the Value data text box. You can make changes to the current string value or replace the entire string with a new string.

Note: *Although the registry displays string values in quotation marks, never type the quotation marks when entering or changing string values with the Edit String Value dialog box.*

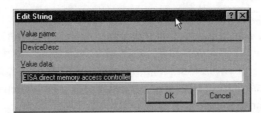

Figure 884 Editing a string value.

885 Taking a Close Look at HKEY_LOCAL_MACHINE\hardware

HKEY_LOCAL_MACHINE contains the hardware subkey that describes your math coprocessor, as well as all serial ports used in programs such as HyperTerminal. When a Windows 95 application gives you a selection list of available serial ports, the application retrieves the available serial hardware information from the HKEY_LOCAL_MACHINE's hardware subkey.

886 Taking a Close Look at HKEY_LOCAL_MACHINE\Config

HKEY_LOCAL_MACHINE contains the Config subkey that holds information about your computer's various hardware profile configurations. The configurations (see Tips 307 through 309) include font and display settings, as well as available printers for each configuration. Windows 95 refers to each user's profile settings to select an appropriate hardware configuration to use. If the user changes his or her profile (using the Control Panel's System Properties sheet to change to a different hardware profile), Windows 95 loads that hardware profile from the Config subkey to reconfigure Windows 95 instantly to that profile's available hardware.

Taking a Close Look at HKEY_LOCAL_MACHINE\Enum — 887

HKEY_LOCAL_MACHINE contains the *Enum* (for *enumerated*) subkey that holds information about your computer's low-level hardware such as the BIOS (*Basic Input/Output System*), bus settings, installed disk drives, network protocol, and floppy disk drives. Enum's subkeys (see Figure 887), show the various categories of information contained in the Enum subkey branch. Figure 887's right-hand window contains additional subkeys that ultimately hold data values rather than specific information.

Each of the Enum's entries, for example, the hard disk entries, contain manufacturer information whenever possible (and when given such information at installation time) so that the Control Panel's System Properties sheet can display manufacturer contact information that you can use when diagnosing problems with your computer.

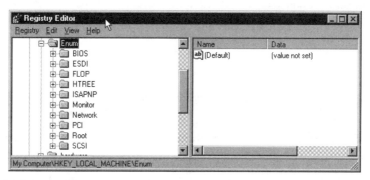

Figure 887 *The Enum subkey branches.*

Taking a Close Look at the HKEY_LOCAL_MACHINE\Network — 888

HKEY_LOCAL_MACHINE contains the Network subkey that holds information about your network. This registry entry changes depending on the user who logs on to Windows 95 and to the network. The Network entry describes the user's profile settings such as the user name, network provider (the client software), server log on validation, and network policies.

Taking a Close Look at HKEY_LOCAL_MACHINE\Software — 889

HKEY_LOCAL_MACHINE contains the Software subkey that holds information about the computer's installed software. This registry entry contains only software that is registry-aware and that can make changes to the registry. No matter who logs on to the computer, the Software subkey contains the same information unless the user changes the software by installing additional software or removing existing software.

One of the most interesting purposes of the Software subkey is its association of filename extensions to applications and descriptions. The Software's Classes subkey contains all registered software filename extensions, such as .AVI and .DOC, and their associated application programs. Therefore, although you should normally use your Control Panel to associate extensions to programs, you can make specific edits to such associations inside the registry, such as changing a word processor file associated with the .DOC extension.

890 Taking a Close Look at HKEY_LOCAL_MACHINE\System

One of the most eclectic subkeys in the registry is the HKEY_LOCAL_MACHINE's System subkey that contains information on the following items:

- Computer network name
- File system
- Keyboard layout (including the language used)
- Multimedia resources
- Network client providers
- Printer and monitor parameters
- System Monitor statistics requested (see Tip 862)
- Time zone information
- Virtual device driver filenames

891 Taking a Close Look at HKEY_LOCAL_MACHINE\hardware

HKEY_LOCAL_MACHINE contains the hardware subkey that holds information on your serial ports and floating-point math coprocessor if your computer's math coprocessor is separate from your CPU. The hardware subkey contains very little information because the Enum, Network, and System subkeys describe most of your computer's hardware components and how those components relate to Windows 95.

892 Taking a Close Look at HKEY_CLASSES_ROOT

HKEY_CLASSES_ROOT points to the branches within HKEY_LOCAL_MACHINE that describe software settings such as filename associations. In addition, HKEY_CLASSES_ROOT describes the user's interface, OLE capabilities and mappings, Briefcase settings, and Windows 95 shortcuts. HKEY_CLASSES_ROOT often comprises the largest registry entry because each of your Windows 95 installed software components (those with some kind of registry support) appear in the entry.

893 Taking a Close Look at HKEY_CURRENT_USER

Whereas HKEY_USERS contains entries for all possible users of the system (those with profiles), HKEY_CURRENT_USER contains the current user's profile information that applications can use such as:

- Control Panel settings
- Event labels (the text that Windows 95 displays when certain events occur)
- Keyboard
- Language
- Network information
- Software settings

894 Taking a Close Look at HKEY_USERS

HKEY_USERS contains information on each user who can log on to the computer's network and Windows 95. Some of the information is *generic* which means that the information is available to all users and includes applications settings and Desktop configurations. Other information is specific to individual users. HKEY_USERS keeps current a list of network computers available or that have been available recently. All HKEY_USERS application settings take precedence over similar settings in HKEY_LOCAL_MACHINE because the current user may require special machine or application settings that the general user does not require.

895 Taking a Close Look at HKEY_CURRENT_CONFIG

Whereas HKEY_LOCAL_MACHINE\Config contains a collection of machine configurations, HKEY_CURRENT_CONFIG describes the current computer configuration obtained for the current user based on the user's profile and settings. The following lists some of the information that HKEY_CURRENT_CONFIG contains:

- Display information, such as resolution
- Default Fonts
- Mouse behavior
- Printer settings

896 Taking a Close Look at HKEY_DYN_DATA

The registry is a large database. The registry is so large, in fact, that Windows 95 cannot possibly load the entire database into RAM and still have room for multitasking with acceptable performance. Therefore, when Windows 95 needs a registry setting, Windows 95 must load that setting from your disk drive. Although caching helps speed the disk access, registry access can be slow. Therefore, Windows 95 keeps several registry data values in RAM at all times. The in-RAM settings are located in the HKEY_DYN_DATA entry. For example, HKEY_DYN_DATA\Config contains a RAM-based copy of the current computer's machine configuration. Windows 95 changes HKEY_DYN_DATA every time the user makes a configuration change so that Windows 95 keeps HKEY_DYN_DATA up to date at all times, both on disk and in RAM memory.

897 Entries You May Actually Edit

Although you can make changes to any registry entry, you should do so with caution. A large portion of Windows 95 users will use Windows 95 for years and never need to change a registry setting or even know that the registry exists. You may have to change the registry, for instance, due to a unique hardware device's installation instructions in order to allow that device behave a particular way under Windows 95. When you make changes to the registry, especially if you share a computer with other users, keep your changes limited to your specific profile's entries, such as those found in the HKEY_LOCAL_MACHINE\System\CurrentControlSet\control which describes your machine and profile settings but does not reflect other users at all. For example, when Microsoft first released Windows 95, users in India could not properly set their Windows 95 time zone using the ordinary Time Zone dialog box. The users could go into the Time Zone Information stored in HKEY_LOCAL_MACHINE\System\CurrentControlSet\control and change their time zone settings.

898 Understanding REGEDIT Command-Line Options

If you want to change the way REGEDIT starts, you can use REGEDIT's command-line options. Instead of typing **REGEDIT** from within the Start menu Run option, you can type one of the following REGEDIT formats:

```
REGEDIT [/L:system] [/R:user] file1.reg [,file2.reg]...

REGEDIT [/L:system] [/R:user] /e file3.reg [regkey]

REGEDIT [/L:system] [/R:user] /c file2.reg
```

Table 898 explains each of REGEDIT's command-line arguments.

Command-Line Argument	Description
/L:*system*	The location of SYSTEM.DAT (the registry's system information backup file created at each Windows 95 startup)
/R:*user*	The location of USER.DAT (the registry's user information backup file created at each Windows 95 startup)
file1.reg	One or more .REG registry files that you want to import into the registry
/c *file3.reg*	The file to which you want the registry to export
regkey	The starting registry key from which to export if you only want to export part of the registry
/c *file2.reg*	The .REG registry file with which you want to replace the current registry

Table 898 REGEDIT's command-line arguments.

899 Using the Registry to Change Your Computer Name

As you have learned, within a network, each computer must have a unique name. If you want to change the name your computer uses for network access, modify the string value found at the following subkey:

HKEY_LOCAL_MACHINE\System\CurrentControlSet\ComputerName\ComputerName

900 Exporting Your Registry Database

If you want to learn more about the registry, perhaps you should export the registry to a file that you can view and edit instead of using REGEDIT to work with (and perhaps harm) the registry itself. When you export your registry, you send your registry to a text file that you can look at with WordPad, another text editor, or a word processor. Exported registry files make good backups because you can import an exported registry file to restore the registry if you wish.

To export the registry file, perform these steps:

1. Start REGEDIT (see Tip 879).
2. Click your mouse on the Registry menu Export Registry File option. REGEDIT will display the Export Registry File dialog box as shown in Figure 900.

3. Select a path and type a filename for the exported registry file.
4. Click your mouse on the Export range's All option if you want to export the entire registry file. Click your mouse on the Export range's Selected branch option and type that branch's key if you want to export only a selected portion of the registry.
5. To start the registry export, click your mouse on the Save button.

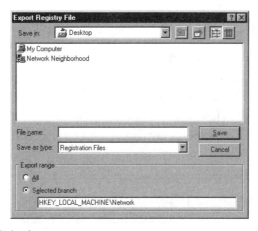

Figure 900 *The Export Registry File dialog box.*

Viewing an Exported Registry Database   901

If you want to view an exported registry file, use WordPad or another text editor to look at the file. The exported registry file is a text file but uses a .REG filename extension to indicate that the file contains registry information. Each entry in the registry appears in the file and each entry contains its associated key. Figure 901 shows a registry file loaded into WordPad. Notice how each value in the file has an associated key. The text file does not visually show the registry's hierarchical levels as well as REGEDIT does because REGEDIT displays the registry as a series of folders and subfolders. Nevertheless, the bracketed values in the exported registry represent keys for each data value that follows.

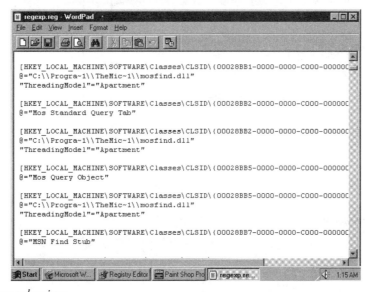

Figure 901 *Viewing an exported registry.*

902 — Importing Your Registry Database

When you import a registry database, you overwrite your registry, or part of your registry, with the imported file that you or someone else previously exported. Perhaps you want to restore part or all of a previous registry. When you want to import a registry file, perform these steps:

1. Start REGEDIT (see Tip 879).
2. Click your mouse on the Registry menu Import Registry File option. REGEDIT displays the Import Registry File dialog box which is nothing more than a standard Windows 95 open dialog box.
3. Select a path and type a filename to import.
4. To start the import process, click your mouse on the OK button. The imported file replaces your registry's contents. If you export only part of a registry into the import file, REGEDIT replaces only that portion of the registry.

903 — Understanding Registry Files

Figure 903 illustrates how the registry gets its database information. The registry is a central repository of information about your system's hardware and software settings. Windows 95 re-examines your system and makes updates to the registry if needed (in case you've installed or removed hardware) every time you start up the system. Given the wide range of registry sources, it's no wonder that the registry is so large.

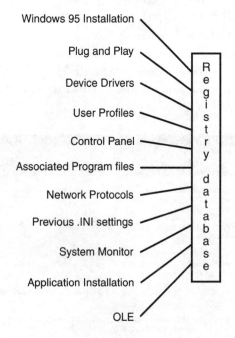

Figure 903 *The registry's information sources.*

Backing Up and Restoring Your Registry Database — 904

As you have learned, your system registry contains information essential to Windows 95. As such, you should always keep a current backup copy of your registry. Before you read further, this is a good time to perform Tip 900 and export your registry to a text file. Save that file to tape or to a diskette so you'll have a copy of your registry as it currently appears. Three ways to back up and restore your registry database:

- Export the registry to a text file and later import the text file to restore the registry.

- If you cannot start Windows 95 because of a badly corrupted registry, use your Windows 95 startup disk to start Windows 95 and run the startup disk's REGEDIT program to import one of your saved registry files.

- Every time you startup your system, Windows 95 makes a backup of your registry in two hidden files named SYSTEM.DA0 and USER.DA0 and places new versions of the files in SYSTEM.DA0 and USER.DA0. If your registry becomes damaged, copy SYSTEM.DA0 and USER.DA0 over your Windows directory SYSTEM.DAT and USER.DAT and you will restore your registry to its most recent successful startup.

Finding a Registry Entry or Value — 905

Due to the large size of your registry, you may want to use the registry's search capabilities to search for specific values to change or view. When you click your mouse on the Edit menu Find option, REGEDIT will display the Find dialog box shown in Figure 905. You can search through the entire registry, through keys only (the name of entries), values only (for binary values), and string data only, by narrowing the search with the "Look at" options.

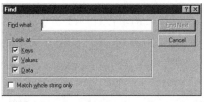

Figure 905 *Finding registry information.*

Renaming a Registry Entry — 906

The Edit menu Rename option lets you rename registry keys. Although you should leave the keys alone in normal situations, renaming a registry key is a good alternative to deleting a key. For example, if you are going to delete a key because you no longer have a certain hardware board but portions of that board's driver still reside in your registry, rename the key to a name such as DELETE_ME, exit REGEDIT, and restart your computer. If everything seems to work for a while then you know that you can probably safely perform Tip 907 and delete the entry.

Deleting a Registry Entry — 907

Use the Edit menu Delete option to delete registry entries. As mentioned in Tip 906, you should leave your registry keys alone in normal situations, although you may have to delete a key because you no longer have certain hardware but portions of that hardware's driver files still reside in your registry.

Note: *The registry does not send deleted keys to the Recycle Bin but deletes the keys as soon as you confirm the delete.*

908 | Adding a Registry Entry

To add a registry entry, right-click your mouse over an existing key name. The registry displays a menu from which you can select the New option. The New option produces an additional menu that contains these options:

- *Key*: Adds a key to your left-hand window so you can add an additional branch to your registry
- *String Value*: Adds a string value (with the string icon) to your right-hand window so you can add a string value to the currently selected key
- *Binary Value*: Adds a binary value (with the binary icon) to your right-hand window so you can add a binary value to the currently selected key
- *DWORD Value*: Adds a DWORD value (with the binary icon) to your right-hand window so you can add a DWORD value to the currently selected key

DWORD values are special binary *double-word values*. A PC's word size is 16-bits or 2 characters wide. Therefore, a double-word is 32-bits or 4 characters wide and holds a hexadecimal value from 0 to 0FFFF hex. Some registry entries require fixed DWORD-sized values instead of the variable-length data size that the binary values provide.

909 | Not Sure About a File Type? See HKEY_CLASSES_ROOT

As you work with files, you may come across a file type you don't recognize by its associated icon, or perhaps, you are not familiar with the file's extension. One operation you can perform with the registry is to learn more about a file's contents. Perform these steps to use the registry to view a file's information:

1. Use the Start menu Run option to start REGEDIT.
2. Open the HKEY_CLASSES_ROOT branch by clicking your mouse over HKEY_CLASSES_ROOT's plus sign.
3. Locate the extension you do not recognize.
4. Open the extension's file folder by clicking that extension's folder icon. The registry's right-hand window will display information about the file. Generally, the right-hand window will explain the associated program for that file. Figure 909 shows that the .GRA filename extension belongs to the MS-DOS Graph 5.0 program. (MS-DOS Graph is a Microsoft product that Microsoft embeds in the Office product line to display graphs.)

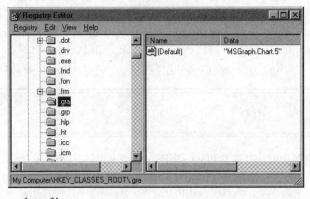

Figure 909 *Use the registry to learn about files.*

Changing the Label Windows 95 Uses to Reference an Event | 910

In Tip 291, you learned how to assign sounds to different Windows 95 events. An event is a mouse click, a window opening, or a keypress. To assign sounds to events, you used the Sounds Properties dialog box shown in Figure 910.1. If you have difficulty remembering what a specific event means, you can change that event's name. To change event names, perform these steps:

1. Use the Start menu Run option to start REGEDIT.
2. Open the HKEY_CURRENT_USER branch by clicking your mouse over HKEY_CURRENT_USER's plus sign.
3. Open the subkey branch named AppEvents by clicking your mouse over the AppEvents plus sign.
4. Open the subkey branch named EventLabels by clicking your mouse over the EventLabels plus sign.
5. Click your mouse over the event you want to change.
6. Right-click your mouse over the right-hand window's event description and select the Modify option.
7. Type a new description for the event. Figure 910.2 shows the Open program event being changed.
8. To save your changes, click your mouse on the OK button and close the registry.

Note: *Most users will never need to rename an event. You might, however, want to use this section of the registry to delete one or more event descriptions that another program added to your registry but you no longer use. To delete the event, simply click your mouse over the event's folder and choose the Edit menu delete option.*

Figure 910.1 *Adding sounds to events.*

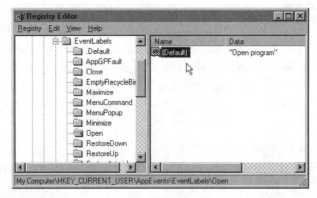

Figure 910.2 Changing an event's description.

911 Using the Registry to Control Your Keyboard's Responsiveness

Windows 95 uses two registry values to control the keyboard's responsiveness. Their descriptions are as follows:

- *Keyboard delay*: The time it takes for Windows 95 to begin repeating a key once you press the key
- *Keyboard speed*: The speed at which Windows 95 repeats a key you hold down

To change these settings, choose the right-click menu Modify option on the following values:

- HKEY_CURRENT_USER\Control Panel\Keyboard\KeyboardDelay
- HKEY_CURRENT_USER\Control Panel\Keyboard\KeyboardSpeed

For maximum performance, set the KeyboardDelay value to 0 and the KeyboardSpeed value to 31. To slow down the keyboard's responsiveness and repeat rate, change KeyboardDelay to 3 and the KeyboardSpeed to 0.

912 Using the Registry to Control the Cursor Blink Rate

You may use the registry to speed up or slow down your text cursor's blink rate. On some laptops, the text cursor is difficult to find until you slow down the blink rate. To slow down the blink rate, set the following registry subkey value to 200:

HKEY_CURRENT_USER\Control Panel\Desktop\CursorBlinkRate

To increase the blink rate's speed, change the value to 1200.

913 Using the Registry to Control the Screen Saver Interval

As you have learned, Windows 95 waits for a specified interval of no activity before it starts its screen saver. The registry contains the time interval, in seconds, which you want Windows 95 to pause before starting the screen saver.

To change the timing of this delay, assign a different value, in seconds, to the following subkey value:

HKEY_CURRENT_USER\Control Panel\Desktop\ScreenSaveTimeout

For example, if you assigned 300 to the subkey (for 300 seconds), Windows 95 starts the screen saver only if keyboard inactivity goes beyond five minutes.

Note: *Two additional subkey values, ScreenSavePower and ScreenSaveLowPowerTimeout, determine the waiting period before the Energy Star's power saving feature (if enabled) begins or enters a stand-by mode.*

Using the Registry to Control Screen Saver Password Protection — 914

As you have learned, Windows 95 lets you password protect your screen saver. If you want to turn on or off the screen saver's password protection, you can do so from within the registry. Change the following subkey value

HKEY_CURRENT_USER\ControlPanel\Desktop\ScreenSaveUsePassword

to 0 to disable the password protection and to 1 to enable the password protection.

Using the Registry to Tile or Center Wallpaper — 915

Figure 915.1 shows a Desktop with tiled wallpaper and Figure 915.2 shows the same wallpaper centered on the Desktop. Set the following registry value to 1 to tile your Desktop's wallpaper and 0 to center your Desktop's wallpaper:

HKEY_CURRENT_USER\Control Panel\Desktop\TileWallPaper

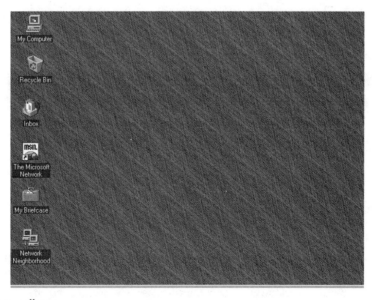

Figure 915.1 *Tiled Desktop wallpaper.*

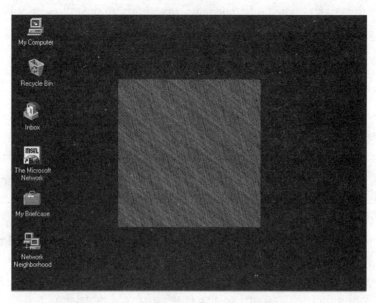

Figure 915.2 The same wallpaper centered.

916 — Using the Registry to Specify the Wall Paper You Desire

As you have learned, Windows 95 lets you specify a file's contents which you want to use for a wallpaper that appears on your system's desktop. When you change the following subkey's string value to a full path and bitmap filename, Windows 95 uses that file for your wallpaper:

>HKEY_CURRENT_USER\Control Panel\Desktop\WallPaper

Although you can change the wallpaper from within the Control Panel's Display Properties sheet, the registry is often quicker, especially if you stay in the registry and update other values while there.

917 — Using the Registry to Control Video Resolution

Although your Control Panel's Display Properties sheet provides a preview of your screen when you change your video resolution, you can also change your screen's resolution from within the registry. You may want to change the registry value if you are already working within the registry and doing something else.

Change the following registry subkey value to your desired screen resolution:

>HKEY_LOCAL_MACHINE\Config\0001\Display\Settings\Resolution

Enter the resolution as a string value that describes both the vertical and horizontal pixels you desire. For example, you would change the resolution to "800, 600" if you wanted to display 800 pixels across the screen and 600 pixels down the screen. Obviously, your video adapter and screen must be capable of supporting the resolution you enter. Figure 917 shows this subkey value window and its resolution, as well as other screen-related values.

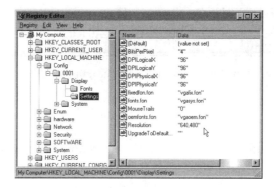

Figure 917 *The screen subkey values.*

918

Windows 3.1 users could use Notepad or a similar editor to display their installed device drivers in the SYSTEM.INI file. With Windows 95, you can view the following subkey window to see your installed device drivers:

HKEY_LOCAL__MACHINE\System\CurrentControlSet\Control\InstalledFiles

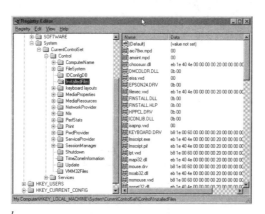

Figure 918 *The device driver subkey values.*

919 Using the Registry to List the Windows 95 32-Bit Virtual Drivers

As you may recall from Tip 858, a virtual device driver, *VxD*, is a 32-bit driver now available for Windows 95 hardware and software. Unlike the 16-bit Windows 3.1 device drivers, the virtual device drivers consume no conventional memory so you have more room for real-mode applications such as MS-DOS applications. The following subkey lets you display the 32-bit virtual device drivers you have currently installed:

HKEY_LOCAL__MACHINE\System\CurrentControlSet\Control\VMM32Files

920 How HKEY_CURRENT_CONFIG Relates to Others

HKEY_CURRENT_CONFIG contains a pointing link to your current system settings. All your system settings, as well as other user's profile settings, appear in the HKEY_LOCAL_MACHINE\Config subkey. When you first log on to Windows 95 (at startup), your user name determines where HKEY_CURRENT_CONFIG points within the HKEY_LOCAL_MACHINE\Config subkey. Therefore, if you want to view your own computer's full and unique settings, display the HKEY_CURRENT_CONFIG subkey branch and scroll through the values.

921 Working with Accessory Program Settings

The registry tracks settings for several of the Accessory menu's programs. If you run the REGEDIT registry editing program and select the following branch:

- HKEY_CURRENT_USER\Software\Microsoft\Windows\CurrentVersion\Applets

then you will be able to view or manipulate the Accessory menu settings. As Figure 921 shows, the Applets branch contains folders for each Accessory menu option as well as for other utility applications, such as Briefcase, that do not appear on the Accessory menu but that are accessory-like programs.

Open the folders from the registry's branch to view some of the settings that you can change, such as the Hearts program's default dealer name or the CD Player's status bar value. You can change virtually every accessory program option using the corresponding program's menu bar, but the registry gives one centralized place in which to modify these program settings.

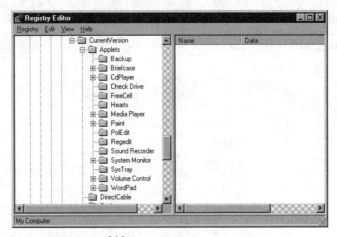

Figure 921 Viewing the registry's accessory program folders.

922 Speeding Up Menu Operations

Windows 95 lets you control the speed at which the Start menu options (such as the Accessory menu and the programs it contains) appear when you point or click on a menu item. As you know, when you display the Start menu, you can display another menu by selecting one of the Start menu's options such as the Programs option. The registry lets you control the speed at which subsequent menu options appear when you select from a menu. To adjust the speed, start REGEDIT and select the following registry branch:

- HKEY_CURRENT_USER\Control Panel\desktop

Create a new Key value (see Tip 908) named *MenuShowDelay* and assign a binary value (from 1 to 10) to the item, with 1 being the fastest and 10 being the slowest menu rate. If you set the rate to 1, the Start menu options appear almost immediately when you select them from the menu. A value of 10 slows down the appearance of the menu options. If you find yourself having to wait too long for menu items to appear, you'll want to increase the speed of the menu rate.

Note: *If you own a fast computer, you may not notice much difference in the menu display rate.*

Turn Off Animated Window Display — 923

You can use the registry to change the speed of windows that you open or minimize. For example, if you click your mouse on a Taskbar button that represents a running program, the program appears to grow quickly from the Taskbar and appears on your screen. When you click your mouse on a window's minimize button, the window shrinks down to a Taskbar button. To control the animation speed of these opened and minimized windows, display the following branch within the registry:

- HKEY_CURRENT_USER\Control Panel\Desktop\WindowMetrics

Create a new entry named *MinAnimate*. If you want to eliminate the animated window's open and minimized states, assign the binary value 0 to MinAnimate. If you want to keep the animated windows, assign 1 to MinAnimate.

Be Aware of WIN.INI — 924

If, when you make changes to the registry, you find that your changes are not taking place, your system's WIN.INI file may be overriding your registry options. Although WIN.INI exists for compatibility to older Windows versions, Windows 95 must respect the values within WIN.INI so that older programs continue to work. For example, Desktop wallpaper, Desktop fonts, and International settings all appear in the file named WIN.INI as well as in your registry. Therefore, if you make a registry change that does not seem to be taking place, open WIN.INI with the Notepad program (WIN.INI appears in your WINDOWS directory) and search for entries that may be overriding the registry's entry. For example, if you make a change to your Desktop wallpaper that does not appear on your Desktop, search WIN.INI for the word Wallpaper to see if a WIN.INI setting counteracts your registry setting.

Note: Before a registry change goes into effect, you must restart Windows 95. Therefore, registry changes never go into effect until you restart whether or not WIN.INI conflicts with the registry. Tip 925 explains how to bypass the restart requirement, however, so that your registry changes goes into effect more quickly.

Updating the Registry without Rebooting — 925

Whenever you make a change to your registry, you must restart Windows 95 for that change to take place. Windows 95 loads all registry settings when you start Windows 95. Instead of restarting Windows 95, however, you can perform the following steps to request that registry settings take place immediately:

1. Click your mouse on the Start menu Shutdown option.
2. When Windows 95 displays the shutdown menu, press the CTRL-ALT-DEL sequence of keystrokes. Windows 95 will display the Close Program dialog box.
3. Close Explorer and select End Task. Windows 95 will display a dialog box stating the program is not responding.
4. To update and load the registry as if you rebooted, click your mouse on the End Task button to update the registry and return to Windows 95.

Removing the Arrow From Shortcut Icons — 926

Figure 926 shows several Desktop shortcut icons. You know the icons represent shortcuts and not actual programs or documents because the icons contain small arrows that represent shortcuts. Some users don't like the small arrows on shortcut icons. If you want to remove the arrows, open the registry's HKEY_CLASSES_ROOT and delete the *lnkfile* and *piffile*'s IsShortCut entries. When you restart Windows 95, your shortcut icons will no longer have the arrows on them.

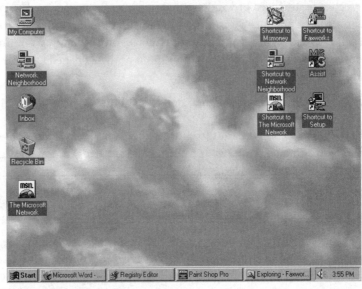

Figure 926 *Shortcut icons usually contain arrows.*

927 Working with Long Filenames From the Command Line

If you use long filenames, and you probably should so that your filenames are as descriptive as possible, Windows 95 converts the long filenames to a pre-Windows 95 8.3-character format when you work with files at the MS-DOS command-line prompt. If you want to work with long filenames from the MS-DOS command-line prompt, simply enclose the long filenames in quotation marks as done in the following commands:

```
DIR  "This is a long filename"

COPY C:\"Program Files"\"My word processor" A:\"Diskette files"\DATA\*.*
```

928 Adding Printers to the Start Menu

In Tip 1,001 you learned how to add the Control Panel to your Start menu so that you could quickly access the Control Panel. You can also add your Printers window to your Start menu by performing these steps:

1. Right-click your mouse on the Taskbar's Start button.
2. Start Explorer by clicking your mouse on the right-click menu Explorer option.
3. Display Explorer's right-click menu by right-clicking your mouse on a blank space within Explorer's right window.
4. Create a new folder by clicking your mouse on the right-click menu New Folder option.
5. Type the following name for the folder:
   Printers.{2227A280-3AEA-1069-A2DE-08002B30309D}
6. Exit Explorer by clicking your mouse on the File menu Close option. As Figure 928 shows, your Start menu now offers one-click access to your printers.

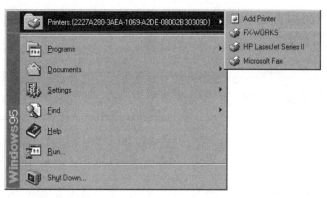

Figure 928 *The Start menu now includes a Printers option.*

Restart only Windows When You Reboot, Not Your System — 929

By default, when you select the Start menu Shutdown option, Windows 95 restarts both your computer (by rebooting) and Windows 95. If you only want to restart Windows 95 without going through your computer's complete reboot process, select the Start menu Shutdown option, click your mouse on the Restart the computer? option, and hold down your SHIFT key when you click your mouse on the Yes button. Windows 95 restarts, without rebooting, your computer's hardware. By restarting Windows 95 without rebooting, your system restarts much more quickly.

Isolating an Error — 930

Windows 95 goes through an exhaustive start-up process when you turn on or reboot your computer. Windows 95 checks its registry, updates Plug-and-Play files, if needed, honors your AUTOEXEC.BAT and CONFIG.SYS requests if you load real-mode drivers in those files, loads programs found in your Start menu's Startup menu, and performs routine Windows 95 clean-up chores such as deleting temporary files you no longer need.

Note: *Temporary files end with the .TMP filename extension. Windows 95 uses temporary files for intermediate storage during normal Windows 95 operations. Never delete temporary files while running Windows 95. If you find several temporary files when scanning your disk with Explorer or the My Computer window, start your computer in a command-line mode the next time you boot your computer (see Tip 184) to an MS-DOS command prompt and delete the .TMP files.*

If you experience errors when you start Windows 95, some things to try that may help you isolate the error are:

1. Use Notepad to insert the letters REM before the first line in your AUTOEXEC.BAT file. Reboot your computer as normal. If the error persists, remove REM and insert REM before the second line. Keep inserting REM between restarts, one line at a time, to see if a particular AUTOEXEC.BAT is causing your troubles. (*REM* is an abbreviation for *remark* and keeps the boot-up process from seeing certain AUTOEXEC.BAT lines.) If you find the offending line, you can often remove the line or keep REM before the line until you can fix the problem. Windows 95 does not need most AUTOEXEC.BAT lines. If you need the line to make a particular device work, check the manual that goes with that line's hardware or software to see if you can change the line to suit your particular computer settings.

2. If AUTOEXEC.BAT does not appear to be the culprit, repeat the REM-inserting process on the CONFIG.SYS file.

3. Have you installed new software recently? If so, the software may have changed your SYSTEM.INI or registry settings. Try uninstalling the software using your Control Panel window's Add/Remove Programs icon. Then, reinstall the software. If the uninstall is not

available for that particular software, try reinstalling a new version of the software on top of the existing version. You may have to contact the software's manufacturer to get a Windows 95 driver file if you think you have the latest version of the software.

931 Using DETCRASH.LOG

If your system freezes up or reboots intermittently, you may have a hardware conflict. Sometimes, Windows 95 detects when a system crash is about to occur. When Windows 95 believes a crash is imminent, or if Windows 95 starts without completing successfully, Windows 95 creates a file named DETCRASH.LOG in your C: drive's root directory. DETCRASH.LOG is not an ASCII text file so you cannot read its information. Windows 95, however, can read the information. When you reboot your system, Windows 95 reads DETCRASH.LOG, if it exists, and attempts to repair damage or side-step the file's problems upon subsequent startups.

932 Disabling 32-bit Disk Access

If your system has a disk that does not support *32-bit disk access*, an advanced high-speed disk I/O mechanism with which your computer can read and write disk data quickly, your system will hang during startup. If you suspect your system may have this problem, perform these steps to verify the conflict and eliminate it:

1. Start the system in the command prompt's safe mode by pressing F8 when you see the Starting Windows 95 message.
2. When you see the MS-DOS prompt, start Windows 95 by typing **WIN/D:F**.
3. If Windows 95 fails to start, the 32-bit access is not the problem. However, if Windows 95 seems to start properly, open Control Panel and double-click on the System icon.
4. Click your mouse on the Performance tab to display the System Properties sheet Performance page shown in Figure 932.1.
5. Click on the File System button to display the File System Properties page shown in Figure 932.2.
6. Click on the Troubleshooting tab to display the Troubleshooting page shown in Figure 932.3.
7. Click your mouse on the Disable all 32 bit protect-mode disk drivers option to disable 32-bit disk access.
8. Click your mouse on the OK button and restart Windows 95 to run Windows 95 using a 16-bit disk access mode.

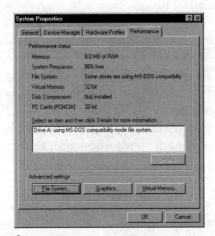

Figure 932.1 The System Properties sheet Performance page.

Windows 95 Advanced Concepts and Operations

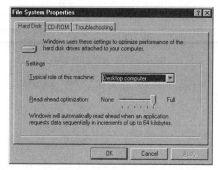

Figure 932.2 The System Properties sheet File System Properties page.

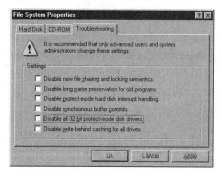

Figure 932.3 The System Properties sheet Troubleshooting page.

Starting Windows 95 without Network Support | 933

If Windows 95 freezes due to a network problem, restart Windows 95 to a safe mode command-line prompt by pressing F8 when you see the Starting Windows 95 message. Type the following to see if Windows 95 works without networking support:

WIN /D:M

If Windows 95 seems to work, restart your computer once again to the MS-DOS command-line prompt and type the following command to start Windows 95's safe-mode networking version:

WIN /D:N

If Windows 95 works and so does your network, you may not have a network problem after all. Try to locate the problem elsewhere. If Windows 95 or your network does fail, however, the network may be your problem and you may have to contact your network card's vendor or recheck your Control Panel's Network Properties sheet settings to make sure they match your network cabling and hardware.

Preventing Windows 95 Use of the ROM Breakpoint | 934

A ROM breakpoint is a location in the PC BIOS that contains instructions Windows 95 uses to change from protected to real mode. Normally, Windows 95 looks for the breakpoint instructions at a specific address. If, however, you are using a third-party memory manager that moves your BIOS to RAM, Windows 95 should not assume that it knows the breakpoint location. If you experience intermittent errors within Windows 95, try disabling Windows 95 use of ROM breakpoints by starting Windows 95 using the following command line:

WIN /D:S

The /D:S command-line switch tells Windows 95 not to use ROM addresses in the range F000:0000 through 1Mb as a breakpoint. You can also disable Windows 95 ROM breakpoint use by placing the following entry within your SYSTEM.INI file:

SystemROMBreakPoint=False

935 Insuring BIOS-based Disk Operations

If your system hangs during disk operations and you've tried Tip 932 without success, you may need to change the way that Windows 95 accesses your disk drives. Perhaps Windows 95 needs to use BIOS-based disk operations (*BIOS* stands for *Basic Input/Output System* and describes the instructions burned into your computer's processor hardware). Restart Windows 95 to a safe mode MS-DOS command-line prompt by pressing F8 when you see the Starting Windows 95 message and type the following line to start Windows 95 with BIOS-based disk I/O:

WIN /D:V

If Windows 95 starts and works successfully, place the following entry in your SYSTEM.INI file (see Tip 934 for SYSTEM.INI editing instructions):

VirtualHDIRQ=False

936 Preventing Windows 95 Video-Adapter Memory Use

If your system hangs when you start Windows 95, you may need to disable Windows 95's use of video adapter memory for I/O going to your screen. Restart Windows 95 at the safe mode's MS-DOS command-line prompt by pressing F8 when you see the Starting Windows 95 message and type the following to start Windows 95 with video adapter memory disabled:

WIN /D:X

To correct the problem, type the following entry in your SYSTEM.INI file (see Tip 990 for SYSTEM.INI editing instructions):

EMMExclude=A000-FFFF

937 Start the Registry from the DOS Prompt

If you have trouble starting Windows 95, your error may be due a Registry entry. In such cases, turn on your computer and press the F8 function during the Windows 95 startup process to start your system DOS mode. Next, from the DOS prompt, invoke the Registry editor by typing **REGEDIT**.

Tip 899 discusses the command line options you can use. After you make your changes to the Registry, restart your system.

Shortcut Keys for the Microsoft Keyboard — 938

If you use Microsoft's keyboard, you can use Table 938's key combinations to perform common Windows 95 tasks.

Key	Description
WIN+R	Displays the Start menu's Run dialog box
WIN+M	Minimizes all open windows
SHIFT+WIN+M	Reverses a minimize all open windows operation by restoring all minimized windows to their original state
WIN+F1	Starts the Windows 95 online help
WIN+E	Starts Explorer
CTRL+WIN+F	Finds files and folders
WIN+TAB	Cycles through Taskbar buttons
WIN+BREAK	Displays the System Properties dialog box

Table 938 The Microsoft keyboard shortcut keys.

Great Resources for the Visually Impaired — 939

If you are visually impaired or know someone who is, you can get Windows 95 special documentation from the following locations:

Recording for the Blind, Inc.
20 Roszel Road
Princeton, NJ 08540
Phone: 800-221-4792 or 609-452-0606
Fax: 609-987-8116

Trace R&D Center
S-151 Waisman Center
1500 Highland Ave.
Madison, WI 53705-2280
Phone: 608-263-2309
Fax: 608-262-8848

National Information System Center for Developing Disabilities
Benson Building
University of South Carolina
Columbia, SC 29208
Phone: 803-777-4434
Fax: 803-777-6058

940 A Good Source for Device Driver Files

Hardware changes all the time. If you acquire hardware after you buy Windows 95, the hardware's manufacturer should supply a Windows 95 driver so the device works with Windows 95. If you need a device driver file, you can phone Microsoft Product Support Services at 206-637-7098 to obtain the *Windows 95 Driver Library* (*WDL*). You can also use your modem to download the file (use Windows 95's HyperTerminal program for a trouble-free connection) from Microsoft's *Download Service* at this data phone number: 206-936-6735.

941 Understanding the System Policy Editor

The System Policy Editor lets you create and manage system policies. A system policy controls the way that people use your computer and its Windows 95 resources. For example, you can limit Control Panel window access so that only certain users can use the window. The system policies can also control which users can and cannot change their Desktop settings. The system policies controls network settings as well. (You would not want just anybody to change network settings because every other network user would be without network access if someone changed something that cripples the entire network.) If you use your own computer at home or if you are the only one who uses your computer in a non-networked office setting, you probably have no need to use the system policy editor to change system policies from their default settings. (By default, no system policy restrictions are in place until you set them.) If you are a network administrator, or if you share your PC with other users, however, you may want to set system policies. Different policies will then be in effect depending on who logs onto the computer. To use the System Policy Editor, install the System Policy Editor from the Windows 95 installation CD. Install the System Policy Editor by performing these steps:

1. Open the Control Panel's Add/Remove Programs window.
2. Display the Windows Setup page by clicking your mouse on the Windows Setup tab.
3. Click your mouse on the Have Disk button.
4. Click your mouse on the Browse button and locate your CD-ROM's ADMIN\APPTOOLS\POLEDIT folder.
5. Click the OK button on the Windows Setup page and the next dialog box that appears.
6. Be sure to check the System Policy Editor in the Have Disk dialog box.
7. Start the installation by clicking the Install button.

942 Running the System Policy Editor

To run the System Policy Editor, select the Start menu Run option and type **POLEDIT**. Figure 942 shows the System Policy Editor's opening window. These are the two modes in which you can run the System Policy Editor:

- *Registry mode*: Directly edit the Registry of local or remote computers so those changes are reflected immediately. This mode is most common and the next few tips use the Registry mode to modify certain Windows 95 settings. Select the File menu Open Registry open to use the Registry mode.

- *Policy File mode*: Change polices for users on local or remote computers but those policies will not take effect until those users subsequently log on to their computers. If a user is currently using one of the local or remote computers, that computer's policy will not change until the user logs on the next time. Select the File menu New File or Open File to use the Policy File mode.

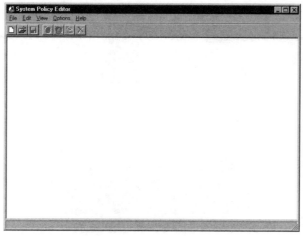

Figure 942 *The System Policy Editor's opening window.*

Turning Off the Network Neighborhood | 943

You can use the System Policy Editor to turn off the Network Neighborhood icon so that users cannot make network adjustments. You'll thus protect the network and keep the user or users from accessing the network. Perform these steps to turn off the Network Neighborhood:

1. Start the System Policy Editor.
2. Select the File menu Open Registry icon. The System Policy Editor will display a list of current users and computers.
3. Select a user or computer by clicking your mouse over one of the user or computer icons in the System Policy Editor's window. The System Policy Editor will display a list of available policies as shown in Figure 943.1.
4. Open the Shell book icon by clicking the Shell's plus sign with your mouse.
5. Open the Restrictions book icon by clicking the Restriction's plus sign with your mouse. Figure 943.2 shows your System Policy Editor window.
6. Hide the Network Neighborhood icon by clicking your mouse on the Hide Network Neighborhood option.
7. Close the Policies window by clicking on the OK button to close the System Policy Editor.
8. Save your changes by selecting the File menu Save command.

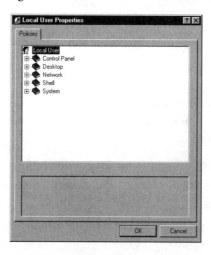

Figure 943.1 *Available policies to edit.*

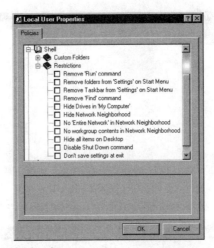

Figure 943.2 Controlling the Network Neighborhood icon.

944 Removing the Taskbar from the Settings Menu

In an office, you may not want users to change the Taskbar or Start menu settings. You can use the System Policy Editor to remove the Taskbar menu options from the user's (or computer's) system policies. To remove the Taskbar menu, perform these steps:

1. Start the System Policy Editor.
2. Select the File menu Open Registry icon. The System Policy Editor will display a list of current users and computers.
3. Select a user or computer by clicking your mouse over one of the user or computer icons in the System Policy Editor's window.
4. Open the Shell book icon by clicking the Shell's plus sign with your mouse.
5. Open the Restrictions book icon by clicking the Restriction's plus sign with your mouse.
6. Hide the Taskbar by clicking your mouse on the Remove Taskbar from Settings on Start Menu option.
7. Close the Policies window by clicking your mouse on the OK button to close the System Policy Editor.
8. Save your changes by selecting the File menu Save command.

945 Disabling the Save Settings at Exit

Normally, Windows 95 saves profile settings when the current user shuts down Windows 95 or logs off. In an office environment where different users share the same computer, you might not want user settings saved when a user logs off the computer. For example, the user may have modified the Desktop for his or her session but you don't want the desktop to remain changed permanently. You can use the System Policy Editor to disable the automatic saving of system settings by performing these steps:

1. Start the System Policy Editor.
2. Select the File menu Open Registry icon. The System Policy Editor will display a list of current users and computers.
3. Select a user or computer by clicking your mouse over one of the user or computer icons in the System Policy Editor's window.

4. Open the Shell book icon by clicking the Shell's plus sign with your mouse.
5. Open the Restrictions book icon by clicking the Restriction's plus sign with your mouse.
6. Click your mouse on the Don't save settings at exit option to turn off Windows 95's automatic saving of settings.
7. Close the Policies window by clicking your mouse on the OK button to close the System Policy Editor.
8. Save your changes by selecting the File menu Save command.

Appreciating the Impact of Energy-Compliant Hardware | 946

As you know from previous tips (such as Tip 259), Windows 95 supports Energy Star hardware such as printers and monitors. According to the EPA, within the government alone, the use of energy compliant hardware is projected to save tax payers $40 million a year and possibly as much as $2 billion a year by the year 2000. If every PC in the U.S. were to power down when not in use, the US would save up to $1 billion a year in electricity and would reduce emission of carbon dioxide (due to the power consumption) by the equivalent of 5 million cars on the road. Be aware of these Energy Star-compliant hardware savings when you next shop for computer equipment.

Is Your Device Driver Using Real-Mode or 32-Bit Mode? | 947

To improve performance, you should use protected-mode 32-bit device drivers whenever possible. Not all your drivers can be 32-bit drivers because some hardware must use real-mode 16-bit drivers. If, however, you are not getting the performance you expect from a disk or other device, you may be using a real-mode device driver when a 32-bit driver is available from the manufacturer or elsewhere. To determine if a device driver is using a real-mode 16-bit or a virtual 32-bit mode device driver, perform these steps:

1. Open the Control Panel window.
2. Open the System Properties window by clicking your mouse on the System icon.
3. Click on the Performance tab to display the Performance page shown in Figure 947.
4. If you see the "Your system is configured for optimal performance" message, you are using all available virtual 32-bit device drivers. If you see a different message, click your tab on the Device Manager and locate device drivers that might be suspect.

Figure 947 The System Properties sheet Performance page.

948 Taking a Close Look at Safe Mode Drivers

Windows 95 maintains a list of real-mode 16-bit device driver files that Windows 95 found and replaced when you first installed Windows 95. You'll find the list in a file named IOS.INI that you can view with Notepad or print by dragging this file to your printer's icon in the Printers window. If you see devices in IOS.INI that have corresponding entries in either your AUTOEXEC.BAT or CONFIG.SYS system files, you can safely remove the lines from those system files that reference those drivers as long as the drivers appear in IOS.INI's *SafeMode* section. The drivers will no longer consume conventional memory space and your system's startup procedure will take slightly less time.

949 Understanding Driver Qualifiers in IOS.INI

IOS.INI lists safe mode drivers next to each of its device driver entries. You may encounter one or more qualifiers in IOS.INI. Table 949 explains each qualifier so you can better understand the IOS.INI entries.

Modifier	Description
do_not_care	Windows 95 loads an available protected-mode driver and does not use a *mapper file* (an equivalent real-mode driver) because there is no I/O request associated with this driver
must_chain	The device driver is safe and Windows 95 can use the protected mode driver but Windows 95 must map any interrupt 13 I/O request through a real-mode mapper. All non-interrupt 13 requests go through the improved 32-bit protected-mode driver.
must_not_chain	As long as there are no interrupt 13 I/O requests to or from the driver, Windows 95 will use protected-mode 32-bit drivers.
non_disk	The driver controls a device that is not a disk such as INTERLNK.
monolithic	Similar to non_disk. The device's manufacturer determines whether the device is monolithic and safe and installs the driver with the monolithic qualifier to let Windows 95 know that the device driver's starting entry point is adjustable so no contention with other devices takes place.

Table 949. The IOS.INI file qualifiers.

950 What Drivers did Windows 95 Load?

A file named IOS.LOG keeps track of all drivers that should use a protected-mode device driver but instead use a real-mode driver because Windows 95 could find no protected-mode driver. IOS.LOG also exists if Windows 95 detects an unknown device driver. Most users whose systems work properly will not find an IOS.LOG file in their Windows directory. If you find such a file, you may have device problems such as conflicts or out-of-date drivers. Even worse, if you see a file named MBRINT13.SYS in the first line, you may have a computer virus and you should immediately get Windows 95-compatible software that checks and corrects computer viruses.

Note: In rare instances, a boot device may use MBRINT13.SYS so such a mention does not always *indicate a virus. Your virus-scanning software should let you know if the mention is safe or not.*

Why Some Multimedia CDs Automatically Run — 951

If you have purchased newer multimedia programs, you may have found that when you insert the program's CD-ROM in your CD-ROM drive, the program automatically runs. As it turns out, when you insert a CD-ROM, Windows 95 searches the CD's root directory for a file named AUTORUN.INF. This file contains instructions that Windows 95 follows to automatically run the CD-ROM's program or the CD-ROM's setup program if you've yet to run the setup. The AUTORUN.INF file triggers Windows 95's AutoPlay feature to start the CD-ROM.

Avoiding Windows Version Problems — 952

If you have an older program that refuses to run under Windows 95 because the program requires a specific Windows 3.1 system file, you may be able to trick the program into running. To try to run the program, use Notepad to edit your WIN.INI file, locate the *Compatibility* section, and type the following on a line by itself:

Name=0x00200000

where *Name* corresponds to the program module that is experiencing the version number error. When you save your WIN.INI changed, attempt to run the program again. The problem now has a good chance of running.

Troubleshooting a Slow Printer — 953

If your printer is printing slowly, things you can check to increase the printing speed include:

1. If your printer is printing raw printed output data as opposed to EMF-spooled data, you'll want to change your printed output to EMF-spooled output. See Tip 805 for instructions.
2. Make sure your disk is not fragmented because Windows 95 may have a difficult time trying to collect all the pieces of your printed output. See Tip 395 for instructions.
3. Check your spooler settings to ensure they are properly set. Tip 274 explains how to check your current settings.
4. Make sure your disk has adequate free space for the temporary spool files. Use Explorer to locate files you can delete. Be sure to empty the Recycle Bin once you delete the files so you get actual free disk space instead of just erased filenames.
5. Turn off your printer's TrueType As Graphics option. Select your printer from your Desktop Printers window, choose the File menu Properties option, and click your mouse on the Fonts tab to display the Fonts page shown in Figure 953. Uncheck the option labeled Print TrueType as graphics if it is active and click your mouse on the OK button to save your changes.
6. Turn off spooling (use the printer's Properties sheet and select the Spool Settings button on the Details page) to print directly to your printer.

Note: *Change these settings one at a time to see if one of them dramatically improves your printing speed. If you change all at once, your printer will be too slow.*

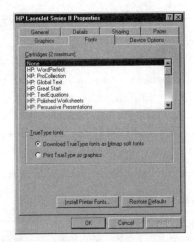

Figure 953 Changing the TrueType print settings.

954 Trouble Shooting Modem Operations

If Windows 95 has trouble working with your modem, you can request that Windows 95 create a modem operation log in a file named MODEMLOG.TXT. You then can use this file to troubleshoot your modem connection and trace the problem. Before Windows 95 can write to MODEMLOG.TXT, you must tell Windows 95 to create the file. To create the file, select your modem from the Control Panel's Modem window. Display the modem's Properties sheet Advanced Connection Settings page (see Figure 954) and check the Record a log file. When you close the modem's Properties window, Windows 95 adds to the MODEMLOG.TXT file every time you access, or attempt to access, your modem.

Figure 954 Requesting a modem log file.

955 Editing the MSDOS.SYS File

As you have learned, Windows 95 places a hidden file in your system disk root directory named MSDOS.SYS that contains entries which control Windows 95 settings. The following tips discuss how you can use the MSDOS.SYS file to customize Windows 95. Before you can edit this file, however, you will need to change several of the file's attributes. To change the attributes quickly, perform these steps:

1. Open an MS-DOS window.
2. Type the following at the MS-DOS prompt: **ATTRIB -r -s -h MSDOS.SYS** and press ENTER.
3. Copy the file to a backup file by typing the following at the MS-DOS prompt: **COPY MSDOS.SYS *.SAV** and press ENTER. You can now change MSDOS.SYS but first, make sure you know exactly what to change. If you damage the MSDOS.SYS file, you can restore the original file from the backup by entering **COPY MSDOS.SAV *.SYS** at the MS-DOS prompt and press ENTER. If you want to overwrite the existing file, type Y when the system prompts you.
4. After you finish making changes to MSDOS.SYS, type the following to convert the file back to a protected read-only system file: **ATTRIB -r -s -h MSDOS.SYS** and press ENTER.

956 Controlling the Windows 95 Boot Delay

The *boot delay* specifies how long Windows 95 will wait for a user to press **F8** once the Starting Windows 95 message appears the screen. During the boot delay time period, the user can press **F8** to start the computer at the MS-DOS prompt or in a Windows 95 safe mode. If the user does not press **F8**, Windows 95 will load itself into memory. The default boot delay is 2 seconds. If you want to change this setting, use Notepad to edit MSDOS.SYS and insert the following line in the [Options] section:

BootDelay=n

Use a boot delay seconds value for n. For example, to set a 5-second delay, you would type the following:

BootDelay=5

957 Turning Off Boot-Key Support

As Windows 95 starts, you can press **F5** or **F8** at the Starting Windows 95 message to display a menu from which you can control the way Windows 95 loads. In an office environment, you may not want users to be able to use **F5** or **F8** to modify the startup behavior of Windows 95. To disable these keys, use Notepad to edit MSDOS.SYS and insert the following line in the [Options] section:

BootKeys=0

If you later want to allow the **F5** or **F8** keys, delete the line or change it to the following:

BootKeys=1

958 Turning Off the Animated Windows 95 Logo

By default, Windows 95 displays an animated Taskbar logo that highlights the Start button (Reading Press here to start Windows 95). If your system hangs during this process, you can turn off the animated logo by placing the following line in the MSDOS.SYS [Options] section:

Logo=1

959 Directing Windows 95 to Double Buffer SCSI Devices

If you use a SCSI disk drive or other bus-mastering disk controller, you may need to use Windows 95 *double buffering* capabilities. Double buffering is a technique Windows 95 uses to copy data to be written to disk into conventional memory and then to the disk. To perform the actual disk operation, Windows 95 changes from protected mode to real mode. In a similar way, for read operations, Windows 95 changes to real mode, then reads the data into conventional memory and then changes back to protected mode, copying the data to a protected mode buffer. By changing to and from protected mode in this way, Windows 95 insures that data is correctly read from and written to disk.

Unfortunately, double buffering slows down your disk operations but some drives require double buffering. To enable double buffering, place the following line in MSDOS.SYS [Options] section:

DoubleBuffer=1

To turn off double buffering, use this line:

DoubleBuffer=0

960 Disabling Windows 95 Graphical User Interface

Depending on your preferences, there may be times when you want Windows 95 to start at the MS-DOS command-line prompt instead of the usual graphical user interface. To control how Windows 95 starts, edit the MSDOS.SYS file and change the BootGUI entry.

Place the following line within the file to use Windows 95 graphical user interface:

BootGUI=0

Use the following line for an MS-DOS command-line startup:

BootGUI=1

961 Controlling the Windows 95 Boot Menu

By default, Windows 95 does not display its startup menu (the menu you see when you press **F8** after the Starting Windows 95 message appears). You can request that Windows 95 always display the menu by inserting the following line in the MSDOS.SYS file:

BootMenu=1

If you remove the line or change the line to the following:

BootMenu=0

Then, Windows 95 starts as usual and you'll be able to display the special startup menu only by pressing **F8** at the Starting Windows 95 message.

962 Controlling the Windows 95 Boot Menu Delay

When you start Windows 95 and display the special F8 startup menu, Windows 95 will, by default, select the default menu choice after 30 seconds if you do not select another choice. (This automatic choice is called the *timeout* value.) If you want to change the amount of time Windows 95 waits before selecting the default choice, change the delay interval time by inserting the following line in MSDOS.SYS:

BootMenuDelay=*n*

where *n* represents the number of seconds you want Windows 95 to wait before selecting the default menu option.

963 Controlling the Boot Menu Default Option

By default, if Windows 95 successfully started properly on the previous boot, the Windows 95 boot menu uses option 1 ("Normal") as its default startup option. If an error occurred on the most recent boot, Windows 95 uses option 3 ("Safe Mode") to start Windows 95. If you want to change the number used for the default option, edit the MSDOS.SYS file's BootMenuDefault entry and specify the option number that you want Windows 95 to select if a timeout (see Tip 962) occurs. The following entry, in the MSDOS.SYS file's [Options] section, directs Windows 95 to use option 2 ("Logged \BOOTLOG.TXT") for the default menu option:

BootMenuDefault=2

964 Controlling Network Software

Even if you require a network and spend the time needed to configure your network software correctly, there may be times when you want to disable the network software for system testing or to free resources that you need for a particular project. If you use the Control Panel to disable the network software, you'll have to reconfigure all the network settings once again when you need the network. Instead of resetting Control Panel settings, you can disable network support by changing the MSDOS.SYS file. The [Options] section entry turns off all network support:

Network=0

When you want your network back, change the MSDOS.SYS entry to the following to restore a working network:

Network=1

965 Supporting BootMulti Operations

If your hard disk has both the full MS-DOS operating system and Windows 95 installed, you can boot either operating system as your needs require. To direct Windows 95 to support multiple boot capabilities, assign the MSDOS.SYS file [Options] section's BootMulti option to the value 1 shown here:

BootMulti=1

After you assign 1 to the BootMulti entry, you can later start MS-DOS by pressing the **F4** function key when your system displays the message Starting Windows 95 message.

966 Loading COMMAND.COM or DRVSPACE.BIN at the Top of 640K

If you are running Novell's Netware software and experience errors, you may need to move either COMMAND.COM or DRVSPACE.BIN to the top of your conventional memory (to the top of 640K) to free more lower memory and make room for Novell's software. To direct Windows 95 to load these programs at the top of 640K, assign 1 to the MSDOS.SYS file [Options] section's LoadTop entry as shown here:

LoadTop=1

967 Controlling Automatic Loading of DBLSPACE.BIN

The DBLSPACE.BIN file controls *DoubleSpace*, the disk compression utility Windows 95 uses to gain more disk space. When Windows 95 starts, Windows 95 looks for the DBLSPACE.BIN file for disk compression instructions. To direct Windows 95 to automatically load DBLSPACE.BIN each time it starts, set the MSDOS.SYS file [Options] section's DblSpace entry to 1 as shown here:

DblSpace=1

968 Controlling Automatic Loading of DRVSPACE.BIN

The *DriveSpace* disk drive compression utility that comes with Microsoft Plus! add-on program lets you compress disk drives as large as two gigabytes (2 billion bytes). (DoubleSpace compresses drives only as large as one-half megabytes.) The DRVSPACE.BIN file controls DriveSpace and specifies compression settings. To direct Windows 95 to automatically load DRVSPACE.BIN each time it starts, set the MSDOS.SYS file's [Options] section's DrvSpace entry to 1 as shown here:

DrvSpace=1

969 Controlling the Default Operating System

If your system has both a full MS-DOS operating system and Windows 95, you can specify which operating system you desire as the default operating system using the MSDOS.SYS file [Options] section's BootWin entry. To specify Windows 95 as the default operating system, set BootWin to 1 as shown here:

BootWin=1

To boot to the MS-DOS operating system, instead of Window 95, assign the BootWin entry 0.

970 Controlling the Safe Mode Warning

When you restart Windows 95 after a system problem, Windows 95 automatically starts in the safe mode so that Windows 95 can start without loading potentially troublesome device drivers. Although you will not always be able to use your full Windows 95 utilities or attached devices, the safe mode helps to ensure that you can start Windows 95 without getting errors or a startup failure. When Windows 95 starts in the safe mode, Windows 95 displays a safe mode startup warning to let you know that Windows 95 is starting in the safe mode. If you want to disable the safe mode startup warning, change the MSDOS.SYS file [Options] section's BootWarn setting to 0, as shown here:

BootWarn=0

To return to the normal safe mode warning, set the BootWarn option to 1 like this:

BootWarn=1

Understanding the MSDOS.SYS Path Entries — 971

The MSDOS.SYS file's [Paths] section contains entries that define directory locations for various Windows 95 files. Table 971 explains each of the [Paths] section's entries.

Entry	Description
HostWinBootDrv	Defines the directory Windows 95 uses for the boot drive
WinBootDir	Defines Windows 95's startup files. If you do not specify a different directory, Windows 95 uses the directory you specified when you first installed Windows 95 (which is usually C:\WINDOWS)
WinDir	Defines the Windows 95 directory

Table 971. The MSDOS.SYS [Paths] section entries.

Running Hover!, a Pretty Cool Game — 972

If you have the Windows 95 CD-ROM, you can play a 3-D animated action game called *Hover!*. To run Hover!, perform these steps:

1. Insert your Windows 95 installation CD-ROM into your CD-ROM drive. Windows 95 will display the CD-ROM's opening window shown in Figure 972.1.
2. Start Hover! by clicking your mouse over the Hover! icon at the right of the window. Windows 95 will start the Hover! game and will display an opening help window shown in Figure 972.2.
3. Clicking your mouse on the OK button to close the window.
4. Click your mouse on the **F2** button to start playing Hover!. Windows 95 will begin a new game. Figure 972.3 shows an in-play Hover! game window.

Note: Press **F3** to pause the game if you need a few extra moments to get started. Hover!'s Help menu contains a How To Play option that explains how to control and win Hover!.

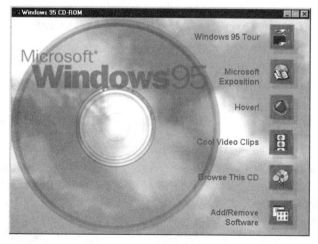

Figure 972.1 The Windows 95 CD-ROM opening window.

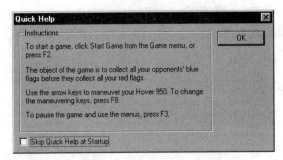

Figure 972.2 Hover!'s opening help window.

Figure 972.3 Hover!'s startup action window.

973 Demonstrating Microsoft Products

The Windows 95 installation CD-ROM contains several demonstrations of Microsoft application programs. If you are interested in purchasing other Windows 95 products, you may want to run a demonstration program first to see how you like the program. To demonstrate a program, perform these steps:

1. Insert your Windows 95 installation CD-ROM into your CD-ROM drive. Windows 95 will display the CD-ROM's opening window shown.

2. Click your mouse on the Microsoft Exposition icon at the right of the window. Windows 95 will display the Product Information window shown in Figure 973.1. The default option, Microsoft Exposition, selects Microsoft products for which you can run a demonstration. The other option, Programs Designed for Windows 95, lists non-Microsoft products.

4. Click your mouse on the OK button to start Microsoft Exposition. Figure 973.2 shows the opening Microsoft Exposition window from which you can select an introduction or a sample execution of several Microsoft products such as Access, Excel, Arcade, Visual Basic, and PowerPoint.

5. Clicking your mouse button over an icon or category to select a sample program to demonstrate.

Note: *You cannot actually demonstrate the non-Microsoft programs. Instead of demonstrating Microsoft programs, the installation CD-ROM contains an online help window of several non-Microsoft product program descriptions you can read to learn more about other vendor's products.*

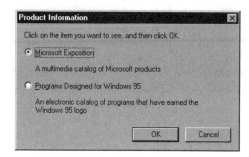

Figure 973.1 The Microsoft Product Information window.

Figure 973.2 The Microsoft Exposition window.

974 Starting Explorer From the Command-Line Prompt

As you get used to working with the Explorer, you will find that you will often use the Explorer to locate files quickly. As it turns out, you can start the Explorer from the MS-DOS command-line prompt using the START command. For example, the following command would direct Windows 95 to start Explorer and display Explorer's folder tree from the root directory:

**START **

The backslash, \\, represents the root directory.

The following command starts Explorer and displays Explorer's folder tree from the current directory:

START .

The period, in this case, represents the current directory.

975 A Quick Way to Maximize DOS-based Memory Use

If you run MS-DOS-based programs, you can quickly maximize the use of memory within an MS-DOS window by assigning the SYSTEM.INI file's LocalLoadHigh entry to 1 as shown here:

LocalLoadHigh=1

Insert the line in the SYSTEM.INI [386Enh] section.

976 Drag and Drop a File to the Command-Line Prompt

If you often work from the MS-DOS command-line prompt, you can drag a file icon or folder to the command-line instead of typing the file's complete path name. For example, if you open Explorer as well as an MS-DOS window, you can start typing an MS-DOS command, such as COPY, then use your mouse to drag a filename from Explorer to the MS-DOS window. When you release the file on the MS-DOS window, Windows 95 types the complete path and filename for the file you dragged. If a file uses a long path and filename, you can often drag the file quicker than typing the full filename specification.

977 Defining Your Own Startup Logo

By default, each time you start Windows 95, Windows 95 displays the logo shown in Figure 977 while Windows 95 loads, reads the registry, and sets up your Desktop. To override the logo with your own graphic file, you can create a file named LOGOS.SYS that contains the graphic image you want to see during the startup process. Store the file in your root directory. The LOGOS.SYS file must be 320x400 pixels with an 8-bit color pattern. Paint can create such graphic files. To help you get the correct graphic specifications, use Paint to edit a file named LOGOS.SYS (the original startup logo graphic) from within the Windows 95 directory and save the file as LOGOS.SYS in your root directory. By using the original LOGOS.SYS file as your starting point, you'll ensure that the file you create will have the correct pixel size and number of colors.

Figure 977 The Windows 95 startup graphic.

978 Bypassing the Windows 95 Logo

Each time you start Windows 95, Windows 95 displays its startup logo (see Tip 977). If you do not want to see a logo graphic, you can bypass the logo's display by pressing Esc immediately after Windows 95 displays the Starting Windows 95 message. Although Windows 95 will not start any faster, Windows 95 does keep the screen clear until your Desktop appears.

979 Change the Shutdown Messages

When you shut down your system, Windows 95 displays two messages. The first message informs you that the shutdown is taking place and that you are to wait before turning off your computer. Once Windows 95 successfully shuts down your system, Windows 95 displays a second message that informs you that you can safely turn off your computer.

These messages are nothing more than graphic bitmap images that you can edit and change using Paint. Therefore, you can create your own customized message screens that you and other users see when you shut down Windows 95. Windows 95 uses the file names LOGOS.SYS and LOGOW.SYS for these two files.

Removing the Control Panel or Printers Option from the Start Menu | 980

Tip 928 describes how you can add a Printers folder to your Start menu so that you have one-click access to your printers. Likewise, Tip 1001 describes how to add the Control Panel window to your Start menu so you can access your system configuration more quickly than you otherwise could through your Desktop icons. If you decide that you want to remove one of these menu items, use Explorer to open the Startup Menu folder and highlight the entry you want to delete by clicking the entry with your mouse. When you press DEL, Windows 95 deletes the menu item and restores your Start menu to its previous state.

There's More to the Windows 95 CD-ROM than Windows 95 | 981

The Windows 95 CD-ROM comes with more files than the floppy disk version. Although both versions provide a full Windows 95 implementation, the CD-ROM contains additional tools you won't find on the floppy disk version. Therefore, if you bought Windows 95 on floppy disks, you still may want to purchase the CD-ROM version to get these extras:

- *Movie clips and a game*: The CD-ROM offers extra .AVI movie clips (see Tip 993) and a 3-D action game called Hover!.
- *Network Monitor*: A program that lets you monitor network traffic statistics.
- *Quick viewers*: The quick viewers let you look at files without loading the file's associated programs (see Tips 817 through 819).
- *System Policy Editor*: A program that lets you specify who has access to Control Panel options, limits Desktop functionality for certain users, customizes the Desktop for individual users, and configures advanced network settings.

To access these extras, just insert your CD-ROM into your CD-ROM drive and let AutoPlay take over from there.

Understanding Font Smoothing | 982

Font smoothing, sometimes known as *anti-aliasing*, improves the appearance of your screen fonts. The Microsoft Plus! Windows 95 add-on program contains a utility that smoothes your screen fonts by giving the fonts a more rounded appearance. If you work with a desktop publishing program, you will certainly want to purchase Microsoft Plus! for its font smoothing ability that makes your screen's text more clear, rounded, and sharp.

Tune Your Start Menus | 983

As you add more and more programs to your system, your Start menu and its submenus can get very cluttered as Figure 983 shows. One solution is to remove all programs from the Start menu (and submenus) except those programs you use on a regular basis. In addition, you may want to group related programs so they do not always display when you access the Start menu. For example, you could create a Work submenu with all your work programs, and a Home submenu with all your home files such as your personal checkbook and budgeting program. Think of the Start menu and its submenus as a hierarchical directory that you organize just as you organize programs and files into folders and subfolders (or, in Windows 3.1 and MS-DOS terminology, like directories and subdirectories).

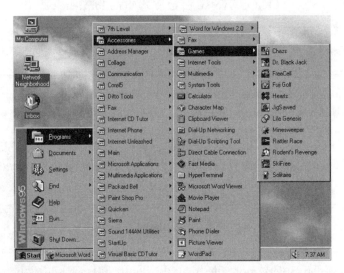

Figure 983 *The Start menu can get complicated.*

984 Offer a Reward for Your PC

If you travel with a laptop, use WordPad to create a README.DOC file in your root directory containing text that someone who finds your laptop will see. The file might look something like this:

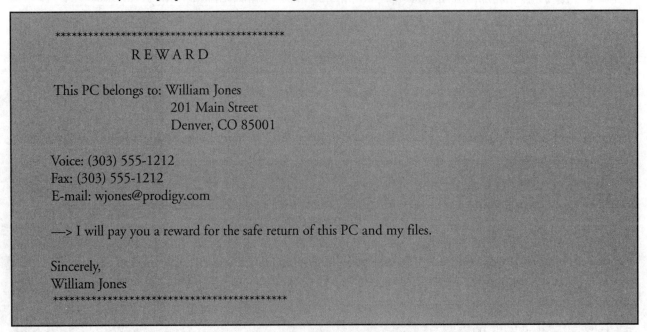

Drag the README.DOC file to your Startup folder so Windows 95 displays the file as soon as someone turns on your lost laptop.

Always Travel with a Startup Disk 985

If you use a laptop, create a startup floppy disk to keep with your system at all times. If Windows 95 ever gets damaged, you can reboot your computer and begin to diagnose the problem. To create a startup, bootable floppy disk, perform these steps:

1. Find a spare 1.2 MB high-density floppy disk. (You do not need to format the disk.)
2. Write Windows 95 Start-up Disk on the floppy disk's label.
3. Open your Control Panel's Add/Remove Programs dialog box.
4. Click your mouse on the Startup Disk tab to display the Startup page shown in Figure 985.
5. Insert your floppy disk in the floppy disk drive.
6. Click your mouse on the Create Disk button. Windows 95 will turn the floppy disk into a bootable system disk.

If you cannot start Windows 95 due to a bad registry file or another problem, insert your startup diskette into your floppy disk drive and reboot. The floppy disk starts your computer and Windows 95. At that point, you can restore the registry and other corrupted files.

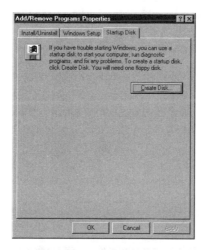

Figure 985 Creating a startup floppy disk.

Finding a Folder that Contains a File 986

As Tip 359 explains, you can use Windows 95's Find tools to locate a particular file. Once you find the file, you may want to open the folder that contains the file. For example, you may only remember one file out of several that you created and stored in a special project's folder. Not only do you want the file whose name you remember, but also the others in the folder. To open the folder in which a file resides, use Explorer's find command to locate the one file. After you click your mouse on the file to highlight the file's name, click your mouse on the File menu Open Containing Folder. Explorer displays a window that lists every file located in the same folder as the found file.

987 | Avoid Common Extensions

Two programs can use the same filename extension. For example, Word for Windows uses .DOC and so does WordPad. If you use both programs, you should change the default extension for one of the programs (the one you use least). For example, you could change the default WordPad extension from .DOC to .PAD by typing the .PAD extension every time you save a file with WordPad. You'll then be able to associate .DOC with Word for Windows and .PAD with WordPad. When you subsequently double-click your mouse over your .PAD document files, Windows 95 starts WordPad and when you double-click your mouse over .DOC document files, Windows 95 starts Word for Windows.

988 | Need to Edit Binary Files? Try Write or EDIT

Programmers often need to edit and view binary files. A binary file, unlike a text file, is compressed and makes very little sense to most people who view the file contents. Programmers, however, can and often need to interpret the compressed information in binary files. Before Windows 95, programmers used the Windows 3.1 Write program to view and edit binary files. Sadly, Windows 95 replaces Write with WordPad and WordPad does not handle binary files. If you want to use Write, you have two options:

- Rename all Windows 3.1 program files that begin with WRITE to other filenames before you install Windows 95. When you finish installing Windows 95, you then can rename those files back to their previous name.
- If you've already installed Windows 95, as you probably have if you're reading this, you can extract Write from your Windows 3.1 installation disks or CD-ROM. Locate your Windows 3.1 diskettes or CD-ROM and perform Tip 998 to copy WRITE files to your Windows 95 folder. You can now execute Write from the Start menu Run option.

Windows 95 supplies an MS-DOS-based EDIT program that lets you view and edit text and binary files. Despite the fact that EDIT is an MS-DOS program, Microsoft greatly improved Windows 95's EDIT program over previous versions. Therefore, EDIT makes viewing and editing binary files simple. To start EDIT, type **EDIT** at the Start menu Run option. Figure 988 shows an EDIT session in progress.

Figure 988 Editing a file with EDIT.

Working with AU Files — 989

If you FTP audio sound files from the Internet or transfer audio sound files using the World Wide Web, the Internet usually provides you with audio files stored in the .AU extension. Your PC, however, plays audio files only in the .WAV extension. Therefore, if you click your mouse on an Internet audio hot spot, neither Sound Recorder nor Media Player can play that file. Usually, you will see garbage (the binary contents of .AU files) instead of hearing the file's audio. If you want to download and play .AU audio files, you must get a program that converts the downloaded .AU file format to the .WAV audio file format that your computer can play. If you anonymously FTP to the ftp.cwi.nl server and get the binary file named pub/audio/sox5dos.zip, you can uncompress the file and use the resulting *SOX* program to convert downloaded .AU files to the .WAV format so you can use Sound Recorder or Media Player to play the audio files.

Note: *To uncompress .ZIP files, download the PKUNZIP.EXE program from Microsoft Network, CompuServe, or America Online, register the program, and use PKUNZIP to uncompress .ZIP files you'll often find on online services.*

Take Advantage of Sysedit — 990

Several of the Tips presented in this book have directed you to edit files such as AUTOEXEC.BAT, CONFIG.SYS, or several Windows-based INI files. Although you can use an ASCII-based editor such as Notepad to edit these files, a better method is to use the SYSEDIT command which opens a window for each of the key configuration files. To start the SYSEDIT command, perform these steps:

1. Select the Start menu Run option. Windows 95 will display the Run dialog box.
2. Type in the command line SYSEDIT and press Enter. Windows 95 will display the SYSEDIT window as shown in Figure 990.
3. Make your changes to each file as required and use the File menu Save option to save your changes.

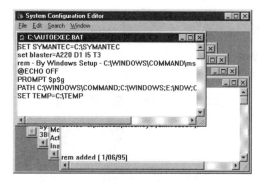

Figure 990 *The SYSEDIT Window.*

A Qucik Way to Explore a Disk or Folder — 991

As you have learned, the Windows 95 Explorer gives you a convenient and powerful way to manage your files and folders. Unfortunately, even though you can get to the Explorer from the Start menu with a few mouse clicks, getting to the folder you desire can often take time. If you know the pathname to the folder you want to explore, a quick way to access the folder within Explorer is to use the Start menu Run option. From within the Run dialog box, type **EXPLORER** followed by the pathname to the folder you desire. For example, to explore the Windows folder, you would type **EXPLORER \WINDOWS** and press Enter.

992 Viewing Wave File Specifics

As Tip 541 explains, audio .WAV files differ in quality depending on their 8-bit or 16-bit sampling rate, high hertz (*hz*) value, and stereo/mono setting. If an audio .WAV does not seem to have the quality that you think it should, you can view the .WAV file quality settings by performing these steps:

1. Start Explorer.
2. Locate the .WAV file you want to analyze.
3. Right-click your mouse over the .WAV file.
4. Select the right-click menu Properties option. Windows 95 will display the file's Properties sheet General page shown in Figure 992.1.
5. Click your mouse on the Details page to display the Properties sheet Details page shown in Figure 992.2.
6. Read the Audio format description to find the file's sampling rate and high hertz value. If the file uses 8-bit sampling (the most critical of a sound file's properties), you have a good indication of why the sound file is poor.

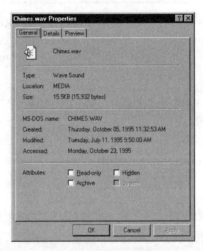

Figure 992.1 Displaying .WAV file properties.

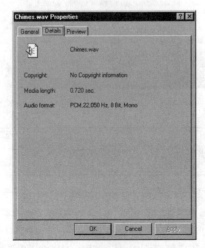

Figure 992.2 Analyzing the sound's quality.

Test Driving Some Cool Video Files   993

Windows 95 builds upon video support you once got from Windows 3.1's Video for Windows utility program. As such, on the Windows 95 CD-ROM, Microsoft includes a few video demonstration files that really bring out the multimedia in your computer. To play these video files, perform these steps:

1. Insert your Windows 95 CD-ROM in your CD-ROM drive. After a few moments, AutoPlay will display the CD-ROM's introductory window shown in Figure 993.1.
2. Open the Videos window by clicking your mouse over the Cool Video Clips button.
3. Double-click your mouse on any of the icons with a video camera on them. These are .AVI files and, depending on your Explorer display options, you may or may not see the .AVI filename extensions on the filenames beneath the icons. As soon as you double-click an icon, Windows 95 will start the Media Player and play the video (see Figure 993.2).
4. When the video clip ends, click on the window's Close button to close the video window.

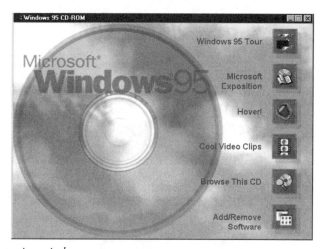

Figure 993.1 *The CD-ROM's opening window.*

Figure 993.2 *Watching a video.*

Viewing AVI File Specifics   994

The video files you play in Tip 993 are .AVI files. The .AVI filename extension means the files are *Audio Video Interleaved* files. Windows 95 uses the .AVI file format to store videos and their associated audio data. If you want to view the settings for an AVI file to determine the sampling and quality of the recording, perform these steps:

1. Start Explorer.
2. Locate the .AVI file you want to analyze.
3. Right-click your mouse over the .AVI file.
4. Select the right-click menu Properties option. Windows 95 will display the .AVI file's Properties sheet General page shown in Figure 994.1.
5. Click your mouse on the Details page to display the .AVI Properties sheet Details page shown in Figure 994.2. The Details page contains a lot of information about the video clip including the file size, audio format, and the video's recording size. If you click your mouse over the items in the Click an item list, you'll learn about the people behind the video's production.

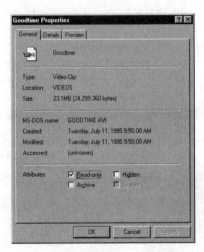

Figure 994.1 Displaying .AVI file properties.

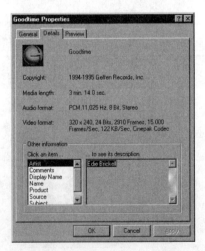

Figure 994.2 Analyzing the video's quality.

995 Previewing an AVI, MIDI, or WAV File

You can use QuickView to look at a text file or a word processor's document file, however, the right-click menu also supports video and sound files. When you right-click over an .AVI, .MID (for MIDI), or .WAV, you can use Explorer to hear or play the file. To hear or play the file, perform these steps:

1. Right-click over the video or audio file.
2. Click your mouse on the right-click menu Play option. This option normally reads Open for text or document files. Audio and video right-click menus do not contain QuickView options. Windows 95 will start the Media Player, load the file, and play the sound or video file.
3. Close Media Player when you finish playing the file.

996 Revisiting the Pentium Bug

One of the biggest items in computing news in 1994 was the discovery that some Pentium processors contain flaws that produce math errors in certain high-precision calculations. Windows 95 lets you know if you have a good or a flawed Pentium. Find out which you have by performing these steps:

1. Open your Control Panel window.
2. Double-click your mouse on the System icon to display the System Properties page.
3. Double-click on the Device Manager tab to display the Device Manager page.
4. Click your mouse on the plus sign next to the System Devices option to open the System Devices branch.
5. Click your mouse on Numeric data processor to highlight the item.
6. Click your mouse on the Properties button to display the Numeric data processor Properties page shown in Figure 996. If the Device Status area displays the message "This device is working properly", your Pentium processor does not have the flaw.

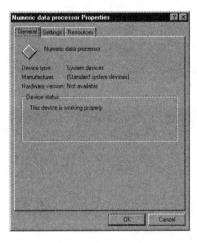

Figure 996 *Checking your Pentium processor.*

997 Understanding Windows 95 CAB Files

If you look at the files on your Windows 95 installation CD-ROM or floppy disks, you'll notice several .CAB files. These files are Windows 95's *cabinet* files. Microsoft developed the .CAB file format to compress installation files into the smallest possible format so that they could squeeze as much information onto one floppy disk or CD-ROM as possible. The .CAB file format lets Microsoft put almost two megabytes of information on a single floppy disk. If you've heard of .ZIP files, the .CAB files are similar but the .CAB format is Microsoft's proprietary format. During the Windows 95 installation, the installation program extracts (decompresses) individual Windows 95 files from the large .CAB files and installs those files. If you want to extract a driver file from your installation floppy disks or CD-ROM manually, you can extract that file from its .CAB file without performing a full installation.

998 | Installing Files from CAB Files

Most of the time, you'll use your Control Panel's Add/Remove Hardware item to add hardware to your computer. However, in rare cases, a hardware device requires special installation intervention which requires that you manually extract a .CAB file. Such instructions describe which installation floppy disk from which to extract. To extract a file from a floppy disk or CD-ROM's .CAB file, perform these steps:

1. Insert the .CAB file's Windows 95 floppy disk or CD-ROM into its drive. If you insert the CD-ROM, hold SHIFT when you slide the CD-ROM into its drive and keep holding SHIFT for a few moments after you close the door to keep AutoPlay from taking over.
2. Click your mouse on the Start menu Run option.
3. Type the command **EXTRACT D:*CABFILE.CAB***. Substitute *CABFILE.CAB* with the .CAB filename from which you want to extract. Windows 95 will read the .CAB file, decompress the file, and store the uncompressed file in your Windows 95 directory.

999 | Renaming Folders and Files within Applications

For years, if you misnamed a document in Word, Excel, or other Windows 3.1 applications, you could do little if you did not know how to use File Manager. The new Windows 95 Open and Save As dialog boxes solve this common problem. If you misname a file that you saved from within an application, display the File Open or File Save As dialog box once again, click your mouse on any folder or file to highlight the folder or file that you want to rename, and press **F2**. Windows 95 then lets you type a new file or folder name over the old one. When you press ENTER, Windows 95 renames the file and you then can return to your application.

1000 | Lose the Tilde (~) in Short DOS Filenames

When you use long filenames, Windows 95 must represent the long filenames with the old 8.3 naming limitation so that both your new Windows 95 and older legacy applications can work with the files. When storing a long filename, Windows 95 also stores a shortened version of the name using a *tilde* (~) character to represent the long right-hand portion of the name that does not fit in the shorter format.

Using a little-known trick, you can turn off Windows 95's use of the tilde so you don't have to type the tilde character when accessing short versions of long filenames from older applications. Perform these steps to turn off the tilde:

1. Start the registry editor by clicking your mouse on the Start menu Run command and typing **REGEDIT**.
2. Click your mouse on the HKEY_CLASSES_ROOT plus sign to open that branch.
3. Scroll the left-hand window down to the Directory folder and click its plus sign to open the Directory branch.
4. Open the shellex branch.
5. Open the CopyHookHandlers branch.
6. Click your mouse on the FileSystem folder to open the folder.
7. If you do not see the NameNumericTail subkey in the right-hand window, select the right-click menu New Binary Value, type **NameNumericTail**, and press ENTER. Windows 95 will automatically assign 0 to the value.

8. If the value of NameNumericTail is not 0, select the right-click menu Modify option and change the value to 0. Your registry window should look something like Figure 1000.
9. To implement your changes, close REGEDIT and restart Windows 95. Windows 95 will no longer use the tilde character for short versions of long filenames.

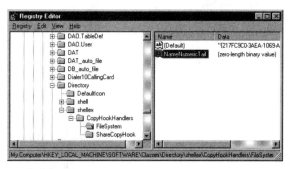

Figure 1000 *Eliminating short filenames' tilde character.*

Creating a Control Panel Folder on the Start Menu — 1001

Windows 95 presents this problem: The only way to access Control Panel entries is to access your Desktop first, open your Control Panel window, and scroll through the entries until you find the one you want to change. A better solution is to put a Control Panel folder on your Start menu. Unfortunately, that's not as easy as it sounds. To place a Control Panel entry on the Start menu (as shown in Figure 1001), perform these steps:

1. Right-click your mouse on the Start button,
2. Click your mouse on the right-click menu Explorer option.
3. Click your mouse on the File menu New Folder option.
4. Type the following long folder name (be careful that you type the name correctly):

Control Panel.{21EC2020-3AEA-1069-A2DD-08002B30309D}

5. Press ENTER.
6. Close Explorer and display your Start menu once again. As you can see from Figure 1001, you can now access the Control Panel and its items from the Start menu.

Note: *The strange Control Panel value comes from a registry entry. The value tells Windows 95 that the entry is a special Start menu value that displays the Control Panel on the Start menu.*

Figure 1001 *The Control Panel entry on the Start menu.*

Index

accessibility option
  keys
    FilterKeys, understanding and using, 211
    MouseKeys, understanding and using, 216
    StickyKeys, understanding and using, 210
    ToggleKeys, understanding and using, 212
  settings, controlling the, 218
  understanding the, 209
accessory programs
  Calculator
    accessing buttons from the keyboard, 580
    performing simple statistics using, 581
    Scientific, using the, 579
    Standard, performing a simple calculation using, 578
    using the standard, 577
  Clipboard
    changing the viewer display on the, 583
    saving the, contents, 584
    using the, viewer, 582
  Games
    FreeCell
      controlling options, 589
      playing instructions, 586
      starting a game, 587
    Hearts
      customizing options, 595
      playing a hand, 593
      playing instructions, 590
      playing network or local, 591
      shooting the moon, 594
      starting a game, 592
    Minesweeper
      marking the mines, 597
      playing instructions, 596
      selecting your level, 598
      showing off your scores, 599
    Running Hover!, playing instructions, 972
    understanding Windows 95, 585
  Paint
    drawing options
      circles and ovals, 607
      curved lines, 603
      filling a shape with a specific color, 609
      filled shapes, 606
      polygons, 608
      rectangles and squares, 604
      straight lines, 602
    program operations
      aligning objects using the grid, 628
      changing an image's attributes, 626
      copying objects to or from a file, 622
      cut and paste, selecting objects for, 621
      drawing with the, 600
      editing the color palette, 627
      flipping or rotating an image, 624
      fonts, controlling in, 620
      foreground and background colors, selecting, 605
      saving your image, 618
      stretching and skewing an image, 625
      undoing an operation within, 610
      wallpaper, using your image for, 619
      zooming in and out using using the Zoom menu, 623
    tools
      airbrush, using the, 616
      brush tool, painting with the, 612
      color picker, 614
      eraser, using, 613
      magnifying glass, using the, 615
      pencil, using for detailed drawing, 611
      text tool, using the, 617
      understanding, 601
      understanding the Windows 95, 575
  WordPad
    Bold, Italics, and Underline attributes, using the, 634
    bullets, using within a, document, 642
    creating, printing, and saving a document, 630
    date and time, inserting into a, document, 638
    font, controlling the current, 635
    format bar, using the, 645
    object, inserting into a, document, 641
    options, controlling, 647
    page attributes, controlling a document's, 650
    paragraph alignment, controlling, 632
    paragraph indentation, controlling, 633
    previewing a, document before printing, 649
    ruler, using the, 646
    ruler, using to set tabs, 648
    separating, paragraphs, by pressing Enter, 631
    tab stops, controlling, 643
    telecommunications, understanding, 651
    text, finding within a large document, 636
    text, moving or copying within a, document, 640
    text, replacing throughout a, document, 637
    text, selecting within a, document, 639
    toolbar, using the, 644
    using the, accessory, 629
Alt-Tab, using, to select a running program, 135
anti-aliasing *See* font smoothing
Apply
  button, using the, 81
  versus OK, understanding, 206
ARP (Address Resolution Protocol), 686
audio *See also* sounds and multimedia
  creating custom settings, 542
  devices, selecting Volume Control's , 565
  files, recording and saving, 558
  understanding digital, 541
audio codec
  prioritizing, 550
  understanding, 549
AU files, working with, 989
AUTOEXEC.BAT
  controlling a program's MS-DOS settings using, 166
  finding your old system files in, 195
  how Windows 95 uses, 151
  in Windows 3.1, 33
AutoPlay, using, to play music CDs, 41
AVI (Audio Video Interleaved) files, viewing specifics, 994
backup files
  compressing, to save tape or floppy disk space, 386
  creating, on floppy disks before you compress, 403
  drag and drop
    incremental, understanding, 384
    operations, understanding and performing, 382
    settings, controlling, 383
  selection, inverting a, 334
  sets
    comparing new files to 393
    saving your file and folder selections to, 380
    selecting files for, 379
    understanding, 378
    understanding your need to create, 375
  tape-based, controlling, 388
  using a tape drive to, 376
  verification, understanding, 385
backup, full-system, understanding a, 377
binary files, editing, 988
BIOS-based disk operations, insuring, 935
BOOTLOG.TXT
  logging your system startup using, 185
  operations, understanding incremental, 384
  verification, understanding, 385
boot
  delay, controlling the Windows 95, 956

key support, turning off, 958
menu
    controlling the Windows 95, 961
    default option, controlling the, 963
    delay, controlling the Windows 95, 962
operations, multiple, supporting, 965
Briefcase
    date-and-time stamps, checking the, 518
    file management, using, 514
    splitting a file from an original, using, 517
    updating a, file, using, 516
    using the toolbar for, 519
    using, to test a file transfer, 515
Browse dialog box, using the, 94
CAB files
    installing files from, 998
    understanding Windows 95, 997
Cancel button, using the, 81
case-sensitive search operations, performing, 365
CD-ROM, Windows 95, learning about the contents of the, 981
CD-ROMS, MSCDEX (Microsoft CD Extension), elimination of the need to use, 810
check boxes, selecting multiple options using, 77
color scheme
    saving your, 123
    using a, to control Desktop colors, 119
command path, and Windows 95, 181
command prompt, starting your system to a, 188
compatibility of non-Windows 95 files, 183
components, viewing details about, 204
CONFIG.SYS
    controlling a program's MS-DOS settings, 166
    finding your old system files in, 195
    how Windows 95 uses, 152
    in Windows 3.1, 33
Control menu, using the, 96
    for screen display settings, 208
Control Panel
    customizing the, CD-ROM, 313
    customizing the, hard-disk, 312
    displaying general System information for the, 301
    getting to the, 45
    graphics acceleration, 315
    multimedia settings, Control Panel, 538
    setting the date-and-time, 207
    trouble shooting, 314
    understanding Apply versus OK in the, 206
    understanding the, 283, 311
    using the, for screen display settings, 208
    using the, to set the date-and-time, 207
Control Panel Device Manager
    file system, understanding the, 311
    removing a device from your device list using, 306
    specifics, locating, 304
    summary, printing the, 305
    understanding the, 302
    view, controlling the, 303
copy and paste operation
    using to copy a file, 343
    using to copy objects, 108
Cover Page Editor, 431 *See also* fax
currency formats, controlling, 285
customizing
    CD Player preferences, 574
    Control Panel
        CD ROM disks, 313
        to control currency formats, 285
        to control date formats, 287
        to control numeric formats, 284
        to control time formats, 286
        to display screen contrast, 215
Desktop
    by assigning a graphic, using a new bitmap, 126
    by assigning a pattern, 124
    by assigning a specific color to an item, 120
    by assigning a specific font to an item, 121
    by assigning a wallpaper, 125
    by creating a custom color, 122
device properties, 556
Explorer, using command-line arguments, 837
graphics acceleration, 315
    CD-ROM file system, 313
hard-disk file system, 312
Help window font size, 67
modem settings, 234
mouse
    by changing your mouse pointer, 249, 251
    by changing your mouse type, 252
    by changing your settings, 246
    by switching between a right- and left-handed mouse, 247
    by using a predefined mouse pointer scheme, 250
multimedia
    advanced settings, 547
    audio settings, 542
    driver, 548
    Multimedia Player options, 555
network components, properties of, 781
printer, 263
reasons for, 197
screen saver settings, 118
sounds, creating a custom audio setting, 542
system, your, 197
cut-and-paste operation, using to move a file, 342
data bits, definition of, 238
data connection preferences, understanding, 238
date formats, controlling, 287
date or time, changing the, 142
day and date, displaying the, 141
default operating system, controlling the, 969
default system settings in 10.SYS, 192
delete operation, undoing a, 134
demand-paging virtual memory system, definition of, 874
Desktop
    arranging icons on the, 101
    color scheme
        saving your, 123
        using a, to control color, 119
    customizing
        by assigning a graphic, using a new bitmap, 126
        by assigning a pattern, 124
        by assigning a specific color to an item, 120
        by assigning a specific font to an item, 121
        by assigning a wallpaper, 125
        by creating a custom color, 122
    lining up icons on the, 102
    management, using Windows 95 accessories, 575
    moving clipboard contents to the, using Scraps, 820
    pasting a, scrap, by dragging a document on to the taskbar, 821
    Properties
        changing the number of colors your monitor displays within, 137
        changing your screen font size within, 139
        changing your screen resolution within, 138
        changing your video card or monitor type within, 140
    understanding, 98, 115
    using the, to undo a delete operation, 134
DETCRASH.LOG, using, 931
device driver files, sources, 940
Device Manager
    specifics, locating, 304
    summary, printing the, 305
    removing a device from your device list using, 306

Index

understanding the, 302
view, controlling the, 303
dialing scheme, 244
dialog boxes
  Browse, using the, 94
  definition of, 75
  Open
    listing files of a specific type using the, 87
    understanding the, 85
    using the, to locate and open files, 86
  options, highlighting, 76
  understanding sheets, pages, and tabs within, 75
  using the OK, Cancel, and Apply buttons within a, 81
directories
  moving up multiple levels of, using the CD command, 196
  organizing your files using, 82
  Windows 95 folders and, 83
disability resources for the visually impaired, 939
disk compression
  of part of your hard drive, 409
  of your entire hard drive, 408
  operations
    adjusting free space on a compressed disk, 412
    changing a host drive's letter for a compressed disk, 416
    controlling automatic loading of DBLSPACE.BIN, 967
    controlling automatic loading of DRVSPACE.BIN, 968
    controlling automatic mounting of a compressed disk, 407
    deleting a compressed disk, 410
    formatting a compressed disk, 415
    hiding or displaying the host drive for a compressed disk, 414
    mounting and dismounting of a compressed disk, 406
    uncompressing a compressed disk, 405
  preparation for
    by backing up files, 403
    by compressing a floppy disk as practice, 402
    by determining the disk space your drive gives you, 404
  properties, viewing, 411
  ratios, understanding and fine-tuning, 413
  understanding, 400
  understanding how DriveSpace accomplishes, 417
  using DriveSpace for, 401
disk drive defragmentation
  advanced settings for Disk Defragmenter, understanding and using for, 399
  pausing, resuming, or ending Disk Defragmenter for, 396
  understanding Disk Defragmenter's detailed display for, 398
  using the Disk Defragmenter for, 395
disk drive errors
  automatic correction of, 425
  correcting with ScanDisk advanced options
    to delete or copy cross-linked files, 429
    to fix lost file fragments, 428
  log for, 427
  ScanDisk, understanding and using, 426
  standard check for, 422
  thorough check for, 423
    using a surface scan, 424
  understanding and repairing, 421
disk drive formatting within Windows 95, 816
disk drive fragmentation, 394
  displaying details of, 397
  understanding how, decreases your system's performance, 394
disk drive space availability, displaying, 839
disk operations, insuring BIOS-based, 935
disk partitioning
  understanding, 814
  using FDISK to create multiple logical drives, 815
display screen contrast, controlling the, 215
DNS (Domain Name System), definition of, 675
docking
  understanding, 522

Windows 95, detection, 524
Documents
  menu
    clearing the, 46
    taking advantage of the, 30
  window, clearing the, 46
DoubleSpace, controlling automatic loading using, 967
Drawing Toolbar, 435 *See also* fax
driver(s)
  determining the device, your system is using, 860
  determining whether your device, is using real-mode or 32-bit mode, 947
  determining which were loaded by Windows 95, 950
  overcoming sluggishness with 16-bit, 861
  protected mode, understanding VxD, 858
  qualifiers in IOS.INI, understanding, 949
  safe-mode, taking a close look at, 948
  16-based, understanding, 859
  source for device, files, 940
DriveSpace
  controlling automatic loading of DRVSPACE.BIN, 968
  understanding, 417
  using, for disk drive compression, 401
ECP (Extended Capability Ports), understanding, 803
ending an application, using a local reboot, 36
energy-compliant hardware, impact of, 946
Energy Star features, understanding and using, 127
EPP (Enhanced Parallel Ports), understanding, 803
errors
  disabling 32-bit disk access before correcting, 932
  isolating, 930
  Pentium bug, revisiting the, 996
  using DETCRASH.LOG to repair, damage, 931
Ethernet, understanding, 756
events, referencing, changing the label Windows uses for, 910
exchanging files with non-windows 95 users, 183
Explorer
  icon display, using the large and small, 347
  selecting quickly all but a few, files, 845
  Send To option, using to send files, 504
  using to move up one level from an open file, 840
Explorer window(s)
  customizing, using command-line arguments, 837
  file extensions and icons, using to display, 355
  files and folders
    finding, by using, 64, 359, 360, 362, 363
    refreshing a list of, in the, 351
  hidden files, controlling which are displayed in the, 352
  large and small icon display in the, 347
  multiple viewer, opening, 370
  parts of the, 320
  running a program from the, 327
extensions, avoiding common, 987
fax cover sheet
  creating a new, 434
  creating a, using lines, fills, and colors, 445
  creating a, using the Cover Page Editor, 431
  creating a, using the Drawing Toolbar, 435
  customizing an existing, 433
  objects
    aligning, 446
    duplicating, 447
    inserting, other than those pre-defined, 444
    placing a graphic, on, 441
    placing text, on, 436
    selecting and working with, 442
    sending, to the front or back, 443
  pasteboard, using the, 449
  text frames
    aligning objects within, 440
    aligning text within, 439
    controlling, fonts, 438

using pre-defined, 437
using an existing, 432
fax operations
  address book entry
    changing an, 460
    creating an, 454
    creating a fax-based, 455
    creating a local area network-based, 458
    creating a Microsoft Network-based, 457
    creating an, for other online services, 459
    creating an Internet-based, 456
    finding an, 461
  calling card, using a, 452
  call waiting, disabling, 453
  in Windows 95, 430
  Microsoft Exchange
    composing a mail message within, 473
    controlling, services, 470
    messages and folders, working with, 471
    toolbar, customizing the, 479
    understanding, 469
    understanding messages and icons within, 472
    working with, messages and folders, 471
  profiles
    creating, 451
    using, 450
fax options
  attaching a file to your fax, 466
  controlling, 463
  receiving a fax, 468
  retrieving a fax, 467
  security keys
    creating and managing, 465
    using, 464
  security, understanding, 463
filenames
  long, MS-DOS-based support for, 182
  long, turning off temporarily, using LFNBK, 823
  short, removing the tilde in, 1000
  understanding and using long, 44
files *See also* backup files
  archive property for, 339
  attributes, displaying details about, 349
    changing location of, using the Save As dialog box, 89
  copying
    cancelling a, operation, 830
    recognizing a, operation, 829
    using a copy and paste operation, 343
    using a drag and drop operation, 371
  deleting a, 329
    by bypassing the Recycle Bin, 836
  determining the number of, in a folder, 844
  exchanging
    understanding host and guest connections for the purpose of, 525
    using a Direct Cable Connection, 524
    with non-windows 95 users, 183
  filtering, understanding and using, 381
  finding, 359
    by contents, 363
    by date, 362
    by name, 360
    by size, 364
  found, using, 361
  hidden files, understanding, 337
  inverting a, selection, 334
  listing, of a specific type using the Open dialog box, 87
  LNK, understanding, 834
  management, using Briefcase, 514
  moving
    cancelling a, operation, 830
    recognizing a, operation, 829
    using a cut-and-paste operation, 342
    using a drag and drop operation, 372
  moving and copying, using the mouse, 344
  multiple
    organizing your, using Directories, 82
    selecting dispersed, for an operation, 332
    selecting successive, for an operation, 331
    selecting, using a lasso, 832
  opening, using the Open dialog box, 86
  operation, undoing a, 345
  overwrite, controlling, operations during a restore, 392
  printing, using a drag and drop operation, 373
  properties, displaying for a, 335
  read-only, understanding, 336
  recognizing types of, using icons, 324
  recovering, from the Recycle Bin, 130
  removing, from the Recycle Bin, 132
  renaming, 330
    from within applications, 999
    safely, 833
  restoring
    from a previous backup, 388
    to a new location, 390
    to their original locations, 389
    verifying an operation, 391
  saving, to a specific format, 90
  selecting
    all but a few, quickly, in Explorer, 845
    all in a folder, 333
    two or more dispersed, for an operation, 332
    two or more successive, for an operation, 331
  specific, going to, 369
  storing, in Windows 95, 847
  swapping
    deleting a Windows 3.1 permanent swap file, 813
    forcing permanent, 812
    understanding, 811
  system
    measurements, improving, 865
    monitoring the Windows 95, 864
    understanding, 338
  transferring
    using the Direct Cable Connection feature, 525
    setting up a guest computer for, 526
    setting up a host computer for, 527
file type(s)
  associating a program with a, 328
  displaying a, 355
  recognizing a, using icons, 324
  registered
    new, establishing a, 357
    removing a, 358
    understand and viewing, 356
  understanding, 23
  unfamiliar, viewing information on, 909
  using drag and drop to delete, 129
  using drag and drop to restore, 131
File Explorer
  using the status bar, 326
  using the toolbar, 325
FilterKeys, understanding and using, 211
flash memory support, 533
folder
  branch, opening within Explorer, 843
  closing multiple in one step, 842
  contents lists and details, displaying, 348
  contents, sorting, 350
  creating and removing, 84
  creating new, 340
  creating, within a file-related dialog box, 92
  creating your own, 112

Index

deleting, 329
    using a drag and drop operation, 129
displaying contents lists and details, 348
expanding and collapsing, 323
files, determining the number of, in a, 844
finding a, 359
    by contents, 363
    by date, 362
    by name, 360
    by size, 364
    that contains a file, 986
improving your organization using, 321
listing icons for, within a file-related dialog box, 93
moving up quickly while traversing, 91
new, creating, 340
opening, 322
    using the same window, 831
organizing your, using subfolders, 113
properties, displaying for, 335
Recent, using to view recently used documents within, 835
recovering, from the Recycle Bin, 130
removing, from the Recycle Bin, 132
renaming, 114, 330, 833
restoring, using a drag and drop operation, 131
saving, to a backup file set, 380
scrolling through the list of, 322
selecting all the files in, 333
specific, going to, 369
understanding, 23
Windows 95, and their relationship to directories, 83
font(s)
    adding, 222
    listing, by similarity, 226
    point sizes, understanding, 221
    removing, 223
    samples, viewing and printing, 220
    screen, changing size of, 139
    size, controlling in an MS-DOS window, 154
    TrueType, understanding, 224
    understanding, 219
    window, reducing clutter in the, 225
font smoothing, understanding, 982
games *See* accessory programs
hardware
    detected, viewing, 850
    energy-compliant, 946
    installing new, 199
    Legacy, understanding, 849
    profiles
        creating your own, 308
        renaming and deleting, 309
        understanding, 307
full-system backup, understanding a, 377
graphical user interface, disabling Windows 95, 960
Help
    building a topic index for, 64
    finding information using Find within, 63
    finding similar topics within, 70
    fine-tuning Find options within, 65
    placing and jumping to a bookmark within, 69
    requesting, using the What's This? option, 57
    starting an operation from within, 68
    starting Windows 95 online, 51
    topic(s)
        annotating (adding your own notes to a), 59
        copying a, to the clipboard, 62
        Index, locating information using the, 60
        links, understanding, 53
        previously displayed, moving back to a, 54
        printing a, 56
        selecting and viewing a, 52
        selecting, using the Help Topics sheet Index tab, 61
        traversing, using browse buttons, 55
    using, to find definitions, 58
    windows
        customizing the, font size, 67
        keeping your, visible, 66
hidden files
    controlling which, the Explorer displays, 352
    understanding, 337
HKEY_CLASSES_ROOT, using to work with unfamiliar files, 909
HKEY_LOCAL_MACHINE
    taking a close look at, 882
    taking a close look at, \config, 886
    taking a close look at _CURRENT-CONFIG, 895
    taking a close look at _CURRENT-USER, 893
    taking a close look at _DYN_DATA, 896
    taking a close look at, \enum, 887
    taking a close look at, \hardware, 885, 891
    taking a close look at, \network, 888
    taking a close look at, \software, 889
    taking a close look at, \system, 890
    taking a close look at _USERS, 894
hot key, understanding, 74
HyperTerminal
    accessing a remote computer using, 670
    text buffer, controlling the size of, 663
    text, capturing to a file or printer using, 662
    toolbar, displaying and using the, 664
icons
    arranging on the Desktop, 59
    changing an MS-DOS-based program's, 163
    Control Panel, understanding, 260
    lining up on the Desktop, 102
    taskbar volume, 539
    using New, Open, Save, and Print, 97
idle sensitivity, using to improve system or program responsiveness, 177
Improving an MS-DOS-Based Program's Video Output, 174
Inbox *See also* Microsoft Exchange
    understanding and repairing, error, 418
    using the, 28
incremental backups, definition of, 339
.INI files
    and compatibility with Windows 95, 877
    and Windows 95, 34
Internet
    accessibility, using Ping to test a site's, 684
    accessing an, account using HyperText, 670
    accessing, preparing your system for, 673
    account naming
        domain name server, configuring your TCP/IP connection's, 676
        domain names, understanding, 675
        IP address, specifying your computer's, 677
        IP (Internet Protocol) addresses, understanding, 674
        WINS (Windows Internet Naming Service), understanding and configuring, 678
    address resolution, controlling using ARP, 686
    connections
        TCP/IP, displaying, using Winipcfg, 696
        tracing a route using Tracert, 685
        understanding PPP and SLIP, 669
    FTP (File Transfer Protocol)
        programs, downloading, 697
        sites, 692
        understanding file transfers using, 691
        using, to download a web browser, 693
    Gopher
        sample, sites, 704
        traversing the, using, 703
    IP (Internet Protocol), definition of, 674
    IRC (Internet Relay Chat), understanding, 699
    JPEG

sample sites, 711
viewer, downloading a, 710
mailing lists, understanding, 702
newsgroups
    accessing through Microsoft Network, 750
    sample, 701
    understanding, 700
online services and the, 666
phone programs, downloading a Windows-based, 709
provider(s)
    dialing your, 682
    properties, configuring, 681
    telling Windows 95 about your, 679
    understanding, 668
SLIP
    script, creating a, 683
    support software, installing, 680
Telnet
    downloading a Windows-based, program, 708
    sites, 690
    using to move from one computer to another, 689
    working on a remote computer using, 689
understanding the, 665
WAIS (Wide Area Information Server)
    sample sites, 706
    traversing the, using, 705
Windows 95 and the, 667
IRC (Internet Relay Chat), understanding, 699
joystick settings, controlling, 227
kernel, understanding the Windows 95, 863
keyboard
    controlling responsiveness of the, 228
        using registry, 911
    languages
        adding and removing, 231
        switching between, 232
        understanding and using, 230
    Microsoft, shortcut keys for the, 938
    type, selecting your, 233
laptop *See* notebook computer
Legacy hardware, understanding, 849
LFNBK, using to turn off long filenames temporarily, 823
local reboot, using a, to end an application, 36
mailing lists, understanding, 702
mapping, to a Network Drive, 366
maximizing a window, 13
Media Player
    customizing, options, 555
    using the, 551
    using, to open a media file, 552
    using, to select a media object, 554
    using, to view tracks, time, or frames, 553
memory
    management, 866
        monitoring Windows 95, 866
    measurements, optimizing, 867
    understanding why adding, improves system performance, 875
    virtual, understanding, 316
Microsoft Exchange
    columns, modifying, 501
    customization of, using the Control Panel, 503
    e-mail
        retrieving remotely, 496
        scheduling Remote Mail operations within, 499
        sending, from a remote computer, 498
        using the Remote Mail toolbar within, 498
    faxes
        composing within, 482
        controlling, formats, 491
        controlling outgoing, 489
        controlling when sent, 490
        defining user, properties, 493
        specifying, redial properties, 492
        viewing outgoing, 488
    folders, sorting contents of, 502
    message
        attaching a file to a, 475
        composing a mail, within, 473
        finding a mail, 486
        forwarding a mail, 485
        inserting a file into a, 474
        inserting an object into a, 477
        inserting or attaching an existing message within a, 476
        performing an advanced, search, 487
        reading a new mail, 483
        replying to a mail, 484
        retrieving from a remote computer's files, 495
        working with, properties, 480
        working with the current, 481
    options, customizing, 494
    services, controlling, 470
    toolbar
        customizing the, 479
        using the mail composition, 478
    understanding, 469
    understanding messages and icons within, 472
    windows, changing, 500
    working with, messages and folders, 471
Microsoft Network (MSN)
    accessing the, 715
    calendar of events, 725
    categories, accessing, 734
    forums
        Arts and Entertainment, 745
        Business and Finance, 746
        chat sessions in, participating in, 737
        computer information-related, 739
        Health and Fitness, 744
        Home and Family, 741
        reading and writing messages in, 736
        Science and Technology, 743
        Sports, 742
        visiting, 735
        Windows 95-related, 740
    favorite locations
        adding, to your list, 727
        visiting, 726
    Go To feature, 722
    Internet
        accessing through, 748
        e-mail, sending and receiving through, 751
        newsgroups, accessing through, 750
    local number, locating a, for, 718
    logging off, 752
    mail, using, 732
    news
        accessing the, using the, Today window, 729
        member assistance for, 731
        moving around, 730
        understanding how to access, 724
    online magazine, *MSN Computing*, reading, 747
    registering the, for the first time, 717
    requirements, 715
    software, installing, 714
    SOHO (Small Office Home Office) site, using the, 733
    suggestion box, 738
    surfing cyberspace with, 27
    toolbar buttons, 721
    traversing, 720
    understanding, 713
    viewing, using Explorer, 728
    welcome window, 719

Index

World Wide Web, browsing using, 749
Microsoft products, demonstrating, 973
MIDI (Musical Instrument Digital Interface)
    creating a custom setting, 545
    understanding, 544
minimizing all open windows at once, 12
minimizing a window, 11
modem
    adding and removing a, 235
    advanced settings for a, understanding, 242
    call preference settings, understanding and using for a, 239
    creating a dialing scheme for a, 244
    customizing settings for a, 234
    dialing properties for a, understanding, 243
    operations, troubleshooting, 954
    properties, controlling, 236
    speed, understanding, 237
    UART
        settings, controlling, 241
        understanding, affect on performance of a, 240
    using your calling card with your, 245
monitor, changing the number of colors displayed on a, 137
monitoring your system's network or disk access using the System Monitor, 862
mouse
    customization
        by changing mouse settings, 246
        by changing your mouse pointer, 249, 251
        by changing your mouse type, 252
        by switching between a right- and left-handed mouse, 247
        by using a predefined mouse pointer scheme, 250
    double-click speed, controlling, 248
    moving and copying using the, 344
    operations, controlling in an MS-DOS-based window, 178
    pointer motion, controlling, 252
MouseKeys, understanding and using, 216
MS-DOS
    activating an, -based program, using a shortcut key, 161
    and Windows 95, 144
    batch file, running a, immediately before an, based program, 160
    changing an, -based program's icon, 163
    commands, locating, 194
    controlling an, -based program's
        AUTOEXEC.BAT and CONFIG.SYS settings, 166
        command line, 158
        conventional memory, 169
        (DPMI) DOS protected mode memory, 172
        expanded memory, 170
        extended memory, 171
        font, 167
        screen and window usage, 173
        window, 162
        working directory in, 159
    controlling termination of an, -based program, 179
    differences between an -based program memory and Windows 95
    memory management, 168
        controlling, by preventing an, -based program from knowing it's
    running within Windows, 164
        getting to an, prompt, 32
        improving an, -based program's video output for, 174
        location of, 5
    program(s)
        FDISK, using to partition a drive, 815
        memory, 168
        that may not run in, 149
        using a shortcut key to activate a, 161
    prompts, getting to, 32
    replaced in Windows 95, 144
    running a batch file immediately before a, -based program, 160
    running, -based programs, 148
    starting your computer in, 150
    suggesting that a, -based program run in MS-DOS mode, 165
    suspending or allowing -based programs in the background, 176
    using a shortcut key to activate a, -based program, 161
    using idle sensitivity to improve system or program responsiveness in, 177
    using the, toolbar, 153
    windows
        closing, 147
        controlling, in an, -based program, 162
        controlling mouse operations in, 178
        controlling the font size in, 154
        copying text to the clipboard, from, 155
        opening, 145
        pasting text to, 156
        sizing, 146
        support for long filenames, 182
MSCDEX (Microsoft CD Extension), elimination of the need to use, 810
MSD, using to troubleshoot hardware, 937
MSDOS.SYS
    path entries, understanding the, 971
    understanding, 191
    understanding and using file entries in, 193
MSDOS.SYS file, editing the, 956
multimedia
    audio
        CD Player
            controlling how tracks play using the, 572
            customizing preferences, 574
            toolbar, using the, 570
            using the, 567
        CD(s)
            creating a playlist for an, 569
            finding a, specific song, 573
            information, viewing, 571
            playlists, understanding, 568
            understanding, 546
            understanding why some, run automatically, 951
        controlling sound formats, 559
        creating custom settings, 542
        files, inserting and mixing, 561
        files, recording and saving, 558
        recording your own sounds using Sound Recorder, 557
        understanding digital, 541
    codecs
        prioritizing, 550
        understanding video and audio, 549
    driver, customizing a, 548
    files
        AU files, working with, 989
        .WAV, viewing specifics, 992
    Media Player
        customizing, options, 555
        using the, 551
        using, to open a media file, 552
        using, to select a media object, 554
        using, to view tracks, time, or frames, 553
    MIDI (Musical Instrument Digital Interface)
        creating a custom setting, 545
        understanding, 544
    settings
        advanced, 547
        Control Panel, 538
    Sound Recorder, achieving special effects with the, 562
    support
        for sound effects, understanding, 536
        understanding Windows 95, 537
    video
        AVI files, viewing specifics, 994
        AVI, MIDI, or WAV files, previewing, 995
        controlling the default, size, 543
        files, taking a look at some, 993
        .WAV files, viewing specifics, 992

volume control
   balance, controlling, 564
   customizing Advanced Volume Control Settings, 566
   devices, selecting Volume Control's, 565
   properties, customizing, 556
   using the Windows 95, 563
multiple directory levels, moving up using the CD command, 196
multiple viewer windows, opening, 370
multitasking
   preemptive, how Windows 95 uses, 827
   smoother, using multithreaded applications, 828
   understanding, 826
My Computer
   quickly exploring, 846
   taking a look at, 22
   traversing drives inside, 24
NetBEUI, understanding, 761
Netstat program, displaying TCP/IP statistics using the, 687
Netware, troubleshooting errors in, 966
network
   drive
      disconnecting from a, 368
      mapping to a, 366
   newsgroups, understanding, 700
   organization, types of, 755
   persistent connection, creating a, 367
   routing tables, controlling using Route, 688
   software, controlling, 964
   support, starting Windows 95 without, 933
   TCP/IP statistics, displaying using Netstat, 687
Network Neighborhood
   getting to know your, 24
   turning off the, 943
NFS (Network File System), understanding, 764
non-Windows 95 programs, avoiding problems running, 952
notebook computer *See also* Briefcase
   deferred printing for a
      understanding, 520
      using, 521
   determining the battery life of your, 261
   docking
      understanding, 522
      Windows 95, detection of your, 524
   file management, using Briefcase, 514
   offering a reward for your lost or stolen, 984
   PC card *See also* PCMCIA
      controlling a 32-bit, support, 532
      displaying the, indicator, 529
      installing a, 531
      installing a, device, 530
      removing a, 531
      understanding the, 528
   testing a file transfer from your, to your desktop computer, 515
   understanding Windows 95's, support for your, 513
   updating a, file, using Briefcase, 516
numeric formats, controlling, 284
object(s) *See also* OLE
   copying, using Copy and Paste, 108
   creating a new, from a file, 857
   embed and link, when to, 855
   embedding, using, 853
   linking
      understanding, 852
      using, 854
   moving and copying, using Drag and Drop, 110
   moving, using Cut and Paste, 109
ODBC (Open Database Connectivity)
   data source(s)
      adding an, 299
      options, controlling, 300
      setting up an, 298
   understanding, 297
   drivers
      adding, 296
      specifics about, 295
      understanding, 294
   general system information, displaying, 301
   understanding, 293
OK button, using the, 81
OLE (Object Linking and Embedding)
   understanding, 852
   understanding how, works, 856
online
   Help, starting, 51
   services
      non-Internet, *See* Microsoft Network
      understanding, 712
   sources of Windows 95 information, 48
Open dialog box
   understanding the, 85
   using the, to locate and open files, 86
option buttons, using, 78
pages, understanding, 75
paging
   performance, improving, 874
   understanding, 317
parity, definition of, 238
password(s)
   changing your Windows, 255
   controlling other, 256
   restricting remote administration using, 257
   understanding how Windows 95 uses, 254
   using, to protect your screen saver, 117
pathname(s)
   complete MS-DOS, displaying in the title bar, 354
   understanding complete, 353
PC card(s)
   controlling a 32-bit, support, 532
   displaying the, indicator, 529
   installing a, 531
   installing a, device, 530
   removing a, 531
   sound effects, understanding, 536
   understanding, 528
Pentium bug, revisiting the, 996
Phone Dialer
   creating a speed-dial entry with, 507
   device, specifying the, 508
   logging calls using, 510
   logs
      controlling the, 511
      purging the, 512
   manually dialing a phone number with, 506
   placing calls using the, 505
   profile, using a, 509
phone programs, downloading a Windows-based, 709
Ping program
   downloading a Windows-based, 707
   using to test a site's accessibility, 684
Plug and Play, understanding, 37
port settings, controlling, 275
power management
   controlling your PC's, settings, 260
   determining your notebook computer's battery life, 261
   understanding, 259
printer
   adding a, 264
   adding, customizing, and removing a, 261
   default, selecting a, 281
   details, viewing and customizing, 269
   driver, removing a, 265
   jobs

Index

changing the order of, 280
purging, 278
viewing the current, 276
viewing the number of, on each, 282
pausing a, 277
pausing or canceling a specific job's printing, 279
ports
    adding and deleting, 270
    capturing and releasing, 271
    controlling settings on, 275
    ECP and EPP, providing support for, 804
    ECP and EPP, understanding, 803
properties, viewing, 267
sharing
    across the network, 272
    understanding and using separator pages for, 268
shortcuts, creating, on the Desktop, 266
spooling
    DOS-based program, understanding, 806
    EMF (Enhanced Metafile) files, to improve printer performance, 805
    settings, understanding and using, 274
    understanding, 273
troubleshooting a slow, 953
printing
    by performing a drag and drop print operation, 373
    deferred
        understanding, 520
        using, 521
    font samples, 220
    Device Manager summary, the, 305
    Help topics, 56
    registry contents, 880
programs
    ending, 8
    multiple, running, 9
    non-Windows 95, avoiding problems running, 952
    rebooting your computer in, 21
    starting, in, 7
    switching between, in, 10
    32-bit and 16-bit, understanding, 822
Properties Menu, using the, to undo a Delete operation, 134
protocol, definition of, 658
pull-down list, selecting items from a, 79
pull-down menus, working with, 73
Quick View
    understanding, 817
    using, to determine the best way to open a file, 819
    using to view a file, 818
read-only files, understanding, 336
rebooting your computer, 21
renaming files from within applications, 999
Resource Meter, understanding the, 419
Resource Monitor, understanding output from the, 420
Recycle Bin
    bypassing the, to delete a file, 836
    emptying (flushing) the, 133
    recovering files and folders from the, 130
    removing a specific file or folder from the, 132
    retrieving objects from the, 26
referencing events, changing the label Windows uses for, 910
REGEDIT command line options, understanding, 898
regional settings, understanding, 283
registered file type(s)
    new, how to establish a, 357
    removing a, 358
    understanding and viewing, 356
registering Windows 95, 40
registry *See also* HKEY_LOCAL_MACHINE
    accessing specific information, using
        to edit an entry's binary value
        to edit an entry's string value, 884

        to view computer's settings information using HKEY_LOCAL_MACHINE 882
    contents, printing, 880
    database
        backing up and restoring your, 904
        exporting your, 900
        importing your, 902
        viewing an exported, 901
    editing the Windows, 878
    editor
        running the Windows 95, 879
        using the, to remove the network, 899
    entries
        adding, 908
        deleting, 907
        editable, 897
        renaming, 906
        understanding the basic, 881
    files, understanding, 903
    finding a, entry or value, 905
    functions
        changing your computer's name, 921
        controlling the cursor blink rate, 912
        controlling the screen saver interval, 913
        controlling the screen saver password protection, 914
        controlling video resolution, 917
        controlling your keyboard's responsiveness, 911
        displaying installed device drivers, 918
        listing the Windows 95 32-bit virtual drivers, 919
        specifying the wallpaper you desire, 916
        tiling or centering wallpaper, 915
    release notes, reading and printing the Windows 95, 91
    understanding the relationship between HKEY-CURRENT-CONFIG and other profile settings, 920
    understanding the Windows 95, 876
remote administration, restricting, 257
ROM breakpoint, preventing Windows 95 use of the, 934
router, definition of, 688
running a program
    from Explorer, 327
    MS-DOS, 148
    multiple, 9
    using the Run option, 31
safe-mode drivers, taking a close look at, 948
safe mode, starting your system in a, 186
safe mode warning, controlling the, 970
Save As
    using the, option, 88
    using the, dialog box to change a file's location, 89
Save settings, disabling at EXIT, 945
Save, using the, option, 88
ScanDisk
    advanced options
        understanding and using, 426
        using, to delete or copy cross-linked files, 429
        using, to fix lost file fragments, 428
    automatic error correction, controlling, 425
    error log, using, 427
    standard check, 422
    thorough check, 423
    surface scan, controlling, 424
Scraps
    moving clipboard contents to the Desktop using, 820
    pasting, by dragging a document on to the taskbar, 821
screen resolution, changing the, 138
screen saver(s)
    customizing your settings, 118
    installing a, 116
    operations, controlling with MS-DOS-based programs in the foreground, 175
    password protecting your, 117

selecting a running program, using Alt-Tab, 135
SCSI devices, directing Windows 95 to double buffer, 959
separator pages, understanding and using, 268
SerialKey devices, understanding and using, 217
Settings menu, removing the taskbar from the, 944
Setup File, viewing the Windows 95, 848
sheets, understanding, 75
shell-based account, understanding, 671
shortcut(s)
   creating a new, 341
   keys
      controlling, for an MS-DOS-based program, 180
      for the Microsoft keyboard, 938
   printer, creating on the Desktop, 266
   understanding and creating, 107
ShowSounds, understanding and using, 214
shutting down your computer, 20
   using one keystroke, 841
software, installing and removing, 201
SOHO (Small Office Home Office) site, using the, 733
sound
   assigning a, to an event, 291
   controlling, speaker volume, 539
   creating a custom audio setting, 542
   digital audio, understanding, 541
   files, inserting and mixing, 561
   formats, controlling, 559
   multimedia support, understanding, 536
   previewing a, event, 289
   recording your own, for Windows events, 292
   scheme, using a predefined, 290
   taskbar volume icon, 539
   understanding, and Windows events, 288
sound card recording, controlling, 540
Sound Recorder, using the, 557
SoundSentry, understanding and using, 213
spool settings, understanding and using, 274
SRAM memory cards, supporting, 534, 535
starting Windows 95
   Online Help, 51
   without network support, 933
starting your computer
   in a safe mode, 186
   in Windows, 100
   to a non-Windows 95 prompt, 184
   to a prompt command, 188
Start command
   understanding the, 824
   using, to control the order in which Windows 95 runs related programs, 825
Start menu
   accessing
      using Ctrl-Esc, 136
      using the Windows system key, 838
   adding an option to the, 47
   adding a program to the, using drag and drop, 128
   controlling the size of, options, 106
   creating a Control Panel folder on the, 1001
   options, controlling the size of, 106
   startup tips, requesting the, 38
   Suspend command, 262
   tuning your, 983
   using Ctrl-Esc to access the, 136
   using drag and drop to add a program to the, 128
start-up disk
   creating a, 205
   understanding the importance of traveling with a, 985
startup process, viewing the Windows 95, 851
status bar, using the File Explorer's, 326
StickyKeys, understanding and using, 210
stop bits, definition of, 238

swapping, understanding, 317
system
   components, kernel, understanding, 863
   files
      finding your old, 195
      understanding, 338
   general, displaying information, 301
   performance, adding memory to improve, 875
   performance settings, displaying, 310
   resources, understanding, 419
   startup
      confirmation of, 187
      logging your, using BOOTLOG.TXT, 185
   tools, understanding the, 374
System Monitor
   changing a measurement's chart options in the, 869
   changing the, chart interval, 870
   graph types, changing, 868
   toolbar, using the, 872
   understanding, 862
   using, to find bottlenecks, 873
   using, to monitor a remote computer, 871
   using, to monitor the Windows 95 file system, 864
System Policy Editor
   running the, 942
   understanding, 941
tabs, understanding, 75
tape drive, understanding the need to backup files using a, 376
taskbar
   clock, displaying or hiding the, 105
   hiding the, after each use, 104
   insuring visibility of the, 103
   moving the, 18
   removing the, from the Settings menu, 944
   sound volume icon, 539
   tracking programs on the, 99
   using the, 15
   using the, to cascade or tile open windows, 35
   using the, to control sound card volume, 42
   widening the, 100
10.SYS
   default system settings in, 192
   understanding, 191
telecommunications
   definition of, 651
   file(s)
      sending, to a remote computer, 661
      transfer protocols, 658
      transferring from a remote computer, 659
      transferring to a remote computer, 660
   operations
      ASCII control, controlling your connection's, 657
      configuring a new connection, 653
      configuring an existing connection, 652
      data communications settings, establishing your, 655
      text buffer, controlling the size of HyperTerminal's, 663
      text, capturing to a file or printer, 662
      toolbar, displaying and using HyperTerminal's, 664
   terminal emulation, understanding, 656
   understanding, 651
Telnet program
   downloading a Windows-based, 708
   sites, 690
   using to move from one computer to another, 689
   working on a remote computer using, 689
terminal, definition of, 656
text
   copying from an MS-DOS window to the clipboard, 155
   cursor blink rate, controlling the, 229
text box, using a, to type in data, 80
32-bit and 16-bit programs, understanding, 822

Index

time zone, changing the, 143
title bar, displaying the complete MS-DOS pathname in the, 354
ToggleKeys, understanding and using, 212
Token ring, understanding, 756
toolbar
    buttons, finding out about the, 71
    using the File Explorer's, 325
    using the MS-DOS window, 153
    using the New, Open, Save, and Print icons on the, 97
topic index, building a, for Help, 64
topology, definition of, 755
Tracert program, using to trace an Internet connection's route, 685
transferring files
    setting up a guest computer for, 526
    setting up a host computer for, 527
    using the Direct Cable Connection feature, 525
Trouble Shooting the Windows 95 File System, 314
TrueType fonts, understanding, 224
TSR, programs, old ones Windows 95 may load during startup, 190
UART settings, controlling, 241
UNIX shell, definition of, 670
user profiles, understanding and controlling, 258
VCACHE, understanding, 808
VFAT (Virtual File Allocation Table), understanding, 807
video-adapter memory use, preventing Windows 95, 936
video codecs
    prioritizing, 550
    understanding, 549
video, controlling the default, size, 543
video files
    AVI files, viewing specifics, 994
    taking a look at some, 993
viewer window, refreshing a, 357
viewing a document, using scroll bars, 72
virtual memory
    controlling Windows 95, 318
    swapping and pasting to increase, 317
    using a swap file to increase, 811
    understanding, 316
visually impaired, resources for the, 939
VxD (Virtual Device Driver), understanding, 858
WAIS (Wide Area Information Server), traversing the Internet using, 705
.WAV files, viewing specifics, 992
web browser, definition of, 672
Welcome Window, features of the, 3
What's This? option, requesting Help using the, 57
windows
    differences between Windows 3.1 and Windows 95, 6
    maximizing, 13
    minimizing, 11
    minimizing all open, at once, 12
    moving, 16
    moving, and INI files, within, 34
    restoring, to original size, 14
    sizing, by dragging a window frame, 17
    types of, 6
    understanding program and document, within, 95
    viewer, refreshing a, 351
Windows Explorer
    case-sensitive search operations, using, to perform, 365
    two parts of the, 320
    understanding the, 319
Windows 95
    accessibility options
        controlling settings for, 218
        understanding, 209
    and TSR programs, 190
    as replacement for MS-DOS, 144
    CAB (cabinet) files
        installing files from, 998
        understanding, 997

CD-ROM, learning about the contents of the, 981
component(s)
    adding and removing, 203
    viewing details about a, 204
Direct Cable Connection, understanding, 525
icons, understanding, 198
information, online sources of, 48
keys, special
    FilterKeys, understanding and using, 211
    MouseKeys, understanding and using, 216
    SerialKey devices, understanding and using, 217
    StickyKeys, understanding and using, 210
    ToggleKeys, understanding and using, 212
network support
    component(s)
        adding a, 775
        adding an adapter, 776
        customizing properties of a, 781
        removing a, 780
        starting, without, 933
        viewing current, 774
    organization, understanding, 755
    terms and concepts
        accessing, 782
        client and server, 759
        consistent connection, specifying a, 789
        dial-up networking
            accessing the Internet through, 762
            using, 792
        direct cable connect networking, 763
        drive letter, assigning to a network computer or folder, 788
        identifying your PC to the network, 777
        IPX/SPX, understanding, 765
        logging off, 799
        NetBEUI, understanding, 761
        Net Watcher toolbar, using the, 797
        network adapter, understanding the, 757
        network interface, determining your, 758
        Network Neighborhood, traversing your, 783
        network password, changing your, 791
        network resources, monitoring using Net Watcher, 794
        network resource use, understanding, 795
        network security, understanding, 772
        network server, creating a, 793
        NDIS (Network Driver Interface Specification), understanding 767
        NFS (Network File System), understanding, 764
        ODI (Open Datalink Interface), understanding, 768
        organization, types of, 755
        password, changing a folder or printer's, 787
        peer-to-peer networking, understanding, 769
        printer, accessing a shared, 784
        remote system administration, understanding, 773
        remote users, disconnecting using Net Watcher, 796
        resources, understanding, 771
        share access, defining your PC, 778
        shared access, ending, to a folder, 790
        shared folder, accessing a, 785
        shared folder or printer, controlling access to a, 786
        sharing, allowing file and printer, 779
        SNMP (Simple Network Management Protocol), understanding, 766
        TCP/IP, understanding, 760
        technology, types of, 756
        UNC (Universal Naming Conventional), understanding, 770
        understanding, 754
        VFAT (Virtual File Allocation Table), understanding, 807
        viewing files opened by network users, 798
    understanding, 753
new features in, 4
online sources of, information, 48

opening screen, viewing the, 2
passwords, understanding how, uses, 254
Quick View
   understanding, 817
   viewing a file using, 818
reboot, using a local, to end an application in, 36
registering, 40
registry, understanding, 876
release notes, reading and printing the, 50
Resource Kit, acquiring the, 49
setup options, understanding the difference between the, 202
10.SYS and MSDOS.SYS, understanding, 191
shortcuts in, 107
ShowSounds, understanding and using, 214
shutting down your computer in, 20
starting, 1
Start menu
   adding a program to the, using drag and drop, 128
   options, controlling the size of, 106
   using Ctrl-Esc to access the, 136
startup tips, requesting the, 38
SoundSentry, understanding and using, 213
switching between programs in, using Alt-Tab, 135
System Tools, understanding, 374
what's new in, 4
World Wide Web sites related to, 698
Windows 3.1
   accessory programs, 576
   AUTOEXEC.BAT and CONFIG.SYS, 33
   command path, 181
   File Manager
      conversion to Explorer in Windows 95, 43
      running the, 801
   MS-DOS, 144
   PIF editor, 157
   program groups, getting to your, 19
Program Manager, using the, 800
   SmartDrive, 189
   swap file, deleting a Windows 3.1 permanent, 813
   Task Manager, using the, 802
WINS (Windows Internet Naming Service), understanding and configuring, 678
wizard(s)
   adding new hardware, using, 200
   understanding, 39
word wraps, definition of, 631
World Wide Web
   browser
      downloading a, using FTP, 693
      understanding, 672
      using a, 694
   sites
      browsing, 695
      Windows 95-related, 698
   understanding the, 671